PRINCIPLES OF BUSINESS ORGANIZATIONS

By

Richard D. Freer

Robert Howell Hall Professor of Law
Emory University

Douglas K. Moll

Beirne, Maynard & Parsons, L.L.P. Professor of Law
University of Houston Law Center

CONCISE HORNBOOK SERIES®

A Thomson Reuters business

Concise Hornbook Series and Westlaw are trademark registered in the U.S. Patent and Trademark Office.

© 2013 Thomson Reuters
    610 Opperman Drive
    St. Paul, MN 55123
    1–800–313–9378
Printed in the United States of America

ISBN: 978–0–314–18133–6

*To Louise, Courtney, and Collin for having
me on the team—RDF*

*To Stefanie, Asher, Samara, Daisy, and Gatsby,
who make it all fun—DKM*

Preface

This book is designed for use in law school courses that focus on Business Organizations. Although course names differ from school to school, the book is ideally suited for courses such as "Business Organizations," "Business Associations," "Agency, Partnerships, and Limited Liability Companies," or "Unincorporated Business Associations." If we have done our jobs, reading this book will provide you with a solid grounding in the law of agency, general partnerships, corporations, limited partnerships, limited liability partnerships, and limited liability companies.

We very much hope that you will find this book to be informative, "user-friendly," and enjoyable. Most importantly, we hope that the book will help you learn about a subject that is of great significance to a tremendous number of companies and individuals—the law of business organizations.

RICHARD D. FREER
DOUGLAS K. MOLL

January 2013

Acknowledgments

Several students provided us with invaluable research assistance during the preparation of this book: Sangeetha Krishnakumar (Emory LL.M. 2013), Dominic Valponi (Emory 2014), and Monica White (Houston 2012). Our families also deserve a tremendous amount of thanks for their patience and support throughout this project.

Summary of Contents

PREFACE v

ACKNOWLEDGMENTS vii

Chapter 1. Introduction 1

Chapter 2. Agency 7
A. Introduction 7
B. The Creation of the Agency Relationship 9
C. Liability From the Agency Relationship 20
D. Duties of the Agent and the Principal to Each Other 57
E. Termination of the Agent's Power 62

Chapter 3. The General Partnership **64**
A. Introduction 65
B. Formation 65
C. Management and Operation 76
D. Financial Rights and Obligations 83
E. Fiduciary Duties 94
F. Ownership Interests and Transferability 113
G. Dissociation and Dissolution 119

**Chapter 4. The Corporation: Overview, Theory, and
History** **139**
A. Characteristics of the Corporation: Overview 139
B. Theoretical Understandings of the Corporation 142
C. Social Responsibility and Political Activity 146
D. Historical Development of Corporate Law in the United
    States 151
E. Relevance of Federal Income Tax Law 155

**Chapter 5. Formation of Corporations (and Related
Pre-Incorporation Activities)** **158**
A. Introduction 158
B. Selecting the State of Incorporation (and Invoking the Internal
    Affairs Doctrine) 159
C. Mechanics of Formation 163
D. Corporate Purposes and Powers (and Ultra Vires Activity) 169
E. Foreign Corporations 172
F. Promoters and Their Activities 173
G. Defective Incorporation 181

Chapter 6. Distribution of Powers in the Corporation 189
A. Introduction 189
B. The Traditional Model 190
C. Shareholders 198
D. Board of Directors 222
E. Officers 240

Chapter 7. Fiduciary Duties 251
A. Introduction 251
B. Who Owes What Duties to Whom? 252
C. The Duty of Care 254
D. The Obligation of Good Faith 269
E. The Duty of Loyalty 271
F. Which Directors Are Liable? 299
G. Duties of Controlling Shareholders 300

Chapter 8. Special Issues in the Closely Held Corporation 311
A. Introduction 311
B. Characteristics of the Close Corporation and the Statutory
    Close Corporation 313
C. Avoiding Outsiders and Ensuring Financial Return 314
D. Shareholder Management 319
E. Shareholder Liability: Piercing the Corporate Veil and
    Related Doctrines 328
F. Fiduciary Duty and Oppressive Behavior 341

Chapter 9. Special Issues in the Publicly Traded Corporation 349
A. Introduction 349
B. Characteristics of Publicly Traded Corporations 350
C. Registration and Stock Markets 359
D. Sarbanes-Oxley and Financial Accountability 362
E. Regulation of Proxy Solicitation 364
F. Hostile Takeovers 368

Chapter 10. Finance, Issuance, and Distributions 379
A. Introduction 379
B. Debt and Equity Financing and Securities 380
C. Issuance of Stock 387
D. Accounting and Financial Records 399
E. Dividends and Other Distributions 404
F. Statutory Limitations on Distributions and Liability for
    Improper Distributions 416

Chapter 11. Potential Liability in Securities Transactions..**422**
A. Introduction.. 422
B. State Law 423
C. Rule 10b–5—Background and Elements............................ 427
D. Section 16(b).. 445

Chapter 12. Fundamental Corporate Changes....................**452**
A. Introduction.. 452
B. Procedure for Fundamental Changes................................ 453
C. Dissenting Shareholders' Right of Appraisal..................... 455
D. Amendment to the Articles of Incorporation 461
E. Different Ways to Combine Businesses: Merger,
        Consolidation, and the Share Exchange 462
F. Disposition of All or Substantially All Assets 467
G. Conversion.. 470
H. Dissolution 470

Chapter 13. Shareholder as Plaintiff: Derivative Litigation **475**
A. Introduction.. 475
B. Determining Whether a Case is Derivative......................... 476
C. Overview of Derivative Litigation 480
D. Prerequisites for a Derivative Suit.................................... 482
E. Motions to Dismiss and Special Litigation Committees 487
F. Discontinuance or Settlement of a Derivative Suit 490
G. Indemnification Statutes... 491
H. Exculpatory Provisions and Insurance 496

Chapter 14. The Limited Partnership...............................**498**
A. Introduction.. 498
B. Formation 503
C. Management and Operation 506
D. Financial Rights and Obligations..................................... 508
E. Entity Status.. 510
F. Limited Liability 511
G. Fiduciary Duties 523
H. Ownership Interests and Transferability 530
I. Dissociation and Dissolution 533
J. A Final Look... 536

Chapter 15. The Limited Liability Partnership **538**
A. Introduction.. 538
B. Formation 540
C. Limited Liability 544
D. The Limited Liability Limited Partnership.......................... 551

Chapter 16. The Limited Liability Company **554**
A. Introduction.. 554
B. Formation 558
C. Management and Operation 561
D. Financial Rights and Obligations............................. 574
E. Entity Status.. 576
F. Limited Liability 581
G. Fiduciary Duties 585
H. Ownership Interests and Transferability 599
I.   Dissociation and Dissolution.................................... 601
J. The Nature of the LLC... 613
K. A Final Look... 616

TABLE OF CASES 619
INDEX... 629

Table of Contents

PREFACE v

ACKNOWLEDGMENTS vii

Chapter 1. Introduction 1

Chapter 2. Agency 7
A. Introduction.. 7
B. The Creation of the Agency Relationship............................ 9
   1. Defining Agency 9
   2. Distinguishing Agency From Other Relationships.............. 12
      a. Agency vs. the Gratuitous Bailment 12
      b. Agency vs. the Creditor-Debtor Relationship................ 15
C. Liability From the Agency Relationship 20
   1. Tort Liability From the Agency Relationship 20
      a. Distinguishing Between Servants and
         Independent Contractors 20
      b. Liability for the Torts of Servants.............................. 25
      c. Liability for the Torts of Independent Contractors 27
   2. Contract Liability From the Agency Relationship............... 28
      a. Liability of the Principal to the Third Party 29
         (1) Actual Authority.. 29
         (2) Apparent Authority.. 31
         (3) Inherent Authority... 38
         (4) Estoppel 43
         (5) Ratification 47
         (6) Summary 51
      b. Liability of the Third Party to the Principal 51
      c. Liability of the Agent to the Third Party 55
D. Duties of the Agent and the Principal to Each Other 57
   1. The Agent's Duties to the Principal................................. 57
   2. The Principal's Duties to the Agent................................. 61
E. Termination of the Agent's Power 62

Chapter 3. The General Partnership 64
A. Introduction.. 65
B. Formation 65
   1. The Definition of Partnership... 65
   2. The Partnership Agreement 71
   3. Entity vs. Aggregate Views 72
   4. Partnership By Estoppel 75
   5. Federal Tax Consequences... 76

C. Management and Operation 76
   1. General Governance and Actual Authority 76
   2. Apparent Authority 81
   3. Inspection and Information Rights 83
D. Financial Rights and Obligations 83
   1. Partnership Accounting 83
   2. Sharing of Profits and Losses 83
   3. Liability to Third Parties 90
      a. Liability of the Partnership 90
      b. Liability of the Partners 91
   4. Indemnification and Contribution 93
E. Fiduciary Duties 94
   1. The Common Law 94
   2. Statutory Developments 98
      a. The Duty of Loyalty 99
      b. The Duty of Care 105
      c. The Duty to Disclose 106
   3. Duties When Leaving a Partnership 107
   4. The Role of Contract 110
F. Ownership Interests and Transferability 113
   1. Partnership Property 113
   2. Transferring a Partnership Interest 114
   3. The Charging Order 117
G. Dissociation and Dissolution 119
   1. Dissolution Under UPA 119
      a. Doctrinal Overview 119
      b. Causes of Dissolution 124
      c. The Winding Up Process 132
   2. Dissociation and Dissolution Under RUPA 136

**Chapter 4. The Corporation: Overview, Theory, and
History** **139**
A. Characteristics of the Corporation: Overview 139
B. Theoretical Understandings of the Corporation 142
C. Social Responsibility and Political Activity 146
D. Historical Development of Corporate Law in the United
   States 151
E. Relevance of Federal Income Tax Law 155

**Chapter 5. Formation of Corporations (and Related
Pre-Incorporation Activities)** **158**
A. Introduction 158
B. Selecting the State of Incorporation (and Invoking the Internal
   Affairs Doctrine) 159
C. Mechanics of Formation 163
D. Corporate Purposes and Powers (and Ultra Vires Activity) 169
E. Foreign Corporations 172

F. Promoters and Their Activities 173
   1. Background 173
   2. Pre-Incorporation Contracts 175
   3. Subscriptions for Stock and Agreements to Form
      a Corporation 177
   4. Fiduciary Duties and the Secret Profit Rule 179
G. Defective Incorporation 181
   1. Personal Liability 181
   2. Defenses to Personal Liability: De Facto Corporation
      and Corporation by Estoppel 183

Chapter 6. Distribution of Powers in the Corporation 189
A. Introduction 189
B. The Traditional Model 190
   1. Introduction 190
   2. Overview of the Role of the Shareholders 191
   3. Overview of the Role of the Board of Directors 193
   4. Overview of the Role of Officers 194
   5. The Spectrum From "Closely Held" to "Publicly
      Held" Corporations: Tension Between the
      Traditional Model and the Real World 195
C. Shareholders 198
   1. Introduction 198
   2. Concepts of the Record Owner and the Record Date 199
   3. Shareholders Act as a Group in One of Two Ways 201
   4. Shareholder Meetings: Notice, Quorum, and Voting 202
   5. Cumulative Voting 207
   6. Voting by Proxy 211
   7. Methods for Combining Voting Power 214
   8. Inspection of Corporate Records 218
D. Board of Directors 222
   1. Introduction 222
   2. Statutory Requirements 222
   3. The Board Must Act as a Group in One of Two Ways 227
   4. Board Meetings: Notice, Quorum, and Voting 229
   5. Compensation 236
   6. Committees of the Board 237
E. Officers 240
   1. Introduction 240
   2. Statutory Requirements 240
   3. Sources of Authority 241
   4. Application of Agency Law 243
   5. Selection and Removal of Officers 248
   6. Fiduciary Duties Owed by Officers 250

Chapter 7. Fiduciary Duties..**251**
A. Introduction.. 251
B. Who Owes What Duties to Whom?.............................. 252
C. The Duty of Care... 254
    1. Overview.. 254
    2. Cases Involving Nonfeasance................................ 255
    3. Cases Involving Misfeasance: Managerial Action and
       the Business Judgment Rule 262
D. The Obligation of Good Faith 269
E. The Duty of Loyalty 271
    1. Overview.. 271
    2. Competing Ventures.. 272
    3. Self-Dealing ("Interested Director" Transactions)............... 274
    4. Usurpation of Business Opportunities 287
F. Which Directors Are Liable? 299
G. Duties of Controlling Shareholders.............................. 300
    1. Transfer of the Controlling Interest 301
    2. Transfer Accompanied by Resignations of Directors.......... 303
    3. Two Famous but Odd Cases.................................. 305
    4. Parent-Subsidiary Corporation Issues 307

Chapter 8. Special Issues in the Closely Held
Corporation..**311**
A. Introduction.. 311
B. Characteristics of the Close Corporation and the Statutory
    Close Corporation 313
C. Avoiding Outsiders and Ensuring Financial Return 314
    1. The Outsider Problem and Stock Transfer Restrictions 314
    2. The Illiquidity Problem and Buy-Sell Agreements 318
D. Shareholder Management... 319
    1. Background 319
    2. Case Law Development 320
    3. Legislative Amelioration: Statutory Close Corporations .. 325
    4. Legislative Rejection of the Traditional Model.................. 326
E. Shareholder Liability: Piercing the Corporate Veil and
    Related Doctrines 328
    1. Background.. 328
    2. Case Law... 331
    3. Piercing the Corporate Veil in the
       Parent-Subsidiary Context 336
    4. Choice of Law Issues 337
    5. Reverse Piercing and Related Issues 338
    6. Enterprise Liability.. 340
F. Fiduciary Duty and Oppressive Behavior 341
    1. Background 341
    2. Common Law Recognition of a Fiduciary Duty.................. 343
    3. The Effect of Involuntary Dissolution Statutes.................. 345

    4. Reasonable Expectations of the Shareholder 347

Chapter 9. Special Issues in the Publicly Traded Corporation **349**
A. Introduction... 349
B. Characteristics of Publicly Traded Corporations.................... 350
    1. Board Structure and Managerial Function........................ 350
    2. Compensation of Managers.. 356
C. Registration and Stock Markets 359
D. Sarbanes-Oxley and Financial Accountability 362
E. Regulation of Proxy Solicitation 364
    1. Background and Federal Regulation................................. 364
    2. Shareholder Proposals.. 365
    3. Private Right of Action 366
F. Hostile Takeovers 368
    1. Background 368
    2. Tender Offers and Leveraged Buyouts.............................. 369
    3. Proxy Contests 370
    4. Defensive Tactics 372
    5. State Anti-Takeover Laws... 377

Chapter 10. Finance, Issuance, and Distributions **379**
A. Introduction... 379
B. Debt and Equity Financing and Securities............................. 380
    1. Background and Definitions 380
    2. Advantages and Disadvantages.. 382
    3. Types of Debt Securities.. 383
    4. Types of Equity Securities.. 384
C. Issuance of Stock.. 387
    1. Background and Definitions 387
    2. Form and Amount of Consideration for an Issuance.......... 388
    3. Determination of Value 391
    4. Watered Stock 392
    5. Dilution and Pre-Emptive Rights 394
    6. Venture Capital and Public Issuance 398
D. Accounting and Financial Records 399
    1. The Income Statement 399
    2. The Cash Flow Statement.. 401
    3. The Balance Sheet 402
E. Dividends and Other Distributions 404
    1. Background 404
    2. Dividends.. 404
    3. Is There a "Right" to a Dividend? 406
    4. Classes of Stock and Dividends 409
    5. Repurchases and Redemptions 413
F. Statutory Limitations on Distributions and Liability for
    Improper Distributions 416

1. Background 416
2. Traditional ("Fund") Limitations 416
3. The Modern ("Insolvency") Approach 419
4. Liability for Improper Distributions.................................. 420

**Chapter 11. Potential Liability in Securities
Transactions**...**422**
A. Introduction... 422
B. State Law 423
1. From Fraud to a Fiduciary Duty to Disclose 423
2. Insider Trading in the Market.. 426
C. Rule 10b–5—Background and Elements................................ 427
1. The Provision and Who Can Enforce It............................ 427
2. Potential Defendants 429
3. Elements in a Rule 10b–5 Claim 430
4. Types of Fraudulent Behavior Covered............................. 436
D. Section 16(b)... 445
1. Differences from Rule 10b–5 445
2. Application of § 16(b) 446

Chapter 12. Fundamental Corporate Changes.................... **452**
A. Introduction... 452
B. Procedure for Fundamental Changes..................................... 453
C. Dissenting Shareholders' Right of Appraisal........................... 455
D. Amendment to the Articles of Incorporation 461
E. Different Ways to Combine Businesses: Merger,
Consolidation, and the Share Exchange 462
F. Disposition of All or Substantially All Assets 467
G. Conversion 470
H. Dissolution 470

**Chapter 13. Shareholder as Plaintiff: Derivative
Litigation** **475**
A. Introduction... 475
B. Determining Whether a Case is Derivative............................. 476
C. Overview of Derivative Litigation 480
D. Prerequisites for a Derivative Suit.. 482
1. Contemporaneous Ownership 482
2. Adequacy of Representation... 483
3. Security for Expenses 484
4. Demand that the Corporation Bring Suit 484
E. Motions to Dismiss and Special Litigation Committees 487
F. Discontinuance or Settlement of a Derivative Suit 490
G. Indemnification Statutes 491
H. Exculpatory Provisions and Insurance 496

Chapter 14. The Limited Partnership...................................... **498**
A. Introduction.. 498
B. Formation 503
C. Management and Operation 506
D. Financial Rights and Obligations..................................... 508
E. Entity Status.. 510
F. Limited Liability 511
   1. The Control Rule... 511
   2. Control of the Entity General Partner 519
G. Fiduciary Duties 523
   1. General Partners 523
   2. Limited Partners.. 528
H. Ownership Interests and Transferability 530
I. Dissociation and Dissolution... 533
   1. Dissociation 533
   2. Dissolution... 535
J. A Final Look 536

Chapter 15. The Limited Liability Partnership **538**
A. Introduction.. 538
B. Formation 540
C. Limited Liability 544
D. The Limited Liability Limited Partnership...................... 551

Chapter 16. The Limited Liability Company **554**
A. Introduction.. 554
B. Formation 558
C. Management and Operation 561
   1. General Governance and Actual Authority........................ 561
   2. Apparent Authority 563
   3. Inspection and Information Rights.................................... 572
D. Financial Rights and Obligations..................................... 574
E. Entity Status.. 576
F. Limited Liability 581
G. Fiduciary Duties 585
   1. The Basic Duties 585
   2. The Role of Contract 592
H. Ownership Interests and Transferability 599
I. Dissociation and Dissolution... 601
J. The Nature of the LLC... 613
K. A Final Look... 616

TABLE OF CASES 619

INDEX.. 629

PRINCIPLES OF BUSINESS ORGANIZATIONS

Chapter 1

INTRODUCTION

The study of business organizations is, broadly speaking, a study of how people engage in business and, more importantly, how the law facilitates and regulates the operation of such businesses. This book examines many of the legal rules and doctrines associated with running a business—from formation to dissolution to everything in between. These rules and doctrines are explored within the context of the various organizational forms in which a business may be operated.

For many years, two or more persons seeking to engage in a commercial venture in this country typically chose between the partnership and corporation structures. These days, however, the number of business forms has proliferated. This book focuses on the general partnership, the corporation, the limited partnership, the limited liability partnership, and the limited liability company. Basic agency principles, which are the building blocks for many of the legal doctrines associated with these business forms, are a focus of the book as well.

Chapter 2 examines the law of agency—the law governing the relationships between principals, agents, and third parties. Although agency law applies to all forms of business, it is frequently invoked when dealing with the most basic (and most common) form, the sole proprietorship. A sole proprietorship is a business owned by a single individual that is not operated as a corporation or other special legal form. The major advantage of a sole proprietorship is that it is easy to establish—the proprietor simply begins to conduct business. In some jurisdictions, a proprietor using an assumed name for the business must also file an "assumed name" or "fictitious name" certificate with the county clerk specifying the name of the owner and the name of the business. The major disadvantage of a sole proprietorship is that the owner is liable for the obligations of the business. Debts of the business, in other words, are viewed by the law as debts of the owner, and the owner's personal assets are at risk in lawsuits arising out of business activities. A sole proprietor may operate the business entirely by himself or, more likely, may employ others to help conduct the venture. When others are involved, the relationships between the proprietor (the principal), the employees (the agents), and third parties are governed, in large part, by agency law. As mentioned, agency law is also important

1

because it serves as the foundation for many of the legal principles associated with the other business forms discussed in this book.

Chapter 3 explores the general partnership—an association of two or more persons to carry on, as co-owners, a business for profit. Among the modern forms of business organization that involve two or more owners, the general partnership is unique in that it can be informally created. Put differently, establishing a general partnership does not require the filing of an organizational document with the state. So long as two or more persons are carrying on, as co-owners, a business for profit, a general partnership is created, regardless of whether the co-owning persons intended that result.

Some statutes view a general partnership as a separate legal entity whose identity is distinct from that of its owners (known as "partners"). Other statutes view a general partnership as an aggregate of the individual partners with no legal differentiation between the business and the partners themselves. Under either view, all of the partners in a general partnership have the right to participate in the management of the business. Moreover, the general partnership form provides partners with a relatively easy exit from the venture, as a partner's withdrawal typically causes a buyout of the partner's interest or the dissolution of the partnership itself.

The general partnership is also characterized by structural flexibility (the partners can contractually arrange to run the business largely as they see fit), restricted transferability of ownership interests (a transferee of a partnership interest can only become a partner with the unanimous consent of the other partners), and pass-through taxation (partnership income is only taxed at the partner level, rather than "doubly taxed" at both the partnership and the partner levels). Like a sole proprietorship, however, the primary downside of a general partnership is that the law imposes personal liability on partners for the obligations of the partnership. Further, the easy exit of the general partnership makes it a rather unstable business form in certain circumstances—a situation which may be unsuitable for particular types of ventures.

Chapters 4–13 examine the corporation. Whether you are taking a course on Corporations, Business Associations, or Business Organizations, the centerpiece of your study will be the corporation. It has been the dominant business form in the United States since the early days of independence. Under all corporation statutes, a corporation is viewed as a separate legal entity whose identity is distinct from that of its owners (known as "shareholders"). In contrast to a general partnership, a corporation is consciously formed by filing an organizational document with the state. Unlike general partners, shareholders have no right to participate in the management of the business (except in certain extraordinary situations, such as mergers). Perhaps most importantly, a corporation provides its shareholders with limited liability for the obligations of the business. In a lawsuit against a corporation, a shareholder's personal assets are not at risk; instead, the most that a shareholder can lose is the amount of his investment.

Many people assume that all corporations are "public" or "publicly held"—that is, that they are large entities, with their stock traded on the New York Stock Exchange or NASDAQ. This is not true. Most corporations are "close" or "closely held," with a handful (or even one) shareholder and no public market for the stock. Unlike publicly traded General Motors, for example, whose stock can be bought and sold on the New York Stock Exchange simply by calling a broker, a closely held business lacks an established market of buyers and sellers for its ownership interests. If a buyer can be found, however, ownership interests in a corporation may, as a default matter, be freely and fully transferred without the consent of the other shareholders. Aside from the possibility of sale, exit rights in a corporation are otherwise restricted. A shareholder has no default right to demand a buyout of his interest or, in most instances, to compel dissolution of the enterprise.

The income of a corporation is taxed twice—once at the corporation level, and a second time at the shareholder level. Stated differently, the corporation pays taxes on its income, and the shareholders pay taxes on that income again when (and if) the income is distributed to them. Whether this tax treatment is advantageous or disadvantageous depends heavily on the individual and corporate tax rates that exist at the time, as well as on the financial circumstances of the shareholders. In today's tax climate, however, this "double taxation" is usually undesirable. Aside from income taxes, corporations (but not partnerships) are also subject to state franchise taxes—taxes imposed for the privilege of organizing a business in a state.

Chapter 14 begins the exploration of the "hybrid" business organizations—i.e., business structures that combine attributes of the general partnership and corporation forms. In particular, Chapter 14 addresses the limited partnership—a partnership comprised of two classes of partners, general and limited, that is formed by filing an organizational document with the state. Like a general partnership, general partners in a limited partnership have personal liability for the venture's obligations (although individual liability concerns are significantly lessened by the common use of limited liability entities as general partners). Like a corporation, limited partners in a limited partnership have limited liability for the venture's obligations (although, under many statutes, that limited liability can be forfeited in certain circumstances if a limited partner participates in the control of the business). In a limited partnership, the limited partners are largely passive investors while the general partners manage the business. As with a general partnership, a limited partnership is characterized by structural flexibility, restricted transferability of ownership interests, and pass-through taxation. Exit rights, however, tend to be more restricted in the limited partnership form.

Chapter 15 addresses the limited liability partnership ("LLP"). The LLP is typically a general partnership that, depending on the relevant statute, provides the partners with limited liability for the partnership's tort obligations or for both its tort and contract obligations. Chapter 15 also addresses the limited liability limited partnership ("LLLP")—a limited partnership that provides LLP-like limited liability protection to some or all of the partners. A state filing is necessary for both of these business forms.

Chapter 16 examines the limited liability company ("LLC"). An LLC is a business organization, formed by a required state filing, that adopts many of the best features of the corporation and partnership forms. Like a corporation, an LLC is a legal entity that is separate and distinct from its owners (known as "members"). An LLC can be structured to provide management rights to members or to a designated group of managers, and it offers limited liability to the members for all of the venture's obligations (regardless of whether the members participate in the control of the business). Exit rights in an LLC tend to be restricted in a corporate-like manner, as many statutes prevent a member from demanding a buyout of his interest or from compelling dissolution of the enterprise. Like a partnership, an LLC is characterized by structural flexibility, restricted transferability of ownership interests, and pass-through taxation. Along with avoiding double taxation with respect to income taxes, LLCs in most states avoid franchise taxes as well. Because of this favorable combination of attributes, the LLC has emerged as the preferred business form for many closely held ventures.

If you are somewhat bewildered by the assortment of business organizations, do not despair. Remind yourself that we are only getting started, and rest assured that you are not alone. The materials in this book are designed to help you understand the differences between the business forms and to recognize when one might be more appropriate than another for a particular client's situation. That said, in determining which form to use, the proprietors of any business—from a front-yard lemonade stand to a multinational hotel chain—should consider eight major issues:

1. How is the business formed and maintained? For example, do we need to file anything with the government or can we just start selling lemonade? Accompanying this question is a legitimate concern about costs, such as whether we will need an attorney to form the business and keep it in good standing.

2. Is the business considered an entity, separate from the person(s) who own it? The answer to this question may be important in answering the next question.

3. Who is liable to third parties for business debts? By business debts, we mean any liability incurred in operating the business. Suppose, for instance, we contract with a third party to provide lemon extract with which we will make lemonade. If the business does not pay for it, will the owners be personally liable? Or if our lemonade is tainted and a customer gets sick, will the owners' personal assets be at risk? This raises the question of "limited liability."

4. Who owns the business? In the corporation, for instance, the shareholders are the owners; the shares of stock are units of ownership.

5. Who makes decisions for the business? For example, do the owners make the business decisions or do they look to others to make the decisions? (This is the question of "management.")

6. If one of the owners wants to get out of the business, can she transfer her interest? If so, does the business survive her leaving, or does it have to be dissolved and a new business formed? (These questions relate to "continuity of existence.")

7. Does the business pay income tax on its profits? If so, this will result in "double taxation" because the owners also pay income tax on the amounts they receive (such as dividends) from the business.

8. What are the needs for capital? At one level, this is a silly question because all businesses need money to get started and grow. We note two things, each of which we discuss in detail later.

First, if somebody furnishes money for our business, what does she expect in return? For instance, does she want a guarantee of repayment plus interest, a share in profits, a voice in management of the business, or some combination of these things? The answer to these questions will determine whether we raise capital through "debt" or "equity." If you majored in sociology in college, these terms may scare you, but they should not. Debt means a loan—the business borrows money and must repay it (with interest as specified in the contract). The person who lends money becomes a creditor of the business, but is not an owner of the business. Equity, in contrast, means ownership—the person invests in the business and gets an ownership interest. The business can raise capital either by getting loans or by selling ownership interests (or by some combination).

Second, if the business gets big enough, can we raise money by selling interests to the public? In other words, will we need (or be able to get) access to the public markets for financing? Registering to sell investments to the public is extremely detailed and expensive.

As you proceed through the various business organizations discussed in this book, you may find it useful to return to this list. Ideally, it will focus your attention on some of the critical issues that determine whether a particular business form is suitable (or unsuitable) for a specific business situation.

Chapter 2

AGENCY

Analysis

A. Introduction
B. The Creation of the Agency Relationship
    1. Defining Agency
    2. Distinguishing Agency From Other Relationships
        a. Agency vs. the Gratuitous Bailment
        b. Agency vs. the Creditor-Debtor Relationship
C. Liability From the Agency Relationship
    1. Tort Liability From the Agency Relationship
        a. Distinguishing Between Servants and Independent Contractors
        b. Liability for the Torts of Servants
        c. Liability for the Torts of Independent Contractors
    2. Contract Liability From the Agency Relationship
        a. Liability of the Principal to the Third Party
            (1) Actual Authority
            (2) Apparent Authority
            (3) Inherent Authority
            (4) Estoppel
            (5) Ratification
            (6) Summary
        b. Liability of the Third Party to the Principal
        c. Liability of the Agent to the Third Party
D. Duties of the Agent and the Principal to Each Other
    1. The Agent's Duties to the Principal
    2. The Principal's Duties to the Agent
E. Termination of the Agent's Power

A. Introduction

The law of agency is the law of delegation—i.e., the legal principles that govern the ability of one person (the principal) to have another person (the agent) act on his behalf. Basic agency relationships underlie virtually all commercial dealings in the modern world. For example, the relationship between a sole proprietor and his employees is governed by the law of agency, as is the relationship between a corporation and its officers. The agency relationship is not a form of business organization in and of itself; instead, agency is the mechanism by which business organizations function. To take an obvious example, a corporation—an artificial legal construct that has no physical being of its own—can act only through agents for everything it does. Whether the corporation is writing a check, selling a product, or entering into a multi-billion dollar merger, the law of agency is involved.

Agency concepts explicitly appear in the statutory schemes of many business organizations. In the general partnership, for example, partners are agents with apparent authority to bind the partnership for acts in the ordinary course of the partnership business.[1] While this principle presents itself as a partnership doctrine (it is in the partnership statute after all), and while it could be studied purely as a matter of partnership law, it is far easier to understand it if one is familiar with the agency concepts from which the principle derived. Even when the relevant business organization statute does not explicitly incorporate an agency concept, the common law of agency will apply unless it is clearly displaced by the statutory scheme at issue. Section 104(a) of the Revised Uniform Partnership Act, for example, indicates that "[u]nless displaced by particular provisions of this [Act], the principles of law and equity supplement this [Act]," and the comment states that the law of agency is encompassed within these supplementary principles. As a further example, § 301 of the Revised Uniform Limited Liability Company Act explicitly defers to the law of agency. In short, the study of agency law is directly related to the study of modern business organizations.

The principal sources of agency law today are the Second and Third Restatements of Agency. The American Law Institute—an association of lawyers, academics, and judges—authored the Restatements of Agency and, like all Restatements, their text and comments represent an effort to capture the law as developed by the courts. The Second Restatement of Agency was published in 1958, and the Third Restatement of Agency was published in 2006. Although the Restatements are not binding authorities, they are very influential and persuasive to many courts.

Because of the relatively recent publication of the Third Restatement, most of the existing case law deals with the Second Restatement. Nevertheless, the basic principles of the Second and Third Restatements are largely the same. The materials in this Chapter will discuss and cite both versions.

---

[1] *See, e.g.*, REV. UNIF. P'SHIP ACT § 301 (1997).

B. The Creation of the Agency Relationship

1. Defining Agency

The Second Restatement defines *agency* as the "fiduciary relation which results from the manifestation of consent by one person to another that the other shall act on his behalf and subject to his control, and consent by the other so to act."[2] The person who is acting for another is the *agent*; the person for whom the agent is acting is the *principal*. Parsing this definition reveals three elements of an agency relationship: (1) consent by the principal and the agent; (2) action by the agent on behalf of the principal; and (3) control by the principal. These elements reveal the general policy thrust of agency law—if there is mutual consent to an arrangement involving an agent acting to further the principal's interest and subject to the principal's control, then it is appropriate to make the principal liable for the agent's actions.

Consent: Consent of both the principal and the agent is necessary to form an agency relationship. More specifically, both the principal and the agent must consent to the agent acting on the principal's behalf and subject to the principal's control. Thus, agency is a consensual relationship in which one person agrees to act for the benefit of, and subject to the control of, another person.

The principal must manifest (or convey) his consent to the agent. This required manifestation of consent may be written, oral, or implied from the parties' conduct. The agent's consent may also be established by written or oral statements, or by implication from the parties' conduct.[3] Thus, if *P* asks *A* to complete a task pursuant to *P*'s instructions, and *A* does so, an agency relationship has been created even if *A* did not expressly communicate to *P* his agreement to perform the task.

On behalf of: The agent must be acting on the principal's behalf. This requirement is generally understood to mean that the agent must be acting *primarily* for the benefit of the principal rather than for the benefit of the agent or some other party.[4] This element is crit-

---

[2] RESTATEMENT (SECOND) OF AGENCY § 1 (1958); *see* RESTATEMENT (THIRD) OF AGENCY § 1.01 (2006).

[3] *See, e.g.*, RESTATEMENT (THIRD) OF AGENCY § 1.03 (2006).

[4] *See* J. DENNIS HYNES & MARK J. LOEWENSTEIN, AGENCY, PARTNERSHIP, AND THE LLC: THE LAW OF UNINCORPORATED BUSINESS ENTERPRISES: CASES, MATERIALS, PROBLEMS 17 (7th ed. 2007) ("'On the principal's behalf' and acting 'primarily' for the principal's benefit are different ways of expressing the same requirement. Merely benefitting another by one's conduct does not qualify. It is too far removed in degree."); *cf.* RESTATEMENT (SECOND) OF AGENCY § 13 cmt. a (1958) ("The agreement to act on behalf of the principal causes the agent to be a fiduciary, that is, a person having a

ical to the agency definition, as it allows courts to distinguish the agency relationship from more garden-variety exchanges of compensation for services where we would not expect an agency relationship to arise. Simply acting in a way that benefits another, in other words, even where there is control, is insufficient to establish an agency relationship; instead, a court must believe that the agent was acting primarily for the benefit of the other person (the principal).[5]

For example, suppose that a homeowner calls an electrician to install a new chandelier. One might plausibly argue that the electrician has agreed to act subject to the homeowner's control in several respects—e.g., the homeowner has specified the particular task, the homeowner may have required a particular time and date for the service, and the homeowner may want the chandelier hung in a particular manner. Nevertheless, absent extraordinary facts, the electrician's services would be considered primarily for his own benefit, largely because the electrician sets the price for his services and retains the profits from his labor. From a policy standpoint, this conclusion is sensible, as we would not expect an electrician to have a fiduciary duty of loyalty to his customer, or for the customer to be liable for the electrician's negligence, or for any of the other onerous obligations of the agency relationship to apply.[6]

Control: The agent must act subject to the principal's control, but the degree of control exercised by the principal does not have to be significant. As one court observed:

> The control a principal must exercise over an agent in order to evidence an agency relationship is not so comprehensive. A principal need not exercise physical control over the actions of its agent in order for an agency relationship to exist; rather, the agent must be subject to the principal's control over the result or ultimate objectives of the agency relationship.

    . . .

---

duty, created by his undertaking, to act primarily for the benefit of another in matters connected with his undertaking.").

[5] Keep in mind, however, the following words of caution: "While this proposition is well accepted, the task of distinguishing between actions that merely benefit persons and actions taken on behalf of persons is not always easy. It sometimes involves drawing a fine line, subject to debate." HYNES & LOEWENSTEIN, *supra* note 4, at 17.

[6] Does the fact that an agent is compensated indicate that the agent is acting primarily for his own benefit rather than that of the principal? A paid agent is in some sense acting on his own behalf in order to earn the promised compensation; nevertheless, "compensation is earned by acting in a manner that advances the interest of the principal, and thus the paid agent is considered to be *primarily* acting for the benefit of another." *Id.*

In sum, the control a principal exercises over its agent is not defined rigidly to mean control over the minutia of the agent's actions, such as the agent's physical conduct... The level of control may be very attenuated with respect to the details. However, the principal must have ultimate responsibility to control the end result of his or her agent's actions; such control may be exercised by prescribing the agents' obligations or duties before or after the agent acts, or both.[7]

Thus, the requisite level of control may be found simply by the fact that the principal has specified the task that the agent should perform, even if the principal has not prescribed the details of how the task should be accomplished.

In addition to these three elements, it is important to note that the agency definition uses the term "person" to refer to both agents and principals. Both the Second and Third Restatements define "person" to include individuals as well as organizations.[8] Thus, agency relationships are not limited to natural persons; indeed, artificial entities such as corporations, trusts, partnerships, or limited liability companies may act as principals or as agents.

Keep in mind that, if the legal definition of agency has been met through satisfaction of the above elements, an agency relationship is present, regardless of whether the parties intended to create such a relationship (and regardless of what they call it):

> Agency is a legal concept which depends upon the existence of required factual elements: the manifestation by the principal that the agent shall act for him, the agent's acceptance of the undertaking and the understanding of the parties that the principal is to be in control of the undertaking. The relation which the law calls agency does not depend upon the intent of the parties to create it, nor their belief that they have done so. To constitute the relation, there must be an agreement, but not necessarily a contract, between the parties; if the agreement results in the factual relation between them to which are attached the legal consequences of agency, an agency exists although the parties did not call it agency and did not intend the legal consequences of the relation to follow. Thus, when one who asks a friend to do a slight service for him, such as to return for credit goods recently purchased from

---

[7] Green v. H&R Block, Inc., 735 A.2d 1039, 1050–51 (Md. 1999); *see also* RESTATEMENT (SECOND) OF AGENCY § 14 cmt. a (1958) ("The control of the principal does not, however, include control at every moment; its exercise may be very attenuated and, as where the principal is physically absent, may be ineffective.").

[8] *See* RESTATEMENT (SECOND) OF AGENCY § 1 cmt. a (1958); RESTATEMENT (THIRD) OF AGENCY § 1.04(5) (2006).

a store, neither one may have any realization that they are creating an agency relation or be aware of the legal obligations which would result from performance of the service.[9]

2. Distinguishing Agency From Other Relationships

It is often difficult to distinguish agency relationships from other types of legal relationships. Much turns on the distinction because, as will be discussed, the agency relationship imposes significant burdens and obligations on both agents and principals that are often absent in non-agency settings.

a. Agency vs. the Gratuitous Bailment[10]

A law school favorite in this area is *Gorton v. Doty*.[11] In *Gorton*, the Soda Springs High School football team was scheduled to play the Paris High School football team on September 21, 1934. Rather than travel by bus, the team was to be taken to the game in private cars. Doty, a teacher at Soda Springs, volunteered the use of her car for transporting some of the players on the condition that Russell Garst, the coach of the football team, drive the car himself. Doty was not paid for the use of her car, and she testified that she merely loaned the car to Garst and that she did not "direct[] his work or his services, or what he was doing."

Unfortunately, an accident resulted while Garst was driving. Garst was killed, and Richard Gorton, one of the student passengers in the car, was injured. Gorton's father sued Doty to recover for his son's injuries on the theory that Garst was acting as Doty's agent when the accident occurred.[12]

The jury returned a verdict in favor of Gorton on the agency theory, and the Idaho Supreme Court affirmed. As to consent, the court stated that Doty consented to Garst acting as her agent "from her act in volunteering the use of her car upon the express condition that he [Garst] should drive it." Similarly, the court concluded that Garst consented to act as Doty's agent "by his act in driving the car." The court further noted that "[i]t is not essential to the existence of authority that there be a contract between principal and agent or that the agent promise to act as such, nor is it essential to

---

[9] RESTATEMENT (SECOND) OF AGENCY § 1 cmt. b (1958); *see* RESTATEMENT (THIRD) OF AGENCY § 1.02 (2006).

[10] A bailment is defined as the "rightful possession of goods by one who is not the owner." 9 SAMUEL WILLISTON, A TREATISE ON THE LAW OF CONTRACTS 875 (3d ed. 1967). A gratuitous bailment is "the transfer of possession or use of property without compensation." Fili v. Matson Motors, Inc., 590 N.Y.S.2d 961, 963 (App. Div. 1992).

[11] 69 P.2d 136 (Idaho 1937).

[12] *See id.* at 138–41. A principal can be liable for the torts of his agent. *See* Chapter 2(C)(1).

the relationship of principal and agent that they, or either, receive compensation." Other than mentioning Doty's "express condition" that Garst should drive the car, the court provided no analysis of the control and "on behalf of" elements of the agency inquiry.[13]

Was Garst the agent of Doty, or was he simply, as the dissent maintained, a "gratuitous bailee?" As in any agency analysis, one should consider the three elements of the agency relationship. First, as to consent, the court's conclusion was based on no more than Doty volunteering the use of her car and Garst driving it in accordance with Doty's instructions. Nevertheless, consent does not require an explicit verbal or written agreement. As mentioned, the parties' conduct may imply consent—a principle that supports the court's conclusion.

Second, as to control, was it enough that Doty conditioned the use of her car on Garst driving it? This evidence was certainly thin, and the dissent downplayed it as "a mere precaution upon her part that the car should not be driven by any one of the young boys—a perfectly natural thing for her to do."[14] Recall, however, that the degree of control exercised by the principal does not have to be significant, and it can be enough that the principal has specified the task (e.g., drive my car to the football game) that the agent should perform. That said, the imposition of liability upon Doty based on such underwhelming control evidence tends to make students (as well as professors) uneasy.

What if the evidence of control were much stronger? What if, for example, Doty prescribed the route that Garst must travel, the speed that Garst must average, the rest breaks that Garst must take, etc.? Would that make the agency conclusion in *Gorton* more palatable? These questions are critical because they highlight the third element of the agency relationship—the "on behalf of" element—that the court largely ignored. Even if consent and control were firmly established, in other words, was there any evidence that Garst was acting primarily for the benefit of Doty? The use of Doty's car benefitted Garst to the extent that he could transport some of his players to the game and could stop looking for alternative vehicles; similarly, it benefitted the school to the extent that public or other private transportation did not have to be provided. But the use of the car appears to have provided no benefit to Doty at all; at the very

---

[13] *See Gorton*, 69 P.2d at 138, 140, 145.

[14] *Id.* at 146 (Budge, J., dissenting).

least, the arrangement was not *primarily* for her benefit. As a result, the court's agency conclusion seems far off the mark.[15]

What are the planning implications of *Gorton*? What should Doty have done to avoid the possibility of a liability finding against her? The court suggested that Doty's failure to communicate explicitly to Garst that she was "loaning" her car to him made a difference, but that omission should hardly matter. The label that the parties give to their relationship (e.g., lender-borrower) is not controlling for agency purposes. The only question is whether the facts and circumstances surrounding the parties' arrangement meet the legal definition of agency. Surely it would have helped if Doty had placed no condition on who could drive, but as the dissent indicated, her desire to keep teenagers from driving her car was a sensible precaution. Doty could have, of course, refused to lend her car at all, which in hindsight would have been ideal. If she truly wanted to lend her car, however, perhaps her best course of action would have been to confirm that her auto insurance policy was in good standing, and that it covered accidents caused by persons driving her car with permission.

This last point may explain what the *Gorton* majority was attempting to accomplish by using agency principles to uphold the liability verdict. The court may have believed that automobile owners were in the best position to insure against this type of loss. By using (abusing?) agency principles to impose liability, the court gives vehicle owners an incentive to obtain insurance that covers themselves as well as other permitted drivers.

One final point is worth mentioning. Students are often amazed that agency liability can be found when one person is simply doing a favor for another. Notice, however, that if one person agrees to do a favor for the other pursuant to the other's instructions, it is entirely consistent with an agency relationship—particularly because the person doing the favor (who would be viewed as the agent) is generally doing it for the benefit of the other person (who would be viewed as the principal).[16] After all, that's what a favor is—something that you do primarily to help someone else out. The reason that *Gorton* does not fit this explanation, of course, is that the person doing the favor (Doty) is characterized as

---

[15] As the dissent observed, "[Doty] loaned her car to Garst, not for her benefit, but for his benefit or for the benefit of the school district." *Id.* at 146 (Budge, J., dissenting).

[16] *See, e.g.*, RESTATEMENT (SECOND) OF AGENCY § 1 cmt. b (1958) ("Thus, when one who asks a friend to do a slight service for him, such as to return for credit goods recently purchased from a store, neither one may have any realization that they are creating an agency relation or be aware of the legal obligations which would result from performance of the service.").

the principal, even though the favor was being done for the benefit of someone else.

b. Agency vs. the Creditor-Debtor Relationship

A leading case addressing the distinction between agency and the creditor-debtor relationship is *A. Gay Jenson Farms Co. v. Cargill, Inc.*[17] In *Cargill*, Warren Seed & Grain Company operated a grain elevator. The business had several components: (1) Warren purchased grain from local farmers and resold it; (2) Warren stored grain for farmers; (3) Warren sold chemical, fertilizer, and steel storage bins; and (4) Warren operated a seed business which involved buying seed grain from farmers, processing it, and reselling it to farmers and other local grain elevators.

Cargill, Inc. (a large international trader of grain products) provided Warren with working capital financing from 1964 to 1977. Cargill effectively provided a $175,000 line of credit to Warren that gradually increased over the years to $1.25 million. Cargill also purchased the majority of Warren's grain for Cargill's own operations. Ultimately, Warren ceased operations in 1977 as a result of mounting financial difficulties. At the time of Warren's collapse, it owed $2 million to 86 farmers for the purchase of their grain, and it owed $3.6 million to Cargill.[18]

The 86 farmers sued Cargill to recover their $2 million. They alleged that Warren incurred the debts as an agent of Cargill and that Cargill was therefore liable as a principal for Warren's obligations. After a jury trial, judgment was entered in favor of the plaintiffs.[19] On appeal, Cargill argued that its relationship with Warren was not that of principal-agent, but was instead merely a creditor-debtor arrangement (or, alternatively, a buyer-supplier relationship).

Relying on the Second Restatement of Agency, the Minnesota Supreme Court held that an agency relationship did exist between Cargill and Warren. The court concluded that Cargill interfered with the internal affairs of Warren, "which constituted de facto control of the elevator." According to the court, factors indicating Cargill's control over Warren included the following: "(1) Cargill's constant recommendations to Warren by telephone; (2) Cargill's right of first refusal on grain; (3) Warren's inability to enter into mort-

---

[17] 309 N.W.2d 285 (Minn. 1981).

[18] *See id.* at 287–90.

[19] It should be noted that Warren was located in the town of Warren, Minnesota and the jury pool was drawn from that community. *See id.* at 288, 295. As mentioned, the plaintiffs were local farmers, while defendant Cargill was a large corporation.

gages, to purchase stock or to pay dividends without Cargill's approval; (4) Cargill's right of entry onto Warren's premises to carry on periodic checks and audits; (5) Cargill's correspondence and criticism regarding Warren's finances, officers salaries and inventory; (6) Cargill's determination that Warren needed 'strong paternal guidance'; (7) Provision of drafts and forms to Warren upon which Cargill's name was imprinted; (8) Financing of all Warren's purchases of grain and operating expenses; and (9) Cargill's power to discontinue the financing of Warren's operations." In addition to control, the court concluded that Warren acted on behalf of Cargill "in procuring grain for Cargill as the part of its normal operations which were totally financed by Cargill." In short, the combination of the control by Cargill and the grain supply benefits to Cargill led the court to conclude that an agency relationship had been established.[20]

The holding of *Cargill* is controversial. With respect to control, when a lender finances a business, it is common for the lender to impose various conditions on how the money can be used and how the business may run its operations—e.g., the funds can be used for expansion purposes only, liabilities cannot be increased above a certain ratio or amount, decisions to sell key assets require the lender's approval, etc. These conditions give the lender a degree of control over the business, but is that control enough to meet the element of the agency definition? Section 14O of the Second Restatement, which the court cited, provides some general guidance by stating that "[a] creditor who assumes control of his debtor's business for the mutual benefit of himself and his debtor, may become a principal, with liability for the acts and transactions of the debtor in connection with the business." The comment to the section, however, is more helpful:

> A security holder who merely exercises a veto power over the business acts of his debtor by preventing purchases or

---

[20] *See id.* at 289–91. Cargill's interest in Warren is easier to understand with some historical context:

> These events occurred in the midst of the "Great Grain Robbery" that occurred after President Richard Nixon authorized grain sales to the Soviet Union and China. Grain firms like Cargill then sold about 25 percent of America's grain harvest to the Soviet[s], pushing up grain prices to unheard of levels ("beans in the teens") and having widespread effects on nearly every area of the economy. "It was one of those economic events . . . that . . . can truly be said to have changed the world." Dan Morgan, *Merchants of Grain* 121 (1979). Cargill badly needed grain to fulfill the contracts it made with the Soviet Union and other purchasers. It needed Warren's supplies, as well as those of other grain elevators.

THOMAS LEE HAZEN & JERRY W. MARKHAM, CORPORATIONS AND OTHER BUSINESS ENTERPRISES 34 (3d ed. 2009).

sales above specified amounts does not thereby become a principal. However, if he takes over the management of the debtor's business either in person or through an agent, and directs what contracts may or may not be made, he becomes a principal, liable as any principal for the obligations incurred thereafter in the normal course of business by the debtor who has now become his general agent. The point at which the creditor becomes a principal is that at which he assumes de facto control over the conduct of his debtor, whatever the terms of the formal contract with his debtor may be.

This section and its accompanying commentary highlight the difference between "affirmative" control (i.e., the power to initiate or direct transactions) and "negative" or "passive" control (i.e., the power to limit, block, or veto conduct that is initiated by others). Whereas affirmative control is substantial and generally goes beyond the control that most creditors possess, negative control, such as the ability to veto transactions that substantially threaten the debtor's prospect of repayment is, as previously mentioned, a very common feature of lending arrangements. The commentary to § 140 recognizes this distinction to the extent that it indicates that the mere exercise of a veto power is typically insufficient to create a principal-agent relationship.[21]

Did Cargill exercise more than "negative" control? Cargill's approval was needed for entering into mortgages, purchasing stock, or paying dividends, but those are just examples of veto power. As mentioned, the court stated that Cargill made "constant recommendations to Warren," it noted "Cargill's correspondence and criticism regarding Warren's finances, officers salaries and inventory," and it highlighted Cargill's determination that Warren needed "strong paternal guidance." Recommendations, correspondence, criticism, and internal determinations, however, are not the same as the existence of an affirmative power to direct the business. After all, a debtor like Warren could just reject the recommendations and criticism and continue to operate its business as it desired. There was some evidence, in fact, that Warren did just that.[22] Without evidence

---

[21] *See also* RESTATEMENT (THIRD) OF AGENCY § 1.01 cmt. f (2006) ("The right to veto another's decisions does not by itself create the right to give affirmative directives that action be taken, which is integral to the right of control within common-law agency. Thus, a debtor does not become a creditor's agent when a loan agreement gives the creditor veto rights over decisions the debtor may make. Moreover, typically a debtor does not consent to act on behalf of the creditor as opposed to acting in its own interests.").

[22] As the court noted:

Between 1967 and 1973, Cargill suggested that Warren take a number of steps, including: (1) a reduction of seed grain and cash grain inventories; (2) improved collection of accounts receivable; (3) reduction or elimination of its wholesale seed business and its specialty grain operation; (4) marketing fertilizer and

that Cargill went beyond recommendations and criticism and actually assumed the power to initiate transactions or to direct changes within Warren, Cargill's input could have been viewed simply as input, and not as evidence of significant control. Thus, although the *Cargill* court states definitively that "Cargill was an active participant in Warren's operations rather than simply a financier," and that "Cargill made the key economic decisions," the basis for these and related statements would seem to be in question.[23]

Even assuming that the control element was met, what about the "on behalf of" element of the agency inquiry? Was Warren acting primarily for the benefit of Cargill? Cargill clearly benefitted from its relationship by receiving interest on the loaned sums as well as a steady supply of grain, but Warren also benefitted by earning money from its grain resale business as well as its other business pursuits.[24] When a debtor is attempting to generate income for itself in its own business, there is a strong argument that it is operating primarily for its own benefit rather than for the benefit of another.[25] (Indeed, the fact that Warren's officer salaries were high enough to prompt complaint by Cargill suggests that Warren's officers were primarily running the business for their benefit and not for Cargill's.) Even if the proceeds from Warren's sales were largely used to repay the Cargill debt, it is not clear why the court did not view the debt as facilitating Warren's own business—a business where Cargill happens to be a primary lender and customer, but a business nonetheless. Instead, the court viewed the financial and customer ties between Cargill and Warren as an indication that Warren lacked an independent business all together.[26]

---

steel bins on consignment; (5) a reduction in withdrawals made by officers; (6) a suggestion that Warren's bookkeeper not issue her own salary checks; and (7) cooperation with Cargill in implementing the recommendations. *These ideas were apparently never implemented, however.*

Cargill, 309 N.W.2d at 289 n.4 (emphasis added).

[23] *Id.* at 291–93.

[24] Even though the court noted that Warren was shipping up to 90% of its cash grain to Cargill, Warren was presumably benefitting from those sales by earning the difference between the price at which it purchased the grain from farmers and the price at which it resold that grain to Cargill. Moreover, Warren also benefitted by selling to customers other than Cargill. *See id.* at 289 (noting that Warren was at one point shipping Cargill 90% of its cash grain, but also stating that "[w]hen Cargill's facilities were full, Warren shipped its grain to other companies," and further mentioning that "[a]pproximately 25% of Warren's total sales was seed grain which was sold directly by Warren to its customers"); *cf. id.* at 288 n.3 (stating that "Cargill hoped that Warren's profits would be used to decrease its debt balance").

[25] *Cf.* RESTATEMENT (THIRD) OF AGENCY § 1.01 cmt. f (2006) (noting that "typically a debtor does not consent to act on behalf of the creditor as opposed to acting in its own interests").

[26] Cargill alternatively argued that its relationship with Warren was that of buyer-supplier rather than principal-agent. The Second Restatement distinguishes an

At bottom, the *Cargill* court seemed to believe that Warren was simply a business being run for Cargill's advantage. In such circumstances, one can make a basic economic argument for liability: a creditor should be required to internalize all of the costs of a business being run for its benefit. Put differently, the court may have believed that Cargill's relationship allowed it to get the benefits of Warren's business without the accompanying obligations—a situation that is rectified by holding Cargill liable as a principal for the debts of Warren.[27]

After *Cargill*, should banks and other lenders have anything to fear? The amici curiae argued in *Cargill* that lenders would decline to make further loans to grain elevators if liability on an agency theory were imposed. The *Cargill* court attempted to alleviate such concerns by distinguishing the Cargill-Warren relationship from an "ordinary bank financing, since Cargill was an active participant in Warren's operations rather than simply a financier." According to the court, "there was a unique fabric in the relationship between Cargill and Warren which varies from that found in normal debtor-

---

agent from a supplier by observing that "[o]ne who contracts to acquire property from a third person and convey it to another is the agent of the other only if it is agreed that he is to act primarily for the benefit of the other and not for himself." RESTATEMENT (SECOND) OF AGENCY § 14K (1958). As mentioned, because Warren was attempting to generate income for itself in its own business, there is a strong argument that it was operating primarily for its own benefit rather than for the benefit of Cargill. Pursuant to § 14K, this would counter an inference of agency.

The commentary to § 14K further observes that "[f]actors indicating that the one who is to acquire the property and transfer it to the other is selling to, and not acting as agent for, the other are: (1) That he is to receive a fixed price for the property, irrespective of the price paid by him. This is the most important. (2) That he acts in his own name and receives the title to the property which he thereafter is to transfer. (3) That he has an independent business in buying and selling similar property." *Id.* § 14K cmt. a. The *Cargill* court stated that "[u]nder the Restatement approach, it must be shown that the supplier has an independent business before it can be concluded that he is not an agent." Because the court determined that Warren lacked an independent business, it concluded that "the relationship which existed between the parties was not merely that of buyer and supplier." *Cargill*, 309 N.W.2d at 292. This conclusion is puzzling. Given that Warren earned money by selling to Cargill as well as other customers, *see* note 24 and accompanying text, it is unclear why the court did not view Warren as an independent business. Moreover, there is nothing in the comment indicating that the "independent business" concept is a *requirement* for supplier status; instead, it is listed only as a factor, and not even as the most important factor.

[27] Indeed, the court noted that "Cargill became, in essence, the owner of the [Warren] operation without the accompanying legal indicia." *See Cargill*, 309 N.W.2d at 292. Because Cargill did not get the profits from Warren's operation, however, the court's conclusion arguably imposes Warren's costs on Cargill without its benefits. *But see* STEPHEN M. BAINBRIDGE, AGENCY, PARTNERSHIPS & LLCs 28–29 n.30 (2004) ("This analysis, however, overlooks the local monopoly typically enjoyed by grain elevators. Cargill's relationship with Warren gave it the benefit of Warren's local monopoly—i.e., sole access to the grain harvested in the area.").

creditor situations."[28] As discussed above, this conclusion is debatable.

Going forward, opinions like *Cargill* would seem to increase the cost of borrowing for debtors. Even if a creditor exercised only negative control over a debtor, *Cargill* suggests that there is some risk of agency liability being imposed. A creditor who appreciates this risk will presumably refuse to make loans that it otherwise would have made or will charge more for the loans to compensate for the increased risk of liability. Another alternative is that a creditor will significantly decrease the level of control exercised over a debtor in an effort to avoid the risk of agency liability. A decrease in control, however, increases the risk of default to the creditor. Correspondingly, the creditor will presumably charge more for the loan to compensate for this heightened default risk.

C. Liability From the Agency Relationship

What liability is created when an agent interacts with a third party? This is the most common question that arises out of a principal-agent relationship. Because the principal's liability for an agent's tortious acts is addressed in many first-year torts courses, most professors give this topic very little coverage (if any) in an upper-level business law class. Instead, a business law course typically focuses on contract liability from the agency relationship. Accordingly, contract liability is emphasized in the materials below, although the basics of tort liability are also discussed.

1. Tort Liability From the Agency Relationship

a. Distinguishing Between Servants and Independent Contractors

A general tenet of agency law is that a principal has the right to control the conduct of an agent with respect to matters entrusted to the agent.[29] The principal can determine what the ultimate goal is, and the agent must strive to meet that goal. The degree of control that the principal has over the acts of the agent may vary widely within the agency relationship. In this respect, the Second Restatement distinguishes between a master/servant relationship and an independent contractor relationship.[30]

A *master* is a principal who "employs an agent to perform service in his affairs and who controls or has the right to control the physical

---

[28] *Cargill*, 309 N.W.2d at 292–93.

[29] *See* RESTATEMENT (SECOND) OF AGENCY § 14 (1958); RESTATEMENT (THIRD) OF AGENCY § 1.01 (2006).

[30] *See* RESTATEMENT (SECOND) OF AGENCY § 2 (1958).

conduct of the other in the performance of the service." A *servant* is an agent so employed by a master.[31] In some sense, the use of the words master and servant for this relationship is unfortunate because those words may imply servility, household service, or manual labor. The relationship is not so limited; indeed, under these definitions, most employment relationships are technically master/servant relationships.[32] An *independent contractor* is a "person who contracts with another to do something for him but who is not controlled by the other nor subject to the other's right to control with respect to his physical conduct in the performance of the undertaking."[33] In general, if a person is subject to the control of another as to the means used to achieve a particular result, he is a servant. By contrast, if a person is subject to the control of another as to his results only (but not over how to achieve those results), he is an independent contractor.

Example: General Motors Corporation employs an individual to serve as head designer of a new automobile. His salary is $300,000 per year. The designer is a "servant" in the Second Restatement terminology and General Motors is his "master." As evidence, consider this possible scenario: the chief executive officer of General Motors comes to the designer and says, "John, the board of directors liked your sketches for the new convertible. They feel, however, that it looks a little boxy and they think the headlights are too conspicuous. Please streamline it a little more and move the headlights into the front fenders." What should the head designer do? He makes the changes that are requested, thereby indicating that he is a servant.

Example: A builder enters into a contract with the owner of a lot to build a house on the lot in accordance with certain plans and specifications prepared by an architect. The builder is an independent contractor. He is employed merely to accomplish a specific result and is not otherwise subject to the owner's control.

Example: A broker enters into a contract to sell goods for a manufacturer. His arrangement involves the receipt of a salary plus a commission on each sale, but the broker has discretion as to how to conduct his business. He determines which cities to visit and who to

---

[31] *See id.* §§ 2, 220(1). Thus, a master is a subcategory of principal, and a servant is a subcategory of agent. *See id.* § 2 cmt. a.

[32] *See, e.g., id.* § 220 cmt. a ("The word [servant] indicates the closeness of the relation between the one giving and the one receiving the service rather than the nature of the service or the importance of the one giving it. Thus, ship captains and managers of great corporations are normally superior servants, differing only in the dignity and importance of their positions from those working under them. The rules for determining the liability of the employer for the conduct of both superior servants and the humblest employees are the same. . . .").

[33] *Id.* § 2(3).

contact. He uses his own automobile to visit prospects. The broker is an independent contractor because the manufacturer does not control the details of how the broker conducts his day-to-day business.[34]

It is often difficult to determine whether a person is a servant or an independent contractor. The Second Restatement includes a somewhat dated provision that lists the following factors to consider in making the determination:

(a) the extent of control which, by the agreement, the master may exercise over the details of the work;

(b) whether or not the one employed is engaged in a distinct occupation or business;

(c) the kind of occupation, with reference to whether, in the locality, the work is usually done under the direction of the employer or by a specialist without supervision;

(d) the skill required in the particular occupation;

(e) whether the employer or the workman supplies the instrumentalities, tools, and the place of work for the person doing the work;

(f) the length of time for which the person is employed;

(g) the method of payment, whether by the time or by the job;

(h) whether or not the work is a part of the regular business of the employer;

(i) whether or not the parties believe they are creating the relation of master and servant; and

---

[34] While all servants are agents, an independent contractor may or may not be an agent. *See id.* § 2. In general, a non-agent independent contractor exists when one or more of the basic elements of the agency relationship are absent—e.g., when there is insufficient control over the contractor, or when the contractor is acting primarily in his own interests. *See, e.g., Kemether v. Pa. Interscholastic Athletic Ass'n, Inc.,* 15 F. Supp. 2d 740, 748 (E.D. Pa. 1998) ("Where prerequisites of agency, such as control, are not satisfied, a non-agent independent contractor relationship may exist: A person who contracts to accomplish something for another or to deliver something to another, but who is not acting as a fiduciary for the other is a non-agent contractor. He may be anyone who has made a contract and who is not an agent." (internal quotation omitted)). In this Chapter, we are concerned only with independent contractors who would also be legally characterized as agents.

(j)   whether the principal is or is not in business.[35]

In which direction do these factors cut? With respect to (a), more control by the principal over the details of the work suggests servant status. For (b), the presence of a distinct occupation or business for the worker leans toward independent contractor status, as there is some business to conduct outside of the principal's operations. A more substantial degree of supervision in (c) indicates servant status. For (d), work which does not require the services of highly skilled individuals suggests servant status. With respect to (e), the employer providing the materials necessary for the work to be accomplished favors servant status (if provided by the worker, independent contractor status is suggested). A longer length of time of employment in (f) indicates servant status, as independent contractor assignments are often one-time engagements. Payment by time in (g) suggests servant status, while payment by the job suggests independent contractor status. The task being part of the employer's regular business in (h) indicates servant status, as servants typically work on assignments related to the employer's business. For (i), the parties' belief that they are creating a master-servant relationship obviously favors servant status. Finally, with respect to (j), the fact that the principal is in business suggests servant status—presumably because, as in (h), servants typically work on assignments related to the employer's business, but also because an operating business is more likely to have the resources necessary to exercise the degree of control that is required for servant status.

Why does the law care (and why should you care) about whether a person is a servant or an independent contractor? The classification of an agent as a servant or an independent contractor is important primarily because different rules apply with respect to the liability of the principal for harm caused by the agent's tortious conduct. While a master is liable for torts committed by a servant within the scope of his employment, a principal is generally not liable for torts committed by an independent contractor in connection with his work.[36] Thus, the determination of whether a person is a servant or an independent contractor can be outcome-determinative in a particular dispute.

---

[35] *See* RESTATEMENT (SECOND) OF AGENCY § 220(2) (1958); *see also* RESTATEMENT (THIRD) OF AGENCY § 7.07 cmt. f (2006) (listing similar factors). A more modern list might include factors such as whether the employer uses a W–4 form for the employee, or whether the employee is listed as such on insurance forms.

[36] *See* RESTATEMENT (SECOND) OF AGENCY §§ 219, 250 (1958); *cf.* RESTATEMENT (THIRD) OF AGENCY § 7.07 (2006) (imposing similar liability rules but not using the terms "master," "servant," or "independent contractor").

Example: *P*, the owner of a successful retail operation with two stores, hires *D* to drive her delivery truck and to deliver goods to her two stores. Before doing so, *P* checks *D*'s driving record and arranges for him to go to a driving school for truck drivers. *D*'s record shows that he has had no accidents for 20 years, and he completes the driving school program without difficulty. Three weeks later, while driving *P*'s delivery truck, *D* is negligent and has a serious accident, injuring *T*. *P* is liable to *T* for his injuries.

In this example, *D* is a servant, and *P*'s liability is independent of whether *P* exercised due care in hiring *D*, or even whether she knew that *D* was her employee at all. *P*'s liability, however, only applies to actions within the scope of *D*'s employment. *P*'s liability in this situation may be described as "vicarious liability" and the consequence of "respondeat superior." *Vicarious liability* refers to the imposition of liability on one person for the actionable conduct of another. *Respondeat superior* is a Latin phrase that means "let the master respond."

Example: The manufacturer's broker, who is selling goods in one of the above examples, has an automobile accident while driving his own car to visit a prospect. The manufacturer is not liable for injuries to third persons arising from the accident. The same would be true of a person injured by the builder in the above example while working on the owner's house. Because the broker and the builder are both independent contractors, the general rule of non-liability for the principal applies.

Of course, the broker and the builder themselves would both be personally liable for the injuries that they caused in these examples, as a person is always responsible for his own torts. *D*, the servant in the above delivery truck example, would also be personally liable for *T*'s injuries, since he too is a tortfeasor. This illustrates the difference between direct liability (a person is always responsible for his own torts) and vicarious liability (a person is sometimes, but not always, responsible for the torts of another).[37]

The Third Restatement does not use the terms "master," "servant," or "independent contractor." Instead, the Third Restatement simply defines an "employee" as "an agent whose principal controls or has the right to control the manner and means of the agent's performance of work," and it provides that "[a]n employer is subject to

---

[37] *See* RESTATEMENT (SECOND) OF AGENCY § 343 (1958); RESTATEMENT (THIRD) OF AGENCY § 7.01 (2006). Similarly, while agency concepts may make a principal vicariously liable for the acts of an agent, the principal may also be directly liable for the principal's own tortious behavior (e.g., negligent hiring or negligent supervision). *See, e.g.*, RESTATEMENT (SECOND) OF AGENCY § 213 (1958); RESTATEMENT (THIRD) OF AGENCY §§ 7.03(1), 7.05 (2006).

vicarious liability for a tort committed by its employee acting within the scope of employment."[38] Under the Third Restatement, therefore, there are "employee agents" and "nonemployee agents," with the latter term analogous to the "independent contractor" language of the Second Restatement.

b. Liability for the Torts of Servants

As mentioned, the general rule is that a master is liable for the torts committed by a servant within the scope of the servant's employment. What is the rationale for this rule of vicarious liability? One basis for its application is that the servant may be judgment proof and have no insurance of his own. As a consequence, the injured party's only recourse is against the principal. As further justification for the doctrine, consider the following:

> What has emerged as the modern justification for vicarious liability is a rule of policy, a deliberate allocation of a risk. The losses caused by the torts of employees, which as a practical matter are sure to occur in the conduct of the employer's enterprise, are placed upon that enterprise itself, as a required cost of doing business. They are placed upon the employer because, having engaged in an enterprise, which will on the basis of all past experience involve harm to others through the torts of employees, and sought to profit by it, it is just that he, rather than the innocent injured plaintiff, should bear them; and because he is better able to absorb them, and to distribute them, through prices, rates or liability insurance, to the public, and so to shift them to society, to the community at large. Added to this is the makeweight argument that an employer who is held strictly liable is under the greatest incentive to be careful in the selection, instruction and supervision of his servants, and to take every precaution to see that the enterprise is conducted safely.[39]

The principal is only liable when the servant acts within the scope of his employment. This "scope of employment" restriction is the subject of numerous published decisions. According to § 228(1) of the Second Restatement, a servant's conduct is within the scope of employment "if, but only if . . . (a) it is of the kind he is employed to perform; (b) it occurs substantially within the authorized time and space limits; (c) it is actuated, at least in part, by a purpose to serve the master, and (d) if force is intentionally used by the servant against another, the use of force is not unexpectable by the mas-

---

[38] RESTATEMENT (THIRD) OF AGENCY § 7.07 (2006).

[39] W. PAGE KEETON ET AL., PROSSER AND KEETON ON THE LAW OF TORTS § 69, at 500–01 (5th ed. 1984) (footnote omitted).

ter."[40] Notice that, as subsection (d) suggests, even an intentional tort committed by an employee can be viewed as within the scope of employment.[41]

With respect to subsection (c), it should be noted that many courts have found that the servant was acting with a purpose to serve the master on very tenuous facts. In *Nelson v. American-West African Line*,[42] for example, a drunken boatswain (the foreman of the crew) started a fight with (and injured) a crew member who was trying to sleep in his bunk. Although Judge Learned Hand acknowledged that "unless there was some evidence that he supposed himself engaged upon the ship's business, the ship was not liable," he concluded that the boatswain might have thought that he was acting in the interest of the ship. As the court noted, "[i]f he really meant to rouse the plaintiff and send him upon duty, if he really meant to act as boatswain and for the ship, however imbecile his conduct it was his master's."[43]

---

[40] For additional guidance on whether a servant/employee's actions are within the scope of his employment, see RESTATEMENT (SECOND) OF AGENCY §§ 229–237 (1958). The Third Restatement's formulation of the scope of employment doctrine is stated in more general terms: "An employee acts within the scope of employment when performing work assigned by the employer or engaging in a course of conduct subject to the employer's control. An employee's act is not within the scope of employment when it occurs within an independent course of conduct not intended by the employee to serve any purpose of the employer." See RESTATEMENT (THIRD) OF AGENCY § 7.07(2) (2006).

[41] See, e.g., RESTATEMENT (THIRD) OF AGENCY § 7.07 cmt. c (2006) ("Intentional torts and other intentional wrongdoing may be within the scope of employment. For example, if an employee's job duties include determining the prices at which the employer's output will be sold to customers, the employee's agreement with a competitor to fix prices is within the scope of employment unless circumstances establish a departure from the scope of employment. Likewise, when an employee's job duties include making statements to prospective customers to induce them to buy from the employer, intentional misrepresentations made by the employee are within the scope of employment unless circumstances establish that the employee has departed from it.").

[42] 86 F.2d 730 (2d Cir. 1936).

[43] *Id.* at 731–32. In *Ira S. Bushey & Sons, Inc. v. United States,* 398 F.2d 167 (2d Cir. 1968), the court went even further by holding the employer liable on a foreseeability theory even though the employee concededly had no purpose to serve the employer. See id. at 170–72; see also RESTATEMENT (THIRD) OF AGENCY § 7.07 cmt. b (2006) (criticizing a foreseeability approach).

Many cases involving the scope of employment concern whether an employee was on a "frolic" (an act of the employee outside the scope of employment because it was done for the employee's own benefit) or whether the conduct should simply be viewed as a "detour" (an act usually considered to be within the scope of employment because it is only a minor deviation from the employee's task). As one authority explains:

Take an employee who is told to drive a truck from city A to city B, fifty miles away. The employee drives thirty miles out of his way to visit a friend in city C and negligently injures someone while engaged in this digression. If the deviation from the assigned route is considered sufficiently great to be classified as a "frolic" on the part of the employee, the employer may not be liable for the accident in these circumstances. But as the relative extent of the deviation dimin-

c. Liability for the Torts of Independent Contractors

As mentioned, a principal is not generally liable for torts committed by an independent contractor in connection with his work. In *Anderson v. Marathon Petroleum Co.*,[44] the Seventh Circuit explained the rationale for this rule:

> Generally a principal is not liable for an independent contractor's torts even if they are committed in the performance of the contract and even though a principal is liable under the doctrine of respondeat superior for the torts of his employees if committed in the furtherance of their employment. The reason for distinguishing the independent contractor from the employee is that, by definition of the relationship between a principal and an independent contractor, the principal does not supervise the details of the independent contractor's work and therefore is not in a good position to prevent negligent performance, whereas the essence of the contractual relationship known as employment is that the employee surrenders to the employer the right to direct the details of his work, in exchange for receiving a wage. The independent contractor commits himself to providing a specified output, and the principal monitors the contractor's performance not by monitoring inputs—i.e., supervising the contractor—but by inspecting the contractually specified output to make sure it conforms to the specifications. This method of monitoring works fine if it is feasible for the principal to specify and monitor output, but sometimes it is not feasible, particularly if the output consists of the joint product of many separate producers whose specific contributions are difficult (sometimes impossible) to disentangle. In such a case it may be more efficient for the principal to monitor inputs rather than output—the producers rather than the product. By becoming an employee a producer in effect submits himself to that kind of monitoring, receiving payment for the work he puts in rather than for the output he produces.

> Since an essential element of the employment relationship is thus the employer's monitoring of the employee's work, a principal who is not knowledgeable about the details of some

---

ishes, so that the digression becomes a mere "detour," the chances of the employer being held liable increase.

GEORGE C. CHRISTIE ET AL., CASES AND MATERIALS ON THE LAW OF TORTS 401 (3d ed. 1997); *see also* KEETON ET AL., *supra* note 39, § 70, at 505 ("Essentially the question is one of major and minor departures, having always in mind that the employer is to be held liable for those things which are fairly to be regarded as risks of his business.").

[44] 801 F.2d 936 (7th Cir. 1986).

task is likely to delegate it to an independent contractor. Hence in general, though of course not in every case, the principal who uses an independent contractor will not be as well placed as an employer would be to monitor the work and make sure it is done safely. This is the reason as we have said for not making the principal vicariously liable for the torts of his independent contractors.[45]

Despite this general rule, there are circumstances where liability is imposed on a principal for the torts of an independent contractor. Examples of such circumstances include non-delegable duties (such as duties associated with abnormally dangerous activities), torts that are authorized by the principal, and fraud or misrepresentation (in some situations) by the agent.[46]

2. Contract Liability From the Agency Relationship

A contractual transaction between an agent and a third party may impose liability upon the principal, the third party, and/or the agent. This liability inquiry is often affected by the type of principal that is present in the transaction: (1) a "disclosed" principal; (2) a "partially disclosed" principal; or (3) an "undisclosed" principal.

A principal is *disclosed* if, at the time of the agent's transaction, the third party has notice that the agent is acting for a principal and has notice of the principal's identity.[47] It may be, of course, that in a specific situation, a third person does not actually know who the principal is, but should be able to reasonably infer the identity of the principal from the information on hand. This is still a disclosed principal situation.[48]

A principal is *partially disclosed* if, at the time of the agent's transaction, the third party has notice that the agent is or may be acting for a principal, but has no notice of the principal's identity.[49]

Example: *A offers to sell goods to T, truthfully advising T that A is the manufacturer's representative for a well-known manufactur-*

---

[45] *Id.* at 938–39.

[46] *See, e.g.,* RESTATEMENT (SECOND) OF AGENCY §§ 212, 214–216, 250–267 (1958); RESTATEMENT (THIRD) OF AGENCY §§ 7.03–7.06, 7.08 (2006). For additional information, see KEETON ET AL., *supra* note 39, § 71, at 509–16 (discussing exceptions to the general rule of non-liability for the conduct of independent contractors).

[47] *See* RESTATEMENT (SECOND) OF AGENCY § 4(1) (1958); RESTATEMENT (THIRD) OF AGENCY § 1.04(2)(a) (2006).

[48] *See* RESTATEMENT (SECOND) OF AGENCY § 9(1) (1958); RESTATEMENT (THIRD) OF AGENCY § 1.04(4) (2006).

[49] *See* RESTATEMENT (SECOND) OF AGENCY § 4(2) (1958). Instead of the term "partially disclosed" principal, the Third Restatement uses the term "unidentified" principal. *See* RESTATEMENT (THIRD) OF AGENCY § 1.04(2)(c) (2006).

er. The identity of the manufacturer is not disclosed. The manufacturer is a partially disclosed principal.

A principal is *undisclosed* if, at the time of the agent's transaction, the third party has no notice that the agent is acting for a principal.[50] In effect, the third party is dealing with the agent as though the agent is the real party in interest.

a. Liability of the Principal to the Third Party

A principal will be liable on a contract between the agent and a third party when the agent acts with actual authority, apparent authority, or inherent authority. Even when the agent lacks one of these three types of authority, the principal may be liable under the doctrines of estoppel or ratification.

(1) Actual Authority

Actual authority (often described as *express authority* or simply by the words "authority" or "authorized") arises from the manifestation of a *principal to an agent* that the agent has power to deal with others as a representative of the principal. An agent who agrees to act in accordance with that manifestation has actual authority to so act, and his actions without more bind the principal.[51] Put differently, if the principal's words or conduct would lead a reasonable person in the agent's position to believe that the agent has authority to act on the principal's behalf, the agent has actual authority to bind the principal.

Example: *P*, the owner of two retail stores, employs *C* to serve as credit manager. *P* has orally given *C* the authority to review and approve requests from customers for the extension of credit. *C* reviews the application of *Y* and approves him for the extension of credit. *C* has actual authority to approve *Y*, and *P* is bound by *C*'s decision.

Example: *P* goes to an office where, as he knows, several brokers have desks, and leaves upon the desk of *A*, thinking it to be the desk of *X*, a note signed by *P*, which states: "I authorize you to contract in my name for the purchase of 100 shares of Western Union stock at today's market." Unaware of the mistake, *A* comes to work, finds the note, and makes a contract with *T* in *P*'s name for the purchase of the shares. *A* has actual authority to make the contract, and *P* is bound by *A*'s action.

---

[50] *See* RESTATEMENT (SECOND) OF AGENCY § 4(3) (1958); RESTATEMENT (THIRD) OF AGENCY § 1.04(2)(b) (2006).

[51] *See* RESTATEMENT (SECOND) OF AGENCY §§ 7, 26, 32–34, 144, 186 (1958); RESTATEMENT (THIRD) OF AGENCY §§ 2.01–2.02, 3.01, 6.01–6.03 (2006).

Actual authority may be *express* (e.g., oral or written statements, including provisions in the company's organizational documents) or *implied* (e.g., inferred from words used, from custom, or from the relations between the parties).[52]

Example: *P* is an elderly person living alone. He is befriended by *A*, a neighbor. *A* does errands for *P*, going to the store, helping *P* go to the doctor, and so forth. *P* has long had a charge account at a local grocery store that *A* has used frequently to charge groceries for *P*. The approval by *P* of *A*'s prior transactions would lead a reasonable person in *A*'s position to believe that he had authority to buy groceries for *P* in the future. This is implied actual authority based on *P*'s acceptance of the groceries in the past.[53]

A common type of implied actual authority is incidental authority. *Incidental authority* is simply authority to do incidental acts that are related to a transaction that is authorized. As the Third Restatement explains:

> If a principal's manifestation to an agent expresses the principal's wish that something be done, it is natural to assume that the principal wishes, as an incidental matter, that the agent take the steps necessary and that the agent proceed in the usual and ordinary way, if such has been established, unless the principal directs otherwise. The underlying assumptions are that the principal does not wish to authorize what cannot be achieved if necessary steps are not taken by the agent, and that the principal's manifestation often will not specify all steps necessary to translate it into action.[54]

---

[52] *See* RESTATEMENT (SECOND) OF AGENCY § 7 cmt. c (1958) ("It is possible for a principal to specify minutely what the agent is to do. To the extent that he does this, the agent may be said to have express authority. But most authority is created by implication. . . . [Such authority may be] implied or inferred from the words used, from customs and from the relations of the parties. [It is] described as 'implied authority.'"); RESTATEMENT (THIRD) OF AGENCY § 2.02(1) (2006) (noting that an agent has actual authority "to take action designated or implied in the principal's manifestations to the agent").

[53] *Cf.* RESTATEMENT (SECOND) OF AGENCY § 43(2) (1958) ("Acquiescence by the principal in a series of acts by the agent indicates authorization to perform similar acts in the future."); RESTATEMENT (THIRD) OF AGENCY § 2.02 cmt. f (2006) ("On prior occasions the principal may have affirmatively approved of the agent's unauthorized act or silently acquiesced in it by failing to voice affirmative disapproval. This history is likely to influence the agent's subsequent interpretation of instructions. If the principal's subsequent instructions do not address the history, the agent may well infer from the principal's silence that the principal will not demand compliance with the instructions to any degree greater than the principal has done in the past.").

[54] RESTATEMENT (THIRD) OF AGENCY § 2.02 cmt. d (2006); *see also id.* § 2.02(1) (stating that "an agent has actual authority to take action . . . necessary or incidental to achieving the principal's objectives"); RESTATEMENT (SECOND) OF AGENCY § 35 (1958) ("Unless otherwise agreed, authority to conduct a transaction includes authority to do

Example: *P* authorizes *A* to purchase and obtain goods for *P* but does not give *A* money to pay for them. Without an arrangement that *A* is to supply the money or is to buy upon his own credit, *A* has authority to buy upon *P*'s credit.

Example: *P* directs *A* to sell goods by auction although, as *P* and *A* know, a statute forbids anyone but a licensed auctioneer from conducting sales by auction. Nothing to the contrary appearing, *A*'s authority includes the authority to employ a licensed auctioneer.

(2) Apparent Authority

Apparent authority arises from the manifestation of a *principal to a third party* that another person is authorized to act as an agent for the principal. That other person has apparent authority and an act by him within the scope of that apparent authority binds the principal.[55] Put differently, if the principal's words or conduct would lead a reasonable person in the third party's position to believe that the agent (or other person) has authority to act on the principal's behalf, the agent (or other person) has apparent authority to bind the principal.[56]

Apparent authority commonly arises when a principal creates the impression that authority exists in an agent when in fact it does not. The theory is that if a third party relies on the appearance of authority, the third party may hold the principal liable for the action of the agent. As mentioned, the principal is bound by the agent's conduct within the scope of the agent's apparent authority, even though the conduct was not actually authorized by the principal.

---

acts which are incidental to it, usually accompany it, or are reasonably necessary to accomplish it.").

[55] *See* RESTATEMENT (SECOND) OF AGENCY §§ 8, 27, 49, 159 (1958); RESTATEMENT (THIRD) OF AGENCY §§ 2.03, 3.03, 6.01–6.02 (2006).

[56] Why the use of the phrase "the agent (or other person)" in the text? The simple answer is that apparent authority can exist even in the absence of a principal-agent relationship. For example, apparent authority can arise when a person falsely represents to a third party that someone else is his agent. *See, e.g.*, RESTATEMENT (THIRD) OF AGENCY § 2.03 (2006) ("Apparent authority is the power held by an agent *or other actor* to affect a principal's legal relations with third parties when a third party reasonably believes *the actor* has authority to act on behalf of the principal and that belief is traceable to the principal's manifestations."); *id.* § 2.03 cmt. a ("The [apparent authority] definition in this section does not presuppose the present or prior existence of an agency relationship. . . . The definition thus applies to actors who appear to be agents but are not, as well as to agents who act beyond the scope of their actual authority."); *see also* RESTATEMENT (SECOND) OF AGENCY § 27 (1958) (describing apparent authority and noting that it is created by the principal's conduct "which, reasonably interpreted, causes the third person to believe that the principal consents to have the act done on his behalf by *the person* purporting to act for him" (emphasis added)).

Example: *P* gives *A*, an agent who is authorized to sell a piece of property on behalf of *P*, specific instructions as to various terms of the sale, including the minimum price ($300,000) *P* is willing to accept. *P* informs possible buyers that *A* is his selling agent but obviously does not communicate *A*'s specific instructions to anyone but *A* (because to do so would be a virtual blueprint to possible buyers as to how to buy the property as cheaply as possible). *A* has actual authority only to enter into a contract to sell the property at a price equal to $300,000 or more. *A* has apparent authority, however, to sell the property at any price given that *P* has represented to possible buyers that *A* is his selling agent. Suppose that *A* signs a contract on behalf of *P* to sell *P*'s property to *T* for $275,000. *P* is bound on that contract because the action was within *A*'s apparent authority. Nevertheless, *A* has violated his instructions and is liable to *P* for the loss incurred.[57]

As the above text emphasizes, apparent authority is based on the principal's manifestations to a third party. Thus, apparent authority cannot be created by the mere representations of an agent or other actor. Not even the most convincing and persuasive person can create an agency or apparent agency relationship entirely on his own.[58]

Example: John is a smooth-talking con man. He becomes friends with *X* and represents to *X* that he is an agent for General Motors seeking possible owners of new car franchises. John is very convincing, showing forged letters on GM letterhead, a forged identification card, and so forth. He persuades *X* that he will obtain a franchise for *X* if *X* will pay $250,000. *X* does so. John disappears with *X*'s money. General Motors is not obligated to grant a franchise to *X* and is not otherwise liable for *X*'s loss.

Apparent authority may be established through an agent's title or position. Indeed, it is somewhat common for a third party to argue that an agent's title or position, which was given to him by the principal, created a reasonable belief in the third party that the agent was authorized to act for the principal in ways that are typical of someone who holds that title or position. This notion that title or position conveys authority can also be used to establish actual authority to the extent that the agent reasonably believes that he has

---

[57] *See* Chapter 2(D)(1).

[58] Interestingly, the Second Restatement states that the manifestation by the principal required for apparent authority can be established by the principal "authorizing the agent to state that he is authorized." RESTATEMENT (SECOND) OF AGENCY § 8 cmt. b (1958). Thus, an agent's representation to a third party—one made with the consent of the principal—should not be considered to be solely an act of the agent that is insufficient for apparent authority.

authority to act based on the title or position given to him by the principal.

For example, if *P* appoints *A* as "Treasurer," and nothing more is stated, *A* will reasonably believe that he has the authority that treasurers typically have, and third parties who deal with *A* (and are aware of his position) will reasonably believe the same. If *P* tells *A* that he will not have authority to write checks on the company's account, *A* will not have actual authority to do so. Assuming that a treasurer typically has the power to write company checks, however, *A* will have apparent authority to write checks with respect to third parties who are aware of his position but are unaware of the limitation on his authority.[59]

The major difference between apparent authority and actual authority is that actual authority flows from the principal to the agent, while apparent authority flows from the principal to the third party. As previously mentioned, if the principal's words or conduct would lead a reasonable person in the *agent's* position to believe that the agent has authority to act on the principal's behalf, the agent has actual authority, but if the principal's words or conduct would lead a reasonable person in the *third party's* position to believe that the agent (or other person) has authority to act on the principal's behalf, the agent (or other person) has apparent authority.[60]

In some circumstances, the scope of an agent's apparent authority will be equivalent to the scope of the agent's actual authority. For example, when a principal sends identical letters describing an agent's authority and its limits to both the agent and the third party, actual and apparent authority are co-extensive (assuming no other facts). As the above examples indicate, however, the scope of actual and apparent authority will not always be the same. It is, therefore, important to distinguish between the concepts and to recognize that liability for a principal may arise from statements or other manifestations made by the principal to an agent (actual authority), and/or

---

[59] *See, e.g.*, RESTATEMENT (SECOND) OF AGENCY § 27 cmt. a (1958) ("[A]s in the case of authority, apparent authority can be created by appointing a person to a position, such as that of manager or treasurer, which carries with it generally recognized duties; to those who know of the appointment there is apparent authority to do the things ordinarily entrusted to one occupying such a position, regardless of unknown limitations which are imposed upon the particular agent."); *id.* § 49 cmt. c ("Acts are interpreted in the light of ordinary human experience. If a principal puts an agent into, or knowingly permits him to occupy, a position in which according to the ordinary habits of persons in the locality, trade or profession, it is usual for such an agent to have a particular kind of authority, anyone dealing with him is justified in inferring that he has such authority, in the absence of reason to know otherwise. The content of such apparent authority is a matter to be determined from the facts.").

[60] Apparent authority cannot arise in an undisclosed principal situation. After all, when a principal is undisclosed, the third party has no idea that a principal is involved in the transaction. *See* notes 77–78 and accompanying text.

from statements or other manifestations made by the principal to a third party (apparent authority).[61]

An excellent example of apparent authority, as well as its relationship to actual authority, is provided by *Essco Geometric v. Harvard Industries*.[62] Harvard manufactured chairs and sold them to private and public entities. Diversified (Essco's trade name) sold foam that Harvard used in its chairs. Frank Best was Harvard's purchasing manager for over twenty years. During that time, Best cultivated a close business relationship with Edsel Safron, the president of Diversified. When Best retired, Michael Gray, the former purchasing agent, became the new purchasing manager for Harvard.

In 1989, Ed Kruske, the president of Harvard, issued two internal memoranda. The first directed that all purchase orders be initialed by Kruske prior to being sent out to a vendor. The second stipulated that all requisitions of fifty dollars or more have both the department manager's approval and Kruske's approval, unless an emergency arose. Gray received both of these directives, but no one outside of Harvard was notified of these changes in internal operating procedures.

In early 1990, Gray and Safron signed a letter that they believed represented an exclusive multi-million dollar contract between Harvard and Diversified for all of Harvard's foam needs over a two-year period. The agreement was different from prior practice to the extent that Harvard had ordinarily issued cancellable purchase orders whenever it needed foam. The letter agreement, however, purported to be an exclusive and non-cancellable requirements contract. Kruske refused to honor the agreement. As a result, Diversified sued Harvard for breach of contract on the grounds that Gray had actual

---

[61] Apparent authority (as well as other agency rules) can be justified through a "least cost avoider" concept. The concept is based on the notion that, in many situations, it makes sense to impose liability on the party who could have taken precautions against the loss in the least expensive manner. By imposing such liability, the party who could most easily and cheaply prevent the loss is incentivized to do so. As an example, recall the hypothetical where P appoints A as "Treasurer" but prohibits A from writing company checks. Assuming that treasurers typically have the power to write such checks, P's prohibition is unusual. One could argue that it will be cheaper for P, and the relatively few idiosyncratic principals like P, to take precautions against A acting beyond his actual authority (such as by providing A with a different title or with no title at all) than to require all potential third parties to investigate A's authority to write checks. If this argument is credited, it is appropriate to impose liability on P when A acts with apparent (but without actual) authority. Indeed, the principal is often the least cost avoider because principals have many tools to control agents acting beyond their actual authority (e.g., better monitoring, clearer instructions, greater care in the selection of agents). For more on the relationship between agency rules and the least cost avoider concept, see generally Eric Rasmusen, *Agency Law and Contract Formation*, 6 AM . L. & ECON. REV. 369 (2004).

[62] 46 F.3d 718 (8th Cir. 1995).

or apparent authority to bind Harvard to the agreement. A jury found for Diversified, and Harvard appealed.[63]

Did Gray have actual authority to bind Harvard to the agreement? The court noted that there was a lack of evidence on express actual authority, as no job description outlined the nature of Gray's responsibilities or the scope of his authority. Nevertheless, the court found sufficient evidence of implied actual authority to support the jury finding. First, Gray testified that he believed that he had the authority to enter into the transaction because of his job as the purchasing manager of the company. Second, in Gray's October 1989 performance evaluation, Harvard encouraged him to take a more active role in managing his department and reducing costs. Thus, Gray could have reasonably believed that he was authorized to act in ways that furthered those objectives (such as entering into a contract with a less expensive supplier like Diversified). Third, the court cited the custom and practice at Harvard and within the industry. Gray testified that, for approximately fifteen years, he had observed Harvard's former purchasing manager selecting vendors for the company. Other witnesses similarly testified that purchasing managers within the industry customarily made unsupervised decisions as to who would be their company's suppliers.

Notice that much of the evidence relied upon by the court focused on Gray's title or position. Because Harvard had given Gray the title of purchasing manager, he believed that he was authorized to enter into an agreement with Diversified. Why? Because Gray knew that Harvard had allowed the prior purchasing manager to enter into agreements with vendors, and because Gray was presumably aware that persons with the title of purchasing manager throughout the industry had similar authority. As a result, Gray could have reasonably believed that his title or position gave him the authority to enter into an agreement with Diversified.[64]

On the other hand, was it reasonable for him to believe that purchasing managers at Harvard could enter into non-cancellable agreements when that had not been the practice in the past? The court noted that, when Harvard selected a vendor, it usually sent between 60% and 70% of its foam needs to that vendor. Moreover, Harvard cancellations were "few and far between." In practice, therefore, the court did not seem to view the non-cancellable nature of the Diversified contract as significantly different from the agreements that Harvard purchase managers had entered into in the past. Thus, it

---

[63] *See id.* at 720–23.

[64] *Cf. id.* at 724 ("Thus, evidence that an agent historically engaged in related conduct, without limitation, would be enough to support a jury question on the issue of actual authority.").

was not necessarily unreasonable for Gray to believe that he had authority to enter into the non-cancellable Diversified contract. This was likely a very close call, however, as even the court admitted that "cancelable purchase orders constitute the daily and weekly routine," and that "an exclusive, non-cancelable requirements contract differs materially from a standard purchase order."[65] The procedural posture of the case becomes important here. Because the jury found that Gray was authorized, and because the court on appeal was simply looking to see if there was sufficient evidence to have submitted the case to the jury, close calls favored Diversified.

What about the two Harvard internal memoranda that seemed to restrict the authority of Harvard employees? Was it reasonable for Gray to think that he had authority to enter into the Diversified contract in light of these restrictions? The court noted that Kruske's directives were issued because he wanted to cut costs and maintain high quality controls. Because Gray believed that Diversified was an inexpensive and high-quality vendor, the court observed that "[a] reasonable jury could thus conclude that Gray's decision to sign the letter [agreement] fully comported with the purpose behind the directives."[66] Thus, the court accepted a "spirit over letter" argument— i.e., the requirement of Kruske's approval was simply to insure that a contract furthered the company's interests. Because there was evidence suggesting that the Diversified contract did further Harvard's interests, a jury could find that Gray was reasonable in believing that he had complied with the directives. One would think, however, that the Kruske memoranda were issued so that he (rather than the employees) could determine if the company's contracts were beneficial, and that the requirement for his approval was not simply a formality that employees could decide to ignore. Once again, this was likely a close call.

What about Gray's apparent authority? Was it reasonable for Diversified to believe that Harvard had given Gray the authority to enter into the letter agreement? The court observed that, for over twenty years, Harvard had allowed its former purchasing manager (Frank Best) to select vendors for Harvard. When Gray replaced Best, the court noted that "no one ever advised Diversified that Harvard had instituted new internal operating procedures or that the purchasing manager would have less authority to negotiate on behalf of the company."[67] Thus, Harvard's acceptance of its purchasing manager's contracts over the years—a course of conduct that Diversified was aware of—reasonably suggested to Diversified that Har-

---

[65] *Id.* at 724–25.

[66] *Id.* at 725.

[67] *Id.* at 726.

vard's purchasing manager had the authority to bind the company. Even though Diversified knew that Harvard had never entered into a non-cancellable requirements contract, the court cited testimony that industry custom presumed without question that the person in the position of purchasing manager possessed the authority to bind the company. Based on this custom, it was not unreasonable for Diversified to believe that the person designated by Harvard as purchasing manager did have authority to enter into a non-cancellable requirements contract, even though such contracts had not been the prior practice between the parties.[68] The court concluded that, "[a]s with actual authority, the evidence and inferences therefrom led to differing conclusions, and were matters for resolution by the jury."[69]

Why were Kruske's internal memoranda not mentioned by the court in its apparent authority discussion? Recall that apparent authority addresses a principal's manifestations and how they affect the reasonable beliefs of a third party. Because Diversified knew nothing about the internal memoranda, they are not relevant to an apparent authority analysis.

Why was the evidence of industry custom regarding the authority of a purchasing manager mentioned in the court's actual authority and apparent authority discussions? Recall that when a principal gives a title or position to an agent, that action can establish actual authority by creating a reasonable belief in the agent that he is authorized to act in ways that are typical of someone in the industry who holds that title or position. Similarly, that action can establish apparent authority by creating a reasonable belief in a third party that the agent is authorized to act in ways that are typical of someone in the industry who holds that title or position.

Going forward, what should Harvard do to protect itself from employees binding it to unwanted contracts? First, to combat actual authority, Harvard should make it very clear that the employees do not have authority to enter into contracts without Kruske's express permission, and that the employees have no discretion to waive or modify this requirement. It would likely help to further convey that this is a change from prior practice and that such prior practice is no longer valid. Second, to combat apparent authority, Harvard should convey this same information to its existing and prospective suppliers. This will help defeat an argument that a

---

[68] Moreover, the court cited testimony from Safron that Diversified had entered into similar contracts with some of its other customers. *See id.* at 727. This testimony was presumably relevant because it suggested that the Harvard-Diversified contract was not so extraordinary that it would have been unreasonable for Diversified to believe that the Harvard purchasing manager could enter into it.

[69] *Id.*

third-party supplier reasonably believed that a Harvard employee had the authority that is typically possessed by a person in the industry with that position. The goal, of course, is to influence the reasonable beliefs of both the employees (actual authority) and the third-party suppliers (apparent authority).

(3) Inherent Authority

According to the Second Restatement, the term "inherent agency power" (typically referred to as *inherent authority*) describes "the power of an agent which is derived not from authority, apparent authority or estoppel, but solely from the agency relation and exists for the protection of persons harmed by or dealing with a servant or other agent."[70] That definition indicates that inherent authority is a distinct type of authority, but it says very little about when it arises.

Later sections, however, provide further guidance. A general agent[71] for a disclosed or partially disclosed principal has inherent authority to bind the principal "for acts done on his [the principal's] account which usually accompany or are incidental to transactions which the agent is authorized to conduct if, although they are forbidden by the principal, the other party reasonably believes that the agent is authorized to do them and has no notice that he is not so authorized."[72]

Example: *P* hires *A* to manage a branch store of *P*'s retail operations. *A* has authority to manage the store on a day-to-day basis but is told expressly that he has no authority to reduce the prices of goods without the prior approval of *P*. *A* nevertheless marks down slow-moving goods which are sold to third persons. There is no actual authority, but *P* is bound by inherent authority if the act of marking down prices usually accompanies managerial duties, and if a third party reasonably believed that *A* was authorized to do such an act.

In the above example, can an argument be made that there was apparent authority? The principal gave *A* the position of "manager," and it may be reasonable for third parties who know that *A* is a manager to believe that he has the authority to mark down prices.[73] In situations involving a disclosed or partially disclosed principal, therefore, the concepts of apparent authority and inherent authority typically overlap.

---

[70] RESTATEMENT (SECOND) OF AGENCY § 8A (1958).

[71] A "general agent" is "an agent authorized to conduct a series of transactions involving a continuity of service." *Id.* § 3(1).

[72] *Id.* § 161.

[73] *See* Chapter 2(C)(2)(a)(2).

A further illustration is provided by the facts of *Kidd v. Thomas A. Edison, Inc.*[74] Edison engaged singers for "tone test" musical recitals, which were designed to show the accuracy with which the singer's voice was reproduced by the record albums made by the company. An Edison employee named Maxwell engaged Fuller to retain the singers. The plaintiff was one of the hired singers who apparently was not paid. She sued Edison for breach of contract. After a jury finding for the plaintiff, Edison moved to set aside the verdict. Maxwell testified that Fuller was authorized to retain singers, but only for performances where record dealers had agreed to pay the singer's fee. Fuller, in other words, was not authorized to enter into contracts where Edison had the primary obligation to pay.[75]

In denying Edison's motion, Judge Learned Hand observed that "while . . . the 'tone test' recitals were new, in the sense that no one had ever before employed singers for just this purpose of comparing their voices with their mechanical reproduction, they were not new merely as musical recitals; for it was, of course, a common thing to engage singers for such recitals." More importantly, Judge Hand noted that "[w]hen . . . an agent is selected, as was Fuller, to engage singers for musical recitals, the customary implication would seem to have been that his authority was without limitation of the kind here imposed, which was unheard of in the circumstances."[76]

Given this analysis, Edison could be held liable on inherent authority grounds because (1) Fuller, its general agent, was authorized to engage singers for musical recitals, (2) the payment of the singer's fees by the engager usually accompanied such authority, (3) the plaintiff reasonably believed, based upon the first two factors, that Fuller was authorized to bind Edison to payment, and (4) the plaintiff had no notice that Fuller's authority in this regard had been curtailed. Notice, however, that these circumstances would also establish apparent authority by virtue of Fuller's position. That is, Edison placed Fuller in the position of engaging singers for musical recitals. According to Judge Hand, it was reasonable for third parties such as the plaintiff to believe that a person in that position had the customary authority of persons in that position— notably, the ability to bind the engager to payment. Because the plaintiff was unaware that Fuller's authority was more restricted, Fuller still had apparent authority to bind Edison. In short, *Edison* reiterates that in situations involving a disclosed or partially disclosed principal, the concepts of apparent authority and inherent authority typically overlap.

---

[74] 239 F. 405 (S.D.N.Y. 1917).

[75] *See id.* at 405–06.

[76] *Id.* at 406.

In an undisclosed principal situation, however, inherent authority has independent significance. After all, apparent authority involves a third party who reasonably believes, based on a *principal's* manifestations, that another person was authorized to act on the *principal's* behalf. [77] In an undisclosed principal situation, therefore, there can be no apparent authority, as the third party has no idea that a principal is involved in the transaction. Stated differently, in an undisclosed principal situation, a third party does not believe that the agent or other person is acting on behalf of someone else—a belief that is necessary for apparent authority. To the third party, the agent or other person appears to be acting for himself.[78] Nevertheless, even in the absence of actual and apparent authority, an undisclosed principal can still be bound via inherent authority.

The case of *Watteau v. Fenwick*[79] is illustrative. In *Watteau*, the defendants were a group of brewers who purchased a "beerhouse" known as the Victoria Hotel from a man named Humble. For reasons that are not explained, the defendants wanted to conceal the fact that they now owned the pub. As a result, although Humble remained employed as the pub's manager, he was also held out as the pub's owner.[80]

With the exception of bottled ales and mineral water, the defendants required Humble to purchase all of the goods needed for the pub from them. Over a period of years, however, Humble violated these instructions by purchasing on credit, in his own name, "cigars, bovril [a non-alcoholic drink], and other articles" from the plaintiffs. Apparently unpaid, the plaintiffs sued to recover.

Did Humble have actual authority as the pub manager to buy the cigars and other items? Clearly not. Despite his position as manager, he was explicitly forbidden by the defendants from purchasing those goods from outsiders. Did Humble have apparent authority to engage in the purchases? This too is a dead-end. The plaintiffs had no idea that a principal-agent relationship was even

---

[77] *See* Chapter 2(C)(2)(a)(2).

[78] *See, e.g.*, RESTATEMENT (SECOND) OF AGENCY § 194 cmt. a (1958) ("Since apparent authority is the power which results from acts which appear to the third person to be authorized by the principal, if such person does not know of the existence of a principal there can be no apparent authority."); RESTATEMENT (THIRD) OF AGENCY § 2.03 cmt. f (2006) ("In contrast, apparent authority is not present when a third party believes that an interaction is with an actor who is a principal. . . . If a third party believes that an actor represents no one else's interests, the third party does not have a reasonable belief in the actor's power to affect anyone else's legal position.").

[79] [1893] 1 Q.B. 346 (Eng.).

[80] *See id.* at 346. The court noted that "[a]fter the transfer of the business, Humble remained as defendants' manager; but the license was always taken out in Humble's name, and his name was painted over the door." *Id.*

involved in the transaction; they thought that Humble was buying for himself.[81] Nevertheless, the court held the defendants liable:

> [O]nce it is established that the defendant was the real principal, the ordinary doctrine as to principal and agent applies—that the principal is liable for all the acts of the agent which are within the authority usually confided to an agent of that character, notwithstanding limitations, as between the principal and the agent, put upon that authority. It is said that it is only so where there has been a holding out of authority—which cannot be said of a case where the person supplying the goods knew nothing of the existence of a principal. But I do not think so. Otherwise, in every case of undisclosed principal, or at least in every case where the fact of there being a principal was undisclosed, the secret limitation of authority would prevail and defeat the action of the person dealing with the agent and then discovering that he was an agent and had a principal.[82]

This holding in *Watteau* is reflected in § 194 of the Second Restatement: "A general agent for an undisclosed principal authorized to conduct transactions subjects his principal to liability for acts done on his account, if usual or necessary in such transactions, although forbidden by the principal to do them."[83] Humble was authorized to manage the bar for the defendants. Purchasing cigars, non-alcoholic drinks, and similar items for patrons can be viewed as "usual or necessary" actions in carrying out the management of a bar. Thus, even though Humble was forbidden to make such purchases, the defendants were liable for Humble's actions.[84]

---

[81] As the court noted, "[t]he plaintiff gave credit to Humble, and to him alone, and had never heard of the defendants." *Id.* at 348; *see id.* at 349 ("There was no holding out, as the plaintiff knew nothing of the defendant[s].").

[82] *Id.* at 348–49.

[83] *See also* RESTATEMENT (SECOND) OF AGENCY § 195 (1958) (discussing the inherent authority of manager-agents in an undisclosed principal situation); *cf.* RESTATEMENT (THIRD) OF AGENCY § 2.06(2) (2006) (preserving what is effectively inherent authority (although not designated as such) in undisclosed principal situations).

[84] A more modern application of inherent authority in the undisclosed principal setting is addressed in *Morris Oil Co. v. Rainbow Oilfield Trucking, Inc.,* 741 P.2d 840 (N.M. 1987). Dawn, the holder of a certificate of public convenience and necessity, was engaged in the oilfield trucking business. Rainbow was permitted to use Dawn's certificate in order to operate a trucking enterprise in Hobbs, New Mexico. Dawn and Rainbow entered into several contracts giving Dawn control over Rainbow's operations and a share of Rainbow's gross receipts. *See id.* at 842.

Rainbow contracted in its own name to buy diesel fuel from defendant Morris. When Rainbow did not pay, Morris discovered Dawn's relationship with Rainbow and ultimately sued Dawn. *See id.* at 842–43. The court held for Morris on several grounds, including the fact that Dawn was bound by Rainbow's inherent authority at the time of the Rainbow-Morris contract. According to the court, Dawn (the undisclosed principal) entrusted Rainbow (the agent) with the management of Dawn's enter-

What is the rationale for inherent authority? The Second Restatement bases the doctrine on the notion that, as between a principal who benefits from an agent's actions and an innocent third party, it is more appropriate for the principal to bear the costs of the agent's conduct:

> The principles of agency have made it possible for persons to utilize the services of others in accomplishing far more than could be done by their unaided efforts... Partnerships and corporations, through which most of the work of the world is done today, depend for their existence upon agency principles. The rules designed to promote the interests of these enterprises are necessarily accompanied by rules to police them. It is inevitable that in doing their work, either through negligence or excess of zeal, agents will harm third persons or will deal with them in unauthorized ways. It would be unfair for an enterprise to have the benefit of the work of its agents without making it responsible to some extent for their excesses and failures to act carefully. The answer of the common law has been the creation of special agency powers or, to phrase it otherwise, the imposition of liability upon the principal because of unauthorized or negligent acts of his servants and other agents. These powers or liabilities are created by the courts primarily for the protection of third persons, either those who are harmed by the agent or those who deal with the agent. In the long run, however, they [i]nure to the benefit of the business world and hence to the advantage of employers as a class, the members of which are plaintiffs as well as defendants in actions brought upon unauthorized transactions conducted by agents.[85]

---

prise in Hobbs. Because purchasing fuel for a trucking enterprise was "in the usual course of business engaged in by the agent," the court found that inherent authority existed. *See id.* at 843–44.

Two peculiarities in *Morris Oil* are worth mentioning. First, the dispute could have been resolved on actual authority grounds. The court explicitly noted that "the agreement [between Dawn and Rainbow] specifically states that Rainbow may create liabilities of Dawn in the ordinary course of business of operating the terminal," and it observed that "[t]here is no question that the liability to Morris was incurred in the ordinary course of operating the trucking business." *Id.* at 843. Second, there is some question as to whether Rainbow was Dawn's agent at all. Dawn collected all fees for transportation services conducted by Rainbow, deducted a $1,000 per month clerical fee and a percentage of the gross receipts, and remitted the balance to Rainbow. *See id.* at 842. This arrangement could be viewed as Rainbow simply paying a fee to Dawn for the use of Dawn's certificate (particularly if the share of gross receipts retained by Dawn was relatively small). With respect to the "on behalf of" element of the agency inquiry, therefore, Rainbow may have been acting primarily for its own benefit rather than for the benefit of Dawn. *See* Chapter 2(B)(1).

[85] RESTATEMENT (SECOND) OF AGENCY § 8A cmt. a (1958); *see also id.* § 161 cmt. a ("The basis of the [inherent authority] liability stated in this Section is comparable to

The Third Restatement does not recognize inherent authority as an independent concept:

> The term "inherent agency power," used in Restatement Second, Agency, and defined therein by § 8A, is not used in this Restatement. Inherent agency power is defined as "a term used . . . to indicate the power of an agent which is derived not from authority, apparent authority or estoppel, but solely from the agency relation and exists for the protection of persons harmed by or dealing with a servant or other agent." Other doctrines stated in this Restatement encompass the justifications underpinning § 8A, including the importance of interpretation by the agent in the agent's relationship with the principal, as well as the doctrines of apparent authority, estoppel, and restitution.[86]

Despite this position, § 2.06(2) of the Third Restatement preserves what is effectively inherent authority (although not designated as such) in undisclosed principal situations: "An undisclosed principal may not rely on instructions given an agent that qualify or reduce the agent's authority to less than the authority a third party would reasonably believe the agent to have under the same circumstances if the principal had been disclosed."

(4) Estoppel

Section 8B of the Second Restatement describes the doctrine of estoppel in the following manner:

> (1) A person who is not otherwise liable as a party to a transaction purported to be done on his account, is nevertheless subject to liability to persons who have changed their positions because of their belief that the transaction was entered into by or for him, if
>
> (a) he intentionally or carelessly caused such belief, or

---

the liability of a master for the torts of his servant. . . . In the case of the master, it is thought fair that one who benefits from the enterprise and has a right to control the physical activities of those who make the enterprise profitable, should pay for the physical harm resulting from the errors and derelictions of the servants while doing the kind of thing which makes the enterprise successful. . . . Commercial convenience requires that the principal should not escape liability where there have been deviations from the usually granted authority by persons who are such essential parts of his business enterprise. In the long run it is of advantage to business, and hence to employers as a class, that third persons should not be required to scrutinize too carefully the mandates of permanent or semi-permanent agents who do no more than what is usually done by agents in similar positions.").

[86] RESTATEMENT (THIRD) OF AGENCY § 2.01 cmt. b (2006).

(b) knowing of such belief and that others might change their positions because of it, he did not take reasonable steps to notify them of the facts.[87]

Estoppel is closely related to the doctrine of apparent authority. Both doctrines focus on holding the principal responsible for a third party's belief that a person is authorized to act on the principal's behalf. The doctrines, however, are distinct. Apparent authority holds the principal responsible for a third party's belief because of the principal's manifestations of authority to the third party. By contrast, the doctrine of estoppel can apply when the principal has not made any manifestations of authority to the third party at all. Instead, the principal is held responsible because the principal contributed to the third party's belief or failed to dispel it:

> The [estoppel] doctrine is applicable when the person against whom estoppel is asserted has made no manifestation that an actor has authority as an agent but is responsible for the third party's belief that an actor is an agent and the third party has justifiably been induced by that belief to undergo a detrimental change in position. Most often the person estopped will be responsible for the third party's erroneous belief as the consequence of a failure to use reasonable care, either to prevent circumstances that foreseeably led to the belief, or to correct the belief once on notice of it. . .[88]

Thus, the estoppel doctrine can apply when apparent authority is unavailable. Consider the following example:

> P has two coagents, A and B. P has notice that B, acting without actual or apparent authority, has represented to T that A has authority to enter into a transaction that is contrary to P's instructions. T does not know that P's instructions forbid A from engaging in the transaction. T cannot establish conduct by P on the basis of which T could reasonably believe that A has the requisite authority. T can, however, establish

---

[87] RESTATEMENT (SECOND) OF AGENCY § 8B (1958); *see also* RESTATEMENT (THIRD) OF AGENCY § 2.05 (2006) (substantially the same). The Third Restatement makes it clear that the estoppel doctrine protects third parties who "justifiably" rely on a belief that an actor is an agent, and who act on that belief to their detriment. Although the Second Restatement lacks the "justifiably" term, the courts often impose a justifiable reliance requirement. *See, e.g.,* McNeil Real Estate Fund XXVI, L.P. v. Matthew's, Inc., 112 F. Supp. 2d 437, 443 (W.D. Pa. 2000).

[88] RESTATEMENT (THIRD) OF AGENCY § 2.05 cmt. c (2006); *see also id.* § 2.05 cmt. d ("The doctrine stated in this section may estop a person from denying the existence of an agency relationship with an actor when the third party would be unable to establish either the existence of a relationship of agency between the actor and the person stopped . . . or a manifestation of authority sufficient to create apparent authority . . . .").

that *P* had notice of *B*'s representation and that it would have been easy for *P* to inform *T* of the limits on *A*'s authority. *T* detrimentally changes position in reliance on *B*'s representation by making a substantial down payment. If it is found that *T*'s action was justifiable, *P* is estopped to deny *B*'s authority to make the representation.[89]

Apparent authority and estoppel also differ to the extent that apparent authority may be created without the need for a third party to establish a detrimental change in position. By contrast, estoppel requires such a showing.[90] The requisite change in position can be demonstrated through "payment of money, expenditure of labor, suffering a loss or subjection to legal liability."[91]

How does estoppel differ from inherent authority? First, inherent authority applies only when a principal-agent relationship has been established. By contrast, estoppel can apply even when a principal-agent relationship is absent.[92] (The discussion of *Koos Bros.* below illustrates this point.) Second, while inherent authority can apply in undisclosed principal situations,[93] estoppel requires the third party to believe that the transaction was entered into on behalf of a purported principal.[94] In disclosed or partially disclosed principal situations, however, the doctrines likely cover similar ground.[95] Third, as with apparent authority, inherent authority

---

[89] *Id.* § 2.05 illus. 1.

[90] *See, e.g.*, RESTATEMENT (SECOND) OF AGENCY § 8B cmt. b (1958); RESTATEMENT (THIRD) OF AGENCY § 2.03 cmt. e (2006).

[91] RESTATEMENT (SECOND) OF AGENCY § 8B(3) (1958).

[92] *Compare* RESTATEMENT (SECOND) OF AGENCY §§ 161, 194 (1958) (establishing inherent authority in relationships between a "general agent" and its "principal"), *with id.* § 8B (describing estoppel more generically as a doctrine that can subject "[a] person who is not otherwise liable as a party" to liability for transactions believed to have been entered into "by or for him"), *and* RESTATEMENT (THIRD) OF AGENCY § 2.05 cmt. d (2006) (noting that the estoppel doctrine can apply "when the third party would be unable to establish . . . the existence of a relationship of agency between the actor and the person estopped").

[93] *See* Chapter 2(C)(2)(a)(3).

[94] *See, e.g.*, RESTATEMENT (THIRD) OF AGENCY § 2.05 (2006) (defining estoppel as involving "a person," "an actor," and "a third party," and noting that liability can be imposed on the "person" when the third party believes that a transaction done by the "actor" was on the "person's" account).

[95] If a disclosed or partially disclosed principal restricts an agent from performing acts that usually accompany transactions that the agent is authorized to conduct, the principal's failure to inform third parties of this atypical restriction should give rise to inherent authority. *See* Chapter 2(C)(2)(a)(3). Moreover, the failure to inform third parties could give rise to estoppel on the grounds that the principal "carelessly caused" a third party's belief that the agent had the typical scope of authority, or that the principal, "knowing of such belief . . . did not take reasonable steps to notify" the third party of the restriction. Technically, however, the doctrines of estoppel and inherent authority will never both apply to a particular situation, as the presence of inherent authority (or any type of authority) precludes the application of the estoppel doctrine. *See, e.g.*, RESTATEMENT (SECOND) OF AGENCY § 8B (1958) (stating that

may be created without the need for a third party to establish a detrimental change in position.

Hoddeson v. Koos Bros.[96] nicely illustrates the independent significance of the estoppel doctrine. Mrs. Hoddeson went to the Koos Bros. furniture store to purchase some bedroom furniture. Upon entering the store, she was "greeted by a tall man with dark hair frosted at the temples and clad in a light gray suit." The man asked if he could be of assistance, and he guided Hoddeson to the furniture that she wanted. He informed Hoddeson that, other than the display models, her desired items were not in stock, but they would be delivered to her in a few weeks. Hoddeson paid him $168.50 in cash—the amount calculated by the man as the purchase price—and she departed the store. After not receiving the furniture, she contacted Koos Bros. to inquire. To her dismay, she discovered that there was no record of her order, as the man was simply an imposter who was not affiliated with Koos Bros. She sued Koos Bros. to recover her $168.50, and a jury found in her favor.[97]

On appeal, Koos Bros. reiterated that the salesman was an imposter who was not affiliated with the store. Obviously, there was no actual authority that could bind Koos Bros. to the sale. What about apparent authority? While apparent authority can be established in the absence of a principal-agent relationship, the doctrine requires the principal—by words, conduct, or other manifestations—to "hold out" another person as someone authorized to act for the principal.[98] The imposter lacked apparent authority, therefore, because there were no manifestations by Koos Bros. indicating that the imposter had authority to act for it. The mere fact that the imposter purported to exercise authority on Koos Bros.' behalf was insufficient.[99] Finally, although the court did not discuss it, inher-

---

estoppel only applies to a person "who is not otherwise liable as a party to a transaction"); RESTATEMENT (THIRD) OF AGENCY § 2.05 (2006) (stating that estoppel only applies to a person "who has not made a manifestation that an actor has authority as an agent and who is not otherwise liable as a party to a transaction").

[96] 135 A.2d 702 (N.J. Super. Ct. App. Div. 1957).

[97] *See id.* at 703–05.

[98] *See* Chapter 2(C)(2)(a)(2).

[99] As the court observed:

The point here debated is whether or not the evidence circumstantiates the presence of apparent authority, and it is at this very point we come face to face with the general rule of law that the apparency and appearance of authority must be shown to have been created by the manifestations of the alleged principal, and not alone and solely by proof of those of the supposed agent. Assuredly the law cannot permit apparent authority to be established by the mere proof that a mountebank in fact exercised it.

Hoddeson, 135 A.2d at 706; *see also* Chapter 2(C)(2)(a)(2) (discussing apparent authority).

ent authority was inapplicable given the absence of a principal-agent relationship between Koos Bros. and the imposter.

Despite this absence of authority, the court ordered a new trial on the question of whether Koos Bros. could be liable under the doctrine of estoppel:

> Our concept of the modern law is that where a proprietor of a place of business by his dereliction of duty enables one who is not his agent conspicuously to act as such and ostensibly to transact the proprietor's business with a patron in the establishment, the appearances being of such a character as to lead a person of ordinary prudence and circumspection to believe that the impostor was in truth the proprietor's agent, in such circumstances the law will not permit the proprietor defensively to avail himself of the impostor's lack of authority and thus escape liability for the consequential loss thereby sustained by the customer.[100]

Using the language of the Second Restatement, if Hoddeson demonstrated at a new trial that Koos Bros. did not take sufficient steps to prevent imposters from posing as salesmen in its store, Koos Bros. would presumably be liable because it "carelessly caused [her] belief" that the imposter had the authority to act for the store. Alternatively, to the extent that Koos Bros. was aware that it had a problem with imposters, Hoddeson could argue that Koos Bros. knew that customers were being fooled into thinking that imposters acted for the store, but it "did not take reasonable steps to notify [the customers] of the facts."

(5) Ratification

Even if an agent acts without authority, a principal will be liable to a third party if (1) the agent purports to act (or, under the Third Restatement, acts) on the principal's behalf, and (2a) the principal affirmatively treats the agent's act as authorized (*express ratification*), or (2b) the principal engages in conduct that is justifiable only if the principal is treating the agent's act as authorized (*implied ratification*).[101] Express ratification most commonly occurs through oral or

---

[100] *Hoddeson*, 135 A.2d at 707; *see also id.* ("Certainly the proprietor's duty of care and precaution for the safety and security of the customer encompasses more than the diligent observance and removal of banana peels from the aisles. Broadly stated, the duty of the proprietor also encircles the exercise of reasonable care and vigilance to protect the customer from loss occasioned by the deceptions of an apparent salesman.").

[101] *See* RESTATEMENT (SECOND) OF AGENCY §§ 82–83, 85, 100, 143 (1958); RESTATEMENT (THIRD) OF AGENCY §§ 4.01–4.03 (2006).

written statements (e.g., a company resolution).[102] Implied ratification most commonly occurs when the principal has knowledge of an unauthorized transaction entered into purportedly on his behalf, but the principal nevertheless accepts the benefits of the transaction.[103]

   Example: *P* owns an advertising agency and employs *A* to service existing accounts by purchasing space in advertising media. *A* does not have authority to set terms with clients. *A* executes an agreement with *T* that commits *P* to develop a new advertising campaign for *T*. *P* learns of the agreement and then accepts and retains advance payment made by *T* for the new advertising campaign. By accepting and retaining the payment, *P* has ratified the unauthorized agreement made by *A*.

   A further illustration of both express and implied ratification occurred in *Evans v. Ruth*.[104] Homer Ruth was awarded a contract to provide crushed stone for certain state highways in Pennsylvania. One of Ruth's foremen, allegedly without authority, hired James Evans to haul stone. After the work was completed, Evans presented his bills to Ruth, who stated: "Well, I see you finished the work for me. . . If you will have a sworn affidavit to that statement, I will pay you." Evans furnished the affidavit, but Ruth refused to pay. The court stated that Ruth "affirm[ed] [the contract] by stating that the work was done for him and that he would pay for it provided an affidavit was furnished." Even without this express ratification, Ruth probably would have been liable via implied ratification, as he received "weigh slips" from haulers, including Evans, indicating the weight of stones that had been hauled. Ruth submitted these weigh slips to the state in order to get himself paid. The weigh slips were evidence, in other words, that Ruth was aware of the contract with Evans, and his submission of those slips to the state for payment suggested that he knowingly accepted the benefits of his contract with Evans.[105]

   Ratification occurs as soon as the principal objectively manifests his acceptance of the transaction, even if the fact of ratification is not communicated to the third party, the agent, or any other person.[106]

---

   [102] *Cf.* RESTATEMENT (SECOND) OF AGENCY § 93 (1958); RESTATEMENT (THIRD) OF AGENCY § 4.01(2) (2006).

   [103] *Cf.* RESTATEMENT (SECOND) OF AGENCY §§ 98–99 (1958); RESTATEMENT (THIRD) OF AGENCY § 4.01 cmt. g (2006) ("A person may ratify an act . . . by receiving or retaining benefits it generates if the person has knowledge of material facts . . . and no independent claim to the benefit.").

   [104] 195 A. 163 (Pa. Super. Ct. 1937).

   [105] *See id.* at 164–65.

   [106] *See* RESTATEMENT (SECOND) OF AGENCY § 95 (1958); RESTATEMENT (THIRD) OF AGENCY § 4.01 cmt. d (2006) ("Ratification requires an objectively or externally observable indication that a person consents that another's prior act shall affect the person's legal relations. To constitute ratification, the consent need not be communi-

The effect is to validate the contract as if it were originally authorized by the principal. Thus, ratification imposes liability upon a principal in the same manner as if the principal had actually authorized the contract in the first place.[107]

Ratification, however, is subject to several restrictions. First, it is ineffective unless the principal, at the time of the ratification, was fully aware of all of the material facts involved in the original transaction.[108] Second, ratification must occur before the third party has withdrawn from the transaction.[109] This rule reduces the risk that the principal will use ratification to speculate at the expense of the third party. We do not want the principal waiting to see if the deal works out to his advantage—ratifying the transaction if it does, and repudiating the transaction if it does not. Third, ratification is ineffective if it would be unfair to the third party as a result of changed circumstances.[110] Finally, ratification cannot operate to prejudice the rights of intervening persons—i.e., persons who are not parties to the transaction, but who acquired rights or other interests in the subject matter of the transaction before the ratification occurred.[111]

Example: Without authority to bind P, A purports to rent machinery from T for P. A delivers the machinery to P, representing that T has loaned the machinery to P without requiring compensation. P uses the machinery. There is no ratification by P because he was unaware of the material facts related to the rental transaction.

Example: P retains A to identify properties that P might purchase. Lacking actual or apparent authority to do so, A enters into a contract that purports to commit P to purchase Blackacre, which is owned by T. T notifies P that T withdraws from the transaction. If P subsequently affirms the contract made by A, ratification will not have occurred. T is not bound by the transaction because his withdrawal preceded P's attempt to ratify.

---

cated to the third party or the agent. This is so because the focal point of ratification is an observable indication that the principal has exercised choice and has consented.").

[107] *See* RESTATEMENT (SECOND) OF AGENCY §§ 82, 100, 143 (1958); RESTATEMENT (THIRD) OF AGENCY §§ 4.01(1), 4.02(1) (2006).

[108] *See* RESTATEMENT (SECOND) OF AGENCY § 91 (1958); RESTATEMENT (THIRD) OF AGENCY § 4.06 (2006).

[109] *See* RESTATEMENT (SECOND) OF AGENCY § 88 (1958); RESTATEMENT (THIRD) OF AGENCY § 4.05 (2006).

[110] *See* RESTATEMENT (SECOND) OF AGENCY § 89 (1958); RESTATEMENT (THIRD) OF AGENCY § 4.05 (2006).

[111] *See* RESTATEMENT (SECOND) OF AGENCY § 101(c) (1958); RESTATEMENT (THIRD) OF AGENCY § 4.02(2)(c) (2006).

Example: Purporting to act for *P* but without power to bind him, *A* contracts to sell Blackacre with an existing house to *T*. The next day the house burns to the ground. *P*'s later ratification does not bind *T*, as a material change in circumstances (the house burning) prior to the ratification makes it inequitable to bind *T*. *T*, however, may elect to be bound by the contract if he chooses.

Example: Purporting to act for *P* but without power to bind him, *A* makes a contract for the sale of *P*'s land to *T*. *B*, not knowing this, offers *P* a lower price than that called for by *T*'s contract. *P* accepts *B*'s offer. *P* then learns of the contract with *T* and attempts to ratify it. *B* is entitled to the land because *B* acquired his rights to the land before *P*'s attempt to ratify.[112]

As mentioned, ratification requires an agent to purport to act on a principal's behalf. Under the Second Restatement, therefore, there can be no ratification by an undisclosed principal. By definition, in an undisclosed principal situation, a third party has no notice that the agent is acting for a principal; thus, the agent is not purporting to act on a principal's behalf. The Third Restatement changes this rule and allows ratification by an undisclosed principal by stating that a person may ratify an act "if the actor *acted or purported to act* as an agent on the principal's behalf."[113] Because an agent for an undisclosed principal acts on the principal's behalf (even though he does not purport to do so), ratification by an undisclosed principal is permissible under the Third Restatement.

What function does ratification serve? Consider the following:

Ratification often serves the function of clarifying situations of ambiguous or uncertain authority. A principal's ratification confirms or validates an agent's right to have acted as the agent did. That is, an agent's action may have been effective to bind the principal to the third party, and the third party to the principal, because the agent acted with apparent authority. If the principal ratifies the agent's act, it is thereafter not necessary to establish that the agent acted with apparent authority. Moreover, by replicating the effects of actual authority, the principal's ratification eliminates claims the principal would

---

[112] Can a principal ratify part of a transaction and repudiate other aspects of it? For example, assume that *A*, acting without authority, purports to enter into a contract on behalf of *P* for the sale of land to *T*. The contract price is for $300,000, and the sale is set to close at the end of next month. Can *P* ratify the price aspect of the transaction because *P* is pleased with the $300,000 sum, but reject the closing date because *P* wishes to finalize the sale earlier? Unfortunately for *P*, ratifying only part of a single transaction is impermissible. An effective ratification must encompass "the entirety of an act, contract, or other single transaction." RESTATEMENT (THIRD) OF AGENCY § 4.07 (2006); *see* RESTATEMENT (SECOND) OF AGENCY § 96 (1958).

[113] RESTATEMENT (THIRD) OF AGENCY § 4.03 (2006) (emphasis added).

otherwise have against the agent for acting without actual authority. The principal's ratification may also eliminate claims that third parties could assert against the agent when the agent has purported to be authorized to bind the principal but the principal is not bound. . .[114]

(6) Summary

What was the point of walking through these authority and related doctrines? (By now, you may have forgotten.) Recall that a principal will be liable on a contract between an agent and a third party when the agent acts with actual authority, apparent authority, or inherent authority. Even when the agent lacks one of these three types of authority, the principal may be liable under the doctrines of estoppel or ratification. Thus, the authority and related doctrines are important because, when they are established, the principal will be liable to a third party for contracts entered into by an agent.

b. Liability of the Third Party to the Principal

When an agent makes a contract for a disclosed or partially disclosed principal, the third party is liable to the principal if the agent acted with authority (actual, apparent, or, under the Second Restatement, inherent), so long as the principal is not excluded as a party by the form or terms of the contract.[115] When an agent makes a contract for an undisclosed principal, the third party is liable to the principal if the agent acted with authority (actual or, under the Second Restatement, inherent), so long as the principal is not excluded by the form or terms of the contract, the existence of the principal is not fraudulently concealed, and there is no set-off or similar defense against the agent.[116] In most situations, therefore, one can assert that a third party will be liable to the principal in circumstances where the principal is liable to the third party.[117]

---

[114] RESTATEMENT (THIRD) OF AGENCY § 4.01 cmt. b (2006) (citation omitted).

[115] *See* RESTATEMENT (SECOND) OF AGENCY §§ 292–293 (1958); RESTATEMENT (THIRD) OF AGENCY §§ 6.01(1), 6.02(1) (2006). Because ratification functions as a substitute for actual authority, ratification by the principal would also seem to bind the third party. *See* RESTATEMENT (SECOND) OF AGENCY § 292 cmt. a (1958); RESTATEMENT (THIRD) OF AGENCY § 6.03 cmt. c (2006); *see also* Chapter 2(C)(2)(a)(5) (discussing ratification).

[116] *See* RESTATEMENT (SECOND) OF AGENCY §§ 302–304, 306, 308 (1958); RESTATEMENT (THIRD) OF AGENCY §§ 6.03, 6.06, 6.11(4) (2006). As mentioned, apparent authority is inapplicable in an undisclosed principal situation. *See* Chapter 2(C)(2)(a)(3). Once again, because ratification functions as a substitute for actual authority, ratification by the principal would also seem to bind the third party. *See* Chapter 2(C)(2)(a)(5).

[117] *See* Chapter 2(C)(2)(a) (discussing when a principal is liable to a third party). This general notion of reciprocal liability does not seem to apply when the principal is liable to the third party on the grounds of estoppel. *See, e.g.,* RESTATEMENT (SECOND) OF AGENCY § 8B cmt. b (1958) ("However, contrary to the rule as to appar-

Example: *A* is a general agent for *P* who manages *P*'s business. With *P*'s consent, the business is conducted in *A*'s name. *A* enters into a contract in his own name to buy goods from *T* which are suitable for the business. The purchase has been authorized by *P*. If *T* fails to deliver the goods, *P* can maintain an action against *T* for such failure because *A* had actual authority to enter into the contract with *T*.

Example: *P* authorizes *A* to buy Blackacre from *T*. *A* goes to *T*, who refuses to deal with *P* in any manner. Although *T* realizes that *A* is acting in *P*'s interest, it is stated in the written agreement that the contract is made solely between *A* and *T* and that *P* is not a party to the agreement. *P* has no cause of action against *T* on the contract because the terms of the agreement exclude *P*.

Example: *P* is the undisclosed principal of *A*. Pursuant to *P*'s instructions, *A* enters into a stock purchase agreement with *T* Corporation on behalf of *P*. The agreement contains a representation made by *A* that *A* acts solely for *A*'s account and that no other person will have any interest in the securities that *A* will acquire from *T* Corporation. *P* cannot enforce the agreement against *T* Corporation because the terms of the agreement exclude *P*.

Example: *P*, who owns a farm, engages *A* to sell cattle owned by *P*. *P* tells *A* to contract in *A*'s own name. *A* sells cattle to *T* for $10,000 (with *T* having no notice that *A* is acting as an agent). At the time of the sale, *A* also independently owes $4,000 to *T*. *P* demands payment of the $10,000 from *T*. Because *A* had actual authority to enter into the contract with *T*, *T* is liable to *P*. *T*'s liability to *P*, however, is only $6,000. *T* is entitled to set off the $4,000 amount that *A* owes *T*.

The fraudulent concealment exception merits some additional discussion. When an agent contracting on behalf of an undisclosed principal falsely represents that he is acting solely for himself (i.e., falsely represents that he is not acting on behalf of a principal), the

---

ent authority, one who is estopped to deny liability upon a contract which was purportedly made for him does not thereby have a right of action against the other party. He may, however, gain rights by ratification if he satisfies the requirements as to formalities." (citation omitted)). Moreover, while the Third Restatement does preserve a vestige of inherent authority in undisclosed principal situations, *see* RESTATEMENT (THIRD) OF AGENCY § 2.06(2) (2006), this provision only makes the principal liable to a third party. For the third party to be liable to the principal, the principal must bind itself through actual authority or ratification. *See* RESTATEMENT (THIRD) OF AGENCY § 6.03 cmt. c (2006) ("If an agent acts without actual authority in making a contract on behalf of an undisclosed principal, the principal may be subject to liability as stated in § 2.06. A principal in such a case may acquire rights against the third party by ratifying the agent's conduct as stated in § 4.03.").

Second and Third Restatements both provide that the third party can avoid the contract if the principal or the agent had notice that the third party would not have dealt with the principal.[118]

Example: *P* is *A*'s undisclosed principal. With authorization from *P*, *A* contacts *T* and offers to sell and deliver to *T* 1,000 shares in a corporation. Neither *P* nor *A* has notice that *T* would be unwilling to deal with *P*. In response to a question by *T*, *A* falsely represents that he is not acting on behalf of a principal. *A* and *T* then enter into a contract for the sale of the shares. *P* can enforce this contract.

Example: Same facts as above, except that *A* has notice that *T* would not enter into any contract if *T* knew that *P* was the principal. *P* cannot enforce the contract if *T* elects to rescind. The same result occurs if *A* had no notice that *T* would be unwilling to deal with *P*, but *P* did have such notice.

This fraudulent concealment exception can be confusing. After all, doesn't an agent contracting on behalf of an undisclosed principal always represent that he is acting solely for himself and not on behalf of a principal? While an agent acting on behalf of an undisclosed principal certainly represents that he is acting for himself, he does not represent that he is acting *solely* for himself—unless that particular representation is affirmatively made in some manner. Thus, the fraudulent concealment exception applies only if the agent does something more than simply sign his name to a contract. In the above examples, the agent does something more by affirmatively denying the existence of a principal.[119]

Hirsch v. Silberstein[120] discusses the fraudulent concealment exception in circumstances suggesting racial discrimination. The Hirsches sold a lot next to their home to the Silbersteins for $10,000. Apparently the Silbersteins had represented that they

[118] *See* RESTATEMENT (SECOND) OF AGENCY §§ 9, 304 (1958); RESTATEMENT (THIRD) OF AGENCY §§ 1.04(4), 6.11(4) (2006). Mere doubts or suspicions about the third party's willingness to deal with the principal do not satisfy this "notice" standard. *See, e.g.*, RESTATEMENT (THIRD) OF AGENCY § 6.11 cmt. d (2006).

[119] *See, e.g.*, RESTATEMENT (THIRD) OF AGENCY § 6.11 cmt. d (2006) ("When an agent deals with a third party on behalf of a principal but does not disclose the principal's existence, the agent does not impliedly represent that the agent does not act on behalf of a principal. . . . If a third party wishes certainty that the party with whom it deals will be the only party with rights and liabilities under the contract . . . [t]he third party may also ask the person with whom it deals whether that person acts as agent for an undisclosed principal. . . . If the agent answers the third party's question falsely, the agent has made a false representation to the third party. This is a basis on which the third party may avoid a contract made with the agent on behalf of the undisclosed principal if the agent had notice that the third party would not have dealt with the principal.").

[120] 227 A.2d 638 (Pa. 1967).

intended to build their own home on the lot and to live there as neighbors of the Hirsches. Mr. Hirsch personally inspected Mr. Silberstein's place of work and investigated Mr. Silberstein's credit. As a result of these investigations, he concluded that the Silbersteins would make desirable neighbors, and he agreed to sell them the lot. The Silbersteins, however, were acting as a "straw party" for the Crosses, an African-American family, and the Silbersteins conveyed the property to the Crosses as soon as they acquired it. The Hirsches sued for rescission, and Mr. Hirsch claimed that he "would not have entered into the agreement of sale had he known that there had been any misrepresentation with reference to who was going to occupy the land." The court rejected the claim, noting that "[t]he Silbersteins were under no legal duty to reveal the existence of their undisclosed principals." According to the court, "[w]hile the instant record may indicate a representation by Silberstein that he was not acting on behalf of a principal, it is nonetheless barren of any evidence that appellants would not have dealt with the Crosses had their existence been known."[121] Although an admission of racial prejudice might have caused the Hirsches difficulties under a variety of civil rights laws, such prejudice, if brought to the attention of the Silbersteins or the Crosses before the contract was entered into, presumably would have been a sufficient basis for rescission under the fraudulent concealment exception.[122]

Despite the general rules stated above, an undisclosed principal cannot bind a third party to a contract if the principal's role in the contract substantially changes the third party's rights or obligations:

> The nature of the performance that a contract requires determines whether performance by an undisclosed principal will be effective as performance under the contract and whether an undisclosed principal can require that the third party render performance to the principal. Performance by an undisclosed principal is not effective as performance under a contract if the third party has a substantial interest in receiving performance

---

[121] *Id.* at 639.

[122] The purchase agreement between the Hirsches and the Silbersteins included an anti-assignment clause. The court held that the clause was not violated because the agreement of sale was not assigned; instead, the Silbersteins conveyed the property in an entirely separate transaction to the Crosses. If the Silbersteins were agents on behalf of an undisclosed principal (the Crosses), however, it is more accurate to say that the Crosses themselves were parties to the original purchase agreement because the Silbersteins had actual authority to enter into the agreement on behalf of the Crosses. *See, e.g.*, RESTATEMENT (THIRD) OF AGENCY § 6.03 (2006) (noting the general rule that "[w]hen an agent acting with actual authority makes a contract on behalf of an undisclosed principal, . . . unless excluded by the contract, the principal is a party to the contract"). Thus, no assignment (or further conveyance) was necessary.

from the agent who made the contract. This limit corresponds to the limit on delegability of performance of a duty . . . The nature of the performance that a contract requires from a third party determines whether an undisclosed principal is entitled to receive that performance. An undisclosed principal may not require that a third party render performance to the principal if rendering performance to the principal would materially change the nature of the third party's duty, materially increase the burden or risk imposed on the third party, or materially impair the third party's chance of receiving return performance. These limits correspond to the limits imposed on assignment of a contractual right.[123]

Example: *T* enters into a contract with *A* in which *A* promises to manage *T*'s investment portfolio. *A* does not disclose that *A* makes the contract on behalf of *P*. *P* offers to manage *T*'s portfolio. *T* is free to accept or reject *P*'s offer of performance. *P*'s offer does not constitute an offer of performance of the contract made by *A*. *T* has a substantial interest in receiving investment-management services from *A*.

Example: *T* enters into a contract to purchase a quantity of coal of a specified kind from *A*. *A* does not disclose that *A* makes the contract on behalf of *P*. *P* tenders coal to *T* of the specified kind and quantity. *P*'s tender has the effect of a tender by *A* because *T* has no substantial interest in receiving the coal from *A*.

Example: *T* agrees to work as a nanny for *A*. *P*, *A*'s undisclosed principal, cannot require *T* to work as a nanny for *P*. The contract between *T* and *A* requires that *T* render personal services in an ongoing close association. Requiring *T* to render the services to *P* would materially change the nature of *T*'s duties.

Example: *T* agrees to sell Blackacre in exchange for cash to *A*, who acts on behalf of *P*, *A*'s undisclosed principal. *P* may require performance from *T* (assuming that neither *P* nor *A* had notice that *T* would not have dealt with *P*). The contract made by *A* requires only the payment of money in exchange for Blackacre.

c. Liability of the Agent to the Third Party

If an agent contracts with a third party on behalf of a disclosed principal, the general rule is that the agent is not a party to the contract and is not liable to the third party.[124] This result is consistent

---

[123] RESTATEMENT (THIRD) OF AGENCY § 6.03 cmt. d (2006); *see* RESTATEMENT (SECOND) OF AGENCY §§ 309–310 (1958).

[124] *See* RESTATEMENT (SECOND) OF AGENCY § 320 (1958); RESTATEMENT (THIRD) OF AGENCY § 6.01(2) (2006).

with the third party's expectations—i.e., the third party expected that he was entering into a contract with the principal and not with the agent.

Example: *P* instructs *A* to purchase a computer on *P*'s behalf. *A* goes to *T*'s computer store and represents to *T* that he is buying for the account of *P*. A contract is entered into. *P* is liable on the contract, but *A* is not.

If an agent contracts with a third party on behalf of a partially disclosed or undisclosed principal, the general rule is that the agent is a party to the contract and is liable to the third party (regardless of whether the principal is also liable to the third party).[125] The third party's right to hold the agent responsible on contracts with partially disclosed principals is based on the common sense notion that a third party normally would not agree to look solely to a person whose identity is unknown for performance of the contract. If the third party does not know the identity of the principal, the third party cannot investigate the solvency and reliability of the principal; thus, the third party probably expected the agent to be liable.[126] Similarly, the third party's right to hold the agent responsible on contracts with undisclosed principals is also consistent with the third party's expectations—i.e., the third party expected the agent to be a party to the contract because the agent presented the deal as if he were acting for himself. Moreover, if the third party is unaware of the principal's existence, the third party must be relying on the agent's solvency and reliability when entering into the contract.

Example: *P*, a well-known manufacturer, instructs *A* to offer to sell goods on *P*'s behalf to *T* without revealing *P*'s identity. *A* makes the offer and truthfully advises *T* that *A* is making the offer on behalf of a well-known manufacturer. *A* does not disclose *P*'s identity. *T* accepts the offer. Both *P* and *A* are liable on the contract. *P* is liable because *A* acted with actual authority in entering into the transaction. *A* is liable because he is an agent acting on behalf of a partially disclosed principal.

---

[125] *See* RESTATEMENT (SECOND) OF AGENCY §§ 321–322 (1958); RESTATEMENT (THIRD) OF AGENCY §§ 6.02(2), 6.03(2), 6.09 (2006). If an agent becomes a party to a contract under the general rule, and if the third party breaches the contract in some manner, the third party may be liable to the agent. *See, e.g.,* RESTATEMENT (THIRD) OF AGENCY § 6.03 cmt. e (2006) ("As a party to a contract made on behalf of an undisclosed principal, an agent may sue the third party in the agent's own name.").

[126] In *Van D. Costas, Inc. v. Rosenberg,* 432 So. 2d 656 (Fla. Dist. Ct. App. 1983), the president of Seascape Restaurants, Inc. signed a contract with his name and the trade name of the restaurant—"Jeff Rosenberg, The Magic Moment." The court cited authority for the proposition that the use of a trade name is not a sufficient disclosure of the identity of the principal to create a disclosed principal situation (which would eliminate the liability of the agent). Instead, Rosenberg was held liable as an agent for a partially disclosed principal. *See id.* at 657–59.

Example: Same facts as above, but *A* offers to sell the goods to *T* without disclosing that they are *P*'s goods and that he is selling the goods on *P*'s behalf. *T* accepts the offer. Both *P* and *A* are liable on the contract. *P* is liable because *A* acted with actual authority in entering into the transaction. *A* is liable because he is an agent acting on behalf of an undisclosed principal.

An agent who purports to act on behalf of a principal makes an implied warranty of authority to a third party. If the agent lacks the power to bind the principal, the agent is liable to the third party for breach of the implied warranty (unless the agent conveyed that he was not making such a warranty or the third party knew that the agent had no authority).[127] The agent may also be liable to the third party under a theory that he has tortiously misrepresented his authority.[128]

Example: *A*, a mortgage broker claiming to act as agent for *P* Corporation, makes an oral contract to sell mortgage-backed securities owned by *P* Corporation to *T* Bank. *A* acted without actual, apparent, or inherent authority. *A* is subject to liability to *T* Bank for loss to *T* Bank resulting from *T* Bank's reliance on *A*'s implied representation that *A* had the power to bind *P* Corporation.

D. Duties of the Agent and the Principal to Each Other

1. The Agent's Duties to the Principal

An agency relationship has the important characteristic of being a *fiduciary* relationship—i.e., an agent is a fiduciary with respect to matters within the scope of his agency.[129] This effectively means that an agent is held to a very high standard of conduct in carrying out tasks for the principal. An agent's fiduciary duties require the agent to act *loyally* and *carefully* when acting within the scope of the agency. Some examples of this loyalty obligation include the following: (1) an agent is accountable to the principal for any profits arising out of the transactions he is to conduct on the principal's behalf;[130] (2) an agent must act solely for the benefit of the principal and not to bene-

---

[127] *See* RESTATEMENT (SECOND) OF AGENCY § 329 (1958); RESTATEMENT (THIRD) OF AGENCY § 6.10 (2006). The Third Restatement explicitly indicates that the agent is not liable for breach of the implied warranty if the principal ratified the agent's conduct. *See id.* § 6.10(1).

[128] *See* RESTATEMENT (SECOND) OF AGENCY § 330 (1958); RESTATEMENT (THIRD) OF AGENCY § 6.10 cmt. a (2006) ("An agent who falsely warrants authority may be subject to liability for fraud or negligent misrepresentation.").

[129] *See* RESTATEMENT (SECOND) OF AGENCY § 13 (1958); RESTATEMENT (THIRD) OF AGENCY §§ 1.01, 8.01 (2006).

[130] *See* RESTATEMENT (SECOND) OF AGENCY § 388 (1958); RESTATEMENT (THIRD) OF AGENCY §§ 8.02, 8.06.

fit himself or a third party;[131] (3) an agent must refrain from dealing with his principal as an adverse party or from acting on behalf of an adverse party;[132] (4) an agent may not compete with his principal concerning the subject matter of the agency;[133] and (5) an agent may not use the principal's property (including confidential information) for the agent's own purposes or a third party's purposes.[134] In general, these prohibitions on an agent's behavior can be trumped by agreement. If a fully informed principal consents to the behavior, in other words, there is usually no problem.[135]

The decision of *Tarnowski v. Resop*[136] involves the agent's duty of loyalty. The plaintiff engaged the defendant as his agent to locate a route of coin-operated music machines that was suitable for purchase. The defendant allegedly investigated a business owned by the sellers and proposed that the plaintiff purchase the business. After the plaintiff did so, he discovered that the defendant had misrepresented the extent of his investigation and had passed along false statements of the sellers. The plaintiff sued the sellers for fraud and received a judgment for $10,000 (which largely served as a return of the $11,000 that the plaintiff had paid for the business). The plaintiff then sued the defendant agent for a $2,000 commission the defendant

---

[131] *See* RESTATEMENT (SECOND) OF AGENCY § 387 (1958); RESTATEMENT (THIRD) OF AGENCY §§ 8.01, 8.06 (2006).

[132] *See* RESTATEMENT (SECOND) OF AGENCY §§ 389, 391 (1958); RESTATEMENT (THIRD) OF AGENCY §§ 8.03, 8.06 (2006).

[133] *See* RESTATEMENT (SECOND) OF AGENCY § 393 (1958); RESTATEMENT (THIRD) OF AGENCY §§ 8.04, 8.06 (2006).

[134] *See* RESTATEMENT (SECOND) OF AGENCY §§ 395–396, 398, 402, 404, 422–423 (1958); RESTATEMENT (THIRD) OF AGENCY §§ 8.05, 8.06, 8.12 (2006). An interesting application of this principle is found in *Reading v. Attorney General*, [1948] 2 K.B. 268 (Eng.). While in uniform, a British soldier stationed in Cairo helped escort a smuggler's trucks through police checkpoints. Because of the presence of the soldier, the trucks were allowed to pass without being inspected. The smuggler paid the soldier approximately 20,000 pounds, but the army discovered his actions and seized the funds. *See id.* at 269–70. The soldier sued to recover his money, but the court rejected the claim. As the court indicated, where "the wearing of the King's uniform and his position as a soldier is the sole cause of his getting the money, and getting it dishonestly, that is an advantage which he is not allowed to keep." *Id.* at 277. The soldier's official uniform and position can be viewed as property of the principal that the soldier improperly exploited for his own personal purposes. *See, e.g.*, RESTATEMENT (SECOND) OF AGENCY § 404 illus. 3 (1958) ("A soldier uses his official uniform and position to smuggle forbidden goods into a friendly country and thereby makes large profits. The country by which he is employed is entitled to the profits.").

[135] For example, why are waiters, bartenders, and other service personnel allowed to retain tips from customers? As agents, they are accountable to the principal for all profits received in the course of the agency relationship. Nevertheless, in most service industries, the principal implicitly or explicitly consents to the agent keeping the tips. *Cf.* RESTATEMENT (SECOND) OF AGENCY § 388 cmt. b (1958) ("An agent can properly retain gratuities received on account of the principal's business if, because of custom or otherwise, an agreement to this effect is found.").

[136] 51 N.W.2d 801 (Minn. 1952).

had received from the sellers, as well as for various amounts of damages.[137]

With respect to the recovery of the $2,000 commission, the court noted that all profits made by an agent in the course of an agency belong to the principal "whether they are the fruits of performance or the violation of an agent's duty." According to the court, "[i]t matters not that the principal has suffered no damage or even that the transaction has been profitable to him." Moreover, the principal's right "is not affected by the fact that the principal, upon discovering a fraud, has rescinded the contract and recovered that with which he parted." The plaintiff had an "absolute right" to the $2,000 commission "irrespective of any recovery resulting from the action against the sellers for rescission."[138] The strictness of this rule is premised on the basic notion that we want the agent committed fully to the principal's interests; correspondingly, we do not want that commitment diluted by the agent's efforts to seek profits for himself. As a consequence, there is a strict rule of disgorgement of profits by the agent.

The plaintiff also sought to recover damages for losses suffered in the business prior to rescission, loss of time devoted to the operation, and the expenses and attorneys' fees incurred in connection with the suit against the sellers. The court allowed the plaintiff to recover all of these damages. Citing agency principles, the court noted that when an agent receives a benefit as a result of violating his duty of loyalty, the principal is entitled to recover that benefit as well as the amount of damages caused by the breach. Citing tort principles, the court observed that a wrongdoer is liable for all of the foreseeable injuries resulting from his tortious acts.[139]

When all was said and done, the plaintiff had recovered (1) almost all of the purchase price that he had paid the sellers; (2) damages caused by the agent's misconduct; and (3) the $2,000 commission the sellers paid to the agent. In other words, the plaintiff was made more than whole—he recovered his losses *and* was allowed to recover the agent's $2,000 profit. What justifies this result? As the court observed, "[f]idelity in the agent is what is aimed at."[140] It bears repeating that, in order to ensure that an agent does not put his interests before those of the principal, the law requires the agent to disgorge all of his ill-gotten gains, regardless of whether the principal has been made whole. If an agent was allowed to retain profits made in the scope of the agency, the agent may be tempted to advance his own interest in maximizing personal profits rather than the interests

---

[137] *See id.* at 802.

[138] *Id.* at 802–03.

[139] *See id.* at 803–04.

[140] *Id.* at 803.

of the principal.[141] Because motivating fidelity in the agent is of paramount importance, the law is not particularly bothered if the principal receives a windfall along the way.

As mentioned, the agency relationship requires an agent to act carefully as well. An agent "has a duty to the principal to act with the care, competence, and diligence normally exercised by agents in similar circumstances."[142] Moreover, "[i]f an agent claims to possess special skills or knowledge, the agent has a duty to the principal to act with the care, competence, and diligence normally exercised by agents with such skills or knowledge."[143] Although the *Tarnowski* court did not focus explicitly on the agent's duty of care, the defendant agent likely breached that duty by conducting only a superficial investigation into the sellers' business and the accuracy of their representations.[144]

In many circumstances, an agent also has a duty to disclose information to the principal. The agent must "use reasonable efforts to give his principal information which is relevant to affairs entrusted to him and which, as the agent has notice, the principal would desire to have and which can be communicated without violating a superior duty to a third person."[145] This disclosure obligation between parties in a fiduciary relationship differs dramatically from the lack of a duty to volunteer information in an arm's length transaction.

Example: *M* is looking for a site for his plant. He learns that *O* has a site for sale. The asking price is $250,000. *M* and *O* negotiate and agree upon a price of $247,500. In this negotiation, *O* does not disclose that he purchased the site for $150,000 a few days before— information that would have been relevant to *M*'s decision to agree to the $247,500 price. *O*'s failure to disclose this information is not a breach of any duty and *M* may not rescind the transaction.

Example: *P* retains *A* to purchase a suitable manufacturing site for him. *A* owns a suitable site which he offers to *P* for $250,000, a fair price. *A* tells *P* all of the relevant facts, but he fails to disclose

---

[141] For example, on the facts of *Tarnowski*, we do not want the agent thinking something along the lines of "Maybe I won't investigate the sellers' representations too much because I won't get the commission if this deal falls through."

[142] RESTATEMENT (THIRD) OF AGENCY § 8.08 (2006); *see* RESTATEMENT (SECOND) OF AGENCY § 379 (1958).

[143] RESTATEMENT (THIRD) OF AGENCY § 8.08 (2006); *see* RESTATEMENT (SECOND) OF AGENCY § 379 (1958).

[144] *See Tarnowski*, 51 N.W.2d at 802.

[145] RESTATEMENT (SECOND) OF AGENCY § 381 (1958); *see id.* § 390 (imposing a duty to disclose on an agent who acts as an adverse party with the principal's consent); RESTATEMENT (THIRD) OF AGENCY §§ 8.06, 8.11 (2006).

that he purchased the site for $150,000 a short time ago. *A* has breached his duty and the transaction may be rescinded by *P*.

An agent also has a duty to act only as authorized by the principal.[146] It should come as no surprise, therefore, that an agent acting without actual authority is liable to his principal for any loss suffered by the principal (e.g., if an agent lacking actual authority binds the principal via apparent authority).[147]

Example: *A* acts as *P* Insurance Co.'s agent for purposes of issuing policies of workers' compensation insurance. *A* issues a binder policy to *T*. *A* acts with apparent authority in issuing this policy but *A* issues it in a manner clearly prohibited by *A*'s agency agreement with *P* Insurance Co. *E*, an employee of *T*, suffers a job-related injury. *P* Insurance Company must pay the claim even though *A* exceeded *A*'s actual authority in issuing the insurance policy to *T*. *A* is subject to liability to *P* Insurance Co. for the amount of *E*'s claim against *P* Insurance Co. *A* is also subject to liability for any costs *P* Insurance Co. incurs in opposing *T*'s claim.

2. The Principal's Duties to the Agent

A principal's duties to an agent are not fiduciary in nature as fiduciary responsibilities run only from the agent to the principal.[148] Nevertheless, a principal has several obligations to an agent. For example, a principal must perform his contractual commitments to the agent, must not unreasonably interfere with the agent's work, and must generally act fairly and in good faith towards the agent.[149] In addition, if an agent incurs expenses or suffers other losses in carrying out the principal's instructions, the principal has a duty to indemnify the agent.[150] Perhaps most importantly, unless the circumstances indicate otherwise, it will be inferred that the principal agreed to compensate the agent for his services.[151]

---

[146] *See* RESTATEMENT (SECOND) OF AGENCY §§ 383, 385 (1958); RESTATEMENT (THIRD) OF AGENCY § 8.09 (2006).

[147] *See* RESTATEMENT (SECOND) OF AGENCY §§ 399, 401 (1958); RESTATEMENT (THIRD) OF AGENCY § 8.09 & cmt. b (2006).

[148] *See* Chapter 2(D)(1).

[149] *See* RESTATEMENT (SECOND) OF AGENCY §§ 432–437 (1958); RESTATEMENT (THIRD) OF AGENCY §§ 8.13, 8.15 (2006).

[150] *See* RESTATEMENT (SECOND) OF AGENCY §§ 438–440 (1958); RESTATEMENT (THIRD) OF AGENCY § 8.14 (2006).

[151] *See* RESTATEMENT (SECOND) OF AGENCY §§ 441, 443 (1958); RESTATEMENT (THIRD) OF AGENCY § 8.13 cmt. d (2006) ("Unless an agreement between a principal and an agent indicates otherwise, a principal has a duty to pay compensation to an agent for services that the agent provides.").

E. Termination of the Agent's Power

As previously discussed, the relationship between an agent and a principal is a consensual one.[152] Actual authority from that relationship terminates when the objective of the relationship has been achieved, when the principal or the agent dies, and in a variety of other circumstances.[153] Actual authority also terminates when the principal revokes it or the agent renounces it.[154] If the agency relationship is based on contract, however, the decision to terminate actual authority may result in a breach of that contract. Nevertheless, actual authority has ended, even though contractual liability may exist for its termination.[155] Stated differently, a principal or an agent always has the *power* to terminate actual authority, but he may not have the *right* to do so.[156]

Example: *P*, who owns a hotel, retains *A* Corp. to manage it. *P* and *A* Corp. enter into an agreement providing that, in exchange for *A* Corp.'s management services, *A* Corp. will receive a commission equal to five percent of the hotel's gross revenues. The agreement further provides that *A* Corp.'s authority shall be irrevocable by *P* for a period of 10 years. Two years later, *P* revokes *A* Corp.'s authority. *A* Corp.'s actual authority is terminated, although *A* Corp. may sue *P* for breach of contract.

Because an inference of apparent authority may be based on the existence of prior actual authority, the termination of actual authority does not itself eliminate the apparent authority of an agent. It may be necessary to give notice of termination to third parties who

---

[152] *See* Chapter 2(B)(1).

[153] *See* RESTATEMENT (SECOND) OF AGENCY §§ 105–124 (1958); RESTATEMENT (THIRD) OF AGENCY §§ 3.06–3.10 (2006).

[154] *See* RESTATEMENT (SECOND) OF AGENCY §§ 117–119 (1958); RESTATEMENT (THIRD) OF AGENCY §§ 3.09–3.10 (2006).

[155] *See* RESTATEMENT (SECOND) OF AGENCY § 118 (1958); *id.* § 118 cmt. b ("The principal has power to revoke [authority] and the agent has power to renounce [authority], although doing so is in violation of a contract between the parties and although the authority is expressed to be irrevocable. A statement in a contract that the authority cannot be terminated by either party is effective only to create liability for its wrongful termination."); RESTATEMENT (THIRD) OF AGENCY § 3.10(1) & cmt. b (2006).

[156] The rationale for this proposition is that an agent can impose tort and contract liability upon a principal. This potential for liability can only be avoided if the principal retains the ability to terminate an agent's authority. Thus, the law always leaves the principal with a termination power, although its exercise may result in a breach of contract. Similarly, an agent who no longer wishes to serve a principal needs a mechanism for ridding himself of the fiduciary obligations imposed by the agency relationship. As a result, the law always allows the agent to renounce his authority, although such a renunciation may result in a breach of contract.

dealt with the agent or who otherwise continue to believe that the principal has authorized the agent to act.[157]

---

[157] *See* RESTATEMENT (SECOND) OF AGENCY §§ 124A, 125 (1958); RESTATEMENT (THIRD) OF AGENCY § 3.11 (2006).

Chapter 3

THE GENERAL PARTNERSHIP

Analysis

A. Introduction
B. Formation
    1. The Definition of Partnership
    2. The Partnership Agreement
    3. Entity vs. Aggregate Views
    4. Partnership By Estoppel
    5. Federal Tax Consequences
C. Management and Operation
    1. General Governance and Actual Authority
    2. Apparent Authority
    3. Inspection and Information Rights
D. Financial Rights and Obligations
    1. Partnership Accounting
    2. Sharing of Profits and Losses
    3. Liability to Third Parties
        a. Liability of the Partnership
        b. Liability of the Partners
    4. Indemnification and Contribution
E. Fiduciary Duties
    1. The Common Law
    2. Statutory Developments
        a. The Duty of Loyalty
        b. The Duty of Care
        c. The Duty to Disclose
    3. Duties When Leaving a Partnership
    4. The Role of Contract
F. Ownership Interests and Transferability
    1. Partnership Property
    2. Transferring a Partnership Interest
    3. The Charging Order
G. Dissociation and Dissolution
    1. Dissolution Under UPA
        a. Doctrinal Overview
        b. Causes of Dissolution
        c. The Winding Up Process
    2. Dissociation and Dissolution Under RUPA

A. Introduction

There are many business organizations that have the partnership structure. This Chapter focuses on the general partnership, which can be thought of as the basic partnership form. Other partnership structures, such as the limited partnership and the limited liability partnership, are discussed in later Chapters.

The law governing general partnerships is largely derived from statute. The National Conference of Commissioners on Uniform State Laws ("NCCUSL") promulgated the Uniform Partnership Act ("UPA") in 1914. With the exception of Louisiana, UPA was adopted in every state. In 1992, NCCUSL promulgated a revision of UPA. This revised act was itself amended in 1993, 1994, 1996, and 1997, and the final 1997 act has become known as the Revised Uniform Partnership Act ("RUPA"). As of this writing, some version of RUPA has been adopted by thirty-seven states as well as the District of Columbia and the Virgin Islands.

Despite the prevalence of RUPA in this country, the materials in this Chapter will discuss both UPA and RUPA. There are several reasons for this dual treatment. First, UPA is still the law in some commercially important states, including New York. Second, UPA and RUPA share many common principles. Because there is far more UPA case law than RUPA case law, however, many of the primary materials that are useful for teaching the basic principles of partnership law are based on UPA. Third, it is easier to understand many of the significant changes in RUPA, particularly the dissociation and dissolution provisions, if one has a working knowledge of how those issues are dealt with under UPA.

B. Formation

1. The Definition of Partnership

The general partnership is unique among business organizations with two or more owners because its formation does not require a public filing with the state. Instead, under UPA, a general partnership is formed whenever there is an "association of two or more persons to carry on as co-owners a business for profit."[1] Both UPA and RUPA contain rules for determining whether a partnership has been formed. The most important of these rules is that a person who receives a share of the profits of a business is presumed

---

[1] UPA § 6; *see* RUPA § 202(a) (defining a partnership as an "association of two or more persons to carry on as co-owners a business for profit . . . whether or not the persons intend to form a partnership"). Both UPA and RUPA recognize that partners need not be individuals; they may be corporations, partnerships, or other types of associations. *See* UPA §§ 2, 6; RUPA § 101(6), (10).

to be a partner in the business, unless the profits were received in payment of a debt, as wages, or for other listed exceptions.[2]

Because the formation of a general partnership simply requires a business relationship to fall within the statutory definition, a general partnership can be created even if the partners do not realize that they are forming such an enterprise.[3] This "surprise" has a serious bite—all of the default rules of the partnership statute will apply to the business, including the rule that partners have unlimited personal liability for the obligations of the partnership.[4]

The well-known decision of *Martin v. Peyton*[5] nicely illustrates this point. Knauth, Nachod & Kuhne ("K.N. & K.") was a banking and brokerage firm. The business had financial difficulties and borrowed $2.5 million in liquid securities from Peyton, Perkins, and Freeman. K.N. & K. was ultimately placed in bankruptcy, and Martin, apparently on behalf of a group of creditors, sought to hold Peyton, Perkins, and Freeman liable as partners in the firm.[6] Other key facts included the following: (1) An offer was made to Peyton, Perkins, and Freeman to become partners, but they refused. (2) Peyton, Perkins, and Freeman were to receive 40% of the firm's profits until the loan was repaid. Those payments had to be at least $100,000, and they could not exceed $500,000. (3) Peyton and Freeman were designated as "trustees" who had to be kept advised as to the conduct of the business and consulted on important matters. They could inspect the firm books and were entitled to any information. Finally, they were able to veto any business that they regarded as "highly speculative or injurious." (4) The firm was to retain Hall as the managing partner until the loaned securities were returned. (5) Each member of the firm was to place his resignation in the hands of the managing partner (Hall). If at any time

---

[2] *See* UPA § 7(4); RUPA § 202(c)(3).

[3] *See, e.g.,* Byker v. Mannes, 641 N.W.2d 210, 215–16 (Mich. 2002) ("The statutory language is devoid of any requirement that the individuals have the subjective intent to create a partnership. Stated more plainly, the statute does not require partners to be aware of their status as 'partners' in order to have a legal partnership. . . . Thus, one analyzes whether the parties acted as partners, not whether they subjectively intended to create, or not to create, a partnership.").

[4] *See* Chapter 3(D)(3)(b) (discussing the liability of partners).

[5] 158 N.E. 77 (N.Y. 1927).

[6] Why was this strategy pursued? If Peyton, Perkins, and Freeman were partners of the firm, they would have unlimited personal liability for the firm's obligations. *See* Chapter 3(D)(3)(b) (discussing the liability of partners). Martin, as a representative of a group of creditors who is owed money by the partnership, would be able to recover what the partnership owes from the personal assets of Peyton, Perkins, and Freeman.

Hall and the trustees agreed that such resignation should be accepted, that member would then be forced to retire.[7]

Given these circumstances, did the relationship between the firm and Peyton, Perkins, and Freeman meet the legal definition of a partnership—i.e., an association of two or more persons to carry on as co-owners a business for profit? Several factors are worthy of discussion:

Sharing of profits: Of what significance was it that the lenders were to receive 40% of the profits of the business? Under UPA § 7(4), the receipt by a person of a share of the profits of the business is prima facie evidence that he is a partner in the business. Similarly, under RUPA § 202(c)(3), sharing profits creates a presumption of partner status. That prima facie inference or presumption can be rebutted, however, if the share of profits is received in payment of a debt, or of interest or other charge on a loan.[8] Given this framework, there is a strong argument that the 40% profit share in *Martin* was in payment of a debt because, unlike a true share of profits, there was a minimum ($100,000) and maximum ($500,000) payment required regardless of the amount of profits. A fixed charge had to be paid, in other words, even if there were no profits, which seems like a mandatory debt payment. In addition, the court indicated that the 40% profit share continued "until the return was made"[9]—i.e., until the loan was paid back—which is suggestive of a loan repayment rather than a profit share. A typical profit share would continue into the future rather than end while the business was still operating.[10]

Express intent not to become partners: Peyton, Perkins, and Freeman expressly declined to become partners. Of course, whether persons think of themselves as partners should be irrelevant. The last clause of RUPA § 202(a), "whether or not the persons intend to form a partnership," makes this point. The only intent that matters is the intent to do the things that meet the legal definition of part-

---

[7] *See Martin*, 158 N.E. at 78–80.

[8] *See* UPA § 7(4)(a), (d); RUPA § 202(c)(3)(i), (v).

[9] *Martin*, 158 N.E. at 79.

[10] If the 40% profit share is viewed as a repayment of a debt, does that mean that it is of no significance in the partnership inquiry? This is a hard question. It certainly means, according to the uniform acts, that no prima facie inference/presumption of partnership may be drawn or imposed. But that does not necessarily mean that the sharing of profits is irrelevant. It may still be a factor in what is a totality of the circumstances inquiry. After all, the carrying on of a business for profit is part of the partnership definition in UPA § 6 and RUPA § 202. For all intents and purposes, however, if it is established that a purported share of profits is really just a loan repayment, then there isn't the same kind of profit-sharing arrangement that a true partner would have. Thus, if there is any significance left to the mere fact that the lender is receiving a share of profits, it is likely minimal.

nership—i.e., the "intent to carry on as co-owners a business for profit, regardless of [the parties'] subjective intention to be 'partners.'"[11]

Aspects of "co-ownership": The partnership definition references carrying on as "co-owners" a business for profit. Anything related to the rights and obligations that owners typically have, therefore, should be relevant to the partnership inquiry.

Sharing of losses: Owners are obligated to bear the losses of the business. Creditors are not. There was no evidence that Peyton, Perkins, and Freeman were responsible for firm losses, other than the notion that if the firm did poorly, the loan might not be repaid. This indirect form of loss sharing, however, is part of every creditor relationship and is not the type of direct profit-and-loss sharing that characterizes an owner relationship.

Ability to inspect books and records of the business: The right to inspect the firm's books and records is a right typically associated with ownership.[12] The trustees were given the right to inspect firm books and were entitled to any information about the business. This is suggestive of partner status.

Control over the partnership's affairs: Perhaps the most important aspect of co-ownership is a partner's right to control the business. The comment to RUPA § 202 states that "[o]wnership involves the power of ultimate control," and "[t]o state that partners are co-owners of a business is to state that they each have the power of ultimate control." (The comment to UPA § 6 is nearly identical.) Any suggestion of control, therefore, is relevant to the co-ownership inquiry, which in turn is relevant to the partnership inquiry.

While this statement is technically correct, control is a spectrum that one might think of as running from "passive" or "indirect" control on one end (i.e., the power to stop things from happening, such as the power to veto decisions) to "active" or "direct" control on the other (i.e., the power to affirmatively make things happen, such as the power to initiate transactions). This idea is important because the typical creditor has a good deal of passive control. For example, it is common for business loans to contain restrictions on the amount of debt that a business can accrue, levels of assets that must be maintained, etc. The specter of default exerts indirect con-

---

[11] RUPA § 202 cmt. 1; *see* Hilco Prop. Servs., Inc. v. United States, 929 F. Supp. 526, 537 (D.N.H. 1996) ("[A]lthough the question of intent is a crucial part of the calculus, the only necessary intent . . . is an intent to do those things which constitute a partnership" (internal quotation omitted)); note 3 and accompanying text.

[12] *See* Chapter 3(C)(3).

trol over the business by making the borrower think twice before violating these debt or asset restrictions. Because this level of indirect control is possessed by the typical creditor, the "partner" label should not be imposed unless the purported creditor possesses *more* control than is present in the typical lending arrangement. Thus, these sorts of disputes often become battles of dueling experts—one side asserting that the control goes beyond the control associated with a typical lending arrangement, and the other maintaining that the control possessed is within lending norms. In general, this means that courts dealing with a partnership inquiry tend to be persuaded by evidence of active control. After all, while an ordinary lending arrangement often provides the creditor with passive or indirect control, such an arrangement does not usually provide the lender with the power to affirmatively initiate transactions for the borrower's business.[13]

What type of control did Peyton, Perkins, and Freeman have? Primarily passive control, as the trustees were merely to be kept advised as to the conduct of the business and consulted on important matters. Such control did not give them the power to initiate action on behalf of K.N. & K. What about the right to veto business that they regarded as too risky? This again is classic passive control. Even the court observed that the trustees "may not initiate any transaction as a partner may do," and "[t]hey may not bind the firm by any action of their own." The trustees' rights were simply "a proper precaution to safeguard the loan," and the court noted that "[n]ot dissimilar agreements have been held proper to guard the interests of the lender."[14]

What about the fact that, until the loaned securities were returned, the firm was to retain Hall as the managing partner? Admittedly, one could view this as Peyton, Perkins, and Freeman controlling the management of the firm, but it is an indirect control, as Hall was still capable of doing (largely) what he wanted. The court stated that this was simply "ordinary caution."[15]

What about the requirement that each member of the firm tender his resignation to Hall? If Hall and the trustees agreed to accept the resignation, the member would then be forced to retire. This sounds like the trustees had control over terminating partners. It is not clear if they could compel a termination over Hall's dissent, or if the decision among the three had to be unanimous. Nevertheless, this seems more like active control (the power to expel a part-

---

[13] A similar distinction between active and passive control arises in the agency context as well. *See* Chapter 2(B)(2)(b).

[14] *Martin*, 158 N.E. at 79–80.

[15] *Id.* at 79.

ner), and the court admitted that it was "somewhat unusual." After considering the totality of the circumstances, the court concluded that it was not enough.[16]

Ultimately, the question of whether a partnership has been formed is a totality of the circumstances inquiry that, as the court noted, involves a "question of degree."[17] Profit sharing and control tend to be the most important factors in this inquiry. Because classic profit sharing was not present, and because the control possessed was mostly passive and indirect, the court could plausibly conclude that the circumstances did not reflect more than creditors taking proper precautions to safeguard their loan. Thus, Peyton, Perkins, and Freeman were not partners in the firm. Nevertheless, the case was likely a close call for the court.

The decision of *Lupien v. Malsbenden*[18] is useful to compare to *Martin*. In *Lupien*, the plaintiff entered into a written agreement with Steven Cragin, doing business as York Motor Mart, for the construction of a Bradley automobile.[19] The plaintiff paid a portion of the purchase price, but the Bradley was never received. After Cragin disappeared, a suit was filed against Frederick Malsbenden on the theory that he was a partner of Cragin in the business. Malsbenden had purportedly loaned $85,000 to the venture, but he admitted that his loan carried no interest and that repayment was only to occur upon the sale of Bradley automobiles. Moreover, unlike a lender, Malsbenden participated in the control of the business on a day-to-day basis. Among other tasks, Malsbenden opened the premises each morning, had final say on the ordering of parts, paid for parts, equipment, and employee salaries, and met with the plaintiff when he visited the business.[20]

What should one make of the $85,000 interest-free "loan" by Malsbenden? Interest-free loans with no regular payment dates are non-existent (or at least highly unusual) in ordinary arms-length lending arrangements. As a result, the $85,000 looks more like a contribution of capital—something that owners do, rather than lenders. Moreover, Malsbenden ran all aspects of the business and apparently made the day-to-day decisions for the venture. According to the court, Malsbenden had an "intent to share [in] the fruits of the enterprise" and, unlike the defendants in *Martin*, he exercised active control over the business. Not surprisingly, the court

---

[16] *See id.* at 80.

[17] *Id.*

[18] 477 A.2d 746 (Me. 1984).

[19] According to the court, a Bradley automobile is "a 'kit car' constructed on a Volkswagen chassis." *Id.* at 747 n.2.

[20] *See id.* at 747–49.

concluded that Malsbenden was liable as a partner for the obligations of York Motor Mart.[21] Although *Lupien* and *Martin* reach different conclusions about whether the defendants are liable as partners, the decisions consistently suggest that a partnership is more likely to be found when active or direct control is possessed.[22]

2. The Partnership Agreement

As a general matter, once a partnership has been formed, the partnership's operation is governed by the provisions of the applicable statute. For example, UPA indicates that partners share equally in the profits and losses of the partnership, and it directs that every partner has the right to participate in the management of the partnership.[23] Nevertheless, almost all of the statutory provisions function merely as default rules that can be altered by the agreement of the partners.[24] Thus, partners in a general partnership can largely structure their business as they see fit.

RUPA makes clear that a partnership agreement may be written, oral, or implied among the partners.[25] (UPA has no analogous provision.) Although it is not necessary for a partnership agreement to be in writing, it is usually desirable. For example, one major advantage of having a written agreement is that it may prevent future disputes over what the actual business arrangement was between the parties. As another example, a partner may wish to lend (rather than to contribute) specific property to a partnership. A written agreement clearly identifying which property is loaned and which is contributed is critical to protect the partner's interest in the loaned property.

When real estate is to be contributed as partnership property or the agreement includes a term of more than one year, a written agreement may also be necessary to comply with the statute of frauds. In *Gano v. Jamail*,[26] Gano claimed that he was made a

---

[21] *Id.* at 749.

[22] It is unclear in *Lupien* whether the business was actually profitable. Nevertheless, so long as it is a business for profit and the partners intend to share any profits, the fact that no profits are actually made is irrelevant. Otherwise, a losing venture could never be a legal partnership.

[23] *See* UPA § 18(a), (e); RUPA § 401(b), (f).

[24] *See* RUPA § 103. UPA has no analogous provision. Nevertheless, some UPA provisions explicitly indicate that they can be altered by an agreement between the partners. *See, e.g.,* UPA §§ 18–19. The hard question in UPA is when the provision does not contain "unless otherwise agreed" or similar language. A strong argument can be made that, because some provisions do contain such language, the absence of the language is material and conveys that the provision is intended to be mandatory. It is, however, not clear. The clarity provided by RUPA § 103 can be seen as an improvement in this regard.

[25] *See* RUPA § 101(7).

[26] 678 S.W.2d 152 (Tex. App. 1984).

partner by oral agreement in Jamail's one-person law practice in
1969, after which the firm was known as "Jamail and Gano." In
1978, Jamail terminated the arrangement. Gano brought suit on
the alleged partnership agreement, but he lost because of the one-
year provision of the statute of frauds. The court accepted the argument that the firm "was involved almost exclusively in a personal
injury practice in which cases were based on contingent fee contracts, and almost always took more than a year to conclude." The
court also found that the agreement contemplated that the partnership was to last until all of the cases signed up during the partnership were resolved.[27]

A written partnership agreement is advantageous to the partnership's attorney as well, as it places suggestions and advice in
concrete form to help prevent misunderstandings. More generally,
and as mentioned, in the absence of a written or other agreement,
the relationship between the partners will be governed by the default provisions of the applicable state partnership statute. It is
unlikely that the provisions of this statute will reflect all of the expectations and understandings among the partners. In short, the
advantages of a written agreement are substantial, and lawyers
should advise their clients to consider a written agreement before
entering into a partnership.

3. Entity vs. Aggregate Views

Is a general partnership a legal entity separate and distinct
from the partners themselves, or is a partnership simply an aggregate of its partners with no separate legal status? Several issues
turn on the answer to this question. For example, can a partnership sue or be sued in its own name? Can it hold property of its
own? Only if the partnership is viewed as a distinct legal entity
would the answer to these questions appear to be yes.

In general, UPA adopts an aggregate view of the partnership
and rejects the notion that a partnership is a legal entity. For example, UPA § 29 indicates that a partnership is dissolved whenever
any partner ceases to be associated in the carrying on of the business. If a partnership were a separate legal entity, the departure of
a partner would not have to affect the existence of the partnership
itself. If a partnership were simply an aggregate of its partners,
however, then the departure of one of the partners would necessari-

---

[27] *See id.* at 154.

ly change the aggregate. It would make sense to conclude, as UPA § 29 does, that the former aggregate partnership no longer exists.[28]

This aggregate view of the partnership has produced some controversial judicial decisions. In *Fairway Development Co. v. Title Insurance Co. of Minnesota*,[29] a general partnership consisting of Thomas Bernabei, James Serra, and Howard Wenger purchased a title guaranty policy. The defendant, Title Insurance Company, attempted to avoid payment under the policy on the theory that the insured partnership (Fairway Development I) no longer existed because two of the partners had left the firm. According to the defendant, a new partnership resulted from this departure (Fairway Development II), and that new partnership was not an insured under the policy. The plaintiff responded, in effect, that nothing changed with the departure of the two partners—the remaining partners continued to operate the firm in the same manner.[30] After reviewing various sections of the UPA-based Ohio partnership statute, the court sided with the defendant insurance company:

> The Court's review of the applicable statutory law supports a finding that the common law rule that "a dissolution occurs and a new partnership is formed whenever a partner retires or a new partner is admitted," survives the enactment of the Ohio Uniform Partnership Law. ... The Court's conclusion accords with the aggregate theory of partnership, which, applied to this case, recognizes Fairway Development I not as an entity in itself, but as a partnership made up of three members, Bernabei, Serra, and Wenger. That partnership ceased when the membership of the partnership changed. ... The Court finds that the law as applicable to the facts of this case supports a finding that the named party guaranteed in the contract in question is not the plaintiff, and that the plaintiff is a new partnership which followed the termination of Fairway Development I. ... [T]he Court holds that the terms of the title guaranty extended only to the named party guaranteed, that party being Fairway

---

[28] UPA § 29 is about a partner leaving the partnership. When a partner joins a partnership, that addition also changes the aggregate. It would necessarily dissolve the former partnership. Although UPA § 29 does not speak to this "addition" scenario, § 41(1) does. It indicates that when any new partner is admitted into an existing partnership, "creditors of the *first or dissolved* partnership are also creditors of the partnership so continuing the business" (emphasis added). The comment to § 41 states the following: "It is universally admitted that any change in membership dissolves a partnership, and creates a new partnership. This section, as drafted, does not alter that rule." *See also id.* § 17 cmt. ("The present section eliminates the difficulty which arises when a new partner is admitted without liquidation of firm debts. The present theory of the common law is that a new partnership is formed . . . .").

[29] 621 F. Supp. 120 (N.D. Ohio 1985).

[30] *See id.* at 121–22.

Development I, and that Fairway Development II therefore has no standing to sue the defendant for breach of the contract in question.[31]

Given the result in *Fairway*, aren't all contracts entered into by UPA partnerships in jeopardy? The answer would appear to be yes. Any change in the composition of the partners leads to the dissolution of the former partnership and the commencement of a new partnership. This problem might be solved by contract by indicating that a particular insurance policy or other contract would cover the partnership "and any successor partnership" or some similar phrase. But presumably that phrase would have to be part of every contract that the partnership signs.

Would it work if the partners agreed that a change in the composition of the partners would not result in dissolution? That is, can UPA § 29 (and § 41(1)) be contractually altered by the partners? The prevailing view under UPA is that dissolution cannot be avoided by agreement. Concluding otherwise would fly in the face of the aggregate conception of the partnership. Indeed, a partner's departure or addition necessarily changes the aggregate and it would be conceptually inconsistent to allow otherwise.[32]

In contrast, RUPA explicitly adopts an entity view of the partnership. RUPA § 201 states that "[a] partnership is an entity distinct from its partners," and the comment mentions that "RUPA embraces the entity theory of the partnership." This entity view simplifies many of the practical problems caused by the aggregate perspective.[33]

---

[31] *Id.* at 123–25 (citations omitted).

[32] *See* II ALAN R. BROMBERG & LARRY E. RIBSTEIN, BROMBERG AND RIBSTEIN ON PARTNERSHIP § 7.01(c), at 7:14 (13th ed. 2005) (stating that "in most jurisdictions the occurrence of a statutory cause of dissolution . . . *necessarily* causes dissolution of the partnership . . . because U.P.A. §§ 29, 31, and 32 are not subject to the contrary agreement of the parties").

UPA is silent on whether a partnership may sue or be sued in its own name, presumably because of the aggregate view of the partnership. Nevertheless, many UPA jurisdictions have enacted provisions—usually in the state's partnership statute or in its rules of civil procedure—that explicitly permit the partnership to sue or be sued in its own name. Absent such provisions, all of the partners would need to be joined as plaintiffs in lawsuits seeking to assert the partnership's rights. Similarly, absent such provisions, some or all of the individual partners (depending upon whether the partners have joint liability or joint and several liability) would need to be sued to recover an obligation owed by the partnership. *See* Chapter 3(D)(3)(b).

[33] *See, e.g.,* RUPA § 307(a) (stating that a partnership "may sue and be sued in the name of the partnership"); *see also id.* § 203 ("Property acquired by a partnership is property of the partnership and not of the partners individually.").

Interestingly, it is not clear that RUPA solves the *Fairway* problem. The partnership in *Fairway* was likely an at-will partnership—a partnership with no definite term or particular undertaking. *See id.* § 101(8). When a partner in an at-will part-

4. Partnership By Estoppel

Among partners or purported partners, a partnership is only formed if the legal definition of partnership is met.[34] As to third parties, however, a partnership can be formed by estoppel—i.e., by representing that a person is a partner to third parties, and by inducing reliance on such a representation. A person who is not a partner, in other words, can be estopped from denying partner status (and the accompanying partner liability) under certain circumstances: "[i]f a person, by words or conduct, purports to be a partner, or consents to being represented by another as a partner,[35] in a partnership or with one or more persons not partners, the purported partner is liable to a person to whom the representation is made, if that person, relying on the representation, enters into a transaction with the actual or purported partnership."[36] If a person is not a partner in fact (a partner by virtue of meeting the legal definition of

---

nership leaves, § 801(1) indicates that the partnership is dissolved and must be wound up. Thus, it would appear that the partnership in *Fairway* would have dissolved even under an entity-conception statute like RUPA. Perhaps the problem is solved by § 802(b), which indicates that, at any time after the dissolution of a partnership and before winding up is completed, all of the partners (including rightfully dissociating partners) can agree to waive the right to have the partnership wound up. In that event, "the partnership resumes carrying on its business *as if dissolution had never occurred.*" *Id.* § 802(b)(1) (emphasis added). Alternatively, under RUPA, the partners can agree in advance that a partner's departure in an at-will partnership will not lead to dissolution of the partnership. *See id.* § 103(b). As mentioned, if a partnership is an entity that is distinct from the partners themselves, it is conceptually consistent for the departure of a partner to not affect the continuation of the partnership itself.

[34] *See* UPA § 6; RUPA § 202; Chapter 3(B)(1).

[35] Does one "consent" to being represented as a partner if he knows about the representation but does nothing about it? RUPA seems to indicate that affirmative consent is required and that "consent by silence" is insufficient. *See* RUPA § 308 cmt. ("As under the UPA, there is no duty of denial, and thus a person held out by another as a partner is not liable unless he actually consents to the representation."). Under UPA, however, conflicting case authority exists, as some courts require a person to take steps to repudiate another's representation of him as a partner, even though the person had no role in the other's decision to make the representation.

[36] RUPA § 308; *see* UPA § 16 (substantially the same). The uniform acts distinguish between public and private representations of partner status. *See* UPA § 16(1); RUPA § 308(a). A number of cases decided under UPA conclude that reliance by the plaintiff third party is not necessary when a public representation is made. *See, e.g.,* Ag Servs. of Am., Inc. v. Nielsen, 231 F.3d 726, 735–36 (10th Cir. 2000); Anderson Hay & Grain Co. v. Dunn, 467 P.2d 5, 7 (N.M. 1970); Gilbert v. Howard, 326 P.2d 1085, 1087 (N.M. 1958). *But see* Cheesecake Factory, Inc. v. Baines, 964 P.2d 183, 187–90 (N.M. Ct. App. 1998) (holding that a showing of reliance is always necessary to establish a partner by estoppel, and containing a nice discussion of the conflicting case law). RUPA makes clear, however, that reliance is required in both private and public representation disputes. *See* RUPA § 308(a) (requiring reliance in the first sentence (private representations) and in the second sentence (public representations) of the subsection).

a partnership), then this estoppel theory is the only basis for holding the person liable as a partner to a third party.[37]

5. Federal Tax Consequences

Under Subchapter K of the Internal Revenue Code, a partnership is taxed on a "pass-through" basis. The partnership is required to compute its taxable income and to file an informational return with the IRS, but the partnership itself does not pay any tax. Instead, the net income or loss from partnership operations is allocated or "passed through" to the partners in accordance with their profit or loss shares. The partnership provides each partner with a statement (Form K–1) informing the partner of his respective share of the partnership's income or loss, and each partner must then include this amount directly on his individual income tax return.

The major advantages of pass-through taxation are (1) partnership profits are not subject to double taxation (i.e., the partnership's profits are taxed only at the owner (partner) level, rather than also taxed at the business or entity (partnership) level), and (2) if the partnership has losses rather than gains, the partners may use the losses to shield other income on their individual returns. The major disadvantage of pass-through treatment is that an individual partner is taxed based on his allocation of partnership income and not on the amount actually distributed in cash to him. In other words, the partners must pay tax based on their share of the business income even if the partnership has not distributed any of that income to them.

In 1997, the "check-the-box" regulations of the IRS became effective.[38] These regulations permit noncorporate entities, including general partnerships, to elect to be taxed like a corporation. If no election is made, pass-through partnership taxation is the default rule. Because a corporation is subject to double taxation (i.e., the corporation itself pays taxes on its income, and the shareholders pay taxes on that income again when and if the income is distributed to them), it would be unusual for a partnership to elect corporate taxation.

C. Management and Operation

1. General Governance and Actual Authority

In a general partnership, ordinary business matters are decided by a majority of the partners (by number).[39] This is a default

---

[37] *See, e.g.,* RUPA § 308(e) & cmt.

[38] *See* Treas. Reg. §§ 301.7701–1 to –3.

[39] *See* UPA § 18(h); RUPA § 401(j).

rule that partners can alter by agreement.[40] Extraordinary matters (matters outside of the ordinary course of business) require a unanimous vote by the partners, although this too is a default rule that may be altered by agreement.[41] If the requisite consent is obtained according to these rules, a partner has actual authority to bind the partnership to the transaction at issue. Actual authority can also be established by other conduct of the partnership (or the partners collectively) that makes it reasonable for the partner to believe that he is authorized (e.g., language in a partnership agreement, a title, or a position).

Is this "majority vote by number" rule (a per capita rule) an appropriate default provision for deciding ordinary business matters? Why not allocate management power by financial contribution—i.e., if you contribute 90% of the financial capital for the business, you are entitled to 90% of the management power? (Indeed, this is the way it works in the corporation.) When owners have unlimited personal liability for a firm's obligations, as in a general partnership, a per capita rule makes sense because the owners are providing more than a mere financial contribution to the firm—they are providing their personal credit as well. In other words, personal liability gives owners a stake in the business that exceeds their contribution of financial capital. Stated more plainly, a person who puts up 10% of the financial capital may expect an equal vote with a person who puts up 90% of the financial capital because the 90% owner can make decisions that put the personal assets of the 10% owner at risk. Consider a wealthy partner who puts up 10% of the financial capital and a nearly insolvent partner who puts up 90% of the financial capital. Given the nearly insolvent partner's lack of personal assets, the wealthy partner is arguably bearing more risk if the partnership finds itself unable to pay its liabilities.

In addition, partners may enter into personal guarantees for the firm or participate actively in the management of the venture. To this extent, they are making service contributions that exceed their contributions of financial capital to the firm, and they may expect voting rights to reflect these additional contributions.

---

[40] UPA § 18 is prefaced with "subject to any agreement between [the partners]," and RUPA § 103(b) does not list § 401 as a section that cannot be altered by agreement.

[41] RUPA § 401(j) explicitly states that "[a]n act outside the ordinary course of business of a partnership and an amendment to the partnership agreement may be undertaken only with the consent of all of the partners." UPA § 18(h) does not speak to extraordinary transactions, other than noting that "no act in contravention of any agreement between the partners may be done rightfully without the consent of all the partners." Comment 11 to RUPA § 401 states, however, that "[a]lthough the text of the UPA is silent regarding extraordinary matters, courts have generally required the consent of all partners for those matters." *See also* note 40 (explaining that UPA § 18 and RUPA § 401 are merely default rules).

In short, pro rata (by financial contribution) is the default rule in corporations because shares are usually sold for cash and not services, and limited liability largely eliminates any credit contributions. Thus, allocating voting rights by financial contribution makes sense. In a general partnership, however, the per capita default rule reflects the financial, service, and credit contributions that partners typically make. Allocating voting rights based purely on financial contributions, in other words, may not reflect the entirety of the partners' contributions.

The decision of *Summers v. Dooley*[42] is often used to illustrate the basic voting rules under the partnership statutes. Summers and Dooley were partners who operated a trash collection business. Summers wanted to hire an additional employee, but Dooley did not. Nevertheless, Summers hired the employee and paid him out of his own pocket.

Summers ultimately sued claiming that he should be reimbursed by Dooley for half of the expenses of hiring the "third man." Citing the statutory equivalent of UPA § 18(h), the court stated that ordinary business matters must be decided by a majority vote of the partners. With only two partners in the business, both needed to consent to establish the requisite majority. Because Dooley opposed the hiring, Summers' conduct was unauthorized. As a result, the court held that Dooley was not liable for any of the hiring expenses.[43]

Distinguishing between ordinary and extraordinary business matters is not always an easy task. For example, is hiring an additional employee in a small, two-man partnership an ordinary business matter? The *Summers* court seemed to think so, as it cited the "ordinary matters" language of the statute and focused on a "majority" vote. One could argue, however, that the hiring of an additional employee in a small business is a significant event—possibly rising to the level of "extraordinary." In a partnership with two partners, of course, this makes little difference, as a majority vote and a unanimous vote wind up being the same. In a partnership with more than two partners, however, this issue can be critical.

One could also argue, as Summers did, that Dooley ratified the unauthorized act of Summers by retaining profits earned by the additional employee. On the other hand, the court pointed out that Dooley "continually voiced objection" and "did not sit idly by and

---

[42] 481 P.2d 318 (Idaho 1971).

[43] *See id.* at 319–21. Stated another way, in a two-person partnership, the requirement of majority approval gives each partner a veto power.

acquiesce in the actions of his partner."[44] Thus, the ratification evidence was, perhaps, mixed. At bottom, the opinion seems designed to deter those in Summers' position from acting improperly, even if those in Dooley's position receive some benefit.[45]

In contrast to *Summers*, consider the decision of *National Biscuit Co. v. Stroud*.[46] Stroud and Freeman were partners in a business that sold groceries. National sold bread to the partnership. Stroud advised National that he would no longer be responsible for any additional bread sold by National to the partnership. Nevertheless, at the request of Freeman, National continued to deliver bread.

The court noted that Freeman had equal rights in the management of the partnership.[47] More importantly, the court concluded that Stroud could not restrict Freeman's authority to buy bread for the partnership because (1) buying bread was an ordinary matter connected with the partnership business, and (2) Stroud was not and could not be a majority of the partners. The court held that Freeman's purchases of bread for the partnership bound the partnership and Stroud.[48]

In *Summers*, majority approval for a transaction was lacking, and the transaction was not held to be a partnership obligation. In *Stroud*, majority approval for a transaction was lacking, but the transaction was held to be a partnership obligation. Are these cases consistent? Part of the problem here is understanding what the *Stroud* court held. *Stroud* could be read to suggest that the combination of UPA § 9 ("[e]very partner is an agent of the partnership for the purpose of its business") and § 18(e) ("[a]ll partners have equal rights in the management and conduct of the partnership business") results in every partner having actual authority to unilaterally bind the partnership to an ordinary business transaction.[49]

---

[44] *Id.* at 321.

[45] General agency principles, such as ratification, do apply in the partnership setting. *See* UPA § 4(3); RUPA § 104(a); *see also* UPA § 9(1) (stating that "[e]very partner is an agent of the partnership for the purpose of its business"); RUPA § 301(1) (substantially the same).

[46] 106 S.E.2d 692 (N.C. 1959).

[47] UPA § 18(e) provides that "[a]ll partners have equal rights in the management and conduct of the partnership business." *See also* RUPA § 401(f) (substantially the same). This provision "has been interpreted broadly to mean that, absent contrary agreement, each partner has a continuing right to participate in the management of the partnership and to be informed about the partnership business, even if his assent to partnership business decisions is not required." *Id.* § 401 cmt. 7.

[48] *See Stroud,* 106 S.E.2d at 694–95.

[49] *Cf.* STEPHEN M. BAINBRIDGE, AGENCY, PARTNERSHIPS & LLCS 117 (2004) ("Since each partner is an agent of the partnership, with an equal right to conduct partnership business, actual authority to bind the partnership is inherent in the position."); RUPA § 301 cmt. 2 ("Section 301(1) retains the basic principles reflected in UPA Section 9(1). . . . The effect of Section 301(1) is to characterize a partner as a

Under this interpretation, Freeman had actual authority to make the bread purchases, even after Stroud's objection. This seems contrary to the *Summers* conclusion that a partner lacks actual authority to bind the partnership to an ordinary business transaction unless a majority of the partners agree. Under this reading, therefore, *Stroud* and *Summers* appear inconsistent.

Reading *Stroud* to say that partners have actual authority to unilaterally bind the partnership to ordinary business transactions is, however, puzzling. UPA § 9 and RUPA § 301 both deal with the relations of partners to third parties—a context that typically invokes apparent authority, but not actual authority. Provisions that deal with the relations of partners to one another, e.g., UPA § 18 and RUPA § 401, should be the relevant actual authority provisions. Even under this reading, however, the cases could be reconciled. Perhaps *Summers* should not be viewed as speaking to the issue of whether a partner has actual authority to unilaterally bind the partnership to an ordinary business transaction because *Summers* involved an extraordinary transaction—a decision to hire an additional employee in a small, two-man partnership. Thus, *Summers* (an extraordinary transaction case) does not necessarily contradict the holding of *Stroud* (an ordinary transaction case). As mentioned, however, the *Summers* court thought it was dealing with an ordinary business transaction—it cited the statutory equivalent to UPA § 18(h) and its discussion of ordinary business matters, and it mentioned the necessity for a majority vote.

Perhaps a better reading of *Stroud* is that it, like *Summers*, holds that the consent of a majority of partners is necessary for a partner to have actual authority to bind the partnership on ordinary business matters. Under that common holding, the cases can be reconciled by arguing that Summers and Stroud were both trying to change the status quo (Summers by hiring an additional employee, and Stroud by attempting to stop bread deliveries)—a status quo that had previously been authorized by the partners. If these changes are viewed as ordinary business matters, majority votes would be needed to authorize them. Such votes were not received; thus, the status quo persisted (the employee could not be hired, and the bread deliveries could not be discontinued). A similar point can be made if we think of the status quo as based on a partnership agreement. That is, perhaps it could be argued that the partners had reached agreement on how their respective businesses would be run (no additional employees and continued bread deliveries).

---

general managerial agent having both *actual* and apparent authority co-extensive in scope with the firm's ordinary business, at least in the absence of a contrary partnership agreement." (emphasis added)).

When one partner wanted to change things, that partner was trying to alter the prior partnership agreement. Amending a partnership agreement requires a unanimous vote, and a unanimous vote was not obtained.[50] Viewed in these terms, *Stroud* does not hold that a partner has the actual authority to unilaterally bind the partnership to an ordinary business transaction. Instead, actual authority is established only if the requisite statutory vote is obtained.

2. Apparent Authority

Stroud can also be used to introduce the concept of apparent authority in the partnership setting. UPA § 9 and RUPA § 301 convey that (1) a partner is an agent of the partnership, and (2) a partner has apparent authority to bind the partnership to transactions within the ordinary course of the partnership's business, unless the third party is aware that the partner lacks actual authority. Did Freeman have apparent authority to continue buying bread for the partnership? From the perspective of National, buying bread would appear to be within the ordinary course of business of a grocery store, and there was a prior relationship of delivering and paying for bread between the parties. Of course, there can be no apparent authority if the third party is aware that actual authority is lacking. Did Stroud's statement that "he personally would not be responsible for any additional bread sold by plaintiff" suggest that Freeman's later purchases were not authorized? Not necessarily. National may simply have understood that the partnership would be responsible for the bread payments, but not Stroud individually if the partnership did not pay. This does not seem to convey that National knew that Freeman lacked actual authority to purchase bread for the partnership. In short, it seems plausible to argue that *Stroud* is simply an apparent authority decision.[51]

Under UPA § 9, a partner has authority to bind the partnership for any act that is "apparently carrying on in the usual way the business of the partnership." This language would presumably encompass an act within the apparent course of business of the partner's firm. It is unclear, however, whether it would also encompass an act that is not within the apparent course of business of the partner's firm, but that is within the apparent course of business of other firms engaged in a similar line of business as the partner's firm. There is authority under UPA for this broader construction.[52]

---

[50] *See* UPA § 18(h); RUPA § 401(j); note 41.

[51] If a partner lacking actual authority binds the partnership through apparent authority, is there a remedy? Presumably the partnership would have an action against the partner for acting without authority and causing it harm. *See, e.g.,* RUPA § 405.

[52] *See, e.g.,* Burns v. Gonzalez, 439 S.W.2d 128, 131 (Tex. Civ. App. 1969) ("As we interpret [UPA] Sec. 9(1), the act of a partner binds the firm, absent an express limi-

RUPA § 301 makes clear that a partner has authority to bind the partnership for any act that is "apparently carrying on in the ordinary course the partnership business or business of the kind carried on by the partnership."

The fact that every partner has the ability to bind the partnership via apparent authority in ordinary business transactions can be a real problem for a partnership. The uniform acts do not appear to allow an elimination of this apparent authority by contract. UPA § 9 is not prefaced by "unless otherwise agreed" or similar language that would suggest that contractual alteration is permissible.[53] Moreover, as a general matter, contract cannot be used to affect the rights of non-parties, and a third party's right to rely on the apparent authority of a partner would seem to be a right that the uniform acts grant. RUPA § 103(b)(10) explicitly states that partners cannot agree to restrict the rights of third parties. Without a contractual solution, the only way to limit apparent authority involves providing notice of a partner's lack of authority to as many creditors as possible. This works under UPA because § 9 states that apparent authority is eliminated if the third party has "knowledge" of the partner's lack of authority. Similarly, under RUPA § 301(1), apparent authority is eliminated if the third party "knew or had received a notification that the partner lacked authority."[54]

RUPA § 303 permits a partnership to file a public "statement of partnership authority." According to the comment, § 303 "provides for an optional statement of partnership authority specifying the names of the partners authorized to execute instruments transferring real property held in the name of the partnership," and it "may also grant supplementary authority to partners, or limit their authority, to enter into other transactions on behalf of the partnership." (UPA has no similar provision.) Although a statement of partnership authority may limit authority, § 303(e) and (f) restrict the effectiveness of any filed limitations to real estate transactions. In non-real estate transactions, limitations on a partner's authority in a filed statement do not bind third parties. Of course, if a third party did check the public filings, and if he became aware of a limi-

---

tation of authority known to the party dealing with such partner, if such act is for the purpose of 'apparently carrying on' the business of the partnership in the way in which other firms engaged in the same business in the locality usually transact business, or in the way in which the particular partnership usually transacts its business.").

[53] In contrast, UPA § 18 does include such language.

[54] UPA § 3 defines knowledge as encompassing actual knowledge and "knowledge of such other facts as in the circumstances shows bad faith." RUPA § 102 defines knowledge and notice, and it limits knowledge to actual knowledge. These distinctions can be meaningful. See RUPA § 301 cmt. 2.

tation on a partner's authority, that actual knowledge would prevent him from relying on the apparent authority of the partner.[55]

3. Inspection and Information Rights

Both uniform acts provide partners with the right to inspect the books and records of the partnership.[56] In addition, both acts provide that partners shall furnish to other partners, on demand, information concerning the partnership's business and affairs.[57] RUPA expands this informational right by imposing an affirmative disclosure obligation on the partners and the partnership to furnish information to other partners even without demand. This affirmative obligation is required for "any information concerning the partnership's business and affairs reasonably required for the proper exercise of the partner's rights and duties under the partnership agreement or [RUPA]."[58]

D. Financial Rights and Obligations

1. Partnership Accounting

From an accounting standpoint, the business of the partnership is distinct from the financial affairs of the individual partners. The partners' financial interests are usually reflected in "capital accounts," which are adjusted periodically for contributions of capital, distributions, profits, and losses. RUPA § 401(a) describes how each partner's capital account is constructed and maintained: the account equals the money and property contributed by the partner, less the amount of any distributions to the partner, plus the partner's share of the profits, less the partner's share of the losses. A partner's capital account may be negative from time to time; upon the final settlement of accounts when the partnership is terminated, a partner with a negative capital account must pay the partnership that amount.[59] The partnership is not required to maintain a formal capital account for each partner, but all except the most informal partnerships do so.

2. Sharing of Profits and Losses

In the absence of a contrary agreement, the uniform acts state that profits are shared equally among the partners (by number), and that the sharing of losses follows the allocation for the sharing

---

[55] *See* RUPA § 303 cmt. 3.

[56] *See* UPA § 19; RUPA § 403(b).

[57] *See* UPA § 20; RUPA § 403(c)(2).

[58] RUPA § 403(c)(1).

[59] *See, e.g., id.* § 807(b) & cmt. 3.

of profits (the "losses follow profits" rule).[60] Thus, the default rules indicate that both profits and losses are shared equally among the partners.

Example: *A* contributes 70% of the capital to a partnership and *B* contributes 30%. Profits and losses are split equally between *A* and *B*. The fact that the partners contributed unequal amounts of capital is irrelevant under the default rules.

Example: *A* contributes 70% of the capital to a partnership and *B* contributes 30%. *A* and *B* agree that profits will be split 70% to *A* and 30% to *B*, but nothing is stated about losses. Because the default rule of equal profit sharing has been displaced, profits will be split according to the agreed 70/30 allocation. Because the default rule for loss sharing is that losses follow profits, losses will also be split according to the 70/30 allocation.

Example: *A* contributes 70% of the capital to a partnership and *B* contributes 30%. *A* and *B* agree that losses will be split 70% to *A* and 30% to *B*, but nothing is stated about profits. Because the default rule of losses following profits has been displaced, losses will be split according to the agreed 70/30 allocation. Because the default rule of equal profit sharing has not been displaced, profits will be split 50/50 rather than 70/30. (In other words, as a default rule, losses follow profits, but profits do not follow losses.)

In many general partnerships, the default rules for profit and loss sharing have been displaced by a partnership agreement. For example, the profits of a business may be divided by agreement in various ways:

(a) The partners may share on a flat percentage basis without regard to any other factor. Profit sharing ratios for each partner may be established in the partnership agreement itself. They may also be established by issuing "partnership units" to each partner and determining the profit sharing or loss sharing ratio for each partner by dividing the number of units owned by that partner by the total number of units outstanding. In this way, if new partners are added, dilution of existing interests occurs automatically without any need to amend the agreement; if old partners depart without new ones being added, the remaining interests are also automatically concentrated. Partnership units also permit the creation of incentive options or unit appreciation rights that permit successful partners to increase their percentage interest in the firm.

---

[60] *See* UPA § 18(a); RUPA § 401(b).

(b) Partners may be entitled to a fixed weekly or monthly "salary." This payment may be treated as a "cost" and subtracted before the "profit" is computed for division on some other basis, or it may be considered an advance to be credited against the amount the partner is otherwise entitled to after division of the profit. In the latter case, the agreement should consider the responsibility of the partner receiving a "salary" if the "salary" exceeds the actual profit allocable to him during any period.

(c) The partners may share on a percentage basis, with the percentages recomputed each year on the basis of the average amount invested in the partnership during the year by each partner. This type of arrangement is appropriate when the business is largely dependent on capital for income generation.

(d) The partners may share on a percentage basis, with the percentages recomputed each year on the basis of total income, the sales or billings by each partner, time devoted to the business, or some other factor.

(e) In large partnerships, each partner may be entitled to a fixed percentage applied against perhaps 80 percent of the income. A committee of senior partners will allocate the remaining 20 percent among the junior partners as a form of incentive compensation on the basis of productivity, billings, or some other factor. Usually committee members are not themselves eligible to share in the "incentive pie."

(f) The partnership agreement may be intentionally silent on the division of profits. The partners will work out the division of profits by agreement on a mutual acceptable basis. In larger firms, a committee or a single managing partner may have the responsibility of making the division of profits.

It is not uncommon in informal ventures for the parties to agree on a sharing of the profits but not to discuss the sharing of losses. There is often some judicial sympathy for the unfortunate partner who is unexpectedly caught in a losing venture with the threat of personal liability for partnership obligations that were incurred by others. In these cases, a court may accept the erroneous argument that the absence of an express agreement to share losses indicates that no partnership was ever created in the first place.[61] Many cases, however, correctly recognize that an express agreement to share losses is not essential for the existence of a partnership—a

---

[61] *See, e.g.,* FDIC v. Claycomb, 945 F.2d 853, 858–59 (5th Cir. 1991); Grimmett v. Higginbotham, 907 S.W.2d 1, 2–3 (Tex. App. 1994).

result that is consistent with the language of UPA §§ 6–7 and RUPA § 202.[62]

The decision of *Kessler v. Antinora*[63] highlights the unfairness that can result when the default rule on loss sharing is applied to service-contributing partners. Robert Kessler and Richard Antinora entered into a partnership agreement for the purpose of building a home for resale. Kessler was to provide the money and Antinora was to act as the general contractor. Profits would be split 60% to Kessler and 40% to Antinora after Kessler had been reimbursed for his financial contributions. There was no agreement on the sharing of losses.

The cost to construct the home over a three-year period was $498,917, but the house only sold for $420,000. Kessler was repaid all but $78,917 of the money he advanced, but he also claimed unreimbursed interest of $85,440. He sued Antinora for 40% of his alleged total loss of $164,357. The New Jersey statute mirrored UPA § 18(a) in stating that the default rule for loss sharing was that losses followed profits. The court, however, found that this default rule was displaced by an agreement between the partners—i.e., Kessler would be repaid his investment solely from the sale of the house and not by Antinora. Antinora, in other words, would lose the value of his services in the event of a partnership loss, but he would not be required to contribute to Kessler's unreimbursed financial losses. The court was heavily influenced by *Kovacik v. Reed*—a California decision concluding that when one partner contributes money and the other services, neither partner is liable to the other in the event of a loss, as each loses his own investment (one in the form of money, and one in the form of labor).[64]

Is the ruling in *Kessler* consistent with the "losses follow profits" default rule of UPA § 18(a) and RUPA § 401(b)? The partners did agree upon a profit allocation—60% to Kessler and 40% to Antinora. Without an agreement as to losses, the default rule should have applied, and the loss allocation should have mirrored the profit allocation. Thus, Antinora should have been responsible for 40% of the partnership's losses. Kessler's argument was rejected, however, because the court interpreted the language governing the allocation of profits in the partnership agreement as an implicit

[62] *See, e.g.*, Parks v. Riverside Ins. Co., 308 F.2d 175, 180–81 (10th Cir. 1962). RUPA § 202(c)(3), for example, indicates that a person who receives a share of the profits is presumed to be a partner in the business. If no other relevant evidence exists, that presumption should result in a finding of partnership even without an agreement to share losses. *See also* UPA § 7(4) (stating that the receipt of profits is prima facie evidence of partner status).

[63] 653 A.2d 579 (N.J. Super. Ct. App. Div. 1995).

[64] *See id.* at 580–82 (citing Kovacik v. Reed, 315 P.2d 314, 315–16 (Cal. 1957)).

agreement that Kessler could recover his financial contribution only from the sale of the residence (and not from Antinora). According to the court, this language in the partnership agreement "evinced a clear intent" that Antinora did not have to contribute to Kessler's losses.[65] Although this conclusion is questionable, it is clear that the court was motivated by equitable concerns, as Antinora had already lost the value of his labor for the three years of construction. Thus, although Kessler lost part of his invested capital, Antinora had already lost the value of his services.

Consider the following modified set of facts: Kessler and Antinora agree that Kessler will contribute $200,000 to the partnership to cover the expenses of constructing the home. They also agree that Antinora will not contribute any capital; instead, he will be responsible for overseeing the construction. Finally, the partners agree that profits will be split 50/50, but nothing is mentioned about losses. The house takes one year to build and, because of a downturn in the market, it is sold for only $125,000. The partnership then dissolves.

What are the consequences of this sequence of events? Kessler's capital account would start with a $200,000 balance to reflect his capital contribution, while Antinora's capital account would start with a zero balance to reflect his lack of a capital contribution.[66] When the house is sold, the partnership suffers a $75,000 loss ($125,000 in sale proceeds minus $200,000 in construction expenses). Without an agreement as to losses, the default rule applies. Because profits are split 50/50, losses should be split 50/50 as well. Thus, each partner must bear $37,500 of the loss. This would result in a debit to each partner's capital account, producing a balance for Kessler of $162,500 ($200,000 − $37,500) and a balance for Antinora of <$37,500> ($0 − $37,500). In general, when a partnership dissolves, its assets are used to repay partnership liabilities and to settle up the partners' capital accounts.[67] There are no partnership liabilities here; thus, settling up is all that is required. The partnership would owe Kessler $162,500, and Antinora would owe the partnership $37,500. Kessler would receive the $125,000 from the sale of the house plus the $37,500 that came from Antinora. This would leave Kessler with a $37,500 loss (contributed $200,000 but only recovered $125,000 plus $37,500). Similarly, Antinora would have lost the $37,500 that he was obligated to pay to the partnership. Antinora, of course, has also lost the value of his labor

---

[65] *Id.* at 581.

[66] *See, e.g.,* RUPA § 401(a)(1) (noting that a partner's capital account is "credited with an amount equal to *the money plus the value of any other property*" contributed by the partner to the partnership (emphasis added)).

[67] *See* UPA § 40; RUPA § 807. *See generally* Chapter 3(G) (discussing dissolution).

during the year of construction, but this loss of a services contribution appears to have no role in the statutory analysis.

Does this result seem consistent with the partners' likely expectations? Antinora lost all of the value of his labor, and he was obligated to contribute $37,500 to minimize Kessler's financial losses. Borrowing from the rationale of *Kovacik*, isn't it logical to assume that Kessler and Antinora had implicitly agreed that the value of their respective contributions to the venture (Kessler's capital and Antinora's labor) was equivalent? Why would the parties have agreed to split profits 50/50 if they didn't consider their contributions to be roughly equivalent in value?

This thinking might lead a court down one of two paths. First, as in *Kessler*, a court might imply an agreement that the services partner does not have to contribute to the financial losses of the capital partner. In the event of a loss, the services partner loses the value of his services, and the capital partner loses the value of his unreimbursed financial contributions. Kessler would receive only the $125,000 from the sale of the home, and Antinora would receive nothing (but would not pay anything either).

Alternatively, a court might credit the capital account of the services partner with the value of his services. In this hypothetical, for example, Kessler's capital account would start with a $200,000 balance to reflect the value of his capital contribution, while Antinora's capital account would start with a $200,000 balance to reflect the value of his services contribution. When the house is sold, the partnership's $75,000 loss would again be shared by the partners. This would result in a debit to each partner's capital account of $37,500, producing a balance of $162,500 for each partner ($200,000 − $37,500). Upon dissolution, the partnership's assets (the $125,000 in sale proceeds) would be insufficient to cover the $325,000 total of the capital account balances ($162,500 + $162,500). This would produce a $200,000 shortfall that the partners would be required to share. Each capital account balance would be reduced by $100,000, producing a final balance of $62,500 for each partner ($162,500 − $100,000). The $125,000 earned from the sale of the house, therefore, would be split evenly between Kessler and Antinora. In the end, each partner has lost $137,500—i.e., Kessler has recovered $62,500 of his $200,000 financial contribution, and Antinora has recovered $62,500 of his $200,000 services contribution.

Notice that this second approach is better for Antinora. He receives $62,500 rather than nothing under the first approach. The second approach is also more precise, as it can account for differences in the value of the partners' contributions. For example, assume that a court credits the capital account of Antinora with the value of his services, but the court values those services at only $100,000. When the house is sold, the partnership's $75,000 loss would again be shared by the partners. This would result in a debit to each partner's capital account of $37,500, producing a balance of $162,500 for Kessler ($200,000 – $37,500) and $62,500 for Antinora ($100,000 – $37,500). Upon dissolution, the partnership's assets (the $125,000 in sale proceeds) would be insufficient to cover the $225,000 total of the capital account balances ($162,500 + $62,500). This would produce a $100,000 shortfall that the partners would be required to share. Each capital account balance would be reduced by $50,000, producing a final balance of $112,500 for Kessler ($162,500 – $50,000) and $12,500 for Antinora ($62,500 – $50,000). The $125,000 earned from the sale of the house, therefore, would be allocated $112,500 to Kessler and $12,500 to Antinora. In the end, each partner has lost $87,500—i.e., Kessler has recovered $112,500 of his $200,000 financial contribution, and Antinora has recovered $12,500 of his $100,000 services contribution.[68] It seems likely that a court desiring to avoid any unfairness to services partners will choose the first approach when the services are difficult to value, but will choose the greater precision of the second approach when there is some basis for estimating the value of the services.

What if Antinora received a salary for his services in overseeing the construction of the home?[69] He would already have been compensated for the value of his services, and it would be double counting to credit the value of those services to his capital account. Moreover, with respect to the first approach, it is difficult to imply an agreement that the services partner does not have to contribute to the capital partner's losses in such circumstances. After all, that agreement is arguably justified when both partners lose the value of

---

[68] Depending on the numbers, the second approach may be worse for Antinora. If his services are valued at only $50,000, for example, the partnership's $75,000 loss would again result in a debit to each partner's capital account of $37,500. Kessler would have a $162,500 balance ($200,000 – $37,500), and Antinora would have a $12,500 balance ($50,000 – $37,500). Upon dissolution, the partnership's assets (the $125,000 in sale proceeds) would be insufficient to cover the $175,000 total of the capital account balances ($162,500 + $12,500). This would produce a $50,000 shortfall that the partners would be required to share. Each capital account balance would be reduced by $25,000, producing a final balance of $137,500 for Kessler ($162,500 – $25,000) and <$12,500> for Antinora ($12,500 – $25,000). Kessler would receive the entire $125,000 from the sale of the house, and Antinora would be obligated to contribute $12,500 to further ameliorate Kessler's losses. In the end, each partner has lost $62,500—i.e., Kessler has recovered $137,500 of his $200,000 financial contribution, and Antinora has lost his $50,000 services contribution plus his $12,500 obligation.

[69] The default rule under the uniform acts is that partners are not entitled to compensation for services outside of the winding up of the business. *See* UPA § 18(f); RUPA § 401(h).

their contributions. When the services partner has been compensated for the value of his contribution, however, the capital contributor is the only one bearing any losses. In the absence of more explicit evidence of the parties' agreement, it is unlikely that the partners intended for the capital partner to be the sole loss bearer. In short, if Antinora received a salary for his services, then the unfairness of a literal application of § 18(a) and § 401(b) is no longer present, as the services partner has been compensated for the value of his contribution.

Keep in mind that the parties in *Kessler* could have avoided their dispute by changing the default loss sharing rule by agreement. They could have explicitly agreed, for example, that Kessler would bear all of the losses of the venture, or that the parties shall share losses in some other designated manner. At the very least, they could have agreed that Antinora's services would be credited to his capital account at a specified value, or that Antinora would receive an agreed-upon salary for his services.[70] That said, it is worth reiterating that UPA § 18(a) provides a default rule for the situation that seems inconsistent with the parties' probable expectations when one partner is providing capital and the other is providing services. RUPA § 401(b) follows the UPA approach, even though the comment indicates that the drafters were aware of the potential unfairness stemming from the rule.[71]

3. Liability to Third Parties

a. Liability of the Partnership

With respect to the partnership's liability in contract, you have already learned that a partnership is liable for contracts entered into on its behalf by partners with actual or apparent authority.[72] With respect to the partnership's liability in tort, UPA § 13 also re-

---

[70] As the preceding discussion has revealed, changing any one of the following default rules would mitigate any perceived unfairness to services partners: (1) change the default loss sharing rule so that a services partner does not have to contribute to the financial losses of a capital partner (UPA § 18(a); RUPA § 401(b)); (2) change the default capital account rule so that the account is credited with the value of a services contribution (RUPA § 401(a)(1)); or (3) change the default "no compensation for services" rule so that a services partner is compensated for a services contribution (UPA § 18(f); RUPA § 401(h)).

[71] *See* RUPA § 401 cmt. 3 ("The default rules apply . . . where one or more of the partners contribute no capital, although there is case law to the contrary. *See, e.g., Kovacik v. Reed.* . . . It may seem unfair that the contributor of services, who contributes little or no capital, should be obligated to contribute toward the capital loss of the large contributor who contributed no services. In entering a partnership with such a capital structure, the partners should foresee that application of the default rule may bring about unusual results and take advantage of their power to vary by agreement the allocation of capital losses.").

[72] *See* UPA § 9; RUPA § 301; *see also* Chapter 3(C)(1)–(2) (discussing actual and apparent authority).

flects agency principles by providing that a partnership is liable to third parties for "any wrongful act or omission of any partner acting in the ordinary course of the business of the partnership or with the authority of his co-partners." UPA § 14 also provides that a partnership is liable in certain circumstances if a partner misapplies money or property of a third person. RUPA § 305 is generally consistent with these UPA provisions.

b. Liability of the Partners

A defining characteristic of the general partnership is that each partner has unlimited personal liability for all of the obligations of the partnership. UPA § 15 provides that partners have "joint and several" liability for all partnership obligations under §§ 13–14 (essentially tort obligations) and "joint" liability for all other partnership obligations (essentially contractual obligations). Joint and several liability permits a plaintiff to sue one or more of the partners without having to sue them all. In contrast, joint liability requires a plaintiff to join all of the partners as defendants in litigation. This joinder requirement may create serious practical enforcement problems when process cannot be readily served on some partners. Thus, as between a partnership's tort and contract liabilities, UPA makes it substantially easier to sue a partner for the tort obligations of the firm.[73]

The distinction between joint liability and joint and several liability is largely one of procedure—i.e., who must be sued in a particular case? When liability is joint, all of the partners must be sued together, but when liability is joint and several, one or more of the partners may be sued. Under either rule, however, a plaintiff with a judgment against the partnership may collect the entirety of the judgment from any partner. Joint liability, in other words, does not change the principle that each partner has unlimited personal liability for all of the partnership's obligations.

RUPA eliminates the reference to joint liability and instead provides that partners are jointly and severally liable for all obligations of the partnership.[74] Although RUPA allows a creditor to sue the partnership and one or more of the partners in a single action, a judgment creditor is first required to exhaust partnership assets

---

[73] Why is UPA § 18 prefaced with the phrase "subject to any agreement between [the partners]," but UPA §§ 13–15 are not prefaced in a similar manner? The distinction is that § 18 provides rules that govern the relationship between the partners themselves, while §§ 13–15 provide rules that govern the relationship between the partners and the outside world. Partners can modify rules that affect the relationship between themselves, but they cannot modify rules that affect the rights of third parties. *See also* RUPA § 103(b)(10).

[74] *See* RUPA § 306(a).

(with certain exceptions) before proceeding directly against a partner's individual assets.[75] This exhaustion requirement (RUPA § 307(d)) is an important change from UPA. It was suggested by an ABA committee which stated that the new requirement "would respect the concept of the partnership as an entity and would provide that the partners are more in the nature of guarantors than principal debtors on every partnership debt."[76]

Both UPA and RUPA provide that a newly admitted partner is not personally liable for partnership obligations that arose before his admission.[77] Both uniform acts also indicate that a withdrawing partner remains liable for partnership obligations incurred before withdrawal. A creditor can agree to release the withdrawing partner, however, from specific obligations.[78]

Continuing partnership obligations can produce confusion when applying these rules. For example, assume that a partnership enters into a long-term loan with monthly installment payments, or a long-term lease with monthly rent payments. Is each monthly payment a separate partnership obligation that is incurred when it is due? If so, partners who join after a monthly due date, or partners who withdraw before a monthly due date, would not be liable for that payment. On the other hand, there is authority for the proposition that "[a] creditor contracting with a general partnership does so in the rightful expectation that all of the general partners stand behind that contract, and that a partner's withdrawal will not release that partner's responsibility on the contract."[79] Under that

---

[75] *See id.* § 307. The typical route under RUPA for collecting a partnership obligation from a partner requires the following steps: (1) a judgment must be obtained against the partnership and the individual partner (§ 307(c)), and (2) efforts to collect the judgment from the partnership's assets are attempted but are wholly or partially unsuccessful (§ 307(d)(1)). A creditor can skip step (2) and proceed directly against an individual partner's assets, however, if (a) the partnership is in bankruptcy; (b) the partner has agreed that the creditor need not exhaust partnership assets; (c) a court grants permission to the creditor to proceed directly against the partner's assets; or (d) liability is imposed on the partner by law or contract independent of the existence of the partnership (e.g., if the partner has signed a personal guarantee). *See id.* § 307(d)(2)–(5).

[76] UPA Revision Subcomm. of the Comm. on P'ships and Unincorporated Bus. Orgs., *Should the Uniform Partnership Act Be Revised?*, 43 BUS. LAW. 121, 143 (1987).

[77] UPA § 17 and § 41(7) reach this conclusion rather indirectly by providing that the liability of the newly admitted partner for pre-admission obligations is to be satisfied only out of partnership property. RUPA § 306(b) is much clearer.

[78] *See* UPA § 36; RUPA § 703. Under RUPA, a withdrawing partner may also be liable for partnership obligations incurred after withdrawal. *See* RUPA § 703(b).

[79] *In re* Judiciary Tower Assocs., 175 B.R. 796, 809 (Bankr. D.D.C. 1994).

view, a partner with the firm when a loan or lease is executed would still be liable for a default that occurred after his withdrawal.[80]

4. Indemnification and Contribution

UPA § 18(b) and RUPA § 401(c) provide that, in the absence of a contrary agreement, a partnership must indemnify a partner for payments made and liabilities incurred by the partner in the ordinary course of the partnership business. While an individual partner may have to pay the entirety of a partnership obligation to a third party, indemnification provides a mechanism for sharing payment of that obligation among the partners.

In an ongoing partnership, an indemnification payment reduces the partnership's profits just like any other partnership payment. As a result, each partner of a profitable venture "suffers" from indemnification in proportion to his profit share. On dissolution, a partnership's obligation to indemnify is paid out of partnership assets like any other partnership obligation. If the partnership has insufficient assets to pay indemnification or other partnership obligations, partners must contribute to make up the shortfall in accordance with their loss shares.[81] Thus, indemnification is an obligation of a partnership, while contribution is an obligation of a partner.

As between partners and the outside world, therefore, an individual partner has unlimited personal liability for the obligations of the partnership.[82] A creditor, in other words, may collect the entirety of a partnership obligation from any partner under UPA, and from any partner under RUPA if the exhaustion requirement of RUPA § 307(d) has been met. As between the partners themselves, however, each partner is only responsible for his share of the partnership obligation. If one partner pays off a partnership obligation, he is entitled to indemnification from the partnership. If the partnership lacks the funds to indemnify the partner, the partners are required to contribute according to their loss shares. The net effect of indemnification and contribution is that, if all parties are solvent, a partner who is rightfully sued for the entirety of a partnership

---

[80] *See, e.g.*, 8182 Md. Assocs. Ltd. P'ship v. Sheehan, 14 S.W.3d 576, 581–82 (Mo. 2000) (concluding that a partner who signed a long-term lease along with other partners, but who withdrew before the lease commenced and before the firm defaulted, was personally liable for the default); *id.* at 583–86 (concluding that partners who joined the firm after the lease was signed, but who withdrew before the firm defaulted, were not personally liable for the default).

[81] *See* UPA §§ 18(a), 40(b)–(d); RUPA §§ 401(b), 807(b)–(c).

[82] *See* UPA §§ 13–15; RUPA § 306(a); *see also* Chapter 3(D)(3)(b) (discussing the liability of a partner).

obligation will ultimately bear only his pro rata share of the obligation.

A simple example is helpful. Consider the facts of *Summers v. Dooley* and assume that Summers did have authority to hire the additional employee.[83] Summers pays the employee's compensation out of his own pocket. Would Summers be entitled to indemnification? Yes. The payment of compensation was made on the partnership's behalf in the ordinary course of the partnership business. The partnership is required to reimburse Summers and, in effect, both Summers and Dooley bear 50% of the expense to the extent that the partnership now has less profits to distribute. What if the partnership lacked sufficient funds to indemnify Summers? Dooley would then have to make a contribution payment of 50% of the obligation (Dooley's loss share) to the partnership, and the partnership would in turn use those funds to indemnify Summers.[84] The net result is that Summers and Dooley would each wind up funding half of the partnership obligation (the employee's salary) out of his own respective pocket.[85]

E. Fiduciary Duties

1. The Common Law

One of the fundamental principles of partnership law is that partners owe fiduciary duties to the partnership and to each other. Justice (then Judge) Cardozo's opinion in *Meinhard v. Salmon*[86] is the classic case on the fiduciary duties owed between partners.[87] It

---

[83] *See* Chapter 3(C)(1) (discussing *Summers*).

[84] Many courts streamline the separate obligations to make indemnification and contribution payments by allowing a partner who is owed indemnity to sue another partner directly for his contribution payment. Rather than having Dooley make his contribution payment to the partnership, in other words, a court might simply allow Summers to recover that payment directly from Dooley.

[85] Notice that a partner with an indemnification claim bears the risk of his fellow partners' insolvency. If Dooley were insolvent, and if the partnership lacked sufficient funds to indemnify Summers, Summers would bear the entirety of the loss. Contrast the situation of a judgment creditor of the partnership. If the partnership has insufficient assets to pay the judgment, the judgment creditor can ignore the insolvent Dooley and can recover the entirety of the judgment from Summers. Thus, Dooley's insolvency affects Summers' right of recovery on his indemnification claim, but not the creditor's right of recovery on his judgment.

[86] 164 N.E. 545 (N.Y. 1928).

[87] In a true fiduciary relationship, the fiduciary acts solely in the best interests of another (e.g., trustee-beneficiary). Indeed, a fiduciary duty imposes an onerous burden that requires the fiduciary to place the interests of the other party before his own. *See, e.g.*, Crim. Truck & Tractor Co. v. Navistar Int'l Transp. Co., 823 S.W.2d 591, 594 (Tex. 1992). Partners, however, have legitimate selfish interests in making money in the venture. As owners, they are allowed to think about their personal interests and not solely about the interests of others. As a result, the fiduciary notion that a partner must put other partners' interests ahead of his own seems inapposite. Despite the fact that a partner's duty is characterized as "fiduciary" in na-

articulates a standard for fiduciary conduct (albeit a very vague one) that has been cited in countless opinions.

In 1902, Louisa Gerry leased the Hotel Bristol to Walter Salmon. The lease was for twenty years, and Salmon undertook to change the property so that it could be used for shops and offices. Needing financial support for the project, Salmon entered into a joint venture[88] with Meinhard to develop the property. Meinhard was to provide much of the necessary funding, and Salmon was to manage the venture. They agreed to split profits 60% to Salmon and 40% to Meinhard for the first five years of the lease, and then profits would be split equally. Losses were also to be split equally.

Elbridge Gerry became the owner of the reversion. He owned other property in the neighborhood, and he desired to combine these properties into one large tract. Gerry wished to find someone who would destroy the existing buildings and would replace them with a new one. In 1922, when the lease on the Salmon-Meinhard joint venture had four months remaining, Gerry leased the larger tract to a corporation owned by Salmon, Midpoint Realty Company. The rent on the new lease was between $350,000 and $475,000, as opposed to the $55,000 rent on the Bristol lease. Salmon entered into the new lease without informing Meinhard.[89]

Meinhard sued Salmon for breach of fiduciary duty and sought to have the new lease placed in a constructive trust for the benefit of the joint venture. The trial court granted judgment for Meinhard, but restricted him to 25% of the new venture, or one-half of the portion of the new venture attributed to the former Bristol site. The Appellate Division modified the trial court's judgment and awarded Meinhard a 50% interest in the new venture. The Court of Appeals affirmed. Chief Judge Cardozo noted that partners owe a "duty of the finest loyalty" to one another—a duty that Salmon breached by negotiating with Gerry in secret and by failing to disclose the existence of the opportunity to Meinhard. The court em-

---

ture, therefore, one can argue that the duty should be understood to focus more on fairness than selflessness.

[88] There is a good deal of older case law suggesting that a "joint venture" is distinct from a general partnership. The modern view rejects this separate characterization and treats a joint venture as simply a general partnership that has a limited purpose. Under the modern view, therefore, general partnership rules govern the formation and operation of joint ventures. *See, e.g.,* Hooper v. Yoder, 737 P.2d 852, 857 n.4 (Colo. 1987) ("A joint venture is a partnership formed for a limited purpose. . . . The substantive law of partnership applies to joint ventures as well as partnerships."); RUPA § 202 cmt. 2 ("Relationships that are called 'joint ventures' are partnerships if they otherwise fit the definition of a partnership.").

[89] *See Meinhard,* 164 N.E. at 545–46.

phasized that Salmon was the managing partner of the old lease and that Gerry approached him as the managing partner.[90]

In one of the most famous passages in business law, Chief Judge Cardozo described the fiduciary relationship between partners as follows:

> Joint adventurers, like copartners, owe to one another, while the enterprise continues, the duty of the finest loyalty. Many forms of conduct permissible in a workaday world for those acting at arm's length are forbidden to those bound by fiduciary ties. A trustee is held to something stricter than the morals of the market place. Not honesty alone, but the punctilio of an honor the most sensitive, is then the standard of behavior. As to this there has developed a tradition that is unbending and inveterate. Uncompromising rigidity has been the attitude of courts of equity when petitioned to undermine the rule of undivided loyalty by the "disintegrating erosion" of particular exceptions. Only thus has the level of conduct for fiduciaries been kept at a level higher than that trodden by the crowd. It will not consciously be lowered by any judgment of this court.[91]

Does this passage make clear when a partner's conduct will breach his fiduciary duty? Not at all. Why would Cardozo write such a broad and amorphous passage? One could argue that this is similar to a rule versus standard debate. There are so many ways that a partner could breach his fiduciary duty that a specific listing of impermissible conduct would inevitably leave something out. In addition, by leaving it purposefully vague, partners have to think twice before doing anything that could be construed as unfair. Put differently, when it is not clear where the line of impermissible conduct is, a partner's best defense may be to stay far away from any area where that line might be drawn. In contrast, if the line were clearly demarcated, partners may act in undesirable ways that technically go right up to the line without crossing it. The downside of such an amorphous passage, of course, is that litigation often results over whether conduct should be characterized as a breach of fiduciary duty.

Although there is a good deal of dicta in *Meinhard*, the holding is actually quite narrow: Salmon violated his fiduciary duty to Meinhard by failing to disclose the existence of the opportunity pre-

---

[90] *See id.* at 546–48. The court modified the Appellate Division's judgment by attaching the constructive trust to the shares of Midpoint Realty, rather than to the lease itself. The court also added one share beyond 50% to Salmon's holdings so that he could continue to control and manage the venture. *See id.* at 548.

[91] *Id.* at 546 (citation omitted).

sented by Gerry. Every partner has a duty to make full disclosure
of all information concerning the partnership's business and affairs
that is reasonably required for the proper exercise of a partner's
rights.[92]

Could Salmon have avoided the outcome by disclosing to
Meinhard in advance what he proposed to do and by giving him an
opportunity to deal directly with Gerry? There appears to have
been little downside to disclosure, as there was no reason to think
that Gerry would have been interested in dealing with Salmon's
silent partner who apparently was merely an investor and not a
property manager. There is language in the opinion indicating that
nondisclosure was the basic vice, and in view of the 4–3 split, disclosure might have changed the result. Nevertheless, one cannot be
positive.[93] After all, it is well accepted that a partner's fiduciary
duty of loyalty includes the obligation to avoid usurping business
opportunities belonging to the partnership.[94] Was the opportunity
to lease the expanded area a partnership opportunity? Perhaps not
if the court viewed the partnership as a venture that was intended
to end at the expiration of the original 20-year lease.[95] On the other
hand, the court might have found that the partnership was intended to last for so long as Gerry would lease the premises. While that
started out as 20 years, Gerry's offer to extend the lease (albeit covering an expanded area and a bigger project) might have been
viewed as a business opportunity for the partnership and not just
for Salmon.

---

[92] *See, e.g.*, RUPA § 403(c); *see also* Chapter 3(E)(2)(c) (discussing the duty to disclose).

[93] Indeed, the opinion seems to take no position on whether a disclosing Salmon
would have been allowed to take the opportunity for himself:

He might have warned Meinhard that the plan had been submitted, and that either would be free to compete for the award. If he had done this, we do not need to
say whether he would have been under a duty, if successful in the competition, to
hold the lease so acquired for the benefit of a venture then about to end, and thus
prolong by indirection its responsibilities and duties. The trouble about his conduct
is that he excluded his coadventurer from any chance to compete, from any chance to
enjoy the opportunity for benefit that had come to him alone by virtue of his agency.
This chance, if nothing more, he was under a duty to concede. The price of its denial
is an extension of the trust at the option and for the benefit of the one whom he excluded.

Meinhard, 164 N.E. at 547.

[94] *See* UPA § 21; RUPA § 403(b)(1); *see also* Chapter 3(E)(2) (discussing fiduciary
duties under the uniform acts).

[95] *See, e.g., Meinhard*, 164 N.E. at 552 (Andrews, J., dissenting) ("It seems to me
that the venture so inaugurated had in view a limited object and was to end at a
limited time. There was no intent to expand it into a far greater undertaking lasting
for many years. The design was to exploit a particular lease. Doubtless in it Mr.
Meinhard had an equitable interest, but in it alone. This interest terminated when
the joint adventure terminated.").

The dispute between Meinhard and Salmon might have been avoided by contract if the partners had clearly stated (ideally in a written partnership agreement) what their obligations were to one another after the expiration of the original lease. Similarly, the partners might have contracted to explicitly allow a partner to compete with the partnership and the other partners (although it is not clear that Salmon's failure to disclose would have been excused under such a provision). Under current law, using contract to define the scope of the partners' fiduciary duties to each other is generally acceptable.[96]

2. Statutory Developments

UPA § 21 is the only provision in UPA that refers to a partner's "fiduciary" duty. It states that "[e]very partner must account to the partnership for any benefit, and hold as trustee for it any profits derived by him without the consent of the other partners from any transaction connected with the formation, conduct, or liquidation of the partnership or from any use by him of its property." An ABA Committee commenting on this section stated that while it "is often cited as establishing a broad fiduciary duty, in fact, as presently worded, [it] is basically merely an anti-theft provision."[97] Nevertheless, many partnership cases cite *Meinhard* and § 21 as establishing a broad fiduciary duty among partners.

RUPA has a much more elaborate treatment of fiduciary duty. RUPA § 404(a) states that the "only" fiduciary duties owed by a partner to the partnership and the other partners are the duties of loyalty and care. Section 404(b) defines the duty of loyalty as "limited to" the following obligations: (1) to account to the partnership for any benefit derived by the partner in conducting the partnership business, using the partnership's property, or appropriating a partnership opportunity; (2) to refrain from dealing with the partnership in the conduct of its business as (or on behalf of) a party having an interest adverse to the partnership; and (3) to refrain from competing with the partnership in the conduct of its business. Section 404(c) defines the duty of care as "limited to refraining from engaging in grossly negligent or reckless conduct, intentional misconduct, or a knowing violation of law."

Section 404(d) imposes an "obligation of good faith and fair dealing" upon partners when discharging duties and exercising rights. The comment indicates that the obligation is a contractual concept that is imposed upon the partners because of the consensual

[96] *See* Chapter 3(E)(4).

[97] UPA Revision Subcomm. of the Comm. on P'ships and Unincorporated Bus. Orgs., *supra* note 76, at 151.

nature of a partnership. The comment further states that the meaning of good faith and fair dealing "is not firmly fixed under present law," although good faith "clearly suggests a subjective element" while fair dealing "implies an objective component."

Section 404(e) indicates that a partner does not violate a duty or obligation "merely because the partner's conduct furthers the partner's own interest." According to the comment, "[a] partner as such is not a trustee and is not held to the same standards as a trustee," and subsection (e) "makes clear that a partner's conduct is not deemed to be improper merely because it serves the partner's own individual interest."[98]

Section 404(f) states that "[a] partner may lend money to and transact other business with the partnership, and as to each loan or transaction the rights and obligations of the partner are the same as those of a person who is not a partner, subject to other applicable law." The comment indicates that this subsection would permit, for example, a partner to purchase the assets of the partnership at a foreclosure sale, upon liquidation, or at a tax sale.

a. The Duty of Loyalty

Enea v. Superior Court[99] provides an excellent vehicle for discussing the relationship between the duty of loyalty obligations in RUPA § 404(b) and some of the other subsections of § 404. More specifically, it raises the question of whether RUPA permits fair conflict of interest transactions in the partnership setting.

Benny Enea, William Daniels, and Claudia Daniels formed a partnership known as 3–D. The partnership's sole asset was a building which was rented to William Daniels and Claudia Daniels. Enea alleged that it was a breach of fiduciary duty for the Daniels to lease the partnership's property to themselves at less than what could be earned in the open market. The trial court granted defendants' motion for summary judgment on the ground that there was not an agreement requiring a fair market rent. The California Court of Appeal reversed.[100]

The Court of Appeal stated that partners owe duties to one another beyond those explicitly provided by contract. Because fiduciary duties are imposed by law, the lack of an agreement requiring a

---

[98] *See also* RUPA § 404 cmt. 5 (noting that subsection (e) "underscores the partner's rights as an owner and principal in the enterprise, which must always be balanced against his duties and obligations as an agent and fiduciary"); *cf.* note 87 (noting that partners, as owners, are not classic fiduciaries).

[99] 34 Cal. Rptr. 3d 513 (Ct. App. 2005).

[100] *See id.* at 514–16.

fair market rent was irrelevant. The court believed that the defendants' conduct violated the California analog to RUPA § 404(b)(1) because below-market rent allowed the defendants to receive a benefit from the use of the partnership's property. The court also concluded that the California analog to RUPA § 404(e) did not cure this breach of duty, as that provision only excused partners from accounting for incidental benefits obtained in the course of partnership activities without detriment to the partnership. According to the court, because the partnership was deprived of a market rent, the defendants improperly obtained this benefit to the partnership's detriment.[101]

Would the result in *Enea* have changed if the defendants had rented partnership property to themselves at a fair market rent? The court suggested that a fair rent would have protected the defendants from liability by stating that "the statute entitled defendants to lease partnership property *at the same rent another tenant would have paid*."[102] The court seemed to believe that, under the analog to RUPA § 404(b)(1), a fair rent would have eliminated any profit or benefit that the defendants were deriving from their use of partnership property. Moreover, the court indicated that § 404(e) protected partners from liability for incidental benefits obtained without detriment to the partnership. A fair rent would not have deprived the partnership of "valuable assets"—i.e., the ability to earn a market rent—and thus would not be at the partnership's expense.

RUPA § 404(b)(2), however, seems to indicate that even a fair market rent would be problematic. A partner's duty of loyalty includes a duty to refrain from dealing with the partnership "in the conduct of the partnership business . . . as or on behalf of a party having an interest adverse to the partnership." The Daniels have an interest adverse to the partnership as they are the lessees generally seeking a lower rent, while the partnership as the lessor is generally seeking a higher rent. Section 404(b)(2) prohibits conflict of interest (also known as "self-dealing") transactions involving a partner and the partnership, and any conflict of interest transaction—whether fair or unfair—would seem to fall within its scope. Strangely, the *Enea* court did not even mention § 404(b)(2).

Is there a statutory argument for validating a fair conflict of interest transaction? In the corporate law context, the typical conflict of interest statute explicitly provides that fairness to the corpora-

---

[101] *See id.* at 518–19.
[102] *Id.* at 518.

tion is a defense.[103] Thus, the lack of an explicit fairness provision in the partnership setting may be significant. On the other hand, perhaps one could argue that payment of a fair rent indicates that interests are not "adverse," and thus § 404(b)(2) is not implicated. This seems like a stretch, however, as even the concept of fairness is a range, and the partner and the partnership would still have adverse interests within that range (the partner wants to pay at the low end of the fairness range, while the partnership wants to charge at the high end of the range).[104]

Does § 404(e) provide support for a fairness defense? The meaning of this subsection is unclear, and it is useful to consider some possible interpretations. First, § 404(e) on its face seems to say that the mere fact that a partner is self-interested in a transaction is not enough for a breach of duty. That suggests that the existence of a conflict of interest transaction, without more, should not subject a partner to liability for breach of the duty of loyalty. (Of course, § 404(b)(2) seems to say just the opposite.) Liability would only be imposed if something more than self-interest were present, such as harm to the partnership. This is the interpretation that the *Enea* court appears to give to § 404(e)—it excuses partners from accounting for incidental benefits obtained in the course of partnership activities without detriment to the partnership. Under this interpretation, § 404(e) modifies § 404(b)(2) such that a fair conflict of interest transaction would not result in liability. In such a transaction, there is a conflict of interest (the partner is seeking a low rent, while the partnership is seeking a high rent), but not one that harms the partnership.

A problem with this interpretation is that the comment to § 404 explains that § 404(b)(2) is based on § 389 and § 391 of the Second Restatement of Agency, and that the rule there "is not based upon the harm caused to the principal, but upon avoiding a conflict of opposing interests in the mind of an agent whose duty is to act for the benefit of his principal." If that interpretation is meant to apply to § 404(b)(2), the absence of harm to the partnership should be irrelevant, as the problem is simply the partner putting himself in a conflicted position.

---

[103] *See, e.g.*, DEL. CODE tit. 8, § 144(a)(3); *see also* Chapter 7(E)(3) (discussing conflict of interest transactions in the corporate setting).

[104] The Daniels argued that the primary purpose of the partnership was not to lease the building. If that argument were credited, would that mean that § 404(b)(2) was not implicated because the Daniels were not dealing with the partnership "in the conduct . . . of the partnership business?" We doubt it, as the partnership would still have an interest in earning rents, and that would seem to be part (although not the primary part) of the business of the partnership.

Second, § 404(e) might simply reaffirm the § 404(b) notion that the duty of loyalty is "limited to" the situations described in subsections (b)(1), (b)(2), and (b)(3). Conduct outside of those subsections—even conduct that furthers the partner's own interest—does not result in liability for breach of duty or breach of the obligation of good faith and fair dealing. As the comment to § 404(e) states, partners are not trustees and are not held to trustee standards— i.e., partners are not required to act selflessly in conduct related to the partnership. Partners are owners of the business and have some legitimate rights to act in ways that further their personal interests.[105] Thus, as the comment describes, a partner who owns a shopping center may vote against a proposal by the partnership to open a competing shopping center. Such a vote is arguably not viewed as a § 404(b)(2) conflict of interest transaction because the partner is not transacting or "dealing with" the partnership by simply exercising his voting rights as a partner. Under this interpretation, § 404(e) simply reaffirms that a partner will not violate his duty or good faith obligation by engaging in conduct designed to further the partner's interest, so long as that conduct does not fall within the scope of § 404(b). Significantly, this interpretation would not validate fair conflict of interest transactions, as such transactions still involve a partner violating § 404(b)(2) by "dealing with the partnership . . . as or on behalf of a party having an interest adverse to the partnership."

If § 404(e) doesn't help, what about § 404(f)? This subsection is equally puzzling. On its face, it seems to suggest that a partner can transact business with the partnership with obligations that are no different from those of a stranger. Because a stranger can act in a self-interested fashion and does not have to pay a fair price, so too can a partner. This interpretation proves too much, however, as it effectively guts most, if not all, of the partner's duty of loyalty. If a partner has no greater duty than a stranger, engaging in unfair conflict of interest transactions and competing with the partnership, for example, would seem to be fine. The comment to § 404(f) suggests a more limited reading by stating that subsection (f) permits a partner to purchase partnership assets at a tax sale or a foreclosure sale, even if the purchasing partner is also the mortgagee. Similarly, the source of subsection (f) has been narrowly interpreted as simply removing restrictions on partner-creditors that previously existed (e.g., limited partners at one time could not make secured loans to the partnership).[106] Although these examples and

---

[105] *Cf.* note 87 (noting that partners, as owners, are not classic fiduciaries).

[106] The comment to § 404(f) indicates that the subsection is based upon § 107 of the Revised Uniform Limited Partnership Act ("RULPA"). In *BT-I v. Equitable Life Assurance Society,* 89 Cal. Rptr. 2d 811 (Cal. Ct. App. 1999), the court indicated that § 107 does not alter a general partner's fiduciary duties:

interpretations suggest that § 404(f) was meant to be construed narrowly and was not meant to significantly undercut the duty of loyalty, the broad language of subsection (f) itself confusingly suggests otherwise.

So where does this leave us? About all one can say is that, although the *Enea* court suggested that liability could be avoided if a fair rent were paid, that suggestion can be questioned. Moreover, uncertainty about the meaning of § 404(e) and (f) adds to the confusion.[107]

It should be noted that, even in the absence of a provision in the partnership agreement, RUPA would validate a conflict of interest transaction with the unanimous consent of the partners.[108] Although RUPA provides this consent defense, it does not provide for an explicit fairness defense. Does it make sense that fair conflict of interest transactions are legal in the corporate setting, but are arguably illegal in the partnership setting? It might. The partnership form of business is generally characterized by a relatively smaller number of owners. In such a setting, it might be feasible to provide that the unanimous consent of the partners is the only way to validate a conflict of interest transaction. After all, with a smaller number of owners, it is possible to obtain unanimous consent without a prohibitive expenditure of time and money.

In the corporate setting, however, particularly in public corporations, the sheer number of owners would make unanimous consent impossible to obtain. Unless some other defense was available, conflict of interest transactions would effectively be illegal as a per se matter. This is an undesirable result, as conflict of interest transactions can be very helpful to a business in certain circumstances (e.g., a fledgling business may not be able to procure loans on favorable terms from conventional sources, but can potentially

---

We cannot discern anything in the purpose of Corporations Code section 15617 [analogous to RULPA § 107] that suggests an intent to affect a general partner's fiduciary duty to limited partners. Under the prior limited partnership rule, limited partners were prohibited from making secured loans to the partnership and any collateral received could be set aside as a fraud upon creditors. Corporations Code section 15617 is identical to Uniform Limited Partnership Act (1976) section 107, which was enacted to remove the fraudulent conveyances prohibition from the limited partnership law and leave the question to the general fraudulent conveyances statute. This change hardly sanctions Equitable's self-dealing.

Id. at 818 (citations omitted).

[107] For what it is worth, the 2006 Revised Uniform Limited Liability Company Act ("RULLCA") refers to RUPA § 404(e) and (f) as "inappropriate," "unnecessary," and "confusing" in the LLC setting, and it eliminates those subsections. In addition, RULLCA explicitly provides for a fairness defense in § 409(e) of that statute.

[108] *See* RUPA § 103(b)(3)(ii).

get favorable terms from an insider of the business). Thus, a fairness defense in the corporate setting may have developed as a matter of necessity given that a unanimous consent defense was not feasible. That necessity for a fairness defense, however, is less compelling in the partnership setting where unanimous consent can be more easily obtained.[109] On the other hand, the lack of harm posed by fair conflict of interest transactions makes it difficult to say that they should be prohibited, and it is hard to understand why the same fair transaction would be legal in the corporate setting but illegal in the partnership context.[110]

As mentioned, RUPA § 404(b) defines the duty of loyalty as "limited to" certain obligations. This effort to cabin the duty of loyalty by creating an exclusive statutory definition of the duty was intentional. The *Meinhard* common-law notion that partners owed a duty of the "finest loyalty" and "the punctilio of an honor the most sensitive" was seen as a vague pronouncement that failed to provide any predictability on what the duty of loyalty covered.[111]

Given this intentional effort to restrict the scope of the duty of loyalty in RUPA, it is worth considering whether there are any aspects of a more general duty of loyalty that might not be encompassed within the three subsections of § 404(b). One possible gap is mandatory disclosure requirements that were implicit in *Meinhard* and that are now covered by RUPA § 403. Although RUPA does not characterize the duty to disclose as a "fiduciary" duty,[112] case law in a number of jurisdictions does characterize it as a fiduciary duty that is related to a partner's duty of loyalty. Moreover, many jurisdictions retain the *Meinhard*-like notion that fiduciary duty requires a partner to act with the "finest loyalty." In such jurisdictions, any unfair conduct towards a partner or the partnership could be characterized as a breach of the duty of loyalty. In some circumstances, the unfair conduct may be difficult to characterize as

---

[109] If fair conflict of interest transactions are impermissible in the partnership setting, what remedy exists for such transactions? Presumably a court could grant equitable relief, such as an injunction to block a not-yet-completed transaction, or perhaps rescission to unwind a completed deal (if feasible). Nominal damages for breach of duty are also a possibility.

[110] *Cf.* J&J Celecom v. AT&T Wireless Servs., Inc., 169 P.3d 823, 825 (Wash. 2007) (concluding, with little statutory analysis, that a fair conflict of interest transaction was permissible in a partnership setting).

[111] *See, e.g.,* Donald J. Weidner, *The Revised Uniform Partnership Act Midstream: Major Policy Decisions,* 21 U. TOL. L. REV. 825, 856 (1990) (noting that the "limited to" language was added because of "a sense that vague, broad statements of a powerful duty of loyalty cause too much uncertainty," and observing that "even if there are no bad holdings, overly broad judicial language has left practitioners uncertain about whether their negotiated agreement will be voided"); *see also* Chapter 3(E)(1) (discussing *Meinhard*).

[112] *See* Chapter 3(E)(2)(c).

conduct that would fit § 404(b)(1)–(3) (e.g., a partner refusing to acknowledge the rights of another partner).

Significantly, some jurisdictions that have adopted RUPA have rejected its efforts to exclusively define the duty of loyalty. California and Texas, for example, omit the "limited to" phrase in their versions of § 404(b) and state instead that the partner's duty of loyalty simply "includes" the obligations in § 404(b)(1)–(3).[113] Jurisdictions like these that "uncabin" the duty of loyalty make it easier for plaintiffs to argue that unfairness of any type violates the fiduciary duty of loyalty. Of course, that returns the duty of loyalty to the vagaries of *Meinhard*-like common law, which undermines RUPA's effort to create more predictability on the scope of the loyalty obligation.

b. The Duty of Care

As mentioned, RUPA § 404(a) describes the duty of care as a fiduciary duty, and § 404(c) defines the duty as "limited to refraining from engaging in grossly negligent or reckless conduct, intentional misconduct, or a knowing violation of law."[114] The decision of *Bane v. Ferguson*[115] provides an opportunity to explore the operation of § 404(c) and its relationship with the business judgment rule. Charles Bane was a partner in the law firm of Isham, Lincoln & Beale. The firm adopted a noncontributory retirement plan that entitled every retiring partner to a pension. The plan instrument provided, however, that the plan and the payments under it would end when and if the firm dissolved without a successor entity.

Bane retired from the firm. His former law firm then merged with another practice. Unfortunately, the merger was a disaster, and the merged firm was dissolved without a successor. Thus, the payment of pension benefits ceased.

Bane sued the members of the firm's managing council and asserted that, among other things, they acted unreasonably in deciding to merge the firm. The trial court granted judgment for the defendants. On appeal, the Seventh Circuit affirmed. The court held that Bane could not sue his former partners for breach of the duty of care because their fiduciary duty to him ended when he left the partnership. More importantly, the court noted that "[e]ven if the defendants were fiduciaries of the plaintiff ... the business-judgment rule would shield them from liability for mere negligence

---

[113] CAL. CORP. CODE § 16404(b); *accord* TEX. BUS. ORGS. CODE § 152.205.

[114] UPA does not attempt to define a duty of care for partners. UPA § 21 is the only provision that references the notion of a partner as a fiduciary.

[115] 890 F.2d 11 (7th Cir. 1989).

in the operation of the firm, just as it would shield a corporation's directors and officers, who are fiduciaries of the shareholders."[116]

The business judgment rule is discussed at length in the corporation materials, but the general concept is that courts do not evaluate the substantive merits of a business decision so long as the decision is not tainted by fraud, conflicts of interest, grossly unreasonable decision-making processes, or bad faith.[117] (The precise articulation of the business judgment rule varies among jurisdictions.) The theory is that the operation of a successful business often involves the taking of appropriate risks, and that managers should not be deterred from taking those risks because of a fear of personal liability if a decision turns out poorly. The rule attempts to mitigate this concern by giving managers substantial room to act with impunity, even if their substantive business decisions are later characterized as unreasonable or unwise. The *Bane* court observed that "[t]he suit does not allege that the defendants committed fraud, engaged in self-dealing, or deliberately sought to destroy or damage the law firm or harm the plaintiff; the charge is negligent mismanagement, not deliberate wrongdoing." In such circumstances, the business judgment rule shields defendants from judicial second-guessing of the merits of a decision. RUPA § 404(c) reflects this notion to some extent by signaling that action that can only be characterized as ordinary negligence does not breach the duty of care—gross negligence or worse is required.

c. The Duty to Disclose

UPA § 20 states that partners "shall render on demand true and full information of all things affecting the partnership to any partner." RUPA § 403 expands the scope of this disclosure obligation by stating that each partner and the partnership shall furnish to a partner "without demand, any information concerning the partnership's business and affairs reasonably required for the proper exercise of the partner's rights and duties under the partnership agreement or this [Act]," and shall furnish "on demand, any other information concerning the partnership's business and affairs, except to the extent the demand or the information demanded is unreasonable or otherwise improper under the circumstances."

Although *Meinhard* and other cases suggest that a partner's disclosure obligation is fiduciary in nature, UPA § 20 does not refer to the obligation as a fiduciary one. Moreover, the use of "only" in

---

[116] *See id.* at 13–15.

[117] *See* Chapter 7(C)(3). It is sometimes helpful to think of the business judgment rule as a rule that shields the "output" (or substantive merits) of a decision from judicial scrutiny as long as the "inputs" to the decision are appropriate.

RUPA § 404(a) clearly indicates that the disclosure obligation in RUPA § 403 is not an independent fiduciary duty.

3. Duties When Leaving a Partnership

A recurring fact pattern implicating fiduciary duties involves a partner's departure from a partnership to start a competing firm. A number of logistical steps usually precede such a departure— securing office space, contacting clients, seeking employees and fellow partners, etc. The line separating permissible logistics for a new firm from a breach of duty to the former partnership, however, is not always clear.

In the Massachusetts decision of *Meehan v. Shaughnessy*,[118] Meehan and Boyle were partners in the law firm of Parker, Coulter, Daley & White. They decided to leave Parker Coulter and to form their own firm. They spoke with several Parker Coulter attorneys about joining them in their new venture, and they executed a lease on office space. Meehan and Boyle also prepared form letters to send to clients and referring attorneys as soon as Parker Coulter was notified of the separation.

Rumors of the departure of Meehan and Boyle began to spread. On three separate occasions, Meehan denied to Parker Coulter partners that he was leaving. On November 30, 1984, Meehan and Boyle gave notice of their impending departure. Starting December 1, 1984, Boyle began calling and mailing the previously prepared form letters to clients and referring attorneys in order to determine which clients could be persuaded to leave. Although the Parker Coulter partners had asked during the week of December 3 for a list of cases that Boyle intended to take with him, Boyle did not provide the list until December 17.[119]

Meehan and Boyle sued Parker Coulter seeking amounts allegedly owed to them under the firm's partnership agreement and a declaration as to amounts they owed Parker Coulter on removed cases. Parker Coulter counterclaimed for breach of fiduciary duty, breach of the partnership agreement, and other actions. The Supreme Judicial Court agreed that partners may make arrangements to compete with a former partnership before leaving the partnership. The court also accepted the trial judge's findings that the departing lawyers continued to do the business of Parker Coulter in an appropriate fashion before leaving. Nevertheless, the court found two breaches of fiduciary duty. First, Meehan lied to his partners about his decision to leave the firm in violation of the Mas-

---

[118] 535 N.E.2d 1255 (Mass. 1989).

[119] *See id.* at 1257–59.

sachusetts version of UPA § 20. Second, Meehan and Boyle acted
inappropriately in competing with the firm for clients prior to leaving the firm.

With respect to this second breach, the court explained that the
communications with firm clients were a breach of fiduciary duty
because Meehan and Boyle did not give Parker Coulter a fair
chance to retain those clients. By misrepresenting their intention
to leave, Meehan and Boyle had time to prepare for obtaining removal authorizations from clients without competition from the
firm. As the court noted, "they were 'ready to move' the instant
they gave notice to their partners." Moreover, even though Meehan
and Boyle immediately began communicating with clients and referring attorneys, Boyle delayed in providing the firm with the list
of clients that he intended to solicit. Finally, as the court explained,
the content of the letter sent to clients was unfairly prejudicial to
Parker Coulter because it did not comply with the American Bar
Association's ethical guidelines for approaching clients when forming a new firm. These guidelines state that, although a departing
lawyer may inform clients that he is leaving and offer his continued
services, he must make clear that staying or leaving is the client's
decision, and he may not encourage clients to sever relations with
the old firm. The court found that the letter sent by Meehan and
Boyle did not clearly present to clients the choice they had between
remaining at Parker Coulter or moving to the new firm.[120]

Despite the conclusion that Meehan and Boyle breached their
fiduciary duties, the court recognized that a certain amount of logistical planning for a new venture is permissible. While still partners, Meehan and Boyle executed a lease for their new firm, prepared lists of clients expected to follow them, and obtained financing on the basis of these lists. The court found that all of this conduct was permissible.[121] Significantly, the court specifically noted
that Meehan and Boyle "continued to work full schedules" while
they were planning their departure and that "[e]ach generally
maintained his or her usual standard of performance." What if this
had not been the case? What if Meehan and Boyle had spent 30% of
their normal working hours on matters related to the organization
of their new firm? This would likely be problematic. As mentioned,

---

[120] See id. at 1256, 1264–65.

[121] Cf. FRANKLIN A. GEVURTZ, CORPORATION LAW § 4.2.9(b), at 385 (2000) ("Numerous courts have faced the question as to how far employees can go to prepare a
competing venture without crossing the line and engaging in impermissible competition before the employee quits. Incorporating the new business and lining up its
finances and facilities seem okay. Soliciting the employer's customers is unaccepta-
ble. Borderline questions involve soliciting one's fellow employees to leave and join
the new venture, and notifying customers of the employee's intentions without soliciting their business.").

logistical activities to form a new business are typically permissible, but that usually assumes that such preparations do not detract from the partners' work at their former firm. Of course, if Meehan and Boyle spent 30% of the work day on their new firm, but they made up this time for Parker Coulter by working at night or on weekends, there is likely no problem. The key is presumably whether the "usual standard of performance" was maintained.[122]

Meehan and Boyle also recruited three associates to leave the firm before they announced their departure. The court, rather controversially, did not find this to be a problem, apparently "[b]ecause Parker Coulter identifies no specific loss resulting from this claimed breach." The court probably considered approaching the associates to be part of the logistics necessary for organizing the new firm. There is a strong argument, however, that recruiting employees while still partners is impermissible competition with the partnership itself:

> [T]he fiduciary restraints upon a partner with respect to client solicitation are not analogous to those applicable to employee recruitment. By contrast to the lawyer-client relationship, a partner does not have a fiduciary duty to the employees of a firm which would limit its duty of loyalty to the partnership. Thus, recruitment of firm employees has been viewed as distinct and "permissible on a more limited basis than . . . solicitation of clients." Pre-withdrawal recruitment is generally allowed "only after the firm has been given notice of the lawyer's intention to withdraw."[123]

Would the result in *Meehan* change if RUPA governed the dispute? Under § 403(c), Meehan's misrepresentations to the partnership about his intention to leave would presumably be viewed as improper.[124] Similarly, under § 404(b)(3), the conduct of Meehan

---

[122] If substandard performance did exist, an appropriate remedy might call for the partners to forfeit a portion of the compensation that they received from their former firm during the relevant time period. For example, if Meehan and Boyle were improperly spending 30% of the work day on logistics for their new firm, they would forfeit 30% of the compensation that they were paid by Parker Coulter during this time.

[123] Gibbs v. Breed, Abbott & Morgan, 710 N.Y.S.2d 578, 582–83 (Sup. Ct. 2000) (citations omitted); *see* note 121. In other words, as the passage indicates, partners are given less leeway with respect to the recruitment of employees than they are with the solicitation of clients. One reason for this may be to protect the important value of client freedom of choice in legal representation. This value may conflict with the duty of loyalty that partners owe to each other as partners. It may be that lawyers must be allowed to notify their clients of their departure in order to allow the clients to have freedom of choice.

[124] *Cf.* GEVURTZ, *supra* note 121, § 4.2.9(b), at 386 ("Courts also often condemn employees for concealing from, or misrepresenting to, their employers, the employees' intention to leave and set up a competing business. . . . [T]here is a bit of unreal-

and Boyle would likely be characterized as impermissible competition with the firm that violated the partners' duty of loyalty. It would also be difficult to characterize the misrepresentations to the firm and the other conduct as good faith under § 404(d).

4. The Role of Contract

A recurring question in the law of business organizations is whether contractual provisions can modify the obligations imposed by fiduciary duties. In *Singer v. Singer*,[125] the Singer family formed an oil production partnership called Josaline Production Co. Andrea and her brother Stanley were partners. On July 25, 1979, the partnership held a meeting where several investment opportunities were discussed. One item of interest was the possible purchase of 95 acres of land owned by IDS. Prior to the meeting, Stanley had been asked to look into the possibility of purchasing the land. At the meeting, however, the partners deferred the decision.

After the meeting, Stanley and Andrea formed a general partnership known as Gemini Realty Company. Gemini Realty purchased the IDS land without further consultation with any of the Josaline partners. A lawsuit was commenced by the Josaline partners, and the district court concluded that the IDS land was to be held in constructive trust for Josaline Production Co.

The Oklahoma Court of Appeals reversed. According to the court, the purchase by Stanley and Andrea would clearly have been a breach of fiduciary duty absent paragraph 8 of the Josaline partnership agreement. That paragraph stated the following:

> 8. Each partner shall be free to enter into business and other transactions for his or her own separate individual account, even though such business or other transaction may be in conflict with and/or competition with the business of this partnership. Neither the partnership nor any individual member of this partnership shall be entitled to claim or receive any part of or interest in such transactions, it being the intention and agreement that any partner will be free to deal on his or her own account to the same extent and with the same force and effect as if he or she were not and never had been members of this partnership.

---

ity to expecting employees to disclose intentions which will prompt the employer to fire them. Indeed, one suspects this is an area in which there may be a substantial discontinuity between legal expectations and customary practice.").

[125] 634 P.2d 766 (Okla. Ct. App. 1981).

The *Singer* court observed that paragraph 8 permitted any partner to engage in outside business transactions even if those transactions competed with the partnership. Thus, the court concluded that the purchase by Stanley and Andrea was, pursuant to contract, not a breach of their fiduciary duties.[126]

Would the *Singer* court have reached the same result if UPA governed the dispute? UPA § 21(1) provides that partners must account to the partnership for any benefit and hold as trustee for it any profits derived "without the consent of the other partners" from any partnership transaction. The provision suggests that the duty can be modified, but only with the consent of all of the Josaline partners.

The conduct of Stanley and Andrea would seem to violate § 21(1) absent paragraph 8. Any gains from the land purchased from IDS would presumably constitute "profits derived . . . from any transaction connected with the . . . conduct . . . of the partnership." Conduct allowed by the partnership agreement, however, would likely be considered conduct that had the "consent of the other partners." Thus, if paragraph 8 were interpreted to allow competition and usurpation of partnership opportunities by partners (an interpretation accepted by the *Singer* court), Stanley and Andrea would have avoided liability under UPA.

Would anything change if RUPA governed the dispute? RUPA § 404(b)(1) expressly prohibits partners from appropriating a partnership opportunity, and § 404(b)(3) prohibits partners from competing with the partnership. Absent contractual modification, therefore, the conduct of Stanley and Andrea would clearly have violated their duties. As § 103(a) indicates, however, all of RUPA's provisions are default rules that can be modified by the parties, except for the provisions stated in § 103(b). Section 103(b)(3) is particularly relevant, as it indicates that the duty of loyalty cannot be eliminated, but it can be limited in several ways.

For example, the partnership agreement "may identify specific types or categories of activities that do not violate the duty of loyalty, if not manifestly unreasonable." This presumably means that the partnership agreement may eliminate aspects of the duty of loyalty so long as the duty is not entirely eliminated. Thus, permitting some or all competition by the partners, or allowing the partners to take some or all partnership opportunities for themselves, would seem to be appropriate. Of course, the "if not manifestly unreasonable" clause is a bit of a wildcard. A court might use such language if it appears that contractual restrictions on the duty of

126 *See id.* at 767–70, 772–73.

loyalty come too close to a wholesale elimination of the duty. Alternatively, a court might use such language to strike down a contractual restriction on the duty of loyalty that has a particularly harmful effect on the partnership.

In short, it appears that paragraph 8 of the partnership agreement would be viewed as a permissible modification of the duty of loyalty. The paragraph identifies a specific type or category of activity (i.e., actions in competition with the partnership) and explicitly authorizes it. It is not a wholesale elimination of the duty of loyalty because, for example, the prohibition on using partnership property for personal purposes in § 404(b)(1) is largely unaffected, as is the prohibition on self-dealing transactions in § 404(b)(2). Because paragraph 8 permits *any* competition with the partnership, however, regardless of the harm to the partnership, one wonders if a court might find the paragraph to be "manifestly unreasonable."

RUPA § 103(b)(3)(ii) also provides that "all of the partners or a number or percentage specified in the partnership agreement may authorize or ratify, after full disclosure of all material facts, a specific act or transaction that otherwise would violate the duty of loyalty." Thus, conduct that would breach the duty of loyalty can be "blessed" by a unanimous partner vote or by a different vote that is designated in the partnership agreement. RUPA, therefore, provides various ways for consent to limit the fiduciary duty of loyalty.

What about the fiduciary duty of care? RUPA § 103(b)(4) says that the partnership agreement cannot "unreasonably reduce the duty of care." This language presumably means that the duty of care cannot be eliminated (as that would surely constitute an unreasonable reduction in the duty), but it can be limited to some reasonable extent. This is a very uncertain standard.

Can the obligation of good faith and fair dealing be eliminated under RUPA? Section 103(b)(5) prohibits elimination of the obligation, but it can be limited in ways that are similar to § 103(b)(3)(i)— i.e., the partnership agreement may prescribe the standards against which performance of the obligation is to be measured, if not manifestly unreasonable.[127]

---

[127] Delaware has adopted RUPA. Delaware's version of RUPA § 103(b), however, omits subsections (b)(3) and (b)(4)—indicating that the duties of loyalty and care can be limited or eliminated as the partners see fit. *See* DEL. CODE tit. 6, § 15–103(b). The statute further states that "[a] partnership agreement may provide for the limitation or elimination of any and all liabilities for breach of contract and breach of duties (including fiduciary duties) of a partner or other person to a partnership or to another partner . . . ; provided, that a partnership agreement may not limit or eliminate liability for any act or omission that constitutes a bad faith violation of the implied contractual covenant of good faith and fair dealing." *Id.* § 15–103(f). Delaware

With respect to the duty to disclose, UPA § 20 is not prefaced by "unless otherwise agreed" or similar language. Thus, it would appear that the section cannot be modified. Under RUPA, the duty to disclose in § 403(c) can be completely eliminated, as it is not on the list of sections in § 103(b). The right of access to books and records under § 403(b), however, cannot be "unreasonably restrict[ed]."

Should the law allow partners to limit or eliminate fiduciary duties by contract? As a general matter, the question of permitting limitations on fiduciary duty is far less controversial than the question of permitting wholesale eliminations of fiduciary duty. Some considerations include the following: (1) It may be efficient for the partners to waive fiduciary duties if there are other ways for the parties to protect themselves. In a general partnership where each partner has the right to actively participate in management, and where relatively easy exit rights are available through dissociation and dissolution, the need for fiduciary duties is arguably lessened.[128] (2) A partnership may not be able to recruit necessary talent unless concessions on fiduciary duties are made. For example, a real estate developer may be unwilling to join a partnership to develop a particular subdivision if that developer will be prohibited from working on other related subdivisions. The legal ability to permit competitive activity, therefore, may be useful to a partnership. (3) Fiduciary duty litigation is uncertain, time consuming, and expensive. The parties may prefer to rely on contractual protections and to avoid the vagaries of fiduciary duty doctrine and litigation. (4) Because it is difficult for partners to foresee all of the ways in which their fellow partners may act unfairly, the notion of permitting the elimination of fiduciary duties is worrisome, as it may leave partners without judicial protection in unexpected situations.[129]

F. Ownership Interests and Transferability

1. Partnership Property

As previously discussed in this Chapter, UPA generally adopts an aggregate theory of the partnership. If that aggregate theory were strictly applied, a partnership itself could not own property. Instead, what we would think of as partnership property would be

---

has similar provisions in its limited partnership and limited liability company statutes.

[128] *See* Chapter 3(C) (discussing partnership management), 3(G) (discussing dissociation and dissolution).

[129] For more on the benefits and costs of fiduciary duties, see Larry E. Ribstein, *Fiduciary Duty Contracts in Unincorporated Firms,* 54 WASH. & LEE L. REV. 537, 546–50 (1997).

held, as a legal matter, by individual partners as tenants in common or joint tenants.

Despite this conceptual problem, UPA effectively treats partnership property as if it were owned by the partnership itself. UPA accomplishes this by stating, in § 25(1), that "[a] partner is co-owner with his partners of specific partnership property holding as a tenant in partnership." Having established this "tenancy in partnership" form of ownership, UPA then proceeds to negate the rights normally associated with individual ownership. A partner has no right to possess partnership property for non-partnership purposes; a partner may not assign his interest in partnership property; a partner's right in partnership property is not subject to attachment or execution on a claim against the partner; on the death of a partner, his right in partnership property vests in the surviving partners; and a partner's right in partnership property is not subject to dower, curtesy, or allowances to widows, heirs, or next of kin.[130] The net result of these provisions is that the partnership, rather than the partners, is effectively treated as the owner of partnership property.

RUPA avoids the conceptual problems and related complexity associated with the UPA approach. RUPA § 201 recognizes the partnership as an entity, and § 203 provides, in a conceptually consistent manner, that "[p]roperty acquired by a partnership is property of the partnership and not of the partners individually." Similarly, § 501 provides that "[a] partner is not a co-owner of partnership property and has no interest in partnership property which can be transferred, either voluntarily or involuntarily."[131]

2. Transferring a Partnership Interest

A partner's ownership interest in a partnership is referred to as a "partnership interest," and owning such an interest confers various rights. RUPA § 101(9) defines "partnership interest" as "all of a partner's interest in the partnership, including the partner's transferable interest and all management and other rights." According to RUPA § 502, a partner's "transferable interest" includes "the partner's share of the profits and losses of the partnership and the partner's right to receive distributions." Broadly speaking,

---

[130] See UPA § 25(2)(a)–(e). Interestingly, with respect to real estate, UPA § 8(3) states rather directly (and seemingly contrary to an aggregate view) that "[a]ny estate in real property may be acquired in the partnership name."

[131] It can be difficult to determine whether property has been contributed to a partnership or whether it remains the personal property of an individual partner. UPA § 8 and RUPA § 204 provide rules for determining when property is considered to be partnership property.

therefore, a partnership interest provides both (1) financial rights (the transferable interest) and (2) management rights.[132]

Can a partner transfer his partnership interest—i.e., his bundle of financial and management rights—to a third party, thereby making that third party into a "partner?" Not without the consent of his fellow partners. Partnership law has long provided a default "pick-your-partner" rule dictating that a person may become a partner only with the consent of all of the existing partners.[133] The policy behind this rule is that a partner's wrongdoing while conducting partnership business can create a partnership obligation, and partners have unlimited personal liability for partnership obligations. Thus, because a partner's actions can create personal liability for other partners, the default rule is sensible—a person can only be admitted as a partner if all of the existing partners agree. In addition, because every partner has a right to participate in the management of a general partnership,[134] partners should have some control over who can enter the partnership and exercise management rights.

Despite the pick-your-partner rule, a partner is entitled to transfer a portion of his partnership interest to a third party without the need to obtain the other partners' consent. That portion is the "transferable interest," or the financial rights aspect of the partnership interest.[135] Such a unilateral transfer would not result in the transferee becoming a partner (with accompanying management rights), but it would provide the transferee with the right to receive distributions to which the transferor partner would otherwise be entitled.[136] At the conclusion of a unilateral transfer, therefore, the transferor remains a partner and "retains the rights and duties of a partner other than the interest in distributions transferred."[137] Correspondingly, the transferee is not a partner, but he has the financial right to receive the transferor-partner's share of any partnership distributions.[138] Keep in mind that these princi-

---

[132] Analogous UPA provisions are §§ 24–26.

[133] See UPA § 18(g); RUPA § 401(i).

[134] See UPA § 18(e); RUPA § 401(f); see also Chapter 3(C) (discussing partnership management).

[135] Indeed, the "transferable interest" is a partner's personal property. See UPA § 26; RUPA § 502.

[136] See UPA §§ 26–27; RUPA §§ 502–503. UPA uses the terminology of "assigning" a partnership interest rather than "transferring" a partnership interest, but the meaning is the same. See RUPA § 503 cmt. 1.

[137] RUPA § 503(d). While it is true that the transferor remains a partner, the nontransferring partners can expel the transferor from the partnership in certain circumstances. See UPA § 31(1)(c); RUPA § 601(4)(ii).

[138] A transferee also gets the right to petition for dissolution of the partnership in certain circumstances. See UPA § 32(2); RUPA §§ 503(b)(3), 801(6). Moreover, recall that a partner's "transferable interest" also includes "the partner's share of the prof-

ples are merely default rules that can be altered by an agreement of the partners.

The operation of these principles is nicely illustrated by the decision of *Rapoport v. 55 Perry Co.*[139] The Rapoports (Simon, Genia, and Ury) and the Parnes each owned a 50% partnership interest in 55 Perry Company. Paragraph 12 of their partnership agreement stated the following:

> No partner or partners shall have the authority to transfer, sell ... assign or in any way dispose of the partnership realty and/or personalty and shall not have the authority to sell, transfer, assign ... his or their share in this firm, nor enter into any agreement as a result of which any person shall become interested with him in this firm, unless the same is agreed to in writing by a majority of the partners as determined by the percentage of ownership ... , except for members of his immediate family who have attained majority, in which case no such consent shall be required.

Without getting the approval of the Parnes, Simon and Genia Rapoport transferred 10% of their partnership interest to their adult children (Daniel and Kalia). The Rapoports then claimed that the transfer resulted in Daniel and Kalia becoming partners in the business. The Parnes disagreed and maintained that their consent was necessary before any new partners could be admitted.[140]

Assuming that paragraph 12 did not exist, the Rapoports would not have been able to make Daniel and Kalia into partners without the Parnes' consent. As mentioned, the default pick-your-partner rule requires the unanimous consent of the existing partners before a new partner can be admitted. Nevertheless, the Rapoports would have been able to transfer their financial rights to

---

its and losses of the partnership." RUPA § 502. As a matter of federal income tax law, a transferee is treated as a partner for tax purposes. As a consequence, the transferee must account for any pass-through profits and losses on his personal tax return in the same manner as a partner. *See, e.g.,* CARTER G. BISHOP & DANIEL S. KLEINBERGER, LIMITED LIABILITY COMPANIES: TAX AND BUSINESS LAW ¶ 8.07[1][a][i]–[ii] (Supp. 2008–2). Viewed from a federal income tax standpoint, therefore, a transferee also receives the right to share in the profits and losses of the partnership at the conclusion of a unilateral transfer. As a matter of state law, however, the transferee is not a partner, and he has no liability for partnership obligations. *See, e.g.,* RUPA § 503 cmt. 4 ("[Section 503(d)] makes clear that unless otherwise agreed the partner whose interest is transferred retains all of the rights and duties of a partner, other than the right to receive distributions. This means the transferor is entitled to participate in the management of the partnership and remains personally liable for all partnership obligations . . . .").

[139] 376 N.Y.S.2d 147 (App. Div. 1975).

[140] *See id.* at 148–49.

Daniel and Kalia without the Parnes' consent. The transferable interest, in other words, can be unilaterally transferred in the absence of a contrary agreement.

The Rapoports argued, however, that paragraph 12 changed the pick-your-partner default rule by allowing them to make their adult children into full partners in the business (with both financial and management rights) without the Parnes' approval. The Parnes disagreed and argued that paragraph 12 did not alter the pick-your-partner rule at all. Instead, paragraph 12 only changed the transferable interest default rule by requiring majority consent of the partners for the transfer of financial rights to a third party, unless that transfer was to the adult children of the existing partners. The Parnes, in other words, argued that paragraph 12 allowed the Rapoports to unilaterally transfer their financial rights, and only their financial rights, to their adult children. If the transferees were not adult children of the partners, the Parnes interpreted paragraph 12 to mean that their consent would be needed before the Rapoports could effectuate any transfer of their financial rights.

Rather strangely, the court held that the partnership agreement could be interpreted as a matter of law. (It would seem that paragraph 12 was at least ambiguous, and that the interpretation of the agreement should have been resolved at a trial.) After citing the default rules regarding the transfer of a partnership interest, the court examined whether those default rules had been altered by the partnership agreement. Ultimately, the court accepted the Parnes' interpretation of the agreement and concluded that the Rapoports' unilateral transfer had the effect of transferring 10% of their financial rights in the partnership to their children, but it did not result in the children becoming partners themselves.[141]

3. The Charging Order

Assume that a partner has an individual creditor who obtains a judgment against the partner. The judgment creditor cannot execute against the partnership's assets because the partner does not have any ownership interest in the partnership's assets.[142] Moreover, allowing the judgment creditor to involuntarily seize and sell the partner's ownership interest (just like any other non-exempt asset of a judgment debtor) would be undesirable, as such a sale would suggest that the buyer is now a full-fledged partner—a result contrary to the pick-your-partner rule. To accommodate the interests of partners and their individual creditors, partnership law de-

---

[141] *See id.* at 148–50.

[142] *See* UPA § 25(2); RUPA § 501; *see also* Chapter 3(F)(1) (discussing partnership property).

veloped the remedy of a "charging order" that a court can impose against a debtor-partner upon the request of that partner's creditor.

A charging order is effectively a lien on the partner's transferable interest (i.e., his financial rights) in the partnership. If a court imposes a charging order, the judgment creditor is entitled to any distributions made by the partnership that would otherwise have gone to the debtor-partner.[143] The entitlement to distributions continues until the judgment creditor has received enough proceeds to pay off the judgment.

What happens, however, if the partnership does not make any distributions? In such circumstances, the charging order is largely useless, and a court can order foreclosure. In effect, the foreclosure of a charging order results in the sale of the debtor-partner's transferable interest in the partnership. The purchaser at the foreclosure sale will become a transferee, and the sale proceeds will go to the judgment creditor in full or partial satisfaction of the judgment.[144]

By becoming a transferee, a purchaser at a foreclosure sale gains a few rights. First, the purchaser now owns the debtor-partner's transferable interest, which entitles the purchaser to any distributions that would otherwise have gone to the debtor-partner.[145] Second, the purchaser obtains the right to petition for dissolution of the partnership in certain situations.[146] If the purchaser at the foreclosure sale is the judgment creditor himself, this right can be particularly useful as leverage to motivate the partnership to make sufficient distributions to pay off the judgment; otherwise, the partnership risks dissolution. Alternatively, if dissolution is ordered, the purchaser (as the owner of the transferable interest) is entitled to the distribution that the debtor-partner would have received. Despite these additional rights, the purchaser, as a mere transferee, is not granted the status of "partner" under state law and is not afforded any of the other rights that partner status conveys.[147]

---

[143] *See* UPA § 28; RUPA § 504.

[144] *See* UPA § 28; RUPA § 504(b). If the partnership is not making distributions, few (if any) persons will be interested in buying the debtor-partner's transferable interest at a foreclosure sale. Thus, a foreclosure sale often generates little or no sale proceeds for the judgment creditor. In fact, the purchaser at a foreclosure sale is often the judgment creditor himself who plans on using the purchase to obtain a right to dissolve the partnership. *See* notes 146–148 and accompanying text.

[145] *See* UPA § 27; RUPA §§ 503(b), 504(b).

[146] *See* UPA § 32(2); RUPA §§ 503(b)(3), 801(6).

[147] *See* text accompanying notes 135–138.

Unfortunately, because a transferee is treated as a partner for federal income tax purposes, a purchaser at a foreclosure sale must also account for any pass-through profits and losses of the partnership on his personal tax return, even if no cash is actually distributed.[148] Thus, the decision to purchase at a foreclosure sale is not one that should be made lightly.

G. Dissociation and Dissolution

The dissociation and dissolution provisions of UPA and RUPA differ significantly from each other and were a principal area of controversy in the drafting of RUPA. These provisions are the most complicated sections in both of the uniform acts. It is easier to understand the changes made by RUPA if one has a firm grasp of the related provisions under UPA. Thus, UPA is where we begin.

1. Dissolution Under UPA

a. Doctrinal Overview

The termination of a partnership as a going concern under UPA generally involves three phases. The first phase is referred to as "dissolution." UPA § 29 defines "dissolution" as "the change in the relation of the partners caused by any partner ceasing to be associated in the carrying on . . . of the business." This definition of the word "dissolution" differs considerably from the lay understanding of the word. It refers to a change in personal relationships among partners within the partnership and has nothing to do with the disposition of assets or the closing down and selling of the business. Put differently, "dissolution" under UPA generally refers to an event which causes a change in the composition of the partners themselves.

The second phase is referred to as "winding up" (also known as "liquidation"). Winding up can be generally defined as the process of ending the partnership's business. It typically involves the sale of the partnership's assets, the repayment of partnership creditors, and the distribution of any remaining proceeds to the partners based on a settling up of profits and losses. In some circumstances, dissolution causes the winding up of the partnership. In other circumstances, it does not. Thus, it is helpful to keep the concepts separate in your mind (dissolution on the one hand, and winding up on the other). A change in the composition of the partners (dissolution), in other words, does not necessarily mean that the business of the partnership must cease (winding up).

---

[148] *See* note 138.

The third phase is referred to as "termination." Termination is simply the moment in time when the winding up of the partnership's affairs is completed.[149] It marks the end of the partnership as a going concern.

Why does § 29 indicate that dissolution is caused by any partner "ceasing to be associated" in the partnership? As previously discussed, under the aggregate conception of the partnership, the aggregate of the partners changes whenever a partner leaves or joins the partnership.[150] Thus, § 29 is correct to say that dissolution—i.e., a change in the aggregate of the partners—is caused whenever a partner leaves the partnership. Interestingly, § 29 does not speak to the addition of a partner, but § 41 does. Section 41(1) discusses the admission of a new partner, and the last clause states that creditors of the "first *or dissolved*" partnership are also creditors of the partnership continuing the business. Thus, when a partner is admitted, § 41(1) stands for the proposition that the partnership dissolves—which makes sense as the aggregate of the partners has changed.[151]

Under UPA, many of the issues associated with partnership dissolution turn on whether the partnership is "at-will" or "term," and on what might be described as whether the act of dissolution is "rightful" or "wrongful." An at-will partnership is one where the partners have not agreed to remain partners until the expiration of a definite term or the completion of a particular undertaking.[152] It is the default form of partnership. A term partnership is the converse—it is a partnership where the partners have agreed, explicitly or implicitly, to remain partners for a definite term or until the completion of a particular undertaking.[153]

Example: A partnership is formed with the agreement that it shall terminate after five years. It is a term partnership because the partners have agreed to remain partners for a definite term.

Example: A partnership is formed to construct an office building. It is a term partnership because the partners have agreed to remain partners until a particular undertaking—the construction of the building—is completed. Alternatively, it is a term partnership because the partners have agreed to remain partners for a definite

---

[149] *See* UPA § 30.

[150] *See* Chapter 3(B)(3).

[151] *See also* UPA § 17 cmt. ("The present section eliminates the difficulty which arises when a new partner is admitted without liquidation of firm debts. The present theory of the common law is that a new partnership is formed.").

[152] *See id.* § 31(1)(b); *cf.* RUPA § 101(8) (defining "partnership at will").

[153] *See* UPA § 31(1)(a); *cf.* RUPA § 101 cmt. (discussing a term partnership and the distinction between term and at-will partnerships).

term—the time required to complete the construction of the building.[154]

Example: A partnership is formed to operate a linen supply business. It is an at-will partnership because the partners have not agreed to remain partners for a definite term or until the completion of a particular undertaking. The partnership is simply conducting a business which may last indefinitely.[155]

The at-will or term characterization of a partnership is important primarily because it determines whether dissolution by a partner's express will (i.e., by a partner's express desire) is rightful or wrongful. As will be explained, there are differing consequences depending upon that determination.

For some acts of dissolution, UPA suggests that the act is rightful—it is "[w]ithout violation of the agreement between the partners." Such acts include the following: (1) the termination of the definite term or particular undertaking in a term partnership; (2) the express will of any partner in an at-will partnership; (3) the express will of all of the partners who have not assigned their interests or had them subject to a charging order; and (4) the expulsion of any partner from the business bona fide in accordance with a power conferred by the partnership agreement.[156]

UPA also specifies an act of dissolution that is, in effect, wrongful—it is "[i]n contravention of the agreement between the partners." That act is when dissolution is caused by the express will of any partner at any time where the circumstances do not permit dissolution under any other provision of § 31.[157] For example, when a partner decides to withdraw from a term partnership before the end of the term or the completion of the particular undertaking, that act of dissolution (the "express will of any partner") typically falls under § 31(2) and is considered wrongful. UPA provides four other acts of dissolution that are not explicitly designated as rightful or wrongful: (1) any event which makes it unlawful for the business of the partnership to be carried on, or for the members to carry it on, in

---

[154] *See, e.g.,* 68th Street Apts., Inc. v. Lauricella, 362 A.2d 78, 89–81, 86–87 (N.J. Super. Ct. Law Div. 1976) (concluding that a partnership to construct an apartment building was a term partnership, and noting that "a number of cases have found agreements to develop real estate to be partnership or joint venture obligations which are to continue until the undertaking is accomplished").

[155] *Cf.* RUPA § 101 cmt. (noting that "[a] partnership to conduct a business which may last indefinitely . . . is an at-will partnership, even though there may be an obligation of the partnership, such as a mortgage, which must be repaid by a certain date, absent a specific agreement that no partner can rightfully withdraw until the obligation is repaid").

[156] *See* UPA § 31(1).

[157] *See id.* § 31(2).

partnership; (2) the death of any partner; (3) the bankruptcy of any partner or the partnership; and (4) a decree of court under § 32.[158]

When an act of dissolution is considered rightful, UPA § 38(1) suggests that each partner has the default right to compel the winding up of the partnership's business through sale. (This point is explored further in the discussion of the *Dreifuerst* case below.) As mentioned, winding up typically involves the sale of the partnership's assets, the repayment of firm creditors, and the distribution of any remaining sale proceeds to the partners. By contrast, an act of dissolution that is considered wrongful subjects the dissolving partner to several negative consequences under § 38(2): (1) the wrongfully dissolving partner is liable for damages for breach of the agreement; (2) the remaining partners can decide to wind up the business of the partnership, or they can forego winding up in favor of continuing the business without the wrongfully dissolving partner; and (3) if the remaining partners decide to forego winding up in favor of continuing the business, the wrongfully dissolving partner has the right to be bought out, but only at a price that does not include the value of the firm's goodwill.[159]

This goodwill "penalty" can be severe. As defined in Black's Law Dictionary, goodwill is "[t]he capacity to earn profits in excess of a normal rate of return due to establishment of favorable community reputation and consumer identification of the business name." The term is "[i]nformally used to indicate the value of good customer relations, high employee morale, a well-respected business name, etc. which are expected to result in greater than normal earning power."[160] In a services-oriented business, a large part of the value of the business may be goodwill. For example, consider a small air conditioning repair company. The value of the assets of that business may be trivial—some tools, and perhaps some air conditioning units that are available for sale. A larger component of the value of that business is its reputation for timely and high-quality service. Thus, depending upon the type of business, a buy-out exclusive of goodwill value may be a significant penalty.[161]

---

[158] *See id.* § 31(3)–(6).

[159] *See id.* § 38(2) (specifying the consequences "[w]hen dissolution is caused in contravention of the partnership agreement").

[160] BLACK'S LAW DICTIONARY 694–95 (6th ed. 1990).

[161] *See, e.g.*, Drashner v. Sorenson, 63 N.W.2d 255, 256, 259–60 (S.D. 1954) (stating that "the most valuable asset" of an insurance and real estate agency was its goodwill, and concluding, in a wrongful dissolution setting, that the lower court properly excluded the goodwill from the valuation of the property of the business).

After dissolution, partners are still liable for pre-dissolution partnership obligations,[162] and they still have lingering apparent authority to bind the partnership in certain circumstances.[163] Moreover, creditors of the dissolved partnership generally remain creditors of the continuing partnership (assuming that winding up has not occurred).[164]

Although this doctrinal framework is complicated, it is important to notice that it reveals a critical characteristic of the general partnership form: partners have easy exit rights from the venture. That is, a partner can always liquidate his partnership interest for cash whenever he desires to do so. If the partnership is at-will, the partner can simply dissolve by express will. That dissolution will be considered rightful and the partner will have the power to compel the winding up of the partnership business (which typically means that the partner will receive his share of the sale of the partnership assets).[165] Alternatively, the partner can use his right to wind up as leverage to motivate a buyout of his interest by agreement of the remaining partners who prefer to continue the business. If the partnership is for a term, the partner can still dissolve by express will, although that wrongful dissolution has some negative consequences. The partnership will either be wound up (in which case the wrongfully dissolving partner will typically receive his share of the sale of the partnership assets), or the remaining partners will purchase the wrongfully dissolving partner's interest in the business (exclusive of goodwill and offset by any damages).[166] Thus, regardless of whether a partnership is at-will or for a term, a partner can always exit the partnership and cash out the value of his interest. This point is important to contrast with other business structures where easy exit rights are absent. It also underscores why courts often state that every partner has the power, but not necessarily the right, to dissolve a partnership. A partner can always dissolve by express will (the power), but such an act of dissolution may not be rightful (the right), as it depends in large part upon the at-will or term characterization of the partnership.

---

[162] See UPA § 36; see also Chapter 3(D)(3)(b) (discussing a partner's liability for partnership obligations).

[163] See UPA § 35. This apparent authority is terminated as to any creditor who has knowledge or notice of the dissolution. A newspaper notice of dissolution is sufficient for parties who knew about the partnership prior to dissolution, but who had not extended credit before that time. For parties who had extended credit to the firm prior to dissolution, more individualized notice of dissolution is required. See id.

[164] See id. § 41.

[165] See id. §§ 31(1)(b), 38(1).

[166] See id. §§ 31(2), 38(2).

b. Causes of Dissolution

Page v. Page[167] is a well-known decision that highlights some of the causes of dissolution specified in UPA § 31. In *Page*, two brothers were partners in a linen supply business. Each brother contributed approximately $43,000 to start the venture. Unfortunately, from 1949 to 1957, the business consistently lost money. In 1958, however, the business turned a profit, and the improved operations continued in the first three months of 1959. Despite this improvement, the plaintiff filed a declaratory judgment action seeking a determination that the partnership was at-will rather than for a term.[168]

Why did the plaintiff brother seek a declaratory judgment that the partnership was at-will? Why didn't the plaintiff simply give the partnership notice of his express will to dissolve? After all, a partner can dissolve by express will regardless of whether the partnership is at-will or for a term.[169] Most likely, the plaintiff was concerned about the consequences of wrongful dissolution. If he dissolved by express will, and if his brother challenged it, a court might find that he wrongfully dissolved before the end of a term partnership. To avoid this possibility, the plaintiff sought a declaration that the partnership was at-will. If the court agreed, the plaintiff could then dissolve by express will knowing that his dissolution would be rightful. If the court disagreed, the plaintiff could step back and rethink his actions without having already triggered a dissolution and its consequences.

Although there was no written partnership agreement, the defendant argued that the partnership was for a term based on an implicit agreement that the partnership would continue until all of its debt obligations were repaid. He testified that the terms of the partnership were to be similar to former partnerships between the brothers where "we went into partnership to start the business and let the business operation pay for itself . . . put in so much money, and let the business pay itself out." The defendant conceded, however, that there was no understanding as to the term of the present partnership in the event of losses. As the defendant admitted, "[w]e never figured on losing, I guess."[170]

The trial court found that the partnership was for a term— "such reasonable time as is necessary to enable said partnership to repay from partnership profits, indebtedness incurred . . . for the

---

[167] 359 P.2d 41 (Cal. 1961).

[168] *See id.* at 42.

[169] *See* notes 156–157, 165–166 and accompanying text.

[170] *See Page*, 359 P.2d at 42–43.

operation of such business." The Supreme Court of California disagreed:

> Viewing this evidence most favorably for defendant, it proves only that the partners expected to meet current expenses from current income and to recoup their investment if the business were successful.

> Defendant contends that such an expectation is sufficient to create a partnership for a term under the rule of Owen v. Cohen, 19 Cal.2d 147, 150, 119 P.2d 713. In that case we held that when a partner advances a sum of money to a partnership with the understanding that the amount contributed was to be a loan to the partnership and was to be repaid as soon as feasible from the prospective profits of the business, the partnership is for the term reasonably required to repay the loan. It is true that Owen v. Cohen, supra, and other cases hold that partners may impliedly agree to continue in business until a certain sum of money is earned, or one or more partners recoup their investments, or until certain debts are paid, or until certain property could be disposed of on favorable terms. In each of these cases, however, the implied agreement found support in the evidence.

> . . .

> In the instant case, however, defendant failed to prove any facts from which an agreement to continue the partnership for a term may be implied. The understanding to which defendant testified was no more than a common hope that the partnership earnings would pay for all the necessary expenses. Such a hope does not establish even by implication a "definite term or particular undertaking" as required by [the California version of UPA § 31(1)(b)]. All partnerships are ordinarily entered into with the hope that they will be profitable, but that alone does not make them all partnerships for a term and obligate the partners to continue in the partnerships until all of the losses over a period of many years have been recovered.[171]

Notice that the *Page* court did not reject the possibility of an implied agreement to continue a partnership until its debts are repaid; indeed, the court favorably cited *Owen* and other cases for the proposition that partners may impliedly agree to continue in business for various periods of time.[172] The court simply found that evi-

---

[171] *Id.* at 43–44 (citations omitted).

[172] *See also* Drashner v. Sorenson, 63 N.W.2d 255, 257–58 (S.D. 1954) (finding a term partnership based on an agreement of the parties that "contemplated an asso-

dence of such an agreement was lacking. Thus, the brothers' linen supply partnership was merely an ongoing business with no defined end—i.e., an at-will partnership. As the decision suggests, partners desiring a term for their partnership should try to make that desire very clear, preferably in a written partnership agreement.

Given that the business had just turned profitable, why was the plaintiff brother thinking about dissolving in the first place? The defendant argued that his brother was attempting to steal the business for himself. The business had started turning a profit, and the establishment of Vandenberg Air Force Base in the vicinity had created a brighter outlook. Because (a) the plaintiff was the sole owner of a separate corporation that supplied the linen and machinery used by the partnership, (b) that corporation held a 47,000 demand note of the partnership, and (c) the plaintiff was the managing partner who knew how to conduct the operations of the partnership, the plaintiff was ideally positioned to purchase the business at a winding up sale. He already owned a source of supply, he could control the terms of the note's repayment, and he knew how to run the business. By contrast, outside purchasers were unlikely to be attracted to the sale of the business. The outside buyer would need to secure a source of supply, would need to resolve the outstanding $47,000 note, and would need to have (or to hire) the expertise to run the operation. Thus, the defendant seemed to suggest that his brother would pay very little (due to the absence of rival bidders) to acquire the business for himself at a winding up sale.[173]

The court noted that there was no showing in the record of bad faith or that the improved profit situation was more than temporary. Moreover, the court pointed out that the issue went beyond the question of whether the partnership was at-will or for a term. Nevertheless, the court stated that any power of a partner must be exercised in good faith. Although the plaintiff had the power to dissolve the partnership by his express will, that power may not be used to "'freeze out' a copartner and appropriate the business to his own use . . . unless he fully compensates his copartner for his share of the prospective business opportunity." The court concluded that if it were "proved that plaintiff acted in bad faith and violated his fiduciary duties by attempting to appropriate to his own use the new prosperity of the partnership without adequate compensation to his co-partner," the dissolution would be considered wrongful under the California version of UPA § 38(2). The defendant's action would be viewed as violating "the implied agreement not to exclude

ciation which would continue at least until the $7500 advance of defendants had been repaid from the gross earnings of the business").

[173] *See Page,* 359 P.2d at 42, 44.

defendant wrongfully from the partnership business opportunity."[174] Based on this analysis, *Page* is often cited for the proposition
that a partner's bad faith dissolution will be considered wrongful,
even if the cause of dissolution otherwise falls within the literal
language of UPA § 31(1).[175]

Collins v. Lewis[176] examines the judicial dissolution provisions
of UPA § 32(1).[177] Lewis and Collins entered into a partnership to
construct and operate a cafeteria on leased premises. Lewis was to
provide management services and supervise construction, while
Collins was to provide the capital. The cafeteria's construction
greatly exceeded both cost and time estimates. As a result, Collins
had spent over $600,000 by the time the cafeteria opened for busi-
ness. After further expenses arose, Collins threatened to cease advancing monies unless Lewis operated the cafeteria on a profitable
basis. Collins ultimately sued and sought, among other requests, a
judicial dissolution of the partnership. The jury found that Lewis
was competent to manage the cafeteria, that Collins had acted negligently, and that but for the conduct of Collins, there would be a
reasonable expectation of profit under the continued management of
Lewis. The trial court entered judgment denying all relief sought
by Collins, and the Texas Court of Civil Appeals affirmed.[178]

Why was Collins seeking to dissolve the partnership? Perhaps
he was simply trying to get leverage against Lewis in an effort to
compel Lewis to operate the cafeteria as Collins wished ("do it this
way or I will seek to wind up the partnership"). Alternatively, Collins may truly have desired dissolution because, if the partnership
business were sold as part of a winding up procedure, he might get
his $600,000 worth of loans and capital contributions back. Indeed,
upon dissolution and winding up, UPA § 40(b) requires partner
loans and partner capital contributions to be repaid before any profits are distributed.

Was the partnership in *Collins* at-will or for a term? The fact
that the partnership was intended to be an ongoing business suggests at-will status. Nevertheless, the court stated that "Lewis and
Collins entered into a partnership agreement to endure throughout
the term of the lease contract," and the lease contract was for thirty

---

[174] *See id.* at 44–45.

[175] RUPA § 404(d) codifies this sentiment to some extent by declaring that a partner must discharge duties and exercise rights "consistently with the obligation of
good faith and fair dealing." *See* Chapter 3(E)(2).

[176] 283 S.W.2d 258 (Tex. Civ. App. 1955).

[177] The *Collins* case arose before Texas enacted its version of UPA. Nevertheless,
the principles and the result are largely the same under UPA.

[178] *See Collins,* 283 S.W.2d at 259–61.

years. Thus, it was a term partnership for the thirty-year term of the lease.

Should Collins have attempted to dissolve the partnership by his express will? Dissolution of an at-will partnership by express will would be characterized as rightful, but dissolution of a term partnership by express will would be characterized as wrongful.[179] Because the partnership was for a thirty-year term, dissolution by express will would have been a bad idea. Along with the other consequences of wrongful dissolution,[180] Collins would have been subject to damages for breach of the agreement with Lewis, and the damages may have been substantial. A court or jury might have based an award on the projected lost profits during the thirty-year period of the partnership. Admittedly, contract law requires that such profits be reasonably certain to be recoverable, but they might be estimable on the basis of any profits actually earned by the cafeteria after it opened. Thus, a dissolution by express will by Collins was too risky. He might have been liable for damages that greatly exceeded his $600,000+ infusion.[181]

Rather than dissolve by express will, Collins attempted to secure judicial dissolution on grounds similar to those provided by UPA § 31(6) and § 32. These sections allow a court to order dissolution if certain circumstances are present: (a) a partner has been declared a lunatic in any judicial proceeding or is shown to be of unsound mind; (b) a partner becomes in any other way incapable of performing his part of the partnership contract; (c) a partner has been guilty of such conduct as tends to affect prejudicially the carrying on of the business; (d) a partner willfully or persistently commits a breach of the partnership agreement, or otherwise so conducts himself in matters relating to the partnership business that it is not reasonably practicable to carry on the business in partnership with him; (e) the business of the partnership can only be carried on at a loss; or (f) other circumstances render a dissolution equitable. Asking for judicial dissolution was safer than dissolving by express

---

[179] *See* notes 156–158 and accompanying text.

[180] *See* note 159 and accompanying text.

[181] As mentioned, one consequence of wrongful dissolution is that the other partners can avoid winding up and can continue the business without the wrongfully dissolving partner. *See* UPA § 38(2)(b). In a two-person partnership, however, this is presumably not possible. When one of the two partners has withdrawn, there is only one partner remaining. A partnership cannot exist without at least two persons owning the business. *See id.* § 6; *see also* Corrales v. Corrales, No. G043598, 2011 WL 3484470, at *1 (Cal. Ct. App. Aug. 10, 2011) ("If a partnership consists of only two persons, the partnership dissolves by operation of law when one of them departs."); Robert W. Hillman & Donald J. Weidner, *Partners Without Partners: The Legal Status of Single Person Partnerships*, 17 FORDHAM J. OF CORP. & FIN. L. 449 (2012) (providing contrasting views on whether a partnership can continue with only one remaining partner).

will because, if judicial dissolution was not ordered, the partnership would still be intact.

Why did the court refuse to grant dissolution? Grounds (c) and (d) above are grounds that a court can use whenever a non-petitioning partner is engaging in misconduct. The *Collins* court concluded, however, that these grounds are unavailable when the petitioning partner (Collins) is the wrongdoer (as the jury found). The same analysis would apply to (f)—there is nothing equitable about helping the wrongdoer. Ground (e) has promise if the partnership was truly a losing venture, but the jury found that the partnership could be run on a profitable basis if Collins would stop misbehaving. In short, although UPA § 32 is a judicial dissolution provision, the court effectively held that the petitioning partner cannot be the one whose own acts are creating the dissolution circumstances.[182]

Based on the jury findings, Lewis would likely have been successful if he had petitioned for judicial dissolution. But why would Lewis do so? He was the manager of a $600,000+ cafeteria in which he had not invested any of his own money and in which he was entitled to half of the profits. It made more sense for Lewis to keep the partnership operating in the hopes of earning large profits in the future. Moreover, and as mentioned, UPA § 40 indicates that if the partnership were dissolved and wound up, loans by partners and partner capital contributions would have to be repaid before any remaining monies could be split between the partners. Thus, Collins would have to be reimbursed his $600,000 before Lewis would see a dime. At the early stage of the cafeteria's operation, it was not clear that a sale of the partnership business would have generated enough proceeds to provide any return to Lewis. In short, for Lewis, dissolution did not make a lot of sense.[183]

---

[182] *See Collins,* 283 S.W.2d at 261.

[183] Does judicial dissolution under § 32 implicate the wrongful dissolution consequences of § 38(2)? Although § 38(2) deals with wrongful dissolution, it is technically triggered only when dissolution "is caused in contravention of the partnership agreement." That phrase, "in contravention of the partnership agreement," is only present in § 31(2) (it isn't identical language, but it is close). Does this mean that only dissolution under § 31(2) should be considered wrongful and subject to § 38(2)? Such a position seems odd, as court-ordered dissolution under § 32(1)(c) or (d) is granted when one of the partners has engaged in misconduct. With respect to § 32(1)(c), a court might find an implicit agreement between partners to avoid conduct that prejudicially affects the business. If dissolution is granted under that subsection, therefore, it could be viewed as a breach of this implied agreement that implicates the "in contravention of the partnership agreement" language of § 38(2). Similarly, with respect to § 32(1)(d), the first clause ("willfully or persistently commits a breach") explicitly refers to a breach of the partnership agreement. With respect to the second clause, a court might find an implicit agreement to avoid acting in ways that make it not reasonably practicable to carry on the business.

Bohatch v. Butler & Binion[184] is a controversial decision involving the expulsion of a partner and related fiduciary duty and dissolution issues arising from the expulsion. Collette Bohatch was a law partner in the Washington, D.C. office of Butler & Binion. After reviewing internal firm reports of billable hours, she became concerned that John McDonald, the managing partner of the office, was overbilling Pennzoil (who was the office's primary client). The firm's management committee commenced an investigation. Pennzoil's in-house counsel—who had a long-standing relationship with McDonald—stated that Pennzoil was satisfied that the bills were reasonable, and the committee ultimately determined that there was no basis for Bohatch's contentions. Bohatch was told to begin looking for other work, and the firm later formally expelled her from the partnership.

Bohatch sued the firm and several of its partners for breach of fiduciary duty and other claims related to her expulsion. On appeal, the Supreme Court of Texas held that the fiduciary duty of partners did not encompass an obligation to remain partners. The court rejected the argument that public policy required, in cases of a whistleblowing partner, a limited duty to remain partners. Although the court acknowledged that permitting a law firm to expel a partner who in good faith reported suspected overbilling would discourage compliance with the rules of professional conduct, the court was more concerned with the problems of forcing partners who no longer trusted one another to continue working together. Thus, the court concluded that the partnership did not owe Bohatch a duty to avoid expelling her for reporting suspected overbilling by another partner. Despite this conclusion, the court emphasized that lawyers must still comply with their ethical duties, even if compliance might result in their expulsion from the firm.[185]

What did Colette Bohatch do wrong? Arguably nothing, and that is what is difficult about this case. In fact, as the court mentioned, she had an ethical obligation to report what she thought was a violation of the rules of professional conduct. The court's decision puts the Bohatches of the world between a rock and a hard place. Compelling lawyers to continue working together, however, is also a difficult position to take.

Because a partner's expulsion results in a change in the aggregate of the partners, it should come as no surprise that UPA § 31(1)(d) states that dissolution is rightfully caused "[b]y the expul-

---

[184] 977 S.W.2d 543 (Tex. 1998).

[185] *See id.* at 544–47; *see also id.* at 547 ("The fact that the ethical duty to report may create an irreparable schism between partners neither excuses failure to report nor transforms expulsion as a means of resolving that schism into a tort.").

sion of any partner from the business bona fide in accordance with such a power conferred by the agreement between the partners."[186] What does "bona fide" mean in this context? It is presumably comparable to the general obligation of all partners to exercise their rights in good faith.[187] As examples of permitted expulsions, courts have held that a partnership may expel a partner for purely business reasons, to protect relationships both within the firm and with clients, and to resolve a "fundamental schism."[188]

UPA § 31(1)(d) contemplates that a partnership agreement will include a right to expel partners. When such a right is present, § 38(1) provides by default for continuation of the business with a cash payment to the expelled partner. Can a partner be expelled in the absence of an expulsion provision in the partnership agreement? As a general proposition, it is risky for partners to try to expel one of their own without support in a partnership agreement. The purported expulsion might be viewed as a breach of fiduciary duty and as an act of wrongful dissolution by those doing the expelling. Perhaps a court would imply a partnership agreement that a partner could be expelled for a serious breach of trust, and would apply § 31(1)(d) on that basis. Otherwise, it may be safer to take alternative action that has the same effect as an expulsion. For example, partners could seek a judicial decree of dissolution for the wrongdoing partner's misconduct under § 32(1). If successful, the wrongdoing partner may be deemed to have wrongfully dissolved such that a buyout and continuation of the firm under § 38(2) would be triggered.[189] The partners could also try to dissolve the firm by express will and to form a new partnership without the "expelled" partner.[190] Such conduct, however, could be viewed as bad faith or a breach of fiduciary duty under principles similar to those articulated in *Page*. In short, the much wiser course is to include an expulsion provision in a written partnership agreement.

---

[186] The *Bohatch* majority noted that, "as provided by the partnership agreement, Bohatch's expulsion did not dissolve the partnership." As previously discussed, this statement would seem to be incorrect, as the prevailing view under UPA is that dissolution cannot be avoided by agreement. *See* note 32 and accompanying text. An agreement purporting to avoid dissolution will likely be construed as an agreement to avoid a forced liquidation of the partnership's business. *See* text accompanying note 203.

[187] Indeed, RUPA § 601(3) and (4) do not include the "bona fide" phrase. This is presumably because RUPA § 404(d) already requires partners to exercise their rights, including the right to expel, in good faith.

[188] *See Bohatch*, 977 S.W.2d at 546.

[189] *See* note 183.

[190] *See, e.g.,* Dawson v. White & Case, 672 N.E.2d 589, 591 (N.Y. 1996).

c. The Winding Up Process

When a partnership is wound up, the assets of the partnership
are typically sold and the proceeds are distributed according to the
scheme provided by UPA § 40: (1) non-partner creditors are paid;
(2) partner creditors are paid; (3) partner capital contributions are
returned; and (4) any remaining monies are split between the partners in proportion to their profit shares. If the proceeds from the
partnership's assets are insufficient to pay the partnership's liabilities (1–3 above), the partners must contribute in proportion to their
loss shares.[191]

As mentioned, when an act of dissolution is considered rightful,
UPA § 38(1) suggests that each partner has the default right to
compel the winding up of the business through sale.[192] This principle is the focus of the court's decision in *Dreifuerst v. Dreifuerst*.[193]
The plaintiffs and the defendant were brothers who formed a partnership to operate two feed mills—one in St. Cloud and one in
Elkhart Lake. There was no written partnership agreement. The
plaintiffs served the defendant with notice that they were dissolving
(rightfully) the partnership.[194] They sought an in-kind distribution
of the partnership's assets, while the defendant sought a sale of the
assets and a distribution of cash. The trial court ordered an in-kind
distribution. Pursuant to a valuation presented by the plaintiffs,
the court granted the assets from the Elkhart Lake mill to the
plaintiffs and the assets from the St. Cloud mill to the defendant.
The Wisconsin Court of Appeals reversed. Applying UPA § 38(1),
the court held that, in the absence of an agreement to the contrary,
the statute required the partnership assets to be sold and the proceeds to be distributed to each partner (after the payment of creditors) in cash.[195]

Why was a sale of the partnership's assets objectionable to the
plaintiffs? The plaintiffs presumably wanted to stay in the feed mill
business without the defendant. They could have accomplished this
goal (and reached the same result as the trial court's in-kind distribution) by purchasing the entire business at a winding up sale, re-

---

[191] *See* UPA §§ 18(a), 40(d). UPA § 37 discusses who has the right to wind up a
partnership. Unless otherwise agreed, this right is given to the partners who have
not wrongfully dissolved the partnership, or to the legal representative of the last
surviving, non-bankrupt partner. Upon cause shown, however, any partner, his legal
representative, or his assignee may obtain winding up by the court.

[192] *See* Chapter 3(G)(1)(a).

[193] 280 N.W.2d 335 (Wis. Ct. App. 1979).

[194] The court held that the partnership was a partnership at will. *See id.* at 337.
Under UPA § 31(1)(b), a partner can rightfully dissolve an at-will partnership by
express will.

[195] *See Dreifuerst*, 280 N.W.2d at 336–39.

taining the assets from the Elkhart Lake mill, and selling the assets from the St. Cloud mill. Nevertheless, the plaintiffs may not have had the financing (or the ability to obtain the financing) to purchase the entire business. Moreover, they might not have been the highest bidders at the sale. If they were not the high bidders, they could have used their share of the cash from the sale to purchase another mill, but they may not have been able to find a comparable mill in the area where they wanted it. Thus, for the plaintiffs, an in-kind distribution of the partnership's assets was preferable.

Why was the in-kind distribution objectionable to the defendant? As an economic matter, the defendant may have objected because the assets of the partnership as a whole may have been worth more than the assets divided up (synergy value). Thus, the defendant may have thought that all of the partners would be better off if the partnership assets were sold together as an operating business. In addition, the defendant may have objected to the in-kind distribution on the ground that a sale was a better way to establish the true worth of the partnership's assets.[196] Finally, because the in-kind distribution of the trial court was based on the plaintiffs' valuation, the defendant may simply have believed that he was awarded the mill (and the related assets) with the lower value.

Aside from economics, the literal wording of § 38(1) gives each partner, in a rightful dissolution setting, the ability to "have the partnership property applied to discharge its liabilities," and to have the surplus distributed "in cash." This wording appears to require the sale of the partnership assets so that liabilities can be paid and the remaining proceeds can be distributed to the partners in cash. Section 38(1), in other words, seems to give each partner, in a rightful dissolution setting, the ability to compel the liquidation of the partnership's business. (Indeed, winding up is often called "liquidation.") As the *Dreifuerst* court stated, "lawful dissolution . . . gives each partner the right to have the business liquidated and his share of the surplus paid in cash."[197]

Does it make sense to give each partner, in a rightful dissolution setting, the ability to liquidate the partnership's business? Why not simply require the partnership to buy out the interest of any departing partner in lieu of a forced sale of the partnership's

---

[196] *See id.* at 338–39 (noting that "a sale provides a more accurate means of establishing the market value of the assets and, thus, better assuring each partner his share in the value of the assets").

[197] *Id.* at 338. The rights provided to partners under § 38(1) extend to the wrongful dissolution setting as well. *See* UPA § 38(2)(a)(i) (extending the rights in § 38(1) to each partner, in a wrongful dissolution setting, who has not caused the wrongful dissolution).

assets? In *Creel v. Lilly*,[198] the court refused to order liquidation after a partner's death caused the dissolution of the partnership:[199]

> . . . [W]hile winding up has often traditionally been regarded as synonymous with liquidation, this "fire sale" of assets has been viewed by many courts and commentators as a harsh and destructive measure. Consequently, to avoid the drastic result of a forced liquidation, many courts have adopted judicial alternatives to this potentially harmful measure. . . . There have been several cases in other jurisdictions . . . where . . . the court elected another option under UPA instead of a "fire sale" of all the partnership assets to ensure that the deceased partner's estate received its fair share of the partnership. These jurisdictions have recognized the unfairness and harshness of a compelled liquidation and found other judicially acceptable means of winding up a partnership under UPA, such as ordering an in-kind distribution of the assets or allowing the remaining partners to buy out the withdrawing partner's share of the partnership.[200]

The *Creel* court describes the liquidation of a partnership's business as a "fire sale" of the partnership's assets. To the extent that this term suggests that the assets are being sold for less than their fair value, a forced liquidation would seem to be detrimental to all partners (assuming that the purchaser at the sale is not one of the partners themselves). A buyout at fair value might be superior, therefore, as it would provide the departing partner with more money while allowing the remaining partners to continue the business. It would also avoid the costs of a sale.[201] The problem with allowing alternatives to a forced liquidation of the partnership's

---

[198] 729 A.2d 385 (Md. 1999).

[199] UPA § 31(4) states that dissolution is caused by a partner's death. There is nothing in UPA indicating that a dissolution caused by death would be viewed as wrongful.

[200] *Creel,* 729 A.2d at 392–93.

[201] *See, e.g.,* Disotell v. Stiltner, 100 P.3d 890, 894 (Alaska 2004) ("We decline to follow the line of cases holding that the statute requires liquidation. . . . The superior court reasoned that a buyout would reduce economic waste by avoiding the cost of appointing a receiver and conducting a sale. Even though there was no ongoing business, the superior court noted that the expense of a sale could total as much as twelve percent of the property's value. . . . Further, properly conducted, a buyout guaranteed Disotell a fair value for his partnership interest. Liquidation exposed Disotell to the risk that no buyer would offer to pay fair market value for the property. A liquidation sale in which no other buyers participated might have given Stiltner an opportunity to buy the property for less than fair market value, to Disotell's disadvantage.").

business, however, is that the language of § 38(1) seems to require such a forced liquidation regardless of the equities.[202]

In *Creel*, dissolution was caused by the death of a partner, while in *Dreifuerst*, dissolution was caused by express will. Does this distinction make a difference? Perhaps an argument could be made that the business of a partnership must end whenever any partner rightfully wants the business to end. When a partner voluntarily decides that he wants to leave a partnership, as in *Dreifuerst*, that voluntary act might be viewed as a desire to end the business. Thus, it may be fair to apply the literal liquidation language of § 38(1) in the absence of agreement. When a partner dies, however, it is not necessarily the case that the deceased partner wanted to leave the partnership. An inference of a desire to end the business cannot be made. In that event, forcing a liquidation is arguably harsher, as there may be no evidence that any of the partners desired the business to end. The fact that § 38(1) states that "each partner" has a liquidation right may support this argument, as a partner's estate is not a partner.

Can partners avoid the result in *Dreifuerst* (i.e., the forced liquidation of the partnership's business upon a rightful dissolution) with appropriate planning? UPA § 38(1) applies "unless otherwise agreed." Thus, the partners can agree to avoid a forced liquidation in favor of an in-kind distribution, a buyout, or some other agreed resolution. Indeed, partnership agreements prepared by attorneys usually make careful provisions for the continuation of the business following dissolution (known as "continuation agreements"). A common provision is that, upon any withdrawal of a partner, the business of the partnership will not be liquidated; instead, the remaining partners will continue the business and will buy out the interest of the withdrawing partner on some predetermined basis.[203]

---

[202] *Cf. Dreifuerst*, 280 N.W.2d at 339 ("[W]e cannot read § 38 of the Uniform Partnership Act . . . as permitting an in-kind distribution under any circumstances, unless all partners agree.").

[203] What if there is no continuation agreement, but a rightfully dissolving partner does not choose to compel liquidation under § 38(1)? For example, in a partnership of three doctors (A, B, and C) that does not have a partnership agreement providing for the continuation of the business, assume that C rightfully withdraws and that A and B decide to continue the same practice at the same location under the same name. C may well acquiesce in this decision by A and B because continuation is usually more sensible as a matter of business economics than a liquidation of the business. In the absence of an agreement as to what C will receive, UPA § 42 provides C with the right to receive the value of his partnership interest at the date of dissolution plus either (a) interest on that amount until it is paid or (b) his share of partnership profits between the date of dissolution and the date that he is paid for his partnership interest.

2. Dissociation and Dissolution Under RUPA

As discussed, the technical definition of "dissolution" set forth in UPA may be traced to the view that a partnership was an aggregate of the partners. By the time of the development of RUPA, courts and business owners had grown comfortable with the entity theory of the partnership, and a new approach towards dissolution was warranted. After all, if a partnership was now viewed as a legal entity separate from the partners themselves, a change in the composition of the partners did not have to affect the partnership. Given this conceptual shift, many commentators argued that "dissociation," or cessation of partner status, was an event that was independent of the question of whether the partnership should be "dissolved" and wound up. In other words, it should be possible for a partner to leave the partnership (i.e., to "dissociate" from the partnership) without affecting the partnership itself. RUPA adopts this approach by providing that a partner's dissociation often leads merely to a buyout while leaving the partnership entity and its business intact.

The major features of the dissociation and dissolution provisions of RUPA are as follows:

(1) "Dissociation" under RUPA refers to the cessation of partner status. The events causing dissociation are specified in § 601. "Dissolution" under RUPA refers to the commencement of the winding up process. The events causing dissolution are specified in § 801. "Winding up" the partnership business under RUPA involves "selling its assets, paying its debts, and distributing the net balance, if any, to the partners in cash according to their interests." When the winding up of the business is completed, the partnership is "terminated."[204]

(2) Section 601 indicates that, among other events, the death, withdrawal, bankruptcy, or expulsion of a partner results in a dissociation of the partner from the partnership. Some of these events were broadened from similar provisions relating to "dissolution" under UPA, such as an expansion of the grounds for expelling partners.

(3) Section 602 retains the basic distinction between "rightful" and "wrongful" dissociation. The list of wrongful dissociation events, however, has been expanded.

(4) When a partner dissociates from a partnership, one of two statutory avenues is implicated. The first avenue provides that the

---

[204] *See* RUPA §§ 601 & cmt. 1, 801 & cmt. 2, 802(a) & cmt. 1.

partnership is dissolved and that its business must be wound up. The second avenue provides that the partnership continues in existence with the dissociated partner becoming entitled to a buyout of his partnership interest. The nature of the event of dissociation dictates which avenue is implicated.[205]

(5) Dissolution and winding up are required only in the limited circumstances set forth in § 801. Two provisions are of particular importance: (a) in an at-will partnership, any partner who dissociates by his express will may compel dissolution and winding up; and (b) in a term partnership, if one partner dissociates wrongfully (or if a dissociation occurs because of a partner's death or otherwise under § 601(6)–(10)), dissolution and winding up of the partnership are required only if, within 90 days after the dissociation, one-half of the remaining partners agree to wind up the partnership.

(6) Section 807 describes the winding up process. Partnership assets must be applied to the discharge of partnership liabilities. If the assets are insufficient, individual partners are required to contribute in accordance with their loss shares. If there are excess assets, they are distributable to the partners in cash in accordance with their profit shares.[206]

(7) If a partner's dissociation does not result in a dissolution and winding up, the partner is entitled to receive a buyout of his partnership interest under the procedures in § 701. If the dissociation is wrongful, any damages will be offset against the buyout price. Moreover, if a partner wrongfully dissociates before the expiration of a definite term or the completion of a particular undertaking, the buyout payment can be deferred until the conclusion of the term or undertaking, "unless the partner establishes to the satisfaction of the court that earlier payment will not cause undue hardship to the business of the partnership." A deferred payment "must be adequately secured and bear interest." Significantly, unlike UPA, RUPA does not impose a "loss of goodwill" penalty when valuing a wrongfully dissociating partner's interest.[207]

---

[205] See id. §§ 603(a) & cmt. 1, 701–705 (second avenue), 801–807 (first avenue).

[206] According to § 802, at any time after the dissolution of the partnership and before the winding up of its business is completed, all of the partners (including any dissociated partner other than a wrongfully dissociating partner) may agree to "waive the right to have the partnership's business wound up." In that event, "the partnership resumes carrying on its business as if dissolution had never occurred."

[207] See id. §§ 602(c) & cmt. 3, 701 & cmts. 1, 3. RUPA does not continue the UPA § 42 election that permitted, in certain circumstances, a former partner in a partnership that did not wind up to take either interest on the value of his partnership stake or a share of the post-dissolution profits. See note 203. Under RUPA § 701(b), a dissociated partner is entitled only to interest on the amount to be paid the dissociated partner from the date of dissociation to the date of payment.

(8) As under UPA, RUPA provides partners with easy exit rights from the venture. A partner's dissociation will always result in either a dissolution and winding up of the business, or in a buyout of the dissociated partner's interest. Dissolution and winding up cashes out the partner's interest through a sale of the partnership's assets, the repayment of creditors, and the distribution of any remaining proceeds to the partners. A buyout cashes out the partner's interest through the partnership's payment of the buyout price. Thus, under RUPA, a partner can always exit the partnership and cash out the value of his interest.[208]

(9) A dissociated partner remains liable for pre-dissociation partnership obligations, and he may be liable for post-dissociation partnership liabilities incurred within two years after the dissociation (assuming that dissolution has not occurred). Moreover, a dissociated partner has apparent authority to bind the partnership for a period of time not exceeding two years (assuming that dissolution has not occurred). Either a dissociated partner or the partnership may file a public statement of dissociation to limit this post-dissociation potential liability and apparent authority.[209]

(10) Similarly, the apparent authority of partners to bind the partnership continues after dissolution, but any partner who has not wrongfully dissociated may file a public statement of dissolution to limit this apparent authority.[210]

---

[208] It bears repeating that, under RUPA, a partner who wrongfully dissociates before the expiration of a term partnership may not be entitled to any portion of the buyout price until the expiration of the term. Thus, while it is true that a partner can always exit the partnership and cash out the value of his interest, it may be a significant period of time before that cash is received. *See* text accompanying note 207.

[209] *See id.* §§ 702, 703(a)–(b), 704.

[210] *See id.* §§ 804–805.

Chapter 4

THE CORPORATION: OVERVIEW, THEORY, AND HISTORY

Anaylsis

A. Characteristics of the Corporation: Overview
B. Theoretical Understandings of the Corporation
C. Social Responsibility and Political Activity
D. Historical Development of Corporate Law in the United States
E. Relevance of Federal Income Tax Law

A. Characteristics of the Corporation: Overview

Many people have the impression that most, if not all, businesses are corporations. And many people have the impression that most corporations are large, multinational affairs such as Coca-Cola or Marriott. Neither impression is correct. Most businesses are sole proprietorships or partnerships. And most corporations are actually small enterprises, often consisting of one or a handful of owners.[1]

All corporations, from the neighborhood bakery to Marriott Corporation, share certain characteristics. First, a corporation can be formed only by satisfying the requirements set forth by state statutes.[2] Every state has statutes regulating corporations. Every one requires that those forming the corporation (the "incorporators" or "organizers") file with the appropriate state officer (usually the secretary of state) a document commonly called the articles of incorporation. In addition, the corporation must appoint a registered agent (on whom process may be served if the corporation is sued), and pay a fee to the state. Operating a business as a corporation imposes continuing formalities, including filing annual reports,[3] holding meetings of shareholders and directors, paying taxes, and the like. Such formalities are a disadvantage over some other business structures, which

---

[1] UNITED STATES CENSUS BUREAU, *Statistics about Business Size (including Small Businesses) from the U.S. Census Bureau*, (May 21, 2012). *See* http://www.census.gov/econ/smallbus.html.

[2] We discuss these requirements in detail in Chapter 5(C).

[3] *See, e.g.,* FLA. STAT. § 607.1622.

can be formed and maintained simply by selling lemonade or renting out hotel rooms (or by doing whatever the business does).[4]

Second, the corporation has always been considered an entity, legally distinct from the person(s) who own it and run it. Third, because it has "entity status," the corporation itself is liable for its contracts, torts, and debts. The people who manage it and those who own it generally are not liable for what the corporation does. This "limited liability" historically has been considered the greatest advantage of the corporate form of doing business.

Fourth, a corporation's shareholders (or stockholders) are its owners. The corporation sells "shares" of stock, which are units of ownership.[5] These shares entitle the stockholder to certain rights and responsibilities. Interestingly, shareholders do not manage the corporation. Rather, they elect the directors, who are responsible for management. Shareholder power is proportionate to the number of shares one owns. So someone holding 50 shares will have five times the ownership stake of someone holding 10 shares. Unless the governing documents say otherwise, she will also have five times as many votes and receive five times as much in dividends than the other. Again, the shareholders enjoy "limited liability." If the corporation does poorly, the shareholder may lose her investment, but she is not liable for what the business does.

Fifth, the corporation is managed by a board of directors. Note, then, that the corporate form separates ownership from management; the shareholders are the owners and the directors are the managers.[6] This separation is not seen, for example, in the general partnership, in which each partner presumptively has equal ownership and management rights. One advantage of the corporation, then, is the possibility of *passive investment*. A shareholder can enjoy the fruits of ownership (hopefully, profits) without being burdened with the responsibilities of management.

Sixth, if one tires of being a shareholder, she can transfer her stock. She can give it away (*inter vivos* or by will) or sell it. If the stock of the corporation is publicly traded, she can sell the stock through a broker or online. If the corporation is not publicly traded, she may have trouble finding a buyer, but, generally, has the right to

---

[4] The sole proprietorship and the general partnership are formed and maintained simply by conducting the business, with no requirement of state imprimatur.

[5] "Issuance" is the formal term for a corporation's selling its own stock. We discuss the process in Chapter 10(C).

[6] It is possible (indeed, quite common) for directors also to be shareholders. Such people play two separate roles. When they act as shareholders, the rules governing shareholders apply. When they act as directors, the rules governing directors apply.

sell whenever she can. This transferability flows from the fact that the stockholder is not a manager. In the general partnership, because the owners are the same as the managers, one cannot simply transfer her entire interest; she does not have a right to force the other partners to accept a new fellow manager.

Transferability also reflects continuity of existence, which is another advantage of the corporation. Because it is an entity separate from those who own and run it, the fact that ownership of the corporation may change is irrelevant. The corporation goes on—no matter who the owners are. A partnership, in contrast, traditionally has been seen as an aggregate of its individual partners; this means that if a partner withdraws, or dies, or becomes bankrupt, the partnership ends. The partners may then have to liquidate the assets, and, if they want, form a new business. The corporate structure avoids these headaches.[7]

Seventh, the corporation, as a general rule, must pay income tax on its profits. In addition, shareholders pay income tax on dividends they receive. This taxation at two levels ("double taxation") is a disadvantage of the corporate form.[8] Partnerships are not taxed at the business level. The partners pay income tax on profits attributed to them, but the partnership itself does not pay income tax. This "flow-through" taxation is an advantage of the general partnership, depending on the marginal taxation rates.

Eighth, every business will need funding. Often, the proprietor (sometimes along with friends and family) provides the initial capital. The corporation (like any form of business) can raise capital either by getting loans or by selling ownership interests (which, as we just saw, consists of stock in the corporation).

The genius of the corporation is that it combines a mechanism for passive investment with limited liability. The shareholder does not bear the responsibility of making management decisions. And while the shareholder might lose the money she invested, generally that is all she can lose. She is not liable for the debts incurred by the business. The development of the corporation unlocked an unprecedented economic engine. This engine created far more than wealth for its investors. It created jobs, spurred innovation, and generated huge amounts of tax revenue. Nearly a century ago, the president of

---

[7] Good planning by partners can avoid these problems.

[8] Corporations can avoid paying income tax at the corporate level by forming an S Corporation, so named because it is provided for in Subchapter S of the Internal Revenue Code. *See* section E.

a major university praised the corporation as "the greatest single discovery of modern times."[9]

B. Theoretical Understandings of the Corporation

For generations, scholars have attempted to explain the characteristics of the corporation by employing different theoretical underpinnings. Their theories are efforts to explain what a corporation "really" is. We might think of them as metaphors for the corporation. None is totally correct, none is totally wrong, and each has its place in defining the corporation.

The traditional theoretical view is that a corporation is an *artificial person* (to be contrasted with a natural person, which is a human being). The corporation is an entity, independent of the people who form it, own it, and run it. It does business, acquires assets, incurs debts, hires and fires people, opens and closes stores, enters contracts—does everything it does—in its own name, rather than in the name of any individual. This artificial person has many of the legal rights of a natural person: it can litigate, apply for business licenses, invest in securities, buy and sell property, and it must also pay taxes and fees for the privilege of doing business.

One consequence of this view is that the corporation, as an independent entity, is liable for its own debts. Indeed, the separate entity concept is so deeply ingrained that many corporation statutes (unlike limited partnership and LLC statutes) never expressly state that shareholders are not liable for corporate obligations. It is simply assumed. Other characteristics can be explained by the artificial person theory. For example, the corporation's continuity of existence—that is, the fact that it can exist notwithstanding the deaths of its owners and managers—can be seen as a consequence of its entity status.

Though well-established, the artificial person theory is highly formalistic. The corporation has no will of its own and cannot really do anything by itself. Everything the corporation "does" is actually done by people. In realistic terms, then, a corporation is a device by which *people* conduct a business. In famous terms, Professor Wesley N. Hohfeld summarized: "[I]t has not always been perceived . . . that transacting business under the forms, methods, and procedure pertaining to so-called corporations is simply another mode by which individuals or natural persons can enjoy their property and engage in

---

[9]Nicholas Murray Butler, *quoted in* JAMES WILLARD HURST, THE LEGITIMACY OF THE BUSINESS CORPORATION IN THE LAWS OF THE UNITED STATES, 1780–1970, at 9 (1970).

business. Just as several individuals may transact business collectively as partners, so they may as members of a corporation—the
corporation being nothing more than an association of such individuals. . ."[10]

Hohfeld's analysis illustrates the fallacy of accepting the artificial person theory uncritically. A corporation may be treated as an
entity for many purposes, but at some point a court may rely on the
reality Hohfeld described to avoid formalistic results. Considerations
of fairness may outweigh arguments grounded solely on the artificial
entity theory. For example, courts developed the doctrine of "piercing
the corporate veil"[11] to impose liability on shareholders for the acts or
debts ostensibly incurred by the entity.

A second metaphorical view is that the corporation is a privilege
from the state that permits the owners and investors to conduct
business in the corporate form. Sometimes people use the terms
"concession," "grant," or "franchise" to refer to this privilege. This
theory may have been more important in earlier times, when state
legislatures granted incorporation to businesses individually. Then,
it was easier to imagine the incorporation as a grant from the state.
Now, all states have enacted "general" incorporation statutes, which
permit anyone to form such an entity by following the steps discussed
in Chapter 5(C). Still, the notion that a corporation receives a "franchise" from the state is the theory on which states apply their franchise taxes to corporations but not to other business forms.[12]

A third view is that the document forming the corporation is a
contract or a compact. A well-known example was Chief Justice John
Marshall's opinion in *Trustees of Dartmouth College v. Woodward*.[13]
He concluded for the Supreme Court that the charter that created
Dartmouth College was a contract between the corporation and the
state.[14] Accordingly, under the Contracts Clause of the Constitution,
the state could not unilaterally change it. In reaction to this decision,
states long ago adopted provisions empowering them to amend their
corporate law and declaring that corporations are subject to the
amendments.[15] Depending on the circumstances, a court may see the
corporate articles as a contract among shareholders or between the
shareholders and the state. For example, courts sometimes use the

---

[10] WESLEY N. HOHFELD, FUNDAMENTAL LEGAL CONCEPTIONS 197 (1923).

[11] *See* Chapter 8(E).

[12] Franchise taxes are levied by the state of incorporation, essentially for the privilege of allowing the company to charter in the state.

[13] 17 U.S. 518 (1819).

[14] *Id. at* 615.

[15] *See, e.g.,* N.J. STAT. § 14A:1–5.

contract theory in disputes between holders of different classes of stock.[16] Because the articles are a "contract," they spell out the rights of the holders.

Over the past half century, law and economics analysis has challenged many of the traditional beliefs about business. This analysis is associated with scholars at the University of Chicago and is often called "the Chicago School." Key among the academic leaders at the University of Chicago were the late Milton Friedman, who won the Nobel Prize for Economics in 1976 and the late Ronald Coase, who won that prize in 1991. Another important pioneer is Dean Henry Manne of George Mason University.

Law and economics scholars talk about the "firm" rather than the corporation to emphasize that their theories apply to businesses generally, no matter what their legal structure. Based on the analysis of Professor Coase in the 1930s, they posit that the firm is a "nexus of contracts."[17] Coase reasoned that every firm is, in essence, a long term relational contract by which each factor of production is affiliated with the others who contribute to the enterprise. Thus a business is not an entity, but a bundle of contracts entered by the managers with persons who provide different "inputs." For instance, shareholders agree to furnish capital, employees provide labor, and suppliers provide materials, etc. The managers are the glue that fits together all the various contributors in the most efficient way.[18]

According to the law and economics model, managers should have broad discretion to structure and run the enterprise. The result is a hierarchical structure of control over employees and agents, perhaps softened by principles of participatory management or team production.[19] The principal problem is control over "agency costs," which are "the sum of the monitoring and bonding costs,"[20] plus "any residual loss,"[21] incurred to prevent shirking by agents. Monitoring costs are the expenses incurred to oversee the business, and bonding

---

[16] *See, e.g.,* Holland v. Nat'l Auto. Fibres, Inc., 19 A. 124, 126 (Del. 1937).

[17] Ronald H. Coase, *The Nature of the Firm,* 4 ECONOMICA 386 (1937). The nexus theory simply views the firm or corporation as a string of different contracts. So a typical corporation will be a series of contracts evidencing limited liability, free transferability of shares, voting power for shareholders, etc.

[18] For more on this subject, *see* Henry N. Butler & Larry E. Ribstein, *Opting Out of Fiduciary Duties: A Response to the Anti-Contractarians,* 65 WASH. L. REV. 1 (1990).

[19] *See* Henry G. Manne, *A Free Market Model of A Large Corporation System,* 52 EMORY L.J. 1381 (2003).

[20] Eugene F. Fama & Michael C. Jensen, *Separation of Ownership and Control,* 26 J.L. & ECON. 301, 304 (1983).

[21] Michael C. Jensen & William H. Meckling, *Theory of the Firm: Managerial Behavior, Agency Costs and Ownership Structure,* 3 J. FIN. ECON., 305, 308 (1976).

costs are devices to assure the fidelity of employees and agents where oversight is impractical or too costly.[22] Shirking is conduct of an individual that diverges from the interests of the enterprise as a whole —including cheating, negligence, incompetence, and culpable mistakes.[23]

In this view, shareholders are not the owners of the corporation. Instead, they are simply contractual suppliers of capital—the group whose "contract" entitles them to the profits of the business and requires them to risk losing their investment. At the same time, however, the goal of the corporation is viewed as the maximization of shareholder wealth in the enterprise. A corporation is thus seen as a set of consensual relationships established by the managers with the goal of maximizing the wealth of those who supplied the capital.[24]

One problem with this model is its use of the term "contract." It is difficult to say that a person who buys 100 shares of McDonald's Corporation through an online brokerage has entered a "contract" with the entity. It is true, of course, that a purchaser of McDonald's stock has certain rights, such as the right to receive any declared dividend. But the shareholder who buys her stock through a stock exchange has not given any money to McDonald's or agreed to do anything for the corporation.[25] And the holder of 100 shares of McDonald's must understand that she has no power to influence the corporate decision-making. After all, over one billion shares of McDonald's stock are held by shareholders throughout the world, so our friend with 100 shares will have no clout among the shareholders.

So did this shareholder enter into a "contract" agreeing to this? To a lawyer, probably not, because "contract" means an agreement the legal system will enforce. But "to an economist, an implied contract is one that is enforced through marketplace mechanisms such as reputation effects rather than in a court, a means of enforcement that may not bring relief to the aggrieved party but will over time penalize parties who welsh."[26]

---

[22] *See* Armen Alchian & Harold Demsetz, *Production, Information Costs, and Economic Organization,* 62 AM. ECON. REV. 777 (1972).

[23] *See id.*

[24] *See* Milton Friedman, *A Friedman Doctrine: The Social Responsibility of Business Is to Increase Its Profits,* N.Y. TIMES, Sept. 13, 1970, § 6 at 33.

[25] The corporation will receive money paid for stock only if there is an issuance, which is when the corporation sells its own stock. After the issuance, when the stock is bought and sold on a stock exchange, the money goes back and forth between the buyer and the seller, not the corporation.

[26] Jeffrey Gordon, *The Mandatory Structure of Corporate Law,* 89 COLUM. L. REV. 1549, 1550 (1989).

Clearly, "contract" may mean something quite different to an economist than to a lawyer. The economist sees the word as encompassing voluntary arrangements generally, even without consensual exchanges. Some of these arrangements "may be implied by courts or legislatures trying to supply the terms that would have been negotiated had people addressed the problem explicitly. Even terms that are invariant—such as the requirement that the board of directors act only by a majority of a quorum—are contractual to the extent that they produce offsetting voluntary arrangements. The result of all of these voluntary arrangements will be contractual."[27]

To law and economics scholars, business law should provide standard default rules which the parties should be free to modify. In other words, the law should not impose mandatory rules; instead, the law should enable businesspeople to structure the business as they see fit. There is no denying the impact of this thinking on modern business law. Contemporary statutes on limited partnerships and LLCs permit the proprietors to contract around most matters, including fiduciary duties. On the other hand, modern corporation law, while clearly permitting more contractual choice than in previous generations, still includes mandatory requirements that the proprietors are not free to waive or modify. And federal law concerning access to public markets is full of mandatory prescriptions that cannot be avoided.

C. Social Responsibility and Political Activity

Business is economic activity aimed at the creation of wealth. In short, people go into business to "make money."[28] But does that mean that everything a business does must be aimed solely at the generation of wealth? Or can businesses engage in philanthropy as well? These are especially apt questions concerning large corporations, the stock of which is traded publicly.[29] On the one hand, many argue that public corporations, because of their immense economic power, should be subject to social control and should be expected to address the social impact of their actions. The argument is often based upon the view of the corporation as privilege or concession, discussed in section B above. Thus, if the state bestows the privilege of

---

[27] Frank Easterbrook and Daniel Fischel, *The Corporate Contract*, 89 COLUM. L. REV. 1416, 1428 (1989).

[28] There are many non-profit businesses, including charitable organizations and universities. They, and the law governing them, are beyond our scope. *See generally* Linda Sugin, *Resisting the Corporatization of Nonprofit Governance: Transforming Obedience into Fidelity*, 76 FORDHAM L. REV. 893 (2007).

[29] The issue is less debated concerning small, closely held businesses. First, those businesses command less wealth. Second, because management and ownership tend to be combined in small businesses, disagreement over philanthropy is less likely.

a corporate charter, through which the corporation generates great wealth, the state ought to be able to impose social responsibilities—to require the corporation to "give back" in some way for societal good.

The contrary argument is that the goal of business is to make money, period. If you want to use the money you make through business to "do good," great—but do it with your money, not the corporation's. This view is essentially *laissez faire*—that the government should leave corporations alone and let them tend to business and the bottom line.

In *A.P. Smith Manufacturing Co. v. Barlow,*[30] a corporation (through its board of directors) made a charitable contribution to Princeton University. Some shareholders objected and argued that charitable giving was not an appropriate corporate goal. After all, the corporation was giving away money that could otherwise go to the shareholders. The court upheld the gift. It noted that in the early days of the Republic, incorporation was permitted only for the social good. Over time, the court said, the goal of private business became focused on profit. When the corporation became the dominant economic force in the country, however, "calls upon the corporations for reasonable philanthropic donations have come to be made with increased public support."[31]

Milton Friedman argued that "social responsibility" is actually a "fundamentally subversive doctrine" in a free society.[32] The corporation, Dr. Friedman asserted, should make its money and let the individual shareholders decide whether to make charitable contributions with their own money.[33] But the *A.P. Smith* view has prevailed. The corporation law of every state permits (but does not compel) corporations to make charitable contributions, and federal income tax law permits the corporation to take a deduction for such gifts. Modern statutes list specific "powers" that corporations automatically have, including the power to make charitable contributions.[34] There are limits, however, on the corporation's largesse. These are for-profit enterprises, and, accordingly, they cannot give away everything.

---

[30] 98 A.2d 581 (N.J. 1953).

[31] *Id.* at 584.

[32] *See* note 24; *see also* Milton Friedman, *The Social Responsibility of Business,* THE ESSENCE OF FRIEDMAN 36, 36–38 (1987).

[33] Individuals might make contributions to institutions less prestigious, less wealthy, and in greater need than Princeton.

[34] *See, e.g.,* RMBCA § 3.02(13).

Charitable contributions must be reasonable.[35] Courts are very deferential to management decisions in this area.[36]

It is worth noting that corporate philanthropy consists of managers giving away money that otherwise might go to shareholders. Warren Buffett, the famous investor, relates an interesting tale about a friend who sought charitable contributions for various organizations. Buffett said: "And in the process of raising . . . eight million dollars from 60 corporations from people who nod and say that's a marvelous idea, it's pro-social, etc., not one [executive] reached in his pocket and pulled out ten bucks of his own to give to this marvelous charity."[37]

Fifty years ago, most people who owned stock in public corporations were relatively wealthy. Stock ownership was for the rich, and the idea that they would forego a dividend so the corporation could give money to Princeton did not cause much concern. Today, however, the majority of Americans are invested in the stock market. If you have money in a pension plan or in a savings-and-loan association, it is invested in the stock market.[38] So today, corporate philanthropy may result in funneling to an institution like Princeton money that otherwise might go into a blue-collar worker's pension.

The social responsibility discussion, however, is much broader than corporate gifts to charity. The discussion focuses in addition on social ramifications of corporate decisions. Decisions about where to locate manufacturing facilities, how many people to hire, etc. carry dramatic consequences for communities, and, sometimes, entire regions. For example, suppose a corporation has an old, obsolete manufacturing plant in a small town in a northern state. The board of directors is considering closing the plant and moving manufacturing to a different region—where labor and land are cheaper, and where a modern, efficient plant could be built. In making this decision, should the corporation take into account the adverse effects on the

---

[35] *See* Theodora Holding Corp. v. Henderson, 257 A.2d 398, 405 (Del. Ch. 1969) (stating that the "test to be applied in passing on the validity of a gift . . . is that of reasonableness"); State v. Chicago, B. & Q.R. Co., 199 N.W. 534, 537 (Neb. 1924) (stating that there is no reason why a corporation may not "to a reasonable extent" donate funds to "aid in good works.").

[36] *See, e.g.,* Kahn v. Sullivan, 594 A.2d 48, 58 (Del. 1991) (noting "limited" options for courts reviewing management decisions on charitable contributions).

[37] KNIGHTS, RAIDERS AND TARGETS: THE IMPACT OF HOSTILE TAKEOVERS 14 (1988) (John C. Coffee, Jr., et al., eds.).

[38] *See* Asset Allocation of Pension Funds and Public Pension Reserve Funds in Organization for Economic Co-Operation and Development, *Pensions at a Glance 2011: Retirement-income Systems* (OECD Publishing 2011), http://www.oecdilibrary.org; Treasury Inspector General for Tax Administration, *Statistical Trends in Retirement Plans* (August 2010), http://www.treasury.gov.

persons currently employed in the plant, their families, the other businesses in the town, the community itself, and the state?

These interests are often described as "other constituencies" of the corporation. Does the corporation "owe" something to these constituencies—who, after all, have supported the business in this community for years? If the company should consider the effect on these other constituencies, how does it balance the possibility that keeping the present plant may result in reduced dividends to shareholders and higher prices to the public? And what if a new plant would be "greener?" Should it change the calculus if the new plant would be built—and people employed—in Honduras instead of another region of the United States? Ultimately, the social responsibility debate raises more questions than answers.

The corporation law in some states reflects the concerns with other constituencies. Pennsylvania law, for example, provides that directors, when making management decisions, are not required "to regard . . . the interests of any particular group affected by such action as a dominant or controlling interest or factor."[39] This permits the board to point to broad societal concerns—and not just the bottom line for shareholders—when making decisions.

More recently, several states have passed statutes allowing the formation of "benefit corporations," or "B Corporations."[40] These entities pursue business purposes, but also expressly commit to benefiting society. The charter of such a B Corporation will set forth its social policy goals, which might be, for instance, paying foreign workers higher wages, or ensuring that workers are discharged only for cause, or promoting environmentally-friendly policies. Managers of such companies are thus shielded from liability if their actions (such as paying higher wages) harm the shareholders' bottom line. In fact, they could be sued for failing to satisfy their social policy objectives. B Corporations are required to publish their performance on social policy goals against third-party standards.[41]

---

[39] See 15 PA. CONS. STAT. § 1715.

[40] In 2010, Maryland became the first state to pass B Corporation legislation. MD. CODE CORPS. & ASS'NS § 5–6C–01 et seq. Since then, Hawaii, Virginia, California, Vermont, New Jersey, and Washington have done so. See HAW. REV. STAT. § 420D–1 et seq.; VA. CODE § 13.1–782 et seq.; CAL. CORP. CODE § 14600 et seq.; VT. STAT. TIT. 11A, § 21.01 et seq.; N.J. STAT. § 14A:18–1 et seq.; WASH. REV. CODE § 24.03.490 et seq. Other legislation is aimed at the same basic goal. For example, California has also passed legislation allowing "flexible purpose" corporations, 2012 Cal. SB 1171 (2012), and some states permit low-profit limited liability companies ("L3Cs"). For convenience, we will address only B Corporations.

[41] A non-profit outfit called B Lab sets standards and offers rating compliance. It charges a fee for helping B Corporations assess whether they are doing as much good

Implicit in some of the discussion in favor of other constituency provisions and B Corporation laws is the idea that it is wrong to focus exclusively on maximizing profits for shareholders. At its bluntest, some of the discussion equates profit maximization with rapaciousness. But, as Milton Friedman and others have argued, doesn't profit maximization benefit society? Why should someone who has risked her capital by investing in a corporation not depend upon the managers to work diligently to provide a return on that investment? And the people thus enriched can decide what to do with that money. People who make money usually spend some portion of it, which spurs economic growth. Even a modest stockholder, blessed with a profit, may expand her house or buy a vacation home or hire gardeners and landscapers. This is all positive economic activity. Moreover, people with more money often make (sometimes stunning) charitable contributions. And, last but not the least, people who make money pay taxes.

Perhaps the move toward B Corporations simply permits everyone to decide what is important to her. If one wishes to invest in a company that gives away 50 percent of the corporate profits for some social cause, she should be able to do so. And the managers should be able to do so. On the other hand, one who wants to invest to maximize her return should be able to do so. She can then decide how that money should be used (including, of course, for social causes).

Another timely issue is the propriety of corporation political activity. It raises the interesting question of the constitutional status of a corporation. Corporations are entitled to some constitutional protections but not to others. For example, the Privileges and Immunities Clause[42] does not apply to corporations.[43] Thus, a state is free to exclude a corporation from entering its territory. On the other hand, the Commerce Clause permits corporations to enter states to engage in interstate commerce.[44] In *Citizens United v. Federal*

---

as they intended. Companies that pass muster with B Lab get to call themselves "certified B Corps."

[42] U.S. CONST. art. IV, § 2. That clause, which provides that the citizens of one state "shall be entitled to all privileges and immunities of citizens in the several states," means (roughly) that Virginia must accord to Pennsylvanians the privileges and immunities it accords its own citizens. Because the clause does not apply to corporations, one state could deny a corporation founded in another state the privilege of doing business. This fact was relevant to the development of personal jurisdiction doctrine. If Virginia could bar a Pennsylvania corporation from entering the state, for instance, Virginia certainly had the lesser power of permitting the corporation to enter, conditioned upon its appointment of an agent for service of process and its consenting to *in personam* jurisdiction. Paul v. Virginia, 75 U.S. 168, 177 (1869).

[43] Paul v. Virginia, 75 U.S. 168, 177 (1869).

[44] International Textbook Co. v. Prigg, 217 U.S. 91, 108–12 (1910).

Election Commission,[45] the Supreme Court affirmed that corporations enjoy First Amendment rights. The Court struck down a federal ban for corporate expenditures on "electioneering communication" or for speech directly advocating the election or defeat of a candidate in a federal election. The decision has prompted considerable debate about the proper role of corporations—more specifically, corporate money—in political discourse.[46]

Because *Citizens United* addressed an absolute ban on corporate expenditures, it probably does not invalidate state statutes that merely cap political contributions. For example, New York law provides that corporations cannot contribute more than $5,000 per year to any candidate or political organization.[47]

D. Historical Development of Corporate Law in the United States

In the pre-revolutionary period, colonial legislatures granted corporate charters on the authority of the British Crown. After independence and the ratification of the Constitution, state legislatures took up the role and continued to grant corporate charters. After the War of 1812, economic activity blossomed, demonstrated by increased numbers of corporations. Reflecting the expansion of the country, many of these were formed to operate banks, canals, roadways, and, later, railroads.

In 1791, the federal government passed legislation creating the Bank of the United States. There was considerable doubt about whether the federal government had the power to incorporate for general economic purposes, but the Supreme Court upheld the legality of the Bank.[48] There are today various federally chartered entities, including the American Red Cross, the United States Olympic Committee, Fannie Mae, Freddie Mac, Boy & Girl Scouts, Federal Deposit Insurance Corporation and Disabled American Veterans.

Nonetheless, incorporation has been overwhelmingly the product of state, not federal, action. Almost all of the law concerning for-

---

[45] 130 S. Ct. 876 (2010).

[46] *See, e.g.,* James Bopp, Jr., et al., *The Game Changer: Citizens United's Impact on Campaign Finance Law in General and Corporate Political Speech in Particular,* 9 FIRST AMEND. L. REV. 251 (2010); Matthew A. Melone, *Citizens United and Corporate Political Speech: Did the Supreme Court Enhance Political Discourse or Invite Corruption?,* 60 DEPAUL L. REV. 29 (2010); Ciara Torres-Spelliscy, *Has the Tide Turned in Favor of Disclosure? Revealing Money in Politics After Citizens United and Doe v. Reed,* 27 GA. ST. U. L. REV. 1057 (2011).

[47] N.Y. ELEC. LAW § 14–116.

[48] *See* McCullough v. State of Maryland, 17 U.S. 316 (1819).

mation and operation of corporations is state law. To be sure, federal legislation affects the corporation world. We will discuss federal laws relating to securities and financial accountability in Chapter 9.

Originally, each corporation was formed by an act of the state's legislature. In other words, people wanting to incorporate a business had to convince the state legislature to pass a statute doing so. It was not until 1836 that Pennsylvania approved a "general" incorporation statute, by which people could form a corporation by action of an administrative agency rather than requiring a specific statute. Connecticut followed suit in 1840. By 1859, more than half the states had general incorporation laws, and by 1890, it was unanimous. To this day, the corporation laws of various states are called "general" corporation laws.[49]

The populist movement that developed primarily in the agricultural states in the Midwest viewed corporations in general (and railroads in particular) with suspicion and mistrust. In many of these states, legislatures restricted the size, duration, purposes, and capital investment of corporations. These restrictions were largely ineffective, especially because businesses formed in states without such limits were permitted to do business in states that did impose restrictions. Over time, such restrictions have fallen by the wayside.

Beginning in the late nineteenth century, several states tried to attract businesses to incorporate or reincorporate even though the corporations planned to do no business there. They amended their statutes to simplify procedures, relax restrictions and limitations, reduce fees, and generally make things more attractive; the goal was to attract incorporation of large corporations. Why would states compete for the incorporation business? Money. States charge fees to incorporate and to maintain corporate status. They also impose franchise taxes on corporations, often based upon the company's assets. And there may be state income taxes as well. Today, between 15 and 20 percent of Delaware's total budget is generated by franchise taxes paid by corporations.[50] Insurance firms, corporation service companies, and major law firms with principal offices in other states maintain offices in Wilmington; these businesses would be a small fraction of their present size if Delaware's corporation business moved to some other state. Indeed, from a financial standpoint, the Delaware corporation business is the envy of other states.

---

[49] The Delaware legislation is the Delaware General Corporation Law.

[50] *See* Delaware Division of Corporations, *2011 Annual Report*, http://corp.delaware.gov; *see also* Mark J. Roe, *Delaware's Shrinking Half-Life*, 62 STAN. L. REV. 125, 140 (2009).

In the late nineteenth century, leaders in New Jersey estimated that their state could retire its entire Civil War debt by attracting incorporations and charging franchise fees.[51] It liberalized its statutes to allow corporations to do things they generally could not do elsewhere—including investing in the securities of other companies. The effort bore fruit. New Jersey became the dominant state for incorporation and generated an enormous amount of money as a result. But it ended in 1911 when Governor Woodrow Wilson led a charge to repeal the changes in New Jersey law.[52]

The beneficiary was Delaware, which became and remains the dominant incorporation state for public corporations. More than half of the Fortune 500 corporations (the 500 largest corporations based upon revenue) are Delaware companies.[53]

Some observers saw the competition among states for corporate charters as unseemly, even inappropriate. Justice Brandeis said that it was a "race not of diligence but of laxity."[54] One observer called it a "race to the bottom."[55] Such critics saw the "race" as leading to the systematic elimination of all regulatory controls on the corporation, the adoption of a "pro-management" stance whenever conflicts arose between managers and shareholders, and the elimination of preemptive rights and cumulative voting, which were widely viewed as pro-shareholder.

Those complaining about the "race to the bottom" assumed that corporate managers can freely impose their will and that the disorganized shareholders could do nothing about it. Scholars have questioned this assumption. Professor Winter (now Judge Winter of the Second Circuit) pointed out that the assumption overlooks the existence of an efficient market for corporate securities.[56] If Delaware actually permits management to profit at the expense of shareholders (and other states do not, or do not as much), we would expect earnings of Delaware corporations that are allocable to shareholders to be less than earnings of comparable corporations that are subject to more rigorous control in other states. Thus, if the "race to the bottom"

---

[51] See Demetrios G. Kaouris, *Is Delaware Still A Haven for Incorporation?,* 20 DEL. J. CORP. L. 965, 970 (1995).

[52] See id.; see also NEW YORK TIMES, *Wilson Says Honest Men Need Not Fear* (February 1913), http://query.nytimes.com/mem/archive-free/pdf?res=F60715FB385 F13738DDDA80A94DA405B838DF1D3.

[53] Delaware Dep't of State Division of Corporations, *Why Corporations Choose Delaware* (2007), available at http://corp.delaware.gov.

[54] See Louis K. Liggett Co. v. Lee, 288 U.S. 517, 559 (1933) (Brandeis, dissenting).

[55] William Cary, *Federalism and Corporate Law: Reflections Upon Delaware*, 83 YALE L.J. 663, 670 (1974).

[56] See RALPH K. WINTER, JR., GOVERNMENT AND THE CORPORATION 7–10 (1978).

theory is correct, Delaware corporations will be at an economic disadvantage, and ultimately this disadvantage should cause shareholders to invest in non-Delaware corporations.[57]

Several statistical studies tend to show, however, that reincorporation in Delaware more often leads to an *increase* in share prices than to a decrease. These studies generally support Winter's thesis and tend to disprove the "race to the bottom" notion. Share prices may be affected by many factors, and it is not possible to say with certainty that Delaware law is the sole, or even the principal, cause of the favorable price movement. Nonetheless, some concluded that the competition for incorporations had actually been a "race to the top," since shareholders benefited from incorporation in Delaware.[58]

So why has the Delaware General Corporation Law been so attractive? The answer seems not to be substantive. Indeed, in many ways Delaware law is more cumbersome than modern codes. But Delaware is successful in attracting incorporation business because it has created an entire system—with legislation, bench, and bar—that understands business and business law. Lawyers know that they will deal with sophisticated state officials. The bench and bar are generally thought to be well versed in corporate law. Undeniably, there is also inertia—lawyers have their clients incorporate in Delaware because they always have done it that way.

Recent scholarship questions the continuing loyalty of big corporations to Delaware. In the past generation, the Delaware Supreme Court has decided several high-profile cases that make the law of that state more indeterminate. In addition, there is a stunningly high reversal rate of trial court decisions, which also leads to indeterminacy. Two scholars, noting this and the relative certainty of the Revised Modern Business Corporation Act, find the continuing hegemony of Delaware vexing.[59]

Trying to capture more business, several states have modernized their statutes. The New York legislature—which must be frustrated at having all those corporate headquarters in Manhattan for businesses incorporated in Delaware—substantially amended its Business Corporation Act in 1998. Massachusetts scrapped its century-old corporation code in 2004 in favor of a modern law, in the process

---

[57] *See id.* at 10 (stating that it is not in the interest of Delaware for corporations chartered there "to be at a disadvantage in raising debt or equity capital in relation to corporations chartered in other states.")

[58] Roberta Romano, *Law As a Product: Some Pieces of the Incorporation Puzzle*, 1 J. L., Econ. & Organization 225 (1985).

[59] William Carney & George Shepherd, *The Mystery of Delaware Law's Continuing Success*, 2009 U. Ill. L. Rev. 1.

sweeping away some bizarre and arcane requirements. Texas completely overhauled its business organization laws in 2010. It is not clear, however, that these efforts are cutting into Delaware's primacy as the state of incorporation for publicly traded entities.

Each state, plus the District of Columbia and Puerto Rico, has its own corporation statutes. There is a considerable degree of commonality among these statutes, but there is great divergence on specific provisions. The Model Business Corporation Act has been quite influential. Over half the states have used some version of it as their template. The Model Act has been through three editions. The first was promulgated in 1969, another in 1984, and the current version (known as the Revised Model Business Corporation Act) was produced in 2008.[60] Throughout this book, we will refer to this version as the RMBCA.

As a general matter, the trend in corporation statutes, reflected in the RMBCA, is toward simplification and the elimination of formalities that have little substantive effect. In particular, modern law routinely permits the shareholders of a closely held corporation to customize management procedures to their needs.[61] In addition, modern statutes show a trend toward "enabling" rather than "regulating." This movement reflects the influence of the law and economics scholars, as discussed in section C above.

E. Relevance of Federal Income Tax Law

In determining what form of business best suits a client's needs, the business lawyer must consider income tax ramifications. Federal income tax law has three basic regimes for taxation of businesses, routinely referred to by the subchapter of the Internal Revenue Code dealing with that regime.

First, "Subchapter C" applies to corporations generally. It considers the corporation to be a separate entity independent of its shareholders. I.R.C. § 11(a) thus imposes a tax on the income of the corporation, while § 301 in effect imposes a tax on shareholders who receive distributions (such as dividends) from corporations. This means that the earnings of a "C corporation" that pays dividends to its shareholders are subject to "double taxation"—there is federal income taxation at the corporate level and a second time at the shareholder level. Every public corporation is subject to Subchapter C. In the 1960s and 1970s, "master limited partnerships" were publicly traded. The goal was to claim that they were not corporations and

---

[60] This is revised from time to time, including 2010.

[61] For more on this topic, see Chapter 8(D).

thus should not be taxed under Subchapter C. It worked until Congress changed the law in 1987. Since then, all publicly traded businesses (even limited partnerships) are treated as Subchapter C corporations for tax purposes.

Second, "Subchapter K" applies to partnerships and "associations taxable as partnerships." It provides that these businesses are not separate taxable units. Instead, any tax consequences of their activities are passed through to the owners of the enterprise (hence the phrase "pass-through" taxation). The partnership files an informational tax return on which it shows its business income (or loss) and allocates gains, losses, income, and deductions to each partner. Each partner then includes those items in her individual income tax return. "K taxation" is an advantage over "C taxation." The partners pay income tax at the individual level, but the business does not pay a separate tax.

Third, "Subchapter C" was passed by Congress after years of hearing complaints from proprietors of closely held corporations. They complained that double taxation was unfair on such non-publicly-traded businesses. Subchapter S allows qualifying corporations to elect "S status," which offers pass-through taxation. Thus, there is income tax at the individual level but not at the business level. Although this looks a lot like "K taxation," technically there are significant distinctions between "K" and "S" businesses. Those distinctions are addressed in the course on corporate tax.

Subchapter S status is available only to closely held corporations that meet the following requirements: (1) they must be formed in the United States, (2) they must have no more than 100 shareholders, (3) the shareholders cannot be corporations, but must be individuals, or decedent's estates, or certain types of trusts, (4) no shareholder may be a nonresident alien, and (5) basically, there can only be one class of stock. An S corporation is a true corporation with all of the attributes of a corporation other than the double tax treatment. Thus, an S corporation has the normal corporate characteristics of limited liability, centralization of management, perpetual existence, and free transferability of interest.

So where do the newer forms of business—the LLP, limited partnership, and LLC—fit into these regimes? For years, the IRS took the position that pass-through taxation was only available for businesses in which owners were liable for business obligations. The theory seemed clear—since the economic benefits and burdens of the partnership business passed directly through to the partners, it was reasonable to impose income taxation on the same basis. By this log-

ic, LLPs, limited partnerships, and LLCs should not be able to take
advantage of Subchapter S.

Over time, however, the IRS changed its tune. In 1997, the IRS
adopted the "check the box" regulations. These require that corporations choose either Subchapter C or Subchapter S. For business
forms other than the corporation, however, the check the box regulations give great flexibility. Such a non-corporate (that has at least
two members) can elect to be classified for tax purposes either as a
corporation (Subchapters C or S) or as a partnership (Subchapter K)
simply by making an election at the time it files its first tax return. If
the entity does not formally elect to be taxed as a corporation, it will
be taxed as a partnership. A non-corporate business with only one
member may elect to be taxed as a corporation or it will be taxed as a
"nothing"—that is, as though it had no existence separate from its
owner.

Finally, we note the impact of income tax rates. Tax minimization strategies will change if tax rates change. For example, for
many years after World War II individual marginal tax rates for
wealthy individuals were as high as 80 percent, while the maximum
corporate tax rate was capped at 52 percent. In such a world, Subchapter K taxation for a profitable business with high-income tax-
payers was to be avoided at all costs, since it subjected all the business income to the very high individual tax rates. The point is simple: lawyers must provide their clients with advice on the pros and
cons of the various business forms, including the income tax regime
best aimed at minimizing taxes in the current tax climate.

Chapter 5

FORMATION OF CORPORATIONS (AND RELATED PRE-INCORPORATION ACTIVITIES)

Analysis

A. Introduction
B. Selecting the State of Incorporation (and Invoking the Internal Affairs Doctrine)
C. Mechanics of Formation
D. Corporate Purposes and Powers (and Ultra Vires Activity)
E. Foreign Corporations
F. Promoters and Their Activities
    1. Background
    2. Pre-Incorporation Contracts
    3. Subscriptions for Stock and Agreements to Form a Corporation
    4. Fiduciary Duties and the Secret Profit Rule
G. Defective Incorporation
    1. Personal Liability
    2. Defenses to Personal Liability: De Facto Corporation and Corporation by Estoppel

---

A. Introduction

In this Chapter we discuss how to form a de jure corporation— that is, a corporation recognized by law. Under modern statutes, formation is a simple process. The first step is to choose the state in which to incorporate. The laws of that state will govern the corporation's internal affairs (section B). Although there is some variation from state to state, the basics of formation are similar, and consist of filing with the appropriate state agency a document (usually called articles of incorporation) and taking various organizational acts, which we discuss in section C. If a corporation engages in activity beyond that stated in its articles, it acts *ultra vires*. Because corporations today generally may engage in all lawful business, however, this doctrine is of waning importance (section D). A corporation formed in one state can transact business in others, so there is no need to incorporate in each state in which the company will do business. Instead, it need only "qualify" to do business as a "foreign" corporation in each of those other states, which is addressed in section E.

In a perfect world, the proprietors would form a corporation on Monday and the corporation would start doing business on Tuesday. But things are not so smooth in the real world. People who plan a corporation often take steps on behalf of the business before actually forming it. The person acting on behalf of the corporation-not-yet-formed is a "promoter." Sometimes, a promoter will enter a pre-incorporation contract on behalf of what everyone knows is a non-existent business (section F). Other times, though, the parties are not aware that there is no corporation. These are cases of defective incorporation, and make proprietors nervous. Because they have failed to form a *de jure* corporation, proprietors will simply be operating a partnership, and thus risk liability for the business's actions. Here, defenses of de facto corporation and corporation by estoppel may permit the proprietor to escape personal liability (section G).

B. Selecting the State of Incorporation (and Invoking the Internal Affairs Doctrine)

There is no general federal law for forming or operating a corporation.[1] State law governs, and each state is free to craft its own legislation on the matter.[2] This law differs from state to state. As a rule of thumb, older statutes tend to impose more formalistic requirements on the formation and operation of the business, while newer statutes (typified by the Revised Model Business Corporation Act (RMBCA)) permit the proprietors to tailor their business to suit their needs. Still, no two states' corporation laws are identical, and the proprietors will incorporate (or "charter") in a state that makes sense for them. The overwhelming majority of corporations are small, closely held businesses, with only a handful of owners (often, in fact, with only one owner). They do business in a single state. Usually, it makes sense to form the corporation in that state.

But a corporation may be formed in any state, even one in which it does no business. As we see in section C, forming a corporation requires only preparing and filing a document and maintaining a registered agent in the state of incorporation. Because one may hire people to do the filing and to serve as agent, a person can form a corporation in a state in which she has never set foot. Most of the large,

---

[1] The federal government can and does form corporations. The American Red Cross and the United States Olympic Committee are examples. Such federally chartered entities are formed by specific congressional action, however, and not pursuant to any general statutory authority to allow the formation of federal corporations.

[2] The fact that federal law does not govern the formation of corporations does not mean that it is irrelevant in the operation of such businesses. In Chapter 11, we will discuss the important topic of federal regulation of securities.

publicly traded[3] corporations in the United States are chartered in Delaware, even though most do little if any business there.[4]

In its state of incorporation, a corporation is a "domestic" entity. In every other state, it is a "foreign" corporation. (So those terms, in the corporate world, do not imply anything about citizenship in a foreign country.) In earlier eras, some states forbade certain corporations (principally railroads) from operating within their boundaries without incorporating there. Generally, these laws were upheld,[5] and required that such companies actually go through the formation process in each state in which they operated. This replication of effort was expensive and led to intractable conflicts. Suppose, for instance, that a corporation is formed in State A and State B. If the laws of those states differ, say, on the shareholder vote required to approve a merger, there could be a significant problem about which state's law governed.

These problems are a thing of the past because states have jettisoned such statutes.[6] Now all states permit a "foreign" corporation to "qualify" to do business within its borders. So today, a company can incorporate in State A and "qualify" to do business in State B (and others). As we will see in section E of this Chapter, such qualification is rather easy.

Why, then, does it matter where we incorporate? Under the "internal affairs doctrine," the law of the state of incorporation applies to matters relating to the governance of the corporation (its "internal affairs.") This concept clearly includes the relationship, rights, and duties of the various players in the corporation—specifically, the shareholders, directors, and officers. So if the company is chartered in State A, the law of State A will determine what duties the directors owe to the corporation, voting requirements for directors and shareholders, etc. This is true even if the corporation does all of its business in State B. So the internal affairs doctrine gives proprietors an

---

[3] This means that the company's stock is traded on a stock exchange. Only corporations whose stock is "registered" under the Securities Act of 1933 are publicly traded. In Chapter 9(C), we discuss the requirements for registration. When we refer to "public corporations" we mean the same thing.

[4] Historically, Delaware has been thought favorable to management, so those forming such businesses have shopped to gain access to what they consider favorable law. *See* Chapter 4(D).

[5] *See, e.g.,* Railway Express Agency, Inc. v. Virginia, 282 U.S. 440, 444 (1931) (upholding Virginia statute against challenge under the Commerce Clause and the Fourteenth Amendment).

[6] Consequently, there are very few corporations today that actually are formed in more than one state. The few that do exist tend to be transportation authorities that operate bridges or tunnels between two states. For political reasons, these entities are usually incorporated in both states.

incentive to shop—to incorporate in a state in which the rules governing internal affairs are most conducive to the manner in which they wish to have the corporation managed.

The internal affairs doctrine is a choice of law rule.[7] As the Supreme Court explains: "(T)he internal affairs doctrine is a conflict of laws principle which recognizes that only one state should have the authority to regulate a corporation's internal affairs—matters peculiar to the relationships among or between the corporation and its current officers, directors, and shareholders—because otherwise a corporation could be faced with conflicting demands."[8]

There are some areas of uncertainty and tension concerning application of the doctrine. First, some scholars have argued that general principles of choice of law doctrine (and not the internal affairs rule) should apply concerning some aspects of corporate governance.[9] Second, and most importantly, some states have chafed at the application of the doctrine to corporations that do not have significant ties with their state of incorporation. The most aggressive state in this regard is California, which provides by statute that the articles of foreign corporations are deemed amended to comply with California law if, *inter alia*, more than half the company's stock is held by California residents and if at least half of its business is done in the Golden State.[10] In *Wilson v. Louisiana-Pacific Resources, Inc.*, the California Court of Appeal used this provision to override the internal affairs rule and thus to require a Utah corporation to provide cumulative voting to all shareholders (even non-Californians).[11]

The Delaware Supreme Court fought back in *VantagePoint Venture Partners 1996 v. Examen, Inc.*[12] In that case, California law would have permitted stockholders to block a proposed merger, but Delaware law would not. The Delaware court applied the internal

---

[7] *See, e.g.*, RMBCA § 15.05; RESTATEMENT (SECOND) OF CONFLICT OF LAWS § 302.

[8] Edgar v. Mite Corp., 457 U.S. 624, 645 (1982).

[9] In particular, there is some question whether the internal affairs rule should apply concerning "piercing the corporate veil." That doctrine, which we discuss at Chapter 8(E), permits a court to impose personal liability on a shareholder for a corporate debt. *See, e.g.*, Gregory Crespi, *Choice of Law in Veil-Piercing Litigation: Why Courts Should Discard the Internal Affairs Rule and Embrace General Choice-of-Law Principles*, 63 N.Y.U. ANN. SURV. 85 (2008).

[10] CAL. CORP. CODE § 2115. New York has a tamer version. *See* N.Y. BUS. CORP. LAW §§ 1317–1320.

[11] 138 Cal.App.3d 216, 229–232 (Cal. Ct. App. 1982). Cumulative voting, which we discuss in Chapter 6(C)(5), helps minority shareholders elect someone to the board of directors. In most states, such as Delaware, it does not exist unless the articles provide for it. In other states, such as California, it applies unless the articles take it away. The California law is more protective of minority shareholders than the Delaware law.

[12] 871 A.2d 1108 (Del. 2005).

affairs doctrine to hold that Delaware law governed. It concluded that the internal affairs doctrine is more than a choice-of-law rule. Because officers, directors, and shareholders have a "significant right . . . to know what law will be applied to their actions,"[13] the court concluded constitutional principles of due process mandated application of the doctrine. Moreover, the court opined, the Commerce Clause forbade California from applying its law to the internal affairs of a Delaware corporation.[14] Despite the interesting federalism issues, the Supreme Court has not weighed in.

Importantly, the internal affairs rule applies only to laws governing the relations of those who own and run a corporation. It does not apply to general laws concerning the relationship of the corporation (or its owners and operators) with the community at large. A corporation formed in State A but doing business in State B is subject to the general regulatory laws of State B. So, if the business commits a tort or breaches a contract or violates the consumer protection law of State B, State B has every right to apply its law to the corporation. In other words, State A has a right to apply its law to the internal affairs of a corporation that was formed under its auspices. But State A has no right to have its contract, tort, and general regulatory rules apply to "its" corporations for acts committed in other states. Thus, the internal affairs doctrine will not protect a corporation in a suit by a third party.

In deciding where to incorporate, then, proprietors will look at several factors. First is where they anticipate the corporation will do business. If it is one state, they will probably incorporate in that state. Chartering in another state increases costs by requiring that it form in one state and qualify in another; it will have to pay fees or taxes to both. Second, they will consider the laws governing internal affairs. Part of this assessment will be the relative flexibility of competing laws. All corporation laws provide for "default" rules that will apply only if the parties do not agree to the contrary. They vary on what those default rules are. The proprietors must assess those default provisions and see whether they fit their needs. Finally, predictability in the law is relevant. In some states, the courts handle corporate issues routinely; this augurs toward judicial (and lawyer) expertise and probably toward clarity in the law. However, in other

---

[13] *Id.* at 1113.

[14] *Id.* at 1116. Other courts have opined that the internal affairs doctrine is rooted in the Commerce Clause. *See, e.g.,* CTS Corp. v. Dynamics Corp. of America, 481 U.S. 69, 90 (1987) ("beneficial free market system depends at its core upon the fact that a corporation . . . is governed by . . . the law of a single jurisdiction, traditionally the corporate law of the State of its incorporation.")

states, courts may not have developed robust jurisprudence, which may create significant uncertainty in the law of such states.

C. Mechanics of Formation

Though the details vary from state to state, the process of forming a de jure corporation follows the same basic pattern: a document (usually called the "articles of incorporation" or simply the "articles")[15] is delivered to the appropriate state official (usually the secretary of state)[16] and a filing fee is paid.[17] The corporation usually comes into existence when the state official accepts the document for filing. The person responsible for forming the corporation is the "incorporator," who usually will be one of the founding proprietors (or perhaps the only proprietor) of the business. Historically, the law required that three incorporators execute the articles. Today, states require only one.[18] States formerly imposed residency requirements for incorporators, but most states now permit anyone of legal age to act as an incorporator, regardless of residence.[19] Most states permit entities (like a corporation) to serve as an incorporator,[20] although some, including New York, do not.[21] At one time, it was common to require that each incorporator agree to buy stock in the corporation, but this is now obsolete.

- The articles may be delivered to the appropriate state official (we will say the secretary of state) in a variety of ways—mail, overnight delivery service, courier, facsimile or, increasingly today, electronic delivery. A member of the professional staff in that office reviews the articles. If the document fails to meet the statutory requirements, the office refuses to file them. If, on the other hand, the document meets the statutory requirements (and the filing fee is paid), the articles are accepted for filing. Today, this is the critical event. It is this acceptance for filing by the state that forms

---

[15] A few states use different terms, including "articles of organization" (Texas), "certificate of incorporation" (Delaware and New York), and "charter" (Maryland).

[16] Some states empower different offices to serve this function. In Maryland, for example, it is the State Department of Assessment and Taxation.

[17] The fee for filing articles is modest in most states, usually under $100.

[18] *See, e.g.,* RMBCA § 2.01 ("[o]ne or more persons"); DEL. GEN. CORP. LAW § 101(a)("[a]ny person . . . single or jointly with others" may form a corporation").

[19] *See, e.g.,* DEL. GEN. CORP. LAW § 101(a)("without regard to such person or entity's residence, domicile, or state or incorporation").

[20] The RMBCA permits a "person" to incorporate. In § 1.10(16), it defines "person" to include individuals and entities. Delaware permits a "person, partnership, association, or corporation" to incorporate. DEL. GEN. CORP. LAW § 101(a).

[21] New York requires that incorporators be "natural persons of the age of eighteen years or over." N.Y. BUS. CORP. LAW § 401. A natural person is a human being. Corporations are examples of "artificial" persons.

the de jure corporation. Indeed, filing by that office constitutes "conclusive proof that the incorporators satisfied all conditions precedent to incorporation."[22] Historically, the secretary of state would issue a formal "charter" or "certificate of incorporation," which was the proof of valid formation.[23] Today, this issuance is unnecessary. The fact of acceptance is shown by a notation on the document that it is accepted for filing. The secretary of state's office usually then mails notification of acceptance to the incorporator.

- The commonest name for the document is the articles of incorporation (or just the "articles)." Though the requirements for articles differ from state to state, every state distinguishes between mandatory information and information which may be included. The trend has been toward far less mandatory information in articles. The leading example of sparse mandatory provisions is § 2.02(a) of the RMBCA, which requires only four items:

- The articles must give the corporate name, which must satisfy the requirements of § 4.01. That statute requires that the name not be misleading about what business the corporation will engage in (for instance, the name should not include the word "bank" if the company will not be engaged in banking). It also requires—as all states do—that the corporate name contain one of the recognized "magic words" or an abbreviation thereof. The RMBCA allows only four such words: company, corporation, incorporated, or limited. [24] The point here is that there must be a prescribed word in the corporate name that alerts the world that this is a corporation (and, therefore, the proprietors have limited liability).[25]

---

[22] *See* RMBCA § 2.03(b). There is an exception, however, for actions "by the state to cancel or revoke the incorporation or involuntarily dissolve the corporation."

[23] The 1950 and 1969 versions of the MBCA provided for such a "certificate of incorporation." The RMBCA, which was promulgated in 1984, did away with that document.

[24] Delaware is more creative, saying that the name must include one of 12 listed words (or their abbreviation) "or words . . . of like import." DEL. GEN. CORP. LAW § 102(a)(1).

[25] The secretary of state maintains a list of corporate names, available online. Because corporate names are handled on a first-come, first-served basis, many states permit the reservation of a proposed corporate name for a limited time for a fee. A corporation may do business under an assumed name, so long as it does not constitute unfair competition. Many states have "assumed name statutes," which permit anyone doing business under a different name to file a statement (sometimes at the county level) disclosing who is actually conducting business under that name.

- The articles must state the number of shares of stock the corporation will be authorized to issue. Shares are units of ownership. Those who hold stock—the shareholders—are thus owners of the corporation.

- The articles must give the street address of the registered office and the name of the initial registered agent. (In some states, this is called the "statutory agent.") This means there will always be someone available at a specific place (during business hours) to receive legal notices (including service of process and tax documents) for the corporation. The registered office may, but need not, be an actual business office.[26] In fact, if the corporation does not do business in the state, corporation service companies provide registered offices and registered agents for a fee. The corporation must inform the secretary of state of any change in the registered agent or registered office address.

- The articles must set forth the name and address of each incorporator.

Virtually every state requires that the articles contain these four items. The RMBCA, unlike many states, requires nothing else! For instance, in addition to the statement of authorized stock, many states require details about different classes of stock, including the characteristics of each class and the number of shares of each.[27] Some states, such as Arizona and Maryland, require a signed document that the registered agent has agreed to serve as such. In some states, the names and addresses of the initial directors must be stated.[28] In most, however, this is an option; the articles may name the initial directors or may allow the incorporators to elect them later.

Historically, states required that the articles make a statement of corporate *purpose*. In the nineteenth century, articles had to state the specific purposes for which the corporation was formed. In a few states, corporations could list only one purpose. These and other limitations, such as restrictions on how much capital a corporation could have, reflected populist fear of concentrated economic power. Corporations acting beyond their stated purpose are acting ultra vires,

---

[26] New York is atypical in requiring a statement of the county in which the corporation will have its "office of corporation," N.Y. BUS. CORP. LAW § 402(3), and a designation of the New York secretary of state as its agent for service of process. N.Y. BUS. CORP. LAW § 402(7).

[27] *See, e.g.,* DEL. GEN. CORP. LAW § 102(a)(4) (requiring details regarding classes of stock).

[28] *See, e.g.,* NEV. REV. STAT. § 78.035(4) (requiring names and addresses of the initial members of the board of directors).

which we will discuss in section D. Today, ultra vires activity is rare. Many states, under the influence of the RMBCA, do not require any statement of purpose.[29] In these states, it is presumed that the corporation can undertake any and all lawful business.[30] In those states that do require a statement of purpose, almost all permit a general statement of purpose—such as, "this corporation may engage in all lawful business."[31] Very few states do not allow such a general statement of purpose. In Arizona, for instance, the articles must include "a brief statement of the character of the business that the corporation initially intends to actually conduct in this state."[32]

Moreover, historically, states required that the articles contain a statement of *corporate duration*. Even where the requirement persists, it creates no difficulty, because the articles may simply provide that the corporation has perpetual existence. This does not mean that the corporation will actually exist until the end of time. Rather, it will exist until the appropriate people decide to end its existence, for example, by dissolution or merger. The clear modern trend, typified by the RMBCA, requires no statement of duration, and simply *presumes* perpetual existence. In any state, the articles may provide for a term of years or that the business is formed for a particular undertaking (such as to build a shopping center). Such "term corporations" seem quite rare.

Beyond these required matters, incorporators must consider a range of permissive provisions in the articles. It is imperative that those forming the corporation know the relevant state's "default" position on this range of topics. The default position is the law that will apply if the articles are silent. These default positions vary from state to state and topic to topic. One important example is cumulative voting, which concerns shareholder election of directors. It is a device to help minority shareholders gain some representation among directors. We will discuss it in Chapter 6(C)(5). In some states, cumulative voting is presumed unless the articles take it away. In other states, as reflected by the RMBCA, cumulative voting exists only if the articles provide for it.[33] Another important topic with regard to

---

[29] The corporation's purpose—as stated in the articles (or presumed to be all lawful purposes)—should be distinguished from its "powers." In every state, a statute lists corporate powers that a corporation in that state automatically has. The list is usually quite broad, as in § 3.02 of the RMBCA. These powers need not be stated in the articles; the corporation has them automatically, simply by being formed in that state.

[30] Of course, the articles may limit the activities in which the corporation may engage.

[31] *See, e.g.,* N.Y. BUS. CORP. LAW § 201.

[32] ARIZ. STAT. § 10–202(a)(3).

[33] RMBCA § 7.28(a).

default rules is preemptive rights. As we will discuss in Chapter 10(C)(5), preemptive rights allow an existing shareholder to maintain her percentage of ownership by buying new stock when the corporation issues stock. This right is relevant only in closely held businesses. In some states, preemptive rights exist unless the articles take them away. In other states, as reflected by the RMBCA, preemptive rights exist only if the articles say so.[34]

The vast majority of states permit the articles to limit a director's monetary liability to the corporation or its shareholders for breach of the duty of care. Here, it is sufficient that we note the possibility of placing such exculpatory provisions in the articles.[35] The articles may also provide for staggered terms for directors, and may change the default provisions concerning quorum and voting requirements for meetings of shareholders and directors. Other matters may be addressed, depending on the specific statute, either in articles or bylaws. In small, closely held corporations, the articles can modify the traditional governance model—for example, by eliminating the board of directors and having shareholders exercise the board's power. We discuss such provisions in Chapter 8(D).

Some states impose additional requirements. In Georgia, for example, the incorporator must arrange to have the formation of the corporation published in a newspaper of general circulation in the county of the registered office.[36] Historically, states required recording in every county in which the corporation would transact business, but this (wasteful) requirement is on the wane. Also, historically, nearly all states required that a minimum capital investment (usually $1,000) must be paid into the corporation before it could start doing business. This requirement has largely disappeared.

The corporation is formed when the Secretary of State accepts the articles for filing. But there are other statutory requirements, aimed at organizing and running the corporation. Every state requires an *organizational meeting*. If the initial directors were named in the articles, they will hold the organizational meeting. If the initial directors were not named in the articles, the incorporators will hold the organizational meeting.[37] The organizational meeting focuses on two things: adopting bylaws[38] and appointing officers. The

---

[34] RMBCA § 6.30(a).

[35] *See, e.g.,* RMBCA § 2.02(b)(4).

[36] GA. CODE § 14–2–201.1.

[37] Either way, in lieu of an actual meeting, the acts may be taken by unanimous written consent. (This is handy when there is only one director or one incorporator in the corporation; the formality of a meeting of one is rather silly.)

[38] Do not confuse bylaws with articles. Articles are filed with the state and are a public document. Bylaws are not. Bylaws can govern the internal affairs of the cor-

board may, of course, conduct other appropriate business there as well, such as accept subscriptions and approve the issuance of stock, contracts, and payment of the costs of incorporation.[39] In addition, every state requires that the corporation hold periodic meetings of the board of directors and the shareholders. There are strict requirements for notice for most of these meetings. The law also requires the corporate secretary to keep records of the actions taken at these meetings.

Failure to satisfy these requirements concerning organization and operation of the corporation does not affect corporate status. In *Brown v. W.P. Media, Inc.,*[40] the plaintiff corporation's articles had been filed. By the time it brought suit, however, the company had not held the organizational meeting, adopted bylaws, selected officers, or otherwise completed its organization. The defendant argued that the corporation could not sue because it had not satisfied these statutory requirements. The court rejected the argument and noted that such requirements of existing corporations have nothing to do with whether the corporation has been properly formed. That was decided conclusively when the state accepted the articles for filing.[41]

Failure to satisfy the requirements of organization and operation may attract the attention of the state itself, which may be empowered to dissolve the corporation for its failures. One requirement is particularly important in this regard. Each state levies a tax on each corporation it charters, to pay for the privilege of conducting business. This "franchise tax" is usually payable annually. There is often a requirement of an annual report, filed with the state. Failure to pay the tax or make the report may subject the corporation to administrative dissolution. We discuss dissolution in Chapter 12(H).

---

poration. In each state, certain things (such as a provision limiting director liability for damages) can only be provided for in the articles, while others can be provided for in either the articles or bylaws. As a practical matter, putting a provision in one or the other document makes a big difference: amending articles is a fundamental corporate change, which requires approval by the board and shareholders (*see* Chapter 12(D)), while amending bylaws is considerably easier, requiring usually action only one group, the board or the shareholders. If the articles and the bylaws conflict, the articles take precedence.

[39] Under RMBCA § 2.05(a)(2), if the organizational meeting is held by the incorporators, they will elect the initial directors. Then the incorporators have a choice: they can either "complete the organization of the corporation" by adopting bylaws and appointing officers, or they can disappear and let the board of directors do those things.

[40] 17 So.3d 1167 (Ala. 2009)

[41] *Id.* at 1172.

D. Corporate Purposes and Powers (and Ultra Vires Activity)

A corporation's "purpose" refers to the reason it is formed, i.e., to the type of business it will transact. So one might form a corporation to operate a restaurant or to manufacture widgets. In the nineteenth century, statutes required the articles to state specific purposes for which the business was formed. Today, almost all statutes permit formation of a corporation to engage "in any lawful business."[42] A corporation's "powers" refer to those things a corporation may do to help it accomplish its purpose. So a corporation has the power to sue and be sued, to buy and sell property, to borrow money, and so forth. In the nineteenth century, courts imposed restrictions on corporate powers, as we discuss below. Today, all states reject such restrictions with broad legislative grants of general corporate powers.

The nineteenth century legislative restrictions on corporate purposes and common law restrictions on corporate powers reflected that era's nervousness about the concentration of economic power. Their nearly complete demise means that corporations today will rarely act beyond their purpose or powers. When they do, however, the act is *ultra vires*. Conversely, when a business acts within its purpose and powers, it acts *intra vires*.

Ultra vires acts, though rare, can happen. The corporation may undertake additional activities, but those activities might be *ultra vires*. Even in the overwhelming majority of states, which allow a general statement of purpose, there may be corporations in which the articles restrict the character of business that may be pursued. Whenever corporate decision makers want to have the business act beyond its stated purpose, they should take steps to amend the articles to ensure those activities will be *intra vires*.

What happens when a corporation acts *ultra vires*? Suppose the articles indicate that the corporation will engage in oil and gas exploration, and the company operates organic-food restaurants. The restaurant activity is *ultra vires*. Now, say the corporation enters a contract in the operation of the restaurant (for example, to buy food). Is the contract enforceable? The law has taken different approaches to the problem over time.

The earliest view was that *ultra vires* transactions were void because the corporation had no capacity to engage in them. This view was unfortunate. It permitted a corporation to accept the benefits of

---

[42] RMBCA § 3.01(a). Under the RMBCA, the ability to engage in any lawful business is presumed if the articles are silent on the matter.

a contract and then to refuse to perform (as *ultra* vires) its own obligations under the contracts.[43] It also threatened the security of title to property, because even a completed real estate transaction might be set aside if a corporation had acted beyond its authority.

Through the years, courts moderated the doctrine by viewing *ultra vires* acts as voidable, rather than void. The case law in this era established some basic rules. Generally, if neither side had performed, either party could void the agreement. On the other hand, if one party had performed fully, the other party could not raise the *ultra vires* defense.[44] And if both parties had fully performed, the transaction could not be attacked as *ultra vires*.[45] Courts were erratic in applying these rules, however, and even under them, *ultra vires* continued to defeat legitimate expectations when neither party had performed on a contract.

The modern view, which appears to be ubiquitous, starts with the general proposition that *ultra vires* contracts are valid and enforceable. In terms of the RMBCA, which typifies the modern approach, "the validity of corporate action may not be challenged on the ground that the corporation lacks or lacked power to act."[46]

Under modern law, however, the fact that an act or proposed act is *ultra vires* is relevant in three situations. First, a shareholder may sue the corporation to enjoin the act.[47] For example, the court issued an injunction to stop a corporation formed for the purpose of providing health care plans from going into the life insurance business.[48] Second, the corporation may sue the responsible individuals for causing the corporation to undertake the *ultra vires* activity.[49] So if the corporation goes into an *ultra vires* activity and loses money, those responsible for the decision will be liable to the corporation for the losses.[50] Third, the state attorney general can seek judicial dissolu-

---

[43] It certainly seems arguable, though, that the other party should have a claim for unjust enrichment.

[44] *See, e.g.,* Joseph Schlitz Brewing Co. v. Missouri Poultry & Game Co., 229 S.W 813 (Mo. 1921).

[45] *See, e.g.,* Whitney Arms Co. v. Barlow, 63 N.Y. 62 (1875) (refusing to rescind a fully executed contract, even though it was *ultra vires* for the corporation).

[46] RMBCA § 3.04(a). Delaware has a similar provision. *See* DEL. GEN. CORP. LAW § 124.

[47] RMBCA § 3.04(b)(1); *see also* DEL. GEN. CORP. LAW § 124(1).

[48] Blue Cross and Blue Shield of Alabama v. Protective Life Ins. Co., 527 So. 2d 125, 128 (Ala. Ct. Civ. App. 1987). RMBCA § 3.04(c) provides that the court "may award damages for loss (other than anticipated profits) suffered by the corporation or another party" because the deal was enjoined.

[49] RMBCA § 3.04(b)(2); *see also* DEL. GEN. CORP. LAW § 124(2) ("for loss or damage due to such incumbent or former officer's or director's unauthorized act").

[50] This principle flows from agency law. Any agent who damages her principal by exceeding her authority is liable to the principal.

tion of the corporation based upon the company's *ultra vires* activity.[51]

As noted, *ultra vires* problems are less likely today than in the past because modern law embraces the view that corporations can undertake any lawful business; in other words, the law does not restrict the purposes for which a corporation can be formed. Similarly, modern law embraces a broad view of powers available to corporations to pursue their business purposes. In earlier times, courts restricted what corporations could do. Earlier, we saw the important evolution of thought on whether corporations may engage in philanthropic giving. Beyond that, courts in earlier eras forbade corporations from serving as partners in partnerships. These courts expressed concern that the corporation's board of directors would be robbed of power over the business's affairs if the business forms were mixed.[52] Similarly, courts forbade corporations from owning stock in other corporations, sometimes because such investment might permit the company to avoid a limited statement of purpose in its articles. Courts forbade corporations from guaranteeing the indebtedness of an individual, usually because of the potential for conflict of interest.

Such restrictions are now a thing of the past. Every state's corporation law contains a list of "general powers" enjoyed by all corporations.[53] These powers are presumed and need not be stated in the articles.[54] The list in most statutes is long, and includes the power to make charitable contributions, to serve as a partner in partnerships, to make and guarantee loans to officers, directors, and others, and to invest in other companies.[55] Similarly, corporations have the power to sue and be sued, to enter contracts, to take out loans, and to establish pension plans for employees.[56] These statutory grants are called "general powers" of the corporation. In addition, courts infer that corporations have incidental or implied powers to do what is necessary and proper to accomplish legitimate goals. Indeed, modern statutes make such incidental powers express, by permitting corpora-

---

[51] RMBCA § 3.04(b)(3). In some states, the attorney general may sue for dissolution or, in the alternative, to enjoin *ultra vires* activities. *See, e.g.,* DEL. GEN. CORP. LAW § 124(3).

[52] *See, e.g.,* Whittenton Mills v. Upton, 76 Mass. 582 (1858).

[53] *See, e.g.,* RMBCA § 3.02.

[54] RMBCA § 2.02(c).

[55] *See, e.g.,* RMBCA § 3.02(6) (investment in other companies), § 3.02(7)(loans), § 3.02(9)(serve as partner), § 3.02(13)(charitable contributions). A loan by the corporation to an officer or director raises duty of loyalty concerns. *See* Chapter 7(E).

[56] *See, e.g.,* RMBCA § 3.02(1), (7), (8), (12).

tions to do "any . . . act, not inconsistent with law, that furthers the business and affairs of the corporation."[57]

E. Foreign Corporations

A corporation formed in one state may qualify to transact business in another state as a "foreign corporation." The requirements for qualifying vary slightly from state to state, but generally are not difficult to satisfy. The foreign corporation is required to qualify only if it is "transacting business" or "doing business" in the state. Under the Commerce Clause of the Constitution, states can only require qualification by foreign corporations that are engaged in *intrastate* activities. They have no authority to exclude (and therefore no authority to require qualification from) corporations engaged in *interstate* business.[58] Intrastate business requires more activity in the state than interstate business.

How do we draw that line? In most states, statutes create safe harbors by listing activities that will not be considered intrastate business. For example, engaging in litigation, holding meetings, maintaining bank accounts, and owning real or personal property do not constitute transacting business.[59] Beyond that, statutes in some states attempt to define intrastate business. The California Corporations Code defines transacting intrastate business as "entering into repeated and successive transactions of its business in this state, other than interstate or foreign commerce."[60] In states lacking such statutory definition, courts have reached the same general conclusion—that transacting business involves more than sporadic activity, and requires some continuous or significant intrastate activity.[61]

Qualifying as a foreign corporation is a relatively easy process. The corporation seeks from the Secretary of State (or other appropriate state official) what most states call a "certificate of authority."[62] The corporation must provide information similar to that required in its articles[63] and must prove that it is in good standing in the state in

---

[57] RMBCA § 3.02(15).

[58] International Textbook Co. v. Pigg, 217 U.S. 91, 108–12 (1910); Alliance Steel, Inc. v. Piland, 134 P.3d 669, 673 (Kan. Ct. App. 2006) ("It is well-established authority that a State cannot require a foreign corporation to qualify to do business within its boundaries if the business of the corporation is limited wholly or entirely to interstate sales.").

[59] This list is taken from RMBCA § 15.01(b), which includes other activities as well.

[60] CAL. CORP. CODE § 191(a).

[61] *See, e.g.,* J.C. Snavely & Sons, Inc. v. Wheeler, 538 A.3d 324, 327 (Md. Ct. App. 1988) ("significant business activity").

[62] The RMBCA uses this terminology. RMBCA § 15.03(a).

[63] *See, e.g.,* RMBCA § 15.03(a)(1)–(6).

which it is incorporated. Good standing depends upon whether the corporation has paid taxes, filed required reports, and done other things required to maintain corporate status in the home state. That state's secretary of state provides this certification.[64] In addition, the foreign corporation usually must appoint a registered agent and have an instate registered office. It must also pay filing and other fees, file annual reports, and may be subject to state taxation.

What happens if a foreign corporation transacts business without qualifying? The corporation is subject to a civil penalty[65] and is barred from asserting a claim in that state until it qualifies and pays the back fees and penalty.[66] The corporation can defend claims made against it without qualifying.[67] The overwhelming majority view is that the failure to qualify does not affect the validity of corporate acts. Accordingly, contracts entered by the foreign corporation will be valid, even though it failed to qualify.[68] In a small number of states, however, contracts entered by a foreign corporation that was transacting business without qualifying are treated as void, at least when the foreign corporation attempts to enforce them.[69]

F. Promoters and Their Activities

1. Background

A promoter is a person who takes the initiative in developing and organizing a new business venture. Promoters are often imaginative entrepreneurs who take an idea and create a profitable business to capitalize on it. Though one person may serve both as incorporator and promoter, the roles are different. As we saw, the incorporator executes the document that forms the corporation and oversees the initial organization of the business. The promoter's role is

---

[64] RMBCA § 15.03(b) (must provide "certificate of existence . . . duly authenticated by the secretary of state").

[65] RMBCA § 15.02(d).

[66] RMBCA § 15.02(a). The court may stay proceedings against the foreign corporation until it does these things. RMBCA § 15.02(c).

[67] RMBCA § 15.02(e) (failure to qualify does not prevent the foreign corporation "from defending any proceeding in this state").

[68] *See, e.g.,* RMBCA § 15.02(e) (failure to qualify "does not impair the validity of corporate acts or prevent it from defending any proceeding in this state").

[69] *See, e.g.,* ALA. CODE § 10A–2–15.02(a) ("All contracts or agreements made or entered into in this state by foreign corporations prior to registering to transact business in this state shall be held void at the action of the foreign corporation . . ."). Section 10A–2–15.02(b) provides that the foreign corporation sued on such a contract "shall be estopped from setting up the fact that the contract or agreement was made in violation of the law"). Thus in *Brown v. Pool Depot, Inc.,* 853 So.2d 181, 187 (Ala. 2002), the foreign corporation's failure to qualify voided the contract and its arbitration clause.

broader. She is responsible for assuring that the corporation is an economic success.

For the most part, promoters focus on two things. First, they arrange for the start-up capital for the business. They may invest their own money, or that of family members, or they may get a bank loan, or arrange for outside investors. With outside investors, the promoter will negotiate their stake in the corporation and arrange either by contract or subscription to ensure that the capital will be available when needed. Second, the promoter must set things up so the corporation can "hit the ground running" once it is formed. This means she arranges for personnel, machinery, and supplies to enable the business to function. For example, a promoter may lease office space for the business.

Promoters expect to be compensated for their efforts. Often, they will get some of the stock initially issued by the corporation. This gives the promoter a "piece of the action"—an equity position in the venture. Subsequent investors will usually purchase stock at a higher issuance price than the shares previously issued to the promoter, which increases the value of the promoter's stock. This increase in value represents compensation to the promoter; it is often a subject of negotiation between promoters and investors. Of course, all stockholders hope that the business does well so the value of everyone's stock will rise.

Let's return to the promoter's activities to ensure that the business hits the ground running. If she does these things after the corporation is formed, the contracts—to lease office space, buy machinery, pay employees, etc.—will be entered by the corporation itself. The promoter will not be a party to the contracts and will not risk liability on them. (Sometimes, third parties will insist that an individual, such as the promoter, personally guarantee the corporation's performance of the contracts, but that will be a separate undertaking from the ones entered by the corporation itself.)

Often, however, the corporation is not formed by the time the promoter enters into these sorts of contracts. The promoter simply needs to act before the incorporator finishes creating the entity. Perhaps, for example, she simply does not want to lose a potential lease or a purchase of machinery at a desirable price. When the promoter enters a contract on behalf of a corporation not-yet-formed, we have a pre-incorporation contract, which raises important issues of liability.

2. Pre-Incorporation Contracts

Suppose the promoter leases office space from a third party thinking that the space will be perfect for the corporation (once it is formed). Who is liable on the deal? We consider three scenarios:

- First, the promoter might sign the lease in her name, without referring to the corporation. She might do this because she assumes that once the corporation is formed, it will accept an assignment of the contract from her. The promoter is liable on this lease because she is a party to it. If the corporation is never formed, the promoter is liable. If the corporation is formed, the promoter is still liable until there is a *novation*. A novation would be an agreement among the corporation, the third party, and the promoter under which the corporation replaces the promoter on the lease. Thus, even if the corporation is formed and accepts an assignment of the lease from the promoter, the promoter is personally liable until the third party agrees—through a novation—to relieve the promoter of liability.[70]

- Second, the promoter might sign the lease on behalf of "XYZ Corporation, an entity not yet in existence." Here, clearly, the promoter and the third party are aware that there is no corporation. Can the third party enforce this contract against the promoter?

The answer depends on the intent of the parties, and a good lawyer will avoid litigation with clear drafting. The contract might expressly provide, for example, that the promoter is not liable. Essentially, this would create an offer to the corporation, which may choose to accept or reject after it is formed. Or the contract may provide that the promoter is liable until the corporation is formed and adopts the lease.

The problem is that many pre-incorporation contracts are silent regarding intent. Courts have developed some general approaches to such cases. For starters, the promoter has a problem—she has purported to act on behalf of a non-existent principal. Under agency law, the promoter is a party to the contract, and thus will be liable.[71] Accordingly, unless the parties intended otherwise, the promoter is per-

---

[70] *See* Isle of Thye Land Co. v. Shisman, 279 A.2d 484, 496 (Md. 1971) (novation requires agreement by third party that promoter is discharged and that she will look only to corporation for satisfaction).

[71] We discussed agency in Chapter 2.

sonally liable on pre-incorporation contracts.[72] If the corporation is never formed, the promoter is liable.

What happens, though, if the corporation is formed? Does its coming into existence make it liable on the contract? The general answer is no. Those in charge of the corporation should have the opportunity to have it accept or reject the deal; after all, in the meantime, perhaps the contract has become less attractive for the corporation. Accordingly, the corporation generally will become liable on the contract only if it adopts the contract.[73] It might do this expressly, by a formal decision of the board of directors. Or it might accept the contract impliedly, by conduct.[74] Essentially, such conduct creates an estoppel: the corporation accepts a benefit of the contract or otherwise treats it as binding upon it, and cannot then be permitted to shun liability.

If the corporation does adopt the contract, it becomes liable on it from that point. But does that fact relieve the promoter of her liability? Generally, the answer is no. The promoter will be liable on the contract until there is a novation—until the third party essentially agrees to have the corporation replace the promoter under the contract.

- • Third, the promoter might sign the lease on behalf of "XYZ Corporation," with no indication that the corporation does not exist. Perhaps the promoter is mistaken and thought the corporation had already been formed. Or perhaps the promoter is lying, purporting to act on behalf of a business she knows does not exist. In general, the liability rules in this scenario will be the same as discussed in the second scenario. Thus, absent some showing of intent to the contrary, the promoter will be liable on the contract, the corporation will become liable only if it is formed and adopts the

---

[72] *See, e.g.,* Clinton Inv. Co. v. Watkins, 536 N.Y.S.2d 270, 272 (N.Y. App. Div. 1989); Van Dyke v. DCI, Inc., 675 N.W.2d 810 (Wis. Ct. App. 2004).

[73] Courts sometimes say that the corporation "ratified" the contract. *See, e.g.,* 02 Dev., LLC v. 607 South Park, LLC, 71 Cal.Rptr.3d 810, 812 (Cal. Ct. App. 2008) (corporation may "enforce any preorganization contract made on its behalf . . . if it adopted or ratified it."). Technically, ratification is impossible in this scenario. It relates back to the time the agent acted—that is, when the contract was entered. Because the corporation did not exist when the contract was entered, it cannot ratify the deal.

[74] *See, e.g.,* Katz v. Prete, 459 A.2d 81, 86 (R.I. 1983) (accepting loan and making payment on it constituted adoption); Moore v. Dallas Post Card Co., 215 S.W.2d 398, 401 (Tex. Ct. Civ. App. 1948) (bringing suit or making demand on contract constitutes adoption); McArthur v. Times Printing Co., 51 N.W. 216, 216 (Minn. 1892) (corporation, aware of pre-incorporation employment contract, employed plaintiff for six months without objection; adoption "may be inferred from acts or acquiescence on part of the corporation . . . .").

contract, and the promoter will be discharged from liability only if the corporation is formed and it and the third party agree to a novation.

3. Subscriptions for Stock and Agreements to Form a Corporation

A subscription is an offer to buy stock that the corporation has not yet sold (or "issued").[75] Promoters may use subscriptions to raise capital for the business. The subscriber agrees to buy a particular number of shares, the consideration for which is invested in the business. Subscriptions are not used in funding large, publicly traded corporations. Indeed, the use of subscriptions in connection with a public offering is unattractive as a practical matter because the subscriptions themselves constitute securities under federal and state securities acts and must be "registered." Since the underlying securities themselves also must be registered, the use of subscriptions would result in two expensive registrations. Accordingly, subscriptions are used, if at all, only in small, closely held corporations.

One legal issue is whether the subscriber may revoke her offer. If she made the offer to buy stock after the corporation was formed, this question is governed by the law of contracts. Consistent with general contract principles, the subscriber may revoke her offer any time before the corporation accepts it. Once the corporation accepts the subscription, the parties will have entered a "subscription agreement."

A more interesting question arises when the subscriber agrees to buy stock from a corporation-not-yet-formed. Can the subscriber revoke a "pre-incorporation subscription?" The problem here is that the subscriber has made an offer to an entity that does not yet exist. At common law, this meant that the subscriber could revoke the offer any time before the corporation was formed and accepted the subscription. This result meant that the proprietors could not rely on having the investment capital. The subscriber was free to pull the rug out from under the venture by revoking the offer immediately before the corporation was formed.

Corporation statutes have changed the common law rule by making pre-incorporation subscriptions irrevocable for a limited period. Though some states differ, the typical period is six months.[76]

---

[75] Stock is "issued" when it is sold by the corporation itself, as we will see in Chapter 10(C). Thus when a shareholder sells to another person, either directly or through a stock exchange, that sale is not an "issuance" and the special "issuance" rules do not apply.

[76] See, e.g., RMBCA § 6.20(a).

During this period, the pre-incorporation subscription cannot be re-voked, which permits the proprietors to rely on the availability of the capital. These statutes merely give a default rule. Thus, the sub-scriber can provide in the pre-incorporation offer that she can revoke the offer at any time. Or the subscriber and the proprietors can agree to a different period of irrevocability. And, under the statutes, even an irrevocable subscription can be revoked if all the other subscribers agree to it.[77]

Beyond this point, subscriptions generally are subject to the general law of contracts. Accordingly, any subscription—pre- or post-incorporation—may be conditioned on the occurrence of certain events, such as obtaining a specified amount of capital, or a loan, or a lease. The fulfillment of each of these is a condition precedent to the obligation of the subscriber. Of course, the subscriber can rescind any subscription that was induced by fraud.

After the corporation is formed, its board of directors may call upon the subscribers to make payment on their subscriptions. Unless they were established in the subscription agreement, the board will determine the payment terms for pre-incorporation subscriptions. As a general matter, the corporation's call for payment must be uniform among all subscribers of the same class of shares.[78] A subscriber does not become a shareholder until she pays the subscription price in full.

As an alternative to subscriptions, those planning to form a closely held corporation may enter a "pre-incorporation agreement," which is simply an agreement to form a corporation. It is entered by proposed shareholders with the goal of developing a business as a corporation. The contribution of each participant and the number of shares each is to receive are specified in this contract. Because it is a contract among the proprietors (and not between the proprietors and an entity-not-yet-formed), it is enforceable in the same manner as any other contract.

Pre-incorporation agreements may be simple, reciting only broad points of agreement, or they may be quite formal, setting forth all aspects of the agreement, including understandings as to employ-ment, capitalization, voting power, and membership of the initial board of directors. Such an agreement may include as exhibits copies of proposed articles and bylaws. These contracts often impose stock

---

[77] See, e.g., RMBCA § 6.20(a) (irrevocable for six months "unless . . . all the sub-scribers agree to revocation.").

[78] RMBCA § 6.20(b) ("uniform so far as practicable as to all shares of the same class or series, unless the subscription agreement specifies otherwise").

transfer restrictions, which we discuss at Chapter 8(C). One potential question is whether the terms of the pre-incorporation agreement (such as a stock transfer restriction) survive the formation of the corporation. Parties to an agreement to form a corporation are joint venturers. The object of their venture is to establish the corporation. Once the entity is formed, perhaps the joint venture ends and the terms of the deal are not enforceable. Ultimately, the question is one of the parties' intent. If they desire that some provisions survive the formation of the corporation, they should make this clear.

4. Fiduciary Duties and the Secret Profit Rule

Pre-incorporation contracts, which we discussed above, are deals between a promoter and a third party. Here, we address something different: a deal between a promoter and the corporation itself. Usually, a promoter will be selling property to the corporation. We are concerned that the promoter will be tempted to put her own interest above that of the corporation. Courts have used high-sounding terms like "fiduciary duties" and "promoter's fraud" in these cases. As a theoretical matter, there is a slight glitch in speaking of fiduciary duties because the promoter, when engaged in promotion, acted on behalf of a corporation that did not exist. Are we willing to say that her pre-incorporation role as a promoter clothes her with a duty to the corporation after it comes into existence? In most instances, the problem is merely theoretical because the promoter will have become a manager in the corporation, and managers (as we will see in Chapter 7) clearly owe fiduciary duties to the corporation.

The law has developed a doctrine here called the "secret profit rule." The most famous example involved promoters of a mining company who bought mining property for $1,000,000. After the corporation was formed, they sold the property to the corporation for stock worth $3,250,000. The promoters had the corporation approve the transaction because at the time they were the sole shareholders and managers of the corporation. Later, they had the corporation sell stock to the public, without disclosing to those buyers that the corporation had paid the promoters an inflated amount for the mining properties. Two suits were filed against the promoters—one in federal court and one in state court. The federal case went to the Supreme Court and the state case went to the Massachusetts Supreme Judicial Court. They reached different conclusions on the legal principle.

The Supreme Court, applying federal law, held for the promoters.[79] It reasoned that the corporation had approved the transaction with full knowledge that the promoters were making a huge profit. How did it have knowledge? Because the very promoters were running the corporation itself. The corporation was not required to agree to the transaction after independent shareholders joined. The entity approved the deal when it was entered, and it does not become a different entity when new shareholders buy in.[80]

The Massachusetts Supreme Judicial Court reached the opposite conclusion.[81] It adopted a broader duty than that under federal law. Specifically, the promoters must disclose the profit to incoming shareholders and get their approval of the deal. Their failure to do so meant that the promoters gained a "secret profit" and required that the profit be disgorged. Thus, the corporation was entitled to recover the profit gained by the promoters.[82] The Massachusetts rule, then, means that the promoter's "fiduciary duty" continues through the time of setting up the corporation fully—all incoming shareholders (and not just those who were shareholders when the deal was approved) must be informed of the profit.

Despite the broad language of "fiduciary duty," the "secret profit rule" established by Massachusetts boils down to a duty to disclose; it is not a broad duty of fair dealing. So if the promoters, when selling property to the corporation, fail to disclose to and get approval from some independent decision makers, the corporation can recover their profit. Conversely, if the promoters disclose their profit, and an independent board of directors or all shareholders approve the deal, there would be no disgorgement.[83] The rule, then, does not say that the promoters cannot profit on their dealings with the corporation. Rather, they cannot make a *secret* profit on those dealings.

---

[79] Old Dominion Copper Mining & Smelting Co. v. Lewisohn, 210 U.S. 206 (1908). The opinion was unanimous and was written by Justice Holmes. The losing lawyer on the plaintiff's side was Louis Brandeis, who was appointed to the Court in 1916.

[80] Id. at 216 (corporation "remains unchanged and unaffected in its identity by changes in its members").

[81] Old Dominion Copper Mining & Smelting Co. v. Bigelow, 89 N.E. 193, 201 (Mass. 1909), *aff'd*, 225 U.S. 111 (1912).

[82] *Id.* at 200–212.

[83] *See* Frick v. Howard, 126 N.W.2d 619, 623 (Wis. 1964) (independent board required); Swafford v. Berry, 382 P.2d 999, 1002 (Colo. 1963) (all shareholders); Topanga Corp. v. Gentile, 58 Cal. Rptr. 713, 717 (Cal. Ct. App. 1967).

G. Defective Incorporation

1. Personal Liability

We have considered some activities that were undertaken when the parties knew that no corporation had been formed. Parties entering pre-incorporation subscriptions and most pre-incorporation contracts understand that a corporation is planned but does not yet exist. Here, we consider a different scenario: the proprietors believe they have formed a *de jure* corporation, but are wrong. The business now commits a tort or incurs a debt, and the question becomes whether the individual proprietors are personally liable.

Defective incorporation was once more common than it is today. Earlier law imposed more requirements for forming a corporation, so there were more opportunities for mistake. For example, earlier law in many states required not only filing the articles with the state, but filing with a court in the county in which the corporation was to have its principal office. Another example was the requirement that a certain amount of capital be invested before the corporation could undertake business. Today, though, as we saw above, forming a corporation is quite simple. Every state provides, in substance, that corporate existence begins either upon the filing of the articles of incorporation or their acceptance for filing by the state.[84] And most states provide that acceptance of the articles is "conclusive" evidence that all conditions precedent to incorporation have been complied with except in suits brought by the state.[85] Accordingly, errors and omissions in the articles, such as failing to provide the registered agent's address, are irrelevant once the articles are accepted by the state.[86]

This means that today the only real problem of defective incorporation will be that the articles did not get filed. For example, suppose the proprietors send the articles to the secretary of state's office and assume they were filed. The office rejected the document, however, because it did not comply with law. In the interim, the proprietors incur a debt on behalf of the business. A more common example is that someone (usually the lawyer for the business) assures the pro-

---

[84] *See, e.g.,* RMBCA § 2.03(a).

[85] *See, e.g.,* RMBCA § 2.03(b).

[86] This is a helpful doctrine. In earlier times, errors in the articles might provide a basis for attacking *de jure* corporate status. For example, in *People v. Ford,* 128 N.E. 479, 481 (Ill. 1920), the state challenged the legal status of a corporation because the proprietors had failed to affix a seal to their signatures in the articles. The court distinguished between "mandatory" provisions, satisfaction of which are conditions precedent to forming a corporation, and "directory" provisions, failure of which did not threaten the corporation's legal status. It concluded that failure to affix a seal was merely directory. Today, if the articles were accepted for filing, there is a *de jure* corporation.

prietors that the articles will be delivered and filed. That person then fails to follow through. The proprietors, unaware of this failure, operate as though a corporation has been properly formed. Are they personally liable for the debts incurred by the business?

Our knee-jerk reaction is "yes." No *de jure* corporation was formed, so there is no entity to absorb the liability. But let's consider the issue in more depth. In many states today, the issue is addressed by statute. For example, RMBCA § 2.04 provides: "all persons purporting to act as or on behalf of a corporation, knowing there was no incorporation under this Act, are jointly and severally liable for all liabilities created while so acting." This language raises two major questions. First, note that it imposes liability only on those who acted "knowing there was no incorporation." In many cases, however, the proprietors will not be aware of the failure to form a *de jure* corporation (as, for example, when their lawyer failed to deliver the documents to the secretary of state). By implication, such people might not be liable for the business acts. Indeed, this argument underlies the defense of "de facto corporation." Second, the statute applies to "all persons purporting to act" for the corporation. What does that mean? One court, applying an earlier version of the statute, concluded that all managers—not just the one involved in the transaction at issue—would be personally liable.[87]

In a good many states, including Delaware, however, there is no statutory provision such as RMBCA § 2.04. One possibility in such states is to view the issue as a matter of agency law.[88] Because no corporation was formed, the person purporting to act for the business acted on behalf of a nonexistent principal and therefore must be liable. Another possibility is to consider the form of business actually created. If the defectively incorporated business has one owner, it is a sole proprietorship. If it has more than one owner, it is a partnership. Neither of those business structures requires filing with the state; each is formed by conduct. And in each, the sole proprietor and the partners are personally liable for business debts in contract and tort. Thus, failure to achieve *de jure* corporate status leaves the proprietors on the hook for personal liability because of the business structure she or they actually created.[89]

---

[87] Timberline Equipment Co. v. Davenport, 514 P.2d 1109, 1114 (Or. 1973). In dictum, the court opined that merely passive investors, who undertook no role in management, would not be liable. *Id.* at 1114.

[88] *See generally* Comment, *An Empirical Study of Defective Incorporation*, 39 EMORY L.J. 523 (1990) (discussing common law treatment of liability in defective incorporation cases).

[89] There may be a question about who should be liable as a partner in the defectively incorporated business. *See, e.g.,* State ex rel. Carlton v. Triplett, 517 P.2d 136,

2. Defenses to Personal Liability: De Facto Corporation and Corporation by Estoppel

Here we assume that the proprietors failed to form a *de jure* corporation, that they are unaware of that failure, and that they are operating the business as though a corporation had been formed. As we just saw, failure to form a *de jure* corporation leads to the starting point that these proprietors will be liable for debts incurred by the business. They may be able to avoid liability, however, by availing themselves of either of two common law doctrines: de facto corporation and corporation by estoppel.

When de facto corporation is invoked, the business is treated as a corporation for all purposes. This means, of course, that the individual proprietors will not be held personally liable. The doctrine applies in all cases, including in tort or contract. The only minor exception to this is that the state may be able to sue it to challenge its capacity to act.[90] In other words, if the doctrine applies, the failure to achieve *de jure* status is ignored, and the proprietors enjoy limited liability in litigation between private parties. As we will see, courts do this because the proprietors came "close enough" to forming a *de jure* corporation that they should escape personal liability. Corporation by estoppel, in contrast, generally applies only in contract cases, and is aimed at avoiding the unfairness of letting someone switch positions about whether a corporation was formed. Both are equitable doctrines, so may be invoked only by those acting in good faith. Principally, this means they must be unaware of the failure to form a *de jure* corporation.

Courts routinely state that there are three requirements for invocation of de facto corporation.[91] Two of these will rarely pose any problem. First, there must be a statute under which incorporation would have been permitted. This requirement is automatically satisfied because every state has such a statute. Second, there must be "an exercise of corporate powers," which simply means that the proprietors are acting as though a corporation existed. This will always be met because the people running the show thought they formed a corporation, and will be acting on behalf of that business.

---

140 (Kan. 1973) ("In those cases imposing liability, if active participation was not present there was at least some stake in the enterprise on the part of those charged.")

[90] Such a case is called *quo warranto,* and asks "by what warrant" these proprietors purport to act. *People v. Ford,* note 86, was a *quo warranto* case.

[91] *See, e.g.,* Matter of Hausman, 13 N.Y.3d 408, 412 (N.Y. 2009) (stating the familiar three requirements to invoke the doctrine in the context of a limited liability company).

The remaining requirement will be the focus for establishing de facto corporation: that the proprietors made a good faith, colorable attempt to form the corporation. This means not only that they are unaware of the failure to form a *de jure* entity, but that they came very close to forming one. A classic example is this: the proprietors execute proper articles and issue a check for the filing fee, but their lawyer, after saying she would file these with the state, fails to do so. Now the business enters a contract or commits a tort or incurs a debt. The co-owners of the business will be personally liable unless they can convince the court to employ de facto corporation. Their argument for de facto corporation is strong on these facts; they did everything we might reasonably expect them to do. Having them avoid personal liability here seems fair. Otherwise, the error of one person would impose liability on people who innocently invested in what they thought was a corporation. Stated another way, allowing the creditors to recover from the individual proprietors seems unfair. They bargained for a deal with the business, and not to look to individual assets for their claim.

When a court refuses to apply de facto corporation, it must then determine which of the proprietors is liable. Multiple proprietors in this situation will have formed a partnership, and will thus face liability as partners. That does not necessarily include everyone with an ownership stake. Rather, courts look to active participation in the business, and hold that those who actually call the shots in the business will bear the liability.[92]

Corporation by estoppel, like de facto corporation, is relevant when there is no de jure corporation, and is available only to those who act in the good faith belief that a corporation had been formed. And, like de facto corporation, this doctrine will save one from personal liability that would otherwise be imposed because the business as operated is a general partnership (or sole proprietorship). But, as noted above, corporation by estoppel is narrower than de facto corporation, as it generally is said to apply only in contract (not tort) cases.

The name of this doctrine is not helpful. Technically, the doctrine has nothing to do with true estoppel, which requires (1) a false representation of a fact to (or concealment from) a person ignorant of the truth, (2) the intention to cause reliance, and (3) actual reliance by the innocent party. Instead, here is the classic scenario for corporation by estoppel: a third party deals with what she believes to be a corporation, relying on its assets and credit; when she does not get paid, she investigates and discovers that no filing had ever been

---

[92] Minich v. Gem State Dev., 591 P.2d 1078, 1081 (Ida. 1979) (liability for those who "actively participate in the corporate affairs").

made, so no corporation existed; she then sues the individual proprietors, arguing that they are personally liable. The defendants, who also were unaware that no filing had been made, may be able to assert that the plaintiff is "estopped" from holding them personally liable, because she treated the business as a corporation and relied upon "corporate" assets and credit.

This is certainly not estoppel in the classic sense because the person who is being "estopped" (the third party) never made a representation that was relied on by anybody. Rather, the person who relied is the one being estopped. Despite the poor label, the doctrine is fundamentally fair. If the plaintiff were permitted to recover from the personal assets of the proprietors, she would be getting a windfall. After all, she dealt only with the "corporation." The plaintiff could have insisted on looking at the books to assess the state of the corporation's financial health. If the financial picture was shaky, she could then have refused to enter the deal or could have insisted on a personal guarantee of the deal by the individual proprietors. She did neither, and thus should be stuck with recovering only from corporate assets.

Some have argued that the doctrine should be applied even if the defendants knew that the corporation had not been formed. After all, reliance by the plaintiff is unaffected by this fact. Recognizing "corporation by estoppel" in such a case, though, might encourage proprietors to save the filing fee and not file articles at all, simply conducting business in the corporate name. Accordingly, corporation by estoppel seems generally to apply when the plaintiff dealt with the "corporation" as such, and the defendants legitimately believed that the corporation had been formed.

Though corporation by estoppel is often used to avoid the imposition of individual liability on proprietors, it can arise in other contexts. For instance, courts have refused to let a corporation defendant avoid the imposition of liability by a plaintiff that was not incorporated at the time it entered a contract. In *Brown v. W.P. Media, Inc.*,[93] Plaintiff and Defendant entered a contract in which each was asserted to be a corporation. It turns out that Plaintiff had not completed incorporation at the time (something its proprietors knew). Later, after Plaintiff was incorporated and Defendant allegedly breached the contract, Plaintiff sued. Defendant asserted that Plaintiff lacked capacity to sue because it was not a properly formed corpo-

---

[93] 17 So.3d 1167 (Ala. 2009).

ration at the time the deal was entered. The Alabama Supreme Court applied corporation by estoppel to permit Plaintiff to proceed.[94]

Another example of the doctrine fits the classic definition of estoppel nicely: proprietors who held out their business as a corporation cannot later avoid corporate contractual liability by asserting that the company was not formed when the deal was entered. A well-known example is *Southern-Gulf Marine Co. No. 9, Inc. v. Camcraft, Inc.* There, what everyone thought was a corporation entered a contract to sell a yacht. Later (after the yacht became more valuable than the contract price), the proprietors of the seller tried to avoid the contract by noting that the corporation had not been formed at the time of the deal. Accordingly, they argued, the now-formed corporation was not a party to the contract. The court employed corporation by estoppel to prevent the seller from denying corporate status.[95] The seller had represented to the world that it was a corporation, and would not be allowed to switch positions for litigation gain.

Both de facto corporation and corporation by estoppel are creatures of common law. An important question is how, if at all, modern statutes affect them. Many states now have statutes setting forth a conclusive presumption of *de jure* formation when the articles are accepted for filing.[96] Those statutes narrow the role of de facto corporation. Courts in those states need not worry about where to draw the line about "how much" compliance with the formation statute is "enough" to qualify as a de facto corporation.[97] If the articles were filed, there is a de jure corporation. So de facto corporation today is limited to cases in which the articles were not filed.

But there is an argument that these statutes—at least by negative implication—abolish de facto corporation. Specifically, because the codes provide that a corporation exists when the articles are filed, they (arguably) imply that no corporation can exist without the state's filing of the articles. Indeed, the comments to the 1969 version of the MBCA expressly state that "a de facto corporation cannot exist under the Model Act."[98] The problem is that no provision of the Act itself expressly said so. Not only that, but even the comments were silent on whether corporation by estoppel should be recognized.

---

[94] *Id.* at 1171 ("[A]t no time during the venture did [Defendant] challenge the validity of the operating agreement [on the ground that it was entered by a nonexistent corporation] until after it was sued for breaching the operating agreement.")

[95] 410 So.2d 1181, 1183–84 (La. Ct. App. 1982).

[96] Not all states have such a statutory presumption. Delaware, for example, does not.

[97] Under older statutes, courts had to decide which formation requirements were "mandatory" and which were merely "directory." *See* note 86.

[98] *See* Comment to § 56 the MBCA (1969).

There is some authority that such statutes have obviated both doctrines. The leading case is *Robertson v. Levy*. There, the defendant "corporation" became obligated under a contract during a two-week delay in forming the corporation (the relevant authority had rejected the articles, which were then fixed and filed). When the corporation then defaulted, the plaintiff sued individual proprietors of the defendant entity. The proprietors sought to apply corporation by estoppel. The court, applying the District of Columbia's version of the MBCA, held that the common law defenses had been abolished.[99]

The matter may be more complicated today. Earlier versions of the Model Act, including that applied in *Robertson v. Levy*, included a section providing for liability of individuals acting on behalf of a corporation not yet formed.[100] Today, under the RMBCA, the statute has been changed in a significant way. Now, as we saw above, it provides: "all persons purporting to act as or on behalf of a corporation, *knowing there was no incorporation under this Act*, are jointly and severally liable for all liabilities created while so acting."[101] This statement—that proprietors who were not aware of the failure to form a de jure corporation will not be liable—may embody the doctrines of de facto corporation and corporation by estoppel.[102] On the other hand, perhaps it creates a new statutory defense in lieu of the common law doctrines. The latter possibility is significant because it might extend corporation by estoppel to tort cases.[103]

At the end of the day, it is difficult to state a blanket rule about the effect of modern statutes on de facto corporation and corporation by estoppel. Suffice it to say that states may approach the topics in different ways, and that lawyers should be aware of case law developments in their states.

---

[99] 197 A.2d 443, 447 (D.C. Ct. App. 1964).

[100] *See* § 146 the MBCA (1969) ("[a]ll persons who assume to act as a corporation without authority so to do shall be jointly and severally liable for all debts and liabilities incurred or arising as a result thereof.")

[101] RMBCA § 2.04 (emphasis added).

[102] The Official Comment to RMBCA § 2.04 notes situations "in which the protection of limited liability arguably should be recognized even though the simple incorporation process established by modern statutes has not been completed." It goes on to discuss five scenarios which would qualify under common law for protection either under de facto corporation or corporation by estoppel. *See, e.g.,* First Cmty. Bank, N.A. v. Youth Ctr., 81 Va. Cir. 416, 421 (2010) ("In light of Virginia's adoption of the 1984 [Revised] Model Business Corporation Act, the Court finds that case law in effect prior to the 1950 Model Business Corporation Act which applied the doctrine of corporation by estoppel is still good law.").

[103] *See* FRANKLIN A. GEVURTZ, CORPORATION LAW 67 (2d ed. 2010) ("unlike estoppel, this new knowledge element can protect participants from liability to torts claimants").

In theory, when the doctrines are recognized, de facto corporation and corporation by estoppel have been considered alternative bases for recognizing corporate status. The first relates to the extent to which incorporators complied with the incorporation statute, and the second relates to the extent the parties have dealt with the business as a corporation.[104] In fact, however, modern scholarship suggests that the two scenarios are not mutually exclusive, and that recognition of corporate status on the facts of a given case may involve factors from both de facto corporation and corporation by estoppel.[105]

---

[104] *Brown v. W.P. Media, Inc.,* note 40, suggests that the two are hermetically separate. 17 So.3d at 1170 ("[A]lthough [Plaintiff] might not have existed as either a de jure corporation or a de facto corporation, [it] contends that [Defendant] is nevertheless estopped from denying [Plaintiff's] corporate existence. We agree.").

[105] *See, e.g.,* Fred McChesney, *Doctrinal Analysis and the Statistical Modeling in Law: The Case of Defective Incorporation,* 71 WASH. U.L.Q. 493, 530–531 (1993) ("[C]ourts will more likely accord defendants limited liability when they have tried to comply and plaintiffs have treated the firm as a corporation. . . . Evaluated by what they do, not by what they say, judges apply one unitary doctrine—that of defective incorporation. . . . The apparent confusion shown by many judges in distinguishing the two doctrines reflects the fact that they are really not two doctrines at all.")

Chapter 6

DISTRIBUTION OF POWERS IN THE CORPORATION

Analysis

A. Introduction
B. The Traditional Model
    1. Introduction
    2. Overview of the Role of the Shareholders
    3. Overview of the Role of the Board of Directors
    4. Overview of the Role of Officers
    5. The Spectrum From "Closely Held" to "Publicly Held" Corporations: Tension Between the Traditional Model and the Real World
C. Shareholders
    1. Introduction
    2. Concept of the Record Owner and the Record Date
    3. Shareholders Act as a Group in One of Two Ways
    4. Shareholder Meetings: Notice, Quorum, and Voting
    5. Cumulative Voting
    6. Voting by Proxy
    7. Methods for Combining Voting Power
    8. Inspection of Corporate Records
D. Board of Directors
    1. Introduction
    2. Statutory Requirements
    3. The Board Must Act as a Group in One of Two Ways
    4. Board Meetings: Notice, Quorum, Voting
    5. Compensation
    6. Committees of the Board
E. Officers
    1. Introduction
    2. Statutory Requirements
    3. Sources of Authority
    4. Application of Agency Law
    5. Selection and Removal of Officers
    6. Fiduciary Duties Owed by Officers

A. Introduction

In this Chapter, we address the question of who does what in a corporation. Corporation statutes ascribe roles to the three constituents of the corporation: the shareholders, the board of directors, and the officers. This legislation varies at the margins, but is remarkably similar from state to state. In particular, statutes generally reflect a single model that lays out the responsibilities and duties of each group. In other words, they seem based on the assumption that "one size fits all"—that every corporation will fit the statutory model. We will call this the "traditional model."

In the real world, however, corporations distribute authority in different ways. The main distinction is between closely held and publicly held corporations, although, as we will see, many corporations falls somewhere in the middle and defy classification as either. There is some tension between the traditional model and the way closely held and publicly held corporations actually do things. We cannot appreciate that tension, however, until we understand the statutory norm.

In section B of this Chapter, we lay out that norm, including broad overviews of the roles it prescribes for shareholders, the board of directors, and officers. We then note the tension between this model and many corporations as operated in the real world. This will require us to define "close," "closely held," "statutory close," and "publicly held" corporations. We will leave detailed discussion of how the traditional model is modified in closely held and publicly held corporations to Chapters 8 and 9. The bulk of this Chapter (sections C, D, and E) consists of a detailed discussion of the nuts and bolts of how the three groups of players do what they do.

B. The Traditional Model

1. Introduction

Under the traditional model, shareholders own the corporation but do not engage in management. They elect (and can remove) the members of the board of directors, which "manages" the corporation. Thus, shareholders elect and in theory monitor the managers. The board of directors makes the policy decisions for the business. It also selects and monitors officers, whose role is to implement the board's policy choices.

The shareholders and the board of directors can act only as groups. Individual shareholders have no power to make the corporation do anything. Individual directors likewise have no power to make decisions or to bind the corporation. The law in each state imposes strict requirements on how each body can take an act. These include mechanical rules about establishing a quorum and voting at meetings. Implicit in such requirements for group action is the assumption that there will be multiple shareholders and directors. In reality, however, there are many corporations with one shareholder and one director (usually the same person).

Officers do not operate in groups. Individual officers—like the president, secretary, and treasurer—are agents of the corporation. Agency law, discussed in Chapter 2, governs the relationship between the principal (the corporation) and the agent (the officer). Stated another way, the question of whether an officer's act binds the corporation is determined by whether she had agency authority to do so.

It is important to appreciate that one person can serve in more than one capacity simultaneously. Thus, one person might be a shareholder, a director, and an officer at the same time. When a person wears more than one hat, do not confuse her roles. When she acts as a director, the traditional norm requires that she satisfy the rules applicable to directors (section D of this Chapter). And when she acts as a shareholder, the model requires adherence to the rules applicable to that role (section C of this Chapter).

2. Overview of the Role of the Shareholders

The shareholders in the statutory norm are the ultimate owners of the corporation, but have only indirect power to affect management. One of the advantages of the corporation is separation of ownership from control. Thus, those who own the business need not be burdened with management responsibilities; they can be passive investors. The traditional model contemplates that shareholders have some decision making authority, but only in discrete areas.

Electing and removing directors. Shareholders elect directors and can remove them before their terms expire. So although shareholders do not make management decisions, they hire those who do. At common law, a director could be removed only "for cause"[1] and only through an intricate procedure known as "amotion."[2] The fact that shareholders could not remove directors "without cause" was consistent with the principle that directors were elected for their independence and that shareholders should not interfere with their discretionary business judgments.

---

[1] Usually, the cause is the director's breach of one of her fiduciary duties, which we discuss in Chapter 7.

[2] "Where stockholders under their traditional common law power have removed a director before the expiration of his term on the basis that he has been guilty of misconduct, such a procedure is reviewable in court. Upon the other hand, the court lacks power at the instance of a stockholder to compel the stockholders to do what they would have had power to do, but have not done, in the exercise of this traditional common law right to remove a director by 'amotion.'" Burkin v. Katz, 136 N.E.2d 862, 865 (N.Y. 1956).

Today, every state allows shareholders to remove directors for cause (such as nonfeasance or misfeasance), and most states allow removal without cause. Typical of the modern view is RMBCA § 8.08(a), which provides that "[t]he shareholders may remove one or more directors with or without cause unless the articles . . . provide that directors may be removed only for cause." Some states (including New York) permit removal without cause only if the articles (which New York calls the "certificate") allow.[3] We discuss election and removal of directors at sections C(4) and (5).

Modern statutes allowing removal without cause fundamentally change the historic relation between shareholders and directors. It is now possible to remove a director for policy or personal reasons. This power may be important when someone acquires a majority of the stock (or at least working control) and wants to put "her people" on the board. To avoid such threats, some corporate articles provide that directors can be removed only for cause. This obviously enhances directors' security, and makes it difficult for new ownership to obtain immediate control over the board.

Amending bylaws. In most states, the initial bylaws are adopted by the board of directors or by the incorporators, whichever group completes the organization of the corporation.[4] Thereafter, states vary on who has the power to amend or repeal bylaws. In some states, the shareholders have the authority,[5] and in some the board does.[6] In still other states, either group may amend the bylaws.[7] Sometimes, statutes provide that the board may not repeal or amend bylaws adopted by shareholders.[8] Under the RMBCA, the shareholders have the power to amend or repeal bylaws,[9] as does the board unless a statutory exception applies.[10] One exception is if the shareholders, in adopting a bylaw, expressly provide that the board may not change it.[11]

Approving fundamental corporate changes. Shareholders generally must approve certain fundamental changes to the corporation. These changes—consisting of amendment of the articles, mergers, disposition of substantially all corporate assets, share exchanges, and

---

[3] N.Y. Bus. Corp. Law § 716(a).

[4] *See* Chapter 5(C).

[5] Del. Gen. Corp. Law § 109(a).

[6] N.D. Cent. Code § 10–19.1–31(2); Minn. Stat. § 302A.181 subd. 2.

[7] Iowa Code § 490.1020; N.C. Gen. Stat. § 55–10–20.

[8] Miss. Code § 79–4–10.20(b)(2).

[9] RMBCA § 10.20(a).

[10] RMBCA § 10.20(b).

[11] RMBCA § 10.20(b)(2).

voluntary dissolution—are so important that the board cannot do them alone. The shareholders' role here generally is reactive. In other words, the shareholders only get a voice because the statutes require shareholder approval of fundamental changes the board decides to pursue. In general, then, the shareholders do not initiate fundamental corporate changes.

Approval of other matters. From time to time, the board of directors may ask for shareholder feedback on matters by requesting a shareholder vote. More importantly, the corporation statutes provide other situations in which a shareholder vote is required. A good example is the interested director transaction—that is, a deal between the corporation and one of its directors. Sometimes, shareholders vote on whether such deals should be validated despite a director's conflict of interest.[12] The modern trend has been to reduce the number of matters on which shareholder approval is required.

Independent of statute, shareholders may make recommendations to the board on various matters. While these have no legal effect, such resolutions express the views of the ultimate owners of the corporation, and therefore may be influential. In *Auer v. Dressel,*[13] the New York Court of Appeals upheld the practice. In that case, shareholders adopted a resolution that voiced approval of an ousted president and demanded his reinstatement. The court said there was "nothing invalid in their so expressing themselves and thus putting on notice the directors who will stand for election at the annual meeting."[14]

Other powers. What we have listed so far are shareholders' powers over decision-making in the corporation. Shareholders have other powers by statute, but they do not relate directly to decision-making or decision-makers. Two are especially significant: the right to inspect books and records of the corporation (section (C)(8) of this Chapter) and the right to bring "derivative suits." These are suits brought to vindicate a corporate claim (and usually consist of a claim that directors or officers have breached a fiduciary duty owed to the business). We discuss this special litigation in Chapter 13.

3. Overview of the Role of the Board of Directors

Corporation statutes have always vested management power in the board of directors. The traditional model envisions that the board

---

[12] *See* Chapter 7(E)(3), where we also note that in some states shareholders may be asked to approve loans of corporate funds to directors.

[13] 118 N.E.2d 590, 597–98 (N.Y. 1954).

[14] *Id.* at 593.

sets policy, manages the affairs of the corporation, selects officers to carry out its directions, and monitors the officers' performance. In recent decades, however, there has been an interesting shift in the language of such statutes. Traditionally, statutes required that the business and affairs of the corporation "shall be managed" by the board. Now, legislation is usually broader, and provides that the business and affairs of the corporation "be exercised by *or under the direction, and subject to the oversight*" of the board.[15]

The italicized language recognizes business reality in large corporations: the board of directors does not "manage" the day-to-day affairs. Its role is more oversight than management. The modern statutes authorize corporations to vest actual management authority in the executive officers, with the board monitoring them. In smaller businesses, the board usually formulates corporate policy and authorizes important contracts. Even in such a company, however, the board may delegate details of daily operation to officers and agents.

The power vested in the board of directors flows from legislation. It is not delegated from the shareholders. As a result, directors may disregard the desires of shareholders and act as they think best. This freedom, however, is subject to the shareholders' ultimate power to remove directors or to elect different directors next time. In addition to the general power to manage and oversee, directors have specific statutory authority in several areas. These include the decisions of when to issue stock[16] and when to declare a distribution.[17] Moreover, with fundamental corporate changes, the shareholders have a voice, but usually only after the board has formulated and approved the proposed change.

Directorial power brings with it directorial responsibility. The directors owe fiduciary duties of care and loyalty to the corporation. Chapter 7 discusses these duties in detail. Violation of a duty not only constitutes cause for removal, but can expose directors to civil liability to the corporation. In addition, there are potential criminal sanctions for violating some laws, notably the federal Rule 10b–5 concerning trading of securities, as seen in Chapter 11(C).

4. Overview of the Role of Officers

Corporation statutes generally do not attempt to define either the authority or role of officers. A typical statutory provision merely

---

[15] RMBCA § 8.01(b) (emphasis added). *See also* DEL. GEN. CORP. LAW § 141(a)(business and affairs "shall be managed by or under the direction" of the board).

[16] RMBCA § 6.21(b).

[17] RMBCA § 6.40(a).

states that each officer "has the authority and shall perform the functions set forth in the bylaws or, to the extent consistent with the bylaws, the functions prescribed by the board of directors or by direction of an officer authorized by the board of directors to prescribe the duties of other officers."[18] In theory, officers administer the day-to-day affairs of the corporation subject to the direction and control of the board. In fact, their authority is often considerably greater, particularly in large publicly held corporations.

As noted, officers do not operate in groups, but are agents of the corporation. Thus, an individual officer can bind the corporation if she has agency authority to do so. Corporation statutes and common law are quite clear, however, on one point: in discharging their responsibilities, officers owe to the corporation the same fiduciary duties as directors.[19]

5. The Spectrum From "Closely Held" to "Publicly Held" Corporations: Tension Between the Traditional Model and the Real World

The statutory model implies that there is one way to operate a corporation. In fact, corporations come in all sizes and the model can be adapted. In most discussions of corporations, there is a basic bifurcation between "closely held" and "publicly held" corporations.

A "closely held corporation" is also known simply as a "close corporation." Though the definition is a matter of some debate, the classic statement is that these entities have three[20] characteristics: (1) there are few shareholders,[21] (2) there is no active market for the company's stock,[22] and (3) there is substantial stockholder participation in management.[23] In other words, those who own the corporation, those who run it, and those who are employed by it are the same few people.[24]

---

[18] RMBCA § 8.41.

[19] RMBCA § 8.42(a).

[20] Donahue v. Rodd Electrotype Co., 328 N.E.2d 505, 511 (Mass. 1975).

[21] There is no magic number. No matter what number we might arbitrarily choose as the maximum, we could undoubtedly find close corporations with one shareholder more.

[22] F. HODGE O'NEAL & ROBERT B. THOMPSON, O'NEAL'S CLOSE CORPORATIONS § 1.02, at 1–4 to 1–7 (3d ed. 2002)(noting possible definitions, including the characteristics noted above).

[23] See Robert B. Thompson, *The Shareholder's Cause of Action for Oppression,* 48 BUS. LAW. 699, 702 (1993) (noting that, in a closely held corporation, "a more intimate and intense relationship exists between capital and labor").

[24] Often, they are friends or family members who form the business and expect to be employed by it.

Functionally, because the owners are the managers, the close corporation looks a lot like a partnership. Indeed, some courts refer to the close corporation as a "chartered" or "incorporated" partnership.[25] But instead of the flexible management provisions available under partnership law, proprietors of a close corporation historically had to toe the line of the traditional model. There had to be board meetings, with notice, quorum, and voting requirements. And there had to be shareholder meetings, with different notice, quorum, and voting requirements. In a corporation consisting of a handful of friends or family members, this elevation of form over substance was silly.

Moreover, the traditional model imposes rigid lines of demarcation between things the board can do and things shareholders can do. For example, we will see in section (D)(3) that directors cannot enter into voting agreements that will bind how they will vote on the board. The law places great importance on directorial independence. Voting agreements among directors violate this public policy. In contrast, shareholders can enter into voting agreements that require them to vote their shares in a particular way. Commonly, these agreements involve voting to elect particular people (often each other) to the board of directors. Under the traditional model, proprietors of a close corporation can encounter problems if they are not assiduous in keeping their roles separate.[26]

- A and B, who are shareholders of Close Corporation, enter into a voting agreement which requires them to vote their shares in an effort to elect each other to the board of directors. So far, so good, because shareholders can agree on how they will vote their shares. As part of the agreement, A and B also say that once they are on the board of directors, they will vote to elect each other as officers. This aspect of their agreement is void under the traditional view because directors cannot enter binding agreements on how they will vote on the board.[27]

---

[25] See, e.g., Meiselman v. Meiselman, 307 S.E.2d 551, 557 (N.C. 1983) ("commentators all appear to agree that close corporations are often little more than incorporated partnerships") (citation omitted); Hartung v. Architects Hartung/Odle/Burke, Inc., 301 N.E.2d 240, 243 (Ind. Ct. App. 1973) ("In addition, the shareholders in a close corporation, also referred to as an 'incorporated partnership,' stand in a fiduciary relationship to each other"); Donahue, 328 N.E.2d at 514 ("incorporated partnership").

[26] Indeed, failing to keep the roles of shareholders and directors separate may open the door to an argument that shareholders should be liable for business debts under the doctrine of "piercing the corporate veil." See Chapter 8(E).

[27] The classic statement of this principle is found in McQuade v. Stoneham, 189 N.E. 234 (N.Y. 1934).

Such formality makes little sense in the close corporation. The proprietors quite rightly think of themselves as owners and managers at the same time. The traditional model, though, does not permit them to meld these roles; it sees the board and the shareholders as groups that act separately, each under its own rules.

In Chapter 8(D), we will see that the law has changed dramatically in this regard. By common law and later through legislation, the strict requirements of the traditional model may be avoided in the close corporation. The result is that the proprietors have virtually as much flexibility in setting up management as they do in a partnership.[28]

In contrast to the close corporation, a "publicly traded" or "public" corporation is one with a sufficiently large number of shareholders—thousands or even scores of thousands—that its stock is traded on an active public market. The existence of that market means that investors can buy or sell shares at will. So a disgruntled shareholder (or one who simply wants to "cash out") can always get out. She may not like the price, but there is a public market and therefore an exit.[29] In terms of numbers, there are probably about 15,000 public corporations and over 4,000,000 close corporations.

Today's public corporation puts its own pressure on the traditional model. The shareholders in a public corporation are so diverse and poorly organized that they do not "elect" directors in a meaningful way. Rather, they ratify selections made by people who control the day-to-day operations. Further, a public corporation's board does not "manage" the business. That job falls to professional managers who usually own a very small fraction (if any) of the company's stock. The board selects the chief executive officer, oversees management, establishes compensation levels, approves major transactions, and perhaps plays an advisory role. We will discuss management and other issues raised by public corporations in Chapter 9.

---

[28] A "statutory close corporation" is one formed under special legislation, found in about half the states, that permits proprietors to select that express status. Such statutes require that the company's stock not be publicly traded and often impose a maximum number of shareholders (usually 30 or 50). As we will see in Chapter 8(B), statutory close corporations are relatively rare. Indeed, such statutes, which were passed to permit flexibility in managing small companies, are to some degree superfluous because all states now provide for such flexibility even in corporations formed under the general corporate statutes.

[29] "In the typical public corporation, the minority shareholders can escape . . . abuses of power by simply selling their shares in the market. This market exit, however, is not available to the close corporation minority shareholder because, by definition, there is no ready market for the stock of a close corporation." Douglas K. Moll, *Shareholder Oppression v. Employment at Will in the Close Corporation: The Investment Model Solution*, 1999 U. ILL. L. REV. 517, 525.

The bifurcation between close and public corporations is artificial. In fact, there is a continuum from closely held companies with one shareholder at one end to public held companies with scores of thousands of shareholders at the other. Characterizing companies at the extremes brings to mind Justice Stewart's famous definition of pornography: "I know it when I see it."[30] Most close corporations are obviously closely held and most public corporations are obviously publicly held.

There are many companies, however, somewhere in between. Typically, they have a hundred or so shareholders and there is at least some limited trading of their stock. A reporting service—called the "pink sheets"—lists these stocks. The stocks are traded "over the counter," which means that one buys directly from the seller or sells directly to the buyer. Unlike public trading, there is no exchange that provides facilities for the transaction.[31]

In the real world, medium sized corporations may most accurately embody the traditional model. Shareholders, because they are not widely dispersed, meaningfully elect directors and the board clearly engages in management. Nonetheless, the statutory norm is the starting point and the focus of this Chapter. This will enable us to appreciate the adjustments to the model made in many small and large corporations, which we address in Chapters 8 and 9. We turn now to the roles of shareholders, directors, and officers under the traditional model.

C. Shareholders

1. Introduction

What do shareholders do? Above, we saw that shareholders are the owners (but not the managers) of the corporation. They elect directors, can remove directors before their terms expire, usually can amend bylaws, and must decide whether to approve fundamental corporate changes. In addition, they sometimes vote on interested director transactions and on other matters referred to them by the board of directors. Here, we address how the shareholders' voice is heard, which involves technical rules about voting. We also discuss other things shareholders might do, such as receive a dividend or other distribution and inspect books and records of the corporation.[32]

---

[30] Jacobellis v. State of Ohio, 378 U.S. 184, 197 (1964) (Stewart, J. concurring).

[31] We discuss stock exchanges in Chapter 9(B).

[32] The shareholder's right to file derivative litigation is so important that it warrants separate discussion. *See* Chapter 13.

2. Concepts of the Record Owner and the Record Date

To be eligible to vote (or to receive a distribution),[33] a shareholder must be a record owner as of the record date. Every corporation keeps a record—called the "stock transfer book" or the "share register"—of those to whom it has issued stock. Traditionally, when a record owner transferred her stock to someone else, she would endorse the stock certificate and deliver it to the transferee. The transferee would then submit the endorsed certificate to the corporation and request that it issue a new certificate in her name. The corporation would do so and cancel the old certificate. If this procedure is not followed, the transferee does not become a record owner. Instead, she is the "beneficial owner" of those shares. A corporation deals only with the record owner, and will not recognize the beneficial owner. The beneficial owner has enough of an interest, however, to sue the record owner to compel her to transfer the stock.

This cumbersome process is still followed in many small corporations. Today, however, states permit the corporation to issue "certificateless" shares.[34] With these, the corporation keeps records of share ownership and provides new owners with a written statement of the information that otherwise would be included on stock certificates.[35]

Regardless of whether it uses certificates, the corporation must ensure that transfers are properly recorded. This presents enormous problems for publicly traded corporations, in which millions of shares may be traded each week. Large companies employ "transfer agents" to perform these functions. Transfer agents are usually independent businesses that perform these duties under a contract with the corporation. Publicly held corporations also use "registrars," who ensure that the corporation does not inadvertently issue more stock than is authorized. In small corporations, the secretary performs the functions of the transfer agent and registrar.

As the volume of securities transactions in public corporations increased in the 1960s, clerical staffs of brokerage firms were unable to keep up. They found themselves awash in stock certificates of uncertain ownership. This resulted in the "book entry" or "street name registration" system in use today. Under this system, stock certifi-

---

[33] As we discuss in Chapter 10(E), distributions are payments by the corporation to shareholders. The classic example is the dividend, which is a distribution of profits to the shareholders. To receive the dividend, one must own stock on the record date—that is, the date the board declares the dividend.

[34] See, e.g., RMBCA § 6.26 ("Shares Without Certificates").

[35] See, e.g., RMBCA § 6.25(b) (listing required contents of stock certificates).

cates are largely irrelevant. Stock ownership is recorded in the records of brokerage firms and not in the share transfer books of the corporations. Most stock certificates are permanently stored in vaults at the Depository Trust Company (DTC) and other clearing offices. Most of these shares are in the name of "Cede & Co.," which is the registered owner of more than 70 percent of all shares traded on the major stock exchanges. DTC maintains accounts for securities owned by hundreds of brokerage firms while the firms maintain accounts for individual customers. Transfers of securities are recorded in the records of the brokers representing the buyer and seller.

The book entry system involves two sets of intermediaries between the corporation and the owner of the stock. The system is efficient not only for trading, but also for the distribution of dividends, which are transferred electronically from the issuer to brokerage firms on the day the dividend is payable. They can then be deposited into the accounts of customers on the same day. With further developments in computerization, the SEC has authorized a variation of a book entry system that permits direct book entries of ownership in the records of the corporation. These shares are certificateless, but readily transferable by the owner.

As noted, to vote or to receive a declared distribution, one must be the record owner as of the record date. The record date is an arbitrary cut off, set as an administrative convenience.

- Corporation sets its annual shareholder meeting for May 30 and establishes a record date of May 10. S is the record owner of the stock on May 10, and on May 11 sells the stock to B. At the meeting on May 30, S has the right to vote the sold shares. Even though she no longer owns the stock on the date of the meeting, she was the record owner on the record date.[36]

Usually, the board of directors sets the record dates for the various events (although, instead, record dates can be set in the bylaws). Statutes set time limits on when the record date may be set. RMBCA § 7.07 is typical, and provides that the record date may not be more than 70 days before the meeting.[37] This interim period allows the corporation to give proper notice of the meeting, to prepare a voting list, and to establish who is entitled to vote. It also permits management and other shareholders to solicit votes informally before the

---

[36] The same would be true for a dividend declared on May 10 but not paid until May 30—S will get the dividend.

[37] The requirements vary somewhat from state to state. See, e.g., N.Y. BUS. CORP. LAW § 604 (record date no fewer than 10 and no more than 60 days before the meeting).

meeting.[38] If the board of directors does not formally set a record date, the corporation is deemed to set a record date as of the date the notice of the meeting is mailed, and eligibility to vote is determined as of that date.[39]

3. Shareholders Act as a Group in One of Two Ways

An individual shareholder has no power to do anything on behalf of the corporation[40] or to take any act entrusted to the shareholders. In other words, the shareholders must act as a group. Whatever act the shareholders wish to take—whether it is electing directors, amending bylaws, or approving a fundamental corporate change—must be the result of consolidated effort. In almost every case, this means that the shareholders act at a meeting. The meeting must satisfy quorum requirements and the question posed to the shareholders must be voted upon pursuant to rules we discuss below. As we will also see, there are strict requirements for giving notice of meetings to the shareholders who are entitled to vote.

Instead of having a meeting and voting, shareholders have long been allowed to take an act if all shareholders who are entitled to vote agree in writing as to what that act should be. This "written consent" procedure is especially helpful in closely held corporations, where many shareholder decisions will be unanimous, and where the requirement of a formal meeting would be a waste of effort. Traditionally, the written consent had to be unanimous; this is still the rule under the RMBCA.[41] Some states, including Delaware, have liberalized the procedure and authorize an act by the written consent of the holders of the number of shares that would be needed to take an act if a meeting were held.[42]

---

[38] With payment of a dividend, the record date determines in whose names checks will be issued.

[39] *See, e.g.*, RMBCA § 7.06(d).

[40] If the shareholder also happens to be an officer, she might have agency authority to bind the corporation. But she would be acting in her capacity as an officer, and not as a shareholder. Remember that the various actors in the corporation may wear different hats simultaneously, and we must focus on which hat she wears when she takes a particular act.

[41] RMBCA § 7.04(a)(shareholder action "may be taken without a meeting if the action is taken by all the shareholders entitled to vote on the action . . . [and is] evidenced by one or more written consents bearing the date of signature and describing the action taken, signed by all the shareholders entitled to vote on the action and delivered to the corporation for inclusion in the minutes or filing with the corporate records").

[42] DEL. GEN. CORP. LAW § 228(a)(written consent "signed by the holders of outstanding stock having not less than the minimum number of votes that would be necessary

4. Shareholder Meetings: Notice, Quorum, and Voting

Assuming the shareholders do not act through written consent, they will take action at a meeting. There are two types of shareholder meetings: annual and special. The principal purpose of the annual meeting is to elect directors, although that meeting may address other issues as well. The annual meeting is required, but failure to hold it does not affect the validity of any corporate action. A shareholder can seek a court order requiring the corporation to hold the annual meeting within the time set by statute. A typical provision is RMBCA § 7.03(a)(1), which permits shareholders to seek an order if no annual meeting has been held "within the earlier of 6 months after the end of the [last] fiscal year or 15 months after its last annual meeting."

A special meeting is any meeting other than an annual meeting. It may be called by the persons specified in the statute or in the by-laws of the corporation. Statutes often permit the board of directors or president to call such a meeting, or the holders of ten percent of the outstanding stock.[43] The latter provision is somewhat controversial because it may result in repetitive or unnecessary meetings called by small factions of shareholders to raise issues that have no chance of passage.[44]

The corporation must give written notice to all shareholders who are entitled to vote at any shareholder meeting (annual or special). Most states now permit such notice by e-mail.[45] Statutes set time limits for notice. Under RMBCA § 7.05, for instance, the notice must be given not fewer than 10 and no more than 60 days before the meeting.[46] Obviously, the notice must state the time and place of the meeting. For special meetings, the notice must also state the purpose for which the shareholders will gather. The stated purpose limits the

---

to authorize or take such action at a meeting at which all shares entitled to vote thereon were present and voted. . . .").

[43] *See, e.g.,* RMBCA § 7.02(a)(2).

[44] The Official Comment to RMBCA § 7.02 suggests that the board of directors has discretion to ensure that the shareholders' power to call special meetings is not abused.

[45] *See, e.g.,* RMBCA § 1.41(a)("Notice under this Act must be in writing unless oral notice is reasonable under the circumstances. Notice by electronic transmission is written notice.").

[46] In some states, the minimum requirement is longer for voting at a meeting where the shareholders will consider a fundamental corporate change. *See, e.g.,* TEX. BUS. ORGS. CODE § 21.456(c)(1) (record date usually no fewer than 10 days before the meeting, but at least 21 days before a meeting to consider a fundamental corporate change).

action the shareholders can take at that meeting; they cannot do anything else.[47]

- Corporation sends notice of a special meeting, the purpose of which is to vote on the removal of a particular director. That is the only item of business they can transact at the meeting. They could not, for example, then vote to approve a plan to merge Corporation with another business.

Notice of the annual meeting, in contrast, ordinarily does not have to state a purpose.[48] Everyone knows the shareholders will be electing directors at the annual meeting. Because it is a general meeting, however, shareholders can act on other items. Note, however, that statutes in many jurisdictions require that the notice state if certain issues will be addressed at the annual meeting. For example, in some states, the notice must inform shareholders whenever they will be voting on whether to approve a fundamental corporate change, such as a merger or sale of substantially all assets. So if such an issue is to be considered at the annual meeting, the notice must say so.

Failure to give the required notice to all eligible shareholders renders voidable any action that was taken at the meeting, unless any shareholder not notified waives the defect.[49] This is true even if that shareholder's vote would not have affected the outcome of the vote.

- XYZ Corporation has three shareholders. X and Y each own 40 percent of the stock. Z owns 20 percent of the stock. The corporation calls a meeting of shareholders but fails to give notice to Z. At the meeting, X and Y vote in favor of a proposal that requires a majority vote of the shares. Even

---

[47] See, e.g., RMBCA § 7.02(d)("Only business within the purpose or purposes described in the meeting notice . . . may be conducted at a special shareholders' meeting.").

[48] See, e.g., RMBCA § 7.05(b)(requiring notice of time and place, but not purpose, of the annual meeting).

[49] Because the act is voidable, and not void, it may be ratified by a properly noticed shareholder meeting. Lofland v. DiSabatino, 1991 WL 138505 at *7 (Del. Ch. July 25, 1991) ("The defect in the Notice of the November 14 Annual Meeting caused the election results of that meeting to be voidable and not void.").

On the other hand, some courts appear to consider lack of proper notice to render the results of the meeting void and not merely voidable. See, e.g., Marine Serv. Unlimited v. Rakes, 918 S.W.2d 132, 135(Ark. 1996) ("Actions taken at a shareholders' meeting of which absent shareholders had no notice are illegal. Further, actions of a majority of the members of a board of directors are invalid if absent directors had no legal notice of the meetings."); Badger v. Madsen, 896 P.2d 20, 23 (Utah Ct. App. 1995) ("Failure to comply with [a statute requiring notice of shareholder meetings] may render any action taken at a meeting . . . null and void.").

though Z could not have stopped this result had she been at the meeting, the failure to give notice to Z renders the decision voidable.

This harsh consequence can be avoided if the shareholder(s) to whom notice was not sent waive that defect. This can be done either in writing or by attending the meeting without objecting to the lack of notice.[50] So in the above hypothetical, Z could validate the result of the shareholder vote by filing with the corporation a written waiver. Or, had Z heard about the meeting, attended, and not objected to the lack of formal notice, the result of the vote at the meeting would presumably be valid.

Whenever any group is to act at a meeting, the first question is whether there is a quorum. The group cannot act unless a quorum is represented at the meeting. This is true of shareholders, the board of directors, the House of Representatives, the city council, the student bar association—any group. With most groups, the quorum is determined by considering how many people are present. With shareholders, however, the focus is different. The quorum and the vote required are determined by considering the number of shares, and not the number of shareholders, who are represented at the meeting. Unless the articles provide otherwise, each outstanding share is entitled to one vote[51] and a quorum consists of a majority of those outstanding voting [52]shares.

- Corporation has 20,000 outstanding voting shares. Corporation has 700 shareholders. That latter fact is irrelevant for shareholder voting (indeed, it is only relevant to the caterer of the meeting). To have a quorum, at least 10,001 shares must be represented at the meeting. If a quorum is not present, the shareholders cannot take an act.

Notice that we spoke of the number of shares "represented" (and not the number of shares "present") at the meeting. This reflects the fact that shareholders are not required to attend the meeting personally. As we will see below, they can appoint an agent—called a proxy—to vote for them. In publicly traded corporations, very few shareholders actually attend meetings; the voting is done almost exclusively through proxies.

---

[50] *See, e.g., Badger,* 896 P.2d at 24 ("[W]hen shareholders attend and participate in a meeting, either in person or by proxy, they cannot later claim that any action taken at the meeting was invalid because of improper notice.").

[51] The articles may provide for classes of stock with voting rights and classes without voting rights. At least one class of stock, however, must have unlimited voting rights. *See, e.g.,* RMBCA § 6.01(b)(1).

[52] By "voting," we refer to shares that have the right to vote.

A greater quorum requirement may be established in the articles.[53] For instance, a corporation could require that a supermajority, such as 2/3 of the shares, be represented to constitute a quorum. In some states, the quorum requirement can be reduced to lower than a majority, although several states impose a limit: the quorum can never consist of fewer than one-third of the outstanding voting shares.[54]

If a quorum is initially present, a disgruntled faction may fear that it will lose a vote, and leave the meeting in an effort to "break" the quorum and prevent a vote. Under the general rule, this will not work. For shareholder voting, once a quorum is present, it is deemed present throughout the meeting; the fact that shareholders leave the meeting is irrelevant.[55]

Assuming a quorum is represented, the next question is what vote will be required to pass a resolution—that is, to approve an act by the shareholders. Again, the focus is on the number of shares and not the number of shareholders. In other words, voting strength among shareholders is measured by their relative ownership of the company. A person with 20 shares has twice as many votes as one with 10 shares. This reflects the fact that her equity stake in the corporation is twice as large.

The vote required for the shareholders to take an act depends on the issue being considered. First, if shareholders are electing directors, all that is needed is a plurality. In other words, the candidate who receives the highest number of votes is elected, even if she does not get a majority of the votes cast.

- Corporation has 1,000 outstanding voting shares, all of which are represented at a meeting to elect directors. Four candidates are nominated for one of the seats on the board. All 1,000 votes are cast. Candidate A receives 300 votes. Candidate B receives 250 votes. Candidate C receives 240 votes. Candidate D receives 210 votes. Candidate A is elected, even though she only received 30 percent of the vote.

---

[53] *See, e.g.,* RMBCA § 7.27(a)(articles "may provide for a greater quorum or voting requirement for shareholders . . .").

[54] *See, e.g.,* N.Y. BUS. CORP. LAW § 608(b); TEX. BUS. ORGS. CODE § 21.358(b)(2).

[55] *See, e.g.,* RMBCA § 7.25(b)("Once a share is represented for any purpose at a meeting, it is deemed present for quorum purposes for the remainder of the meeting . . ."). The rule is different for directors. At meetings of the board, a quorum can be broken if the number of directors present at any point in the meeting does not constitute a quorum. *See* RMBCA § 8.24(c) ("If a quorum is present *when a vote is taken,* the affirmative vote of a majority of directors present is the act of the board of directors . . .").

Second, for routine matters that may be put up for shareholder vote, most states today require only a majority of the votes actually cast on the issue.[56] The older traditional rule—still followed in Delaware[57]—requires a majority of the shares present or represented at the meeting. The traditional rule, in other words, essentially counts abstentions (shares not cast either for or against a provision) as a vote of "no."

- Corporation has 20,000 outstanding voting shares. At a meeting, 12,000 shares are present (so there is a quorum). Of those 12,000 shares, 10,000 actually vote on a particular proposal. In Delaware and other states following the traditional rule, at least 6,001 would have to vote "yes" to pass a resolution—that is, a majority of shares present. Under the modern RMBCA view, only 5,001 would have to vote "yes"— a majority of those that actually vote on the proposal.

Third, if shareholders are voting to remove a director before her term expires, most states appear to require the affirmative vote of a majority of the shares *entitled* to vote.[58] This is a more stringent requirement than what we just saw.

- Corporation has 20,000 outstanding voting shares. At a meeting, 12,000 shares are present. Of those 12,000 shares, 10,000 actually vote on whether a director should be removed before her term expires. The measure cannot pass. In most states, a vote to remove a director must be approved by a majority of the shares *entitled to vote*—not a majority of shares present or a majority of shares that actually vote. Because there are 20,000 outstanding voting shares, a majority of that number—at least 10,001—would have to vote in favor of removing the director. Because only 10,000 showed up, the requirement cannot be met.

On the other hand, an increasing number of states appear to treat the vote on removal of directors as a routine matter. Thus, the director is removed from office if a majority of shares that actually vote are in favor of removal.[59]

---

[56] *See, e.g.,* RMBCA § 7.25(c)("if the votes cast within the voting group favoring the action exceed the votes cast opposing the action . . .").

[57] DEL. GEN. CORP. LAW § 216 ("[T]he affirmative vote of the majority of shares present in person or represented by proxy at the meeting and entitled to vote on the subject matter shall be the act of the stockholders.").

[58] *See, e.g.,* DEL. GEN. CORP. LAW § 141(k)("majority of the shares then entitled to vote at an election of directors. . . .").

[59] *See, e.g.,* RMBCA § 8.08.

Fourth, if shareholders are voting to approve a fundamental corporate change, such as a merger, most states require the affirmative vote of a majority of the shares entitled to vote. The traditional view here—still followed in some states—is that the fundamental change must be approved by two-thirds of the shares entitled to vote. On the other hand, in some other states, fundamental changes are treated no differently from routine matters. In such states, the fundamental change need be approved only by a majority of shares actually voting on the matter. We will discuss this point in detail when we consider fundamental changes in Chapter 12.

Anytime shareholders will be voting, the corporation must prepare a "voting list," which is simply the roster of those entitled to vote.[60] Commonly, the list must be made available to shareholders. Because the corporation must compile a list of shareholders entitled to receive notice of the meeting before the notice is actually given and so it is no burden to prepare the voting list at the same time. Some states require that the voting list be available only at the meeting itself. Failure to prepare the voting list does not affect the validity of any action taken at the meeting.

5. Cumulative Voting

Cumulative voting is relevant when shareholders are electing directors. It does not apply when shareholders are voting on other matters—for example, on whether to approve a fundamental corporate change. Cumulative voting is intended to allow minority shareholders to gain representation on the board of directors. It is to be contrasted with "straight" voting in the election of directors. So when shareholders elect directors, they will either use straight voting or cumulative voting.

With straight voting, each director position is filled in a separate election at the meeting. Suppose there are five directorship positions on the board. There will be five elections at the meeting: one for each seat on the board. Unless the articles provide otherwise, each shareholder will cast one vote for each share she holds, and she will do so in each of the five elections.

- X and Y are the only shareholders of Corporation. X has 51 shares and Y has 49 shares. They attend the annual meeting to elect three directors. For each of the three seats on the board of directors, X has proposed her candidates (probably herself for one seat and two of her friends for the others) and

---

[60] *See, e.g.,* RMBCA § 7.20(a).

Y has proposed her candidates (also probably herself for one and two friends for the others). What happens?

- For Seat #1, X will cast her 51 votes for herself and Y will cast her 49 votes for herself. X wins.

- For Seat #2, X will cast her 51 votes for her friend and Y will cast her 49 votes for her friend. X's friend wins.

- For Seat #3, X will cast her 51 votes for another friend and Y will cast her 49 votes for another friend. X's friend wins.

Obviously, with straight voting, if one shareholder owns a majority of the stock (or if a group can pool the voting power of a majority of the stock), she will elect *every* director. This may seem unfair to Y, who, after all, owns a considerable equity position in the firm.

Minority shareholders like Y are in better shape if cumulative voting is in effect. With cumulative voting, the shareholders do not hold a separate vote for each seat on the board. Instead, there is one "at-large" election at the meeting. In that at-large election, the three candidates who receive the most votes would be elected to the board.[61] Not only that, but each shareholder gets to multiply the number of shares owned times the number of directors to be elected. She may allocate those votes in any way she likes. So she may, if she chooses, "cumulate" her votes by putting three seats' worth of votes on one candidate.

Let's demonstrate by taking a more extreme example. Assume that X and Y are the only shareholders in Corporation. X has 74 shares. Y has 26 shares. There are three directors. Clearly, under straight voting, Y has no chance of gaining representation on the board; X can elect all three directors. With cumulative voting, however, we determine each shareholder's voting power by multiplying the number of shares she owns times the number of directors to be elected at the meeting. So here X has 222 votes (74 shares multiplied by 3 directors). Y has 78 votes (26 shares multiplied by 3 directors).

Now suppose Y casts all 78 of her votes for one candidate (probably herself). On the facts here, that candidate will finish in the top three and thus be elected to the board. Remember, under cumulative voting, there is only one election, and it is at-large. So one need not finish in first place to be elected. Those who finish in the top three (or whatever number is being elected) will become a director.

---

[61] This assumes that the shareholders are electing three directors at the meeting; if they were electing five, the five candidates with the most votes would be elected, etc.

How do we know that Y will finish in the top three? Let's see what X can do to try to stop that. If X casts 79 votes for herself and 79 votes for a friend of hers, those two would have more votes than Y. After casting those votes (totaling 158), though, X has only 64 votes left. She cannot stop Y from being elected because Y has 78 votes.

The difference between cumulative and straight voting may be vividly illustrated by the deadlock situation where all shares are owned equally by two shareholders—say fifty shares each. If straight voting is applied and each shareholder votes only for her own candidates, a deadlocked election is inevitable. If there are three places to be filled, X will vote 50 shares for herself, 50 shares for one of her pals, and 50 votes for another of her pals. Y will vote 50 shares for herself, 50 shares for one of her friends, and 50 shares for another of her friends. Six candidates will have 50 votes. No one is elected (because no one got more votes than anyone else).

Now let's try it with cumulative voting. Here, X and Y each have 150 votes to play with (50 shares times three directorships up for election). X can put 76 votes on herself and guarantee election. Why? Because Y cannot put more than 76 on more than one person (she only has 150 votes). So Y will probably put 76 votes on herself. That guarantees her election. Now each has 74 votes left, which means there is a deadlock for the third seat on the board.

This assumes, however, that X and Y voted intelligently. Suppose X casts 76 votes for herself and Y puts 100 votes on herself. Now what happens? Both X and Y are elected because they will finish in the top three. But here X will be able to elect her friend to the board because she has 74 votes to put on her friend. Y, in contrast, has only 50 votes to cast for her friend (because she cast 100 for herself). Here, then, the three highest recipients of votes are Y, X, and a friend of X. Y made a mistake by casting more than she needed (76) to guarantee her own election. She wasted votes she could have put on a second candidate.

The effective allocation of votes among multiple candidates under cumulative voting can become complex.[62] Various formulas may be employed. For instance, to determine the number of shares required to ensure the election of one director, you need one *share* more than this fraction: Shares voting divided by number of directors to be elected plus one.

- Assume that 500 shares will vote and three directors will be elected at the meeting. The fraction above puts 500 in the

---

[62] *See* Lewis R. Mills, *Mathematics of Cumulative Voting*, 1968 DUKE L.J. 28.

numerator, divided by four. Why four? Because that is the number of directors to be elected plus one. 500 divided by four equals 125. We need one *share* more than 125 to elect a director. In other words, we need 126 shares.

A related formula tells us how many shares one needs to elect a certain number of directors (we will call that number "n"). You need one *share* more than this fraction: Shares voting multiplied by the number of directors you want to elect divided by number of directors to be elected plus one.

- So let's say 500 shares will vote and five directors will be elected at the meeting. Say also that we want to elect three directors. The fraction puts 1500 in the numerator. Why? It is 500 shares to be voted multiplied by the three directors we want to elect. The denominator is 6. Why? Because that is the number of directors to be elected plus one. So it's 1500 divided by 6, which equals 250. So we need one *share* more than 250 to elect three directors. In other words, we need 251 shares.

Cumulative voting has a strong emotional appeal. The notion that people with considerable but minority holdings should have a voice in management resonates with American values. It seems "fair" and brings diversity of viewpoint to the board. Moreover, the presence of a minority director on the board may discourage conflicts of interest or other abuses by the majority.

The impact of cumulative voting is minimized when the corporation has a "staggered" board. Usually the entire board of directors is elected each year at the annual meeting. But corporations may choose to give directors staggered terms by dividing the board in half or thirds. Then, each year, only half or one-third of the seats are open for election. The result of reducing the number of directors to be elected is clear—it requires more votes to elect one person to the board.

We can prove this by revisiting the formula for determining how many shares are necessary to elect one director under cumulative voting. Recall that the denominator in that formula consisted of the number of directors to be elected plus one. Any time we reduce the denominator, we will increase the number needed to elect a director. Suppose, for instance, there are 1000 shares to be voted and we will be electing nine directors. To elect one director, we need one share more than 1000 divided by 10 (the 10 consists of the nine directors to be elected plus one). So that means we need one share more than 100, or 101.

But suppose the board is staggered and we are only electing three directors this year. Here, the 1000 shares voting is divided by four (three directors to be elected plus one). To elect one director, then, we need one share more than 250, or 251. So staggered boards—by reducing the number of directors being elected each year—blunt the impact of cumulative voting.

As a practical matter, cumulative voting in a factionalized close corporation may be of considerable importance. It is irrelevant, of course, in one-shareholder corporations or when parties readily agree upon who should serve on the board of directors. In large, publicly held corporations, cumulative voting is generally thought to be a nuisance. It complicates matters and rarely affects the outcome of an election. On the other hand, on large boards, cumulative voting may permit institutional investors or public interest groups to gain representation. It may facilitate takeovers by giving an aggressor a "toe hold" on the board (although there is debate over this).

In a few states, cumulative voting is mandatory. For example, the Arizona Constitution requires corporations formed in that state to provide cumulative voting.[63] In most states, however, it is a matter of choice. Most states have "opt in" provisions, meaning that if the articles are silent, cumulative voting does not exist. The corporation can choose to adopt it, but must provide for it in the articles.[64] Other states have "opt out" provisions, so that if the articles are silent, cumulative voting applies.[65]

When cumulative voting does apply, some states impose a requirement that at least one shareholder give notice to the corporation of her intent to cumulate her votes. If one does so, then all have the right to vote cumulatively.[66] This is a desirable provision because it allows the shareholders to forego cumulative voting if no one wants to use it. In addition, it warns the shareholders when it will apply so they can dust off the formulas and vote intelligently.

6. Voting by Proxy

Shareholders can appoint an agent to cast their votes. The shareholder is the principal, and the agent is usually called a "proxy." Actually, the word "proxy" can be confusing. Sometimes it is used to refer to the document that creates this authority; sometimes it is used to refer to the person to whom the authority is given; and some-

---

[63] ARIZ. CONST. art. XIV, § 10.

[64] The RMBCA adopts this approach in § 7.28(d).

[65] See, e.g., 15 PA. CONS. STAT. § 1758(c).

[66] TEX. BUS. ORGS. CODE § 21.361(c).

times it is used to refer to the grant of authority itself. The RMBCA limits use of "proxy" to the person with the power to vote.[67] It refers to the grant of authority as the "appointment" of a proxy,[68] and to the document creating the appointment as an "appointment form."[69]

Our focus here is the rather mundane subject of state law relating to proxies.[70] Every state permits shareholders to vote "in person or by proxy."[71] The proxy appointment must be in writing. Beyond that, however, the states are not picky about form. Courts have upheld appointments that omitted the name of the proxy, the date of the meeting, or the date on which they were executed.

The standard rule is that appointment of a proxy is effective for 11 months unless the document states otherwise. Thus, in most states, a proxy can be appointed for a longer or shorter time, but the standard is 11 months.[72] The theory is that a new appointment form should be executed before each annual meeting. Although some states limit the duration of a proxy appointment,[73] most do not. Because a proxy is an agent, her appointment generally is revocable at the pleasure of the record owner. Thus, even if a long period is designated as the duration of the proxy appointment, it may be revoked.

A proxy appointment may be revoked either expressly or by implication. For example, the execution of a later appointment constitutes a revocation of an earlier, inconsistent one. Because later proxy appointments revoke earlier ones, it is important that such documents be dated. The shareholder's attendance at a meeting may also constitute revocation of a proxy appointment, although this depends on the intention of the shareholder, and she may be required to express the intent to revoke at the meeting. Death of the shareholder will result in revocation of the appointment, at least when the corporation is informed of the fact.

Can a proxy appointment be made irrevocable? Generally, the mere statement in the appointment form that it is irrevocable is

---

[67] RMBCA § 7.22(b)(shareholder "may appoint a proxy to vote or otherwise act for the shareholder"). The proxy need not be a shareholder of the corporation.

[68] RMBCA § 7.22(c).

[69] RMBCA § 7.22(b).

[70] In public corporations, almost all shareholders participate, if at all, by proxy. Federal law—§ 12 of the Securities Exchange Act of 1934—governs the solicitation of proxies in public corporations. *See* Chapter 9(E).

[71] *See, e.g.,* RMBCA § 7.22(a).

[72] *See, e.g.,* RMBCA § 7.22(c).

[73] NEV. STAT. § 78.355(4) ("Except as otherwise provided in subsection 5, no such proxy is valid after the expiration of 6 months from the date of its creation unless the stockholder specifies in it the length of time for which it is to continue in force . . .").

meaningless. As a matter of agency law, as noted, the appointment is revocable by the principal at will. On the other hand, as established in the old case of *Hunt v. Rousmanier's Administrators*,[74] a proxy purporting to be irrevocable will be irrevocable if it is "coupled with an interest." This means that the proxy has some interest in the stock other than the interest in voting as the shareholder's agent. For example, if the proxy appointment is given to someone who has agreed to buy the stock, or to whom the stock has been pledged (for example, as collateral for a loan), it will be "coupled with an interest."

- S is a shareholder of Corporation on the record date of the annual meeting, and thus is entitled to vote at that meeting. After the record date, but before the meeting itself, S sells the stock to P. S executes a proxy appointment authorizing P to vote the shares at the annual meeting, which provides that it is irrevocable. This proxy is irrevocable because it is "coupled with an interest"—the proxy owns the shares, and thus has an interest in it other than simply voting.

Although the "proxy coupled with an interest" doctrine developed at common law, in recent decades there has been a trend toward codification. For example, RMBCA § 7.22(d) lists five non-exclusive situations in which a proxy holder will be considered to have a sufficient interest in the stock to support irrevocability.[75]

Finally, we emphasize that appointment of proxies is permitted for voting by and as shareholders. It is not allowed for voting by and as directors. Directors owe the corporation certain non-delegable fiduciary duties, which require that they exercise their independent judgment in voting. Thus, proxies among directors for voting as directors are void. Remember that people can serve simultaneously as shareholders and directors; thus, be sure to apply the rule appropriate to the hat they are wearing at the time they take an act.

- X and Y are shareholders and directors of Corporation. X may appoint Y as her proxy for voting at shareholder meetings on matters considered by shareholders. But X may not appoint Y as her proxy for voting at a meeting of the board of directors.

---

[74] 21 U.S. 174, 203–06 (1823).

[75] *See also* CAL. CORP. CODE § 705 (similar); N.Y. BUS. CORP. LAW § 609(f) (listing the same situations, but appearing to consider them exclusive).

7. Methods for Combining Voting Power

Shareholders, particularly in close corporations, may want to pool their voting power. One way to do this is to solicit proxy appointments from other shareholders. As we saw in the preceding section, though, this is often not effective because the proxy usually can be revoked. In this section, we consider two other methods for combining voting power: the voting trust (which is effective but cumbersome), and the voting agreement (which is easy but not effective in some states).

A "voting trust" is a true trust, so it requires the shareholder to separate legal and equitable title to her stock. She does this by transferring the legal title to a voting trustee. That transfer empowers the trustee to vote the stock. The trust agreement instructs the trustee regarding how to vote. The original (now erstwhile) shareholder retains the equitable (or beneficial) title to the stock. This interest is usually reflected in "trust certificates," which can be transferred. And though she no longer holds legal title to the stock, the erstwhile shareholder generally retains all other shareholder rights. Thus, she will receive any dividend declared on that stock, can institute derivative litigation, can inspect the books and records of the corporation, etc.

Both as a matter of contract and as a fiduciary, the trustee is required to vote the shares as instructed in the trust document. A court can compel her to do so. Thus the voting trust can be an effective way to pool voting power. The goal of most voting trusts probably is to allow shareholders to combine their voting power in electing directors. But the voting trust can serve other purposes as well. For instance, creditors of a corporation may insist upon a voting trust to ensure that the corporate management is acceptable to them (until the loan is repaid). At the end of the trust, the trustee returns legal title of the stock to the erstwhile shareholder.

Voting trusts are effective, but they are cumbersome. First, as noted, the parties must enter into a formal trust agreement and spell out some method to instruct the trustee on how to vote. Generally, these agreements must be in writing.[76] Second, the shareholders must identify and recruit an appropriate trustee and transfer legal title to her. Third, statutes generally require that something be filed with the corporation—sometimes it is the agreement itself, some-

---

[76] RMBCA § 7.30(a). The parties should also carefully address issues such as whether the trustee can transfer shares to third parties, compensation of the trustee, whether the trustee can elect herself to the board, and whether and how the trustee may be replaced.

times it is the transfer of legal title to the trustee.[77] That means the trust cannot be a secret because these documents are subject to inspection by shareholders. Fourth, in most states, there is a temporal limit on the lifespan of a voting trust—usually 10 years—and in some states there are rather odd limitations about when the trust can be renewed. For instance, in some states, the trust can only be renewed within a specific time of its original existence.[78] Section 7.30(c) of the RMBCA adopts the simpler rule that the trust may be extended at any time during its existence.

Some states also require that the trust be formed for a proper purpose. This requirement adds little, since few people are so obtuse that they would state an improper purpose, such as "we are forming this trust to ensure that we secure for ourselves lucrative employment in the corporation." In most states, motive is not an issue, and the trust is valid if it meets the statutory requirements.

A "voting agreement" is a contract between or among shareholders to vote their shares as a block on certain matters. These are often called "pooling agreements" because they pool the voting power of the shares affected by the agreement. These are far more convenient than voting trusts. First, there is no separation of legal and equitable title—the shareholders retain both, so there is no need to transfer anything and no disruption to ownership. Second, usually, there is no requirement that the parties file anything with the corporation.[79] Third, in most states, pooling agreements are simply treated as contracts, with no special provisions in the corporate law (except, in some states, voting agreements must be in writing).[80]

Generally, pooling agreements are used to maintain control, to maximize the voting power of the shares (especially when cumulative voting is permitted), or to ensure that some objective is obtained in the corporation. The manner in which the shares are to be voted—for or against a specific proposal—may be specified in the agreement it-

---

[77] Under the RMBCA, the names and addresses of the beneficial owners of the stock, as well as a copy of the trust agreement itself, must be filed with the corporation. RMBCA § 7.30(a).

[78] See, e.g., N.J. STAT. § 14A:5–20(4) (allowing renewal at any time within two years of the original expiration date).

[79] See, e.g., RMBCA § 7.31(a)(requiring only that the agreement be signed). On the other hand, some states impose a filing requirement. In Texas, for example, voting agreements must be filed with the corporation. TEX. BUS. ORGS. CODE § 6.252(b)(1)("A copy of a voting agreement . . . shall be deposited with the domestic entity . . . ").

[80] See, e.g., RMBCA § 7.31(a). On the other hand, the corporate law of some states imposes a temporal limitation on pooling agreements. See, e.g., GA. CODE § 14–2–731(c) ("The duration of any agreement created under this Code section shall not exceed 20 years.").

self. The parties must anticipate disagreement and provide a method for determining how the shares will then be voted. Commonly, they provide that the stock will be voted as a majority—or some higher percentage—decides. Agreements may provide for arbitration in the event of deadlock. Thus, although a party to a voting agreement retains legal and equitable title, she has bargained away her right to vote her shares as she pleases; she is required to vote as the agreement provides.

We have seen that voting agreements are less cumbersome to establish than voting trusts. But they can suffer from a significant drawback. In some states, voting agreements are not specifically enforceable. That means that a court will not force a party to vote her shares in accordance with the agreement. The most famous case is *Ringling Bros.-Barnum & Bailey Combined Shows v. Ringling*,[81] which involved management of the famous circus and featured a family battle for control. There were 1,000 outstanding shares, held by three shareholders: John Ringling North held 370 shares, Edith Ringling held 315, and Aubrey Haley held 315. Cumulative voting was in effect, and there were seven directors. Thus Mr. North had 2,590 votes to allocate, while each of the ladies had 2,205 votes.[82]

Mrs. Ringling and Mrs. Haley entered into a voting agreement. They did so because of a dispute between themselves, on the one hand, and John Ringling North, on the other. They wished to ensure that Mr. North not retain control of the operation of the corporation. The agreement required Mrs. Ringling to vote for herself, her son, and another candidate on whom she and Mrs. Haley would agree (or who would be chosen by their lawyer). Mrs. Haley was required to vote for herself, her husband, and for the additional candidate on whom she and Mrs. Ringling would agree (or who would be chosen by their lawyer). If they followed the agreement, the ladies could pool their power and elect five of the seven directors. This ensured them of control and, more importantly perhaps, ensured that Mr. North would not run the show.

The ladies voted in accordance with the agreement for several years. In 1946, however, Mrs. Haley refused to go along. Instead of voting as agreed, she cast half her votes for herself and half for her husband. Mrs. Ringling voted, as required by the agreement, for herself, her son, and a Mr. Dunn. Mr. North voted for himself and Messrs. Griffin and Woods.

---

[81] 53 A.2d 441 (Del. 1947).

[82] Cumulative voting strength, as we saw above, is determined by multiplying the number of shares held by the number of directors to be elected at the meeting.

At the time, Delaware had only a statute allowing voting trusts. There was no statute permitting voting agreements. Nonetheless, the court upheld the agreement. The big question was the remedy to be ordered. One option would be specific performance—in other words, to force the breaching party (Mrs. Haley) to vote as she agreed to vote. Doing so would result in the election of Mrs. Ringling, her son, Mrs. Haley, her husband, Mr. Dunn (friendly to Mrs. Ringling), Mr. North, and one of Mr. North's candidates. In other words, North and his friends would have only two seats on the board.

The court did not order specific performance. Instead, it held that the votes cast by the breaching party should be ignored.[83] As a result, Mrs. Haley and her Husband were not elected. Indeed, only six people were elected: three on the Ringling side of the dispute (Mrs. Ringling, her son, and Mr. Dunn) and three on the North side of the dispute (Messrs. North, Woods, and Griffin). The court recognized that it is not desirable to have a vacant position on the board, but noted that the 1947 annual meeting was imminent and would likely remedy the situation.[84] In the interim, though the board was evenly split between the Ringling faction and the North faction, Mr. North was able to wrest control.[85]

In other states, such as New York, the remedy for a breach is not clear. Although the New York Business Corporation Law allows voting agreements, it is silent on enforceability. On the other hand, it

---

[83] *Id.* at 448 ("The Court of Chancery may, in a review of an election, reject votes of a registered shareholder. The votes representing Mrs. Haley's shares should not be counted. . . . [W]e have concluded that the election should not be declared invalid, but that effect should be given to a rejection of the votes representing Mrs. Haley's shares. No other relief seems appropriate in this proceeding.").

The fact that the court did not order specific performance on the facts of *Ringling* does not necessarily mean that Delaware courts will not order such relief for breach of a voting agreement. It seems clear that parties may provide in the agreement that specific performance will be the sole remedy. *See, e.g.,* Grayson v. Imagination Station, Inc., No. 5051–CC, 2010 WL 3221951, at *1 (Del. Ch. Aug. 16, 2010) ("The Voting Agreement further provides for specific performance as the sole remedy for breach. . . .").

[84] *Id.*

[85] The story behind Mrs. Haley's breaching the agreement with Mrs. Ringling is interesting. In the era when the case arose, the circus performed under huge canvas tents ("the big top"), which were hauled from town to town and erected by use of elephant power. During World War II, fire-retardant canvas was not available for this purpose because it was being used in the war effort. Mr. North counseled that the circus should suspend operations because using regular canvas posed too great a fire hazard to the public. The Ringling-Haley contingent ignored his advice. On July 6, 1944, an arsonist set fire to the tent during a performance in Hartford, Connecticut. Over 160 people were killed and 700 injured (it was estimated that 7,000 people were attending the show). *See* "Hartford Circus Fire," WIKIPEDIA, available at http://en.wikipedia.org/wiki/Hartford_circus_fire. Mr. Haley was convicted of criminal negligence and imprisoned. Mr. North visited him in prison and befriended him, which is what led Mrs. Haley to side with Mr. North and to breach the voting agreement.

provides that a proxy granted under a voting agreement will be irrevocable.[86] So if the parties to an agreement in New York appoint a
proxy to vote the shares, the proxy cannot be revoked; thus, the
would-be breaching party cannot vote her shares in violation of the
deal. If the parties do not appoint a proxy, though, it is not clear
what remedy a court would provide for a breach.

Led by the RMBCA, many states now expressly provide that voting agreements are specifically enforceable.[87] This means, of course,
that the court will force the parties to vote according to their deal. It
is the superior remedy because it avoids the uncertainty of the New
York approach and the possible unfairness of the Delaware view. In
states providing for specific performance, presumably, parties will
never use a voting trust. The pooling agreement is far easier to execute than a trust, and the availability of specific performance means
that it will work as well as a trust.

It is important to note that a shareholders' pooling agreement
can extend only to voting on matters that are within the province of
shareholders, such as the election and removal of directors and approval of fundamental corporate changes. Directors are forbidden to
tie themselves down to agreements on how they will vote as directors.
Such an agreement would violate the public policy requiring directors
to exercise their independent judgment on each issue. Thus, shareholders will generally not be permitted to enforce provisions in a voting agreement that govern acts to be taken if they are elected to the
board of directors.

- X and Y enter into a pooling agreement to vote their stock to
  elect each other to the board of directors. That is fine, because shareholders elect directors. There would be a serious
  problem, however, if they also agreed what acts they would
  take as directors once they were on the board—such a deal
  would violate the public policy against voting agreements
  that govern director voting.

8. Inspection of Corporate Records

Corporations routinely maintain certain records, such as articles, bylaws, records of actions taken at meetings of shareholders and
of the board of directors, lists of directors, officers, and shareholders,
and a range of financial information.[88] Because many small busi-

---

[86] N.Y. BUS. CORP. LAW §§ 609(e), 620.

[87] RMBCA § 7.31(b)("A voting agreement created under this section is specifically
enforceable.").

[88] See, e.g., RMBCA § 16.01.

nesses do not have accountants, corporation laws may require maintenance of only basic financial statements, made on the basis of generally accepted accounting principles.[89] All corporate documents may be retained in hard copy or in electronic format, with the latter being printable if needed.

Here, we address shareholders' rights to inspect records maintained by the corporation. It is important to make five prefatory comments. First, we deal here with shareholders, not directors. Because directors are managers of the corporation, they have unfettered access to the corporation's papers. Their fiduciary duties require that they be able to inspect the entire gamut of records in the corporation.[90] Shareholders, in contrast, are owners but not managers. Accordingly, their right to inspect is narrower.

Second, speak here of a right to inspect *records*, and not a right to observe the operations of the corporation. Shareholders do not have a right to go to the factory and look over the assembly line.

Third, the shareholder may inspect records personally or may appoint an agent (such as her lawyer) to do so. She may choose to be accompanied by her agent at the inspection. The right to inspect usually includes the right to obtain copies of the documents (though the corporation can charge her for the copies).

Fourth, the right to inspect is usually held by the beneficial, or equitable, owner of the stock, and not simply the record owner. So, for example, a shareholder who has transferred legal title of the stock to a voting trustee usually retains the right to inspect.

Finally, in many states, there is a common law right to inspect, which exists alongside a statutory right. In most of these states, the scope of this common law right is unclear. In most instances, inspections are made pursuant to statutory provisions.

Statutes vary from state to state in a variety of particulars. For starters, they differ on which shareholders are eligible to demand access to the records. The traditional view—still followed in some states—requires that a shareholder meet certain minima of ownership. Usually, this means either that she (1) has owned stock (any amount) for at least six months or (2) currently owns at least five percent of the outstanding stock (for any time).[91] The modern view,

---

[89] Federal law requires publicly traded corporations to maintain and publish various forms of financial information. *See* Chapter 9(C).

[90] *See, e.g.,* RMBCA § 16.05(a).

[91] *See, e.g.,* TEX. BUS. ORGS. CODE § 21.218(b).

typified by the RMBCA, grants inspection rights to "any shareholder"—regardless of how long she has owned her stock or how much she holds.[92]

Assuming the shareholder is eligible, statutes also vary regarding procedure and the types of records that can be reviewed. In some states, a shareholder has a right to review some routine documents (like articles, bylaws, lists of officers and directors, and records of shareholder actions) simply by appearing at the corporation's office during business hours and demanding to see them. In other states, however, she may see such routine documents only after making a written demand—usually five business days in advance—describing the documents sought.[93]

To gain access to more sensitive materials—such as financial information and the record of directors' actions—most states require an eligible shareholder to make a written demand (usually at least five business days in advance) describing the documents desired and stating a "proper purpose" for the inspection.[94] She may also be required to state how the requested documents relate to her proper purpose. In some states, this assertion of a proper purpose is required for *any* inspection—even of routine documents.[95]

Whether a shareholder has stated a proper purpose is sometimes hotly contested. As a general rule, the corporation is likely to see a demand for access to the records—particularly sensitive records such as financial books and director actions—as hostile. For many years, corporations routinely rejected such demands, forcing the shareholder to seek an injunction ordering the corporation to permit access. Some statutes dissuade corporations from doing this by imposing a fine for improper denial of access to a shareholder who has made a proper demand.[96] In addition, generally, if the corporation refuses access, it may bear the burden in litigation of showing that the shareholder had an improper purpose in demanding access (this is especially likely if the demand concerned routine documents).

---

[92] *See, e.g.,* RMBCA § 16.02(a) ("A shareholder . . . is entitled to inspect and copy. . . .").

[93] *Id.*

[94] *See, e.g.,* RMBCA § 16.02(c)(1).

[95] *See, e.g.,* TEX. BUS. ORGS. CODE § 21.218(b)("Subject to the governing documents and on written demand stating a proper purpose . . . ").

[96] *See, e.g.,* NEV. STAT. § 78.105(3)("Every corporation that neglects or refuses to keep the records required by subsection 1 open for inspection, as required in this subsection, shall forfeit to the State the sum of $25 for every day of such neglect or refusal.").

A "proper purpose" is one that relates to the shareholder's interest as a shareholder. In other words, it must relate to some role shareholders play. Determining the value of the shareholder's interest in the corporation is a proper purpose. This is obviously most important in closely held corporations, in which there is no public market for the stock. Unless the shareholder can review the financial information, she is unable to determine the value of her stock.

Kortum v. Webasto Sunroofs, Inc.[97] involved a closely held corporation with two shareholders, each of which was a corporation. One, Magna, was in charge of daily operations and the other, WAG, provided technical support. When profits were 90 percent lower than anticipated, WAG sought access to the books and records to determine the value of its stock. Magna claimed that WAG's purpose in seeking the materials was improper. Specifically, it argued that WAG was trying to gain information to allow it to go into competition with the business. Even though WAG had acquired an interest in a competitor and had sued for dissolution, the court concluded that its purpose in seeking inspection was proper. Regardless of whether the corporation was dissolved or WAG attempted to sell its stock, it would need to know the value of its holdings.[98]

Importantly, a proper purpose may be one that is hostile to management. For instance, it is proper to investigate the reason for a decline in profits or to ascertain whether there has been mismanagement or questionable transactions. Such things affect the value of the shareholder's stock. Moreover, as we see in Chapter 13, shareholders may bring derivative suits against directors and officers who breach fiduciary duties to the corporation (by, for example, making egregious errors of judgment or engaging in self-dealing). Inspection may be important to this right to sue derivatively. Similarly, it may be proper for a shareholder to gain access to the list of shareholders so she can seek proxy appointments to elect new directors. Because shareholders elect directors, this would be a proper purpose.

On the other hand, some demands are not for a proper purpose, and should be rejected. Inspections aimed at harassment of managers or to obtain trade secrets for competitors are obviously improper. One concern, especially in earlier days, was that a shareholder would gain access to the list of shareholders to sell it—for example, to marketers. New York law allows the corporation to require a shareholder demanding access to the shareholder list to give an affidavit that she

---

[97] 769 A.2d 113 (Del. Ch. 2000).

[98] *Id.* at 115–25. The case also involved a demand for access by a director of the corporation.

has not sold a shareholder list in the recent past.[99] This concern is less important today than it once was because the shareholder list often does not reflect who actually owns the stock. As noted above, shares of publicly traded stocks are usually held in a "street name"— i.e., the name of a brokerage firm—rather than in the name of the actual shareholder.

The issue of proper purpose boils down to subjective motivation, which is always difficult to establish definitively. Courts are aware of the need to balance the shareholders' right of access with the corporation's right to be free from "fishing expeditions" by shareholders hoping to get lucky in sifting through records.

D. Board of Directors

1. Introduction

In some states, the corporation's initial directors are named in the articles. In others, the incorporators elect the initial directors. Thereafter, as we discussed above, the shareholders elect directors at the annual meeting. Earlier in this Chapter, we discussed the role of the board of directors in the traditional corporate model. In Chapter 7, we will discuss the important fiduciary duties that directors owe to the corporation. Here, we discuss the nuts and bolts of how the board operates.

Statutes give great leeway regarding the number of directors and their qualifications. They permit election of the entire board each year or, instead, two-or three-year terms with a "staggered board." Statutes also address what happens when a director cannot serve the entirety of her term. The board, like the shareholders, acts as a group, which means that an individual director has no authority to bind the corporation. The board usually takes action at one of two types of meetings: regular or special. The requirements for these meetings are technical and must be strictly observed. We also address directors' compensation and whether the board can delegate its authority to committees.

2. Statutory Requirements

Historically, states required that a board of directors have at least three members. Today, it is likely that every state has rejected this requirement and permits a board of "one or more" directors.[100] In a few states, there may still be a requirement of three directors if

---

[99] N.Y. BUS. CORP. LAW § 624(c).

[100] *See, e.g.,* RMBCA § 8.03(a); DEL. GEN. CORP. LAW § 1.41(b).

the corporation has at least three shareholders. These states set up a sliding scale: if there is one shareholder, it may have one or more directors; if there are two shareholders, it must have at least two directors; and if there are three or more shareholders, there must be at least three directors.[101] This sliding scale seems based on a presumption that every shareholder will be a director, which may be harmless enough in most close corporations. But the sliding scale can create unnecessary problems. Suppose, for example, we have a corporation with one shareholder, who is also the sole director. If she wants to give stock to her two children, as gifts, the sliding scale rule would require that the corporation elect two more directors because there will (after the gift) be three shareholders. Fortunately, this is an issue in very few states.

There is considerable variation among the states regarding where the number of directors is set. Many states provide, as § 8.03(a) of the RMBCA does, that the number may be "specified in or fixed in accordance with the articles of incorporation or the bylaws." This allows considerable flexibility; either the number is set in the articles or bylaws or a procedure for fixing it is set up there. That means that under the RMBCA the board or shareholders can be permitted to change the size of the board. In some states, the number must be set in the articles. This carries the disadvantage that amending the articles is a fundamental corporate change and requires assent from both the board and the shareholders; bylaws are easier to amend, as we discuss in section (B)(2). In a few states, such as Maryland, even though the number of directors is set in the articles, it can be amended by bylaws.[102]

Some states, such as Arizona, permit the corporation to have a variable-sized board, and provide a mechanism for setting the actual number within that range.[103] Wherever the number is set, most corporations have an odd number of directors to lessen the possibility that the board will split evenly when voting on some measure.

---

[101] The Massachusetts provision on this applies only if the articles do not provide for a different number of directors. MASS. GEN. LAWS ch. 156D, § 8.03(a) ("[U]nless otherwise provided in the articles of organization, if the corporation has more than 1 shareholder, the number of directors shall not be less than 3, except that whenever there shall be only 2 shareholders, the number of directors shall not be less than 2").

[102] MD. CODE CORPS. & ASS'NS § 2–402(b)("[A] Maryland corporation shall have the number of directors provided in its charter until changed by the bylaws").

[103] ARIZ. STAT. § 10–803(B) ("The articles of incorporation or bylaws may establish a variable range for the size of the board of directors by fixing a minimum and maximum number of directors. If a variable range is established, the number of directors may be fixed or changed from time to time, within the minimum and maximum, by the shareholders or the board of directors").

For many years, statutes routinely required that each director meet certain qualifications, such as being a shareholder or a resident of the state. These requirements have been almost universally eliminated.[104] So long as a person is of legal age, she can be a director. The corporation is free, of course, to impose qualifications for directors—such as stock ownership—usually in either the articles or the bylaws. In the United States, directors must be human beings.[105] In some countries, corporations or other entities may serve as directors, but this practice never caught on in the United States. In countries that permit artificial entities to be directors, an individual must be designated to represent the entity at board meetings and for voting purposes.

The norm is that the entire board is elected at the annual meeting of shareholders. Accordingly, the usual term for directors (unless the articles provide otherwise) is one year. We will see below that directors may serve longer terms if the corporation has a "staggered" board. Whatever the length of the term, however, in all states a director holds office—even after expiration of the term—until her successor is "elected and qualified."[106] As a result, the failure to hold annual meetings of shareholders does not affect the power of a corporation to continue to transact its business; directors remain in office, with power to act.

The holdover director provision is particularly important when shareholders are deadlocked in voting power and thus unable to elect successors to directors whose terms have expired. When that happens, those who are currently on the board remain in office, for however long the impasse lasts.[107] Of course, a director can resign her position whenever she wishes.[108]

Most states permit corporations to establish "staggered" terms for directors.[109] With a staggered (or "classified")[110] board, the direc-

---

[104] *See, e.g.,* DEL. GEN. CORP. LAW § 141(b)("Directors need not be stockholders unless so required by the certificate of incorporation or the by-laws.").

[105] *See, e.g.,* RMBCA § 8.03(a)(board consists of one or more "individuals," which is defined at § 1.40(13) as "natural person[s]"); DEL. GEN. CORP. LAW § 141(b)(each director "shall be a natural person").

[106] *See, e.g.,* RMBCA § 8.05(e).

[107] One way out of this unfortunate situation would be involuntary dissolution of the corporation, which we address in Chapter 12(H).

[108] *See, e.g.,* DEL. GEN. CORP. LAW § 141(b)("Any director may resign at any time upon notice given in writing or by electronic transmission to the corporation.")

[109] *See, e.g.,* RMBCA 8.06.

[110] In some states, statutes speak of dividing the board into "classes," with one class being elected each year. *See, e.g.,* N.Y. BUS. CORP. LAW § 704. There is some terminological confusion here because "classified" can refer to something else. Sometimes, the articles will provide for different classes of stock. Under RMBCA § 8.04 and

torships are divided into two or three groups, with as nearly equal numbers as possible. Then, one half or one third of the board is elected each year.

- Corporation has nine directorships. Its board could be staggered into three classes of three directorships each. In 2013, the shareholders would elect directors to seats A, B, and C. In 2014, they would elect directors for seats D, E, and F. And in 2015, they would elect directors for seats G, H, and I. Here, each director would serve a three-year term.

- Alternatively, the nine directorships could be divided into two classes, with five elected in year 1 and the other four in year 2, and each director serving a two-year term.

Historically, statutes permitted staggered boards only if there is a relatively large number of directors—usually nine or more. Smaller boards could not be staggered, but were elected in full each year. The trend, however, typified by RMBCA § 8.06, permits staggering a board of any size.

The theoretical justification for a staggered board is that it promotes continuity of leadership. With only a fraction of the directorships open for election each year, it is more difficult for someone to take over the board. Thus, if an aggressor has acquired a majority of the stock, she will only be able to elect new directors to one-third (or one-half) of the seats in one year. The directors elected by the old ownership regime will remain in office for another year or two. In publicly traded corporations formed under Massachusetts law, a staggered board is required, apparently to promote this sort of continuity.[111]

Staggered boards also minimize the effect of cumulative voting. Above, we saw that cumulative voting helps smaller shareholders get representation on the board. As we saw, with cumulative voting, one multiples the number of shares times the number of directors to be elected; the total is the number of votes a shareholder may cumulate on a single candidate if she chooses. A staggered board means that fewer directors are elected each year. This, in turn, reduces the

---

statutes in many states, the articles can provide that a class of stock will elect a certain number of directors. So, for example, the articles may provide that Class A stock may elect two directors. Some people call this a "classified" board. Sometimes, then, "classified" means the stock is divided into different classes, with each having the power to elect a given number of directors. On the other hand, sometimes "classified" is used to indicate that the directors serve staggered terms.

[111] MASS. GEN. LAWS ch. 156D, § 8.06(b).

number of votes a shareholder will have. It takes a larger minority interest to elect one of three directors than it does to elect one of nine directors.

- Corporation has nine directors. If the entire board is elected each year, one share more than ten percent of the stock can elect one director. (We did the math on this in section (C)(5) above).

- If the same company has a staggered board, divided in thirds, it will take one share more than twenty five percent of the stock to elect one director. Clearly, then, it is more difficult for minority interests to get representation on the board if the directors serve staggered terms.

A director might not serve her full term. For instance, a director might resign, die, or be removed by shareholders. It is in the corporation's interest to elect someone to fill out the remainder of the term, so the board stays at full strength. Who selects the new person? States take different approaches here, but the clear modern view, reflected in RMBCA § 8.10(a), is to allow either the shareholders or the directors to elect the new director. In some states, however, the cause of the vacancy will determine who should elect the replacement. If a director dies or resigns, in some states, the remaining directors will select the person to fill out that director's term.[112] If, on the other hand, the director was removed from office by the shareholders, the shareholders will elect the successor.[113]

There is another possibility. A vacancy may be created by amendment to the articles or bylaws to increase the size of the board. If there are five directors and the articles or bylaws are changed to increase the board to seven, there are two new "vacancies." Traditionally, such newly created vacancies can only be filled by the shareholders and not by the remaining directors. The increasingly prevalent view is that the replacement for any vacancy—even one created by an increase in the number of directors—may be elected by the shareholders or by the directors.[114]

If the directors are to select a replacement at a meeting, we must apply the general quorum and voting rules discussed below. Sometimes, though, the fact that there are vacancies will make it impossi-

---

[112] *See, e.g.*, N.Y. BUS. CORP. LAW § 705(a).

[113] *See, e.g.*, N.Y. BUS. CORP. LAW § 705(b) ("Unless the certificate of incorporation or the specific provisions of a by-law adopted by the shareholders provide that the board may fill vacancies occurring in the board by reason of the removal of directors without cause, such vacancies may be filled only by vote of the shareholders.").

[114] RMBCA § 8.10(a).

ble to garner a quorum of the board. A common way to deal with the problem is through a statute allowing election "by the affirmative vote of a majority of all directors remaining in office."[115]

- Corporation has seven directors. Four of the directors leave office before their terms expire, leaving only three directors actually serving. Those three cannot take an act, such as elect new directors, under the normal quorum rules. Why? Because there are only three directors serving, which does not constitute a majority of the seven board positions. Under statutes such as that quoted, the remaining directors may act by majority vote, even though they do not constitute a quorum. Thus, if the remaining directors vote two-to-one (or three-to-zero) to elect replacement directors, they are elected.

Sometimes the articles provide that separate classes of stock are entitled to elect specified numbers of directors. In such a corporation, if a vacancy is to be filled by the shareholders, only shareholders of that class of stock may vote. So if Class A stock elects three directors to the board, and one of those directors is disqualified from service by mental incapacity, on a shareholder vote to fill the vacancy, only those owning Class A stock can vote. Similarly, if the directors are to select the replacement, generally only the remaining directors elected by Class A shareholders can vote.[116]

Finally, note that any director elected to replace one who has left office serves the remainder of the term. So if Director A is removed from office in the eighth month of a one-year term, her replacement will serve only until the end of that year.[117] She may then stand for election to a new term in her own right.

3. The Board Must Act as a Group in One of Two Ways

The power held by directors is held jointly. Accordingly, directors can act only as a body—i.e., as a group. An individual director has no power, simply by virtue of that position, to bind the corporation or to take a corporate act. In most instances, the board takes an act at a meeting, which must satisfy statutory requirements for notice, quorum, and voting. The theory is that shareholders deserve a board decision that is reached after group discussion and deliberation. Views may be changed as a result of discussion, and the sharp-

---

[115] RMBCA § 8.10(a)(3).

[116] *See, e.g.,* RMBCA § 8.10(b).

[117] *See, e.g.,* RMBCA § 8.05(b). If there were a staggered board, with three-year terms, and the original director was replaced in the eighth month of the first year, her replacement would serve through the end of the third year of the term.

ening of minds as a result of joint deliberation improves the decision-
al process.

There are four corollaries to the requirement that the board
must act as a group.

- First, independent, consecutive agreement on a course of action by directors does not work. Thus, if each of the directors
  agreed with a proposition in individual conversations, there
  is no valid board act; the group must decide as a group.

- Second, directors may not vote by proxy.[118] To do so would
  violate the public policy that demands the independent
  judgment of each director. It also would violate the fact that
  directors owe non-delegable fiduciary duties to the corporation.

- Third, directors may not enter into voting agreements tying
  themselves down as to how they will vote.[119] Such an agreement (like a proxy for director voting) would violate the same
  public policies just discussed.

- Fourth, the formalities about notice, quorum, and voting at
  directors' meetings are very strictly enforced.

These corollaries make little sense in the closely held corporation
in which all shareholders are active in the business. There, even the
requirement of a formal meeting of the board will likely be considered
a meaningless formality. Accordingly, as we discussed in section (D)
below, in many close corporations, the shareholders enter management agreements, which can abolish the board and permit more informal decision-making. When this is not done, however, and management rests in the board, the proprietors and their lawyers should
be scrupulous in following the rules.

Instead of holding a meeting, the board of directors can take an
act if they enter a unanimous written consent. Section 8.21(a) of the
RMBCA is typical. It provides that unless the articles or bylaws require a meeting, a board action "may be taken without a meeting if
each director signs a consent describing the action to be taken and
delivers it to the corporation." Such consent is considered an act of

---

[118] Shareholders can vote by proxy. Remember that one person might play more
than one role in the corporation at a time. So if one person is simultaneously a shareholder and a director, she may vote *as a shareholder* by proxy; she cannot vote, however, *as a director* by proxy.

[119] Again, *shareholders* may enter into voting agreements on how to vote as shareholders. But directors may not enter into agreements on how they will vote as directors.

the board, just as if the action had been taken after a formal meeting.[120]

Statutes allowing such written consents are salutary. First, they permit approval of routine matters without a formal meeting. Second, by requiring unanimous approval, they do not foster the stifling of minority sentiment. Any director who is opposed to taking the action proposed, or who believes that the board would benefit from full discussion, can require a formal meeting by refusing to sign the written consent.

Because statutes require that these consents be signed and filed with the corporation, they must be in writing. An increasing number of states permit director consent by electronic transmission.[121] Though all directors must agree to the action, they may do so on separate pieces of paper or in separate emails. For instance, in a corporation with five directors, each could sign and file with the corporate records a separate document.

4. Board Meetings: Notice, Quorum, and Voting

Unless the board acts through unanimous written consent, it will act at a meeting. Technically, the board takes an act by adopting a "resolution" at the meeting. In this section, we discuss the exacting requirements for board meetings. A board meeting (like a meeting of shareholders) can be held anywhere and need not be held in the state of incorporation.

Types of Meetings and the Notice Required for Each. There are two types of board meetings: regular and special. The time and place of regular meetings usually are set in the bylaws, or the bylaws can empower the board to determine when to call such a meeting. Regular meetings are usually held at specific intervals, and the interval can be set for whatever makes sense for the particular board (weekly, monthly, quarterly, etc.). As a general rule, public corporations tend to have fewer regular meetings than smaller corporations, with routine functions delegated to an executive committee. It is customary to hold a regular meeting of directors immediately after the annual meeting of shareholders.

Any board meeting other than a regular meeting is a special meeting. The difference between regular and special meetings of the

---

[120] *See, e.g.,* RMBCA § 8.21(b).

[121] RMBCA § 8.21 permits action without a meeting "if each director signs a consent describing the action to be taken and delivers it to the corporation." RMBCA § 1.40(22A) defines "sign" or "signature" to include "any manual, facsimile, conformed or electronic signature."

board has nothing to do with what matters may be considered. Rather, the difference concerns notice.

Generally, the corporation is not required to give notice to directors of a regular meeting,[122] but must give notice of a special meeting.[123] The details of the notice requirement for special meetings vary a bit from state to state with regard to three things: (1) when it must be given, (2) what it must state, and (3) how it may be given.

Section 8.22(b) of the RMBCA requires that the corporation give notice at least two days before the special meeting. Some states require five days' notice.[124] The statutory standard in this regard is a default rule, however, and the corporation may change it in the articles. New York has a statutory requirement for notice of special meetings, but it says nothing about when it must be given.[125]

In terms of content, states largely agree that the notice must state the date, time, and place of the meeting, but that it need not state the purpose for which the meeting is called.[126] This is different from notice of shareholders' meetings, which often require a statement of purpose. The reason for this difference is that board meetings routinely consider a wide variety of business matters, often under differing degrees of urgency, while shareholders meet only to consider a limited number of important matters.

Section 8.22(b) of the RMBCA says nothing about the form of the notice of special meeting. The Official Comments to the RMBCA make it clear, though, that the notice can be written or oral. This conclusion is consistent with § 1.41, which provides that notice under the RMBCA "must be in writing unless oral notice is reasonable under the circumstances." That section also makes clear that notice by electronic transmission constitutes written notice. An increasing number of states allow e-mail notice. New York again is unusual in that its Business Corporation Law says nothing about the form of notice.[127]

---

[122] *See, e.g.*, RMBCA § 8.22(a).

[123] *See, e.g.*, RMBCA § 8.22(b).

[124] *See, e.g.*, PA. CONS. STAT. § 1703(b)("[W]ritten notice of every special meeting of the board of directors shall be given to each director at least five days before the day named for the meeting.").

[125] N.Y. BUS. CORP. LAW § 711.

[126] *See, e.g.*, N.Y. BUS. CORP. LAW § 711(b) (notice need not state the purpose unless the bylaws require that it does).

[127] N.Y. BUS. CORP. LAW § 711(b) (bylaws may prescribe what will constitute notice of board meetings).

What happens if the corporation fails to give the required notice? As with shareholders, any purported action taken at that meeting is void or voidable, unless those not given notice waive the notice defect.[128] There are two ways a director may waive the defective notice. First, they may do so expressly, by filing in the corporate records a written notice of their intent to waive the defect. They may do this anytime (before, during, or even after the meeting).[129] In many corporations, it is routine to have directors sign waivers of notice at every meeting. Second, a director may waive the notice problem impliedly by attending or participating in a meeting without "object[ing] to holding the meeting or transacting business at the meeting."[130]

- Corporation has seven directors. It gives notice of a special meeting of the board to six of the seven (Directors A, B, C, D, E, and F). It fails to give notice to Director G. Despite this, Director G learns of the meeting by talking to Director A. If Director G attends the meeting and does not object to the fact that he was not given notice, the defect is waived, and acts taken at the meeting are valid.

- In contrast, suppose Director G did not learn of the meeting, and did not attend. The board took various acts at that meeting. Those acts can be rendered void by the fact that notice was not given to Director G. This is true even if his vote seemingly would not have mattered. So if Directors A, B, C, D, E, and F all voted in favor of a resolution, Director G's vote in opposition would not have mattered; he would have lost on that vote, six-to-one. Remember the theory: directors are to exercise independent judgment; the interaction and discussion at a meeting may lead some directors to change their minds. By failing to give notice to Director G, the board was bereft of that interaction. So the act taken can be voided and brought up at another meeting, unless Director G waives the defect in writing. He may well do so. For instance, he might agree with the act, or might be convinced that his presence would have made no difference in the outcome. He may file his written waiver anytime, and thereby protect the corporate act.

---

[128] *See, e.g.,* Neri v. Neri, No. 330627, 1993 WL 7649, at *6 (Conn. Super. Jan. 12, 1993) ("Thus, the court concludes that by virtue of the failure to give John Neri proper notice, the action taken at the 1979 and 1986 meetings was void."); Fogel v. U.S. Energy Systems Inc., No. 3271-CC, 2007 WL 4438978, *3 (Del. Ch. Dec. 13, 2007)(quoting Schroder v. Scotten, Dillon Co., 299 A.2d 431, 435 (Del. Ch. 1972)) ("To the extent that such a [special board] meeting is held without notice, the meeting and 'all acts done at such a meeting are void.'").

[129] *See, e.g.,* RMBCA § 8.23(a).

[130] RMBCA § 8.23(b).

Statutes are usually silent about who may call a special meeting of the board. The matter is usually addressed in the bylaws, and often it is the chief executive officer who will call such a meeting.

At all meetings of the board—regular and special—the corporation's senior executive officer presides. This officer usually holds the title "president" but might instead be the "chief executive officer" or "chairperson of the board." The duties of the chairperson of the board may be described in the bylaws but are largely determined by tradition and practice. She usually determines the agenda of the meeting and may also be involved in preparing information distributed to directors before the meeting. A vice-chair may be named to perform these functions when the chairperson is absent.

    Quorum and Voting. Assuming that any required notice has been given, the board will hold its meeting. The first thing to do is ensure that a quorum is present. Indeed, as a general matter, the board cannot take an act at a meeting in the absence of a quorum.[131] Assuming there is a quorum, the second thing to focus on is the vote required to pass proposed resolutions. In determining a quorum and counting votes, director voting is _per capita,_ which means each person gets one vote.[132]

    If the board is of a fixed size, a quorum consists of a majority of that fixed number. If the board does not have a fixed size—for example, if it has a variable range—a quorum consists of a majority of the directors in office immediately before the meeting begins.[133] The quorum figure can be changed in the articles. Under the traditional view, the quorum requirement can be raised but cannot be lowered. Accordingly, a quorum cannot consist of fewer than a majority of the directors.[134] Increasingly, though, states permit corporations to raise or lower the quorum, with one restriction: a quorum can never be fewer than one-third of the directors described.[135]

---

[131] There are occasional exceptions to this rule. As we saw above, a majority of the directors in office, even if less than a quorum, may elect someone to fill a vacancy on the board. In addition, in some states, the quorum and voting rules are different for board approval of an interested director transaction. We will discuss this in Chapter 7(E)(3).

[132] This is different from shareholder quorum and voting, where the focus is _pro rata,_ which means that shareholders' voting power is determined by their ownership interest. A shareholder with ten shares gets ten times as many votes as a shareholder with one share. In considering quorum and voting by directors, the number of shares each owns is irrelevant. Indeed, directors are not required to be shareholders at all (though they often are).

[133] _See, e.g.,_ RMBCA § 8.24(a).

[134] _See, e.g.,_ N.Y. BUS. CORP. LAW § 707.

[135] _See, e.g.,_ RMBCA § 8.24(b); TEX. BUS. ORGS. CODE § 21.413(b).

- Corporation has nine directors and no relevant corporate document defines the quorum. That means at least five of the nine must attend the meeting to constitute a quorum and conduct business. If only four directors attend, they simply cannot conduct corporate business.

Assuming a quorum is present, an act is taken by passing a resolution. This requires the majority vote of the directors present at the meeting. The articles (and in some states the bylaws) can raise that requirement to a supermajority but generally cannot lower it to less than a majority.[136]

- Corporation has nine directors. Five of them attend the meeting, so a quorum is present. Suppose a resolution is presented and three directors vote (two do nothing but sit there), each of the three voting in favor. The resolution passes because it was approved by a majority of the directors present.

Section 8.24(c) of the RMBCA, and the statutes of most states, require that a quorum actually be present when the vote is taken. In other words, under the general rule, a directors' quorum can be lost, or "broken." Once a quorum is no longer present, the board cannot take an act at that meeting. This rule encourages management to present important issues early in the meeting, when a quorum is more likely to be present rather than toward the end of the meeting.

- Corporation has nine directors. Five attend a meeting, so there is a quorum. They vote on various resolutions. Now one of the five leaves the meeting. That destroys the quorum because only four of the nine are present. Those remaining four cannot take a corporate act.[137]

In some close corporations, the articles define a quorum as all directors and, further, require a unanimous vote to approve a resolution. Proprietors should think long and hard before adopting such provisions. De facto, they give to each director a veto power. This lets any director prevent action to which the others unanimously agree. This may not seem like a problem when the business is being founded. Later, however, after there have been some disagreements, it may lead to spiteful acts and corporate paralysis.

---

[136] *See, e.g.,* RMBCA § 8.24(c)("[T]he affirmative vote of a majority of directors present is the act of the board . . . unless the articles or bylaws require the vote of a greater number of directors.").

[137] This latter rule is different from shareholder voting. With shareholders, a quorum is not lost; once it is present, it is deemed to exist throughout the meeting even if some shareholders leave the meeting.

When analyzing the quorum and voting requirements, we address how many directors are "present" at a meeting. This does not mean, however, that they will all be sitting in the same room. States routinely permit directors to participate in regular or special meetings "by any means of communication by which all directors participating may simultaneously hear each other during the meeting."[138] This includes voice over internet protocols and meeting facilities like gotomeeting.com and Skype. Video capacity is not required. A conference telephone call will suffice—just so all participants can hear and be heard by the other participants.

- Corporation has nine directors. Four are physically present in the board room, and five join in a conference telephone call. The five are on different continents at the time. All nine are "present," and the quorum requirement is met.

Though these provisions are ubiquitous now, the law was surprisingly stubborn in resisting them. In New York, it was not until 1998 that the Business Corporation Law provided as a default provision that communications such as conference telephone calls were allowed. The initial reluctance to embrace technological changes reflected the common law notion that directors must act in a group through communal participation. For many generations, this meant they had to be in the same room.

Rigid application of the rules about quorum and voting could, in some cases, permit a corporation to use its own procedural defects to undo transactions that turn out to be disadvantageous. For example, suppose Corporation enters into a transaction based upon the board's approving a resolution. Suppose now that it quickly becomes apparent that the transaction is a "loser" for Corporation. Can Corporation now try to rescind the transaction because (it now admits) there was no quorum at the board meeting, or because some director was not given required notice and did not waive the defect?

Allowing the corporation to escape the transaction is morally repugnant. It is also unfair to the party with whom the corporation entered the transaction. In most cases, there is no way for that party to know whether the formalities of board action were followed. Thus, principles of estoppel should apply to require the corporation to live up to its end of the transaction.

Registering Dissent or Abstention. If a director disagrees with proposed action at a meeting, she must be careful to ensure that her position is properly recorded. RMBCA § 8.24(d), which reflects the

---

[138] *See, e.g.,* RMBCA § 8.20(b).

common view, provides that any director who is present when corporate action is taken is "deemed to have assented to the action taken" unless she does one of three things. In other words, there is a presumption that if a director was present at the meeting,[139] she agreed with any resolutions that were passed. If one of those resolutions turns out to be improper, or to constitute a breach of fiduciary duty, she will be liable.

Under RMBCA § 8.24(d)(1), a director will not be presumed to have assented to board action if she objects to the transaction of business. This is rather rare—the best example being a failure to give notice of a special meeting.

The other two provisions of § 8.24(d) are more likely relevant. Under § 8.24(d)(2) and (3), the presumption of concurrence does not attach if her "dissent or abstention from the action . . . is entered in the minutes of the meeting" or if she "delivers written notice of [her] dissent or abstention to the presiding officer at the meeting before its conclusion or to the corporation immediately after adjournment of the meeting." Provisions such as this give the director three ways to record her dissent: in the minutes (by requesting such entry at the meeting), or in writing to the presiding officer (for example, a note to the president during the meeting), or to the corporation itself (for example, a letter to the corporate secretary "immediately" after adjournment). Some states are more precise about the third option, and require a registered letter within a set time after adjournment.[140]

All three of these methods involve a writing, which demonstrates that an oral dissent by itself is meaningless.

- Corporation has five directors, all of whom attend the meeting. After discussion, they are to vote on whether the corporation should pay a dividend. Director X, convinced that the

---

[139] If a director was not present at the meeting where the questionable act was taken, generally, she is not liable. So, for instance, if a director missed a meeting at which the board declared an improper dividend—say, because she was sick that day—she would not be liable. An increasing number of states require, however, that the absent director file with the corporation a written dissent within a "reasonable time" of learning of the action taken at the meeting. See, e.g., N.Y. BUS. CORP. LAW § 719(b)("A director who is absent from a meeting of the board . . . when such action is taken shall be presumed to have concurred in the action unless he shall deliver or send by registered mail his dissent thereto . . within a reasonable time of learning of such action."). In such a state, then, the absent director must be careful to dissent once she learns of what happened at the meeting.

[140] See, e.g., MD. CODE CORPS. & ASS'NS § 2–410(a)(2)(iii)("A director of a corporation who is present at a meeting of its board of directors at which action on any corporate matter is taken is presumed to have assented to the action unless: He forwards his written dissent within 24 hours after the meeting is adjourned, by certified mail, return receipt requested, bearing a postmark from the United States Postal Service, to the secretary of the meeting or the secretary of the corporation.").

dividend is improper, announces that she is opposed to the dividend because it is improper. She makes it very clear that she wants to have nothing to do with this act. The other directors then vote four-to-nothing in favor of the dividend. Director X fails to get her dissent recorded in writing in one of the three ways permitted by statute.[141] If the directors are later sued and a court finds that they are personally liable for an improper dividend, Director X is liable.

Filing a written dissent not only eliminates liability, but also obviates later questions of proof. It may also have a desirable psychological effect upon the other directors when they realize that one of their colleagues considers the action questionable. It also gives notice to shareholders and others examining the corporate records that at least one director seriously questioned the propriety of the specific decision.

Rather than filing a notice of dissent, a director may take other steps to delay an action believed to be unwise. She may request that the corporation obtain an opinion of counsel as to the propriety of the proposed transaction. She may resign from the board before the action is taken; if the resignation occurs after the transaction is approved, liability may be avoided only if the director files the appropriate written dissent. (Though it is strongly arguable that a written resignation because of disagreement over an action taken by the board of directors would be viewed as a dissent from that action.) Finally, a director who assented to some act that turned out to be improper may escape liability if she relied in good faith on a report or opinion of a competent officer, employee, or lawyer. This suggests another reason for a director to ask for a delay to allow the corporation to get the opinion of a lawyer, financial expert, etc.

5. Compensation

Traditionally, directors were not compensated for ordinary services as a director. The idea was that they acted as trustees or were motivated by their own financial interest in the corporation. We will see below that officers, in contrast, have traditionally been entitled to compensation. Remember that one person can serve in more than one capacity. Under the traditional view, a person who served both as director and officer would expect compensation only as an officer. Of course, the corporation and the director could agree on compensa-

---

[141] Ordinarily, the corporate secretary would record the dissent in the minutes of the meeting. For some reason, in this hypothetical, this was not done. If you are dissenting, make sure the secretary records it as such.

tion when she was elected or for some extraordinary service beyond normal directorial functions.

In the public corporation, about a century ago, large corporations started paying small honoraria to "outside" (or "non-management") directors for attending meetings. This practice grew, as did the payments. It is now universal for public corporations to provide substantial compensation to outside directors (those who are not also officers). Indeed, such director compensation in large corporations routinely exceeds $200,000 per year. Some corporations even provide retirement plans for outside directors. Corporations believe these compensation plans improve the quality and interest of outside directors, though shareholder-oriented groups have sometimes complained that these plans are too generous.

All states expressly authorize director compensation. Under § 8.11 of the RMBCA, for example, unless the articles or bylaws provide otherwise, "the board of directors may fix the compensation of directors." This raises an inherent conflict of interest because the board is setting the compensation of its members. As fiduciaries of the corporation, they cannot use this opportunity to line their pockets. They must act in good faith and the compensation must be reasonable.

Directors' compensation was long paid in cash. Increasingly, public corporations pay directors in stock or options to buy stock. The National Association of Corporate Directors suggested this move in the 1990s on the theory that it would align the outside directors' interest with that of the shareholders.

At one time, it was not uncommon to find a few people who served on the boards of five or six large corporations simultaneously. This is rare today because of increased focus on the fiduciary duties owed by directors to the corporation. It is difficult to discharge these significant duties to more than one or two corporations at a time. Not only is one nervous about spreading oneself too thin, but serving on boards of different corporations opens the possibility that a director will have an interest on both sides of a particular transaction. Such an interested director transaction raises serious fiduciary issues, as we discuss in Chapter 7(E)(3).

6. Committees of the Board

Like any group, a board of directors might find it helpful to delegate some of its functions to a subset. It may be cumbersome, especially with a large board, to muster a quorum and hold a meeting on short notice. Or there may be long-term questions before the board that call for expertise or interest that only a few members of the board may have. In such instances and many others, the board may delegate to a committee.

There is something inherently problematic about such committees. After all, the board is the repository of managerial power. If it can delegate its authority to a committee, the concern is that the board members—who were elected to manage the corporation—are abdicating their responsibilities to a subset.

In recognition of this concern, the common law imposed limits on delegation to committees. Essentially, it allowed the board to delegate only "routine" functions. Today, there is no need to worry about what constitutes "routine" functions because the matter is handled by statute. Such legislation routinely starts with the broad statement that the board can form committees and then carves out exceptions, tasks that a committee simply cannot perform.[142] In a few states, including Nevada, delegation to a committee is permitted without limit.[143]

The exceptions are non-delegable matters that must be undertaken by the full board. These vary from state to state, but the RMBCA is typical in providing that committees may not: (1) authorize distributions (like dividends), (2) recommend to shareholders a fundamental corporate change, (3) fill a board vacancy, or (4) amend or repeal bylaws.[144] Some states add to this list that a committee cannot set director compensation.

Two observations are in order at this point. First, the fact that a board may delegate does not mean that it will. The authority to create committees is voluntary, and need not be used. Second, though committees cannot do any of the tasks listed as non-delegable, they can recommend such acts for full board action. Thus, the board may create a committee to determine whether dividends ought to be declared and, if so, how large they should be. Although the committee cannot declare a dividend, the full board might accept the committee's recommendation on the issue.

The most common type of committee is the "executive committee," which performs the functions of the board between meetings of the full board. For instance, if the full board meets only a few times each year—say, once per quarter—the executive committee enables

---

[142] For example, RMBCA § 8.25(b) sets out the general power to create committees, and § 8.25(e) provides four tasks that committees may not perform.

[143] *See, e.g.,* NEV. STAT. § 78.125(1).

[144] RMBCA § 8.25(c).

discharge of board functions without having to call the full board for special meetings. Executive committees are usually composed of inside directors (that is, those who are also officers or otherwise employed by the corporation). Because these people work fulltime for the company, they are most likely to be available on short notice as needed.

Other kinds of committees are also routine, especially in publicly held corporations.[145] The three ubiquitous standing committees are the audit committee, the compensation committee, and the nominating committee. These committees are generally composed of outside directors who are not affiliated with management. Other committees that may predominantly be composed of outside directors include strategic planning, public policy, environmental compliance, information technology, and employee benefits.

In addition to these standing committees, the board may create special ad hoc committees to consider the merits of specific sensitive issues, such as derivative litigation filed by shareholders on behalf of the corporation, requests for indemnification for expenses incurred by directors or officers in connection with that litigation, or the ratification of conflict of interest transactions between a director and the corporation.

Historically, the board could delegate to a committee only if the articles allowed it to do so. This remains true in only a handful of states today.[146] In the overwhelming majority of states, the board may appoint committees (within the limits discussed above) unless the articles or bylaws forbid it.[147] Traditionally, statutes required that committees consist of at least two members. This rule, too, has been rejected by the clear majority, which, like RMBCA § 8.25(a), provides that a committee consists of "one or more members of the board of directors."

Although board committees are widely used, some concern about delegation of board functions is reflected in how they are selected. For most board decisions, all that is required is a majority vote of those directors present at a proper meeting (assuming there is a quorum). Appointment of committees, however, generally requires a majority of all directors in office.[148]

---

[145] Indeed, federal law requires certain committees in public corporations. *See* Chapter 9(B)–(C).

[146] *See, e.g.,* TEX. BUS. ORGS. CODE § 21.416(a)(1).

[147] *See, e.g.,* RMBCA § 8.25(a).

[148] *See, e.g.,* RMBCA § 8.25(b)(1)(requiring that the creation of a committee and the appointment of members must be approved by "a majority of all the directors in

Committees operate under the same quorum and voting requirements as the board itself.[149] Importantly, the creation of a committee does not relieve other directors of their duties to the corporation.[150] A director who is not a member of a committee still owes the fiduciary duties discussed in Chapter 7, and can be held liable for breaching them.

E. Officers

1. Introduction

Officers are employees and agents of the corporation. In section B(4), we discussed their role in the traditional model of corporate management. Here, we address officers in greater detail. We start with statutory requirements regarding how many and what types of officers are mandated. We discuss the sources of officers' authority, which usually will be the bylaws instead of the articles. One key issue is whether an officer can bind the corporation to a transaction. The answer depends upon agency law. As we will see, directors generally hire, monitor, and discharge officers. Like directors, officers owe the corporation various fiduciary duties. These are so important that we devote Chapter 7 to them. Issues of officer compensation are important and of considerable contemporary political interest. We discuss compensation in a larger context of increasing regulation in light of notable financial disasters in the early twenty-first century.

2. Statutory Requirements

Traditionally, statutes required that every corporation have three or four officers, consisting of a president, a secretary, a treasurer, and in some states a vice president. The statutes have always permitted the corporation to name additional officers. It would be cumbersome (in fact, unworkable) in many close corporations to have three or four people serving as officers. Legislatures foresaw the problem long ago and statutes have for decades provided generally that one person may hold multiple offices simultaneously. Even here, though, many states continued until recently to impose an old limitation: that the president and secretary had to be separate people. This restriction was based upon the idea that the law might require the president to sign a contract binding the corporation and the secretary to verify the president's signature. A few states may still recognize this limitation, while some states impose other restrictions. In

---

office when the action is taken"). Instead, the articles or bylaws can provide a number of directors that can approve delegation to a committee. RMBCA § 8.25(b)(2).

[149] *See, e.g.*, RMBCA § 8.25(c).

[150] *See, e.g.*, RMBCA § 8.25(d).

Maryland, for instance, one person can hold multiple offices only if the bylaws allow, and even then the same person cannot be president and vice president at the same time.[151]

The modern view, reflected in RMBCA § 8.40(d), is that "[t]he same individual may simultaneously hold more than one office in a corporation." Moreover, contemporary statutes tend not to require three or four officers. Section 8.40(a) of the RMBCA leaves the matter up to the corporation, providing that "[a] corporation has the offices described in its bylaws or designated by the board of directors in accordance with its bylaws." RMBCA § 8.40(c) requires the existence of only one officer—the person who is responsible for "preparing minutes of the directors' and shareholders' meetings and for maintaining and authenticating the records of the corporation. . ." Although these functions describe the corporate secretary, the RMBCA does not require that the person be given that title.

Most smaller corporations tend to use the traditional titles for their officers. The senior executive is likely called the "president," the principal financial officer the "treasurer," and the keeper of the records the "secretary." In publicly held corporations, titles usually reflect their executive function. Thus, the chief executive officer (CEO) is at the head of managerial control, responsible for a team that usually includes the chief financial officer (CFO), chief operating officer (COO), chief accounting officer (CAO), and chief legal officer (CLO or general counsel). In states still requiring a president, in public corporations it is usually an intermediate management position, though sometimes one person serves as both CEO and president.

Fortunately, there is no need with officers (as there was with shareholders and directors) to discuss meetings and quorum and voting. While shareholders and directors act only as groups, officers function as individuals. In the traditional view of the corporation, they carry out the orders of the board and administer the day-to-day affairs of the corporation subject to the direction and control of the board. In reality, officers in public corporations are a focus of managerial decision making, as we see in Chapter 9(B)(1).

3. Sources of Authority

Officers are employees of the corporation. Interestingly, statutes generally do not define the authority or role of an officer. Section 8.41 of the RMBCA is typical; it provides that each officer "has the authority and shall perform the functions set forth in the bylaws or, to the extent consistent with the bylaws, the functions prescribed by

---

[151] MD. CODE CORPS. & ASS'NS § 2–415(a).

the board of directors or by direction of an officer authorized by the board of directors to prescribe the duties of other officers." This statute gives the corporation notable freedom. It can handle the question of officer authority in bylaws or can delegate to an officer the task of prescribing what the other officers shall do.

The articles are not likely to say much about officers. Indeed, in Chapter 5(C), we saw that modern law does not require the articles to say anything at all about officers.[152] On the other hand, the articles may set forth basically any provision about running the corporation. So it is possible that the articles might address officers. For example, in close corporations, the articles may set forth a shareholder management agreement which, in turn, may grant or limit the authority of officers.

Generally, the important sources of authority for officers in a closely held corporation will be the bylaws and board resolutions that authorize an officer to enter into particular transactions approved by the board. The following are typical boilerplate descriptions of the roles of officers as used in many smaller corporations. These are the sorts of things one commonly finds in bylaws of closely held corporations. The board or bylaws may assign additional duties to any officer, and may provide for other officers, such as an assistant treasurer.

The president is often referred to as "the principal executive officer of the corporation." Subject to the control of the board, she usually "supervises and controls the business and affairs of the corporation." She is the proper officer to execute corporate contracts, certificates for securities, and other corporate instruments. The vice president performs the duties of the president when the president is absent or unable to perform. She may also execute share certificates and other corporate instruments.

The corporate secretary has several functions. She keeps the minutes of the proceedings of both the board and the shareholders, and ensures that the required notice is given for meetings of those groups. She acts as custodian of the corporate records and of the corporate seal, and should affix the seal to all authorized documents. The secretary keeps a register of the name and address of each shareholder, and signs, along with the president or vice president,

---

[152] There is a good reason not to have provisions about officers in the articles—once things are in the articles, it is rather difficult to amend them. Amendment of articles is a fundamental corporate change that requires action by the board and the shareholders, as we will see in Chapter 12(D). Bylaws, on the other hand, can usually be amended by one group or the other.

certificates for shares of the corporation. She is also in charge of recording transfers of the corporation's stock.

Finally, the treasurer generally is in "charge and custody of and is responsible for" all funds and securities of the corporation. She receives, gives receipts for, and deposits, all money payable to the corporation. The treasurer may be required to give a bond to ensure faithful performance.

In publicly held corporations, the roles of the CEO, CFO, COO, CAO, and others usually will not be described in the articles or bylaws. Instead, they are often found in organization manuals that describe the corporation's structure. These manuals typically are prepared by management and may be approved by the board of directors.

4. Application of Agency Law

As an artificial entity, a corporation can operate only through the actions of humans. Officers are agents of the corporation (other employees may be agents of the corporation as well). Agency is the law of delegation by which a principal (P) permits an agent (A) to act on its behalf in transactions with a third party (TP). Here, the corporation is P and the officer is A. The officer, like any agent, may have actual or apparent authority to bind P.

Actual authority, as we saw in Chapter 2, is created by manifestations from P to A. In the corporate context, such manifestations may be in the articles or (more likely) the bylaws or (most likely) created by board act.[153] Typically, the board will pass a resolution authorizing A to do something on the corporation's behalf, such as negotiate and enter into a deal with TP to provide supplies for the corporation. Actual authority includes the implied power to bind the corporation to acts that—while not expressly spelled out by the board— are reasonably necessary to perform the task given.[154]

In dealing with a representative of a corporation, TP has a dilemma: how does she know whether that person can bind the corporation? If the corporation is not bound, TP can look only to A for satisfaction on the contract, and A may be a person of limited means. Usually, TP will insist that the officer produce a certified copy of a

---

[153] See, e.g., Miller v. A. & N. R.R. Co., 476 S.W.2d 389, 393–94 (Tex. Ct. Civ. App. 1972) (bylaws may authorize the president to appoint a general manager, whose appointment does not require approval by the board).

[154] "If the agent is reasonable in inferring the existence of such unspoken permission, then the agent has implied actual authority." FRANKLIN A. GEVURTZ, CORPORATION LAW 181 (2d ed. 2010).

board resolution authorizing the transaction. The resolution should direct a named officer to enter into the transaction on behalf of the corporation. If the corporate secretary executes the certificate and the corporate seal is affixed, the corporation is bound because keeping and certifying corporate records is within the actual authority of the secretary.[155]

This is true even if the secretary lies to TP. In *In re Drive-In Development Corp.*,[156] a bank agreed to lend money to Company A only if a related corporation, Company B, guaranteed the loan. The corporate secretary of Company B prepared a fake set of minutes that purported to show that the board had guaranteed the loan. In fact, however, the board knew nothing about it. Company B was bound by the minutes, however, because its corporate secretary has actual authority to certify corporate documents.[157]

Apparent authority, as we saw in Chapter 2, is created by manifestations from P to TP. For example, in the general partnership, each partner has authority to bind the partnership to deals in the ordinary course of business. In the corporate context, this means conduct by the corporation that would lead a reasonably prudent TP to believe that the officer had authority to bind the corporation to the deal. For example, if an officer has entered into transactions with TP in the past, and the corporation paid the bills, TP is likely protected. The corporation will be liable on the new transaction because the officer had apparent authority to bind it.[158]

In the corporate world, there is much discussion of the president's authority to bind the corporation to contracts she enters into on behalf of the entity. Clearly, the president has actual authority to do what the board gives her express power to do. Beyond that, though, does the president have implied actual authority or apparent authority to bind the corporation? One common approach is to say that the president can bind the corporation to contracts entered into

---

[155] Of course, the corporation could remove this authority—for example, in a bylaw provision stating that the secretary lacks any such authority. Even then, it is likely the corporation would be liable under apparent authority because the corporation manifested to TP (by bestowing the position of "secretary" on this person) that TP had the authority customarily held by such officers.

[156] 371 F.2d 215 (7th Cir. 1966).

[157] *Id.* at 219 ("Generally, it is the duty of the secretary to keep the corporate records and to make proper entries of the actions and resolutions of the directors. Therefore it was within the authority of [the secretary] to certify that a resolution such as [that] challenged here was adopted."). This result protects TP, which is appropriate. It is hard to imagine what else TP could have done here to avoid liability.

[158] The corporation may have a right to be indemnified by the officer because she exceeded her actual authority.

in the "ordinary" course of business.[159] Thus the president cannot bind the corporation to "extraordinary" contracts. The dividing line between ordinary and extraordinary is not always clear, and depends to a degree on the custom for people holding that title in like-sized corporations in that geographical areas. For instance, a president might not have authority to enter lengthy employment contracts with employees or to settle litigation involving the corporation.[160]

Other doctrines may be relevant when an officer purports to act on behalf of the corporation. Suppose, for instance, that the board learns that an officer has entered into a deal with TP for which the officer had no authority. The corporation can agree to be bound by the contract (despite the lack of authority). The corporation will then be liable on the deal via ratification. The same result would follow if the corporation accepted the benefit of the transaction entered into by the officer.

What happens, instead, if the corporation does nothing? Generally, ratification requires an affirmative act by P. So if the corporation does nothing, it will not be bound by ratification. On the other hand, if the corporation accepts a benefit of the contract, a court will probably find that the corporation is liable on the contract. In doing so, the court may use terms such as "estoppel" or "unjust enrichment." Courts are often imprecise in using these terms, but the results of the cases are usually consistent with common sense.

- Officer has actual authority to bind Corporation to contracts for supplies not exceeding $3,000 per month. Officer enters into such a contract for $4,000. The supplies are delivered and Corporation accepts and uses them. Common sense tells

---

[159] *See, e.g.,* Bloom v. Nathan Vehon Co. 173 N.E. 270, 272 (Ill. 1930) ("The general rule is that the president of a corporation, as agent and representative, has power, in the ordinary course of business, to execute contracts and bind the corporation in so doing."); Bell Atlantic Tricon Leasing Corp. v. DRR, Inc., 443 S.E.2d 374, 376–77 (N.C. Ct. App. 1994) ("Generally, when the president acts for the corporation with respect to matters outside the corporation's ordinary course of business, in the absence of express authorization for such acts by the board of directors, the corporation is not bound.").

Some courts speak of the president's "inherent" authority to bind the corporation to contracts in the ordinary course of business. *See, e.g.,* Menard, Inc. v. Dage-MTI, Inc., 726 N.E.2d 1206, 1210–15 (Ind. 2000). The Restatement (Second) embraces the concept under the rubric "inherent agency power." The Restatement (Third) rejects the concept, as we discussed in Chapter 2.

[160] *See, e.g.,* Templeton v. Nocona Hills Owners Ass'n, Inc., 555 S.W.2d 534, 538 (Tex. Ct. Civ. App. 1977) ("The execution of an employment contract binding the corporation to employ a person in a managerial position for a period of one year could not be considered a matter in the ordinary and usual course of appellee's business."). And, of course, the president does not have power to do things that are required by statute to be performed by the board, such as recommending a fundamental corporate change to shareholders.

us that Corporation should be liable on that deal. Courts get to that result, but the theoretical basis is often unclear.

We have considered whether an officer can bind the corporation to deals with TPs. Now we turn to a related question—will the officer be personally liable on these deals? The answer again is found in agency law. The starting point is that the officer (or any agent of the corporation) who acts within her authority is not personally liable on the transaction. This is because she has acted as an agent for a disclosed principal, and thus is not a party to the contract. The officer must be careful, however, to avoid liability under any of five theories.

First, an officer may expressly guarantee the performance by the corporation. TPs often insist on such personal guarantees, which may be written or oral, and must be supported by consideration or reliance if it is to be enforceable. Whether it must also be in writing depends on the statute of frauds.

Second, an agent can bind herself by creating the impression that she is negotiating as an individual, rather than as an agent of the corporation. She must be careful about how her capacity is represented on the contract. Even if the existence of the corporation is disclosed, she may be jointly liable with the corporation because of informality in the manner of execution. The proper manner for a corporate officer or agent to execute a document in the name of, and on behalf of, a corporation is the following:

XYZ Corporation

By: _____

President

Any variation from this form could be problematic. Merely designating the corporate office may be deemed simply as an identification of the signer, and not as an indication that she signs as an agent. For example, this form is ambiguous:

XYZ Corporation

_____

President

Here, it is not clear whether (1) the corporation and the president are joint obligors or (2) the president is signing as an agent of the corporation. The word "president" does not resolve the ambiguity because it may be either an identification of an individual co-obligor, or an indication that she signed as an agent of the corporation.

Third, if an officer negotiates a transaction without disclosing that she is acting solely on behalf of the corporation, she is personally liable to TP on general agency principles relating to undisclosed principals.

Fourth, if the agent is acting beyond the scope of her authority, she may be personally liable on the transaction unless the corporation relieves her from liability by ratifying the transaction. An agent implicitly warrants that she has authority to bind P to the transaction. (This principle would not apply, though, if TP were aware that A lacked authority.)

Fifth, liability might be imposed by statute. Failure to pay franchise taxes or to publish a notice of incorporation may lead (depending on the state) to individual as well as corporate liability on corporate obligations.

As a general rule, knowledge acquired by an officer while acting in furtherance of the business or in the course of employment is imputed to the corporation. So, for example, if an officer learns that an employee is stealing from the corporation, that knowledge is imputed to the corporation even though the officer fails to disclose the information to the board or responsible officers.[161]

On a related matter, usually an officer's wrongful intention may also be imputed to a corporation. This fact may open the business itself to civil liability or even criminal prosecution. In the criminal arena, most such cases involve "white collar crime," which generally concerns the theft of money. Corporations have occasionally been indicted for "personal" crimes such as murder, but actual prosecutions are extremely rare. For a corporation to be prosecuted for such conduct, the conduct itself must have been connected with, or in furtherance of, the corporation's business, and the officer's position with the corporation must have been such as to justify imputation of criminal intent to the corporation.[162]

---

[161] *See, e.g., In re* Sunpoint Securities, Inc., 377 B.R. 513, 562–64 (Bankr. E.D. Tex. 2007) (finding that knowledge of theft and misrepresentation can be imputed to the corporation if the officer was acting in furtherance of the corporation's business).

[162] *See, e.g.,* Center v. Hampton Affiliates, Inc., 488 N.E.2d 828, 830 (N.Y. 1985) (concluding that, for there to be no imputation of liability to the corporation, "the agent must have totally abandoned his principal's interests and be acting entirely for his own or another's purposes. [The adverse interest exception] cannot be invoked merely because he has a conflict of interest or because he is not acting primarily for his principal.").

5. Selection and Removal of Officers

Normally, the board of directors hires and discharges officers. The bylaws may permit an officer to appoint other officers. If so, that officer will also have authority to remove the officers.[163] Section 8.43(b) of the RMBCA is typical of modern statutes in providing that "[a]n officer may be removed at any time with or without cause" either by the board or the appointing officer. Accordingly, officers serve at will. The point is driven home by statutory provisions that "[t]he appointment of an officer does not itself create contract rights."[164]

On the other hand, an officer may have contract rights if she and the corporation enter into an employment contract for a term. Such terms might be found in a bylaw provision, for example, indicating that officers will serve for one year. The board has authority to grant an officer a long-term employment contract, even though it will tie the hands of future boards. Doing so might be necessary, for example, for the corporation to lure a particular person to serve as an officer. When an officer has such an arrangement, the corporation may be liable for breach of contract if it removes the officer before the term expires (assuming the officer is not removed for cause). The typical remedy for breach of an employment contract is damages, and not specific performance.

Can a corporation enter into a lifetime contract with an officer? The issue tends to arise in family-run closely held businesses where a contract provides the founder of the business with lifetime income. There is nothing inherently illegal about such deals, as long as they are expressly authorized by the board. Some cases involving claims of lifetime contracts are based upon oral statements. When the facts are ambiguous, courts tend to be hostile to claims of a lifetime contract. Things can change dramatically over the years, and some courts seem to treat a claim of a lifetime contract as inherently implausible. Sometimes, such deals are not enforced because the court concludes that the person ostensibly authorizing the arrangement lacked authority to do so.[165]

---

[163] The RMBCA is typical in providing that the board of directors will "elect" officers and that an appointing officer will "appoint" officers. RMBCA § 8.40(b). The difference in terminology reflects the fact that the board of directors will make its decision as a group—generally by majority vote—whereas an officer with authority to appoint will do so herself.

[164] RMBCA § 8.44(a).

[165] See, e.g., Masters v. Cobb, 431 So. 2d 540, 541–42 (Ala. 1983) (holding that an agent lacked actual or apparent authority to hire anyone on a lifetime basis); McInerney v. Charter Golf, Inc., 680 N.E.2d 1347, 1353 (Ill. 1997) (holding that contracts for lifetime employment must be in writing).

It is clear that an officer or employee with a valid employment contract may be discharged for cause without breaching the contract. "Cause" includes dishonesty, negligence, refusal to obey reasonable orders, refusal to follow reasonable rules, or a variety of other acts such as engaging in sexual harassment or an unprovoked fight. Such conduct constitutes a breach of an implied covenant of good faith in any employment contract. As noted above, officers without a contract for term employment are at will employees and may be discharged at any time.

In closely held corporations, employment contracts are often part of the basic planning arrangement among shareholders. Terms relating to employment may be placed in shareholders' management agreements. Courts may be more willing to order specific performance of a shareholders' management agreement than of an employment contract per se.[166] In fact, a shareholders' management agreement may expressly provide that specific performance should be available if there is a breach.

The board is responsible for monitoring the officers. The level of detail involved in monitoring will depend upon the size and structure of the corporation. In the large public corporation, the board cannot engage in a hands-on, "I'm looking over your shoulder" kind of monitoring. In close corporations, however, it can. In any corporation, however, the board must engage in appropriate review. Failure to do so can constitute a breach of the board's duty of care. Indeed, one especially important current issue involving the duty of care is the establishment of appropriate oversight procedures to allow the board to monitor the officers.

Finally, matters of officer compensation, especially in large public corporations, have commanded attention in recent years. Employment contracts for high-ranking personnel in public corporations often provide for deferred compensation, pension plan benefits, options to purchase shares at bargain prices, reimbursement of business expenses, and other tax-related benefits.

---

[166] For example, in *Wasserman v. Rosengarden,* 406 N.E.2d 131 (Ill. Ct. App. 1980), the appellate court reversed a summary judgment that had been entered in favor of the defendant corporation. The court explained: "In the present case, plaintiff's well-pleaded facts state that he agreed to become an employee, director, officer and shareholder of the defendant corporation. He further agreed to pay into the corporation a sum of $20,000 and enter into a share agreement. In return, he was to receive 20 percent ownership interest in the corporation, be reelected as director and officer and share equally in salaries and bonuses. This agreement was to remain in full force and effect as long as plaintiff remained a shareholder or the corporation remained in existence. . . . [W]e see no reason for precluding the parties from reaching arrangements concerning the management of the closely held corporation which were agreeable to the three shareholders." *Id.* at 134.

6. Fiduciary Duties Owed by Officers

Chapter 7 is devoted to fiduciary duties traditionally referred to as "directors' duties." They include duties of good faith, care, and loyalty. Directors owe these duties to the corporation and to the shareholders. It is clear today, however, that officers also owe these duties. Section 8.42(a) of the RMBCA codifies the same basic standards for conduct of officers as § 8.31(a) does for directors. Accordingly, Chapter 7 addresses the potential liability of officers as well as directors.

Beyond these basic fiduciary duties, RMBCA § 8.42(b) imposes on officers an important duty to disclose to superiors (for example, a superior officer or the board) any information that is material to the superior or that involves "any actual or probable material violation of law involving the corporation or material breach of duty to the corporation. . ." Accordingly, an officer who becomes aware of such problems is required to come forward. She cannot remain silent and at the same time remain faithful to her duty to the corporation.

Chapter 7

FIDUCIARY DUTIES

Analysis

A. Introduction
B. Who Owes What Duties to Whom?
C. The Duty of Care
    1. Overview
    2. Cases Involving Inaction
    3. Cases Involving Misfeasance: Managerial Action and the Business Judgment Rule
D. The Obligation of Good Faith
E. The Duty of Loyalty
    1. Overview
    2. Competing Ventures
    3. Self-Dealing ("Interested Director" Transactions)
    4. Usurpation of Business Opportunities
F. Which Directors Are Liable?
G. Duties of Controlling Shareholders
    1. Transfer of the Controlling Interest
    2. Transfer Accompanied by Resignations of Directors
    3. Two Famous But Odd Cases
    4. Parent-Subsidiary Corporation Issues

———

A. Introduction

Those who manage a business are fiduciaries to the business. A fiduciary is "[a] person who is required to act for the benefit of another person on all matters within the scope of their relationship. . ."[1] With the fiduciary's power comes responsibility. Accordingly, the managers owe to the corporation two bedrock fiduciary duties—those of care and loyalty. We discuss those duties in detail in sections C and E of this Chapter. In addition, fiduciaries must act in good faith. Although some courts and professors consider good faith to be a third "fiduciary duty," the emerging view, led by the Delaware Supreme Court, is that good faith is not a separate duty; it is, instead, a component of the duty of loyalty, as we discuss in section D.

Directors and officers owe these fiduciary duties to their corporation. Shareholders, in contrast, do not, because they are not managers. We will see in Chapter 8(D), however, that shareholders can

---

[1] Black's Law Dictionary 702 (9th ed. 2009).

manage a closely held corporation directly. When they do so, they will owe the fiduciary duties discussed in this Chapter. For convenience, we will speak of the duties owed by directors. Throughout the Chapter, however, this discussion should be understood also to encompass officers and shareholders who manage a closely held corporation.

The fiduciary duties with which we are concerned are owed to the corporation. Breach of the one of the duties gives rise to a claim by the corporation to recover from the breaching directors for harm caused to the business. In section F, we will address circumstances in which particular directors can be held liable for these breaches.

Section G addresses the common law concerning "controlling" shareholders. A controlling shareholder is one who owns enough stock to permit functional control over the business, whether it is closely or publicly held. Courts increasingly impose responsibilities on such persons, even if they do not serve as managers (and therefore are not subject to the classical fiduciary duties).[2]

B. Who Owes What Duties to Whom?

Fiduciary duties are imposed upon those who have the power to manage. Thus, directors and officers always owe fiduciary duties to the corporation. Because shareholders usually have no power to manage, they owe no fiduciary duties.[3] They can pursue their self-interest at the expense of the business and other shareholders. As noted above, however, when shareholders assume management responsibilities—as they may in a closely held corporation—they will owe fiduciary duties to the business. Functionally, then, those who manage the corporation owe the duties.

Occasionally, courts refer to directors as "trustees" of the corporation and suggest that they owe the duties of a trustee.[4] This char-

---

[2] Thus, a "managing" shareholder and a "controlling" shareholder are not the same thing. The former is one who has the de jure authority to make corporate decisions. The latter has the de facto power to elect a controlling portion of the managers of the business. Of course, one person might be a managing and a controlling shareholder simultaneously. But we will separate the discussions of the two.

[3] *See, e.g.,* Ringling Bros.-Barnum & Bailey Combined Shows v. Ringling, 53 A.2d 441, 447 (Del. 1947) ("Generally speaking, a shareholder may exercise wide liberality of judgment in the matter of voting, and it is not objectionable that his motives may be for personal profit, or determined by whims or caprice . . ."); Harris v. Carter, 582 A.2d 222, 234 (Del. Ch. 1990) ("First, is the principle that a shareholder has a right to sell his or her stock and in the ordinary case owes no duty in that connection to other shareholders when acting in good faith.").

[4] *See, e.g.,* Woodruff v. Cole, 269 S.W. 599, 600 (Mo. 1925) ("The directors are the agents or trustees of the corporation for the management of the corporate property, and are charged with the duties and are subject to the liabilities and disabilities of fiduciaries."); Kim v. Grover C. Coors Trust, 179 P.3d 86, 91 (Colo. Ct. App. 2007) ("The fiduciary duties of a director or controlling shareholder are equivalent to the

acterization has never been accurate. True, trustees and directors are fiduciaries. That does not mean, however, that they are equivalent. Trustees are given legal title to property so they can manage it to the advantage of the beneficiaries (who hold equitable title to the property). Trustees are required to preserve and maintain the assets for the beneficiaries. They are expected to be conservative and may be held liable if they commit trust assets to speculative ventures. Directors, in contrast, are expected to maximize the return to shareholders, which may require boldness, audacity, and risk-taking.

Directors owe duties of care and loyalty. It is important to remember that they owe these duties *to the corporation.*[5] Courts occasionally say that directors also owe these duties to the shareholders.[6] By this, however, they mean that the duties are owed to the shareholders collectively, and not individually. This is simply another way of saying that the duties run to the corporation.[7] A breach of duty gives rise to a claim by the corporation against the director. Such claims are often vindicated through shareholder derivative suits, which are the focus of Chapter 13.

The fiduciary duties discussed in this Chapter differ from that implicated by unfair dealing in closely held corporations. In Chapter 8(F), we will discuss the strong trend toward recognizing a fiduciary

---

'high standard of duty required of trustees.'" (*quoting* Kullgren v. Navy Gas & Supply Co., 135 P.2d 1007, 1010 (Colo. 1943))).

[5] *See, e.g.,* Schautteet v. Chester State Bank, 707 F.Supp. 885, 888 (E.D. Tex. 1988)("Officers and directors owe fiduciary duties only to the corporation. Therefore, [a shareholder] has no individual fiduciary right to enforce against any officer or director [of the company]'.").

One interesting question is whether corporate fiduciaries owe any duties to creditors of the corporation. The general answer is no. This changes, however, when the company files for reorganization under Chapter 11 of the Bankruptcy Code. Then, management must protect the interests of the creditors. The board is able to protect itself in these cases by seeking court approval for its various acts. The court order will protect directors from liability for breaching fiduciary duties to the creditors.

A more difficult situation arises when the corporation may be insolvent but has not filed for bankruptcy protection or reorganization. Directors must be quite careful. In Geyer v. Ingersoll Publications Co., 621 A.2d 784, 790 (Del. Ch. 1992), the court recognized a director fiduciary duty to the creditors so long as the corporation is "in fact" insolvent. And in Credit Lyonnais Bank Nederland, N.V. v. Pathe Communications Corp., No. 12150, 1991 WL 277613 (Del. Ch. Dec. 30, 1991), the court held that directors of a corporation "in the vicinity of insolvency" owe fiduciary duties to shareholders and creditors to "maximize the corporation's long-term wealth-creating capacity." *Id.* at * 1155–1157.

[6] *See, e.g.,* Malone v. Brincat, 722 A.2d 5, 10 (Del. 1998) ("The directors of Delaware corporations stand in a fiduciary relationship not only to the stockholders but also to the corporations upon whose boards they serve.").

[7] *See, e.g.,* Favour v. Faour, 789 S.W.2d 620, 621–22 (Tex. Ct. Civ. App. 1990) ("A corporate officer owes a fiduciary duty to the shareholders collectively, i.e. the corporation, but he does not occupy a fiduciary relationship with an individual shareholder, unless some contract or special relationship exists between them in addition to the corporate relationship.").

obligation not to oppress fellow shareholders in small corporations. Those duties run from shareholder to shareholder, and are vindicated by direct personal claims by and for the benefit of the oppressed shareholder against the controlling shareholder.

The duty of care requires directors to take their jobs seriously. A typical statement, found in RMBCA § 8.30(b), is that directors discharge their duties "with the care that a person in a like position would reasonably believe appropriate under the circumstances." As we will discuss in section C, directors may breach this duty through nonfeasance or misfeasance. The former occurs when a director simply does not do much of anything; if her dereliction causes harm to the company, she may be liable for breach of the duty of care. Misfeasance refers to an act by the board on behalf of the company that turned out to harm the company. The "business judgment rule" limits judicial inquiry into such action. As we will see, courts generally review the quality of the decision making process used by the managers rather than the substantive "correctness" of the decision.

The duty of loyalty requires that directors act "in a manner the director reasonably believes to be in the best interests of the corporation."[8] The duty is typically implicated by a director's conflict of interest. For instance, suppose Corporation enters into a contract with a business owned by one of its directors. That director is in a conflict-of-interest situation; she has an incentive to maximize the return on both sides of the transaction. We will see in section E that the business judgment rule does not apply in conflict-of-interest cases. Accordingly, courts readily review the merits and second-guess directorial action.

These duties developed at common law, but, increasingly, states have codified at least the basic framework of the duties. Even in states with statutes such as these, the courts have had to work out important details. So the law of fiduciary duty in most states is an amalgam of statutory and case law.

C. The Duty of Care

1. Overview

Section 8.30 of the RMBCA states standards of conduct for directors.[9] Section 8.30(b) contains a general statement of the duty of care, providing that directors "shall discharge their duties with the care that a person in a like position would reasonably believe appropriate under the circumstances." An earlier version of the Act spoke

---

[8] RMBCA § 8.30(a)(2).

[9] RMBCA § 8.42 applies the standards to officers.

of the care that an "ordinarily prudent person" would use. Many states continue to use that older phrase.[10] The present version of the RMBCA deleted "ordinarily prudent" because the drafters feared that it made directors too conservative—afraid to be bold and take appropriate risks.[11] Moreover, they felt that a focus on prudent persons might lead courts to assess the substantive correctness of business decisions, which would undermine the business judgment rule.[12] The terminology will not matter in most cases. The idea is clear: a director must do her homework and undertake a reasonable effort.

RMBCA § 8.30(b) makes clear that the duty of care applies to directors "when becoming informed in connection with their decision-making function or devoting attention to their oversight function." This is helpful language because it points out that the board of directors performs two sets of tasks. First, it causes the corporation take acts, such as declare distributions, recommend fundamental changes to shareholders, issue stock, and hire and fire officers. Second, it oversees things that other people do. The board of a publicly held company generally is not engaged in day-to-day decision making. Senior officers do that. The board must oversee, or monitor, to ensure that those making the day-to-day decisions are discharging their duties. On the other hand, in a closely held corporation, the board may well make all the day-to-day decisions and have less of an oversight role.

Directors may breach the duty of care in two generic ways: by nonfeasance (or inaction or inattention) and by misfeasance (which is when the board makes a decision that results in harm to the corporation).

2. Cases Involving Nonfeasance

Nonfeasance is "the failure to act when a duty to act existed."[13] A director who is inattentive or disengaged is guilty of nonfeasance. An example is *Francis v. United Jersey Bank*,[14] which involved a reinsurance business that had been run by a father and sons. The father died, and his widow, Mrs. Pritchard (the sons' mother), was elected to the board. She knew nothing about business generally or about the reinsurance business in particular. Mrs. Pritchard attend-

---

[10] *See, e.g.,* MD. CODE, CORPS. & ASS'NS § 2–405.1(a)(care that "an ordinarily prudent person in like position would use"); NEB. STAT. § 21–2099 (same).

[11] "The use of the phrase 'ordinarily prudent person' in a basic guideline for director conduct, suggesting caution or circumspection vis-à-vis danger or risk, has long been problematic given the fact that risk-taking decisions are central to the directors' role." Official Comment, RMBCA § 8.30.

[12] *See* section (C)(3) of this Chapter.

[13] BLACK'S LAW DICTIONARY 1153 (9th ed. 2009).

[14] 432 A.2d 814, 816 (N.J. 1981).

ed no meetings and did nothing to acquaint herself with even the rudiments of the business. She was a figurehead. With their father out of the way and their mother doing nothing, the sons allegedly siphoned large sums of money from the corporation, mostly through improper payments to members of their families.

The company went bankrupt, and the trustee in bankruptcy sued Mrs. Pritchard for breach of the duty of care. (Actually, the trustee sued her estate because she had died by this time.) The New Jersey Supreme Court upheld a judgment of more than $10,000,000 based upon Mrs. Pritchard's breach. The sons' misdeeds were so obvious that a person in a like position—paying *any* attention to the business—would have seen that there was something wrong and would have taken some action to stop the harm to the company.[15] The duty of care required Mrs. Pritchard to acquire some understanding of the company's business, to keep informed, and to monitor activities.

Mrs. Pritchard had plenty of excuses for her dereliction. She was elderly, alcoholic, and devastated by her husband's death. She was at the mercy of her sons. Indeed, Mr. Pritchard had once told her that their sons "would take the shirt off my back." But nobody made Mrs. Pritchard assume a position on the board of directors. When she accepted the job, she accepted the responsibilities that went with it. Mrs. Pritchard breached her duty of care by failing to exercise the diligence, care, and skill that someone in a like position would use.[16]

The *Francis* case involved the reinsurance business, which is a specialized field. This does not mean, however, that every director must have expertise in the particular business engaged in by the corporation. Indeed, in *Barnes v. Andrews*,[17] a case we will consider in detail shortly, Judge Learned Hand noted:

> Directors are not specialists, like lawyers or doctors. They must have good sense, perhaps they must have acquaintance with affairs; but they need not—indeed, perhaps they should not—have any technical talent. They are the general advisers

---

[15] *Id.* at 825–26 ("Thus, if Mrs. Pritchard had read the financial statements, she would have known that her sons were converting trust funds. When financial statements demonstrate that insiders are bleeding a corporation to death, a director should notice and try to stanch the flow of blood.").

[16] *Id.* at 829 ("To conclude, by virtue of her office, Mrs. Pritchard had the power to prevent the losses sustained by the clients of Pritchard & Baird. With power comes responsibility. She had a duty to deter the depredation of the other insiders, her sons. She breached that duty and caused plaintiffs to sustain damages.").

[17] 298 F. 614 (S.D.N.Y. 1924).

of the business, and if they faithfully give such ability as they have . . . it would not be lawful to hold them liable.[18]

What happens, though, if a director does have special expertise? The general rule is that she brings it with her to the board. For example, suppose Director X is an experienced antitrust lawyer. When the board considers whether the corporation should enter into a transaction that may implicate the antitrust laws, she must voice her concerns.[19] Stated another way, the duty of care imposes a floor for all directors, but special expertise or experience may "raise" that floor for an individual director.[20]

The plaintiff has the burden of showing that the defendant failed to meet the standard of care. Making that showing, however, does not result in the director's liability. Under the clear majority view, the plaintiff must also show causation. That is, she must demonstrate that the defendant's failure to meet the duty of care resulted in harm to the corporation. In *Francis*, the court found causation. If Mrs. Pritchard had not been so completely inattentive, she would have seen that something was terribly wrong and taken ameliorative steps.

Francis may be unusual, however.[21] Many plaintiffs fail because they cannot show causation. An example is *Barnes v. Andrews*,[22] a federal court decision by Judge Learned Hand, applying New York law. The case involved a corporation formed to make engine starters for Ford motors. About a year after the company was formed, the defendant became a director. He served for nine months, at which point the company was put into receivership because it had no assets. When the defendant became a director, though, the company had money, a manufacturing plant, and employees. During his directorship, the company simply failed to produce starters and used up all

---

[18] *Id.* at 618.

[19] *See, e.g., In re* Emerging Communications, Inc. Shareholders Litigation, No. 16415, 2004 WL 1305745, at *40 (Del. Ch. May 3, 2004) (because a director "possessed a specialized financial expertise and an ability to understand [the business's] intrinsic value, . . . it was incumbent upon [him], as a fiduciary, to advocate that the board reject the $10.25 price" not incumbent on other directors, who lacked such expertise).

[20] The nature of the business conducted by a corporation may similarly raise the level of care required of directors. As one scholar has noted: "[C]ourts seemingly have been much more willing to find a breach of the directors' duty of care when dealing with bank directors than with directors of corporations engaged in non-financial businesses." FRANKLIN A. GEVURTZ, CORPORATION LAW 280 (2d ed. 2010).

[21] The facts were atypical, as noted, because Mrs. Pritchard had died by the time judgment was entered. The judgment was enforced against her estate, and not against her personally. Presumably, that estate would otherwise have gone to Mrs. Pritchard's sons, who had caused the problems in the first place. The finding of liability meant that the sons would not profit.

[22] 298 F. 614 (S.D.N.Y. 1924).

the money in salaries. Apparently, plant managers disagreed constantly, which paralyzed the business.

The defendant had been put on the board as a favor to the president of the company, who was a friend. The two saw each other frequently, but the defendant never bothered to investigate why a company so well capitalized and staffed failed to produce any products. The receiver sued the defendant for breach of the duty of care and tried to recover money for the benefit of the corporation's creditors.

Without doubt, the defendant breached the duty of care. The duty, as we know, requires directors to act with the care, diligence, and skill that a person reasonably would employ in a like case. The court made clear that this encompasses a requirement that the director "keep advised of the conduct of corporate affairs," which the defendant failed to do.[23] Faced with the fact that the company was not producing anything, the defendant neglected to ask questions or to investigate in any way. He, like Mrs. Pritchard in *Francis*, failed to do what a reasonable person would have done under the circumstances.

Nonetheless, the court held that the defendant was not liable because the plaintiff did not show causation. In the words of Judge Hand, the plaintiff failed to show that "the performance of the defendant's duties would have avoided loss, and what loss it would have avoided."[24] Even if the defendant had done his job, it is not clear that it would have made a difference. The disagreement and dysfunction among officers may have been intractable.[25] It is usually difficult for a plaintiff to show causation in a nonfeasance case because it is often not clear that the director—had she paid attention—could have stopped the bad things from happening. As Judge Hand said in *Barnes*:

> Suppose I charge Andrews with a complete knowledge of all that we have now learned. What action should he have taken, and how can I say that it would have stopped the losses? The plaintiff gives no definite answer to that question. It is easy to say that he should have done something, but that will not serve

---

[23] *Id.* at 616.

[24] *Id.*

[25] *Id.* at 616–17. *Francis* provides an interesting contrast. There, because the problem was caused by obvious illegality, it is easy to imagine that one person's blowing the whistle will rectify the problem. In *Barnes,* however, which involved general business failure, it is tougher to say that increased astuteness could easily have fixed what was wrong.

to harness upon him the whole loss, nor is it the equivalent of saying that, had he acted, the company would now flourish.[26]

In *Barnes*, Judge Hand considered placing the burden regarding causation on the defendant. Specifically, he thought about requiring the defendant to show that her breach did not harm the company. He rejected the idea, and imposed on the plaintiff the burden to show both (1) that the defendant breached the duty of care, and (2) that the breach caused harm to the corporation.[27] *Barnes* is the majority view.

The RMBCA is consistent with the *Barnes* approach. Section 8.30(b), as we saw, codifies the duty of care. But it does not define when a defendant will be held liable. That task is performed by § 8.31.[28] Section 8.31(a) places the burden squarely on the plaintiff to establish any of several things. Specifically, § 8.31(a)(2)(iv) requires the plaintiff to show the defendant's failure to devote attention to the business or to make appropriate inquiries. Additionally, § 8.31(b)(1)(ii) requires the plaintiff to show proximate causation.[29]

But this is not the universal view. Delaware does it differently. In *Cede & Co. v. Technicolor, Inc.*,[30] the Delaware Supreme Court set up a system of shifting burdens. The initial burden is on the plaintiff to demonstrate that the defendant breached the duty of care. Once she has done that, the burden shifts to the defendant to show that that her actions were fair to the corporation.[31] Note that *Cede & Co.* does not require the defendant to show the absence of [32] Instead, she must show that she dealt fairly with the corporation.

The classic nonfeasance fact pattern—like *Francis* and *Barnes*—involves a suit against an individual director who is derelict. Closely related is the claim for failing to engage in appropriate oversight of employees. This claim, however, is likely brought against the entire

---

[26] *Id.* at 618.

[27] *Id.* at 616–17.

[28] Thus, RMBCA § 8.30 is entitled "Standards of Conduct for Directors" while RMBCA § 8.31 is entitled "Standards of Liability for Directors."

[29] RMBCA § 8.31(b)(iv)("The party seeking to hold the director liable . . . for money damages, shall also have the burden of establishing that (i) harm to the corporation or its shareholders has been suffered and (ii) the harm suffered was proximately caused by the director's challenged conduct.").

[30] 634 A.2d 345 (Del. 1993).

[31] *Id.* at 361.

[32] *See generally* Lyman Johnson, *Rethinking Judicial Review of Directors,* 24 DEL. J. CORP. LAW 787 (1999) (discussing *Cede*); E. Norman Veasey & Christin DiGuglielmo, *What Happened in Delaware Corporate Law and Governance from 1992–2004? A Retrospective on Some Key Developments,* 153 U. PA. L. REV. 1399, 1425–28 (2005) (same). To our knowledge, no court has imposed upon a defendant the burden of proving that her act did not cause the harm suffered by the corporation.

board, and not just a single lazy director. The board is charged with breaching the duty of care by failing to oversee those who are engaged in the day-to-day operation of the corporation.

- Mid-level employees of Corporation are indicted for fixing product prices in violation of the federal antitrust laws. The individuals are also indicted and sentenced to prison time. The indictment against Corporation exposes it to substantial criminal penalties. Suppose Corporation is found guilty and ordered to pay $50,000,000 in fines. Now a shareholder brings a derivative suit against the directors to recover that $50,000,000 on behalf of the corporation. The theory is that the directors failed to monitor what the employees were doing, and thereby breached the duty of care. Further, their failure to keep tabs on what their subordinates were doing has caused Corporation to lose $50,000,000.

This fact pattern is surprisingly common. In *Graham v. Allis-Chalmers Manufacturing Co.*,[33] the Delaware Supreme Court held that the directors in such a fact pattern were not liable. The corporation had over 30,000 employees in several states. The court concluded that the board could not be held responsible for the immediate supervision of the day-to-day activities of mid-level employees.[34] The plaintiff did not contend that the defendants personally should have uncovered the wrongdoing. They asserted instead that directors have a duty to establish a monitoring system to ensure corporate compliance with criminal and regulatory laws. The court, in overly broad language, hinted that the board had no responsibility to set up a monitoring system until it had reason to suspect that the employees were doing something illegal.[35]

That broad language in *Graham* is no longer the law in Delaware (or anywhere else). The Delaware Chancery Court established a more responsible approach in *In re Caremark International, Inc. Derivative Litigation.*[36] There, criminal activity by mid-level employees cost the corporation $250,000,000 in fines for violations of Medicare and Medicaid rules. In upholding a settlement of the resulting derivative suit against the directors, the court held that the board of directors must implement reporting or information systems to monitor operations, even in the absence of knowledge of illegal behavior.[37] The board must not only prescribe such a system, but must ensure that it is reasonably designed to determine whether employees are

---

[33] 188 A.2d 125 (Del. 1963).

[34] *Id.* at 128–29.

[35] *Id.* at 130.

[36] 698 A.2d 959 (Del. Ch. 1996).

[37] *Id.* at 970.

complying with law. On the other hand, under *Caremark*, the board has great discretion. Thus, "the level of detail that is appropriate for such an information system is a question of business judgment."[38]

The Delaware Supreme Court embraced *Caremark* in *Stone v. Ritter*.[39] There, a bank was held liable for fines and civil penalties because employees had failed to file reports of suspicious activity as required by federal law. Shareholders filed a derivative suit seeking to impose personal liability on the directors for failing to satisfy their *Caremark* duty. The court said:

> We hold that *Caremark* articulates the necessary conditions predicate for director oversight liability: (a) the directors utterly failed to implement any reporting or information system or controls, *or* (2) having implemented such a system or controls, consciously failed to monitor or oversee its operations thus disabling themselves from being informed of risks or problems requiring their attention. In either case, imposition of liability requires a showing that the directors knew that they were not discharging their fiduciary obligations. Where directors fail to act in the face of a known duty to act, thereby demonstrating a conscious disregard for their responsibilities, they breach their duty of loyalty by failing to discharge that fiduciary obligation in good faith.[40]

Note three things about "oversight liability." First, *Caremark* and *Stone* clearly require boards of directors to establish monitoring mechanisms aimed at assessing compliance throughout the corporate ranks. They cannot feign ignorance. These systems usually consist of periodic reporting requirements up the chain of command to compliance officers on a variety of issues. Moreover, it is not enough simply to draft such a system and put it on the shelf. It must be implemented and assessed periodically.

Second, it is difficult for a plaintiff to prevail on these claims. Directors will be in trouble only if they fail completely to implement some mechanism or "consciously" fail to use one that is set up. As long as the board implements an information system and monitors it periodically, directors should be protected from liability.

Third, failure of the board's oversight function has morphed from a duty of care problem to a duty of loyalty problem. The Delaware courts have addressed the oversight issue in three major cases; the animating normative principle of each is different. In *Graham*, the

---

[38] *Id.*

[39] 911 A.2d 362 (Del. 2006).

[40] *Id.* at 370 (emphasis original; footnotes omitted).

court addressed only the duty of care. The words "loyalty" and "good faith" do not appear in the opinion. In *Caremark*, the plaintiffs asserted only a claim for breach of the duty of care.[41] The court's language concerning liability (adopted by the court in *Stone* in the quotation above), however, did not appear to establish the standard for breach of the duty of care. Rather, it established what would constitute an act not taken in "good faith." In *Stone,* the Delaware Supreme Court held that a violation of the *Caremark* standard constituted a failure to act in good faith. Good faith, that court continued, is not a fiduciary duty separate from the duty of care and the duty of loyalty. It is, instead, a component of the duty of loyalty.

This journey from the duty of care to the duty of loyalty reflects a development we discuss in Chapter 13(H)—statutes that allow corporations to exculpate directors from liability for damages for breach of the duty of care. Most of these statutes do not apply, however, if directors failed to act in "good faith." Because of the ubiquity of such provisions by the time *Stone* was decided, the plaintiffs could prevail only if they could show a lack of good faith. We will discuss this increased focus on good faith in section D of this Chapter.

3. Cases Involving Misfeasance: Managerial Action and the Business Judgment Rule

Background. We have considered directorial inattention to business and its implications for the duty of care. Now we move on to cases in which the board of directors caused the corporation to take an act (or caused the company to decline to take an act). In other words, the board made a decision—and the decision turned out badly for the corporation. Perhaps the board did something that exposed the company to regulatory or criminal sanction or to civil liability. More typically, the board had the corporation pursue a new product line or advertising campaign that proves disastrous in the market.

When this happens, directors get nervous about being sued for breach of the duty of care. The plaintiff[42] in such litigation will assert that the directors failed to use that degree of care, diligence, and skill that someone in their position would reasonably have used.[43] In such cases, unlike cases of nonfeasance, the plaintiff need not worry about causation—it is absolutely clear. The board made a decision that

---

[41] 698 A.2d at 960 ("The suit involves claims that the members of Caremark's board of directors breached their fiduciary duty of care to Caremark in connection with alleged violations by Caremark employees of federal and state laws. . . .").

[42] The plaintiff might be the corporation itself or a shareholder suing on behalf of the corporation in a derivative suit. *See* Chapter 13.

[43] We assume throughout this discussion that there is no allegation that any director had a conflict of interest. As we will see in section E of this Chapter, conflicts of interest implicate the duty of loyalty, and not the duty of care.

harmed the corporation. Instead, the plaintiff in a misfeasance case faces the formidable barrier of the "business judgment rule."

The Business Judgment Rule. The business judgment rule is a presumption that when directors make a decision, they act "on an informed basis, in good faith, and in the honest belief that the action taken was in the best interests of the company."[44] The rule embodies the principle that directors are not guarantors of success. They are not liable simply because a decision turned out badly for the corporation. The rule allows leaders to be bold. If directors were subject to liability any time a decision fared badly, directors would rarely deviate from the beaten path and qualified people would be dissuaded from accepting directorship positions.

The business judgment rule reflects the fact that judges are not trained in product development, marketing, sales, or any other aspect of business. Consider these issues in the context of the Coca-Cola Company's 1985 introduction of "New Coke." Coke had long been the best-selling soft drink in the world; by the 1980s, though, its market share was falling. The board of directors decided to replace the iconic drink with a reformulated (sweeter) beverage called "New Coke." The new product had done well in taste tests and the board was convinced that it would boost sales. The board failed to appreciate the public's attachment to the original product. After some strong negative reaction to the new drink, the board reversed course and brought back the original formula under the rubric "Classic Coke."

In the short term, the introduction of New Coke was a loser. It did not spur an increase in market share and, in the eyes of many, it damaged the company's reputation. In the long term, however, the machinations resulted in increased market share for the company, apparently because it reinvigorated sales of the original drink. Some observers speculate that the whole thing was planned, and that discontinuing original Coke while introducing New Coke was a marketing ploy designed to cause a public outcry for the older drink. In response to that assertion, the company's president said: "We're not that dumb. And we're not that smart."[45] Under the business judgment rule, courts do not address whether a decision was dumb or smart; they do not second-guess business decisions.

In the face of such judicial deference, how, then, can a plaintiff prevail? The best way is to establish that the business judgment

---

[44] Aronson v. Lewis, 473 A.2d 805, 812 (Del. 1984).

[45] Stephanie Clifford, *Coca-Cola Deleting "Classic" From Coke Label*, N.Y. TIMES (Jan. 30, 2009), available at http://www.nytimes.com/2009/01/31/business/media/31coke.html (quoting Donald Keough).

rule does not apply at all. There are three types of cases in which the rule is irrelevant. First, because the rule applies to business judgments, it does not apply in nonfeasance cases.[46] Second, it does not apply when directors have a conflict of interest. We will see in section E of this Chapter that conflicts of interest implicate the duty of loyalty, and not the duty of care. Hence the business judgment rule protects directors from liability for claims based upon alleged mismanagement or misjudgment, but plays no role when they sought personal gain from the transaction. Third, the rule does not protect decisions that are made with a lack of good faith. Thus courts routinely say that the business judgment rule will not protect fraud, illegality, gross overreaching, and the like.[47]

That means that the business judgment rule applies only when the directors made a decision in good faith and without conflict of interest. In such cases, courts presume that the directors acted with due care. The burden is on the plaintiff to overcome that presumption. This is simply a corollary of the duty of care. That duty requires directors to act with appropriate care, diligence, and skill. It does not require them to be flawless or prescient. People make mistakes. And sometimes, no matter how careful directors are, decisions turn out badly. As the Official Comment to RMBCA § 8.31 notes, "as a general rule, a director is not exposed to personal liability . . . for an unwise decision."

In these cases, how can a plaintiff win? She must prove that the directors breached the duty of care—that is, that they did not act with the care, diligence, and skill that a reasonable person in a like position would have employed. This would appear to require a showing of "ordinary" or "simple" negligence—the breach of the duty of due care that we remember from Torts. Although some courts say that the duty of care implicates "negligence," that word is misleading. A well-known opinion explains:

> Whereas an automobile driver who makes a mistake in judgment as to speed or distance injuring a pedestrian will likely be called upon to respond in damages, a corporate [manager] who makes a mistake in judgment as to economic conditions, consumer tastes or production-line efficiency will rarely, if ever, be

---

[46] *Aronson*, 473 A.2d at 813 ("[T]he business judgment rule operates only in the context of director action. Technically speaking, it has no role where directors have either abdicated their functions, or absent a conscious decision, failed to act.").

[47] *See, e.g.*, Sinclair Oil Corp. v. Levien, 280 A.2d 717, 722 (Del. 1972) ("fraud or gross overreaching"); Warshaw v. Calhoun, 221 A.2d 487, 492–93 (Del. Ch. 1966) ("bad faith . . . or a gross abuse of discretion"). As we saw above, *Stone v. Ritter* held that lack of good faith in the board oversight function constitutes a breach of the duty of loyalty, as to which the business judgment rule is irrelevant. *See* notes 39–40 and accompanying text.

found liable for damages suffered by the corporation. Whatever the terminology, the fact is that liability is rarely imposed upon corporate directors or officers simply for bad judgment . . . [48]

The Delaware Supreme Court states it more pointedly: "director liability is predicated upon concepts of gross negligence."[49] Although that court has continued to adhere to the "gross negligence" mantra, its most controversial business judgment rule decision, *Smith v. Van Gorkom*,[50] upheld liability on facts that, in the eyes of many observers, did not rise even to simple negligence.

The Van Gorkom *Decision*. *Van Gorkom* imposed personal liability on directors of a publicly held corporation (Trans Union). The board had agreed to sell the company in a deal that paid the corporation's shareholders $55 per share. That price was about $18 more than the stock was selling for at the time. Nonetheless, the court concluded, they breached the duty of care, which meant that the business judgment rule did not protect them.

Van Gorkom was the chief executive officer of Trans Union. In reaction to economic changes, Trans Union management had been considering various options, including the sale of the corporation to an outsider. Van Gorkom, who was approaching retirement age, reached an intuitive judgment based on his knowledge of the corporation and the relevant economic sector that $55 per share would be a good price. Financial officers made studies to determine whether Trans Union generated enough cash flow to support a leveraged buyout at that price.[51]

With no further investigation, and without seeking other possible buyers, Van Gorkom approached Jay Pritzker, who was a well-known corporate takeover specialist and a social acquaintance of Van Gorkom's. Pritzker offered to have one of his companies buy the corporation (in a deal structured as a cash-out merger)[52] for $55 per share but demanded a decision within three days. Van Gorkom called a special meeting of the Trans Union board. Only Van Gorkom and the chief financial officer had advance knowledge of the purpose of the meeting. With no documentation, and based upon Van Gorkom's 20-minute oral presentation, the board approved the deal. Board members were given no written summary of the terms of the

---

[48] Joy v. North, 692 F.2d 880, 885 (2d Cir. 1982).

[49] Smith v. Van Gorkom, 488 A.2d 858, 873 (Del. 1985) (*quoting* Aronson v. Lewis, 473 A.2d 805, 812 (Del. 1984)).

[50] 488 A.2d 858 (Del. 1985).

[51] In a leveraged buyout, cash flow of the business is used to service the debt that was incurred to fund the purchase. *See* Chapter 9(F)(2).

[52] *See* Chapter 9(E).

merger and no documents supporting the $55 price as adequate. Directors did not ask Van Gorkom how he had arrived at the $55 figure.[53] The board approved the deal and submitted it to the shareholders, who approved the merger overwhelmingly;[54] indeed, nearly 70 percent of the shares voted in favor, with only seven percent opposed (the rest did not vote).

The Delaware Supreme Court concluded that the plaintiffs had proved that the Trans Union directors were *grossly* negligent in approving the merger. A feisty dissenting justice argued that the directors should be able to evaluate a proposed sale based upon their own experience and in reliance on Van Gorkom's experience and background. The directors were sophisticated business people who knew what they were doing.[55] The scholarly reaction to *Van Gorkom* was overwhelmingly negative. As noted above, many observers concluded that the plaintiffs had failed to show even simple negligence. One distinguished commentator called *Van Gorkom* "one of the worst decisions in the history of corporate law."[56]

Van Gorkom shook up the business community and changed the concept of acceptable practice.[57] The court was far less deferential to board decisions than courts usually had been. Indeed, courts historically seemed willing to uphold board action if they could imagine a rational basis for the decision. An example is *Shlensky v. Wrigley*.[58] There, a shareholder sued the management of the Chicago Cubs baseball team to challenge the decision to continue having the Cubs

---

[53] The board did establish a "market test" to see if another company might pay more to acquire Trans Union. The Delaware Supreme Court dismissed the effort, however, finding that the test was so encumbered with restrictions as to render it meaningless. 488 A.2d at 878–80.

[54] Fundamental corporate changes such as mergers must be approved by the shareholders. *See* Chapter 12(E).

[55] "The majority has spoken and has effectively said that Trans Union's directors have been the victims of a 'fast shuffle' by Van Gorkom and Pritzker. That is the beginning of the majority's comedy of errors. The first and most important error made is the majority's assessment of the directors' knowledge of the affairs of Trans Union and their combined ability to act in this situation under the protection of the business judgment rule." 488 A.2d at 894 (McNeilly, J., dissenting).

[56] Daniel R. Fischel, *The Business Judgment Rule and the Trans Union Case*, 40 BUS. LAW. 1437, 1455 (1985).

[57] The potential liability to the directors was stunning. The matter was remanded to the trial court to determine what would have been a fair price for the merger. If that exercise concluded, for instance, that sale to another suitor would have fetched $60 per share ($5 per share more than the merger price), based upon the number of shares represented in the plaintiff class, the directors would have been jointly and severally liable for $64,000,000. The case settled, apparently for around $22,000,000. Though all Trans Union directors were found liable, the judgment was actually paid off using a combination of insurance funds and money proffered by Van Gorkom and Pritzker. Thus, Van Gorkom and Pritzker agreed to hold the other directors harmless.

[58] 237 N.E.2d 776 (Ill. Ct. App. 1968). Under the internal affairs doctrine, *see* Chapter 5(B), the Illinois court applied Delaware law.

play all home games in the afternoon. Every other major league team played increasing numbers of games at night. (Today, the overwhelming majority of games are at night.) Evidence showed that night baseball drew larger crowds than day baseball. Thus, the plaintiff argued, the board's decision was hurting the team financially.[59] The court dismissed the complaint at the pleading stage, explaining:

> [W]e do not mean to say that we have decided that the decision of the directors [to refuse to play night home games] was a correct one. That is beyond our jurisdiction and ability. We are merely saying that the decision is properly one before directors and the motives alleged in the amended complaint showed no fraud, illegality or conflict of interest in their making of that decision.[60]

Merits and Procedure. One way to reconcile the deference shown by the court in *Shlensky* with the imposition of liability in *Van Gorkom* is to focus on the nature of the challenge in each. In *Shlensky*, the plaintiff was saying, in effect, "the board's decision to play only day games is stupid." In contrast, the plaintiffs in *Van Gorkom* effectively were saying "the decision to merge at $55 per share was made sloppily." Stated another way, *Shlensky* was a challenge to the merits—the substance—of the decision, while *Van Gorkom* was a challenge to the procedure by which the board made its decision.

Pragmatically, it is not surprising that courts more readily second guess procedural matters than substantive matters. As we said above, judges have no training in business. Each judge, however, is a proceduralist. Though courts are in no position to know whether a business should open an office in Sacramento, they are equipped to determine whether the board engaged in appropriate homework when it made the decision to open an office in Sacramento.[61] Thus the *Van Gorkom* decision had little (if anything) to do with the $55 per share merger price. If the board had gotten a fairness assessment from investment bankers, pushed Pritzker for more time, and undertaken a meaningful market test for other potential buyers, the

---

[59] The Cubs finally installed lights at Wrigley Field in 1988. They have not helped. The team has not been to the World Series since 1945 and has not won the World Series since 1908.

[60] *Shlensky*, 237 N.E.2d at 780.

[61] Speaking in the context of a board decision that derivative litigation should be dismissed, the court made this point in *Auerbach v. Bennett*, 393 N.E.2d 994, 1002 (N.Y. 1979): "As to the methodologies and procedures best suited to the conduct of an investigation of facts and the determination of legal liability, the courts are well equipped by long and continuing experience and practice to make determinations. In fact they are better qualified in this regard than are corporate directors in general."

court presumably would have upheld a decision to merge at $55 per share (or maybe even less).[62]

In *Shlensky*, though, the plaintiff had no complaint about the way in which Cubs management made its decision. The attack was on the substantive wisdom of the decision. The court was willing to uphold the decision because there was some rational explanation for it. In the words of another court, the business judgment rule protects "conduct by directors that can be attributed to any rational business purpose."[63] Other courts speak of gross abuse of discretion, which has been interpreted as "a decision so removed from the realm of reason or so unreasonable as to fall outside the permissible realm of sound discretion."[64]

These courts recognize that some decisions are so objectively unreasonable—manifest such "galactic stupidity"[65]—that they cannot be saved by the business judgment rule. They are rare, but they do exist. For example, in *Litwin v. Allen*,[66] the court imposed liability on directors for having their corporation purchase $3,000,000 worth of securities in another entity. The agreement gave the seller the option to repurchase the securities at the sales price within six months. Accordingly, the corporation would bear the loss if the notes declined in value but would not reap the benefits of an increase in value (because the seller would buy them back at the sales price). Similarly, in *Joy v. North*,[67] a bank continued to lend money to a commercial real estate venture long after it was clear that the venture would fail. Though the initial loan was defensible, at some point the developer's inability to complete the project should have been obvious.

Statutes Relating to the Business Judgment Rule. Courts, not legislatures, created the business judgment rule. Increasingly,

---

[62] Some skeptics conclude that the *Van Gorkom* decision has simply led to longer meetings, more documentation, and lucrative employment for investment bankers, whose detailed opinions have become an expected part of the board's assessment. *See, e.g.*, Charles M. Elson, *Courts and Boards: The Top Ten Cases,* American Law Institute/American Bar Association Continuing Legal Education, Nov. 12, 1998 (*Van Gorkom* "was responsible for the now common use of third-party advisers to provide expert opinions to boards. And it has led to far more elaborate decision making procedures, involving lengthy meetings, voluminous documentation and the like.").

[63] Janssen v. Best & Flanagan, 662 N.W.2d 876, 882 (Minn. 2003)

[64] This language is from Official Comment, RMBCA § 8.30.

[65] David Rosenberg, *Galactic Stupidity and the Business Judgment Rule,* 32 J. CORP. LAW 301, 322 (2007); *see also* David Millon, *Redefining Corporate Law,* 24 IND. L. REV. 223, 253 (1991) ("An obvious example of objectively irrational behavior not entitled to business judgment rule protection would be a decision that, at the expense of the corporation's shareholders, conferred a benefit on some third party not legitimately entitled to management's largess.").

[66] 25 N.Y.S.2d 667 (Sup. Ct. 1940).

[67] 692 F.2d 880 (2d Cir. 1982).

though, statutes address the topic and provide guidance on its application. The American Law Institute's Principles of Corporate Governance sets forth the concept in traditional language. Section 4.01(a) states the general duty of care. Section 4.01(c) provides that a "director or officer who makes a business judgment in good faith fulfills his or her duty" under § 4.01(a) if she (1) "is not interested in the subject of the business judgment," (2) "is informed with respect to the subject of the business judgment to the extent the director or officer reasonably believes to be appropriate under the circumstances," and (3) "rationally believes that the business judgment is in the best interests of the corporation."

Section 8.31(a)(2) of the RMBCA also reflects the business judgment rule. In cases not involving a conflict of interest, that statute places on the plaintiff the burden to demonstrate that a managerial decision "was not informed to an extent the director reasonably believed appropriate in the circumstances," or that there was a "sustained failure . . . to devote attention to ongoing oversight of the business and affairs of the corporation. . ."

Every state has responded to *Van Gorkom* legislatively by allowing corporations to provide (usually in the articles) that directors (and in some states officers) will not be personally liable for damages for breach of the duty of care. We mention these statutes in the next section and address them in detail in Chapter 13(H).

D. The Obligation of Good Faith

It has always been clear that fiduciaries must act in good faith. RMBCA § 8.30(a)(1) codifies this unremarkable point. Historically, this principle has had little content beyond the obvious case in which a fiduciary acted intentionally to harm the corporation. In the past generation, the duty of good faith has been invigorated. The activity is the result of statutes passed in every state in the wake of *Smith v. Van Gorkom*, which we discussed in the preceding subsection. These statutes allow corporations to eliminate director (and in some states officer) liability for damages.[68] They include exceptions, however, designed to limit such exculpation to cases involving a simple breach of the duty of care. The wording varies from state to state, but most list as exceptions various things that would violate the duty of loyalty. In addition, some—like § 102(b)(7) of the Delaware General Corporation Law—provide that a corporation cannot exculpate "for acts or omissions not in good faith."

In reaction to exculpation clauses adopted under such statutes, plaintiffs started bringing claims for breach of the duty of good faith.

---

[68] *See* Chapter 13(H).

As a consequence, there has been increased litigation, and more case law, about that duty. The initial question is whether a "duty of good faith" constitutes a third fiduciary duty (in addition to the duties of care and loyalty). The Delaware courts demonstrated some uncertainty on the point until that state's Supreme Court decided *Stone v. Ritter*[69] in 2006. The court concluded: "[A]lthough good faith may be described colloquially as part of a triad of fiduciary duties that includes the duties of care and loyalty, the obligation to act in good faith does not establish an independent fiduciary duty that stands on the same footing as the duties of care and loyalty."[70] It is now clear, as we saw in discussing *Stone* in section (C)(2) of this Chapter, that Delaware considers the obligation of good faith to be a component of the duty of loyalty.

Stone involved a claim that directors had failed in the board's oversight function to monitor corporate employees.[71] The court held that the plaintiff in such a case must show either that the directors failed completely to implement any reporting or information controls or that they consciously failed to monitor the operation of an extant system. The Delaware Supreme Court returned to the obligation of good faith in the context of a board decision in *In re The Walt Disney Company Derivative Litigation.*[72] It held that the directors of Disney did not breach the duty of care or the obligation of good faith when it approved a deal that paid Michael Ovitz $130,000,000 for 14 months' service as an officer. (Ovitz was fired without cause after only 14 months on the job.)

The court criticized the directors for not using "best practices" either in deciding to hire Ovitz or in setting his compensation package and its lucrative severance terms. Nonetheless, unlike the directors of Trans Union in *Van Gorkom,* the Disney board had done enough homework and reviewed enough expert analysis to engage the protection of the business judgment rule. The court also held that the defendants had not violated the obligation of good faith. More importantly for present purposes, it defined the limits of that duty.

As a matter of logic, the duty of good faith and the duty of care cannot be co-extensive. If they were, the duty of good faith would have no independent status, and the Delaware legislature's reference to "acts or omissions not in good faith" in § 102(b)(7) would be meaningless. In *Disney,* the court concluded that an act is not in good faith (and therefore cannot be exculpated) if it was made in "intentional dereliction of duty, [or with] a conscious disregard of one's responsi-

---

[69] 911 A.2d 362 (Del. 2006).

[70] *Id.* at 369.

[71] *See* notes 39–40 and accompanying text.

[72] 906 A.2d 27 (Del. 2006).

bilities."[73] It gave three examples: (1) acting with a purpose other than that of advancing the best interests of the corporation, (2) acting with the intent to violate applicable law, and (3) intentionally failing to act in the face of a known duty to act, thereby demonstrating a conscious disregard of the director's duties.[74]

In Delaware, then, breach of the obligation of good faith appears to require intentional wrongdoing. Thus, Delaware courts seem to equate a lack of good faith with affirmative bad faith. This enmeshes courts in assessing directors' motives, a topic on which there is unlikely to be anything but circumstantial evidence. Likely, breaches of this duty will be rare and obvious. And because the duties of good faith, care, and loyalty are not hermetically sealed, it is likely that any breach of the duty of good faith will also constitute a breach of the duty of care or (more likely) the duty of loyalty. It remains to be seen how much independent heft the duty of good faith will have. Observers seem to think that it will not prove significant.[75]

E. The Duty of Loyalty

1. Overview

One scholar summarizes the difference between the duty of care and the duty of loyalty colorfully. He says that the former involves directors who "were lazy or dumb" while the latter involves directors who "were greedy and put their own financial interests ahead of the interests of the corporation and its shareholders."[76] Stated another way, the duty of loyalty involves a fiduciary with a conflict of interest. This arises whenever a fiduciary is tempted to put her interest above that of the corporation or shareholders. In litigation, once the plaintiff shows such a conflict, two related consequences follow. First, the business judgment rule does not apply.[77] Second, the burden usually shifts to the defendant to show that the decision was entirely fair.

The duty of loyalty developed at common law. Every state now has legislation that deals with at least some aspects of the duty of loyalty. Most states have a counterpart to RMBCA § 8.30(a)(2), which defines the general duty of loyalty: a fiduciary must discharge her duties "in a manner [she] reasonably believes to be in the best interests of the corporation." Beyond this, most states also have ra-

---

[73] *Id.* at 67.

[74] *Id.*

[75] *See, e.g.,* Jaclyn J. Janssen, *In re* Walt Disney Company Derivative Litigation: *Why Stockholders Should Not Put Too Much Faith in the Duty of Good Faith to Enhance Director Accountability*, 2004 WIS. L. REV. 1573.

[76] GEVURTZ, *supra* note 20, at 257.

[77] The business judgment rule does not apply in cases involving conflict of interest. *See* note 47 and accompanying text.

ther detailed provisions about one classic duty-of-loyalty fact pattern, usually called "self-dealing" or the "interested director" transaction. Some states have legislation on other aspects of the duty of loyalty as well. In general, though, topics other than self-dealing are addressed by case law. Even in self-dealing, case law usually augments statutory provisions.

Because of the ingenuity of selfish people, there are limitless ways to breach the duty of loyalty. A fiduciary who steals money from the business obviously cannot be acting in a way she "reasonably believes to be in the best interests of the corporation." She has breached the duty of loyalty. Speaking very generally, however, there are three classic fact patterns implicating the duty of loyalty: (1) competing ventures, (2) self-dealing, and (3) usurpation of a business opportunity. We turn to them now.

2. Competing Ventures

It is proper for a person to have more than one business interest. So a director of a corporation that makes widgets may also own a company that makes video games. The problem is when a fiduciary of the widget company wants to own or manage another widget company. For starters, it seems clear that a fiduciary for Company A should not be engaged[78] in a business that competes directly with Company A. Doing so breaches the duty of loyalty because operating a competitor cannot qualify as an act taken "in a manner [she] reasonably believes to be in the best interests of [Company A]."

Nonetheless, some cases say that a fiduciary of Company A may go into competition with Company A if she acts in good faith and does not injure the corporation,[79] or perhaps if the disinterested directors of Company A consent. Neither scenario seems realistic. First, the whole point of going into competition would seem to be to hurt Company A. That is, the fiduciary thinks she can make money in the competing venture, and that money comes at the expense of Company A. Second, disinterested directors would never approve such a plan. We cannot imagine competent directors of Company A saying, in effect, "Sure, Jim, we think it will be great for you to form a com-

---

[78] By engaged, we mean in some capacity that would allow her to direct corporate action. In other words, a director of Coca-Cola Company can own stock in Pepsi Cola Corporation (although she probably would not want anyone at Coke to know). She is merely a passive investor in Pepsi and cannot do anything as a shareholder of Pepsi that would harm Coke.

[79] *See, e.g.,* Parsons Mobile Prods., Inc. v. Remmert, 531 P.2d 428, 433 (Kan. 1975) ("This is a country of free enterprise based upon competition. The essential inquiry on any charge of unfair competition is good faith. Good faith will insulate a former officer or director from liability unless it is shown the rival business was intentionally operated for the purpose and in such a way as to be unfair and detrimental to the former employer-corporation.").

peting venture and try to take money away from Company A." Directors who did that could be sued for doing something not in the best interests of Company A.

Accordingly, fiduciaries should avoid direct competition. On the other hand, a fiduciary for Company A is not required to stay with Company A forever. She has a right to leave. She has a right to go into business with others or for herself. Public policy favors such mobility. Competition is a social good that creates choice and lowers prices for consumers. This is why covenants not to compete—i.e., agreements that one will not go into competition with her former employer—must be tailored geographically and temporally.[80]

If a fiduciary resigns from Company A on Monday and forms Company B on Tuesday, she will likely encounter no problems—at least concerning the duty of loyalty.[81] The problem is that no one ever does anything that cleanly. Common sense dictates that no one will resign to form a new business until she has taken some steps to set up the new business. So the law allows people to "prepare to compete" before resigning.[82] So forming a corporation, leasing office space, arranging for telephone service, and the like may be permitted.

The big problems arise with soliciting clients and employees to go to the new business.[83] *Jones Co. v. Burke*[84] involved a successful Madison Avenue advertising agency, Duane Jones Co. The company started to falter when its founder and leader began to act erratically. At that point, some of its directors and officers—while still fully en-

---

[80] *See, e.g.*, Reed, Roberts Assoc., Inc. v. Strauman, 353 N.E.2d 590, 592 (N.Y. 1976).

[81] Contract and tort law, however, may create problems. The fiduciary must abide by a valid covenant not to compete. And any employee who misappropriates trade secrets or steals company property will be liable in tort (as well as for breaching the duty of loyalty).

[82] *See, e.g.*, Taser Int'l, Inc. v. Ward, 231 P.3d 921 (Ariz. 2010) (fiduciary may prepare to compete but cannot use corporate property or confidential information for her own purposes); Abetter Trucking Co. v. Arizpe, 113 S.W.3d 503, 510 (Tex. Ct. Civ. App. 2003) ("A fiduciary relationship, however, does not preclude the fiduciary from making preparations for a future competing business venture; nor do such preparations necessarily constitute a breach of fiduciary duties.").

[83] A well-known case is Bancroft-Whitney Co. v. Glen, 411 P.3d 925, 935 (Cal. 1965), in which the court noted: "There are only a few cases cited by the parties which involve the specific question whether an officer may offer employees of his corporation jobs with a competing enterprise he is preparing to join. These cases are not consistent in their results and appear to rest on general principles relating to the obligations of the fiduciary. . . . The mere fact that the officer makes preparations to compete before he resigns his office is not sufficient to constitute a breach of duty. It is the nature of his preparations which is significant. No ironclad rules as to the type of conduct which is permissible can be stated, since the spectrum of activities in this regard is as broad as the ingenuity of man itself."

[84] 117 N.E.2d 237 (N.Y. 1954).

gaged at Duane Jones—set up a competing agency. Not until the other business was up and running did they resign from Duane Jones. Immediately, the new company started representing several of Duane Jones's major clients, a fact that strongly implied that they had solicited those clients while still at Duane Jones. They also enticed many lower-level employees to jump ship. Duane Jones sued the erstwhile directors and officers and won a substantial jury verdict. The New York Court of Appeals affirmed the judgment, and held that the defendants had breached the duty of loyalty. Even though the new agency did not make any money until the defendants had left Duane Jones, they breached their duties by arranging everything while still working there.[85]

A corporation should be able to seek a range of appropriate remedies when one of its fiduciaries engages in a competing venture. Injunctive relief to stop the person from competing may be available. A court may impose a constructive trust on profits made by the fiduciary in the competing enterprise. The legal remedy of damages may be appropriate if, for example, the competing venture harmed the corporation in some way.

3. Self-Dealing ("Interested Director" Transactions)

Background. Self-dealing refers to transactions entered into by the corporation in which one or more of its directors has an interest on the other side. These are also known as "interested director" transactions.

- X is a director of XYZ, Inc. X also owns Supply Corp. If XYZ, Inc. enters into a contract with Supply Corp., there is self-dealing (and we have an interested director transaction) because X is on both sides of the deal.

The concern in cases of this sort is that X, in her role as director of XYZ, Inc., has an incentive to have XYZ overpay because doing so lines X's pockets in her role as owner of Supply Corp. Recognizing this conflict, the common law allowed XYZ to void self-dealing contracts at will. Indeed, the rule for some time was that the contract could be voided if even one shareholder objected to it. This rule did not fit business needs. Many self-dealing transactions are good for the corporation—a fiduciary may give her corporation a benefit that

[85] *Id.* at 245 ("The inferences reasonably to be drawn from the record justify the conclusion reached by the jury and by a majority of the Appellate Division that the individual defendants-appellants, while employees of plaintiff corporation, determined upon a course of conduct which, when subsequently carried out, resulted in benefit to themselves through destruction of plaintiff's business, in violation of the fiduciary duties of good faith and fair dealing imposed on defendants by their close relationship with plaintiff corporation.").

it cannot get elsewhere. For example, a director might lend money to a corporation when its credit rating makes it impossible to get a loan from a bank. Such transactions should be encouraged.

States moved away from the traditional rule early in the twentieth century. Increasingly, as a matter of common law, courts began to uphold interested director transactions if the director established that (1) the deal was approved by the disinterested directors (those having no stake in the transaction) and (2) the deal was fair to the corporation.

Thereafter, throughout the twentieth century, most states enacted statutes concerning self-dealing transactions. So what evolved as a matter of common law is now handled in most states by statute. These statutes differ, as we will see, but have some common features. First, they do not allow a corporation (or shareholder) to void a contract simply because it involves self-dealing. Second, an interested director transaction will not be set aside because of self-dealing if the director shows one of three things:

- The transaction was fair to the corporation when entered, or

- The transaction was approved in good faith by disinterested directors, or

- The transaction was approved in good faith by disinterested shareholders.[86]

As one scholar points out, these three choices reflect the law's insistence that self-dealing transactions be approved (if at all) by people who do not have a personal interest. In the first option, a judge makes the assessment. In the latter two, disinterested constituencies of the corporation make the assessment.[87]

Placing the burden on the defendant to demonstrate satisfaction of the statutory requirements makes sense. Because of the conflict of interest, the business judgment rule cannot apply, so the burden must be on the director.[88] The leading approach is probably that found in RMBCA §§ 8.60–8.63, which is Subchapter F of the RMBCA.

---

[86] Actually, in some states, including Delaware, the statute allows "shareholders" to approve the transaction. The omission of the adjective "disinterested" opens the door for an argument that the interested director herself may vote her shares (if she owns stock) in favor of the contract. Modern statutes such as the RMBCA leave no doubt that the approval must come from disinterested (or, as the RMBCA says, "qualified") shareholders. *See* RMBCA § 8.62.

[87] GEVURTZ, *supra* note 20, at 344.

[88] There are a few aberrations. In Arizona, for instance, the burden is on the plaintiff to show that none of the three things listed is true. ARIZ. STAT. § 10–863(C).

A significant number of states, however, embrace an earlier version of the Model Act, from 1975, then codified at § 8.31.

The effect of complying with an interested director transaction is to remove the "taint" of self-interest. We might think of these as "curing" provisions—they cure the conflict of interest and (in most jurisdictions) generally eliminate the need for intrusive judicial review. Once this is done, the corporation must still take the appropriate corporate act to adopt the proposed transaction. In other words, satisfying the statute typically puts the transaction on an equal footing with a transaction that is not tainted by a conflict of interest, but it does not adopt it as a corporate act. Actually entering into the deal, however, is a separate step, to be undertaken by the appropriate corporate mechanism—maybe board resolution if it is a big deal, maybe officer decision if an officer has authority to bind the corporation.

When applying any interested director statute, the following questions should be addressed.

What Transactions Are Covered? The older (1975) version of the Model Act, still applicable in some states, defines a self-dealing transaction as one "with the corporation in which the director of the corporation has a direct or indirect interest."[89] A director has an "indirect interest" if the deal is between the corporation and "another entity in which [she] has a material financial interest," or in which she is a general partner, or in which she is an officer or director and the deal should be considered by the board of directors.[90] In Delaware, an interested director transaction is one between the corporation and (1) one or more of its directors, or (2) a business or organization in which one of its directors also serves as a director, or (3) a business or organization in which one of its directors has "a financial interest."[91] Does this definition cover a transaction between the corporation and a director's spouse? It does not seem to, but most people would probably consider such transactions to raise serious issues of self-interest.

The current version of the RMBCA features a broader and clearer definition of self-dealing. It is any transaction to which the director (1) is a party or (2) in which she has a known "material financial interest," or (3) in which a "related person" is a party or has a material financial interest.[92] A material financial interest is one that rea-

---

[89] MBCA § 8.31(a) (1975).
[90] MBCA § 8.31(b) (1975).
[91] DEL. GEN. CORP. LAW § 141(a).
[92] RMBCA § 8.60(1).

sonably would be expected to impair one's objectivity.[93] A related person includes the fiduciary's spouse or relative (defined very broadly in RMBCA § 8.60(5)(ii)),[94] or even a relative of a spouse. It also includes a person living in the fiduciary's home, and an entity controlled by the fiduciary.[95]

This definition makes clear, for instance, that a deal between the corporation and a director's spouse or sibling is self-dealing. Older statutes, as noted about Delaware, were not clear on this, although case law in some states filled in the gap. Such transactions should be considered self-dealing because of the obvious lack of objectivity one may be expected to have concerning his or her spouse. Moreover, the parties should know what steps to take to avoid having the transactions set aside. And by requiring a "material" financial interest, this statute shields routine transactions in which the only possible self-dealing is that the two corporations have a common director (they have "interlocking directorates"). Because the interest likely would not be material for the director, it should not be subject to approval under the statute.

Approval by Disinterested Directors. Assuming that a transaction falls within the statutory definition of self-dealing, one approach is for the director to have the taint cured by a vote of the disinterested directors. We will compare Delaware and the RMBCA.[96]

In Delaware, for board approval, the conflict of interest and material facts of the transaction[97] must be "disclosed or . . . known" and the deal approved by "a majority of the disinterested directors, even though the disinterested directors be less than a quorum."[98] Interested directors count toward the quorum,[99] may participate in the meeting, and may even vote (but their votes do not count toward curing the taint of self-interest).[100]

This is a poorly drafted statute. First, it is not clear what is required to establish a quorum. The provision that interested directors

---

[93] RMBCA § 8.60(4).

[94] It includes the director's spouse, child, stepchild, grandchild, parent, stepparent, grandparent, sibling, step-sibling, half sibling, aunt, uncle, niece, nephew (or any such relatives of the director's spouse), as well as anyone else "living in the same home" as the director.

[95] RMBCA § 8.60(5).

[96] Under each statute, the approval by disinterested directors must be made in "good faith." We discussed the general obligation of good faith in section D.

[97] Some states appear to require only the disclosure (or knowledge) of the conflict of interest, and not of the material facts of the transaction itself. *See, e.g.,* N.Y. BUS. CORP. LAW § 713(a)(1).

[98] DEL. GEN. CORP. LAW § 144(a)(1).

[99] DEL. GEN. CORP. LAW § 144(b).

[100] DEL. GEN. CORP. LAW § 144(a).

count toward the quorum may imply that "regular" quorum rules apply. In other words, a majority of *all* directors (interested and disinterested) must attend the meeting.[101]   Such an interpretation, though, would create an odd incentive to have interested directors attend the meeting.

- There are seven directors, four of whom are interested in a self-dealing contract. Can the three disinterested directors cure the taint by calling a meeting amongst themselves and voting? As a matter of common sense, the answer should be yes. Those three should meet alone, without possible influence from the interested directors. But if the statute requires a "regular" quorum, these three cannot have a meeting amongst themselves. Why? Because three does not constitute a quorum of a seven-member board. Under this view, one of the interested directors would be required to attend to create a quorum.

The idea that "regular" quorum rules apply arises by implication from § 144(b), which provides that interested directors count toward the quorum. If we did not need a "regular" quorum—in other words, if the disinterested directors could act amongst themselves—why would we care about counting interested directors toward the quorum? One possibility is that the statute mixes two things—that § 144(a) deals with curing the taint of self-interest, while § 144(b) deals with the subsequent approval of the transaction by the corporation (through the board) to enter into the contract. It is one of many uncertainties in the statute.

Second, the Delaware provision is not clear about what vote is required amongst the disinterested directors. Specifically, to cure the taint of self-interest, does § 144(a)(1) require a majority of all disinterested directors on the board, or only a majority of the disinterested directors that actually vote on the matter?

- There are eleven directors, six of whom are interested in a self-dealing contract. At the meeting to consider curing the taint, three of the five disinterested directors and three interested directors attend. Even under "regular" quorum rules, there is a quorum (because six of the eleven board members are in attendance). After appropriate disclosure (or knowledge), the three disinterested directors vote two-to-one in favor notwithstanding the conflict. Does that vote satisfy § 144(a)(1)? If the statute requires a majority of disinterested directors who actually voted, yes. Only three such people

---

[101] This assumes that there is no provision setting a different quorum. *See* Chapter 6(D)(4).

voted, and two of them voted yes. On the other hand, if the statute requires approval by the majority of all disinterested directors on the board, there is no approval. Why? Because only two of the five disinterested directors who are on the board approved.

There is yet another problematic aspect to the Delaware statute:

- There are seven directors, six of whom are interested in a self-dealing contract. At the board meeting, the one disinterested director and three interested directors attend. So we have a quorum even under "regular" quorum rules (four of the seven directors are in attendance). Then the one disinterested director votes in favor of the deal. It is approved for purposes of § 144(a)(1) because it was authorized "by a majority of the disinterested directors." (Indeed, it was unanimous among the disinterested directors, because there was only one.) This result is clear under § 144 but seems questionable as a matter of policy. It puts a great deal of faith in the one disinterested director to stand firm in the face of six interested colleagues.

The RMBCA avoids all of these problems. For starters, some of the RMBCA provisions are consistent with Delaware. Thus, approval under RMBCA § 8.62 must be by "qualified" directors. This is the same idea as Delaware's requirement of approval by "disinterested" directors, except the RMBCA definition is broader and clearer. RMBCA § 1.43(a)(3) defines a qualified director as one who does not have a conflicting interest and does not have a "material relationship" with such a director. Material relationship, in turn, means "a familial, financial, professional, employment or other relationship that would reasonably be expected to impair the objectivity of [her] judgment." Such a relationship with a self-dealing fiduciary renders a director unqualified to vote on the transaction.

And, consistent with Delaware, § 8.62 requires the self-dealing fiduciary to inform the qualified directors of her interest and of the material facts of the transaction, unless those matters are "already known by [the] qualified directors."

But the RMBCA quorum and voting rules are far superior to those in Delaware.

First, the quorum requirement clearly focuses not on a majority of all directors (as Delaware apparently does), but mandates only "[a] majority (but no fewer than two) of all the qualified directors on the board of directors."[102]

Second, as to voting, the transaction must be approved by "a majority (but no fewer than two) of the qualified directors who voted on the transaction."[103] This does not require a majority of all the qualified directors on the board—only a majority of those on the board or committee who actually voted on approval of the interested director deal. Note also that the RMBCA requires at least two qualified directors to vote to approve an interested director transaction, which avoids the problem of permitting approval by a lone director.[104]

Third, under § 8.62(a)(1), the qualified directors must deliberate and vote outside the presence and without the participation of the non-qualified directors.

- There are eleven directors, six of whom are interested in a self-dealing transaction. Assume that the other five are "qualified." Now assume that three of the five qualified directors show up at a meeting. (Remember, under the RMBCA, the interested directors cannot attend this meeting.) That is a quorum under § 8.62(c) because all that is needed is a majority (at least two) of the qualified directors (not of all directors). After proper disclosure (or knowledge), they vote two-to-one to cure the transaction of the taint of self-interest. It is proper because it was approved by a majority of the qualified directors who actually voted (even though not a majority of all qualified directors).

Finally, can the director approval take place after the deal has been entered? Suppose, for example, that an officer with authority to do so approved the corporation's entering into this particular contract. After the corporation has obligated itself to the deal, a director becomes aware that he has a conflict. Can he seek approval from disinterested directors now? Under the RMBCA, the answer is yes. Section 8.61(b)(1) expressly allows approval "at any time."[105] The Delaware statute speaks of the disinterested directors' "authoriz[ing]"[106] the transaction, without reference to when. In contrast, that part of the Delaware statute that allows deals to be upheld

---

[102] RMBCA § 8.62(c). The provision also allows approval by a committee of qualified directors. The quorum would be a majority of the qualified directors on the committee.

[103] RMBCA § 8.62(a).

[104] When there is only one disinterested director on the board, the board simply cannot cure the taint of self-interest.

[105] Some states allow "ratification" by disinterested directors, which would permit *ex post* approval. *See, e.g.,* CAL. CORP. CODE § 310(a)(2).

[106] DEL. GEN. CORP. LAW § 144(a)(1).

if "fair" requires that it be fair when "authorized, approved or ratified,"[107] which seems to allow *ex post* assessment of fairness. Some
scholars have argued that this implies "that an after-the-fact ratification by disinterested directors will not cure the conflict."[108]

Approval by Shareholders. An alternative is to seek approval by
shareholders. Again, we will contrast the Delaware and RMBCA approaches. Delaware § 144(a)(2) requires that the conflict of interest
and material facts be disclosed to or known by the shareholders.
Then the transaction must be approved by "the shareholders entitled
to vote thereon."[109] It is not clear whether the quorum and voting
rules of a regular shareholder meeting apply. If they do, unless the
articles provide otherwise, a majority of shares entitled to vote must
be represented at the meeting. Then a majority of those shares present at the meeting must vote in favor to cure the interested transaction.[110]

The statute is poorly drafted. It does not require approval by
"disinterested" shareholders—only by "shareholders entitled to vote
thereon." What does that mean? Literally, it seems to say that all
shareholders whose stock has voting rights may participate. But that
would mean that the interested director may vote her shares in favor
of the transaction. That is problematic. After all, if an interested
director cannot vote to approve her self-dealing, why should she be
allowed to vote her shares in favor of the deal? On the other hand, if
the legislature meant that such shares could not be voted, it could
have provided for approval by the majority of "disinterested" shares.
It managed to use that word when addressing director voting in
§ 144(a)(1), so its failure to use it in § 144(a)(2) may signal a different
intent.

Maybe the provision's referring to shareholders "entitled to vote
thereon" means disinterested shareholders. Or maybe the fact that
the statute requires approval to be made in "good faith" means that
only disinterested shareholders can vote. These arguments are worth
making, but are pretty weak. Again, if the legislature meant "disinterested," it could have said "disinterested." It did not.

So what do the courts do in the face of this poor statutory drafting? Courts in some states whose statutes are modeled on Delaware

---

[107] DEL. GEN. CORP. LAW § 144(a)(3).

[108] GEVURTZ, *supra* note 20, at 257. As a matter of policy, this position is defended
by the psychological likelihood that disinterested directors will have a difficult time
disapproving of a deal involving one or more of their peers that has already been
undertaken. *Id.* at 353–54.

[109] DEL. GEN. CORP. LAW § 144(a)(2).

[110] *See* Chapter 6(C)(4).

conclude that approval must come from disinterested shareholders.[111] In Delaware, the situation is somewhat unclear. In *Marciano v. Nakash*,[112] the Delaware Supreme Court said in passing that approval by "disinterested stockholders" would satisfy § 144(a)(2).[113] But the statement is arguably inconsistent with other language in the opinion.[114] More importantly, the statement was dictum because no shareholder approval was sought. In the earlier case of *Fliegler v. Lawrence*,[115] the same court arguably suggested that approval by "shareholders" (including the shares held by the interested director) constituted approval under § 144(a)(2).[116] Nonetheless, there is lower court authority in Delaware for the proposition that § 144(a)(2) requires approval only by the disinterested shareholders.[117] This discussion opens another question on which the Delaware statute is deficient: what constitutes "disinterested" shareholders? The director whose conflict triggered the application of § 144 obviously is not disinterested. But what if the stock is held by her spouse? Her children? Another business that she owns? Neither the statute nor case law provides clear answers.

There are no such problems, however, under the RMBCA. Section 8.63 requires approval by a majority of the "votes cast" by the holders of "qualified shares."[118] Qualified shares are those held by folks who are themselves qualified.[119] In other words, the RMBCA makes it clear that the interested fiduciary's shares (if any) may not be voted.

There are special quorum and voting rules under the RMBCA. A quorum consists of a majority of the qualified shares.[120] And the transaction must be approved by a majority of the qualified shares that actually vote.

---

[111] *See, e.g.*, Rivercity v. American Can Co., 600 F. Supp. 908, 919–21 (E.D. La. 1984) (interpreting the Louisiana provision).

[112] 535 A.2d 400 (Del. 1987).

[113] *Id.* at 405 n.3.

[114] In *Marciano*, each shareholder family held fifty percent of the stock. One was interested and one was disinterested. The court said that shareholder approval was impossible because of the deadlock. *Id.* But if only the disinterested shareholder's vote is relevant, there would not have been a deadlock.

[115] 361 A.2d 218 (Del. 1976).

[116] It nonetheless found the transaction unfair. Professor Gevurtz refers to the court's handiwork on this score as "judicial sleight of hand." GEVURTZ, *supra* note 20, at 257.

[117] *See, e.g.*, *In re* Wheelabrator Technologies, Inc. Shareholders Litig., 663 A.2d 1194, 1203 (Del. Ch. 1995).

[118] RMBCA § 8.63(a).

[119] RMBCA § 8.63(c)(2).

[120] RMBCA § 8.63(d).

- The corporation has 50,000 outstanding voting shares. The interested director holds 20,000 of these shares. So there are 30,000 "qualified shares." At the meeting, 18,000 of the qualified shares are represented. There is a quorum, because a majority of the qualified shares is represented at the meeting. Of those 18,000 shares, only 14,000 actually vote—7,500 in favor and 6,500 opposed. The statute is satisfied because the transaction was approved by a majority of the qualified shares that actually voted on the issue. Thus the taint of self-interest is removed.

Fairness and the Effect of Approval by Directors or Shareholders. The statutes we are addressing give three choices for removing the taint of self-dealing. We have discussed two: approval by disinterested directors or shareholders. The third is that the transaction was fair to the corporation at the time it was entered into.

Obviously, if neither of the two options already discussed is met, the only option for the interested director is the fairness route. It seems equally obvious that the burden in this scenario is on the director—she must demonstrate that the deal was fair, and this will be assessed under the "intrinsic" (or "entire") fairness doctrine. We discuss that in detail in (G)(4) below. For now, suffice it to say that this test raises a significant burden for the defendant. It involves assessment of both procedural and substantive fairness. So the court will inquire about whether the structure of the deal and the merits of the deal were equitable. It is a searching inquiry and an exacting test. Applying the intrinsic fairness test here makes sense. By definition, the taint of self-dealing has not been removed—neither disinterested directors nor disinterested shareholders have blessed the transaction. Whenever there is such a taint, the burden is on the director to show fairness. The business judgment rule cannot be invoked.

Now we get to the more difficult question: what happens if disinterested directors or shareholders properly approve the transaction? There are two basic approaches. In some states, approval by one of the groups removes the taint of self-dealing. It "sanitizes" or "cures" the conflict of interest. Stated another way, approval is a "safe harbor" for the director. This means that the director is not required to demonstrate that the deal was fair to the corporation. This approach is consistent with the statutory language, which requires a showing of fairness as an alternative to (not in addition to) approval by one of the groups. The RMBCA embraces this approach.[121]

---

[121] The Official Comment to §§ 8.61 and 8.62 refer to approvals as "safe harbor procedures."

Does that mean that the transaction is beyond judicial review? No. The interested director transaction statutes do not offer blanket amnesty to the director who can invoke them. They provide only that the deal is not subject to attack *on the basis of self-dealing.* So a court can review the transaction to the same extent it can review others that do not involve self-dealing. The burden will be on the plaintiff, but she is free to challenge the deal for a host of other reasons. For example, there may be a viable claim that the deal was not properly approved, constituted a usurpation, was not entered into in good faith, or that it is not entitled to protection under the business judgment rule because it was irrational or constituted a waste of corporate assets.

There is another approach to the matter. Some courts conclude that approval by disinterested directors or shareholders is not a safe harbor; it does not remove the taint of self-interest. Presumably, approval by disinterested directors or shareholders at least shifts the burden of proof from the interested director to the plaintiff, but courts are none too clear on this point. What they insist on is that they have the ultimate say on whether the deal was fair.[122] This conclusion is inconsistent with the clear language of the statutes—which, again, provides that a showing of fairness is an alternative to a showing of approval by one of the two groups. These courts also manifest significant distrust of the process that allows disinterested directors or shareholders to approve self-dealing transactions.

Delaware law seems rather confused. On the one hand, after some hemming and hawing, the Delaware Supreme Court finally held that disinterested director approval does constitute a safe harbor for a transaction between a corporation and an interested director.[123] Such deals are thus reviewed by the forgiving business judgment rule. On the other hand, that court has never expressly overruled its authority that stockholder approval does not provide a safe harbor, at least when the shares of interested stockholders were necessary to approve the deal.[124] Moreover, that court seems to have decided that approval by disinterested directors does not preclude a searching fairness review of a transaction between a corporation and a controlling shareholder.[125]

---

[122] *See, e.g.,* Cookies Food Products, Inc. v. Lakes Warehouse Dist., Inc., 430 N.W.2d 447, 452–53 (Iowa 1988) (involving a transaction with a controlling shareholder).

[123] Benihana of Tokyo, Inc. v. Benihana, Inc., 906 A.2d 114, 120 (Del. 2006).

[124] Fliegler v. Lawrence, 361 A.2d 218, 222 (Del. 1976).

[125] Kahn v. Lynch Comm. Sys., 638 A.2d 1110, 1116 (Del. 1985).

Let's end this foray with discussion of an interesting case, *HMG/Courtland Properties, Inc. v. Gray*.[126] In that case, HMG sold realty to a company called NAF. Gray and Fieber, two of the five directors of HMG, held substantial interests in NAF, so the transaction was self-dealing for those two. Not only that, but Gray negotiated the sale on behalf of HMG. Before the transaction, Fieber disclosed his conflicting interest, but Gray did not. Even though Fieber knew of Gray's conflicting interest, he did not disclose it to the HMG board. The board approved the sale by a vote of four to zero (Gray voted; Fieber did not). More than a decade later, the company became aware that Gray had been interested in the transaction. It sued Gray and Fieber for breach of fiduciary duty.

Gray was obviously in hot water. Although the transaction was approved by disinterested directors, the approval was defective because they were unaware of Gray's conflict of interest. Section 144 in Delaware, like all interested fiduciary statutes, requires that the approval be by disinterested directors or shareholders who were knowledgeable—that the conflict of interest be "known" or "disclosed." Because he had failed to tell his fellow directors about his interest (and because they did not know about it independently), Gray was unable to rely on approval by the disinterested directors. Thus, he had the burden to demonstrate that the transaction satisfied the "entire fairness" test.[127]

What about Fieber? At first blush, he seems to be in good shape. After all, he disclosed his conflict of interest in the transaction, after which the disinterested directors approved. But this approval did not help Fieber; he failed to inform the board of Gray's conflict of interest. This failure meant that Fieber was in no better shape than Gray. By failing to disclose Gray's interest, Fieber could not rely on approval by the disinterested directors. He, like Gray, had to shoulder the burden of demonstrating fairness under the entire fairness test.[128] One part of this test, as we will see in more detail in section (G)(4) of this Chapter, assesses whether the process followed was fair. Neither Gray nor Fieber could satisfy this, however, because they did not inform the board of Gray's interest.[129] So even if the price were substantively fair, Gray and Fieber may still be liable.

---

[126] 749 A.2d 94 (Del. Ch. 1999).

[127] *Id.* at 112–15.

[128] *Id.* at 114.

[129] There is a tough double-whammy here. By failing to inform the board of Gray's interest, Fieber was relegated to the entire fairness test. For the very same reason (failing to inform of Gray's interest), Fieber flunked the first part of that test; he could not show that the procedure he followed was fair to the corporation. The lesson is stark: inform your colleagues on the board of your conflicting interest and of any other of which you are aware.

Compensation and Loans. The board of directors is responsible for setting executive compensation, including the directors' own compensation.[130] We discussed director compensation in Chapter 6(D)(5). There is an inherent conflict when directors set their own compensation, and courts are occasionally asked to second-guess such compensation.

These cases arise in at least two ways. One is a challenge by the Internal Revenue Service. As we saw in Chapter 4(E), C Corporations (as opposed to S Corporations) must pay federal income taxes. In calculating their taxable income, they are entitled to deduct salaries, but cannot deduct dividends paid to shareholders. Thus, corporations have an incentive to label money paid to a director/officer/shareholder as "compensation," rather than as a dividend. The IRS sometimes claims that a corporation has overpaid someone, and thereby taken too generous a deduction.[131]

For us, the more important challenge to director compensation is that the directors have breached their duty of loyalty by overcompensating themselves. In general, director compensation is treated like other forms of self-dealing and will be upheld if the relevant interested director statute is met. Generally, this requires the directors to show that the figure is fair. If they have voted themselves excessive pay, they are guilty of stealing from the corporation, which, of course, is a breach of the duty of loyalty.[132] Courts are reluctant to second-guess executive compensation.[133] Still, it is best practice to have an independent committee of the board determine compensation levels. This approval by disinterested directors could earn the benefit of the interested director statutes such as RMBCA § 8.62.

Can a corporation make a loan to one of its directors? Every state seems to include in its list of general corporate powers the power "to lend money. . ."[134] But making a loan to a director makes us nervous, because the company is putting at risk corporate assets that otherwise would be available for something that would seem to benefit the shareholders more directly—such as dividends or to expanding the business. Traditionally, and perhaps in most states still, these loans are treated as interested director transactions.

---

[130] RMBCA § 8.11.

[131] *See, e.g.,* Exacto Spring Corp. v. Commissioner, 196 F.3d 833 (7th Cir. 1999).

[132] Rogers v. Hill, 289 U.S. 582, 591–92 (1933).

[133] *See, e.g.,* Heller v. Boylan, 29 N.Y.S.2d 653, 679 (Sup. Ct. 1941) ("Yes, the Court possesses the power to prune these payments, but openness forces the confession that the pruning would be synthetic and artificial rather than analytic or scientific . . . Courts are ill-equipped to solve or even to grapple with these entangled economic problems. Indeed, their solution is not within the juridical province.").

[134] RMBCA § 3.02(8).

Increasingly, however, states address these loans by specific statute. Older versions of such statutes permitted loans to directors (and in some states officers and other employees) only if approved by the shareholders. Usually, that meant approval by a majority of the disinterested shares (i.e., shares held by persons other than the person getting the loan). More recently, these statutes have been amended to allow the board of directors to approve such loans if the board concludes that the loan is reasonably expected to benefit the corporation.[135] Some states offer a choice—approval by a majority of the disinterested shares or by a board finding that the deal is reasonably expected to benefit the corporation.[136]

4. Usurpation of Business Opportunities

Background. Here we address a director's taking for herself something that "belongs" to the corporation—or, more precisely, that should have been offered to the corporation so it could decide whether to pursue it. By seizing the property herself, the director "usurps" a corporate or business "opportunity." Unlike interested director transactions, as to which every state appears to have legislation, here there are few statutes. The law of corporate opportunity is largely common law and, unfortunately, courts have failed to forge a clear definition on what constitutes an opportunity. We illustrate the problem with three hypotheticals:

- *Hypothetical A*: X is a director of Candy Co., which manufactures hard candies. X discovers that Confectioner Co., a separate corporation that manufactures a competing brand of hard candy, is for sale. Without informing Candy Co., X buys Confectioner Co. By acquiring a business that puts her in direct competition with Candy Co., she has breached her duty of loyalty to Candy Co. Indeed, notice how closely related the various duty of loyalty scenarios are. Here, once she starts operating Confectioner Co., she will be engaged in a competing venture. Even before that, however, she has usurped for herself a business opportunity in which Candy Co. would be interested. After all, Confectioner Co. was in the same business line and makes a competing brand. Clearly, Candy Co. might have wished to buy Confection Co.

- *Hypothetical B*: X, a director of Candy Co., discovers that Chocolate Co., a separate corporation that manufactures chocolate candy, is for sale. If X buys Chocolate Co. for her-

---

[135] *See, e.g.*, MICH. COMP. LAWS § 450.1548(1) ("A corporation may lend money to . . . an officer or employee of the corporation . . . if, in the judgment of the board, the loan . . . may reasonably be expected to benefit the corporation.").

[136] *See, e.g.*, TEX. BUS. ORGS. CODE § 2.101(13).

self, has she usurped an opportunity? On the one hand, we might say no because Candy Co. and Chocolate Co. are in different business lines—one sells hard candy and one sells chocolate candy. On the other hand, we might say yes because the two companies are in the same generic business of selling sweets. Indeed, if the Candy Co. board had been made aware of the availability of Chocolate Co., it might have chosen to have Candy Co. expand into chocolates.

- *Hypothetical C*: X, a director of Candy Co., knows that Candy Co. wants to expand its manufacturing capacity and needs land on which to do so. X learns of some land that would be perfect for Candy Co.'s needs. If X buys the land for herself, has she usurped an opportunity? On the one hand, we might say no because Candy Co. is in the candy business and not in the business of real estate investment. On the other hand, Candy Co. needs land on which to operate.

Should our answers change if X learned about the availability of the other company or the land while she was discharging her duties to Candy Co.? Or, put differently, would the answer differ if X learned of the other company or the land on the weekend, while surfing the internet on her own time? What if the owner of the company or the land contacted X? Would it matter if the owner contacted X because X is a director of Candy Co.? Would it matter if Candy Co. did not have enough money to buy the other company or the land?

These hypotheticals and questions suggest the uncertainty that characterizes this area of the law. The court's first job in usurpation cases is to determine whether what the director took was a corporate opportunity. If it is, then taking it constitutes a breach of the director's duty of loyalty. She will be liable unless she has some defense, which we will discuss below. On the other hand, if what she acquired is not an opportunity, the director is home free; taking it on her own account does not implicate her duty of loyalty.

Defining Corporate Opportunity. Because the issue is so important, we might expect the definition of an opportunity to be clear. At first glance, though, the area is hopelessly confused; courts use a dizzying array of terms. On closer inspection, though, things may actually be much clearer. Professor Gevurtz has synthesized the topic and concludes that most cases are explained by how three major factors are implicated on the facts of a given case.[137] (In discussing

---

[137] Professor Gevurtz speaks of "triangulating" the relationships (1) between the property and the director, (2) between the director and the corporation, and (3) between the property and the corporation. GEVURTZ, *supra* note 20, at 257.

them, we will refer to the potential opportunity as the "property.") The three factors are: (1) the level of the corporation's interest in the property; (2) the manner in which the fiduciary became aware of the property; and (3) the fiduciary's relationship to the corporation. A particularly strong showing on one factor (such as the fact that the corporation asked the fiduciary to find the property for it) may justify the conclusion that the property is an opportunity, even with relatively weaker showings on the other factors.

Factor One. The corporation's level of interest in the property will fall somewhere on a continuum. At one end are things the corporation must have to survive; some courts thus speak of an opportunity as something "essential" to the corporation.[138] For example, a company might not be able to manufacture its product without securing a license from the patent holder. At the other end of the spectrum are things the company might some day consider pursuing, perhaps when it expands its product line. Common sense tells us that the former (something essential to the business) is more likely to be deemed an opportunity than the latter.

Most cases fall somewhere between the two extremes. Here, courts have adopted two general formulations. One of these, set forth by the Delaware Supreme Court in its 1939 decision of *Guth v. Loft, Inc.*,[139] is the "line of business" test. In *Guth*, the corporation (Loft) ran a chain of retail candy stores. The stores manufactured syrup for candies. Loft also sold soft drinks at the stores. For years, its cola drink had been Coca-Cola. Loft severed its ties with Coke, however, because the syrup, in Loft's judgment, was too expensive. Guth was the president and a director of Loft. The management of the Pepsi-Cola Company approached Guth in his role as president of Loft and informed him that the assets of Pepsi could be acquired rather inexpensively (Pepsi was in bankruptcy). Though the Pepsi people were trying to get the corporation (Loft) to buy the assets, Guth was interested personally. He failed to inform Loft of the chance to buy Pepsi and, instead, teamed up with a Pepsi insider to acquire the soft drink company's assets as their personal investment.

The Delaware Supreme Court held that Guth breached his duty of loyalty to Loft. He usurped a corporate opportunity. Pepsi was an opportunity for the candy company, at least in part because the cola company was in the candy company's "line of business." But, as we

---

[138] *See, e.g.*, Rapistan Corp. v. Michaels, 511 N.W.2d 918, 921 (Mich. Ct. App. 1994) ("so indispensably necessary . . . that the deprivation . . . threaten[s] [the company's] viability); Adams v. Mid-West Chevrolet Corp., 179 P.2d 147, 160 (Okla. 1946)(doctrine applies when a fiduciary obtains "property essential for the business of the corporation").

[139] 5 A.2d 503 (Del. 1939).

saw in Hypothetical B at the beginning of this subsection, this just begs the question: was Loft's "line of business" to be defined narrowly (as operating candy shops) or broadly (as preparing and dispensing sweets, including soda pop)? In *Guth*, the facts made the court's decision a bit easier because Loft already manufactured syrups and served soft drinks. On the other hand, one could argue that while acquiring a source of cola syrup was in Loft's line of business, going into the cola business was not. The court took a broad view and held that the assets of Pepsi fit into Loft's business line. Courts employing this "line of business" test sometimes speak of an opportunity as something "logically related to the corporation's existing or prospective activities."[140]

The other phrase commonly encountered is "interest or expectancy"—something is an opportunity if the company has an "interest or expectancy" in it. The words are elastic. Sometimes (particularly in older cases) it is interpreted narrowly to mean that the company must have a legal interest, such as an option to buy the property.[141] Typically, it is interpreted more broadly as something the company might like to pursue. This broad approach to "interest or expectancy" starts to look like the line of business test: a company will be interested in acquiring something only if it is relevant to its present or prospective business activities.

Consider Hypothetical C above. Arguably, acquiring land is not in the line of business of a candy company. On the other hand, the candy company needs land on which to manufacture its product. In such a case, a court might focus more on interest or expectancy to conclude that land on which the company could expand its plant is an opportunity. Even so, as noted, in some cases courts insist on a legally protectable interest.[142]

As this discussion suggests, "line of business" and "interest or expectancy" are not hermetically sealed. Courts do not tend to adopt one to the exclusion of the other, but routinely throw both into the discussion. Indeed, *Guth* employed both.[143] Instead of worrying

---

[140] Hill v. Southeastern Floor Covering Co., 596 So. 2d 874, 877 (Miss. 1992).

[141] *See, e.g.*, Lagarde v. Anniston Lime & Stone Co., 28 So. 199, 201–02 (Ala. 1900) (corporation operating a quarry did not have an expectancy in land on which it operated and which it had sought unsuccessfully to buy because it lacked a legally protectable interest).

[142] *See, e.g.*, Southeast Consultants, Inc. v. McCrary Eng. Corp., 273 S.E.2d 112, 117–18 (Ga. 1980) (corporation had an interest or expectancy in particular property because of its relationship with the seller, with which it had entered into a preliminary study contract, and on which the corporation had been invited to bid).

[143] 5 A.2d at 510. This becomes clearer in *Broz v. Cellular Information Systems, Inc.*, 673 A.2d 148 (Del. 1996), in which the Delaware Supreme Court listed both line of business and interest or expectancy in its assessment of opportunity. *See* notes 1568–161 and accompanying text.

about which test (or which version of a test) is "right," it is important to remember that there are other factors to be assessed. When the question of whether something is an opportunity is a close call, the outcome will depend on the other factors.

Factor Two. It is important to assess whether the director discovered the property in her "official" capacity or her "individual" capacity. Again, there is a continuum. At one end are cases in which the corporation instructed the person to find something for it. If the person then buys the property for herself, courts will easily find the property to be an opportunity. Indeed, this is a simple proposition of agency law: the agent has been disloyal to the principal. At the other end of the spectrum are cases in which the fiduciary is on vacation and, spending her own money, seeks out property for a personal investment, with no knowledge that her corporation is looking for such property. It is difficult to imagine that courts would find such property to be an opportunity.

Most cases fall between the extremes. In *Guth*, for example, the court concluded that the representative of Pepsi-Cola approached Guth not as an individual, but in his role as manager of Loft, Inc. The representative wanted to have the corporation purchase the assets of Pepsi and market the product.[144] Another example is *Northeast Harbor Golf Club, Inc. v. Harris*,[145] in which a golf club sued its fiduciary for usurping real property that abutted the club. In remanding the case to the trial court, the Maine Supreme Judicial Court noted that the broker who listed the property testified that he approached the fiduciary because she was a representative of the corporation—that is, in her official capacity. "If the fact finder reached that conclusion," the court said, "then at least the opportunity to acquire the . . . property would be a corporate opportunity."[146]

A closely related matter is whether the defendant used corporate resources to find or develop the property. If she did, the court is more likely to find usurpation of an opportunity. In *Guth*, for instance, the

---

[144] *Guth*, 5 A.2d at 513 ("[The Pepsi representative] sought to interest someone who controlled an existing opportunity to popularize his product by an actual presentation of it to the consuming public. Such person was Guth, the president of Loft.").

[145] 661 A.2d 1146 (Me. 1995).

[146] *Id.* at 1151. The court adopted the American Law Institute's Principles of Corporate Governance regarding usurpation of opportunities. Section 5.05(b)(1)(A) defines an opportunity as something of which the fiduciary becomes aware "[i]n connection with the performance of functions as a director or senior executive, or under circumstances that should reasonably lead [her] to believe that the person offering the opportunity expects it to be offered to the corporation." *See* text accompanying notes 165–169.

defendant used corporate funds and personnel to develop the Pepsi-Cola business.[147]

Factor Three. Courts must also consider the fiduciary's relationship to the corporation. All else being equal, one who is higher up the corporate ladder is more readily found to have usurped than a lower-rung employee.[148] With greater power comes a stricter fiduciary duty.[149] Although the American Law Institute's Principles of Corporate Governance limits liability for usurpation to directors and senior executives,[150] some courts find that lower level employees owe duties that preclude them from seizing potential opportunities.[151]

Recap. We believe that the results of most cases can be explained by balancing the three factors discussed. Realizing that each factor involves a continuum of possibilities, the facts of a given case may tip one way or the other either slightly or significantly. Reconsider *Guth*. There, the defendant was the manager of Loft, Inc., so Factor Three tilts toward imposing a broad duty. He learned that the assets of Pepsi-Cola were available for sale while acting in his official capacity—that is, he was approached specifically because he was the animating figure for Loft. Moreover, he used Loft resources to develop the property into a viable source of product. Thus, Factor Two tilts strongly toward finding a breach as well.

Factor One is more interesting and a closer call. Specifically, what was Loft's level of interest in acquiring Pepsi? Loft operated candy stores and made syrups. It offered soft drinks at its stores. It had severed its relationship with Coca-Cola, so it needed a source of cola syrup. But that was not what was offered for sale. Rather, it was the entirety of Pepsi-Cola's assets. By buying those, Loft would

---

[147] *Guth*, 5 A.2d at 510 ("That Guth did not use his own funds and risk his own resources in acquiring and developing the Pepsi business is equally demonstrated.").

[148] "Perhaps the notion is that those higher up must devote all of their waking hours working for the corporation, leaving no time for pursuing opportunities on their own. A simpler explanation may be that senior executives get paid more and, therefore, should give more to the company." GEVURTZ, *supra* note 20, at 257.

[149] Some scholars have suggested that senior executives in publicly traded companies may not take any property for themselves, but must offer all potential opportunities to their corporation. Victor Brudney & Robert C. Clark, *A New Look at Corporate Opportunities,* 94 HARV. L. REV. 997, 1024 (1981). Some courts apply a narrower test for opportunities for outside directors than for inside directors. *See, e.g.,* Johnston v. Greene, 121 A.2d 919, 924 (Del. Ch. 1956)(where defendant was an outside director who served on boards of several other companies and foundations, court refused to find usurpation: "How . . . can it be said that Odlum was under any obligation to offer the opportunity to one particular corporation? And if he was not under such an obligation, why could he not keep it for himself?"). *See* Chapter 9(B)(1)(discussing inside and outside directors).

[150] ALI, PRINCIPLES OF CORPORATE GOVERNANCE § 5.05.

[151] *See, e.g.,* BBF, Inc. v. Germanium Power Devices Corp., 430 N.E.2d 1221, 1228 (Mass. Ct. App. 1981) (plant manager owed duty).

not have been buying a source of syrup. It would have become a producer of cola syrup. One can argue that these are different "lines of business" or that Loft would not have an "interest or expectancy" in going into syrup production. On the facts of the case, though—given how strongly Factors Two and Three tipped toward finding a breach of duty by Guth—the court readily concluded that Pepsi was in the same business line as Loft.

The Fairness Focus. Most opinions employ the phrase "line of business" or "interest or expectancy"—or both—in cases charging usurpation of corporate opportunities. Some, however, purport to employ an overall "fairness" test. Essentially, they ask whether, on the facts of the case, it is fair that the defendant took property for herself without offering it to the corporation.[152] This verbal formulation is not significant because the fairness assessment examines precisely the same factors discussed above. So whether the fiduciary's act was fair depends upon the corporation's level of interest, how the fiduciary became aware of the property, and how high-ranking the fiduciary is in the corporation.

Can the Director Take Advantage of An Opportunity? If a court concludes that something is a corporate opportunity, a fiduciary is not necessarily precluded from acquiring it for herself. She may have a defense or justification for taking the property.

The safest thing for the fiduciary to do is to offer the opportunity to the corporation and wait for the company to reject it before acting on her own accord. If she does this, she should be protected from second-guessing litigation. In essence, the corporation is estopped from challenging her action. When a director is the person involved, however, we worry about conflict of interest—that is, she who takes the opportunity is also one of those deciding whether the corporation should turn it down. The statutes we studied regarding interested director transactions do not apply here because there is no transaction between the corporation and the director (the transaction is between a third party and the director). With no statutory provision on point, what should courts do?

They should be guided by the principles of the interested director transactions and require that the corporation's rejection be approved by disinterested directors or disinterested shareholders. Failing either of these, courts should insist that the fiduciary who claims that the corporation rejected the opportunity demonstrate that such

---

[152] *See, e.g.,* Phoenix Airline Servs. v. Metro Airlines, 397 S.E.2d 699, 702 (Ga. 1990) (once plaintiff shows that the property is an opportunity based upon line of business and interest or expectancy factors, defendant assumes burden of showing that she acted fairly, in consonance with her fiduciary duties); Miller v. Miller, 222 N.W.2d 71 (Minn. 1974) (same).

rejection was fair to the corporation. Indeed, the 2010 version of the RMBCA added § 8.70, which permits "qualified directors" (a term relevant in self-dealing too) or shareholders to "disclaim" the corporation's interest.

Of course, if fiduciaries offered the opportunity to the corporation and waited for appropriate corporate rejection before taking it, there would be no usurpation cases. Most fiduciaries simply take the opportunity. When sued for usurpation, they then seek to raise one of two defenses.

First, they may claim that the corporation was incapable for some non-financial reason of taking advantage of the opportunity. One reason might be that the opportunity would be ultra vires.—i.e., beyond the scope of its articles; ultra vires is rare today because statutes routinely permit formation of a company for all lawful purposes. Even when it does come up, the defense is not necessarily a winner. The fiduciary should endeavor to have the corporation amend its articles to permit pursuit of the opportunity. A better argument is that the corporation cannot engage the opportunity because regulations prohibit it from undertaking that business.[153] Another argument is that the third party simply would not deal with the corporation. Even in these cases, it would seem appropriate to require the fiduciary to tender the opportunity to the corporation. This would allow the corporation to try to persuade the third party to deal with it.[154]

Second, the fiduciary may claim that the corporation could not have pursued the opportunity because of financial constraints. Some courts appear to conclude that fiduciaries should never be permitted to assert as a defense the corporation's inability to pay for the opportunity.[155] This approach may be justified on the basis that a fiduciary should try to help her company raise or borrow the money to pursue the opportunity. Other courts, however, permit fiduciaries to take the opportunity if the corporation truly lacked independent assets to take advantage of it.[156] The Oregon Supreme Court took an

---

[153] For example, banks may be prohibited from engaging in certain non-banking activities.

[154] See, e.g., Energy Resources Corp. v. Porter, 438 N.E.2d 391, 394 (Mass. Ct. App. 1982) ("[T]he firmness of a refusal to deal cannot be adequately tested by the corporate executive alone.").

[155] See, e.g., Irving Trust Co. v. Deutsch, 73 F.2d 121, 124 (2d Cir. 1934) ("If the directors are uncertain whether the corporation can make the necessary outlays, they need not embark it upon the venture; if they do, they may not substitute themselves for the corporation any place along the line and divert possible benefits into their own pockets.").

[156] See, e.g., CST, Inc. v. Mark, 520 A.2d 469, 472 (Pa. Super. 1987) (putting burden on the defendant to show financial inability, which "must amount to insolvency to the point where the corporation is practically defunct"); Ellzey v. Fyr-Pruf, Inc.,

interesting approach in *Klinicki v. Lundgren*.[157] It concluded that a director may not rely on the company's financial inability unless she first presented the opportunity to the corporation.

The (Confused) Delaware Approach. Logically, it seems that the court's first inquiry in a usurpation case should be whether the property constitutes an opportunity at all. If it does, the second inquiry ought to be whether the defendant has a defense such as those just discussed. The Delaware courts do not follow this logical sequence. Rather, they pour various factors into the mix with no particular guidance. As a result, it is unclear whether certain factors are relevant as defenses or as part of the basic definition of whether something constitutes an opportunity.

The Delaware Supreme Court's most recent handiwork in this area is *Broz v. Cellular Information Systems, Inc.*[158] There, Broz was a director of CIS, a company that provided cellular telephone service. He was also the sole owner and president of RFBC, which competed with CIS.[159] A third company, Mackinac, owned a cell phone license for part of Michigan, which was adjacent to an area served by RFBC. Mackinac approached Broz to see if RFBC would be interested in acquiring its license. Without informing CIS or seeking its acquiescence, Broz had RFBC acquire the license.[160] CIS then sued him for usurping a corporate opportunity.

The trial court found that Broz breached his duty of loyalty to CIS by failing to present the opportunity to CIS. The Delaware Supreme Court reversed. Part of its opinion is quite clear. Under Delaware law, presentation of the opportunity to the corporation is not required. It is, however, a good idea. If the board rejects the opportunity after presentation by the director, the director has a "safe harbor" from liability.[161] Failing to pursue that course (as Broz failed) means that the defendant has the burden of showing either that the property was not an opportunity or that he was entitled to seize it.

---

376 So. 2d 1328, 1335 (Miss. 1979) (appearing generally to put the burden on the plaintiff to show that the corporation could have afforded financially to pursue the opportunity).

[157] 695 P.2d 906 (Or. 1985).

[158] 673 A.2d 148 (Del. 1996).

[159] The court makes nothing of this fact. It does not mention any claim against Broz for entering into a competing venture.

[160] Broz did mention his plan to buy the license to a couple of CIS directors, who indicated that CIS would not want the license because it did not do business in Michigan.

[161] "[P]resenting the opportunity to the board creates a kind of 'safe harbor' for the director, which removes the specter of a post hoc judicial determination that the director or officer has improperly usurped a corporate opportunity." *Broz*, 673 A.2d at 157.

Here the opinion gets murky. The court refers to its "classic statement" of usurpation law in the "venerable" case of *Guth v. Loft*, which we discussed above.[162] It then sets out what may be four elements for determining whether something is an opportunity:

> [A] corporate officer or director may not take a business opportunity for his own if: (1) the corporation is financially able to exploit the opportunity; (2) the opportunity is within the corporation's line of business; (3) the corporation has an interest or expectancy in the opportunity; and (4) by taking the opportunity for his own, the corporate fiduciary will thereby be placed in a position inimical to his duties to the corporation.[163]

This is all rather confused. Is the court saying that if the four elements are satisfied, the property is an opportunity? Or is it saying that if the four are not true, the defendant may take the property even though it is an opportunity? The initial line—that a fiduciary may not "take a business opportunity"—seems to assume the very fact we are trying to ascertain—i.e., whether it is an opportunity. Does the inclusion of element (1) mean that the plaintiff must show financial ability? Or is the corporation's lack of financial ability a defense for the defendant to raise?

The court then follows with "a corollary"[164] from *Guth*:

> [A] director or officer may take a corporate opportunity if: (1) the opportunity is presented to the director or officer in his individual and not his corporate capacity; (2) the opportunity is not essential to the corporation; (3) the corporation holds no interest or expectancy in the opportunity; and (4) the director or officer has not wrongfully employed the resources of the corporation in pursuing or exploiting the opportunity.[165]

Are these four factors relevant to determining whether something is an opportunity, or are they defenses to a claim of usurpation?

---

[162] Though it praises *Guth* in these terms, the court later noted that the *Guth* "line of business" test is "less than clear." 673 A.2d at 157 n.7. The Delaware Supreme Court seems to think highly of its efforts. For example, in *Malone v. Brincat*, 722 A.2d 5, 10 (Del. 1998), it noted that it "has endeavored to provide the directors with clear signal beacons and brightly lined channel markers as they navigate with due care, good faith, and loyalty . . . ." Ironically, in *Malone*, the court failed to make clear whether the claim it recognized was direct or derivative. And, of course, this is the same court that decided *Van Gorkom*, which Dean Fischel of the University of Chicago Law School called "one of the worst decisions in the history of corporate law." Daniel R. Fischel, *The Business Judgment Rule and the* Trans-Union *Case*, 40 BUS. LAW. 1437, 1455 (1985).

[163] 673 A.2d at 155.

[164] As we will see, the court then lists four things. If the four things constitute one corollary, do all four have to be demonstrated to invoke the corollary?

[165] 673 A.2d at 155.

Does the fact that the court lists the four with an "and" mean that a defendant must demonstrate all four of these to escape liability? Or will one suffice? Why does the first excerpt above speak of whether the corporation has an "interest or expectancy," while this refers to whether the property is "essential" to the company?

On the facts, *Broz* was easy and can be explained using the factors we discussed above. First, CIS had no interest in the property. It had completely forgone the effort to provide service in the Midwest. Second, Broz was approached in his capacity as representative of RFBC. Mackinac had no interest in talking to CIS about the license—not only because it did not do business in the region, but also because CIS had no money. Third, Broz was a director of CIS, which means that he has a broad fiduciary duty. But given the clarity of the first two factors, it was an easy call that Broz was not liable. Moreover, even if the license were an opportunity, it was absolutely clear that CIS had no assets with which to pursue the license. Whether this meant that the license was not an opportunity—or, instead, that Broz had a defense even though it was an opportunity—is not at all clear. The Delaware court, with its mélange approach, has not advanced the cause of clear analysis.

The ALI Approach. In section 5.05 of its Principles of Corporate Governance, the American Law Institute essentially codifies the doctrine of corporate opportunity. Some courts have referred to it and at least one—the Maine Supreme Judicial Court in *Northeast Harbor Golf Club, Inc. v. Harris*[166]—has adopted it as state law. The section applies to directors and senior executives.

Section 5.05(b) defines a corporate opportunity as something the director or senior officer becomes aware of:

- In connection with the performance of her functions as a director or senior executive; or

- Under circumstances that reasonably should lead her to believe that it is being offered to the corporation; or

- Through the use of company information or property; or

- In any capacity (that is, even in her individual capacity) if the business activity is "closely related to a business in which the corporation is engaged or expects to engage."

---

[166] 661 A.2d 1146 (Me. 1995). The court praised the ALI for "providing long-needed clarity and guidance for corporate decision makers." *Id.* at 1150.

The latter phrase, which seems to capture the idea of the "line of business" test, applies only to senior officers, and not to persons who serve solely as directors.[167] Moreover, as noted, it applies even if such an executive officer becomes aware of the opportunity in her individual capacity—for example, while on vacation. The first three phrases apply to directors as well as to senior officers and are consistent with the factors we discussed above in synthesizing the case law.

If something is an opportunity under § 5.05(b), then § 5.05(a) requires three things, the first two of which are straightforward. First, the fiduciary must offer the opportunity to the corporation (and disclose her conflict of interest). Second, the corporation reject the opportunity.

The third requirement of § 5.05(a) gets involved because it must be read in conjunction with § 5.05(c). Under § 5.05(a)(3), one of three things must also be true: (A) the rejection of the opportunity is fair, or (b) disinterested directors rejected the opportunity in advance, or (c) disinterested shareholders rejected the opportunity either in advance or by ratification. This is where § 5.05(c) comes in. If the plaintiff shows that the rejection was not made by disinterested directors or disinterested shareholders, the fiduciary has the burden of proving that the corporation's rejection and her taking the opportunity were fair to the company. On the other hand, if the opportunity was rejected by disinterested directors or disinterested shareholders, then the plaintiff has the burden of proving that the rejection was not fair.

We emphasize three things about § 5.05. First, it is reminiscent of interested director transaction statutes, discussed in section (E)(3). Those statutes allow interested transactions in the same three ways: either by disinterested directors or by disinterested shareholders, or by a showing of fairness to the corporation. This simply emphasizes that these two doctrines are species of the same concern about self-dealing.

Second, there is no provision for *ex post* presentation of the opportunity to the corporation. If a fiduciary takes the property without first offering it to the corporation and having it rejected, he is in trouble.[168] His only hope at that point will be to convince the court

---

[167] The idea is that this provision would apply to inside directors but not to outside directors. *See* Chapter 9(B)(1)(discussing inside and outside directors).

[168] Section 5.05(e) cuts back on this slightly. It provides that failure to offer the opportunity first to the corporation will not be determinative if two things are true. First, the failure to get approval arose from a good faith belief that the property did not constitute an opportunity. Second, within a reasonable time after suit is filed,

that the property was not an opportunity. This requirement (and the *Guth* recognition that rejection by the corporation is a safe harbor) should result in more fiduciaries doing the wise thing and disclosing before acquiring.

Finally, though § 5.05 does not mention the corporation's financial inability to pay for the opportunity, the Comment to that section indicates that this may be relevant in considering whether the corporation's rejection of the opportunity was fair.

Remedies. Generally, the remedy for usurpation is the imposition of a constructive trust.[169] This equitable tool results in the fiduciary's holding the property for the benefit of the corporation. The usurper must put the corporation in the position it should have been in absent her breach. This usually boils down to two possibilities. First, if she still has the property, she must sell it to the corporation at her cost. The corporation is not entitled to get the property for free, but should pay what it would have paid if the fiduciary had made it aware of the opportunity. Second, if the fiduciary has sold the property at a profit, the corporation is entitled to recover that profit. Of course, other remedies, including damages, may be appropriate depending on the facts of the case.

F. Which Directors Are Liable?

In the preceding sections, we have spoken of director liability for breach of the duties of care, good faith, and loyalty. If the elements of liability are shown, is every director liable? Not necessarily. As we saw in Chapter 6(D)(4), there is a presumption that all directors present at a board meeting concurred with action taken at the meeting unless their dissent or abstention was entered in writing in the corporate records. So a director who feels that the board's act is wrong, or that the board has not done sufficient homework, may insulate herself from liability by recording her dissent or abstention.

Even a consenting director may avoid liability, however, if she relied in good faith on a report or opinion of an appropriate competent person. Statutes in every state embody this principle, which is typified by RMBCA § 8.30(e). That section provides that in discharging her duties, a director "is entitled to rely on information, opinions, reports or statements, including financial statements and other financial data, prepared or presented by any of the persons specified in subsection (f)." That subsection, in turn, allows reliance on employ-

---

the director or senior officer offers the opportunity to the corporation "to the extent possible" and it is rejected pursuant to § 5.05(a).

[169] *See, e.g.,* Coupounas v. Morad, 380 A.2d 800, 803 (Ala. 1980).

ees, professionals (such as lawyers and accountants), and on a board committee of which the relying director is not a member.

It bears emphasis that this must be good faith reliance. Thus, the director must reasonably believe that the person on whom she relies is competent and acting within the scope of her expertise.[170] She cannot use this defense if she has "knowledge that makes reliance unwarranted."[171] So a director cannot bury her head in the sand and rely on information or advice that she knows may be problematic.

Various defendants in the *Van Gorkom* case raised this defense by arguing that they had a right to rely on the CEO's assessment of the appropriate merger price.[172] The court rejected the defense, however, because the defendants should have been aware that Van Gorkom had not done sufficient homework to arrive at a meaningful price. As fiduciaries, they should have asked how the CEO arrived at the number.

Section 8.30(e) also reflects the fact that while directors are usually generalists,[173] each brings her own expertise with her to the boardroom.[174] Suppose the board receives a detailed financial report from a corporate officer. A director with a background in patent law may legitimately rely on the report because she has no expertise that might gainsay it. But a director with a background in finance may reasonably be expected to apply it in assessing the reliability of the report.

G. Duties of Controlling Shareholders

To this point, we have considered duties imposed upon someone because of her management responsibilities. Thus, directors, officers, and managing shareholders (in close corporations) owe the duties of good faith, care, and loyalty. Now we shift gears to consider what duties a "controlling shareholder" might owe to the corporation and the other shareholders. A controlling shareholder is different from a managing shareholder.[175] The latter is someone who, under a shareholder management agreement in a closely held corporation, is enti-

---

[170] RMBCA § 8.30(f)(1)–(2).

[171] RMBCA § 8.30(e).

[172] *See* notes 50–60 and accompanying text.

[173] The notion of the director as generalist was captured in Judge Learned Hand's statement in *Barnes v. Andrews,* 298 F. 614, 618 (S.D.-N.Y. 1924), that "[d]irectors are not specialists, like lawyers or doctors. . . . They are the general advisers of the business. . . ." *See* text accompanying note 18.

[174] Remember, RMBCA § 8.30(e) allows reliance only by a director "who does not have knowledge that makes reliance unwarranted."

[175] We made this distinction in note 2.

tled to call the shots for the business. She need not own a substantial amount of stock (though she usually does). She is the functional equivalent of a director. We discuss this in Chapter 8(D).

A controlling shareholder, in contrast, is one who owns either (1) an outright majority of the voting stock or (2) a substantial minority of the stock with the remaining shares so dispersed that she is able to select the majority of management. For purposes of this section, she does not have an official management position in the corporation.[176] She has significant "clout" in the corporation, however, because of her substantial ownership. Though controlling shareholders are encountered most frequently in close corporations, it is possible to have such a powerful owner in a public corporation. In this section, we address a grab bag of topics relating to controlling shareholders.

1. Transfer of the Controlling Interest

The controlling shareholder's stock is called a "control block."[177] It will almost always be sold as a unit because holding that much stock enables a person to control the management of the corporation. Accordingly, the controlling shareholder can sell her block for more than its simple economic value. For example, suppose the net asset value of the business is $1,000,000 and the controlling shareholder owns 51 percent of the stock. The economic value of that stock is $510,000. But because owning it carries the ability to elect the management, a buyer will pay more than $510,000. The excess she receives over the raw economic value is called the "control premium."

Let's say, for example, the controlling shareholder sells this block for $600,000. The control premium is $90,000. Can the selling shareholder keep that $90,000? Through the years, some have argued that the premium should be shared with other shareholders. To our knowledge, no case has ever so held. In other words, no case imposes a duty to allow the minority shareholders to share in the premium[178] or to purchase her stock.[179] Thus, for starters, a controlling

---

[176] Of course, she may also be a director or officer or managing shareholder. We are concerned here only with the duties imposed upon her because of her controlling shareholder status.

[177] In contrast, "bloc" refers to a group of people agreeing to act as a group, for example, in voting.

[178] The confusing (and confused) case of *Perlman v. Feldmann*, 219 F.2d 173, 175–76 (2d Cir. 1955), to be discussed in section (G)(3) below, hinted at a fiduciary duty to the corporation and the minority shareholders in this situation, but it is hardly clear and has not inspired a following.

[179] This assumes that there is no valid stock transfer restriction requiring the controlling shareholder to offer the stock first to the corporation or the other shareholders. *See* Chapter 8(C)(1).

shareholder who sells her control block at a premium may keep the premium.[180]

Economists argue that transfers of control often benefit minority shareholders by bringing in fresh leadership. Sometimes, however, such transfers result in disaster. The best example is when the controlling shareholder sells her block to a "looter." Suppose the third party buys the interest and then takes control of the company for her personal gain. She converts corporate assets to cash (which she pockets), fails to have the corporation pay bills, has the corporation run up debts—basically "loots" the company. Does the controlling shareholder who sold to this "looter" bear any responsibility?

The answer is yes—but only if she breached a duty owed to the corporation and the minority shareholders. Everyone agrees that the controlling shareholder owes such a duty, but there is some debate about its scope. The American Law Institute's Principles of Corporate Governance suggests that it is a duty to disclose to the corporation and other shareholders if "it is apparent" that the third party "is likely to violate the duty of fair dealing."[181] Courts, however, seem to be more exacting by imposing a duty on the controlling shareholder to investigate the character and reputation of the buyer. If that investigation raises red flags about whether the third party is a crook, she should take further steps to allay her fears, or refuse to sell. There are various red flags, such as the third party's willingness to pay an excessive price, or an excessive interest in the liquid or immediately sellable assets of the business.

A good example is *DeBaun v. First Western Bank & Trust*.[182] There, a bank, as executor for the deceased founder of the corporation, held 70 percent of the corporation's stock. The bank sold the control block to a crook named Mattison, even though the bank was aware that Mattison had failed in several attempts to run businesses profitably. He had 38 unsatisfied judgments against him, including at least one for fraud and punitive damages.[183] Moreover, Mattison could not pay the purchase price without using the corporation's assets. Yet, in part because Mattison was an impressive luncheon companion, the bank sold to him. Any reasonable person would either have demanded explanations for Mattison's track record or walked

---

[180] "A controlling shareholder has the same right to dispose of voting equity securities as any other shareholder, including the right to dispose of those securities for a price that is not made proportionally available to other shareholders. . . ." ALI, PRINCIPLES OF CORPORATE GOVERNANCE § 5.16.

[181] *Id.*

[182] 120 Cal. Rptr. 354, 355 (Cal. Ct. App. 1975).

[183] *Id.* at 357.

away from the deal. In less than a year, Mattison took a company worth $220,000 and turned it into one that owed $218,000.[184]

The two minority shareholders (one owned 10 percent and the other owned 20 percent) sued. The appellate court affirmed a judgment that the bank was liable for selling a control block to a looter without making reasonable investigation. The remedy consisted of monetary recovery for all harm caused. Thus, the bank was liable for the (1) stolen assets, (2) future earnings (based upon the company's clear track record of profits) projected forward for ten years,[185] and (3) claims of creditors. Thus, a seller who breaches the duty and sells to a looter is liable for all harm caused.

But who recovers this money? Is the claim direct (that is, asserted by minority shareholders individually for harm done to them), or is it derivative (that is, asserted on behalf of the corporation for harm done to it)? Logically, a derivative claim does not make sense here. Recovery in a derivative suit is by the corporation itself. On the facts of *DeBaun*, this would mean that 70 percent of the recovery effectively would "belong" to the looter (because he owned 70 percent of the stock)! Instead, the recovery should go to the minority shareholders.[186] But if this is true, would not the proper recovery be 30 percent of the damage caused? After all, the minority shareholders owned only 30 percent of the company's stock. Why should they recover the entire amount of harm caused to the corporation? Their recovery should be pro rata.

The answers to these questions are not entirely clear. In other words, there is confusion about whether the duty is owed to the corporation or to the minority shareholders. The confusion is reflected in *DeBaun*. The plaintiffs asserted both a derivative claim and a direct claim. The trial court dismissed the direct claim and the case proceeded on a derivative basis. The court made no effort to explain, however, how (if at all) the monetary recovery would be allocated between the harmed minority shareholders and the looter.

2. Transfer Accompanied by Resignations of Directors

Suppose there is a sale of the controlling interest in which there is no looting. As part of the deal, and to facilitate the takeover by the

---

[184] *Id*. at 359.

[185] The evidence showed consistent earnings of eight percent. Based upon the facts of the case, the court concluded that this profit stream would have continued for at least ten years.

[186] *See, e.g.*, Yanow v. Teal Indus., 422 A.2d 311, 314 (minority shareholder has individual claim for looting); Caswell v. Jordan, 362 S.E.2d 769, 771 (Ga. Ct. App. 1987) (same).

buyer, the controlling shareholder agrees that she (if she is a director) and directors friendly to her will resign from the board. This practice—called delivering a "stacked" board to the buyer—allows the buyer to step in and fill the vacant board positions with people friendly to her. The alternative would be for the buyer to wait until the next annual meeting to elect "her" directors, or to call a shareholders' meeting to remove the sitting directors without cause. Either of those courses takes time.

When the sale of a control block is accompanied by resignations of directors, it appears that the control premium was paid in part for the resignations. This makes it look as though the buyer "bought" seats on the board, which seems antithetical to public policy; fiduciary offices should not be for sale. Arguably, then, the premium should be recovered by the corporation or shared with the minority owners.

There is very little case law on the topic. The best known case may be *Essex Universal Corp. v. Yates*,[187] though it fails to give definitive guidance. There, the seller held 28.3 percent of the stock in a widely held public corporation. Because the other shares were so broadly dispersed, the seller was a controlling shareholder. He contracted to sell his stock, accompanied by resignations of friendly directors. Later (apparently because the value of the stock increased), the seller tried to get out of the deal and claimed that it violated public policy. The three judges on the appellate panel took different positions. One concluded that the agreement was enforceable because, on the facts, ownership of 28 percent constituted sufficient control to permit the resignations as part of a transfer of control.[188] Another judge "was inclined" to uphold such deals as acceptable only if they accompanied the sale of a true majority of the stock.[189] The third judge concluded that the matter should be remanded for trial.[190]

Another case was easier—the president of the corporation, who owned four percent of the stock, sold his shares as part of an agreement to resign and to have the buyer's pals appointed to the presidency and to two director positions. The court found the sale contrary to public policy as a sale of office because the ownership of four

---

[187] 305 F.2d 572, 580 (2d Cir. 1962).

[188] *Id.* at 579 ("[I]f Essex had been contracting to purchase a majority of the stock of Republic, it would have been entirely proper for the contract to contain the provision for immediate replacement of directors. Although in the case at bar only 28.3 percent of the stock was involved, it is commonly known that a person owning so large a percentage [in a widely owned corporation] is almost certain to have control as a practical matter.")(Lumbard, J.).

[189] *Id.* at 581 (Friendly, J.).

[190] *Id.* at 579–80 (Clark, J.). All three judges purported to apply New York law.

percent would not allow the buyer legitimately to install that many managers.[191]

3. Two Famous but Odd Cases

Here we address two cases that arguably involve payments of a control premium. We say "arguably" because neither opinion is a model of clarity. Yet each has gotten considerable attention through the years and each has found its way into most Business Associations casebooks. In *Jones v. H. F. Ahmanson & Co.*,[192] defendants owned 87 percent of the stock in a savings and loan association (S&L), which was closely held. The defendants wanted to create a public market for the S&L stock because, they felt, it would increase the value of their holdings. It would also guarantee a public market should they want to sell.[193] They could have had the S&L stock registered and therefore qualified to trade publicly, but the defendants pursued a different plan.

They created a holding company, which is a corporation that does not "do" anything—it just owns a majority of the stock of different companies. The defendants then transferred their S&L stock to the holding company. In exchange, they received the stock of the holding company. The minority shareholders of the S&L were not permitted to participate in this deal. The holding company then "went public," which resulted in public trading of its stock. As a result, the defendants had stock (in the holding company) that was publicly traded, while the minority shareholders of the S&L remained locked into a minority position (13 percent) in a closely held subsidiary of the holding company.[194]

The California Supreme Court held that the defendants breached a fiduciary duty owed directly to the minority shareholders. The duty imposed was of the *Donahue* variety[195]—owed by one shareholder to another, and not to the corporation.[196] According to the court, there is a "comprehensive rule of good faith and inherent fairness to the minority in any transaction where control of the corporation is material."[197] Even if the defendants had offered the plaintiffs a chance to sell their stock to the holding company, the court

[191] Brecher v. Gregg, 89 Misc.2d 457, 460 (N.Y. Sup. Ct. 1975).

[192] 1 Cal.3d 93, 102 (1969).

[193] *Id.*

[194] *Id.* at 103.

[195] *Donahue* is the leading case recognizing a fiduciary obligation among shareholders in a closely held corporation. *See* Chapter 8(F)(2).

[196] *Jones*, 1 Cal.3d at 109–110.

[197] *Id.* at 112.

said, they would have to demonstrate good faith or a strong business reason for doing things the way they did.

The other case is *Perlman v. Feldmann*,[198] which involved stock in a company called Newport. That company manufactured steel during the Korean War, when supplies were scarce because of military need. Feldmann and his family owned 37 percent of Newport. Newport was publicly traded, and the 37 percent stake permitted Feldmann to elect a majority of the board (because the rest of the stock was so widely held). Feldmann devised a brilliant plan to help Newport compete in the tight wartime market. Under the "Feldmann plan," Newport would agree to sell steel, but only to buyers who agreed to make interest-free loans to Newport. The company would use the loans to expand its capacity. The plan was an enormous success and Newport profited from it. Feldmann then sold his 37 percent stake to Wilport for $20 per share. The market price for the stock at the time was $12 (meaning that Feldmann's control premium was $8 per share).

Minority shareholders sued derivatively and claimed that the sale of control to Wilport was effectively the sale of a corporate asset—namely, the ability to control the allocation of steel in a period of short supply. As such, plaintiffs argued, the control premium belonged to the corporation. The court's reasoning is muddy at best. The opinion meanders through a discussion of general fiduciary duties and usurpation of corporate opportunities.[199] The court goes out of its way to note that "[w]e have here no fraud, no misuse of confidential information, and no outright looting of a helpless corporation."[200] Yet, somehow we have liability. And though the case was derivative, for reasons not made clear, the court allowed recovery directly by the minority shareholders.[201]

To the extent the court was saying that a fiduciary cannot sell something that belongs to the corporation and pocket the proceeds, *Perlman* makes sense. Indeed, it is a garden variety breach of the duty of loyalty. Feldmann arguably sold a corporate asset—i.e., Newport's ability to charge above-market prices for its steel through its interest-free loans—and kept the proceeds for himself. The remedy there, though, would be recovery by the corporation, and not by the minority shareholders. It is difficult to see why *Perlman* has gotten the attention it has. At the end of the day, it is a strange and confused opinion, and the case should probably be chalked up to the unusual facts of the dispute.

---

[198] 219 F.2d 173, 175 (2d Cir. 1953).

[199] *Id.* at 175–76.

[200] *Id.* at 176.

[201] *Id.* at 177–78.

4. Parent-Subsidiary Corporation Issues

The controlling shareholder of one corporation is often another corporation. By definition, this is true every time there is a parent and subsidiary relationship. The parent owns a controlling block of stock in the subsidiary. When the subsidiary is wholly owned, there are no fiduciary duty problems. Whatever the parent corporation decides to do with its control of the subsidiary can only affect the parent. But when the subsidiary has minority shareholders, the parent must be careful not to breach a fiduciary duty in its dealings with the minority.

In *Sinclair Oil Corp. v. Levien*,[202] Sinclair (a large publicly traded company) owned 97 percent of Sinclair of Venezuela (Sinven). Sinclair dominated Sinven completely—it elected the directors, who were executives of Sinclair. The plaintiff owned some of the other three percent of Sinven. He brought a derivative suit on behalf of Sinven against Sinclair and alleged that the parent corporation had breached its fiduciary duty to the subsidiary. Everyone agreed that Sinclair, as parent, owed a fiduciary duty to Sinven.[203]

The plaintiff asserted three claims. First, he argued that Sinclair caused Sinven to pay huge (though legal) dividends for the purpose of funneling money to Sinclair (Sinclair evidently needed cash). As a result, Sinven lacked funds to develop its own business. Second, the plaintiff argued that Sinclair usurped corporate opportunities belonging to Sinven. Third, he asserted that Sinclair caused a wholly owned subsidiary to breach contracts with Sinven and then prevented Sinven from enforcing the contracts..

The court addressed the appropriate standard for reviewing Sinclair's acts. For starters, a court will employ the business judgment rule unless there is self-dealing. In cases of self-dealing, the court indicated, it would apply the "intrinsic fairness" test (which is sometimes called the "entire fairness" test and sometimes just the "fairness" test).[204] This is consistent with what we saw in section (E) of this Chapter—that the business judgment rule does not apply in cases in which the fiduciary has engaged in self-dealing. Once the plaintiff demonstrates self-dealing, the burden shifts to the defendant to satisfy the "intrinsic fairness" test. As we know from our earlier dis-

---

[202] 280 A.2d 717 (Del. 1971).

[203] *Id.* at 720 ("A parent does indeed owe a fiduciary duty to its subsidiary when there are parent-subsidiary dealings.").

[204] In *Weinberger v. UOP, Inc.*, 457 A.2d 701 (Del. 1983), discussed below, the Delaware Supreme Court applies what it called the "fairness" test. In *HMG/Courtland Properties, Inc v. Gray*, 749 A.2d 94 (Del. Ch.), the Delaware Chancery Court applied what it called the "entire fairness" test. All three cases seem to be talking about the same thing.

cussion, the business judgment rule involves very little judicial oversight of the fiduciary's action. The intrinsic fairness test, as we will see, features very searching judicial review.

Did Sinclair engage in self-dealing? The court defined self-dealing as "when a parent is on both sides of a transaction with its subsidiary." More specifically, "[s]elf-dealing occurs when the parent, by virtue of its domination of the subsidiary, causes the subsidiary to act in such a way that the parent receives something from the subsidiary to the exclusion of, and detriment to, the minority stockholders of the subsidiary."[205]

Regarding the claim of excessive dividends, the court concluded that there was no self-dealing. The allegations—that Sinclair caused Sinven to declare large dividends simply to channel cash to Sinclair—did not involve self-dealing. Why? Because the minority shareholders of Sinven received the same pro rata dividend that Sinclair did. Because the parent got nothing more than the minority shareholders, there was no self-dealing, and the transaction was reviewed under the deferential business judgment rule.[206] Not surprisingly, Sinclair won on that claim.

On the second claim—regarding usurpation of opportunities—the court also rejected application of the intrinsic fairness test. Because Sinclair had received nothing from Sinven (its subsidiary) to the exclusion of its minority shareholders, there was no self-dealing. According to the court, none of the potential opportunities was in Venezuela. Thus, they did not constitute corporate opportunities for Sinven. The court thus applied the business judgment rule and Sinclair prevailed on this claim.

On the third claim—inducing breach of contract—the plaintiff finally had a winner. Sinclair's use of another subsidiary to deal with Sinven, causing it to fail to pay for products bought from Sinven, and thwarting Sinven's ability to enforce the contracts, constituted self-dealing. By those acts, Sinclair (through its other subsidiary) received a benefit (not having to buy so much oil, and not paying on time) to the detriment of the minority shareholders of Sinven. Thus, the intrinsic fairness test applied. Under that test, Sinclair would have to prove that its causing Sinven not to enforce its contracts with the other subsidiary was intrinsically fair to Sinven. Sinclair failed to meet this burden.[207]

---

[205] *Sinclair Oil*, 280 A.2d at 720.

[206] Plaintiffs could invoke the intrinsic fairness test, for example, by showing that the parent corporation held one class of stock, which was paid dividends, while the minority held a different class, which was denied dividends. *Id.* at 721.

[207] *Id.* at 723.

A transaction between a controlling shareholder and its corporation is self-dealing and the business judgment rule simply does not apply. It is the functional equivalent of the interested director transaction that we studied in section (E)(3) of this Chapter. For those, as we saw, statutes provide for approval by disinterested directors or shareholders—occasionally in lieu of a showing of fairness. Those statutes generally do not apply expressly to transactions between a corporation and its controlling shareholder (who is not also a director or officer). Accordingly, such transactions are reviewed under the intrinsic fairness test.

The Delaware Supreme Court shed more light on that test in *Weinberger v. UOP, Inc.*[208] It held that a cash-out merger of a partially owned subsidiary did not satisfy the intrinsic fairness test (which it called simply the "fairness" test). Signal owned 50.5 percent of the stock of UOP. It wanted to acquire the remaining 49.5 percent. Signal dominated the UOP board of directors. It had two of its directors (Arledge and Chitiea)—who were also UOP directors—undertake a "feasibility study." This study used UOP information for the benefit of Signal, to determine a favorable price range for Signal to pay. The feasibility study concluded that Signal's acquiring the remaining UOP stock for up to $24 per share would be a good investment for Signal. Instead, Signal proffered a merger price of $21, which the (Signal-dominated) UOP board (predictably) accepted. After shareholder approval,[209] the UOP shareholders were cashed out at $21 per share.

Plaintiff was a UOP stockholder who brought a class action on behalf of all minority shareholders of Signal, claiming that Signal breached a fiduciary duty owed to the minority shareholders.[210] By the time the suit was filed, the merger had been consummated. It could not be undone, so rescission was not a remedial option. Instead, the plaintiff class sought "rescissory damages" consisting of the difference between the $21 merger price and what would have been the fair value of the stock as of the merger. The lower court entered judgment for the defendants and the Delaware Supreme Court reversed. It established that "entire fairness" consists of two basic elements: fair dealing and fair price. Fair dealing focuses on procedural matters, such as how the transaction was timed, initiated, structured, disclosed, and approved. Fair price focuses on substantive

---

[208] 457 A.2d 701 (Del. 1983).

[209] Mergers are fundamental corporate changes, which must be approved by the shareholders. *See* Chapter 13.

[210] The suit was direct, not derivative, because it asserted breach of a duty owed to the minority shareholders. In contrast, a derivative suit asserts a claim for breach of a duty owed to the corporation.

matters, including the economic and financial considerations of the transaction.

On the facts of the case, the merger failed the entire fairness test. First, it did not satisfy "fair dealing" because the parent corporation (Signal) set all the terms of the merger. It initiated and structured the transaction, including the imposition of severe time constraints. It dictated the terms; there was little in the way of negotiation. More importantly, Signal never disclosed the feasibility study, which concluded that a merger would be favorable for Signal for as much as $24 per share.

Second, the court had misgivings about the fairness of the $21 per share merger price. Some evidence indicated that the stock was worth $26 at the relevant time. The court instructed the trial court on remand to assess the issue. The court emphasized that fair dealing and fair price were not to be considered in a bifurcated fashion. Rather, "all aspects" of the issue must be examined as a whole since the question is one of entire fairness. And, importantly, as noted above, the parent corporation (Signal) had the burden to establish entire fairness.

In a footnote, the court said "the result here could have been entirely different" if the subsidiary (UOP) had appointed an independent negotiating committee of outside directors to deal at arm's length with Signal. It added that "fairness in this context can be equated to conduct by a theoretical, wholly independent, board of directors acting upon the matter before them."[211] In a parent-subsidiary context, this requires a showing that the action taken would have been entered into if each of the contending parties had been unrelated and had dealt at arm's length. Such facts would be "strong evidence" that the transaction meets the entire fairness test.[212] The message of *Weinberger* is that independent directors should be added to the boards of partially owned subsidiaries to permit arm's-length bargaining with the parent. Of course, these independent directors must discharge their duties to the subsidiary.

---

[211] *Weinberger,* 457 A.2d at 709 n.7.
[212] *Id.*

Chapter 8

SPECIAL ISSUES IN THE CLOSELY HELD CORPORATION

Analysis

A. Introduction
B. Characteristics of the Close Corporation and the Statutory Close Corporation
C. Avoiding Outsiders and Ensuring Financial Return
   1. The Outsider Problem and Stock Transfer Restrictions
   2. The Illiquidity Problem and Buy-Sell Agreements
D. Shareholder Management
   1. Background
   2. Case Law Development
   3. Legislative Amelioration: Statutory Close Corporations
   4. Legislative Rejection of the Traditional Model
E. Shareholder Liability: Piercing the Corporate Veil and Related Doctrines
   1. Background
   2. Case Law
   3. Piercing the Corporate Veil in the Parent-Subsidiary Context
   4. Choice of Law Issues
   5. Reverse Piercing and Related Issues
   6. Enterprise Liability
F. Fiduciary Duties and Oppressive Behavior
   1. Background
   2. Common Law Recognition of a Fiduciary Duty
   3. The Effect of Involuntary Dissolution Statutes
   4. Reasonable Expectations of the Shareholder

A. Introduction

We introduced the closely held (or close) corporation in Chapter 6(B)(5). It is one with few shareholders, the stock of which is not publicly traded, and in which the shareholders usually are engaged in management. Most close corporations are founded by friends or family members, whose expectations are the same as those of people who enter into a partnership: they want to own the business, to share in profits and losses, to share in management, and (probably) to be employed by the business. The shareholders do not see their investment as liquid; that is, they do not expect to make money by selling their interest in the business. Rather, their principal financial reward will be realized not as a shareholder but as an employee.[1]

These expectations are radically different from those of shareholders in a public corporation. Those investors are "owners" only in a tangential sense, have no effective voice in management, and do not expect to work for the company. They view their investment as liquid; that is, they hope to make money by selling the stock on the public market for more than they spent to buy it, and perhaps by receiving dividends in the interim.

Because the expectations of those founding a close corporation are so similar to those of proprietors founding a partnership, we might expect the two forms to feature similar characteristics and rules for governance and liability. But, as we discussed at Chapter 6(B)(5), there is considerable tension between the expectations of the parties and the traditional model of the corporation.

In this Chapter, we focus on four specific areas of that tension, and how the law has evolved to deal with it. First concerns the clash between the fact that stock is freely transferable and the fact that in a close corporation there is no market for the stock. The former means that a shareholder, by transferring her stock (even by gift), may force the other shareholders to deal with a new owner. This may prove disruptive, and proper business planning requires that the parties address the issue in advance, perhaps with a stock transfer restriction, as we discuss in section C of this Chapter. The fact that there is no market for the stock means that a shareholder in dire need of cash may be unable to raise it because she can find no one to buy her stock. Again, the problem should be avoided by good planning, such as the use of "buy-sell" agreements, which we also see in section C.

Second, we consider problems regarding management. While partnership law permits proprietors to structure management as they see fit, the traditional corporate model imposes separate roles for shareholders and the board of directors, each with rigid mechanical rules of operation. In section D, we will see that the legal landscape has changed dramatically, so that today those operating a close corporation have the same sort of flexibility enjoyed in partnership law.

---

[1] *See* Wilkes v. Springside Nursing Home, Inc., 353 N.E.2d 657, 662 (Mass. 1976) ("The minority shareholder typically depends on his salary as the principal return on his investment, since the earnings of a close corporation . . . are distributed in major part in salaries, bonus, and retirement benefits.").

Third is the question of liability for business debts. While partners generally are liable for debts incurred in the operation of the business, the corporation, in contrast, features limited liability. Thus, generally, shareholders are not liable for business debts. On the other hand, though, if the corporation is run like a partnership, there may be circumstances in which limited liability will not apply. As we will see in section E, under the doctrine of "piercing the corporate veil," shareholders may be personally liable for what the business does.

Finally, we address the relationship among shareholders. If the business functions as a partnership, should the shareholders owe each other the fiduciary duties customarily applied to partners? In section F, we will see that some courts have said yes, at least in some circumstances.

B. Characteristics of the Close Corporation and the Statutory Close Corporation

A close corporation is a true corporation, formed as discussed in Chapter 5(C). There is no magic number of shareholders. In all states, there can be as few as one, and there is no general statutory or common law imposition of a maximum number.[2] One consequence of the small number of shareholders, of course, is that there is no public market for the stock of the corporation.

Historically, the law of close corporations consisted of common law glosses on the operation of an "ordinary" corporation. In the past generation, about 20 states have enacted "statutory close corporation" provisions. These are not separate codes, but are "supplements" to the general corporation statute in the particular jurisdiction, with express provision that the general statute applies in areas not addressed by the supplement.[3] Thus:

- A "closely held" (or "close") corporation is one formed under a state's general corporation statute. Its stock is not registered for public trading. There is no maximum number of shareholders, and much of the law about governance and liability is common law.

- A "statutory close corporation" is one formed under special legislative provisions. The stock is not registered for public

---

[2] *See, e.g.*, 15 PA. CONS. STAT. § 2304(b)(1) ("The articles of incorporation may set forth the maximum number of persons who are entitled to be record holders."). This is not the case, however, with "statutory close corporations," as to which legislation usually prescribes a maximum number of shareholders. *See* section D(3).

[3] *See, e.g.*, RMBCA Close Corporation Supplement.

trading. Most of these statutes impose a maximum number of shareholders—commonly the number is 50.[4]

The distinction between a close and a statutory close corporation is of waning significance. Even in states permitting the formation of a statutory close corporation, that form is not exclusive. Thus, the proprietors can simply charter a corporation, which they operate under common law glosses on ordinary corporation law. For some years, statutory close corporation status carried a significant advantage because statutes provided great flexibility in management. Today, however, as we discuss in section (D)(4), the same flexibility is available under general corporation statutes. Accordingly, there is not much incentive to form a statutory close corporation (and, in fact, there are relatively few such entities).

In a few areas, however, the choice between the regular close corporation and the statutory close corporation will carry consequences. These differences vary from state to state. In some states, for instance, forming a statutory close corporation will affect the default provision on the existence of pre-emptive rights.[5] In most states, pre-emptive rights do not exist if the articles are silent. With the statutory close corporation, however, in some states the default position is the opposite: shareholders have pre-emptive rights unless the articles provide otherwise.[6] Some other distinctions between close and statutory close corporations will be noted below. For the most part, though, as mentioned, the distinction is not important.

C. Avoiding Outsiders and Ensuring Financial Return

1. The Outsider Problem and Stock Transfer Restrictions

Stock is freely transferable. The shareholder may sell her stock or give it away (*inter vivos* or by will) to whomever she chooses. Doing so transfers her entire interest, so the transferee will receive not just the financial interest, but all shareholder rights—the right to vote, to inspect corporate books and records, to bring derivative suits, etc. This is not true in the partnership. As we saw in Chapter 3, a partner ordinarily may transfer only her financial interest in the business. The transferee does not receive any rights of management.

---

[4] *See, e.g.*, CAL. CORP. CODE § 158(a).

[5] Pre-emptive rights, discussed at Chapter 10(C)(5), allow existing shareholders to maintain their percentage of ownership by buying more stock when the corporation issues new stock. Pre-emptive rights thus protect shareholders from having their interests diluted when the company sells more stock.

[6] *See* 15 PA. CONS. STAT. § 2321(b)(1).

Moreover, unless the partnership agreement provides otherwise, a new partner can be admitted only by unanimous vote of the existing partners. Partnership law thus recognizes the special relationship among the partners. They have chosen to do business with each other, and cannot be forced to accept a different partner unless they all agree.

In the close corporation, the free transferability of stock runs the risk of disrupting the relationship among the original proprietors.

- X, Y, and Z form XYZ Corp., a close corporation. Each owns 100 shares of the 300 issued shares of the stock. Each is a director on the three-person board of directors. Each has a job with the corporation and draws a salary. X needs money to pay college tuition bills for her children. She finds a buyer, A, who will pay for X's interest in XYZ Corp.

If X sells to A, A will become a full-fledged shareholder. She will be able to attend shareholder meetings, propose candidates for election to the board of directors, inspect the books and records, and bring derivative suits if Y or Z get out of line. Y and Z did not bargain for this (indeed, they may not even know A).

This "outsider" problem can be avoided with a stock transfer restriction. Such restrictions often are found in the articles or bylaws, though they may also be established by contract between the corporation and the shareholders or among the shareholders themselves. They are common in closely held corporations.[7] In some states, the statutory close corporation provisions impose automatic restrictions on the power of shareholders to transfer their stock.[8]

A typical stock transfer restriction obligates each shareholder to offer her stock to the corporation (or to the other shareholders) when

---

[7] In a publicly held corporation, stock transfer restrictions may be helpful to avoid violations of federal securities law. For instance, when a corporation issues "unregistered" shares in connection with a merger, a stock transfer restriction can prevent the resale of those shares into the public market. Similarly, a restriction may ensure that a corporation remains exempt from a requirement that it must register under federal law. Such an exemption may be lost, for instance, if stock is offered for resale to nonresidents. Similarly, a closely held corporation may impose such a flat restriction on resale to others to ensure that it continues to qualify as an S Corporation for income tax purposes. An S Corporation cannot have more than 100 shareholders. A stock transfer restriction may prevent transfers that will jeopardize that status.

[8] *See, e.g.*, WIS. STAT. 180.1805 ("No interest in shares of a statutory close corporation may be transferred without the written consent of all shareholders holding voting stock, unless the interest is transferred . . . to the corporation or to any other holder of the same class . . . of shares. . . ."). In other states, stock transfer restrictions in statutory close corporations must be spelled out. *See, e.g.*, GA. CODE § 14–2–910 (requiring conspicuous notice of any transfer restrictions on the stock certificates of shares in a statutory close corporation).

a particular event occurs. Common triggering events are retirement, disability, and death. There are three classic stock transfer restrictions in the small corporation. First is an option, exercisable by the corporation or the other shareholders, to buy the stock at a set price upon a triggering event. Second is a right of first refusal, which gives the corporation or the shareholders a chance to meet the best legitimate price offered by an outsider for the stock of a current investor. Third is a mandatory "buy-sell" agreement, which requires the corporation or the shareholders to buy the stock at a set price upon a triggering event. We will discuss buy-sell agreements in the next subsection.

Stock transfer restrictions usually benefit all shareholders. They allow those who leave the business to liquidate their interests at an acceptable price. An option or a right of first refusal does not guarantee the shareholder a specified price, whereas a buy-sell agreement does. Stock transfer restrictions also allow those remaining in the business to determine whether to allow outsiders to become stockholders. They may also ensure stable management and protect the corporation and other shareholders against an unexpected change in the respective proportionate interests of the shareholders that might occur if one shareholder is able to purchase shares of other investors quietly. Moreover, by reducing the interest to cash, a stock transfer restriction may enable the heirs of a deceased shareholder to pay estate taxes.

Reflecting general antipathy toward restraints on alienation, courts historically were hostile to stock transfer restrictions. The common law would enforce them only if they did "not unreasonably restrain or prohibit transferability."[9] Under this test, an outright prohibition on transferability would certainly be invalid. Similarly, a restriction that prohibited transfer without the consent of directors or shareholders would be suspect because such consent could be withheld arbitrarily. A stock transfer restriction imposing a penalty, such as a loss of voting rights as a consequence of transfer, would also be suspect.

Today, the validity of restrictions is addressed by statute. Almost universally, they are enforceable if "reasonable."[10] Statutes routinely provide a safe harbor for restrictions aimed at (1) maintaining the status of the corporation when it is dependent on the number

---

[9] Ling & Co., Inc. v. Trinity Sav. & Loan Ass'n, 482 S.W.2d 841, 844 (Tex. 1972); *see also* Miller Waste Mills, Inc. v. Mackay, 520 N.W.2d 490, 494–95 (Minn. Ct. App. 1994) (imposition of right of first refusal or option for corporation to buy stock not unreasonable).

[10] *See, e.g.*, RMBCA § 6.27(c)(3).

or identity of shareholders, and (2) preserving exemptions under federal or state securities law. Such restrictions are valid without investigation into their reasonableness.[11] On the other hand, consent restrictions and prohibitory restrictions are valid only if "the requirement is not manifestly unreasonable."[12]

Restrictions are sometimes imposed after the corporation has issued stock. Are previously issued shares subject to the restrictions? The general rule appears to be that found in RMBCA § 6.27(a), which provides that restrictions will apply to previously issued shares only if the holders of those shares are parties to the agreement creating the restrictions, or if they voted in favor of imposing them.[13]

Statutes generally require that stock certificates include notation of any stock transfer restriction.[14] They usually do not mandate that the entire text of the restriction appear; only the fact of its existence must be noted. The notation usually must be "conspicuous," which, in the language of the RMBCA, means "so written that a reasonable person against whom it is to operate ought to have noticed it."[15] Inclusion of a conspicuous notation will charge third parties with knowledge of the restriction.[16] Absent such notation, a third party is not bound by a stock transfer restriction unless she has actual knowledge of it.

Generally, statutes do not impose a time limit on the lifespan of stock transfer restrictions. They may be terminated by express agreement of the shareholders involved[17] or by abandonment. A shareholder who breaches a stock transfer restriction waives the right to enforce the restriction.[18] Depending on the language of the restriction, courts may order transfers that otherwise would not be permitted. For example, in *Castonguay v. Castonguay*,[19] the Minne-

---

[11] *See, e.g.,* RMBCA § 6.27(c)(1)–(2). In other words, the purposes set forth in § 6.27(c)(1) and (2) are conclusively presumed to be reasonable.

[12] DEL. GEN. CORP. LAW § 202; *see also* RMBCA § 6.27(d).

[13] *See, e.g.,* B&H Warehouse, Inc. v. Atlas Van Lines, Inc., 490 F.2d 818, 825–26 (5th Cir. 1974) (after-imposed restriction not enforceable).

[14] *See, e.g.,* RMBCA § 6.27(b)("A restriction . . . is valid and enforceable...if the restriction . . . is noted conspicuously on the front or back of the certificate . . .").

[15] RMBCA § 1.40. For example, "printing in italics or boldface or contrasting color, or typing in capitals or underlined, is conspicuous. A printed heading in capitals . . . is conspicuous." *Id.*

[16] *See, e.g.,* Roof Depot, Inc. v. Ohman, 638 N.W.2d 782, 785–87 (Minn. Ct. App. 2002) (lien given on stock subject to restriction invalid because restriction was conspicuously noted and transferee was therefore charged with notice).

[17] For example, all the shareholders may agree to sell to a third party.

[18] *See, e.g.,* Thomson v. Anderson, 498 P.2d 1, 8 (Kan. 1972) (shareholder who assisted a third party to acquire stock in breach of a right of first refusal not permitted to enforce the restriction against others).

[19] 306 N.W.2d 143, 145 (Minn. 1981).

sota Supreme Court upheld an order commanding the shareholder husband to transfer half his stock to his ex-wife in a divorce proceeding. Though the stock was subject to a stock transfer restriction, the court noted that its terms did not expressly apply to transfers by operation of law.

2. The Illiquidity Problem and Buy-Sell Agreements

Though stock is freely transferable, a shareholder in a close corporation may find it difficult to find a buyer. Unlike stock in a public corporation, she cannot simply go online and liquidate the holding. In other words, the investment in a close corporation is "illiquid"—it cannot readily be converted into cash.[20]

- Again, X, Y, and Z form XYZ Corp., a close corporation. Each owns 100 shares of the 300 issued shares of the stock. Each is a director on the three-person board of directors. Each has a job with the corporation and draws a salary. Now X needs money to pay tuition bills for her children, but cannot find a buyer for her stock. Alternatively, suppose that X becomes disabled, cannot work, and needs money for medical bills. Or suppose Z dies and her estate cannot find anyone to purchase the stock.

Proprietors of a close corporation can avoid these problems with a "buy-sell" agreement. This requires either the corporation or the other shareholders to purchase an investor's shares upon the occurrence of a triggering event, such as retirement, disability, or death. The choice of whether the corporation or the other shareholders will purchase the stock is a matter of preference. Often, the corporation is the better option because it will have greater access to the cash needed for the purchase.[21] Buy-sell provisions requiring purchase by the other shareholders can lead to problems. For instance, one of them might be unable or unwilling to purchase. In such a case, the agreement may require that the shares be offered to willing shareholders proportionately.

It is common to fund buy-sell agreements triggered by the death of a shareholder with life insurance. The proceeds of the policy pro-

---

[20] In the partnership, a partner might be able to force the business to dissolve and liquidate. In contrast, as we will see at Chapter 12, shareholders have no general right to force dissolution and liquidation. At any rate, dissolution and liquidation may not be preferred because the process will cease the existence of what could be a very profitable business.

[21] Such a repurchase by the corporation is a distribution, and must satisfy the legal requirements for such transactions, which we discuss in Chapter 10(F).

vide funds to purchase shares on the death of the shareholder. In these arrangements, it is usually simplest to have the corporation pay the premiums and own the policies on the lives of each shareholder. The alternative is to have each shareholder insure the life of every other shareholder. This can become prohibitively complicated and expensive. If there were 25 shareholders, for example, a complete cross-purchase arrangement with life insurance would require 600 policies.

The price provisions of buy-sell agreements often raise the most difficult problems. Because there is no market for stock in a closely held corporation, there must be some other metric for valuation. There are various options, including a stated price or the best offer by an outsider. The most popular method of valuation, however, is "book value." This is computed by dividing stockholders' equity on the balance sheet by the number of outstanding shares. Book value is relatively easy to calculate. The problem is that it may have no relationship with the actual value of the stock. Why? Basic accounting conventions require that most assets be valued at cost and that they not be reappraised upward or downward to reflect current market values. Thus, a corporation that owns real estate acquired decades earlier at low prices may have a book value that greatly understates the true value of the assets.[22]

Instead of using book value, the agreement may provide that the stock will be appraised at the time of purchase. Appraisal of the value of stock in a closely held corporation is often a difficult thing.[23] We will discuss it in Chapter 12(C) in connection with a shareholder's right of appraisal, which is the right to force the corporation to buy one's stock in reaction to certain fundamental corporate changes. The exercise of that right presents the same valuation problems encountered with buy-sell agreements.

D. Shareholder Management

1. Background

In the traditional model of corporate governance, "shareholder management" is an oxymoron. Shareholders do not manage. Shareholders elect the directors and must approve fundamental changes,

---

[22] Accounting conventions allow corporations to include as assets some things that may never be realized. For example, the costs of formation or the value of "goodwill" acquired in connection with the purchase of another business may be included in book value. It may be appropriate to eliminate such things from the balance sheet before computing book value.

[23] *See* Douglas K. Moll, *Shareholder Oppression and "Fair Value": Of Discounts, Dates, and Dastardly Deeds in the Close Corporation,* 54 DUKE L.J. 293 (2002).

but they do not have a direct voice in running the corporation. That is the job of the board of directors.[24] Under the traditional model, there must be board meetings with notice, quorum, and voting requirements. And there must be shareholder meetings with different notice, quorum, and voting requirements. These formal requirements of corporate law are inconsistent with the managerial flexibility of the partnership. Because shareholder expectations in a close corporation are so similar to partner expectations in a partnership, however, there has long been a sense that some of the corporate formality should yield in the close corporation.

Today, the proprietors of a close corporation can structure management largely as they see fit. They can even abolish the board of directors and seize management power themselves. Getting to that point, however, was a tortuous journey involving case law development and two waves of legislative innovation.

2. Case Law Development

In Chapter 6(B)(5), we saw a hypothetical that demonstrates nicely the formality of the corporate model of operation. We return to it now:

- A and B are shareholders of Close Corporation. They enter into a voting agreement which requires them to vote their shares in an effort to elect each other to the board of directors. The agreement further provides that once the three are on the board of directors, they will vote to elect each other as officers at specified salaries.

  This hypothetical is similar to the facts in the famous case of *McQuade v. Stoneham*,[25] which involved an agreement among three of the (very few) shareholders of the New York Giants baseball team.[26] After a falling out, one of the parties to the agreement, McQuade, was not retained as a corporate officer. He sued the other two for breaching the voting agreement.[27] The New York Court of Appeals upheld judgment for the defendants and concluded that the agreement

---

[24] *See* RMBCA § 8.01(b) ("All corporate powers shall be exercised by or under the authority of the board of directors . . . .").

[25] 189 N.E. 234, 235 (N.Y. 1954).

[26] The team moved to San Francisco in 1958 and (finally) won the World Series in 2011.

[27] The two defendants are members of the Baseball Hall of Fame. One was Charles A. Stoneham, who was the principal owner and whose family controlled the franchise for decades. The other was John J. McGraw, a colorful and very successful manager of the Giants. McGraw's managerial prowess led many to overlook his extraordinary career as a player.

concerning the appointment of officers (and the setting of their salaries) was void. The agreement as shareholders to vote their shares to elect each other to the board was valid.[28] But when the parties agreed in advance as to what they would do *as directors*, the agreement violated public policy.[29] Appointing officers and setting their compensation are jobs for the board of directors. Because they owe non-delegable fiduciary duties to the corporation, directors are required to exercise their independent judgment and may not agree in advance to management decisions.[30] Even the directors are not shareholders themselves, the shareholders cannot agree in advance on matters that are properly within the purview of the board of directors.

This is an example of what is often called a "sterilization" agreement. By fettering the directors' hands in advance, the deal "sterilizes" the board by robbing the company of the benefit of each director's judgment, which is to be forged in consultation with the other directors at board meetings. But this level of formality makes little sense in the closely held corporation. The proprietors quite rightly think of themselves as owners and managers at the same time.

Just two years after *McQuade*, the New York Court of Appeals relented a bit in *Clark v. Dodge*.[31] There, Clark owned 25 percent and Dodge owned 75 percent of the stock of two corporations manufacturing medicinal preparations by secret formulae. Dodge was a passive investor; Clark actively managed the business, and was the only one who knew the formulae for the medicines. The two agreed— as shareholders—that Clark would be general manager of the business and would receive one-fourth of the business's income. Clark, in turn, agreed to disclose the secret formulae to Dodge's son and, upon Clark's death without issue, to bequeath his interest in the corporation to Dodge's wife and children.

---

[28] *Id.* at 236 ("Stockholders may, of course, combine to elect directors. That rule is well settled.").

[29] *Id.* ("[T]he stockholders may not, by agreement among themselves, control the directors in the exercise of the judgment vested in them by virtue of their office to elect officers and fix salaries.").

[30] *Id.* at 236. *See also* RMBCA § 8.30(a) ("*Each* member of the board of directors, when discharging the duties of a director, shall act: (1) in good faith, and (2) in a manner *the director* reasonably believes to be in the best interests of the corporation.")(emphasis added).

In *McQuade,* there was an alternative basis for the holding. The plaintiff was a city magistrate, and was prohibited from having another job. *Id.* at 237.

[31] 199 N.E. 641, 642 (N.Y. 1936).

This entirely sensible business arrangement ran afoul of *McQuade* because the two were making decisions as shareholders that the board of directors should have made (whom to hire as an officer and how much to pay him). Nonetheless, the court upheld the agreement. It criticized its own *McQuade* opinion, and characterized its doctrinal basis as "nebulous."[32] The court continued: "If the enforcement of a particular contract damages nobody—not even, in any perceptible degree, the public—one sees no reason for holding it illegal, even though it impinges slightly upon the broad provision [vesting directors with the sole powers of management]. Damage suffered or threatened is a logical and practical test and has come to be the one generally adopted."[33] Because Clark and Dodge were the only shareholders in the corporation, their agreement could not harm a shareholder. Neither was there any suggestion that the arrangement harmed a public interest. The court recognized that its holding was an inroad on the traditional model, but it characterized that inroad as "so slight as to be negligible."[34]

Interestingly, the court in *Clark v. Dodge* did not overrule *McQuade*. Rather, it purported to limit *McQuade* to its facts.[35] But what does that mean? Scholars have distinguished the cases.[36] First, in *Clark*, all of the corporation's shareholders were parties to the agreement; this was not so in *McQuade*. Certainly, non-consenting shareholders may be injured if directors fail to exercise their "honest and unfettered" judgment, so it seems reasonable to reconcile the two cases on this ground. On the other hand, the agreement in *McQuade* was not attacked by a non-consenting shareholder; instead, it was challenged by a person who was a party to the arguably unenforceable agreement.[37] Second, in *Clark*, the court stressed that the arrangement harmed no one, and that "damage suffered or threatened" is a *practical* test.[38] The *McQuade* court, on the other hand, seemed to find such a test impractical, and said there would be problems if judges were called upon to evaluate the motives of directors who make particular decisions.[39]

---

[32] *Id.*

[33] *Id.*

[34] *Id.* at 643.

[35] *Id.* ("The broad statements in the *McQuade* opinion, applicable to the facts there, should be confined to those facts.").

[36] Steven N. Bulloch, *Shareholder Agreements in Closely Held Corporations: Is Sterilization an Issue?*, 59 TEMP. L.Q. 61, 63–66 (1986).

[37] Indeed, McQuade was trying to enforce the agreement. The defendants did not contend that they complied with the agreement. Rather, the argument was that the agreement was void.

[38] *Clark*, 199 N.E. at 642.

[39] *McQuade*, 189 N.E. at 236–37.

If "damage suffered or threatened" were the sole test for evaluating impingements on the traditional model, the courts might accept quite substantial variations. Later cases in New York, however, stressed instead the statement that the impingement in *Clark v. Dodge* was "slight" or "innocuous." In *Long Park, Inc. v. Trenton–New Brunswick Theatres Co.*,[40] all shareholders agreed (1) that one shareholder should have "full authority and power to supervise and direct the operation and management" of certain theaters, and (2) that he could be removed as manager only through arbitration. The court held the arrangement invalid under *McQuade*. It explained: "We are not confronted with a slight impingement or innocuous variance from the statutory norm, but rather with the deprivation of all the powers of the board insofar as the selection and supervision of the manager of the corporation's theaters, including the manner and policy of their operation, are concerned."[41]

Decades later, however, the same court upheld a similar provision in *Zion v. Kurtz*.[42] The case involved a complex financing arrangement in which a creditor obtained a minority interest in a closely held corporation as part of the security for a loan. He also received a commitment from the dominant shareholder that the corporation would not enter into transactions or new business without the consent of the creditor.

Of course, management decisions such as these are to be made by the board of directors, and not by the shareholders. Under New York legislation, however, such a shareholder agreement would have been valid if the corporation had elected "statutory close corporation" status, which would have required public notice that such deals could be made. Although the corporation in *Zion v. Kurtz* had failed to elect this status, the court upheld the agreement. To the majority, the failure to adopt statutory close corporation status was merely "technical," which it could reform.[43]

In *Nixon v. Blackwell*,[44] the Delaware Supreme Court rejected this New York approach. It refused to apply special statutory close corporation rules to a corporation that had failed to elect them.[45]

---

[40] 77 N.E.2d 633, 634 (N.Y. 1948).

[41] *Id.* at 635.

[42] 50 N.Y.2d 92, 95 (N.Y. 1980).

[43] *Id.* at 110–11.

[44] 626 A.2d 1366, 1378 (Del. 1993).

[45] *Id.* at 1380–81 ("It would run counter to the spirit of the doctrine of independent legal significance, and would be inappropriate judicial legislation for this Court to fashion a special judicially-created rule for minority investors when the entity does not fall within those statutes").

Note the important underlying premise in *Nixon*: failure to satisfy a statutory inroad on the traditional model leaves that model in place.

Earlier, in *Burnett v. Word, Inc.*,[46] a Texas appellate court applied *McQuade* strictly. In that case, the agreement provided that the company could borrow money beyond a certain amount only if all shareholders approved. The agreement prescribed how the parties would vote both as shareholders and as directors. The court invalidated that portion of the agreement relating to directors. In language reminiscent of *McQuade*, it explained: "An agreement by which directors abdicate or bargain away in advance the judgment the law contemplates they shall exercise over the corporation is void. The agreement of the parties to bind themselves as directors is void."[47] It was void because the veto power held by each shareholder abrogated the directors' authority to decide when the corporation should take a loan.[48]

On the other hand, in *Galler v. Galler*,[49] the Illinois Supreme Court rejected *McQuade* and enforced a complex shareholders' agreement containing various impingements on managerial power. Among them was a requirement that the corporation pay a dividend. The court upheld the entire agreement and concluded that "any arrangements concerning the management of the corporation which are agreeable to all" should be enforced if (1) no minority shareholder complains, (2) there is no fraud or injury to the public or creditors, and (3) no clearly prohibitory statutory language is violated.[50] It is not readily apparent what constitutes "clearly prohibitory statutory language." More to the point, it is not clear why the legislative requirement that management be discharged by the board of directors is not "clearly prohibitory statutory language."

The common law retreats slightly from the strict corporate model typified by *McQuade*. But it does not go very far, and it is not entirely clear. Meaningful change toward flexible management in the close corporation would require legislation.

---

[46] 412 S.W.2d 792, 795 (Tex. Ct. Civ. App. 1967).

[47] *Id.*

[48] Though the facts are not entirely clear on the point, it appears that the agreement in this case was signed by all shareholders.

[49] 203 N.E.2d 577, 587 (Ill. 1964).

[50] *Id.* at 584.

3. Legislative Amelioration: Statutory Close Corporations

In the *Galler* case, the Illinois Supreme Court urged a legislative solution. The Illinois legislature responded with the first "statutory close corporation" scheme. It permitted not only sterilization agreements but the complete abolition of the board. Thus, it permitted shareholders to manage the corporation directly. Over the years, about 20 states have passed such statutes. They vary from state to state. There are, however, some common provisions. First, statutory close corporation status applies only if the shareholders affirmatively elect statutory close corporation status. The articles must expressly state that the entity is a statutory close corporation. Second, the corporation's stock cannot be registered for public trading. Third, most states impose a maximum number of shareholders—usually 50.[51]

Corporations electing statutory status can adopt informal internal procedures. They can eliminate the board of directors and permit the shareholders to conduct business, either by following the partnership format (one person, one vote) or by adopting some other system of governance. Bylaws, meetings, and elections of managers may be dispensed with. Shareholders' agreements are validated even if they deal with management issues.

Statutory close corporation legislation brought the flexibility of partnership management to the close corporation. But this advantage was available only if the proprietors expressly adopted the status and satisfied the requirements. What would happen if proprietors attempted to set up shareholder management in a "regular" close corporation, without qualifying as a "statutory close corporation?" States have taken different approaches. In New York, it doesn't matter. In *Zion v. Kurtz*,[52] the Court of Appeals held that the flexibility allowed for statutory close corporations could be claimed by a "regular" close corporation. Delaware has reached the opposite conclusion, however, in *Nixon v. Blackwell*.[53] There, the Delaware Supreme Court refused to apply "statutory close corporation" rules to a corporation that had failed to organize as such an entity.

Ultimately, the question is of little practical importance. In the real world, surprisingly few businesses elect statutory close corporation status. Nor is that likely to change because, as we will see, every state now permits non-traditional governance by provisions in their

---

[51] *See, e.g.*, GA. CODE § 14–2–902(b) (50 or fewer).

[52] 50 N.Y.2d 92, 100–03 (N.Y. 1980).

[53] 626 A.2d 1366, 1379–81 (Del. 1993).

general corporation statute. In other words, flexible management is now available to any close corporation, not just a statutory one.

4. Legislative Rejection of the Traditional Model

General corporation statutes now universally embrace non-traditional governance in close corporations. These statutes usually refer to governance by "shareholder agreements." To avoid confusion with shareholder voting agreements (Chapter 6(C)(7)), we will refer to these as "shareholder management agreements."

The provisions vary from state to state, but there are common themes. We focus on § 7.32 of the RMBCA. All of the statutes apply only in close corporations, but there is no need for the corporation to call itself a close corporation. Indeed, the sole statutory criterion is that the stock is not publicly traded.[54]

Under § 7.32(a), an agreement among shareholders is effective even though it is "inconsistent with one or more other provisions of this Act." This is a reference to those parts of traditional corporation law that vest management authority in the board of directors. The statute lays out a series of stunning usurpations of board power, which, the Official Comment to § 7.32(a) makes clear, are simply illustrative and not exhaustive. Thus, for instance, proprietors can do away with the board and vest management in shareholders or in others (e.g., some hired professional manager). Such agreements would have been unthinkable a generation ago.

Of course, shareholders are not required to do any of this. They can retain a board structure entirely or divide up management prerogatives. For example, they could decide that certain functions, such as hiring officers or declaring dividends, will be discharged by shareholders, with the remaining management power exercised by the board.

To a degree, statutes such as § 7.32 reflect the influence of law and economics scholars, who have long argued that businesspeople ought to be free to structure their companies or firms in the way that makes most sense to them. The freedom, however, is not absolute. Section 7.32(a)(8) provides that an agreement may not violate public policy. The Official Comment spells out, for example, that an agreement providing that managers owe no duties of care or loyalty to the corporation or the shareholders would not be upheld.

---

[54] RMBCA § 7.32(d)(shareholder management agreement "shall cease to be effective when the corporation becomes a public corporation").

The statutes in every state impose strict rules about the permissible forms a shareholder management agreement must take. Section 7.32(b) of the RMBCA is typical, and it gives two choices. First, the agreement may be set forth in the articles or bylaws, but only if it is approved by all shareholders. Second, it can be set forth in a written agreement (not in the articles or bylaws), but again only if it is signed by all shareholders. Either way, the agreement must be in writing and must be adopted unanimously by the shareholders.

The need for a writing was emphasized in *Villar v. Kernan*,[55] which interpreted the Maine statute. There, all three shareholders agreed orally that none of them would receive a salary from the business.[56] After a falling out, the board of directors (dominated by Shareholders A and B) voted to pay a salary to Shareholder A. Shareholder C (the one on the outs) sued, arguing that they had entered into a binding shareholder management agreement providing for no salaries. The court held that the agreement was unenforceable because it was oral.[57] Accordingly, the traditional model of governance was in place, the board could vote a salary for Shareholder A, and there was nothing that Shareholder C could do about it. To our knowledge, all states require that shareholder management agreements be in writing.[58]

In most states, shareholder management agreements may be amended only by unanimous consent and are valid for 10 years, unless the agreement says otherwise.[59] Most states also require that the existence of the shareholder management agreement be noted on the stock certificates, although failure to comply with this requirement usually does not affect the validity of the agreement.[60]

Importantly, § 7.32(e) provides that if the agreement eliminates the board of directors, those who actually run the show owe the duties of care and loyalty to the corporation. We discuss these important duties in Chapter 7. They apply to fiduciaries such as directors. The fact that technically there are no directors—because the shareholders eliminated the board—does not mean that no one owes these duties. Whoever manages the corporation must do so in consonance with those duties.

---

[55] 695 A.2d 1221, 1221–22 (Me. 1997).

[56] *Id.* at 1222.

[57] *Id.* at 1223–24.

[58] *See, e.g.,* N.Y. BUS. CORP. LAW § 620.

[59] *See, e.g.,* RMBCA § 7.32(b)(2)–(3).

[60] *See, e.g.,* RMBCA § 7.32(c).

It bears repeating that provisions of the type discussed here are part of the general corporation statute. One need not satisfy the requirements of forming a statutory close corporation to take advantage of them. In other words, statutory close corporation provisions are not exclusive—one may simply form a general corporation and take advantage of shareholder management by satisfying the state equivalent to RMBCA § 7.32.

On the other hand, statutory close corporation schemes may provide some benefits. In Texas, for example, shareholders who set up a statutory close corporation may file a statement with the secretary of state noting that governance is by shareholder management agreement. Doing so constitutes notice to the world that the traditional model of governance is not followed. That suggests that transferees of the company's stock are bound by the shareholder management provisions even if they lacked actual knowledge of it.[61]

Finally, most statutes provide expressly that shareholders are not personally liable for business debts, even if the business is run the way a partnership is run. The entity is still a corporation, and the entity—not the individual proprietors—is liable for what it does.[62] This means that a shareholder management agreement is not a basis for imposing personal liability on the shareholders through the doctrine of piercing the corporate veil, to which we now turn.

E. Shareholder Liability: Piercing the Corporate Veil and Related Doctrines

1. Background

The principal advantage of the corporation over the sole proprietorship and the partnership is limited liability. The owners are not liable for debts incurred by the business. This is true even if there is only one shareholder; the entity, not the shareholder, is liable for debts incurred by the business. Shareholders may lose the money they invested if the business does poorly, but they are not liable for the corporation's breaching a contract, incurring a debt, or committing a tort. Because of limited liability, a creditor must seek payment only from the corporation.

There are ways around this general rule. A shareholder may voluntarily guarantee the performance of a corporation's obligation. Merchants and lenders may refuse to extend credit to the corporation without a personal guaranty of payment from one or more sharehold-

---

[61] *See, e.g.,* TEX. BUS. ORGS. CODE § 21.701 et seq.

[62] *See, e.g.,* RMBCA § 7.32(f).

ers. And a shareholder—like anyone else—will be liable for torts she commits and contracts she breaches in her individual capacity.[63]

The focus of this section is "piercing the corporate veil," a long-recognized exception to the principle of limited liability. With piercing, a court may impose personal liability on shareholders for business debts. Piercing the corporate veil is an apt description of what happens: a plaintiff is permitted to reach through the corporation and impose personally liability directly on shareholders. In nearly every case, the corporation will lack assets to pay any judgment the plaintiff might win. (Otherwise, if the plaintiff could satisfy her judgment from the corporation, she would simply pursue that remedy.) The question for the court will be whether the loss should fall on the plaintiff (by recognizing the corporate entity) or on the shareholders (by ignoring the corporate entity and piercing the corporate veil).

We emphasize four points at the outset:

- First, piercing is exceptional. It happens rarely because it is antithetical to the entire legal theory of the corporation as an entity. It applies when shareholders have abused the privilege of incorporation so that limited liability would be fundamentally unfair.

- Second, piercing the corporate veil typically imposes liability on shareholders, not directors or officers.[64] True, a shareholder may also be a director or officer at the same time, but piercing is generally aimed at misdeeds by shareholders in their shareholder capacity.

- Third, piercing occurs only in closely held corporations. It has never been applied in the context of a publicly held corporation. Indeed, one empirical study found that no court had pierced the corporate veil in a corporation with more than nine shareholders.[65]

---

[63] For example, suppose that a shareholder punched a customer of the business. The shareholder would be personally liable. The fact that she is also a shareholder in the business will not shield her from direct tort liability.

[64] Some cases speak of imposing liability on individual officers or directors, but it appears that the defendants were shareholders as well. In *Christopher v. Sinyard*, 723 S.E.2d 78, 81 (Ga. Ct. App. 2012), the court discussed piercing to impose liability on corporate officers. It appeared, however, that the corporation had never issued stock, so, technically, there were no shareholders. The defendants clearly were the only two people involved in founding, funding, and operating the corporation.

[65] Robert B. Thompson, *Piercing the Corporate Veil Within Corporate Groups: Corporate Shareholders as Mere Investors*, 13 CONN. J. INT'L LAW 379, 383–85 (1999).

- Fourth, the case law on piercing the corporate veil is impossible to reconcile, and uses a dizzying array of terminology.[66] Many courts say that they will pierce to "avoid fraud or to achieve equity," or to "avoid illegality," or something equally nebulous.[67] They speak of piercing when the corporation is the "alter ego" of shareholders, or is a "mere instrumentality," or when there is "unity of ownership," "excessive control," or "domination," or when the corporation is a "dummy," "shell," or "sham." None of these terms has any content. Judge (later Justice) Cardozo said the entire area is "enveloped in the mists of metaphor."[68] Each phrase is a conclusion for when a court might impose personal liability on shareholders.[69]

Though the case law makes it impossible to predict whether a court will pierce the corporate veil on given facts, certain policy bases for the doctrine are clear. They suggest different approaches to contract and tort cases. In a contract case, the plaintiff usually has dealt directly with the corporation. In the absence of fraud, then, she should assume the risk of loss. She could have insisted on a personal guaranty from the shareholders. If she failed to do so, it is not clear why shareholders should ultimately bear the loss.

Tort cases are different. Here, the plaintiff interacted with the corporation involuntarily—for instance, by getting struck by the company's delivery truck. The question here is whether the shareholders should be able to transfer a risk of injury to members of the general public. The answer should depend on whether the corporation was adequately capitalized to cover the reasonably foreseeable risks in its particular business. If the corporation was plainly undercapitalized, the plaintiff should be able to pierce the corporate veil and recover from the assets of the shareholders.

Policy thus suggests (1) that contract and tort cases should be treated differently and (2) that capitalization of the corporation should be an important (indeed, perhaps the central) factor in determining whether a court should pierce. Most cases are consistent with these conclusions. Unfortunately, though, many cases are not.

---

[66] "[W]e are faced with hundreds of decisions that are irreconcilable and not entirely comprehensible." PHILIP L. BLUMBERG, THE LAW OF CORPORATE GROUPS: PROCEDURAL LAW 8 (1983).

[67] See, e.g., Ross v. Auto Club Group, 748 N.W.2d 552, 546 n.1 (Mich. 2008) ("A court may look through the veil of corporate structure to avoid fraud or injustice.").

[68] Berkey v. Third Avenue Railway Co., 155 N.E. 58, 61 (N.Y. 1926).

[69] One scholar aptly refers to the doctrine as "jurisprudence by metaphor or epithet." BLUMBERG, note 66, at 8; see also ROBERT CLARK, CORPORATE LAW 38 (1983) (case law "hardly gives you any concrete idea about which conduct does or does not trigger the doctrine—not enough of an idea, at least, to give you the ability to counsel clients in a meaningful way").

2. Case Law

We just suggested that capitalization should be the key factor in deciding whether to pierce the corporate veil. Indeed, cases routinely address capitalization, as we will see below. The case law is notable, however, for discussing a great deal more. Many courts adopt what has been called a "template" approach—listing a large number of factors, seeing how many are present in the case, and deciding whether piercing the corporate veil is justified. This approach is unpredictable because courts use different factors and there are no clear rules for how they should be weighted.

Anyone reading piercing the corporate veil cases will be struck by the routine discussion of corporate formalities. Specifically, courts often discuss whether those running the corporation ran it by the book. Countless opinions—in contract and tort cases—bemoan the failure to follow procedures such as appointing officers, holding board and shareholder meetings, keeping financial records, and maintaining corporate assets separate from those of shareholders. Based upon such things, courts may conclude that the corporation was the "alter ego" or "mere instrumentality" of the shareholders.[70] Essentially, by failing to respect the separate corporate form, shareholders equated themselves with the business. That being the case, courts may permit the plaintiff to equate the shareholders with the business and to sue the shareholders directly for the business debts.

There are two significant problems with these alter ego cases. First, the list of factors used is often redundant and nonsensical. One of hundreds of possible examples is *Dewitt Truck Brokers, Inc. v. W. Ray Flemming Fruit Co.*[71] There, fruit growers engaged Corporation to sell their fruit, for which Corporation received a commission. Corporation hired plaintiff to haul the fruit, but failed to pay, so plaintiff sued the principal shareholder of Corporation (at this point, Corporation had no money).[72] The court pierced and imposed personal liability.

Setting aside the question of capitalization, the court noted these factors: (1) failure to observe corporate formalities, (2) non-payment of dividends, (3) insolvency of Corporation when the claim arose, (4) siphoning of corporate assets by the principal shareholder, (5) "non-functioning" of the officers or directors, (6) absence of corporate rec-

---

[70] *See, e.g.*, Deutsche Credit Corp. v. Case Power & Equip. Co., 876 P.2d 1190, 1195 (Ariz. Ct. App. 1994) (discussing factors relevant to the "formalities prong" of the piercing the corporate veil doctrine, including such things as a lack of minutes, meetings, and voting).

[71] 540 F.2d 681 (4th Cir. 1976).

[72] *Id.* at 683.

ords, and (7) Corporation was a façade for the dominant shareholder.[73] That seems like a daunting list, but look again. Factors 1, 5, and 6 are the same—failure to run the business by the book. Factor 7 is a conclusion, not a fact. Factor 3 is meaningless—of course the corporation is insolvent now—if it were not, it would pay the bill and there would be no need to pierce the corporate veil. And factor 2 is absurd—the fact that the corporation does *not* pay dividends is great news for the creditors. It means there is more money in the corporate coffers instead of the shareholders' pockets. The only remaining factor, then, was siphoning of assets, which may relate to inadequate capitalization (which is what we thought was the key anyway).

This demonstrates the second problem with the alter ego cases. It is not clear why informality in running the corporation should result in liability. In most cases, the fact that the business is poorly run has nothing to do with the claim being asserted. For this reason, some courts refuse to pierce for mere sloppiness regarding formalities.[74] One may argue that piercing is appropriate when the corporation is not run by the book because shareholders should not be allowed to ignore the rules of corporate behavior and then, when sued, claim the advantage of the corporate shield. In the absence of harm to anyone *from that behavior,* though, it is difficult to see why the premise should lead to this conclusion.

To be sure, if a failure to follow procedures results in harm, piercing the corporate veil may be appropriate. For instance, if activities in the business are so undifferentiated that a person reasonably believes she is dealing with a shareholder *individually* rather than with the corporation, personal liability may make sense. Fraud also should support piercing the corporate veil.[75] For example, a shareholder who misleads the plaintiff regarding the financial status of the corporation in an effort to induce the plaintiff to enter the deal should be liable. Instead of piercing the corporate veil in such cases, it would seem appropriate to hold the defendant liable as a tortfeasor.

As suggested above, a significant issue in piercing cases is whether the corporation was adequately capitalized. Moreover, we

---

[73] *Id.* at 686–87.

[74] *See, e.g.,* Keams v. Tempe Technical Institute, Inc., 993 F. Supp. 714, 723 (D. Ariz. 1997) ("Even if true, the lack of corporate formalities is not sufficient, standing alone, to pierce the corporate veil under Arizona law.").

[75] In *Christopher v. Sinyard,* note 64, homeowners pierced the corporate veil to impose liability on shareholders of a homebuilding corporation. The court noted that one defendant executed an affidavit at closing knowing that it was false. In addition, the court relied on the fact that the corporation had failed to file its annual registration, to issue stock, to hold meetings or keep minutes, and that individuals had commingled corporate and personal funds. 723 S.E.2d at 81.

noted that this factor might be more important in tort than contract cases. After all, a contract claimant had the right, before entering the deal, to demand assurance that the corporation had sufficient assets (or to demand a personal guaranty from a shareholder). For this reason, observers long assumed that courts would pierce more readily in tort than in contract cases. But empirical research has provided surprising findings: in reported cases, piercing occurs more frequently for contract claims than for tort claims.[76]

Inadequate capitalization (or "undercapitalization") means that the company lacks sufficient resources to cover prospective risks. It is assessed based upon likely economic needs in the specific line of business. This assessment is more art than science. It seems clear that the company need not be capitalized to ensure that it can pay for every conceivable liability. Capitalization should be reasonable in light of the nature and risks of the business. In making the assessment, liability insurance "counts" as capital because it is available to compensate plaintiffs injured by the business.[77]

There is a question as to when the adequacy of capital should be measured. There are two possibilities, which reflect different views of the duty to capitalize a corporation. Suppose a corporation was adequately capitalized initially, but suffered unavoidable losses and now is unable to pay its debts. One view is to measure adequacy at the time the company was formed (or perhaps when it expanded into a new line of business). Under this view, the corporation was not undercapitalized and piercing would not be appropriate. Implicit in this view is the idea that the law does not guaranty that every creditor will be paid. Instead, shareholders "purchase" limited liability by parting with capital—reasonably related to potential risks in the business—when they form the corporation .

The second view assesses adequacy of capital when the claim arises.[78] This approach seems to augur toward piercing.[79] As noted,

---

[76] The original empirical study, which reached this conclusion, was Robert B. Thompson, *Piercing the Corporate Veil: An Empirical Study,* 76 CORNELL L. REV. 1036, 1068–70 (1991). A more recent statistical study is consistent. John H. Matheson, *Why Courts Pierce: An Empirical Study of Piercing the Corporate Veil,* 7 BERKELEY BUS. L. J. 1, 20 (2009)(findings "consistent with Professor Thompson's finding that courts pierce more often in contract cases than in tort cases").

[77] *See, e.g.,* Haynes v. Edgerson, 240 S.W.3d 189, 197 (Mo. Ct. App. 2007) (inadequately capitalized because insurance did not cover the period in question).

[78] There is case law support for both of these approaches to undercapitalization. *Compare* Consumer's Co-op of Walworth County v. Olsen, 419 N.W.2d 211, 219 (Wis. 1988) ("It is clear, therefore, that adequacy of capital must be measured at the beginning period of corporate existence.") (citations omitted), *with* Laya v. Erin Homes, Inc., 352 S.E.2d 93, 101 (W. Va. 1986) ("The obligation to provide adequate capital begins with incorporation and is a continuing obligation thereafter during the corporation's operations.").

if the corporation were not undercapitalized now, the plaintiff would not have to attempt to pierce. She could recover from the corporation. This view assumes that shareholders have an ongoing duty to *maintain* adequate capital for the nature of their operations, at the risk of personal liability.

An especially powerful case for piercing is made if business assets have been siphoned off to line the pockets of the shareholders. For example, these assets—which might be used to buy liability insurance or to pay claims of creditors—might be paid to the shareholders as exorbitant salaries for their labor or in dividends. Such action will be a red flag for most courts. Indeed, this was a factor in *Dewitt Truck Brokers.*

One point stressed in many cases is that the shareholders commingled their own money with corporate funds. Often, this is just a sign of confusion or sloppiness, unrelated to the plaintiff's claim. On the other hand, it may show "stripping" of corporate assets—the shareholders may be draining business assets for their personal use. This enrichment of shareholders at the expense of creditors justifies piercing the corporate veil. Conversely, evidence that the corporation did the best it could to provide a cushion for creditors will likely protect shareholders.

All courts agree, then, that there must be some abuse of the corporate form. The shareholders must have stepped over the line in some way—be it treating the corporation as their alter ego or undercapitalizing or defrauding the plaintiffs (or some combination). Importantly, however, showing such abuse is not enough by itself to justify piercing. In addition, the court must find that the shareholders' behavior results in some basic unfairness to the plaintiff. Stated another way, piercing the corporate veil is appropriate only when recognition of the separate corporate existence will lead to injustice or an unfair or inequitable result.[80] The mere fact that creditors are not now being paid may not be enough. As just discussed, there is a strong school of thought that shareholders are not guarantors that the corporation will always have sufficient capital to pay every debt.[81]

---

[79] In a statistical study of case law, Professor Matheson distinguished between "insufficient funds to start a business" and "draining of funds." Matheson, *Why Courts Pierce*, note 76, at 34. These categories correspond to the two schools of thought on when lack of funding should be measured.

[80] *See, e.g.,* NLRB v. Greater Kansas City Roofing, 2 F.3d 1047, 1051 (10th Cir. 1993) ("Piercing the corporate veil is an equitable action and as such is reserved for situations where some impropriety or injustice is evident.").

[81] In some cases involving undercapitalization and other misconduct, the "Deep Rock" doctrine" may allow courts an alternative to piercing the corporate veil. Deep

We finish this broad overview of case law with two observations. First, while some courts seem to treat "alter ego" and "undercapitalization" as different theoretical bases for piercing, most see them simply as factors to be weighed on the facts of a given case.[82] Thus, as noted above, courts tend to discuss a mélange of factors in a rather ad hoc way.[83]

Second, courts piercing the corporate veil impose liability on "active" (as opposed to "passive") shareholders. For example, in *Dewitt,* only the principal shareholder—who actually ran the corporation and was responsible for its operation—was liable. The shareholders who

---

Rock applies only when the shareholder who might be liable under piercing the corporate veil is also a debt holder of the corporation. In other words, that shareholder also lent money to the company. Under the Deep Rock doctrine, a court will "subordinate" that shareholder's debt to that of other creditors. That means it will put the shareholder last in line when it comes to paying off creditors. It is an example of courts' broad equitable power to subordinate debts of creditors who are guilty of some misconduct.

The doctrine was established in *Taylor v. Standard Gas & Electric Co.*, 306 U.S. 307, 309 (1939). In that case, the Deep Rock Oil Company, which was a subsidiary of Standard Gas & Electric Company (Standard), was in bankruptcy. Standard had caused the bankruptcy of Deep Rock by mismanaging the company for its own benefit. It had engaged in the kind of misdeeds one sees in piercing cases. It forced the subsidiary to pay exorbitant lease amounts and large management fees to it and to other subsidiaries, to pay exorbitant interest, and to declare excessive dividends. When Deep Rock went into bankruptcy, Standard filed its claims, just as other creditors did. The Court held that the debts owed to Standard should be subordinated to those owed to other creditors. Indeed, the debt to Standard was subordinated even to the interests preferred shareholders of Deep Rock.

Deep Rock is almost exclusively encountered when a company is in bankruptcy. A few courts, however, have entertained the argument that debt owed to an abusive controlling shareholder should be subordinated even outside bankruptcy, as an alternative to piercing the corporate veil. *See, e.g.,* Bryan v. Western P. R. Corp., 28 Del. Ch. 13, 20 (Del. Ch. 1944) (entertaining the argument but finding it inapplicable on the facts). *See generally* FRANKLIN A. GEVURTZ, CORPORATION LAW 149 (2d ed. 2010)("Equitable subordination serves simply as a milder remedy [than piercing the corporate veil], since it does not involve personal liability of the controlling shareholder for the corporation's debts.").

On the other hand, some court reject the argument that the Deep Rock doctrine should apply outside the bankruptcy context. *See, e.g.,* 1250 Broadway Parking Corp. v. 38–32 Assocs., 655 N.Y.S.2d 958 at * 12 (N.Y. Sup. Ct. Feb. 2, 1996)(doctrine "developed as an equitable tool in bankruptcy, not in the context of fraudulent transfers").

[82] *See, e.g.*, Salem Tent & Awning Co. v. Schmidt, 719 P.2d 819, 903 (Or. Ct. App. 1986) ("[P]laintiff was entitled to present proof on the issue of piercing the corporate veil to establish the factors to be considered in determining whether to pierce. Undercapitalization is one of those factors; it is not a separate piercing theory which they must plead.")

[83] Professor Matheson's regression analysis found partial support for the hypothesis that "[e]ach piercing factor identified by the courts is independently significant; that is, the presence of any one factor should be enough to cause a court to pierce." Matheson, *Why Courts Pierce*, note 76, at 59. He found that the absence of certain factors—notably fraud, commingling, and unfairness—decrease the likelihood of piercing. *Id.* at 60.

owned the other 10 percent of the stock were entitled to limited liability.

3. Piercing the Corporate Veil in the Parent-Subsidiary Context

Piercing the corporate veil imposes liability on shareholders. In many cases, those shareholders are human. But entities can also own stock, so the shareholders on whom liability is imposed may be other corporations. Indeed, one fairly common fact pattern involves piercing to impose upon a parent corporation liability incurred by a subsidiary. In general, courts look to the same sorts of factors here as they do in "regular" piercing cases.[84]

One example is *In re Silicone Gel Breast Implants Liability Litigation*.[85] There, the subsidiary, MEC, manufactured breast implants. The parent, Bristol (which owned 100 percent of the stock of MEC), did not.[86] Plaintiffs sued Bristol on a piercing theory regarding personal injuries suffered from use of the product. The court denied defendant's motion to dismiss and permitted the claim to proceed. It stressed that MEC's board of directors was controlled by Bristol (many people didn't know MEC even had a board), MEC budgets were approved by Bristol, cash received by MEC went into an account maintained by Bristol, which set employment policies and wage scales for MEC.[87] The court also noted that the subsidiary may have been inadequately capitalized in view of the business risks in manufacturing breast implants. In other words, the court applied the same sort of template approach discussed above. Based on the "totality of the circumstances," the court concluded that it would be "inequitable and unjust" to allow Bristol to have the limited liability ordinarily enjoyed by shareholders.[88]

Other cases have used piercing to hold the parent liable when it operates the subsidiary in an "unfair manner," such as allocating accumulating subsidiary profits to the parent and losses to the subsidiary. This is the functional equivalent of undercapitalization, which, as we saw, is often a critical factor in piercing the corporate veil. The

---

[84] A statistical study found that courts pierce roughly twice as frequently when the defendant is an individual than when the defendant is another corporation. Matheson, *Why Courts Pierce*, note 76, at 14–15 (39.29 percent of cases in which defendant is an individual; 20.56 percent of cases in which defendant is an entity).

[85] 887 F. Supp. 1447, 1452 (N.D. Ala. 1995).

[86] *Id.* at 1450.

[87] *Id.* at 1452–53.

[88] *Id.* at 1453.

parent that impoverishes the subsidiary in this way may answer for debts incurred by the subsidiary.[89]

The lesson of such cases is clear. Parent corporations should maintain clear delineation between its affairs, assets, and operations, and those of its subsidiaries. In many instances, ties between the two companies are inherently close—they may, for instance, be housed in the same offices, with common employees, auditors, and lawyers. These ties are not necessarily inconsistent with the separate existence of the subsidiary, but problems can arise from carelessness and an overly casual attitude about the separateness of the entities.

4. Choice of Law Issues

The courts of some states pierce the corporate veil more readily than others. Delaware and New York are known as difficult states in which to get a court to pierce. A generation ago, Texas codified aspects of piercing law in response to a liberal application of piercing by the Texas Supreme Court.[90] Under Texas law, failure to follow corporate formalities will not support a finding of shareholder liability. Moreover, to pierce in contract cases, the plaintiff must show actual fraud for the personal benefit of the shareholder.[91]

- Corporation is incorporated in State A, where it is very difficult to invoke piercing the corporate veil. Corporation does business in various states, including State B, where it is relatively easy to pierce. Plaintiff's claim arises in State B, and she sues in State B to pierce. Which state's law applies regarding piercing the corporate veil?

There is surprisingly little case law on this important choice-of-law issue. In most cases, courts appear to assume that they should apply the law of the state of incorporation. In some cases, they expressly apply the internal affairs doctrine to reach that conclusion.[92] That doctrine, discussed at Chapter 5(B), declares that the law of the state of incorporation governs on internal matters. Arguably, the law

---

[89] *See, e.g.,* U.S. v. Bestfoods, 524 U.S. 51, 62 (1998) ("But there is an equally fundamental principle of corporate law, applicable to the parent-subsidiary relationship as well as generally, that the corporate veil may be pierced and the shareholder held liable for the corporation's conduct when, *inter alia,* the corporate form would otherwise be misused to accomplish certain wrongful purposes, most notably fraud, on the shareholder's behalf.").

[90] Castleberry v. Branscum, 721 S.W.2d 270 (Tex. 1986).

[91] TEX. BUS. ORGS. CODE § 21.233.

[92] *See, e.g.,* Judson Atkinson Candies, Inc. v. Latini-Hohberger Dhimantec, 529 F.3d 371, 378 ("Texas has the same choice-of-law rule for veil-piercing claims as Illinois, namely that the law of the state of incorporation governs such claims.").

of shareholder liability is an "internal affair."[93] Legislatures in some states have removed the uncertainty by providing that shareholder liability is governed by the law of the in which the corporation was formed.

In the absence of statute, there is a contrary argument. Choice of law rules generally provide for application of the law of the state with the most significant relationship to a dispute. It is not clear that a corporation should be able to "capture" favorable piercing law by forming in one state to avoid piercing for activities in another state. There is some thought that the law may be moving in this direction.[94]

5. Reverse Piercing and Related Issues

As we have seen, piercing the corporate veil arises when a creditor of the corporation seeks to impose liability on a shareholder. In other words, a third party sues a shareholder to recover money that should be paid by the corporation. "Reverse piercing" involves the flip side. Here, a creditor of a shareholder seeks to impose liability on the corporation. So a third party sues the corporation to recover money that should be paid by the shareholder. Reverse piercing is based upon the same general notion as piercing the corporate veil— i.e., based upon the actions of the shareholder, the corporation and the shareholder effectively can be treated as one being.

In *Towe Antique Ford Foundation v. Internal Revenue Service*,[95] an individual owed the IRS a considerable sum in income taxes. When the IRS could not collect from the individual, it placed a lien on property held by a nonprofit corporation that the individual formed and operated. The Ninth Circuit held that the IRS could recover the individual's tax delinquency from the assets of the corporation.[96] The court, consistent with "regular" piercing, noted that the shareholder had dominated the corporation by treating it as his alter ego.

Reverse piercing has generated considerable commentary,[97] but is not invoked as frequently as "regular" piercing. At best, it suffers from all of the uncertainties of the piercing doctrine generally.

---

[93]On the other hand, because the liability is to a corporate outsider (a creditor of the corporation), arguably it is not "internal" affair.

[94] *See* Gregory S. Crespi, *Choice of Law in Veil-Piercing Litigation: Why Courts Should Discard the Internal Affairs Rule and Embrace General Choice-of-Law Principles,* 64 N.Y.U. Ann. Surv. Am. L. 85 (2008).

[95] 999 F.2d 1387 (9th Cir. 1993).

[96] *Id*. at 1389–90.

[97] *See generally* Gregory S. Crespi, *The Reverse Piercing Doctrine: Applying Appropriate Standards,* 16 J. CORP. LAW 33 (1990); Elham Youabian, *Reverse Piercing the*

In *Cargill, Inc. v. Hedge*,[98] the Minnesota Supreme Court applied what it called reverse piercing. A Minnesota family formed a corporation to own and operate its farm. The family encountered financial trouble, and a creditor sued and won a judgment against the corporation. When the judgment was not paid, the plaintiff sought to execute on the farm. Minnesota has a homestead statute making farms exempt from execution. It applies, however, only if the farm is owned by individuals—not by an entity.[99] By law, then,, the creditor should have been allowed to execute its judgment against the corporation. The Minnesota court avoided that result by equating the shareholder and his corporation. At the behest of the shareholder (not the creditor), the court held that the corporation did not exist as a separate entity.[100] Thus, the court was able to say that the family owned the farm and the judgment could not be enforced against the homestead.[101]

Other courts seem skeptical about allowing a shareholder to ask that she be equated with her corporation. They conclude that one who forms a corporation must take the bad with the good. For example, in *Sims v. Western Waste Industries*,[102] the court refused to invoke what it called reverse piercing. There, an employee of a subsidiary sued the parent corporation. Under workers' compensation law, an employee cannot sue her employer. The parent corporation was not the employer, but argued that it should be seen as the employer (and therefore be immune from suit) under reverse piercing.[103] The court pointed out that the parent had "accepted the benefits of establishing a subsidiary corporation in Texas and will not be allowed to disregard that entity now that it is in [its] gain to do so."[104]

Corporate Veil: The Implications of Bypassing "Ownership" Interest, 33 SW. U. L. REV. 573 (2004); Note, *Reverse Piercing of the Corporate Veil: A Straightforward Path to Justice*, 85 ST. JOHN'S L. REV. 1147 (2011); Note, *Reverse Piercing the Corporate Veil: Should Corporation Owners Have it Both Ways?*, 30 WM. & MARY L. REV. 667 (1989).

[98] 375 N.W.2d 477, 478 (Minn. 1985).

[99] *See* MINN. STAT. § 510.01.

[100] "Here there is a close identity between the Hedges and their corporation. While the Hedges maintained some of the corporate formalities, such as keeping corporate minutes, filing corporate tax returns, and dealing with the Production Credit Association as a corporation, realistically . . . they operated the farm as their own." *Cargill*, 375 N.W.2d at 479.

[101] *Id.* at 480.

[102] 918 S.W.2d 682, 686 (Tex. Ct. Civ. App. 1996).

[103] *Id.* at 683.

[104] *Id.* at 686.

6. Enterprise Liability

As we have seen, piercing the corporate veil permits a plaintiff to impose upon shareholders liability for a corporate debt. Enterprise liability is different. It is a theory under which separate corporations are treated as one economic unit. This would allow a plaintiff to recover against the aggregate assets of all the companies, even though she only dealt with one. The leading case is *Walkovszky v. Carlton*.[105] The holding in that case is not entirely clear,[106] but the fact pattern is ideal for discussing the theory.

> • Carlton is the sole shareholder of ten corporations, each of which is properly formed. Each corporation owns two taxicabs and holds the minimum insurance required by state law for operating a taxicab. Carlton has the ten corporations operate their cabs from a single garage and use a common dispatching system. A cab owned by one of the ten corporations, Seon Cab Corp., is driven negligently and strikes Plaintiff. Plaintiff's claim for personal injuries vastly exceeds the assets (including insurance) of Seon Cab Corp.

A piercing the corporate veil claim would seek to impose liability against Carlton (the shareholder) for the sorts of reasons we discussed above. Enterprise liability, in contrast, would allow the plaintiff to treat all ten of Carlton's corporations as one entity and to recover from the aggregated assets of all the corporations.[107] In essence, enterprise liability pierces the walls of one corporation to go after the assets of related companies. The theory is that because the ten corporations were operated as one enterprise, the assets of the entire enterprise ought to be available to the plaintiff.

The theoretical underpinning of enterprise liability makes sense. In economic reality, if there is one business, the law should not allow

---

[105] 223 N.E.2d 6 (N.Y. 1966).

[106] The case was decided on the pleadings. The plaintiff evidently attempted to assert enterprise liability and a claim for piercing the corporate veil against the shareholder. The Court of Appeals held that the complaint failed to state a claim on the latter ground. *Id.* at 10 ("In sum, the complaint fall short of adequately stating a cause of action against the defendant Carlton in his individual capacity."). This holding apparently left the enterprise liability theory intact. After remand, however, the parties settled the case, so there is no court order permitting recovery from the various corporations allegedly involved in a single enterprise.

[107] One interesting question is whether this would allow a plaintiff access to insurance coverage from the related companies. Because insurance policies cover individual automobiles, the answer may be no. It is one thing to say that the assets of the proprietor's related businesses should be available to satisfy a plaintiff's judgment. It is quite another to argue that insurance companies ought to pick up the tab for an incident involving a vehicle they did not insure.

the owner to subdivide liability (and limit a plaintiff's ability to obtain compensation for harm) by chopping the business into small parts. That is why enterprise liability is sometimes called "horizontal piercing"—the court essentially pierces through one corporation to get at the assets of sibling corporations. "Regular" piercing, in contrast, can be seen as "vertical"—the court goes through the corporation to get at the assets of the shareholder. Though enterprise liability has had some traction in case law,[108] it has not had a major impact.[109]

F. Fiduciary Duty and Oppressive Behavior

1. Background

Partners owe each other a duty of utmost good faith and fair dealing. In the corporation, however, the traditional view is that shareholders do not owe fiduciary duties to one another. Even in the close corporation, the standard notion is that the managers owe no special fiduciary duties to minority shareholders.[110] But these views have changed significantly in the past few decades, as courts and legislatures recognize the potential plight of the minority shareholder in the close corporation. When people start a business, no one anticipates disagreement. But disagreements often arise.

- Assume that X, Y, and Z form XYZ Corp., a close corporation. Each owns 100 shares of the 300 issued shares of the stock. Each is a director on the three-person board. Each has a job with the corporation and draws a salary. Everything goes great for a while. Then there is a disagreement over business policy (or maybe over personality). X is on one side of the dispute. Y and Z are on the other. On every matter considered by the board, X will lose by a vote of two-to-one. On every matter considered by shareholders, X will lose by a vote

---

[108] Courts occasionally confuse matters. In *Goldberg v. Lee Express Cab Corp.*, 634 N.Y.S.2d 337 (Sup. Ct. 1995), which involved facts similar to *Walkovsky*, the plaintiff seemed to allege facts aimed at enterprise liability. For instance, he alleged that various corporations purchased supplies collectively, as well as dispatched and garaged cabs centrally, and that the corporations were operated as a single entity. *Id.* at 338–39. Oddly, the court concluded that the complaint stated a claim against the owner in his individual capacity. *Id.* at 339.

[109] *See, e.g.*, Miners, Inc. v. Alpine Equip. Corp., 722 A.2d 691, 695 (Pa. Sup. 1998) (contrasting enterprise liability with piercing the corporate veil and pointing out that the former has not been adopted in Pennsylvania).

[110] Of course, managers in all corporations owe fiduciary duties to the entity itself. Those duties are the focus of Chapter 7. What we address in this section is quite different. These are not fiduciary duties owed to the business itself, but to the other shareholders in the business. Thus, a breach of these duties gives rise to a personal claim by the shareholder who is harmed by the breach.

of 200–100. Now it gets even worse—let's say the corporation terminates X's employment. She argues that the corporation should declare a dividend for shareholders. But Y and Z vote to have the corporation use the profits to expand the business (or maybe even to increase their salaries).

If the business were a partnership, X might have a strong argument that Y and Z have breached their fiduciary duty of good faith and fair dealing.[111] Traditionally, though, in the corporation, there would be little X could do. Note that her plight is the same no matter what the business structure: X has no effective voice in management, is receiving no return on her investment and no salary, and has no ready way out because there is no market into which she can sell her interest. Absent a buy-sell agreement, X is at the mercy of the controlling shareholders (Y and Z in our hypo).

Y and Z might buy X's stock, but they may do so for a very low price (because there is probably no other potential buyer). Doing so might be a good idea for X and Y—to get rid of the nettlesome minority shareholder. X's ownership entitles her to inspect corporate books and records and, if Y and Z are guilty of breaching duties to the corporation, X has the right to bring a derivative suit on behalf of the entity. Moreover, buying out X's interest at a bargain-basement price will allow Y and Z later to dissolve the corporation without having to give X her proportionate interest at liquidation. Recognizing the plight of the minority shareholder, and likening the close corporation to the partnership, courts started considering the imposition of partner-type fiduciary duties in the corporation.

---

[111] It is important to appreciate, however, that X's situation here is not necessarily the result of ill will or a desire to oppress. It could result from honest disagreement over business policy. Either way, though, X is only slightly better off than an orphan in a Dickens novel. She owns stock, but has no voice in management decisions. She has invested her money, but is getting no financial return on her investment: she does not draw a salary, there are no dividends, and it is unlikely that she can find anyone willing to buy her stock.

It is also important to see how X could have protected herself from this situation. She might have negotiated an employment contract that required the corporation to employ her for a given period, terminable only upon cause. She might have negotiated a buy-sell agreement. In setting up the business, the proprietors might consider corporate mechanisms that would avoid problems such as those faced by X. For example, the articles could require unanimous attendance for a quorum or unanimous votes for various corporate acts. This poses its own risks, though, because it gives every shareholder a veto over every act. This, in turn, increases the possibility of deadlock—of the corporation being unable to act because one shareholder refuses to play ball.

The underlying point is clear: the proprietors must think through how to handle problems such as those discussed in the text and plan for them.

2. Common Law Recognition of a Fiduciary Duty

We noted in Chapter 8(B) that many close corporations are the functional analog of a partnership. Indeed, courts routinely refer to close corporations as "incorporated partnerships."[112] Not surprisingly, then, some courts have imported fiduciary concepts from the partnership to the close corporation. The Massachusetts Supreme Judicial court has been the leader in this regard.

The seminal case, decided in 1975, is *Donahue v. Rodd Electrotype Co.*[113] In *Donahue*, management caused the corporation to buy about half the stock owned by the founder of the company. The founder was 77 years old, wanted to retire, and needed the money. Management (which consisted of his children) was happy to oblige, and had the corporation pay $36,000 to buy the founder's stock.[114] Shortly thereafter, a minority shareholder offered to sell her stock to the corporation at the same price per share that was paid to the founder. Management refused, and the minority shareholder sued the managers.[115] Analogizing the close corporation to the partnership, the Massachusetts court concluded:

> [W]e hold that stockholders in the close corporation owe one another substantially the same fiduciary duty in the operation of the enterprise that partners owe to one another. In our previous decisions, we have defined the standard of duty owed by partners to one another as the "utmost good faith and loyalty." Stockholders in close corporations must discharge their management and stockholder responsibilities in conformity with this strict good faith standard.[116]

Among other things, that duty required the corporation to provide an equal opportunity to the minority shareholder to resell her stock.[117] This provides the minority shareholder with the same re-

---

[112] *See, e.g.,* Meiselman v. Meiselman, 307 S.E.2d 551, 557 (N.C. 1983) ("commentators all appear to agree that close corporations are often little more than incorporated partnerships")(citation omitted); Hartung v. Architects Hartung/Odle/Burke, Inc., 301 N.E.2d 240, 243 (Ind. Ct. App. 1973) ("In addition, the shareholders in a close corporation, also referred to as an 'incorporated partnership,' stand in a fiduciary relationship to each other"); Donahue v. Rodd Electrotype Co., 328 N.E.2d 505, 514 (Mass. 1975) ("incorporated partnership").

[113] 328 N.E.2d 505, 508 (Mass. 1975).

[114] *Id.* at 510.

[115] *Id.* at 511.

[116] *Id.* at 515.

[117] *Id.* at 518–19. This has become known as the "equal opportunity" (or sometimes the "equal access") doctrine.

turn on investment that the company's managers gave to their father.[118]

Donahue creates a significant risk of judicial overreaching by permitting courts to review business decisions. Consider again the hypothetical above, in which X, the minority shareholder, was fired from her employment with the corporation. It is possible that she was fired oppressively, for an improper motive. But it is also possible that the firing was justified. Perhaps, for example, she was incompetent, or maybe the company did not need so many employees, or maybe different skills were required in the job. These are all business decisions to which courts usually extend a presumption of correctness through the business judgment rule. A broad interpretation of *Donahue* would convert these from matters of business judgment to litigable matters of fiduciary duty.

The Massachusetts court recognized this problem and recalibrated its fiduciary duty concept in *Wilkes v. Springside Nursing Home, Inc.*[119] There, the court said that an "untempered application of the strict good faith standard" might impose undesirable "limitations on legitimate action by the controlling group in a close corporation which will unduly hamper its effectiveness in managing the corporation in the best interests of all concerned."[120] In other words, management in a close corporation "ha[s] certain rights to what has been termed 'selfish ownership' in the corporation which should be balanced against the concept of their fiduciary duty."[121]

In *Wilkes,* the four initial shareholders (one of whom became the plaintiff) were employed by the corporation, which operated a nursing home. After a falling out, the other three had the plaintiff fired.[122] He sued for breach of fiduciary duty. The court established a regime of shifting burdens.[123] First, the plaintiff must show that the controlling shareholders treated her oppressively. Second, if she does, the burden shifts to the defendants to show a legitimate business reason for the action. This step protects management prerogatives, such as firing for cause or because of the need to downsize. Third, if the defendants make such a showing, the plaintiff may still win if she shows that the legitimate business purpose could have been met by a

---

[118] The court gave Rodd Electrotype two options: either the father would remit the $36,000 paid for his stock plus interest, or Rodd Electrotype would purchase all of the plaintiff's shares for $36,000. *Id.* at 520–21.

[119] 353 N.E.2d 657, 661 (Mass. 1976).

[120] *Id.* at 663.

[121] *Id.*

[122] *Id.* at 659–61.

[123] *Id.* at 663–64.

less restrictive alternative. In other words, is there some way the corporation could achieve its purpose without harming the plaintiff? Thus, Massachusetts has backed off a strict reading of *Donahue.*

Other courts have found *Donahue* and *Wilkes* persuasive and recognize a common law claim for breach of fiduciary obligation between shareholders in the close corporation.[124] But it is a mistake to assume that the claim meets with universal approval. In most states, the matter is not completely clear. And in some states, courts have expressly rejected such a claim.[125] In *Nixon v. Blackwell*,[126] the Delaware Supreme Court rejected the idea that shareholders owe each other a fiduciary duty akin to that among partners. The court did so on grounds of separation of powers: if the state is going to recognize the claim, it should be created by the legislature and not by the courts. In Texas, there is no fiduciary duty between shareholders as a matter of law. [127]

3. The Effect of Involuntary Dissolution Statutes

The main legislative impact in the area has come from statutes addressing involuntary dissolution. Today, the majority of states provide for involuntary dissolution of close corporations based upon "illegal, oppressive, or fraudulent" behavior by corporate managers.[128]

While these statutes address the problem of oppression in the closely held corporation, they appear to provide only for involuntary dissolution. In other words, on their face they appear to offer little help to the oppressed shareholder who wishes to sue directly for harm done to her. Indeed, some courts have interpreted these stat-

---

[124] *See, e.g.,* W&W Equip. Co. v. Mink, 568 N.E.2d 564, 570–71 (Ind. Ct. App. 1991); Evans v. Blesi, 345 N.W.2d 775, 779 (Minn. Ct. App. 1984); Fought v. Morris, 543 So. 2d 167, 170–71 (Miss. 1989); Crosby v. Beam, 548 N.E.2d 217, 220–21 (Ohio 1989). Some federal courts have also recognized the claim. *See, e.g.,* Guy v. Duff & Phelps, Inc., 672 F. Supp. 1086, 1090 (N.D. Ill. 1987); Byelick v. Vivadelli, 79 F. Supp. 2d 610, 614 (E.D. Va. 1999) (purporting to apply Virginia law).

[125] Some scholars of the law and economics school decry judicial intervention here. To them, businesspeople are adults able to negotiate for their own benefit. An investor who fails to protect herself contractually has no one else to blame. This view of the business as a series of contracts was influential in the development of flexible management provisions for the close corporation. It recognizes that businesspeople should be able to structure the governance of their business in the way that makes most sense to them.

[126] 626 A.2d 1366, 1380–81 (Del. 1993).

[127] *See, e.g.,* Hoggett v. Brown, 971 S.W.2d 472, 488 (Tex. Ct. Civ. App. 1997) ("[A] co-shareholder in a closely held corporation does not as a matter of law owe a fiduciary duty to his co-shareholder.").

[128] *See, e.g.,* RMBCA § 14.30(2). We discuss involuntary dissolution in Chapter 12(H).

utes in that fashion. In *Gianotti v. Hamway*,[129] the Virginia Supreme Court rejected the plaintiff's effort to sue for damages caused by her alleged oppression. To the court, the legislature only provided a right to seek involuntary dissolution based upon "oppression."[130] If the legislature wanted to create a right of action for one harmed by oppression, it could have done so. In the absence of such a statute, the court concluded, dissolution was the exclusive remedy.

But most states reject the notion that dissolution is the sole remedy for oppression in the close corporation. In some of these states, the dissolution statute itself permits courts to offer other remedies, such as a buy-out of the complaining shareholder's interest.[131] Even in the absence of such statutory provisions, some courts have not hesitated to order remedies other than dissolution.[132] Indeed, as courts have adopted a broader view of remedies, orders of dissolutions under these statutes have become infrequent. Accordingly, "oppression has evolved from a statutory ground for involuntary dissolution to a statutory ground for a wide variety of relief."[133]

This development is salutary. In many instances, dissolution is not to be preferred because it terminates the existence of what may be a terrific business. This can cause great dislocation to the entire community, which may rely on the business as a source of employment. The clear trend is toward statutory provisions in the general corporation law allowing the court to order a buy-out at a "fair value" (to be set by the court).

Where courts recognize a fiduciary claim in the close corporation, they tend to use terms such as "oppression," "freeze out" and "squeeze out" in describing the treatment of minority shareholders. They use the terms pejoratively to label behavior that breaches the duty of utmost good faith and loyalty. In involuntary dissolution statutes, as noted, the question generally is whether there has been "oppressive" behavior. Because such behavior was not a basis for involuntary dissolution at common law, courts initially interpreted the statutory term narrowly. Now, however, what is "oppressive" conduct for statutory purposes is largely equated with conduct that would breach the duty of utmost good faith and loyalty in Donahue-like jurisdictions. In other words, regardless of whether a court po-

---

[129] 387 S.E.2d 725, 734 (Va. 1990).

[130] *See, e.g.*, VA. CODE § 13.1–747(A)(1)(b).

[131] *See, e.g.*, RMBCA § 14.34; MINN. STAT. § 302A.751 subd. 1–2 ("any equitable relief"); N.J. STAT. § 14A: 12–7(1)(providing a nonexclusive list of remedies, including a buy-out).

[132] *See, e.g.*, Baker v. Commercial Body Builders, Inc., 507 P.2d 387, 395–96 (Or. 1973) (listing "alternative remedies").

[133] Moll, *supra* note 23, at 319.

lices oppressive conduct through a common-law fiduciary duty doctrine or a statutory oppression framework, the results in litigated cases tend to be the same.

4. Reasonable Expectations of the Shareholder

In the past generation, courts have forged consensus on a "reasonable expectations" approach to determine whether behavior is oppressive under a dissolution statute.[134] The New York Court of Appeals explained that "oppressive actions . . . refer to conduct that substantially defeats the 'reasonable expectations' held by minority shareholders in committing their capital to the particular enterprise."[135] This requires the court to assess what the majority shareholders should have known to be the minority's expectations for entering the corporation. Mere disappointment is not sufficient. Rather, the claim requires a showing that the majority "seek[s] to defeat those expectations and there exists no effective means of salvaging the investment."[136]

Those reasonable expectations of the minority include the sorts of things mentioned in the first paragraph of this Chapter: people may invest in close corporations because they want an ownership stake, to share in profits and losses, to share in management, and (probably) to be employed by the business. Thus, oppressive behavior is conduct that unfairly deprives a minority shareholder of meaningful participation. It may concern her participation in governance, distributions, employment, or a combination. An example is the unequal distribution of corporate assets in *Donahue*.

Not all courts adopt the "reasonable expectations" approach to what constitutes oppressive conduct. For example, South Carolina "places emphasis not upon the minority's expectations but, rather, on the actions by the majority."[137] Some courts appear to base their decisions on the subjective intent of the majority shareholders. In other words, actions that harm minority shareholders are not oppressive unless motivated by bad faith.[138]

---

[134] *See, e.g.,* Stefano v. Coppock, 705 P.2d 443, 446 n.3 (Alaska 1985); Maschmeier v. Southside Press, Ltd., 435 N.W.2d 377, 380 (Iowa Ct. App. 1988); Fox v. 7L Bar Ranch Co., 645 P.2d 929, 933–34 (Mont. 1982); Brenner v. Berkowitz, 634 A.2d 1019, 1029 (N.J. 1993); Meiselman v. Meiselman, 307 S.E.2d 551, 563–64 (N.C. 1983); Ritchie v. Rupe, 339 S.W.3d 275, 289 (Tex. Ct. Civ. App. 2011).

[135] *In re* Kemp & Beatley, Inc., 473 N.E.2d 1173, 1179 (N.Y. 1984).

[136] *Id.*

[137] Kiriakides v. Atlas Food Sys. & Servs., Inc., 541 S.E.2d 257, 265 (S.C. 2001).

[138] This appears to be the approach in *Ziddell v. Ziddell*, 560 P.2d 1086, 1090 (Or. 1977)(focusing on "motivating causes" of behavior). Professor Mitchell concludes that this approach "reduces fiduciary analysis to nothing more than the avoidance of un-

The terms "squeeze out" and "freeze out" usually refer to the corporation's efforts to dilute the interest of minority shareholders.

- Controlling Shareholder (CS) makes a loan to Corporation to finance its operations. Thereafter, CS causes Corporation to issue new stock at a set price to all shareholders, including Minority Shareholder (MS). So far, it looks fair. Then, however, CS pays for her additional stock by forgiving the debt to the corporation. MS now has to come up with cash to buy her new stock. If she does not, her holdings will be diluted because of the new stock issued to CS.

Another example is mergers that unfairly cash out minority shareholders, which we will consider at Chapter 12(E). Similarly, in *Byelick v. Vivadelli*,[139] majority shareholders engineered an amendment to the articles that reduced the plaintiff's ownership from 10 to one percent. The court held that the "dilutive transaction can be challenged under the Virginia common law of fiduciaries," and imposed upon the defendants the burden of demonstrating that the amendment was fair.[140]

While nearly every case of oppressive conduct will feature controlling shareholders mistreating minority shareholders, it is possible for a minority shareholder to breach her fiduciary duty to the majority. For example, if the corporate documents require unanimous approval for decisions, even a minority shareholder will have the power to harm others by acting in bad faith.

It is important to note that not every disadvantage to minority shareholders is the result of a breach of duty. To a considerable degree, a person buying a minority stake in a close corporation takes the chance that she will be outvoted on matters of management, that there will be no dividends, and that it will be difficult to sell her shares. This points out the importance of planning, including the negotiation of a buy-sell agreement.

fair treatment of the minority, rather than exclusive pursuit of the minority's interest." Lawrence E. Mitchell, *The Death of Fiduciary Duty in Close Corporations,* 138 U. PA. L. REV. 1675, 1716 (1990).

[139] 79 F. Supp. 2d 610, 614 (E.D. Va. 1999).

[140] *Id.* at 627.

Chapter 9

SPECIAL ISSUES IN THE PUBLICLY TRADED CORPORATION

Analysis

A. Introduction
B. Characteristics of Publicly Traded Corporations
    1. Board Structure and Managerial Function
    2. Compensation of Managers
C. Registration and Stock Markets
D. Sarbanes-Oxley and Financial Accountability
E. Regulation of Proxy Solicitation
    1. Background and Federal Regulation
    2. Shareholder Proposals
    3. Private Right of Action
F. Hostile Takeovers
    1. Background
    2. Tender Offers and Leveraged Buyouts
    3. Proxy Contests
    4. Defensive Tactics
    5. State Anti-Takeover Laws

A. Introduction

In this Chapter, we address some characteristics of and problems encountered in a publicly traded (or public) corporation. By this, we mean a "registered" corporation—one that has gone through the exacting process under § 12 of the Securities Act of 1933. Only these entities—and there are about 15,000 of them—can tap the vast investment potential of the public markets. These are what most people think of when they hear the word "corporation"—a large economic entity with millions of dollars in assets, tens of thousands of employees, and millions of shares outstanding, owned by tens of thousands of shareholders.[1] The list includes such iconic giants as Ford Motor, Procter & Gamble, Apple, Walmart, Consolidated Edi-

---

[1] Even though this is the popular conception, and even though there are several thousand publicly traded corporations, the overwhelming majority of corporations are not publicly traded. There are *millions* of closely held corporations. Most closely held corporations are Mom and Pop businesses operating the neighborhood bakery, grocery, gas station, etc.

son, McDonald's, Coca-Cola, and Delta Air Lines. Among them are the "Fortune 500," which are the 500 largest companies in the world, ranked each year by Fortune magazine.

In section B of this Chapter, we address the characteristics of these companies, particularly the roles of "inside" and "outside" directors and the problems of executive compensation. In section C, we review the requirements of "going public"—of registering to sell securities to the public—and discuss the operation of the stock markets. In section D, we consider problems of financial accountability that led to the collapse of Enron and other corporations in the early part of the twenty-first century, and we consider the congressional response to that collapse. Section E of this Chapter describes why public corporations usually need to solicit proxies from shareholders to allow the shareholders to take any act. These proxy solicitations are regulated by federal law, which (among other things) requires the corporation to include in its solicitations various proposals for shareholder action made by shareholders themselves. This fact can create (or at least reflect) considerable tension between shareholders and management. Finally, section F addresses methods by which one corporation may take over another, and the fireworks that can result from such efforts.

B. Characteristics of Publicly Traded Corporations

1. Board Structure and Managerial Function

The most obvious characteristic of a public corporation is that its stock is publicly traded. Every trading day, we can track what the stock exchanges "say" about the stock of a particular company by how the traders "vote." They vote by buying or selling, and the price reflects supply and demand for the stock. Not all publicly traded corporations are the huge businesses we mentioned above. There are many mid-sized and smaller corporations whose stock is publicly traded.

Public companies—those registered under the Securities Act of 1933—must make available to the public a great deal of information. While they do not exactly live in a goldfish bowl, the reporting requirements do promote transparency and are intrusive. These companies are often called "reporting" corporations because the Securities and Exchange Commission requires them to report periodically. Each files a "10–K," which is a detailed annual report of the business and financial performance, and includes such information as stock options awarded to executives.[2] Each also files a "10–Q," which is a quarterly report of similar information. The company must divulge the bad with the good; the idea is that the public should have access to all relevant data. These documents are available through the company's website, through a service called EDGAR (freeedgar.com), and on the website of the Securities and Exchange Commission (SEC) (that website is SEC.gov). In addition, companies usually produce a rather showy annual report for shareholders, with pictures of new plants, the management team, etc.

The boards of directors of public corporations usually feature "inside" and "outside" directors.[3] Inside directors are those who also hold an employment position with the company, invariably as an officer; they are often called "management directors." Functionally similar are directors who, while not employed by the company, have a significant professional or family relationship with it. For example, a lawyer who is a partner in the law firm retained by the corporation as its principal outside counsel would be considered an inside director. Sometimes, such people are called "affiliated outside directors."

Outside directors do not have other employment or affiliation with the company. They are also called "independent" directors. Today, the boards of public corporations are dominated by independent directors. This is a significant change over earlier times, when board members tended to be insiders or "in the hip pocket" of the president or other officers. The point of this shift is to create a board of directors that is independent of (and therefore can provide a meaningful check on) managing officers.

Inside and outside directors are held to the same fiduciary duties, which we discussed in Chapter 7. In discharging those duties, however, their capacity is relevant. An inside director has greater access to the day-to-day workings of the corporation than an outside director. Outside directors often rely on information provided by officers. Such reliance is appropriate, as long as it is in good faith and is reasonable under the circumstances. This does not mean that outside directors may bury their heads in the sand and avoid responsibility for bad board decisions. As the court explained in *Joy v. North*,[4] "lack of knowledge is not necessarily a defense, if it is the re-

---

[2] *See, e.g.,* Heit v. Weitzen, 402 F.2d 909, 914 n.3 (2d Cir. 1968)("The '10K' report is a detailed document, similar to an annual report, which must be filed annually by all issuers of securities registered pursuant to Section 12 of the Securities Exchange Act of 1934 and by all registrants under the Securities Act of 1933 . . . .").

[3] *See* Donald C. Clark, *Three Concepts of the Independent Director*, 32 DEL. J. CORP. L. 73 (2007).

[4] 692 F.2d 880, 896 (2d Cir. 1982).

sult of an abdication of directional responsibility. Directors who willingly allow others to make major decisions affecting the future of the corporation wholly without supervision or oversight may not defend on their lack of knowledge, for that ignorance itself is a breach of fiduciary duty."

In Chapter 6(B)(5), we noted that management of the public corporation did not fit precisely into the traditional model of corporate governance. This fact is reflected in modern statutes that speak of boards engaging less in direct management and more in overseeing the management team.[5] In the public corporation, direct management functions are discharged by professional managers, who receive the bulk of their compensation in salary and bonuses, and not from stock ownership.[6] The management structure is highly bureaucratic, and the officers at the pinnacle have enormous discretion.

At the top, a management team of officers directs the enterprise. These managers usually have responsibility for specific functional areas. Familiar examples are the chief financial officer (CFO), chief operations officer (COO), chief accounting officer (CAO), and chief legal officer (CLO or, more commonly, general counsel). At the apex of managerial control is the chief executive officer (CEO). She is responsible for the management team and is ultimately responsible for the success of the enterprise. If the CEO loses confidence in the chief financial officer (CFO), she replaces the CFO. In theory, the CEO has power to call the shots in the bureaucracy on all issues, narrow and broad. In practice, though, the CEO, as the head of a large bureaucratic organization, cannot hope to know, let alone direct, the operational details. To be effective, she must delegate authority over day-to-day operations, including personnel, financing, advertising, and production. The CEO should concentrate on the broadest issues relating to the business.

Because the CEO has ultimate responsibility for the success of the corporation, she—and quite possibly she alone—may make the final decision on business strategy. The CEO may decide, for example, to close several plants in an effort to redirect the primary emphasis of the corporation or to develop a new product line. The CEO makes such decisions usually after consultation with the board of directors. The board has the power to reject the CEO's proposal. Such rejection is fairly rare and often signals that the board has lost

---

[5] *See, e.g.,* RMBCA § 8.01(b)(managerial power is "exercised by or under the direction, and subject to the oversight" of the board).

[6] While managers are encouraged to own stock in the company, and may even be given options to purchase shares at below-market prices, typically they own a fraction of one percent of the voting stock.

confidence in the CEO. (This is often followed by the CEO's resignation.)

Until the 1970s, most public corporations had management-dominated boards composed primarily of inside directors and the CEO. In corporations that included some independent directors, the CEO would interview candidates she did not know personally and would develop a social and personal relationship with them. The CEO could usually drop independent directors from the board at the next election simply by not including them on the slate of candidates. A CEO might therefore limit outside directors to friends, college roommates, and the like. Members of such a board acted independently only when faced with a dire emergency such as the unexpected death or disability of the CEO, or when faced with a financial disaster of such a magnitude that it threatened the existence of the corporation. Moreover, the CEO usually also served as chairperson of the board of directors. She thus controlled the agenda and information flow of board meetings.

Those days are gone. Starting in the 1970s, the SEC required public corporations to create audit committees composed of independent directors to review financial reporting and the relationship with outside auditors, and to assess the company's compliance with various laws and regulations. They were responsible for implementation of "best practices" by the corporation. Most companies had to add independent directors to meet this requirement. Moreover, the New York Stock Exchange, American Stock Exchange, and National Association of Securities Dealers amended their listing rules to require that a majority of directors be independent. The Sarbanes-Oxley Act, passed in 2002 in the wake of enormous financial scandals, has further increased the requirements of independent auditing, as we will see in Chapter 9(D).

By the 1990s, it was commonplace that the job of selecting candidates for the board was vested in a nominating committee composed predominantly of independent directors. Although the CEO often had some involvement with that selection process—on the theory that she must be able to work effectively with the outside directors—there is no question the CEO's influence in the actual selection process had declined markedly by then.[7] That trend has continued.

---

[7] Jeffrey N. Gordon, *The Rise of Independent Directors in the United States, 1950–2005: Of Shareholder Value and Stock Market Prices,* 59 STAN. L. REV. 1465, 1496–99 (2007); Nicola Faith Sharp, *Process Over Structure: An Organizational Behavior Approach to Improving Corporate Boards,* 85 S. CAL. L. REV. 261 (2012).

The average board today may consist of 9 or 11 directors. Larger boards of 15 or 17 are less common and the trend is toward smaller boards. Usually, fewer than one-third will be inside directors. The majority, obviously, are independent directors—not employed by the company and therefore not beholden to the CEO. Typical independent directors are present or retired CEOs of other publicly held corporations, university presidents or other prominent academic officers, former public officials, and independent investors. Thus, today the CEO deals with a sophisticated board, members of which she did not appoint.

It is quite common for independent directors to meet separately from the CEO and inside directors at least once a year to discuss the performance of management. Increasingly, the chairperson of the board of directors is an outside director and not the CEO. Such an arrangement would have been unthinkable a generation ago. These changes in board composition and role had an undeniable impact. Certainly starting in the 1990s, it became clear that an underperforming CEO's "head could roll." More Fortune 500 CEOs have been fired in the past 15 years than during any other similar period.[8]

The traditional norm tells us that the shareholders elect the directors. The reality in the public corporation is not that simple. Virtually all shareholders in publicly held corporations vote by proxy; a very small percentage actually attends meetings. The election of directors is by a vote taken at the shareholders meeting. The decision is really made earlier, when shareholders fill out their proxy forms. These proxies are mailed in and tabulated, and the result is announced at the meeting. Shareholders voting by proxy do not normally have the right to select whom to vote for from a list of candidates. Proxy solicitations usually list only those candidates who have been selected by corporate management. The only effective choice the shareholder has is to vote for those people or to withhold her vote.[9]

It is thus questionable whether small investors—those with 500 shares of Procter & Gamble—should be viewed as the "owners" of the business at all. Contrary to the traditional norm, they are passive investors with no real voice in what the corporation does. If they become dissatisfied with management or with their investment, their only real recourse is to sell their stock.

---

[8] Lucian A. Taylor, *Why Are CEOs Rarely Fired? Evidence From Structural Estimation*, THE JOURNAL OF FINANCE (Dec. 2010) ("The degree of entrenchment is significantly lower in recent years (1990 to 2006).").

[9] It is possible for a group of non-management shareholders to organize and solicit proxies in competition with management—a "proxy contest"—which we will discuss at Chapter 9(F)(3).

This does not mean that all shareholders are powerless. In the early 1930s, Professors Berle and Means, in a famous book called THE MODERN CORPORATION AND PRIVATE PROPERTY, concluded that the fragmented ownership of public corporations meant that managers held virtually dictatorial power. There has been a revolutionary change in the ensuing decades. Today, "institutional investors"—an unimportant group half a century ago—dominate stock ownership of public corporations and transactions on major securities markets. These institutions include pension funds, mutual funds, banks, university endowments, life and casualty insurance companies, and private investment funds. Such institutional investors own the majority of stock of the one thousand largest corporations in the United States. In some very large corporations, institutional investors as a group may own 80 percent of the voting stock.[10]

Obviously, the collective influence of institutional investors on management can be enormous. The decision by several institutions to buy or sell the stock of a particular company can have a dramatic (and possibly traumatic) effect on the market price of that company's stock. It is common for institutional investors to communicate directly with independent directors (rather than the CEO) about problems they perceive with a company. They generally do not hesitate to evaluate corporate stock performance and management. TIAA/CREF, the California state employees' pension, the New York State Retirement Fund, and other institutional investors screen the performance of hundreds of public corporations each year and make governance recommendations for companies viewed to be underperforming. Implicit is the not-so-veiled threat that the institutional investor will divest itself of stock in companies that refuse to consider making changes in governance procedures.

The typical board of directors of a public corporation will meet six or eight times a year, for perhaps an average of three or four hours. Much of that time is devoted to discussion of financial status and reports of committees. Director involvement is not limited to formal meetings. There may be periodic communications to board members, informal discussions, and committee meetings. Nevertheless, it is not realistic to expect that outside directors will have exhaustive, continuous involvement in board affairs (after all, they usually have full-time jobs of their own).

---

[10] We say "as a group" because there are legal impediments to one investor owning more than five percent of the voting stock of a corporation. Moreover, institutional investors— investing other people's money (like retirees' pensions)—will want to diversify and not put all of their investment eggs in a small number of baskets.

In Chapter 6(D)(6), we discussed the creation and function of committees of the board. These bodies, which are subsets of the board, are especially important in the public corporation. We noted some of these committees above and will see that others—including audit and compensation committees—are mandated by federal law.[11]

The board should have a succession strategy to replace officers. It must have accounting and reporting systems to ensure that transactions are being appropriately recorded and monitored by responsible managers. Indications that there are breakdowns in the accounting and reporting system must be taken as seriously as breakdowns in the command structure. The board must also ensure that there is an information system that assures that responsible officers are informed about problems as they develop. And, of course, the board must monitor the performance of the CEO. In short, boards of publicly held corporations do not "manage." The management team, led by the CEO, "manages." The board oversees and monitors.

2. Compensation of Managers

One visible and controversial aspect of the modern corporate world is the level of compensation of senior executives, particularly the CEO.[12] From 1993 to 2008, CEO compensation in the Fortune 500 companies quadrupled. In 2008, the average compensation for such a CEO was $11,400,000, including salary, bonus, and stock options. The gap between CEO's compensation and that of the average worker in the company also increased. In 1993, CEOs made 131 times as much as the average worker. In 2005, they made 369 times as much.

Executive compensation has long been a political issue in this country. It has been much debated, for instance, in connection with government "bailouts." For instance, under the Troubled Asset Relief Program (TARP), the United States Treasury purchased assets and stock of companies that had lent money on "subprime" mortgages— mortgages that had little chance of being repaid. TARP was aimed at keeping such companies afloat and allowing them to restructure to repay the federal funds. One aspect of the law limits the compensation of the five highest-paid executives of corporations that received significant TARP funds.

Long before this, however, the federal government tried in various ways to curb executive pay, even in companies receiving no fed-

---

[11] For example, the Sarbanes Oxley Act requires publicly traded companies to have an independent audit committee. *See* Chapter 9(D).

[12] *See* Franklin G. Snyder, *More Pieces of the CEO Compensation Puzzle*, 28 DEL. J. CORP. L. 129 (2003).

eral money.[13] The efforts failed. For example, the SEC required greater disclosure of executive compensation, on the theory that increased awareness of the stunning numbers would curb excess. The plan backfired. If anything, CEOs came to demand greater compensation when they found out what their competitors were making.

Public corporations pay income tax on their net income. In calculating that figure, they are permitted to deduct compensation. In 1993, Congress limited the income tax deductibility of salaries over $1,000,000 per year. This effort failed to curb compensation. Undaunted, Congress then tried to limit "golden parachutes" by imposing taxes on them. These are severance packages for CEOs whose companies are taken over. The CEO loses the job but gets a huge amount of money. The idea is to induce CEOs not to oppose takeover attempts that would benefit shareholders. Again, the effort failed, as increased publicity apparently has caused more executives to demand such parachutes.[14]

Other parts of tax law affect rules of corporate governance. Federal law requires a public corporation to create a compensation committee consisting only of outside directors. The committee must develop performance criteria at the beginning of the performance period. The compensation arrangement must be adequately disclosed to, and approved by, the shareholders before compensation is paid. In addition, the outside directors must certify in writing that the performance criteria have been met before compensation may be paid. But critics argue that the compensation committees are ineffective. They tend to hire consultants and follow the consultant's recommendations. Then the board tends to rubber-stamp what the committee says. Warren Buffet characterizes compensation committees as "tail-wagging puppy dogs meekly following recommendations by consultants."[15]

---

[13] See Tracy Scott Johnson, *Pay For Performance: Corporate Executive Compensation in the 1990s*, 20 DEL. J. CORP. L. 183, 194–206 (1995).

[14] It is worth asking why the federal government tries to curb executive compensation in corporations while showing no concern about the amount of money made by movie stars, professional athletes, and others in the entertainment business. (Many baseball players make far more than $11,000,000 a year. Movie stars can make $20,000,000 per film and can have long careers.) If compensation in the private sector is any business of the federal government, why has it singled out corporate compensation?

As another example, given that virtually every college and university in the United States receives federal funding, why has the government shown no concern with salaries (often more than $1,000,000 per year) of university presidents? This question is especially pertinent in view of the relentless rise of tuition year after year, which, it would seem, has an impact on the lives of ordinary citizens.

[15] Joann Lublin & Scott Thurm, *Behind Startling Executive Pay, Decades of Failed Restraints*, WALL STREET J., Oct. 6, 2006, at A–1.

Harvey Golub was the CEO of American Express from 1993 to 2000, for which he was paid $250,000,000. Michel Eisner, who was CEO at Walt Disney Company, received $576,000,000 for a single year (1998). For context, however, consider that Oprah Winfrey routinely makes hundreds of millions of dollars, including $385,000,000 in 2008.[16] Though some people, including members of Congress, are upset at the CEO compensation, no one is clamoring for government intervention in the case of entertainers.

Consider, too, the possibility that highly paid CEOs create wealth for shareholders. Golub, recognizing that his compensation was generous, pointed out that during his tenure as CEO of American Express, the market value of the company's stock increased from $10 billion to $65 billion. "My stockholders became even wealthier. How much of the $55 billion [increase in value] should I get?," he asked.[17] And that increase was not enjoyed only by wealthy people. Given that institutional investors hold a considerable percentage of the American Express stock, much of the increased value benefited pension and retirement plans of ordinary people.

What is more difficult to understand are huge paydays for CEOs whose companies do not do well. One CEO of Home Depot, for example, received $245,000,000 over five years, while the company's stock declined 12 percent; during the same period, the stock of its archrival Lowe's increased 176 percent.[18] Perhaps the most stunning example of payment for nonperformance involved Eisner's choice of his successor at Disney. After Eisner had suffered a heart attack, he urged the board to hire Michael Ovitz, one of the founders and a leading partner of the preeminent Hollywood talent agency. Ovitz negotiated a deal that included a severance package if he were fired without cause. After 14 months, the Disney board fired Ovitz without cause. Things just were not working out. Disney paid Ovitz $130,000,000—essentially to leave. Shareholders sued, claiming that the board had wasted corporate assets in paying this sum. As seen in Chapter 7(D), the Delaware Supreme Court held that the Disney board had not breached any duties in approving the compensation.[19] The case

---

[16] www.modernminority.com/index.php/2008.

[17] Lublin & Thurm, note 15, at A–1.

[18] *See Home Unimprovement: Was Nardelli's Tenure at Home Depot a Blueprint for Failure?,* www.knowledge.wharton.upenn.edu/article.cfm?articleid=1636 (January 10, 2007)("After years of declining stock price—and a now-legendary 2006 shareholders meeting where an imperious Nardelli refused to answer questions— Home Depot announced the CEO's resignation on January 3. He walked away with a package worth $210 million.").

[19] *In re* Walt Disney Company Derivative Litig., 906 A.2d 27 (Del. 2006). The litigation lasted more than nine years.

shows that courts are reluctant to second-guess decisions concerning executive compensation.

C. Registration and Stock Markets

In Chapter 10(C)(6), we address funding the corporation by selling securities to the public. That process involves financial questions about how much money to try to raise, pricing the securities, and selecting an underwriter. In this section, we briefly discuss the public stock markets and how a corporation qualifies to offer securities to the public.

Registration is part of the federal regulation of securities. Securities are investments. They might be "debt" or "equity" securities. When a corporation sells securities of either type, whether to the public or privately, it is an "issuance," and the corporation is called the "issuer" or "issuing company." Though the laws we discuss apply to issuances of debt and equity, for simplicity, we will talk about stock. Again, whenever there is an issuance (to the public or to a few people in a private placement), the money goes to the corporation.[20] Indeed, that is why the company decided to issue stock—to raise capital. But subsequent sales of that stock do not bring money to the company. It's just like when you buy and sell a car.

- You buy a new Ford Explorer from a Ford dealer. Ford Motor Company gets the net income from that sale. But when you sell the Explorer to your friend Bob, Ford does not get that money. You do. And when Bob sells the Explorer through e-bay, Ford does not get that money. Bob does.

The same thing happens with stock. After the issuance by the corporation, the shareholder can dispose of the stock as she sees fit. If it is a close corporation, she can give the stock away or sell it (if she can find a buyer). If it is publicly traded, she can give the stock away or sell it on the stock market. Either way, though, the corporation will not get anything from subsequent sales.

So why do public companies care about their stock price on the market? Healthy stock prices are seen as good signs for companies. Moreover, managers may earn bonuses based upon stock price. They also usually own stock, so anything that increases the stock price increases their personal wealth. For all these reasons, managers may adopt strategies to ensure a high price. One example is the announcement by the corporation that it will buy back shares from the

---

[20] *See, e.g.,* RMBCA § 6.21.

public market. Such announcements are intended to signal to the
market that management believes that the company's stock is undervalued. Such announcements often have a positive effect on the stock
price. In addition, managers of publicly traded companies often are
rewarded with stock options to buy stock at a given price. They thus
have an incentive to have the market set a higher price for the stock.

These incentives can lead to fraudulent reporting of financial
numbers. Indeed, fraud in some large public corporations in the early part of the twenty-first century led to a financial crisis, which led
to passage of the Sarbanes-Oxley Act, which we discuss in the next
subsection of this Chapter. We do not suggest that management's
interest in stock price is unhealthy—just that some people cheat.

The stock in public corporations is traded on stock exchanges,
such as the New York Stock Exchange, the American Stock Exchange, NASDAQ, and regional exchanges like the Pacific Stock Exchange. These markets set prices in each stock on each trading day,
based upon supply and demand. Investors willing to buy at a certain
price match up with shareholders who are willing to sell at that price.
Historically, stock trades involving the public were handled through
professional securities brokerage firms, which charged substantial
commissions. Technology has had an enormous impact on this, with
most trades today executed online, for minimal commissions. Online
trading made it possible to engage in "day trading," in which speculators execute numerous transactions during the day in an effort to
capture profits from modest variations in securities prices.

There are some smaller, non-public companies, the stock of
which is not publicly traded, but for which there is something of a
market. These can be bought and sold. The transactions are recorded on the "Pink Sheets."[21] This is an electronic system that displays
prices for "bid" and "ask" (prices at which people will, respectively,
buy and sell). The Pink Sheets is not an exchange, and is not registered with the government.[22] The Pink Sheets are used by brokers
who trade stocks "over the counter," which means not on a public exchange. Not all close corporations are traded on the Pink Sheets. Indeed, for the vast majority of close corporations, there is no plausible
quasi-public market for the stock at all.

---

[21] In the days before electronic communication, these transactions were published
on pink paper, which is where the name comes from. *See* "Pink Sheets,"
WIKIPEDIA, available at http://en.wikipedia.org/wiki/OTC_Markets_Group.

[22] *See* Michael K. Molitor, *Will More Sunlight Fade the Pink Sheets? Increasing
Public Information About Non-Reporting Issuers with Quoted Securities,* 39 IND. L.
REV. 309 (2006).

In reaction to the stock market crash of 1929, Congress passed the Securities Act of 1933 (which everyone calls "the '33 Act") and the Securities Exchange Act of 1934 ("the '34 Act"). Speaking broadly, the '33 Act concerns the initial issuance of securities by the corporation. It is not aimed so much at buying and selling in the public market. Rather, the '34 Act focuses on providing information to the securities markets.

Under § 12 of the '33 Act, certain corporations must "register." These "registered corporations" are those (1) with shares listed for trading on a national securities exchange or (2) with $10,000,000 in assets and with a class of securities held by at least 500 shareholders. It is not the total number of security holders that is significant, but the number of holders of the specific class of security for which registration is required. For example, a corporation with 400 shareholders of one class of stock and 450 shareholders of a different class of stock is not required to register either class under § 12.

A corporation cannot offer securities to the public until it has "registered." This is an exacting and expensive process, undertaken by lawyers who specialize in the area. (This is not an area for novices.) It is also a very intrusive process, in which the company must place a great deal of information before the public. The company must file an extensive "registration statement" with the SEC. It must also provide a copy of the "prospectus," which is part of the registration statement and will be given to potential purchasers. The prospectus describes the security being sold, the company selling the security (the "issuer" or "issuing company"), and discusses the risks of investing. The SEC staff reviews the registration statement before permitting the company to offer securities to the public. The American system is based upon disclosure. The idea is that an informed public can protect itself, to some degree. Accordingly, the SEC checks for completeness of the information provided, and does not assess the underlying merits. The '33 Act has various exemptions from the registration requirements. Sophisticated lawyers spend a great deal of time trying to fit their client's securities within an exemption to avoid the expense and intrusiveness of registration.

The issuing company must also comply with various state-law requirements under "blue sky" laws.[23] The name comes from early attempts by crooks to sell pieces of the blue sky to an unsuspecting and naïve public.

---

[23] *See, e.g.,* KY. REV. STAT. § 292.530; NEB. REV. STAT. § 8–1118.

D. Sarbanes-Oxley and Financial Accountability

The financial world was rocked in the early part of the twenty-first century by accounting scandals in several public corporations, most infamously Enron and WorldCom.[24] The companies engaged in fraudulent accounting practices in an effort to paint a rosy picture, which, it was hoped, would keep the stock prices high. As noted above, managers of public corporations have plenty of incentive to report good financial numbers—it creates good publicity, may make them eligible for bonuses and increases the value of their own stock.

In Chapter 10(D), we review the basic accounting documents, including the balance sheet. Companies at the center of the accounting scandal engaged in "off-balance-sheet" accounting, which was an effort to move liabilities from the balance sheet through a series of complicated accounting steps. Though each step may have had some legitimacy, the overall result clearly misrepresented the corporate financial health. This fraud was pervasive—not only did it seem to permeate various layers of management, but the internal and external auditors seemed to turn a blind eye to the shenanigans. For one thing, external accounting firms that were hired to oversee the auditing were permitted to provide other services to the corporations. This created an incentive not to blow the whistle—to ignore accounting irregularities—so that the accounting firm would not jeopardize this other lucrative business.

When the house of cards fell, and the financial reality became apparent, the price of the stock of these corporations plummeted. Retirement funds were wiped out. Lives were ruined. Throughout the companies, the finger-pointing began—the CEO did not know what was going on because he relied on what the CFO told him. The CFO did not know what was going on because he relied on the auditors to catch things, etc.

Congress reacted in 2002 with the Sarbanes-Oxley Act, or "Sarbox," or "SOX." It applies only to public corporations. Though partnerships and close corporations can be wracked by fraudulent accounting practices, Congress was principally concerned with fraud perpetrated on the public. SOX is aimed at financial accountability and corporate governance. It was intended to clarify duties of various players and to impose process and responsibility.

Under SOX, every public company must have an independent audit committee. And each company must disclose that it has an

---

[24] *See, e.g., In re* Enron Corp. Securities, Derivative & ERISA Litigation, 235 F. Supp. 2d 549 (S.D. Tex. 2002).

"audit committee financial expert" on the board, as well as affirm that all other members of the audit committee have a degree of financial literacy not previously required. Section 404 of SOX requires the corporation to evaluate its internal audit controls and to test their effectiveness. It also requires hiring public accounting firms for external audits of the internal controls. Further, the CEO and CFO must attest to the accuracy of the financial statements by signing a document under threat of criminal liability. Other parts of SOX address the perceived conflict of interest in accounting firms by limiting the amount of non-auditing work they can do for a corporate client.

SOX also created the Public Company Accounting Oversight Board, a five-person private, non-profit corporation that acts as an agency supervised by the Securities and Exchange Commission. The Board sets standards for the public accounting firms and reviews their work, with authority to discipline them. Under SOX, members of the Board can be removed by the Commission only for cause. In *Free Enterprise Fund v. Public Company Accounting Oversight Board*,[25] the Supreme Court declared the Board unconstitutional under principles of separation of powers. The Board was too independent of the executive branch of the federal government. Rather than abolish the Board or undermine SOX broadly, however, the Court held that the Commission may remove members of the Board without cause. With this change, the Court held, the Board members would not be insulated unduly from control of the executive branch.

The *Free Enterprise* decision was a disappointment to the critics of SOX, some of whom had engineered litigation efforts to challenge the legislation on separation-of-powers grounds. After the decision, SOX remained in place. Even the Board remained in place, with the change mentioned.

Though many agreed that the accounting scandals required some federal legislative response, it is widely thought that the costs imposed by SOX are greater than the benefits it brings. In particular, many relatively small publicly traded companies have found the expense of the internal controls and employment of the external auditing firm daunting. Critics charge that SOX has resulted in fewer initial public offerings in the United States and increased incidents of public corporations "going private," i.e., ceasing to be publicly traded to avoid SOX.[26] Solid data on this point, however, are hard to find.

---

[25] 130 S.Ct. 3138 (2010).

[26] There is no lack of criticism for SOX. "Cooked up in the wake of accounting scandals earlier this decade, [SOX] has essentially killed the creation of new public companies in America, hamstrung the [New York Stock Exchange] and NASDAQ (while making the London Stock Exchange rich), and cost U.S. industry more than

E. Regulation of Proxy Solicitation

1. Background and Federal Regulation

In Chapter 6(C)(6), we considered shareholders' voting by proxy. We noted that "proxy" usually refers to the person appointed to vote the shares for the record shareholder at the shareholder meeting,[27] and that the state-law rules for appointing a proxy are rather uniform.[28] In many closely held corporations, proxies are not often used; all the shareholders attend the meeting and vote their own shares. When proxies are used in small companies, they tend to be people the shareholder knows. Many closely held businesses are family affairs, so appointing a proxy often consists of asking Uncle Fred to vote your shares at a meeting that you cannot attend.

Things are different in the public corporation. Remember that for any shareholder meeting in any corporation, there must be a quorum.[29] That is, a majority of the shares entitled to vote must be represented at the meeting. Otherwise, no action can be taken. In public corporations, usually the shareholders who show up do not represent anything close to a majority of the shares entitled to vote. So management must solicit proxy appointments to ensure that there will be a quorum. When management does this, it will ask the shareholders to vote in a particular way on the various issues to be considered at the meeting. Federal law attempts to ensure that the corporation provides accurate information in this process.

Specifically, § 14(a) of the '34 Act allows the SEC to develop regulations "necessary or appropriate in the public interest or for the protection of investors" in connection with the solicitation of proxy appointments in registered corporations. Section 14 makes it unlawful for any person to use an instrumentality of interstate commerce or the facilities of a national securities exchange "in contravention of" such regulations.[30] Congress gave the SEC this broad and largely undefined rulemaking authority because it was concerned about abuses in the proxy process, but was uncertain about remedies.

$200 billion by some estimates." Michael S. Malone, *Washington is Killing Silicon Valley*, WALL STREET J., available at www.Wsj.com/article/SB1229904725207.html (Dec. 8, 2008).

[27] *See* RMBCA § 7.22.

[28] *See, e.g.*, DEL. GEN. CORP. LAW § 212(b); ARIZ. STAT. § 10–722.

[29] *See, e.g.*, RMBCA § 7.25; DEL. GEN. CORP. LAW § 216.

[30] As a practical matter, it is impossible to solicit proxies in a registered corporation without using an instrumentality of interstate commerce, such as the mail.

The SEC has issued detailed regulations under § 14, including Rule 14a–3, which requires that solicitations be accompanied by a "proxy statement." These statements are an important source of shareholder information about corporate affairs. They give details about the business, directors and nominees to the board (including compensation), and about other issues to be voted upon at the meeting. Rule 14a–3(b) provides that if a solicitation is made on behalf of management for an annual meeting at which directors will be elected, the proxy statement must be accompanied or preceded by an annual report of the corporation. Further, Rule 14a–9 makes it unlawful to distribute a false or misleading proxy solicitation. As we will see below, violation of this Rule can give rise to a private right of action for damages. Beyond this, the SEC can assess penalties and seek other remedies for non-compliance with its Rules.

2. Shareholder Proposals

Rule 14a–8 permits shareholders to submit proposals for inclusion in the company's proxy solicitation material. If the proposal deals with something appropriate for shareholder action, and is submitted in a timely way, the corporation must include the proposal, even if the board of directors is opposed to it. This mechanism gives minority shareholders an effective way to communicate with other shareholders. Shareholder proposals have addressed a variety of topics, including executive compensation, affirmative action policies, and environmental concerns. For example, one proposal asked for shareholders to vote to force the corporation to comply with various human rights provisions in its dealings in China.

Shareholder proposals almost never "win"—that is, they almost never get the support of a majority of the shares voted at the meeting. But winning in this sense is usually not the point. Management must take a position on the proposal—usually, it solicits proxies to vote against it. This process of engaging management is usually the shareholder's goal. Even unsuccessful proposals, then, may have an indirect educational effect by calling management's attention to the issue. Sometimes, when management receives a serious shareholder proposal, it will reach a mutually agreeable accommodation, and thereby obviate the need to send the proposal to all shareholders.

The most famous practitioner of Rule 14a–8 was Lewis Gilbert, a shareholder of various corporations, who submitted proposals about corporate governance and generally nettled management for over half a century. In *Securities & Exchange Comm. v. Transamerica Corp.*,[31] he won his fight to have the corporation include in its proxy materials

---

[31] 163 F.2d 511, 517–18 (3d Cir. 1947).

his proposal that shareholders (rather than the board) select the company's external financial auditors.

Rule 14a–8 is subject to express exceptions. The corporation may omit shareholder proposals, for example, that address a personal grievance of the shareholder, that deal with something not significantly related to corporate business, that relate to specific amounts of dividends, or when substantially the same proposal has been made within five years and failed to garner significant support.

Another exception is for a proposal that is "related to an election to office." In *AFSCME v. American International Group, Inc.*,[32] the court held that a proposal seeking to amend bylaws to allow shareholder-nominated board candidates on the ballot had to be included. The SEC reacted by amending Rule 14a–8(i)(8) to exclude proposals allowing shareholders to include nominees in the proxy materials.

If management concludes that the proposal falls within an exception and thus need not be included in the proxy materials, it may seek a "no action letter" from the SEC. This communication reflects a decision by the SEC staff that it will recommend to the Commission that no action be taken if the proposal is omitted. A no-action letter does not offer watertight protection. In some circumstances, a disgruntled shareholder may be able to sue. If a proposal opposed by management is included in the proxy statement, the proposing shareholder may include a statement of not more than 500 words supporting the proposal. Management is free to explain its opposition to the proposal, with no word limit.

3. Private Right of Action

It is important to remember our context. Here, management is sending out proxy solicitations—it is asking shareholders to give it their proxy to vote on a particular issue. Management will try to "sell" the shareholders on the idea by telling them why the shareholders should go along and give the proxy. Sometimes, management will stretch the truth, which can lead to liability.

Rule 14a–9 makes it unlawful to distribute proxy solicitation information that contains "any statement which, at the time and in the light of the circumstances under which it is made, is false or misleading with respect to any material fact, or which omits to state any material fact necessary in order to make the statements therein not false or misleading."[33] We noted that Congress, in passing § 14, was

---

[32] 462 F.3d 121, 125–27 (2d Cir. 2006).

[33] We will see similar language in Rule 10b–5, discussed in Chapter 11(C)(1).

unclear about what remedies should be available in case of violation. Nowhere in the legislation did Congress provide for a private claim for violation of § 14.

Nonetheless, in *J.I. Case Co. v. Borak*,[34] the Supreme Court held that Congress intended to allow private civil enforcement of § 14. Specifically, there is an implied right of action to sue for violation of Rule 14a–9. The Court concluded that "private enforcement of the proxy rules provides a necessary supplement to Commission action. As in antitrust treble damage litigation, the possibility of civil damages or injunctive relief serves as a most effective weapon in the enforcement of the proxy requirements."[35] *Borak* has led to a considerable amount of litigation, and three more significant Supreme Court cases.

First, in *TSC Industries, Inc. v. Northway, Inc.*,[36] the Court held that a fact omitted from a proxy statement is "material" if "there is a substantial likelihood that a reasonable shareholder would consider it important in deciding how to vote."[37] The holding rejected a competing test, which would have defined "material" as anything "a reasonable shareholder might consider appropriate."[38] This distinction sent a message to lower federal courts to limit Rule 14a–9 to substantial misstatements.

Second, in *Mills v. Electric Auto–Lite Co.*,[39] the Court held that shareholder reliance on the misstatement or omission in the proxy materials is presumed. A contrary holding would make it impossible to proceed in most cases—one would have to show that each shareholder read the proxy materials and relied upon the misstatement or omission in deciding to give her proxy to management. Under *Mills,* a plaintiff must show that the misstatement or omission in the proxy statement was material and that the proxy solicitation was an essential step in the accomplishment of the transaction being challenged.

Third is the interesting case of *Virginia Bankshares, Inc. v. Sandberg*.[40] There, Virginia Bankshares (VB) owed 85 percent of the stock of a bank, and wanted to acquire the other 15 percent. It proposed a cash merger, which was approved by the boards of both cor-

---

[34] 377 U.S. 426, 435 (1964).

[35] *Id.* at 432.

[36] 426 U.S. 438, 449 (1976).

[37] The same definition of materiality applies to Rule 10b–5, discussed in Chapter 11(C)(3).

[38] *Id.* at 445–49.

[39] 396 U.S. 375, 380 (1970).

[40] 501 U.S. 1083, 1087–89 (1991).

porations. Under the merger, VB would pay $42 per share for the remaining 15 percent of the bank's stock. Virginia law did not require approval by the bank's minority shareholders. Nonetheless, VB insisted on having the matter put to a vote by those shareholders. Management sent proxy solicitations to them indicating that the board had approved the plan "because it provides an opportunity for the Bank's public shareholders to achieve a high value for their shares."[41]

This statement was misleading. Though the $42 merger price was more than the stock was trading for, and was more than its book value, there was a credible estimate that the stock was worth $60 per share. The merger was approved and the plaintiff, a minority shareholder who refused to give her proxy, sued for violation of Rule 14a–9. The plaintiff sought damages consisting of the difference between the merger price and the true value of the stock. Certainly, the statement in the proxy materials that the board considered $42 to be a "high value" was something a reasonable investor would consider important. Thus, it was material.

Defendants argued that the statement did not violate Rule 14a–9. That rule addresses, *inter alia,* misstatements "with respect to any material *fact.*" Defendants contended that the statement that the merger price gave "high value" was not a statement of fact, but of *opinion,* and therefore not within Rule 14a–9. The Court rejected the contention, at least on the facts of the case. A plaintiff complaining about a statement of opinion in proxy materials must show, first, that the board disbelieved it and, second, that the opinion was not supported by fact. The plaintiff prevailed on these points at trial, as the jury concluded that the directors did not believe that $42 was a "high value," and that the facts did not support the $42 price. Ultimately, however, the plaintiff lost in *Virginia Bankshares.* Because applicable law did not require the shareholders' approval for the merger, the plaintiff could not show causation—i.e., could not show that the proxy solicitation was an essential step in the accomplishment of the transaction.[42] The merger would have gone through anyway, even if no proxies were solicited and no minority shareholders voted.

F. Hostile Takeovers

1. Background

There are various ways in which a board of directors can be ousted. If the shareholders have sufficient votes, in most states they

---

[41] *Id.* at 1089.
[42] *Id.* at 1106–07.

may remove directors with or without cause. A controlling share-holder, by definition, has this kind of clout. When she sells the controlling block of stock to someone, that buyer may then use her voting power to remove the incumbent directors and elect directors she prefers. The buyer would do this because she feels that her new slate of directors will manage the company better and increase the value of the stock.

Controlling shareholders are rare in public corporations. Usually, the ownership is so dispersed that no one shareholder can effect a change in management. So trying to seize power in a public corporation will usually require concerted effort, particularly if the incumbent management does not want to give up. In this section, we talk about "hostile takeovers," which are exactly what they sound like. They are the efforts by one person or business—called the "acquirer" or "bidder" (or "insurgent" or "raider" or "shark," depending on one's point of view)—to take control of a corporation (called the "target"). When the target is a public corporation, there are two basic methods of takeover: the tender offer and the proxy fight.

2. Tender Offers and Leveraged Buyouts

In a tender offer, the bidder makes a public offer of cash (or, if it is a corporation itself, perhaps it will make an offer of its stock) to the shareholders of the target. Those who accept the offer then tender their stock to the acquirer for the specified price. They do this because the tender price is substantially higher than the market price. The goal for the bidder is to obtain a majority of the stock. Accordingly, tender offers are conditioned upon a given percentage of the shares actually being tendered. If that number is not reached, the deal falls through and the bidder does not buy anybody's stock.

When a cash tender offer is made, the open market price for the stock will rise. Speculators known as "arbitrageurs" buy the target company's stock in the open market and then tender it at the offer price, making a profit on the difference between the two prices. This activity drives up the market price of the stock.

Tender offers are deals between the bidder and the individual shareholders of the target. They are not fundamental corporate changes for the target. So, unlike a merger or a sale of substantially all the assets of the corporation, tender offers do not require the target board's approval. That is why they are "hostile"—the bidder acquires a majority of the voting stock, right under the target board's nose. Below, we will see defensive measures the target's board might use to avoid the takeover.

In a wave of cash tender offers in the 1960s, the incumbent management never got a chance to employ defensive tactics. This was because they did not see what was happening until it was too late to fend off the takeover. The acquirer made the tender offer and snapped up enough shares to seize control before management knew what hit them. Congress largely eliminated the possibility of such surprise with the Williams Act in 1968 (and amended in 1970). This legislation, which amends the '34 Act, requires anyone making a cash tender offer for a registered corporation to disclose various things, including the source of funds used in the offer, the purpose for which the offer is made, and any contracts or understandings the acquirer has regarding the target. The target company must respond publicly to the offer. The Williams Act also imposes various restrictions on the mechanics of these offers and prohibits the use of false, misleading, or incomplete statements.

The 1980s brought the "leveraged buyout," or LBO. With this, the acquirer got the money to buy shares of the target by issuing "junk bonds" and through temporary ("bridge") loans from commercial banks. The junk bonds were IOUs from the acquirer to the lender, and were (as the name implies) quite risky. If the takeover worked, the bonds and other loans were repaid by the earnings of the target corporation (which had assumed the obligation to repay them). LBOs thus are called "bootstrap" acquisitions, which means that the target company provides the funds to finance its own purchase. In many instances, incumbent management participated in the buyout, and managed the business after the public shareholders were eliminated.

The era of LBOs and unsolicited takeover attempts came to a crashing halt at the end of the 1980s with the collapse of the Drexel Burnham Lambert securities firm. Many companies failed after being acquired in this fashion because their cash flow was not sufficient to pay the debt load of the LBO. When sources of cash for such takeover bids dried up, proxy contests started to look more attractive.

3. Proxy Contests

In a proxy contest, the bidder competes with the incumbent management of the target to obtain enough proxy appointments to elect a majority of the board. The targets tend to be relatively small public corporations. An example was the proxy contest by which TIAA/CREF, a huge pension manager and investment firm, ousted the entire board of a struggling publicly held restaurant chain. Before that, institutional investors had managed only to elect a few directors, but not to seize control of an entire board. Proxy fights may be used (or threatened) to encourage the incumbent board to consider a consensual merger of the target into the acquirer.

A proxy contest may be used in conjunction with a tender offer or with purchases on the market. For example, a bidder may buy a substantial minority position in the target through the stock market. Then, having a toehold in the corporation, the acquirer can use a proxy contest to obtain enough additional shares to replace incumbent management. Or it may get the initial toehold through a proxy fight and complete the takeover with a tender offer. As with a tender offer, a proxy fight may be threatened as a way to get incumbent management to consider a friendly takeover, perhaps through a merger.

Proxy fights for registered corporations cannot be undertaken with stealth. A solicitation from more than ten shareholders requires compliance with the SEC proxy regulations we discussed in the preceding subsection. Other SEC regulations require that "participants" (other than management) file information with the Commission and securities exchanges at least five days before a solicitation begins. "Participant" includes anyone who contributes more than $500 to finance the contest. The information that must be disclosed relates to the identity and background of the participants, their interests in the corporation and when they were acquired, financing arrangements, participation in other proxy contests, and understandings with respect to future employment with the corporation. In addition, the Williams Act requires anyone who acquires more than five percent of the voting stock of a public corporation to file a disclosure statement within ten days thereafter. These requirements, again, reflect the theory underlying the '34 Act generally—that widely dispersed information provides the best protection for the investing public.

Those waging a proxy contest are swimming upstream. Incumbent management has access to corporate assets to fight the contest, and usually has access to defensive tactics discussed below. Moreover, shareholder apathy generally favors management. Many shareholders who might respond to a cash offer for their stock may be less likely to answer a call for their proxy.

The expenses of a proxy contest—of soliciting proxy appointments from thousands of shareholders—can be daunting. It seems clear that the corporation should pay for printing and mailing the notice of meeting, the proxy statement required by federal law, and the proxy appointments themselves. These are legitimate corporate expenses, because without the proxy solicitation it is unlikely that the quorum requirement for a meeting can be met. Many courts have allowed the corporation to pay the reasonable expenses of the incumbent management in defending against the bidder. The theory is that such expenses are for the purpose of educating shareholders when the controversy involves a policy question rather than a mere personal struggle for control. Since virtually every proxy fight may be dressed up as a policy dispute, the corporation will usually pay all management expenses.

If the bidder is successful, it may ask that the corporation reimburse it for its expenses. Though there is some reluctance to allow this, courts have allowed such reimbursement if the dispute involved policy rather than personalities, and if the shareholders approve. In such cases, the corporation ends up paying the expenses of both sides of the dispute (because the losing management will normally reimburse itself before leaving office). Some economics scholars suggest that reimbursement should be routine because successful bidders perform a socially useful function of ridding the business of lousy managers.

4. Defensive Tactics

There was a great deal of tender offer and leveraged buyout activity in the 1970s, which led lawyers to consider defensive tactics to thwart takeover efforts. Innovative counsel devised a host of approaches.[43] Generically, these are sometimes referred to as "shark repellants." Among them are:

- Finding a more congenial bidder (a "white knight").

- Buying a business that increases the chances that the threatened takeover will give rise to antitrust problems by concentrating too much power in a business area.

- Adopting voting procedures that make it difficult for a bidder who acquires a majority of the voting shares to replace the board of directors.

- Suing for an injunction to stop the proposed takeover, alleging violations of the Williams Act or antitrust laws (or anything else that might be plausibly claimed).

- Issuing additional shares to friendly persons to make a takeover more difficult (a "lockup").

---

[43] *See* Albert O. Saulsbury, IV, *The Availability of Takeover Defenses and Deal Protection Devices for Anglo-American Target Companies,* 37 DEL. J. CORP. L. 115 (2012).

- Increasing the dividend or otherwise driving up the price of shares to make the takeover price unattractive.

- Buying off the bidder by paying "greenmail."[44]

- Repurchasing the corporation's stock in the market to drive up the price (thereby hopefully making it too expensive for the acquirer to get control).

- Running up debt obligations to make seizing the company less attractive.

The most effective (and best named) defensive tactic is the "poison pill," which is also called a "shareholder rights plan."[45] This provides that upon a triggering event—which is usually the bidder acquiring a given percentage of the target's stock—the target corporation will issue debt or equity securities to the remaining shareholders at a bargain price. This dilutes the bidder's ownership interest and makes it impractical for her to take control. Poison pills usually provide that the board of directors of the target corporation may voluntarily "disarm" the pill before it is triggered. This ingenious device essentially forces the bidder to negotiate with the incumbent management of the target.

Theoretically, a bidder could buy shares slightly below the number that triggers the poison pill, and then use a proxy fight to replace enough directors to cause the target to disarm the pill. To prevent this maneuver, lawyers have added a "dead hand" provision, to the effect that only the directors in office at the time the pill was approved may vote to disarm it. In *Quickturn Design Systems v. Shapiro*,[46] the Delaware Supreme Court held that such a "dead hand" feature violates the basic principle that the current board of directors has control of corporate affairs. Such "dead hand" plans may fare better in other states.[47] Some corporations have adopted a "no hands" poison pill, which cannot be disarmed by anyone. And there

---

[44] This term, obviously a play on "blackmail," refers to buying back the would-be acquirer's stock at an inflated value. In other words, the corporation pays the would-be acquirer an inflated amount to make it go away.

[45] *See, e.g.,* Versata Enterprises, Inc. v. Selectica, Inc., 5 A.3d 586 (Del. 2010) (upholding the use of the poison pill).

[46] 721 A.2d 1281, 1291 (Del. 1998).

[47] *See* Comment, *Death Toll for the Dead Hand?: The Survivability of the Dead Hand Provision in Corporate America*, 48 EMORY L.J. 991, 1019–20 (1999) (surveying states likely to uphold dead hand provisions).

is a "chewable poison pill," which gives the target's board a set time to negotiate before the pill becomes effective.[48]

Courts have addressed the validity of various defensive tactics. In Chapter 7, we address the fiduciary duties owed to corporations by their directors. One of these is the duty of care, which means that a director must discharge her duties as a reasonable person would in similar circumstances. Board action is judged under the "business judgment rule," which is a presumption that directors used due care in arriving at a business decision. Courts will not second-guess the wisdom of that decision unless the plaintiff can show that the directors were uninformed or that their action was essentially irrational. One of the hallmarks of the business judgment rule, however, is that it applies (and therefore protects directors from liability) only if there is no conflict of interest. It does not apply if there is a conflict—if the director is tempted to put her own interest above that of the company.

Board reactions to takeover attempts raise an important question. On the one hand, they look like any other business decision, so the board's choice should be protected by the business judgment rule. On the other hand, though, the defensive tactics might be seen as efforts by directors to hold onto their own positions. After all, if the bidder is successful, she will likely replace the present board. So fending off a hostile takeover might be seen as a conflict-of-interest situation, in which the business judgment rule would not apply.

So what have courts done? Many have simply applied the business judgment rule. For example, in *Panter v. Marshall Field & Co.*,[49] a department store chain defeated an unwanted takeover bid by another retail chain. It did so by opening additional stores that created serious antitrust problems for the bidder—that is, if the bidder had succeeded, it would have gotten into trouble for having too much concentrated business power in that field. The bidder withdrew the offer. Then the price of the target company's stock fell precipitously, in part because the company had overextended itself in acquiring so many additional stores. Minority shareholders sued the directors for damages. The majority opinion exonerated the board by applying the business judgment rule. A vigorous dissent argued, however, that incumbent managers should not be able to entrench themselves in office to the detriment of shareholders.[50]

---

[48] *See* Mark Klock, *Dead Hands: Poison Catalyst or Strength-Enhancing Megavitamin? An Analysis of the Benefits of Managerial Protection and the Detriments of Judicial Interference,* 2001 COLUM. BUS. L. REV. 67.

[49] 646 F.2d 271, 278–81 (7th Cir. 1981).

[50] *Id.* at 299–312 (Cudahy, J., dissenting in part).

The Delaware Supreme Court has addressed takeover defenses more than any other court, and it recognizes the potential conflict of interest. Most of the cases were decided in the 1980s and 1990s (there was far more merger and acquisition activity then than now). It is fair to say that the Delaware court has not earned high marks for its efforts. Many observers, including Delaware lower court judges, conclude that the Delaware Supreme Court has not provided clear guidance.[51]

For starters, in *Moran v. Household International, Inc.*,[52] the Delaware Supreme Court upheld the board's adoption of a poison pill before any specific takeover attempt had arisen. Because there was no suggestion that the pill was used to entrench the existing board, however, the matter was simply one of the directors' business judgment. The court was dealing, however, with an abstract plan—the board had not actually invoked the pill.

In *Unocal Corp. v. Mesa Petroleum Co.*,[53] in contrast, the court addressed a defensive tactic taken in response to a specific takeover threat. The board of the target, having concluded that a tender offer was inadequate, instituted a selective stock repurchase plan, the clear purpose of which was to defeat the tender offer. The repurchase offered stockholders considerably more than the bidder was offering, and was not made to the bidder (hence "selective stock repurchase"). The court upheld the effort. Though it spoke of the board's "duty" to oppose a takeover it considers harmful to the corporate enterprise, the court noted the inherent danger that directors might undertake a defense merely to protect their own positions.

Accordingly, the court in *Unocal* imposed "enhanced judicial scrutiny." It shifts the burden to directors to show a justification for their conduct. In addition, it requires that the board have "reasonable" grounds for believing that a threat exists, and that the defense adopted is "reasonable" in relation to that threat.[54] The court thus injected the notion of balance—if a defensive measure is to be upheld, "it must be reasonable in relation to the threat posed. This entails an analysis by the directors of the nature of the takeover bid and its ef-

---

[51] *See, e.g., In re* Gaylord Container Corp. S'holders Litig., 753 A.2d 462, 477 n.46 (Del. Ch. 2000) ("Delaware's doctrinal approach [to defensive tactics] is premised on the assumption that the world can be viewed clearly by simultaneously wearing three pairs of eye glasses with different prescriptions (*Unocal*, business judgment, and entire fairness). It is not apparent that this approach works any better in the law than it does in the field of optics.").

[52] 500 A.2d 1346, 1357 (Del. 1985).

[53] 493 A.2d 946, 949 (Del. 1985).

[54] *Id.* at 954–55.

fect on the corporate enterprise."[55] The board may act to avoid danger to "corporate policy and effectiveness."[56] *Unocal* appears to call for a review of the board decision under a rather objective standard, and is less deferential to the board than the business judgment rule.

The court discussed the balancing aspect of *Unocal* in *Unitrin, Inc. v. American General Corp.*[57] There, the board of the target initiated a repurchase of its stock in the open market to fend off a merger proposal. The lower court enjoined the tactic as disproportionate to the minimal threat posed. The Delaware Supreme Court reversed. When considering proportionality, it instructed, a court must first determine whether the board's response to a takeover attempt is "coercive" or "preclusive," in that it would render a later acquisition impossible. If so, the court may enjoin the act. If not, the court may enjoin the act only if it is outside the "range of reasonableness" under the circumstances.[58]

The Delaware Supreme Court adopted another twist in *Revlon, Inc. v. MacAndrews & Forbes Holdings, Inc.*[59] There, despite efforts to thwart a takeover, it became clear to the board of Revlon that sale of the company to one of two bidders was inevitable. In this situation, the court held, the board may not exercise its business judgment to prefer one bidder over the other. Instead, its role becomes that of auctioneer. The board's duty is to obtain the best possible price for the company (this is called the "*Revlon* duty").[60] The decision to defeat a higher bidder and favor a lower bidder violates this duty.

Courts and commentators speak of a "*Revlon* claim"—to enforce the *Revlon* duty to maximize price. If *Revlon* applies, the board cannot favor one bidder over another, but must maximize the sale price. The problem is determining when *Revlon* applies, on the one hand, and when *Unocal* applies, on the other. In *Paramount Communications, Inc. v. Time, Inc.*,[61] Time negotiated a stock-for-stock merger with Warner. After the agreement, but before consummation, Paramount showed up with an uninvited (and, to the Time board, unwelcome) offer to buy the Time stock for cash. Time and Warner restructured their deal to have Time launch a tender offer to acquire 51 percent of the Warner stock for cash.

---

[55] *Id.* at 955.
[56] *Id.*
[57] 651 A.2d 1361, 1367 (Del. 1995).
[58] *Id.* at 1386–88.
[59] 506 A.2d 173 (Del. 1985).
[60] *Id.* at 184–85.
[61] 571 A.2d 1140, 1143–46 (Del. 1989).

Plaintiffs argued that the original Time-Warner stock merger triggered *Revlon* because it resulted in a change of control. Thus, they asserted, Time management could not take sides. The defensive tactics against Paramount, according to plaintiffs, breached the *Revlon* duty to maximize the sale price for the company. The court concluded that *Revlon* did not apply, and limited *Revlon* to cases in which either (1) the target initiates active bidding to sell itself or to effect a reorganization resulting in "a clear break-up" of the company, or (2) the target reacts to a takeover bid by abandoning its long-term strategy and seeks another transaction that involves the break-up of the company.[62] The Time–Warner merger may have put Time "in play," but it did not result in its break-up. Under *Unocal,* then, the defensive tactic was upheld.

Four years later, the court was back at it in *Paramount Communications, Inc. v. QVC Network, Inc.,*[63] in which the target board favored one of the competing bidders and imposed defensive mechanisms against the other. The court concluded that *Revlon* applied because the target pursued a deal that would result in a "change of control." More recently, in *Lyondell Chemical Co. v. Ryan,*[64] the court emphasized that "there is only one *Revlon* duty—to [get] the best price for the stockholders at a sale of the company." It explained when that duty arises: "*Revlon* duties do not arise simply because a company is 'in play.' The duty to seek the best available price applies only when a company embarks on a transaction—on its own initiative or in response to an unsolicited offer—that will result in a change of control."[65] Because the board of the target in *Lyondell* had adopted a wait and see attitude to a proposed takeover, it had not undertaken any act that would result in a change of control.

5. State Anti-Takeover Laws

Above, we discussed the Williams Act, which is federal law requiring various disclosures by potential bidders in takeovers. Here we discuss state law on takeovers.[66] Public corporations are often important to the economy of the states in which they are formed.[67] Accordingly states have tried to hamper takeovers of corporations

---

[62] *Id.* at 1150.

[63] 637 A.2d 34, 42 (Del. 1994).

[64] 970 A.2d 235, 242 (Del. 2009).

[65] *Id.*

[66] *See generally* Michal Barzuza, *The State of State Antitakeover Law,* 95 VA. L. REV. 1973 (2009).

[67] This is true even when the corporation does not do business in the state of formation, because the corporation nonetheless pays fees and taxes in that state. If the corporation also does business in the state, it is even more important to that state's economy, because it hires people and buys things there.

formed there, especially by out-of-state corporations.[68] They have enacted anti-takeover statutes in response. The first generation of these statutes was aimed largely at notification by potential bidders, review of the proposal, and approval or rejection by a state. The U.S. Supreme Court dealt a serious blow to such statutes in *Edgar v. MITE Corp.*,[69] which held that the Illinois statute of this type violated the Commerce Clause.

States shifted gears and moved to the second generation of anti-takeover statutes. These "control share acquisition" laws provide that a purchaser of stock who increases its percentage of ownership above a certain level will be prohibited from voting those additional shares without approval of the board or the other shareholders. If the bidder cannot vote the stock that made it a majority owner, there is no possibility of a takeover. The Supreme Court upheld Indiana's version of such a statute in *CTS Corporation v. Dynamics Corp. of America.*[70] The Court rejected the argument that the Commerce Clause creates an area concerning the market for corporate control that is beyond state regulation. It also held that the Williams Act did not preempt the Indiana statute. In the wake of *CTS*, nearly every state now has adopted such a statute to thwart the takeover of public corporations formed there.[71]

There is a third generation, called "business combination" statutes. These restrict persons who acquire more than a specified percentage of stock from engaging in certain transactions (such as mergers) with the corporation for a specified period (usually three years) without the consent of the pre-acquisition board of directors.[72] States have adopted these statutes widely, and—based largely on *CTS*—these have withstood challenge under the Commerce Clause and against the argument that they are preempted by the Williams Act.[73]

---

[68] If a corporation formed in State A merges into a corporation formed in State B, it ceases to exist. That means that it will no longer pay fees and taxes to State A. Moreover, the State B company may decide to downsize any business locations in State A, further harming the State A economy.

[69] 457 U.S. 624, 646 (1982).

[70] 481 U.S. 69, 93–94 (1987).

[71] *See, e.g.*, MINN. STAT. § 302A.671; VA. CODE § 13.1–728.4.

[72] *See, e.g.*, DEL. GEN. CORP. LAW § 203.

[73] *See, e.g.*, Amanda Acquisition Corp. v. Universal Foods Corp., 877 F.2d 496, 508–09 (7th Cir. 1989) (upholding the Wisconsin statute in an opinion by Judge Easterbrook, who is a noted law and economics scholar and former professor at the University of Chicago Law School).

Chapter 10

FINANCE, ISSUANCE, AND DISTRIBUTIONS

Analysis

A. Introduction
B. Debt and Equity Financing and Securities
    1. Background and Definitions
    2. Advantages and Disadvantages
    3. Types of Debt Securities
    4. Types of Equity Securities
C. Issuance of Stock
    1. Background and Definitions
    2. Form and Amount of Consideration for an Issuance
    3. Determination of Value
    4. Watered Stock
    5. Dilution and Pre-Emptive Rights
    6. Venture Capital and Public Issuance
D. Accounting and Financial Records
    1. The Income Statement
    2. The Cash Flow Statement
    3. The Balance Sheet
E. Dividends and Other Distributions
    1. Background
    2. Dividends
    3. Is There a "Right" to a Dividend?
    4. Classes of Stock and Dividends
    5. Repurchases and Redemptions
F. Statutory Limitations on Distributions and Liability for Improper
    Distributions
    1. Background
    2. Traditional ("Fund") Limitations
    3. The Modern ("Insolvency") Approach
    4. Liability for Improper Distributions

A. Introduction

Every business needs money (also known as "capital"). Whether it is a front-yard lemonade stand or a multinational conglomerate, the business cannot get started without money. The company needs to buy supplies, ingredients, to have office or retail space, pay for deliveries, etc. In general, there are two ways to get this money: borrow it or allow investors to buy ownership interests. These two sources of start-up funds—borrowing and selling ownership interests—represent "debt" interests and "equity" interests in the business. If you majored in sociology in college, these terms may scare you, but they should not. In section B of this Chapter, we will define debt and equity and discuss how businesses use each.

Even after a business is up and running, it may need more money to maintain or expand operations. It may be generating earnings that it can "plow back" into the business for these purposes.[1] Even then, though, it may seek capital from the outside world, and the question will be the same as it was initially: do we borrow or do we sell ownership interests in the business? In other words, do we use debt or equity financing (or a combination)?

In section C, we will consider a corporation's raising capital by issuing stock. This discussion will include concern with issuances that are intended to dilute certain shareholders' interests, and the protection potentially afforded by pre-emptive rights. In section D, we will look at accounting and financial records, which help measure the fiscal health of the business. Section E discusses distributions to shareholders, including dividends. Section F addresses options available to businesses that wish to distribute some of their earnings to investors.

B. Debt and Equity Financing and Securities

1. Background and Definitions

To get capital to start the business (or later, to expand the business), a corporation can either borrow money or sell ownership interests. If it borrows, it is using "debt." If it sells ownership interests, it is using "equity." It is important to understand the difference.

In the business world, debt means exactly what it means in our everyday world—you borrowed money and must pay it back, with interest, on terms specified in the contract. Whoever lends capital to the business is a creditor (not an owner) of that business. She is entitled to be repaid, but will not share in a proportionate way if the business is successful. Even if the business does poorly, the creditor has a right to repayment. Equity, in contrast, means ownership. One who makes an equity investment in a corporation gets stock in the business. She is an owner (not a creditor) of the corporation. She

---

[1] Or, as we shall see in section G, the business could distribute those earnings to investors in the form of dividends.

is entitled to share in the success of the business, but may lose her investment if the company does poorly.[2]

Your friend is forming a corporation to manufacture widgets. She needs $20,000 to get the business going. She will put in $10,000 of her own money and wants you to provide the other $10,000. You agree. Now, do you lend the money to the business or do you buy an equity interest in the business?

First, let's say you lend $10,000 to the corporation. It will issue a document that obligates it to repay you $10,000 plus (let's say) four percent interest, due on demand one year from now.

- Suppose the business does poorly—it makes no money at all. A year from now, you have a right to be repaid your $10,000 loan plus four percent interest.

- Instead, suppose the business does spectacularly well—in fact, after one year, your friend sells the business for a million dollars. Do you share in that good fortune? No. You are not an equity holder. You are a debt holder. You get your $10,000 plus interest. Your friend gets the million dollars (minus the payment to you).

Second, let's say instead of lending, you invested the $10,000 in stock. You get 50 percent of the stock in the corporation (your friend, who also invested $10,000, gets the other 50 percent).

- The business fails completely. It uses up the $20,000 you and your friend invested. You get nothing. You were an equity holder and you have no right to payment. You have lost $10,000.

- But if the business does spectacularly well—and is sold for a million dollars—you, owner of half the company, would get $500,000.

Most businesses use a combination of debt and equity financing. Our purpose is to understand the basics. Hitting the right mix of financing for a given business is sophisticated work, and is the focus of the course on Corporate Finance. We should also know that the line

---

[2] When a company goes out of business, or goes bankrupt, the holders of debt must be paid before any assets are distributed to stockholders. In other words, holders of debt have priority over holders of equity. One investor might hold both debt and equity, by lending money to the business as well as buying a stake in it. The fact that she is a shareholder generally does not affect her status as a debt holder. Thus, she will be entitled to repayment of her debt, along with other creditors, before shareholders recover. *See In re* AutoStyle Plastics, Inc., 269 F.3d 726, 745 (6th Cir. 2001).

between debt and equity is not always clear. Corporations can issue "hybrid" interests that have some characteristics of one and some of the other.[3]

We need two more background vocabulary terms. First, a "security" is an investment. So we will speak of "debt securities," which are loans to the corporation, and "equity securities," which are ownership interests (stock) in the corporation. Second, when a corporation takes a loan or sells an ownership interest, it "issues" the security. So "issuance" is a sale by the corporation itself, and the "issuer" is the corporation. The corporation may issue debt securities or equity securities (or both).

2. Advantages and Disadvantages

In general terms, debt is riskier for the business because it must be repaid. On the other hand, if the business does well, the gain does not have to be shared with the lender. Equity is riskier for the investor because she can lose her investment. So why wouldn't businesses always use equity financing? For one thing, it may be difficult to get. People (and banks) may be more willing to lend to an unproven business than to own a piece of it. For another, owners of stock usually have the right to vote. So issuing stock means sharing power with others. A founder of a business may want to retain control and thus choose not to have the corporation issue stock to others.

There are tax consequences to the choices as well. In general, the corporation can deduct interest payments on debt, but cannot deduct distributions (such as dividends) made to shareholders. So interest payments (on debt) reduce the corporation's income tax liability, but dividend payments (to equity holders) do not.

Debt financing allows the corporation to use "leverage"—that is, to use borrowed money to increase its return on investment. Assume a business that was started with $200,000, which you invested. Assume the business generates $20,000 per year, which is 10 percent of the investment. You are making a 10 percent return on your $200,000 investment.

Instead, suppose you started the business with $100,000 of your own money and $100,000 that you borrowed. Assume you borrowed that $100,000 at five percent interest. The business generates $20,000 per year. Of that $20,000, you have to pay $5,000 to the person from whom you borrowed the $100,000. That means you "netted" $15,000 income. But you only put at risk $100,000 of your own mon-

---

[3] The taxation consequences of these hybrids are often subject to debate. That is beyond our scope.

ey. So your return on investment is $15,000 on a $100,000 investment—that is, 15 percent. So by using borrowed money, you "levered" your return on investment from 10 percent to 15 percent.

This sounds great, but we must remember the *risk* of using debt financing. The loan has to be repaid, with interest. If the business's cash flow falls to $5,000 one year, you will be getting no return on your investment, because that $5,000 goes to pay interest on the loan (or to "service" the loan).

3. Types of Debt Securities

Holders of debt securities have made a loan to the business. Repayment of that loan may be secured or unsecured. There are two main types of debt securities: the debenture and the bond. The debenture is an unsecured corporate obligation, while repayment of a bond is secured by a lien or mortgage on some (or all) of the corporate property. In practice, many people use "bond" as a generic term for debt securities. Typical debt securities are issued in multiples of $1,000, pay interest at a fixed rate for the life of the security, and have a specified maturity date that may be many years in the future.

Historically, debentures and bonds were reflected by certificates printed on heavy paper with elaborate designs, lettering, and figures. The purpose was to deter forgeries. They were "bearer" instruments, so whoever held them on the due date could receive payment by delivering the certificate to the corporation. Interest payments were represented by coupons on the certificate. The bearer "clipped" the coupons with scissors as they matured, and submitted each to the company for payment, usually through a bank or broker.

Because debt instruments were payable to the bearer, it was difficult for the government to ensure that income tax was paid on the interest. With the Tax Equity and Fiscal Responsibility Act of 1982, Congress stepped in to deny corporations income-tax deductions for interest they paid on bearer instruments. As a result, ownership of these instruments is now reflected either by certificates registered in the name of the owner and transferable only by endorsement, or, increasingly, by book entries on the records of the corporation or brokerage firms.

Interest payments on debt securities are usually fixed obligations, expressed as a percentage of the face amount of the security. Thus a five percent bond means that a $1,000 investment will pay $50 per year. Not all debt instruments carry a fixed interest rate. Some corporations have issued "income bonds," on which the obligation to pay interest is conditioned on adequate corporate earnings. Somewhat rarer are "participating bonds," with which the amount of interest increases or decreases with corporate earnings. Such bonds start to look like equity investments.

Indeed, debt securities may have rights analogous to those provided for preferred stock.[4] As we will see in detail in section E of this Chapter, preferred stock has the right to be paid first, before distributions are made to other shares. Similarly, bonds with a "sinking fund" provision require the corporation to set aside cash to redeem a part of those bonds each year. In some instances, sinking funds accumulate until the entire issue matures. The proceeds of the fund are then used to pay off the entire principal. And in some states, the line between debt and equity is further blurred—holders of debt securities may be given the right to vote for directors, usually on some contingency, such as failure to pay interest on bonds.[5] Many debentures are made convertible into equity securities, usually common stock, on some predetermined conversion ratio. When convertible debentures are converted, they, and the debt they represent, disappear and the new equity securities take their place.

What we have discussed are corporate bonds. Municipalities, states, and state agencies frequently issue debt securities as well. The interest on some of these may be exempt from income tax under federal or state or municipal law. This feature makes them attractive investments, but also explains why they usually carry a low interest rate.

4. Types of Equity Securities

Most courses spend more time on equity securities than debt. We already know that "equity security" means stock, and it represents an ownership interest in the corporation. Now we focus on some terminology.

Authorized stock is the maximum number of shares the corporation can issue. This number is set in the articles.[6] There is no statutory limitation on the number of shares that may be authorized by a corporation and no requirement that all the authorized shares actually be issued. The number of authorized shares should be high enough to accommodate future efforts to raise capital.[7] On the other hand,

---

[4] One example is loan "covenants," which force the borrowing company to keep its business within certain standards of financial health or be forced to pay the loan back immediately.

[5] *See, e.g.* DEL. GEN. CORP. LAW § 221.

[6] *See* RMBCA § 6.01; DEL. GEN. CORP. LAW § 102(a)(4).

[7] The corporation cannot issue more shares than are authorized by the articles of incorporation. *See* RMBCA § 6.03(a). Amending the articles to increase the number of authorized shares is a fundamental change, which requires shareholder approval, as we will see in Chapter 12(D). Better to avoid that if possible.

there are practical constraints on setting the number too high. First, some states impose franchise or stock taxes on the basis of authorized shares.[8] Setting the number too high increases this tax with no corresponding benefit. Second, a large number may make investors nervous that their interests could be diluted if a great many shares were later sold to other people. The persons drafting the articles balance such factors.

Issued stock is the number of shares the corporation actually sells. Again, the corporation is not required to issue all of its authorized shares; what it actually does sell is called "issued." Whether and when to issue stock is a management decision, usually made by the board of directors, which also sets the price at which stock is issued.

Outstanding stock consists of shares that the corporation has issued and not reacquired. Often, this is the same number as issued. Assume the corporation has 10,000 authorized shares. It issues 4,000 shares and has not reacquired any of them. The number of issued shares and the number of outstanding shares are the same— 4,000. Now assume that the corporation reacquires 500 of the shares it has issued. Here, the number of issued shares is 4,000. The number of outstanding shares is 3,500. Stated another way, issued stock is historical—that is, how many shares the corporation has sold over time. And outstanding stock is a snapshot at this moment of how many shares are held by persons other than the corporation itself.

Treasury stock consists of shares the corporation has issued and then reacquired. In the example we just saw, the 500 shares that the corporation reacquired would be treasury stock. The theory is that the corporation gets the stock and puts it in its "treasury." This is a strange theory, because there is no such thing! Economically, treasury stock is the equivalent of authorized and unissued stock. Thus, the corporation can reissue it. Until it is reissued, the corporation holds this treasury stock. Because the stock is not considered "outstanding," however, the corporation is not considered an owner of that stock. Thus, the corporation does not vote those shares at shareholder meetings (nobody does) and the corporation does not get any dividend declared (nobody does). The RMBCA has abolished the term "treasury," and simply treats all reacquired stock as authorized and unissued, consistent with the rules we've just discussed.[9]

Every state permits the corporation to establish different *classes* of stock.[10] The principal distinction is between *common* and *preferred*

---

[8] *See, e.g.,* DEL. GEN. CORP. LAW § 503; CONN. GEN. STAT. § 33–618.

[9] "A corporation may acquire its own shares, and shares so acquired constitute authorized but unissued shares." RMBCA § 6.31(a).

[10] RMBCA § 6.01(c).

stock. This distinction is important when we get to distributions in section E. Distributions are payments by the corporation to shareholders. The best example is the dividend. Preferred stock is entitled to be paid first, before any other shares. The other stock—without the right to be paid first—is entitled to the rest of the distribution, and is called common stock.

If there is only one class of stock, by default it is common stock. It has the right to receive distributions (if there are any) and the right to vote. Indeed, under the law of every state, there must be at least one class of stock entitled to receive distributions and one entitled to vote. Though these do not have to be the same class of stock, they usually are—common stock.

But other classes can be created. The corporation can have nonvoting stock. The corporation can have weighted voting stock—for example, with two votes per share, as opposed to one vote per share. While this usually happens in closely held corporations, it can be tried in public corporations as well. A good example is the corporation that published the New York Times. Though publicly traded, this corporation was long associated with a single family. The corporation had a special class of stock, held by family members, with super voting power. This helped ensure that the family could continue to run the show. The Securities and Exchange Commission adopted rule 19c–4 (the "one share one vote" rule) to prevent such unequal divisions in voting power in public corporations, but did not affect companies that were already doing such things. Nonetheless, the District of Columbia Circuit held the rule invalid as exceeding the power of the Commission.[11]

A *series* of stock is a sub-class. So a corporation that wants to give different characteristics within a class of stock may sub-divide that class into, say, Series A and Series B.

Corporations can give stock *options* to employees as an incentive.[12] The option gives the holder the right to purchase stock at the option price. She does not become a shareholder, however, until she exercises the option and pays the purchase price. At that point, the corporation issues the stock to her. *Puts* and *calls* are particular kinds of options. A *put* is the option to sell stock at a set price. A *call* is the option to buy stock at a set price. These terms are used with regard to securities in publicly traded corporations. Puts and calls are created by securities traders as speculation on price movements.

---

[11] The Business Roundtable v. SEC, 905 F.2d 406, 408–17 (D.C. Cir. 1990).
[12] RMBCA § 6.24.

Historically, a shareholder's ownership interest in a corporation has been represented by stock certificates.[13] Many are interesting artistically. For example, the certificate for Disney has a picture of Walt Disney and of various cartoon characters, including Bambi and Winnie the Pooh. In closely held corporations, stock certificates are common, and statutes prescribe the required content.

With publicly traded corporations, however, very few shareholders ever see a stock certificate. Starting in the 1960s, in response to increased trading volume, firms developed the "book entry" or "street name" system. Under this, most certificates are stored in the vaults of the Depository Trust Company (DTC) and its clearing offices. Most of these are registered in the name "Cede & Co.," which is the registered owner of most publicly traded stock. The individual owner's name and information is held by brokerage firms. More recently, statutes have permitted the issuance of stock without certificates.[14]

C. Issuance of Stock

1. Background and Definitions

"Issuance" is a term of art. It refers to the corporation's selling its own stock. It is, as we know, a way to raise capital for the business. The corporation sells the stock (maybe to a small group, maybe to the public) and receives consideration for that issuance. An issuance is contrasted with buying or selling stock on a stock exchange. When an investor goes to an online brokerage and purchases stock in McDonald's, she is not buying that stock from the corporation. Rather, she is buying it from another member of the trading public. Accordingly, the money she pays does not go to McDonald's, but to the person who sold those shares (less a commission for the brokerage firm). In other words, that sale was not an issuance. Only the initial sale by McDonald's was an issuance. The corporation received the money from that sale. After that, publicly traded stocks are bought and sold on an exchange—and the money goes from the buyer to the seller.

Corporations can issue stock through subscriptions. These are offers to buy stock from the corporation. In most states, subscriptions must be in writing.[15] Once the corporation accepts the subscription,

---

[13] Statutes prescribe what information must be set forth in the certificates. At a minimum, each certificate must state the name of the issuing corporation and which state law it is organized under, the name of the person to whom the stock is issued, the number and class of shares, and the designation of the series. RMBCA § 6.25(b).

[14] *See, e.g.,* RMBCA § 6.26; DEL. GEN. CORP. LAW § 158; N.Y. BUS. CORP. LAW § 508.

[15] *See, e.g.,* N.Y. BUS. CORP. LAW § 503(b) ("A subscription, whether made before or after the formation of a corporation, shall not be enforceable unless in writing and signed by the subscriber.").

the parties have a "subscription agreement." The subscriber does not become a shareholder, however, until she has paid the issuance price in full. Failure to pay for the stock constitutes default. If the subscriber does not remedy the default after written demand by the corporation, depending on the state, the corporation may be able to keep the money paid (if any) and sell the stock to someone else.[16]

Consistent with the general rule of contract law, a subscriber may revoke her offer before the corporation accepts it. This may not be true, however, if the subscription is made before the corporation is formed. In many states, a pre-incorporation subscription cannot be revoked for six months[17] unless the subscription itself provides that it is revocable or unless all other subscribers agree to the revocation.[18] This rule allows people forming the company to rely on the money's being there when the corporation comes into existence. If pre-incorporation subscriptions were revocable, promoters—buoyed by what appear to be commitments to invest—might do a great deal of work to prepare for incorporation, only to have the funding pulled out at the last minute.[19]

2. Form and Amount of Consideration for an Issuance

Ordinarily, a corporation will issue stock to obtain money. But suppose the company needs a building or wants to hire someone with special expertise. Can it issue stock in exchange for these forms of consideration? The answer has always been yes. In every state, a corporation has long been permitted to issue stock for any of three forms of consideration: (1) money, (2) tangible or intangible property, or (3) services that had already been performed for the corporation.

"Money" includes cash or its equivalent (like a check). Generally, patents, goodwill, contract rights, and computer software qualify as intangible property under these statutes. There is some debate about whether services rendered *before* the corporation is actually formed can constitute services performed for the corporation. Suppose, for instance, that a lawyer does all the work to form a corporation. Can the company then issue stock to the lawyer as compensation for that service? Some courts may say no, because when the

---

[16] *See, e.g.*, FLA. STAT. § 607.0620; N.Y. BUS. CORP. LAW § 503(d) (if the subscriber has paid at least half of the subscription price at the time of the default, the corporation must attempt to sell the stock to a third party at a price to pay the remaining balance).

[17] In New York and some other states, the period of irrevocability is three months. *See* N.Y. BUS. CORP. LAW § 503(a).

[18] RMBCA § 6.20(a).

[19] *See* Balfour v. Baker City Gas & Elec. Light Co., 41 P. 164, 166 (Or. 1895) (noting the policy reason for irrevocability).

work was done, there was no corporation in existence. Other states, however, permit the practice. For instance, a New York statute provides that such pre-incorporation efforts can be compensated with stock.[20]

Under the historic view, a corporation could not issue stock in exchange for a promise of future payment (i.e., a promissory note) or a promise of future services. If the corporation purported to do so, the stock was said to be "unpaid," with liability imposed as if it were "watered" stock (which we will see below). A generation ago, these limitations were virtually universal.[21]

The law has changed. Today, most states, influenced by the RMBCA, permit issuance for "any tangible or intangible property or benefit to the corporation."[22] This permits a corporation to issue stock in exchange for promissory notes, future services, discharge of a debt, and release of a claim (in addition to the traditional forms of money, tangible or intangible property, and services already rendered). Indeed, it is difficult to imagine a form of consideration that would not satisfy this broad standard.

What happens if the corporation issues stock for a promissory note or a promise of future services and the note is never paid or the services are not performed? The shares are considered outstanding and validly issued, and the corporation has whatever claims it can assert under the contract or for the future benefits. Section 6.21(e) of the RMBCA permits the corporation to place the stock in escrow until the note is paid or the services performed, and to cancel the shares if there is a default.

The new, more permissive, rules on consideration are not universal. Several states adhere to the historical limitations and do not permit issuances for promissory notes or future services. Arizona provides an especially interesting example. Though it adopts the RMBCA definition for permissible forms of consideration—"any tangible or intangible property or interest"—it then specifically provides that promissory notes and future services are prohibited.[23]

---

[20] N.Y. BUS. CORP. LAW § 504(a) ("Consideration for the issue of shares shall consist of . . . labor or services actually received by or performed for the corporation . . . in its formation. . . .").

[21] Indeed, in Texas, these rules about the form of consideration for an issuance were enshrined in the state constitution. *See* Cope v. Pitzer, 166 S.W. 447, 452 (Tex. Ct. Civ. App. 1914) ("It will be noted that the inhibition prescribed by the Constitution and statutes is against the issuance of stock without the payment therefor in money, labor, or property . . .").

[22] *See, e.g.,* RMBCA § 6.21(b).

[23] ARIZ. STAT. § 10–621(B).

Remember that all of the rules discussed here concern an issuance—that is, the sale of stock by the corporation itself.

- Shareholder gives her stock in XYZ Corp. to her daughter as a gift—for *no consideration*. Is this valid? Yes. Remember, the rules we are learning about in this section are "issuance" rules—so they apply only when the corporation is selling its own stock. They do not apply to transfers by anyone other than the corporation itself.

Assuming the issuance is made for a valid form of consideration, the next question is whether it was made for a proper amount of consideration. This raises the subject of "par" and "no-par" stock. Par means that there is a minimum price at which the stock must be issued. No-par means there is no minimum issuance price; with no-par, the board of directors simply sets the issuance price.

Par value is set arbitrarily, and has no necessary correlation with the actual value (or even the issuance price) of the stock.

- XYZ Corp. issues 1,000 shares of $2 par stock. It must receive at least $2,000 for this issuance (because par is the minimum issuance price). If it receives less than $2,000, there will be liability for "watered stock," which we discuss below. Because par does not connote "maximum," however, the corporation may sell this stock for more than $2,000. The board will set the actual issuance price when it authorizes the issuance.

In theory, par stock protects creditors. The par value of any issuance goes into a fund called "stated capital," which can never be used to pay a distribution (like a dividend) to shareholders. Stated capital is a fund—a cushion—from which creditors can be paid. The problem is that the law never required par to be a particular amount. So corporations have always been free to set par at a nominal amount—say, at one-tenth of a penny.[24] Setting a low par gives the board greater flexibility in setting the actual issuance price, and avoids potential liability for "watered stock." It also means that the "stated capital" fund might be very small and offer no real protection to creditors. Recognizing this, most states—led by the RMBCA—have moved away from the "stated capital" requirement and, instead, imposed "insolvency" limitations on distributions to shareholders.[25]

---

[24] *See, e.g.*, Sample v. Morgan, 914 A.2d 647, 650 (Del. Ch. 2007) (discussing an amendment to articles that reduced the par value of stock from $1.00 per share to a tenth of a cent).

[25] RMBCA § 6.21.

We discuss this in section F, which deals with the validity of distributions.

Historically, corporations were permitted to issue only par stock. This started to change in the early twentieth century, when corporations were permitted to issue some par and some no-par. Today, however, no state requires that corporations have par stock, although companies may elect to have it.[26] The RMBCA has basically abolished the notion. So par is a concept of waning importance.

3. Determination of Value

Generally, the board of directors is responsible for determining the value of the consideration received for an issuance.[27] This is not a problem when the payment is made in money. Payments in property or services present the need for appraising the value of such consideration. Traditionally, the board's determination on the matter has been conclusive as to actual value, so long as the board acted in good faith (or, in some states, without fraud). This rule protects directors from liability if the board acted in good faith but set an erroneously high valuation.

This modern trend, typified by RMBCA § 6.21(c), does not require the board actually to set a price tag on consideration received for an issuance. Rather, it must merely determine that the consideration to be received "is adequate." This determination of adequacy is presumed when the board authorizes issuance at a given price and "is conclusive insofar as the adequacy of consideration for the issuance of shares relates to whether the shares are validly issued, fully paid, and nonassessable."[28] This provision emphasizes the decline in importance of par value.

- The board authorizes the corporation to issue 10,000 shares of $2 par to Shareholder in exchange for land worth $16,000. The board's approval of the issuance constitutes a finding that the land is "adequate" consideration for the issuance, and that finding is conclu-

---

[26] The number of par shares and the par value, like other characteristics of stock, is stated in the articles. *See* DEL. GEN. CORP. LAW § 102(a)(4). Because par is not required, why would anyone elect to have it? In part, the answer is force of habit. Lawyers have drafted articles containing provisions for par stock for generations, and some older lawyers are comfortable doing it that way. Moreover, for many years, federal stamp taxes were based upon the issuance price of no-par stock, but only on the par value of par stock, so there was once a tax advantage to issuing nominal par value stock. (Stamp taxes require payment for a government stamp, which must be affixed to a legal document to make it effective.)

[27] The articles of incorporation may grant the powers regarding issuances to shareholders instead of the board of directors. *See* RMBCA § 6.21(a).

[28] RMBCA § 6.21(c).

sive. So the issuance is valid and the stock is fully paid, notwithstanding that it is for less than par.

Remember from section B that the corporation might reacquire some of the stock it has issued. This reacquired, or "treasury" stock, is considered unissued, so the company can resell it. If it does, there is no minimum issue price, even if the original issuance was par stock.

- XYZ Corp. issued $2 par stock for $2 per share. Later, the corporation reacquired this stock. Now the corporation wants to issue this treasury stock. There is no minimum issuance price. The fact that this was $2 par stock was relevant to its original issuance, but is irrelevant now. This is an issuance of treasury stock, not par stock.

4. Watered Stock

We have just seen that the concept of par is less important than it used to be. In states not adopting the modern view on valuation, however, issuance of par stock gives rise to the problem of watered stock. Indeed, even under modern statutes, there is a modern analog to liability in this area.

Watered stock is a generic term, applicable when the corporation issues stock for an improper form of consideration or issues par stock for less than par value.[29] Technically, courts have used different terms for the various situations. The terms "unpaid" or "bonus" refer to stock issued for no consideration or for an improper form (such as for future services in a state that does not permit that form of payment for an issuance). "Discount" is par stock issued for money for less than par value, and "watered" (technically) is par stock issued for property for less than par value. These specific terms are rarely used anymore.

- The board of XYZ Corp. authorizes the issuance of 10,000 shares of $2 par stock to Shareholder for $16,000. Under the par rules, the corporation should have received $20,000. It actually received $16,000. So there is $4,000 of "water." The corporation can sue to recover that amount. Or, if the corporation is insolvent, creditors can sue to recover the $4,000.

---

[29] "Watered stock or fictitiously paid-up stock is stock which is issued as fully paid-up stock, when in fact the whole amount of the par value thereof has not been paid in." Lee v. Cameron, 169 P. 17, 20 (Okla. 1917).

Who is liable for the water? In other words, from whom can the $4,000 be recovered? First, directors who approved the issuance are jointly and severally liable. Second, the purchaser

is also jointly and severally liable, even if she did not actually know about the par value.[30] The reason for this relentless rule is that par value is established in the articles and printed on the stock certificates. Accordingly, the purchaser is charged with notice of par value and has no defense. Third, a transferee from the purchaser is not liable if she acts in good faith.[31] That means that she did not know about the issuance problem. She does not have to give value; she could, for instance, receive the stock by gift from the purchaser. As long as she is unaware of the problem, she is not liable for the water.

At common law, these liability rules were clear, although the theoretical basis for liability of the purchaser was not. Some courts spoke of par value creating a "trust fund" for the benefit of creditors and others imposed liability because the corporation has "held out" that the stock would not be issued for less than par. The theory is less important today because the general liability is imposed by statute.

Section 6.22(a) of the RMBCA provides that a shareholder who buys stock from the corporation is not liable to the corporation or its creditors "except to pay the consideration for which the shares were authorized to be issued" or to which she and corporation agreed in a subscription agreement. This statute means that the shareholder is liable if she pays less for the stock than the consideration set by the board when it authorized the issuance. So it imposes liability for the *issuance* price, and not for par value. It embodies the commonsense notion that one should pay what she agreed to pay.

---

[30] "Holders of watered stock are generally held liable to the corporation's creditors for the difference between the par value of the stock and the amount paid in." Bing Crosby Minute Maid Corp. v. Eaton, 297 P.2d 5, 7 (Cal. 1956).

[31] "[O]ne who is only a transferee of watered stock, and did not participate in the transaction whereby it was originally issued and who took his stock unaware of the character of that transaction, cannot be compelled to make good the false representation as to the capital of the company which he had no part in making. . . ." Rhode v. Dock-Hop Co., 194 P. 11, 16 (Cal. 1920).

5. Dilution and Pre-Emptive Rights

Within the limitations seen above, the board determines the price at which the corporation will issue stock.[32] The board has great discretion here.

> • The articles of YZ Corporation authorize it to issue 2,000 shares. Suppose the business wants an initial capitalization of $100,000. Y and Z—the individuals engaged in the business—agree that each will invest $50,000 and each will own one half of the stock. The board may issue each person one share, at an issuance price of $50,000. Or it may issue each person 10 shares, at an issuance price of $5,000. Or it may issue each person 100 shares, at an issuance price of $500. Y and Z probably do not care how many shares they have, so long as they each have the same number.

Assume Y and Z each get 100 shares at the issuance price of $500 per share. Later, suppose the corporation needs more capital to maintain or expand operations. Do Y and Z care about the issuance price of this stock? Absolutely. Suppose the corporation sells 100 shares to A at $50 per share. A will have gotten 100 shares—and will thus hold one-third of the equity in the corporation. He will be on an equal footing with Y and Z. Yet he will have paid only $5,000, which is one-tenth as much as Y and Z paid. This is an example of "dilution." The value of Y and Z's stock has been diluted by this low-priced issuance to A.

To a degree, this is a risk that any investor takes. But management may go too far if its dilutive issuance is oppressive. Dilutive issuance may be part of an effort to "freeze out" or "squeeze out" some shareholders, and may be actionable. Courts are understandably reluctant to second-guess business decisions, and will generally uphold issuances—even if they dilute present shareholders' interests— if they appear to be undertaken for corporate purposes. They will interfere, however, if the purpose is oppressive.

An example is *Byelick v. Vivadelli*,[33] which involved a corporation with three shareholders. Plaintiff owned 10 percent of the stock and defendants (a married couple) owned the other 90 percent; defendants were the only directors. There was a falling-out between the married couple, on the one hand, and the plaintiff, on the other.

---

[32] Statutes in some states permit the shareholders to do this if the articles allow. *See, e.g.,* MINN. STAT. § 302A.405, subdivision 1(a). Evidently, such provisions are rare.

[33] 79 F.2d 610, 613 (E.D. Va. 1999).

Defendants had the corporation issue additional stock—but only to themselves. The result was to reduce plaintiff's ownership from 10 percent to one percent. In denying summary judgment for the defendants, the court held that managers owe the minority shareholder a fiduciary duty not to cause the corporation to take an act that benefits themselves at the expense of the minority. This "dilutive transaction" was such an act.

One way the existing shareholder might be protected from dilution is with pre-emptive rights. These rights allow a shareholder to maintain her percentage of ownership by buying stock when there is a new issuance. She may buy her proportionate interest of the new issuance. The shareholder is not required to exercise her pre-emptive right, and she may waive it in writing.[34] If she exercises her right, she does not have to do so fully; thus, for instance, if she owns 20 percent of the company's stock, she may buy 20 percent or less of the new issuance. Like anyone else, she must pay the issuance price for the stock, as set by the board.

- X owns 1,000 shares of XYZ Corp. There are 4,000 shares outstanding. The board of directors of XYZ Corp. announces that it will issue an additional 1,000 shares. Right now, X owns 25 percent of the stock of the company (1,000 out of 4,000 outstanding shares). If the new issuance is made to others, X's percentage of ownership will be diluted to 20 percent (she will own 1,000 out of 5,000 outstanding shares). But if X has a pre-emptive right, she may buy her current percentage (25 percent) of the new issuance. The new issuance is 1,000 shares, so she may buy up to 250 shares of the new issuance.

Pre-emptive rights developed at common law. They are now a matter of statute in all states. Today, in most states, pre-emptive rights are permissive and not mandatory. That means that they exist only if the articles provide for them—if the company "opts in."[35] In some states, however, the opposite is true and pre-emptive rights apply unless the articles take them away—if the company "opts out."[36] In still other states, the general presumption is against pre-emptive rights unless the corporation qualifies as a "statutory close corporation."[37] In such specially-formed businesses, the presumption is that pre-emptive rights exist unless the articles say otherwise.

---

[34] *See* Gord v. Iowana Farms Milk Co., 60 N.W. 2d 820, 831 (Iowa 1953) (plaintiff did not waive pre-emptive right).

[35] *See, e.g.,* RMBCA § 6.30(a).

[36] *See, e.g.,* S.C. CODE § 33–6–300(a); MINN. STAT. § 302A.413, subdivision 1.

[37] *See, e.g.,* PA. CONS. STAT. § 2321(b).

The argument in favor of pre-emptive rights is a democratic one: those who buy the initial issuance should be entitled to maintain their percentage interest. In many instances, though, pre-emptive rights are a nuisance. Suppose, for example, that a corporation with a fairly large number of shareholders needs capital on short notice, and wants to obtain it by issuing stock. Having to offer it first to existing shareholders (to honor their pre-emptive rights) can be expensive and time-consuming. Accordingly, pre-emptive rights tend to apply in small closely held corporations. Even here, though, it may be easier and more effective to have shareholders enter agreements with the corporation concerning the right to purchase stock from a new issuance.

Moreover, as a practical matter, the protection afforded by pre-emptive rights is sometimes illusory. A minority shareholder may not be able to pay for the additional stock. Sometimes, the dominant shareholder will have lent money to the business. She can buy her allotment of a new issuance by forgiving the debt; that way, she can buy new stock without having to make a cash outlay. A minority shareholder will rarely be in that position. Unless she can make a plausible claim of oppression, the minority shareholder who cannot afford to pay for the additional shares is just out of luck—her interest will be diluted.[38]

In addition, there are statutory restrictions on pre-emptive rights. These vary somewhat from state to state, but here are some common limitations, applicable unless the articles provide otherwise. First, pre-emptive rights generally do not apply between different classes of stock. For instance, a holder of preferred shares will not have a pre-emptive right to buy common stock.[39]

Second, states disagree on whether pre-emptive rights attach to the issuance of treasury stock. Some deny pre-emptive rights on the issuance of treasury stock, apparently on the theory that issuing such stock does not injure existing shareholders because it merely restores ownership levels to what they were before the corporation reacquired the treasury stock.[40] Today, however, the majority view appears to be that pre-emptive rights attach to the issuance of "unissued" stock. Because treasury shares are "unissued," pre-emptive rights do attach.

---

[38] *See* Gentile v. Rossette, 906 A.2d 91, 103 (Del. 2006) (holding that a majority shareholder breached a fiduciary duty to minority shareholders by exchanging his debt for stock that had a greater value).

[39] *See* RMBCA § 6.30(b)(4)–(5).

[40] *See* FLA. STAT. § 607.0630(1).

Third, pre-emptive rights often do not apply to the issuance of stock originally authorized in the articles and issued within a set period—often six months—of incorporation.[41] This permits the corporation to raise capital early in its existence with multiple issuances without having to worry about honoring pre-emptive rights.

Fourth, pre-emptive rights generally do not attach to the issuance of "shares sold otherwise than for money."[42] Applying pre-emptive rights when there is an issuance for property or services could frustrate the corporation's ability to issue stock in exchange for specific property or services.

- Shareholder owns 20 percent of the outstanding stock of Corporation. Corporation is issuing stock to X to acquire land from X. The land is perfectly situated for Corporation's needs, and the price is fair. If Corporation were required to honor pre-emptive rights, and sell 20 percent of the new issuance to Shareholder, it would not be able to pay for the property with the issuance. So Shareholder should not and does not have a pre-emptive right on this issuance. Pre-emptive rights only make sense when a new issuance is for money. This is because money is fungible.

Sometimes, a shareholder may argue that an issuance for consideration other than money was undertaken to deprive her of pre-emptive rights. For example, Shareholder in the preceding hypothetical may argue that Corporation should have issued stock for money and used the money to buy the land from X. Issuing stock for money would mean, of course, that Shareholder's pre-emptive rights would be honored. Thus, some courts suggest that pre-emptive rights should attach unless the corporation can show a need for particular property and that issuing stock is the only feasible way to get it.

Fifth, pre-emptive rights usually do not apply to stock issued to directors, officers, or other employees as compensation. This includes stock issued pursuant to options held by such people.[43] Without this limitation, existing shareholders could claim some or all of the stock that was intended to be compensation for particular people.

---

[41] *See, e.g.,* RMBCA § 6.30(b)(3)(ii)(six months). In New York, pre-emptive rights do not attach to issuances of originally authorized shares sold within two years of formation. N.Y. BUS. CORP. LAW § 622(e)(5).

[42] RMBCA § 6.30(b)(3)(iii).

[43] RMBCA § 6.30(b)(3)(i)–(ii).

6. Venture Capital and Public Issuance

Most corporations are small affairs, with, at most, a handful of owners. The management authorizes issuance as the need for capital arises, and, usually, the existing shareholders purchase the stock. Here, we consider two other possibilities for issuance: use of venture capital (VC) and issuance to the public.

VC is a form of equity financing. Though VC funding was instrumental in high-tech companies for many years, it is not limited to such companies. VC is most often used to get businesses started when other sources of funds are not available. So if a bank will not make a loan and there is insufficient interest among the entrepreneur's circle of friends to get the business started, one might turn to VC. A VC firm buys a large portion of the company's stock. The issuance is private—not on the public market—and the VC firm is gambling that the business will succeed. Many do not. As a rule of thumb, one-third of VC-backed companies fail, one-third succeed, and one-third end up in "limbo"—getting by, but not excelling.[44] Because of the poor batting average, VC firms insist on high rates of return and demand a voice in management, which is usually guaranteed by their holding the majority of the voting stock.

Of course, the largest potential source of business funding is the public. So companies "go public" to raise capital by selling their stock on the public markets. Usually, such companies have a track record and profitability that warrants the conclusion that the public will buy the stock. So though the company has issued stock before, those were private placements. Now it plans its initial public offering (IPO).

Going public is expensive and time-consuming. The company must go through the "registration" process by which it qualifies to sell stock on the public markets. This requires a registration statement and prospectus filed with and approved by the Securities and Exchange Commission (SEC). Preparing these documents is sophisticated legal work, fraught with potential peril. There can be criminal and civil liability under federal law for misstatements or omissions in the prospectus.

In addition, the company must determine how much money it needs and how many shares to offer. This process is more difficult than it may sound because the company will attempt to hit a "sweet spot" for pricing in the market. It also must be careful to raise enough money without overreaching. It is troublesome for a corporation to announce an issuance target and then fail to raise that much

---

[44] *See generally* George W. Dent, *Venture Capital and the Future of Corporate Finance*, 70 WASH. U. L.Q. 1029, 1031–33 (1992).

money; the markets may react negatively to this fact. The company must engage an underwriter. This is typically an investment bank, which manages the process of drafting the offering memorandum to be filed with the SEC. The underwriter advises on structuring the offering, pricing, and maintaining a market for the company's stock.

Underwriters act on either a "firm commitment" or a "best efforts" basis. In the former, the underwriting firm itself buys all the stock in the public offering at the issuance price (minus a negotiated discount). The underwriter then resells the stock to the public. Here, the underwriter bears the risk that the public will not buy the stock at the offering price. It reduces the risk by not setting the issuance price until the last possible moment, when it has its best information on market interest. In a "best efforts" underwriting, the money invested comes from the public, and not the underwriter. Here, the corporation bears the risk that the stock will not fetch the offering price.[45]

D. Accounting and Financial Records

Every corporation is required to keep "appropriate accounting records," which generally are available for shareholder inspection.[46] Without accurate financial accounting, managers may fail to see problems until it is too late. There are three principal financial statements, and it is important to understand not only what they tell us about the business's fiscal health, but their limitations as well.[47]

1. The Income Statement

This record tells whether the business was profitable over a given period—usually one year. In short, it tells us if the business is "making money." The goal is to determine the profit before taxes (PBT) of the corporation. This is calculated by subtracting costs incurred from revenue generated during the period.

Assume that Corporation buys widgets at wholesale and sells them at retail. Assume for a given year that Corporation sold 10,000

---

[45] Whenever any corporation raises capital by selling shares, it is important that the offering not inadvertently become a public one (thereby triggering the registration requirements of these statutes) or that some exemption from registration under these statutes is available. The definition of a "public offering" and the scope of exemptions from registration raise complex legal issues. As a result, the risk of an inadvertent violation of these statutes is often very real.

[46] RMBCA § 16.01(b). Shareholders have the right to inspect other documents too. *See* Chapter 6(C)(8).

[47] In the real world, these documents may be far more difficult to understand than the examples we will see. In addition, there are other records that will be of use in assessing a business's fiscal health. These advanced considerations are covered in the course on Business Accounting.

widgets at $5 apiece. It had purchased those 10,000 widgets for $3 apiece. Corporation's revenue for the year was $50,000 (10,000 widgets multiplied by $5). Its costs for those widgets was $30,000 (10,000 widgets multiplied by $3). Thus, its PBT was $20,000, and its income statement would look like this:

Revenue	$50,000
minus Costs	$30,000
	————
PBT	$20,000

Now let us say the business was subject to income tax of 30 percent. Based upon its profit of $20,000 for the year, the tax would be $6,000. So to determine net income, we would take PBT ($20,000) minus taxes ($6,000), with the result being $14,000.

Next, let's suppose Corporation purchases a widget-making machine for $25,000. The machine will last for five years. If we executed the income statement as we did for the preceding year, we would subtract a cost of $25,000. This would be quite misleading, though, because even though Corporation spent $25,000 on the machine, it will be using the machine over five years. So it is not accurate to "cost" the entire machine this year. Instead, Corporation will use *depreciation*—it will record only one-fifth of the cost of the machine this year, and one-fifth next year, and so on for five years. This ensures that the income statement reflects that part of the machine "used up" each year.

This method is called "straight-line" depreciation, with equal amounts recorded each year for the five years. There is also something called "accelerated" depreciation, which is more appropriate for equipment that is "used up" unevenly, with more of the cost recorded in earlier years than later. We will stick with straight-line depreciation here.

So Corporation bought the machine for $25,000 and will depreciate it over five years. Now let us assume that Corporation manufactured and sold 40,000 widgets at $5 apiece, and paid $35,000 for raw materials and $60,000 in salary. The income statement of the year would look like this:

Revenue	$200,000 (40,000 widgets at $5)
minus Costs	$35,000 (raw materials)
minus Salary	$60,000
minus Depreciation	$5,000
	————
PBT	$100,000
Minus Taxes	$30,000 (30 percent)
	————
Net Income	$70,000

The income statement is helpful, but it has an important limitation. It does not necessarily tell us how much cash on hand the business has. This statement shows the company made $70,000 in the year. But the company does not have $70,000 in the bank. Why? Because it spent $25,000 on the widget-making machine, but only depreciated $5,000 of it. So it was out of pocket $20,000 more than appears in the income statement. To capture that reality, we turn to a second document.

2. The Cash Flow Statement

This statement tells us how much more (or less) cash the business actually has at the end of the year than it had at the beginning of the year. The cash flow statement and the income statement will be identical except when we have an item—like the widget-making machine—for which we take depreciation. When we have depreciation, we need to adjust the income statement to reflect that we depreciated a portion of the expense of the machine, but were actually out-of-pocket substantially more than that amount.

To make this adjustment, we start with the income statement's bottom line (net income) and *add* the amount we recorded as depreciation. Then *subtract* the amount actually paid for the machine. So here, we would start with the $70,000 net income figure. Add to that the depreciation we took on the income statement. Because that was $5,000, we now have $75,000. Now, we subtract the amount we actually paid for the machine—the out-of-pocket expense, which was $25,000. So the figure we end up with is $50,000. That means that though the corporation made $70,000 during the year, it has only $50,000 cash on hand.

Now let's suppose that the following year, the company performs in exactly the same way it did above. So its revenue is $200,000, from which we deduct costs of $35,000, salary of $60,000, and depreciation of $5,000. As last year, that gives us a PBT of $100,000. We pay the same tax as last year ($30,000), so we have the same net income of $70,000 as we did last year.

So the income statements for the two years are identical. But what about the cash flow statement for this more recent year? Start with the net income of $70,000. Then add the amount we took in depreciation, which was $5,000, so we are at $75,000. Now we subtract the amount we were out-of-pocket for the widget-making machine this year. That number is zero because the business paid nothing for that machine this year—the entire cost was out-of-pocket last year. So our bottom line on the cash flow statement is $75,000.

In sum, then, the company was equally profitable in each of these two years. But its cash flow position was much better in the second year. Though it had $50,000 cash on hand after the first year, it had $75,000 cash on hand after the second year. The difference is due to its getting the benefit of the widget-making machine for which it paid last year.

3. The Balance Sheet

As we just saw, the income and cash flow statements measure fiscal health over a period—usually a year. The balance sheet, in contrast, is a picture of how things stand at a particular moment. Thus, the balance sheet is a snapshot, and it records three things.

First are the business's *assets*. In this part of the balance sheet, we total the value of everything that belongs to the business. For example, its assets include the company's cash, land, buildings, accounts receivable, and equipment (minus any amount of depreciation on it that was reflected on the income statement). Accounts receivable consist of the money owed to the company by its customers.[48]

Second are the corporation's *liabilities*. This consists of everything the company owes, such as accounts payable, wages owed to employees, and indebtedness from borrowing.

Third is the *equity* in the business. This is what is left after subtracting liabilities from assets. It is equity because it is what the

---

[48] Accounts receivable are not depreciated, but may be "written off"—for example, if one of the customers has filed for bankruptcy.

owners of the business (the shareholders) "own." Equity is a number that will change over time, as the assets and liabilities change.

The assets appear on the left side of the balance sheet. The liabilities appear on the right side. Equity appears under the liabilities, also on the right side. It is a "balance" sheet because the left side (assets) and the right side (liabilities plus equity) always balance. By definition, they must balance because equity is the difference between the assets and the liabilities.

Suppose the business starts with $10,000 of cash invested by shareholders. The business assets consist of that $10,000, which is put on the left side of the balance sheet. What are the liabilities? There are none—because the business did not borrow the money, so it need not be paid back. So liabilities are zero. What is the equity? It is $10,000 (assets minus zero liabilities). So the balance sheet looks like this:

Assets		Liabilities
Cash	$10,000	$0
		Equity
		$10,000

Instead, assume the business started with $10,000, which it *borrowed*. That $10,000 is debt, and must be repaid. Therefore, it is a liability. So borrowing money increases the business assets— because it gives the business money. But it creates a liability too. The balance sheet would look like this:

Assets		Liabilities
Cash	$10,000	$10,000
		Equity
		$0

In the first scenario, if the business were liquidated today, the shareholder(s) would get the $10,000 in equity. In the second, the shareholders would get nothing. Remember that the balance sheet tells us the relationship of assets to liabilities at a specific moment. Using it in combination with the income statement and cash flow statement can give a sophisticated observer a great deal of information about the value and viability of a business.

E. Dividends and Other Distributions

1. Background

When a corporation is profitable, it faces a choice about what to do with the money it makes. It can plow that money back into the business—maybe to upgrade machinery or to expand into different cities or product lines—or it can give some of that money to its share-holders. This choice presents an issue on which reasonable people may disagree. It also presents an issue of basic corporate manage-ment, to be resolved by the board of directors.

A corporate payment to a shareholder is a "distribution." It is important to emphasize that a distribution is made to a shareholder in her role as shareholder—in other words, *because* she is a share-holder. Suppose a shareholder also happens to be an employee of the corporation. The corporation's paying wages to her is not a distribu-tion, because it is not being paid to her in her capacity as a share-holder.[49]

There are four types of distributions: dividends, repurchases of stock, redemptions of stock, and liquidating distributions. In this Chapter, we deal with the first three.[50] Some states do not employ different terms for the different types of distributions. For instance, the RMBCA does not use "dividend" at all, referring generically only to distributions.[51] Every state imposes statutory limits on when a corporation can make a distribution, which we see will in section F of this Chapter.

2. Dividends

The most common form of distribution is a dividend, which is a distribution of earnings to the shareholders. It is paid pro-rata by share, so someone with 100 shares will get twice as much in dividend payments as someone with 50 shares (assuming they hold stock in the same class).

What kinds of corporations pay dividends, and why do they do it? We tend to think of dividends as being paid by large publicly traded corporations. And, indeed, many do, but not all of them. Google does not pay dividends, and for many years, neither did Mi-crosoft. So if you invest in such companies, you hope to make money by selling the stock for more than you paid for it. Many large compa-

---

[49] Instead, this type of payment would be included on the income statement as an expense such as "salary" or "wages."

[50] The liquidating distribution is made to shareholders during dissolution, after creditors have been paid.

[51] RMBCA § 1.40(6).

nies, though—usually in more "traditional" businesses—have long histories of paying dividends. McDonald's, Consolidated Edison, and Procter & Gamble are a few of hundreds that have long paid dividends. These payments make the stock more attractive to investors. Not only might you make money by appreciation of the stock price, but the company will pay you in the meantime. And some of these dividends beat returns on such mundane investments as money markets and certificates of deposit. In the summer of 2012, Consolidated Edison, for instance, paid a dividend of nearly four percent, which is more than one can make with certificates of deposit at a bank.

Those public corporations that pay dividends usually do so every quarter, though some pay every six months and a few pay every month. These are called "regular" dividends. A "special" dividend, in contrast, is a one-shot, non-recurring payment. A special dividend that accompanies the payment of a regular dividend is called an "extra." In 2010, the clothing manufacturer Hot Topic declared a special dividend of $1 per share in addition to its regular dividend of seven cents per share. The special dividend was extraordinary because the stock was selling for about $7 per share—meaning that the special dividend constituted a 14 percent return, just for owning stock on the day the dividend was declared. The company received a great deal of positive press from this dividend policy because it showed management's confidence in the corporation.

Most closely held corporations do not pay dividends. But, again, this is a management decision, and the owners of a small business may decide to have the company declare dividends if they wish (assuming the legal tests (section F of this Chapter) are met).

Dividends are usually paid in cash, but can be paid in property (sometimes called "in kind" dividends). Regular dividends are almost always in cash, and special dividends are often in property. Property dividends must be paid in fungible property, such as shares of stock in a subsidiary or some other company in which the corporation has an investment. Or the corporation may issue debt instruments (essentially IOUs) to the stockholders, making them creditors for that amount.

Dividends may also be paid, however, in additional shares of the corporation itself. This "share dividend" is not a true distribution because no assets leave the corporation. With cash and property dividends, the corporation is actually giving up something of value. With share dividends, it is not. Instead, the share dividend merely increases the number of ownership units outstanding without affecting the corporate assets and liabilities. If a shareholder receiving a share dividend sells the new shares, she may view the transaction essentially as a cash dividend, since she owns the same number of shares as before and has, in addition, the cash received from the sale of the new shares. In fact, though, she now owns a slightly smaller percentage of the enterprise than she owned before the dividend. This is because the number of outstanding shares has increased by the number of new shares distributed. In most cases, this dilution will be so slight as to be unimportant.

Instead of a share dividend, the corporation might issue "rights" or "warrants." These are options to buy additional shares from the corporation at a set price (usually below the current market price). Like share dividends, these are also not true dividends. The shareholder who exercises the option must give capital to the corporation to maintain her percentage of ownership. If she does not do so, or if she sells the option (there is a public market for rights and options in publicly held corporations), her interest in the business will be diluted.

A share dividend should be distinguished from a stock "split." With a split, the corporation issues more stock to the shareholders, but the price of each share is correspondingly lowered.[52] Indeed, public companies often use stock splits to maneuver their stock price into its historical trading range. The economic effect of a stock split is nil.

- Corporation has 1 million outstanding shares, trading at $90 per share. This gives it a market capitalization of $90 million (outstanding shares multiplied by price per share). Corporation approves a 2-for-1 split. Each shareholder gets an additional share for every share she now has (so each will have two for every one she had before the split), but the market price of the stock is cut in half, to $45 per share. Thus, the market capitalization is still $90 million (two million outstanding shares multiplied by the new $45 per share price).

3. Is There a "Right" to a Dividend?

Shareholders have no right to a dividend until management declares it. At that point, the dividend becomes a debt of the corporation and cannot be rescinded.[53] The corporation owes the payment to the shareholders; they are creditors to that extent.

---

[52] *See* RMBCA § 6.23. Because the RMBCA eliminates the concept of par value, the distinction between a "split" and a "dividend" has not been retained and both types of transactions are referred to as "share dividends."

[53] *See* Staats v. Biograph Co., 236 F. 454, 458 (2d Cir. 1916) ("But if a board of directors should declare a cash dividend and make a public announcement of the fact,

If management declares a dividend, it is payable to shareholders as of the record date. We discussed record dates with regard to shareholder eligibility to vote in Chapter 6(C)(2). If the board fails to fix a record date, the date on which it authorized the dividend will be treated as the record date.[54] There will be a gap between the record date and the "payable date," which is when payment is actually made. A gap of two or three weeks is common. Transfers of stock during that gap are irrelevant to the corporation—it pays the shareholder as of the record date.

- The board of Corporation declares a dividend on April 7, to be paid on April 24. X owns stock in Corporation on April 7, and sells it to Y on April 8. On April 24, Corporation will pay X because she owned the stock on the record date. The fact that Y owns it as of the payable date does not matter.

Minority shareholders in closely held corporations are often unhappy with management's dividend policy. For one thing, as minority shareholders, they have no "say" in managing the company. For another, because there is no public market for the stock, it is difficult for them to sell their stock at all, much less at a profit. Unless the corporation hires this person and pays her a salary, the only way a minority shareholder in a closely held corporation can get any return on her investment is through dividends.[55] And, as noted, these are declared in the discretion of management.

We saw in Chapter 4(E) that "C Corporations" pay income tax on their earnings, while "S Corporations" do not. In determining their income tax liability, C Corporations can deduct salaries paid to corporation employees, but they cannot deduct dividends. Accordingly, managing shareholders of a closely held corporation have an incentive to use earnings to pay themselves salaries rather than to declare dividends: they get the money, and the company gets a tax deduction.

But even with the S Corporation, there is a problem for the minority shareholder. In an S Corporation, each shareholder must include as income on her personal income tax return her share of corporate earnings. This is true even if she received no dividends. Thus, the fact that the corporation made money will increase the

---

the courts have held that thereafter the board has no right to reconsider and rescind its action.").

[54] *See, e.g.*, RMBCA § 6.40(b).

[55] This assumes that the business is not sold or dissolved, in which case all shareholders would receive their pro-rata share of the net assets.

shareholder's tax liability, and the lack of dividends means that she receives no cash to help pay that tax liability. So minority shareholders in closely held corporations can find themselves with serious cash-flow problems. One solution is a provision in the articles or by-laws that requires the corporation (assuming it meets the legal test for declaring a distribution) to pay a dividend at least equal to the amount of additional taxes incurred by each shareholder as a result of the allocation of S Corporation income to them. These dividends are called "tax distributions."

Like any management decision, the determination of whether to pay dividends will be assessed under the business judgment rule.[56] This means that courts are reluctant to second-guess such a decision. Judges lack expertise concerning optimal dividend policy in a particular business. Clearly, then, shareholders who sue to compel the declaration of a dividend are fighting an uphill battle.

On the other hand, the business judgment rule can be overcome in cases of self-dealing, bad faith, or other egregious circumstances.[57] So it is possible for a minority shareholder to prevail, but only on a strong showing. For instance, if she can show that the corporation is thriving and the board continually refuses to declare dividends while paying its members (who are the majority shareholders) large salaries or bonuses, she might convince a court to compel the declaration of a dividend. In such a case, the majority is oppressing the minority by diverting earnings to themselves at the expense of the minority.

Even in such cases, the plaintiff is swimming upstream, unless the defendants have been brazen or outspoken in their efforts to freeze out the minority shareholders. Courts have no ready standard for deciding how much may be paid in dividends and how much should be retained for contingencies and future growth. So even when there is a finding of bad faith in refusing to pay a dividend, judges will be cautious in setting the amount to be paid.

To our knowledge, there is only one case in which a court forced the declaration of a dividend without a strong showing of abuse or bad faith. It involved the relatively early years of the stunningly successful Ford Motor Company. For years, it paid phenomenal dividends—in some years exceeding the price of the stock itself! After years of regular and special dividends, Henry Ford had the company

---

[56] *See* Gabelli & Co. v. Liggett Group, Inc., 479 A.2d 276, 280 (Del. 1984) ("It is settled law in this State that the declaration and payment of a dividend rests in the discretion of the corporation's board of directors in the exercise of its business judgment; that, before the courts will interfere with the judgment of the board of directors in such matter, fraud or gross abuse of discretion must be shown.").

[57] *See* Maul v. Kirkman, 637 A.2d 928, 938–39 (N.J. Super. Ct. App. Div. 1994) (holding that directors acted in bad faith when they refused to declare dividends).

stop making the distributions. He wanted to use the money to expand corporate manufacturing capacity with its River Rouge plant in Detroit. Minority shareholders sued. They were brothers, named Dodge. They sued to force Ford to resume the payment of dividends. They were using their Ford dividends to start their own automobile company. It became Dodge Motors, which is now a division of Chrysler.

In *Dodge v. Ford Motor Co.*,[58] the Michigan Supreme Court ordered Ford to pay dividends. In part, Henry Ford sealed his own fate when he testified at trial about his desire not to make money but to do social good. Had he gotten on the stand and said the company would make more money if it invested earnings in expanded capacity, it is doubtful that any court would have compelled the dividend. But Ford, obsessed with his legacy and with not being seen as a robber baron, testified that it was his social duty to make low-priced cars, and said little about business judgment. That, combined with the court's own view of desirable social policy, led to the result.

4. Classes of Stock and Dividends

Of course, all corporations issue stock. In most corporations, there is only one class—called common stock. Each share carries one vote on those matters on which shareholders get to vote, and if there is a dividend, each share gets a pro-rata part of it. But the articles can create different classes of stock with different rights to a declared distribution. Even though the business can have different classes of stock, at least one class must have the right to receive the net assets upon dissolution. In other words, the articles cannot provide that when the company dissolves, no shareholders will get what is left after creditors are paid off. Usually, the class that is entitled to vote and the class that is entitled to net assets upon dissolution are the same class (called common stock), but this need not be so. In determining which shareholders receive dividends, we expand our vocabulary by discussing "preferred," "participating," and "cumulative." Stock that is not given one or more of these characteristics is "common" stock.

Preferred Stock. "Preferred" means "pay first." (It does not mean "pay more.") So a class of stock with a dividend preference must be paid first, before the common stock. Depending upon the size of the dividend pool, the preferred shares may end up getting more than the common shares, or perhaps not. The preference is usually stated in dollar terms (though it could be stated as a percentage, for example, of par value).

---

[58] 170 N.W. 668, 685 (Mich. 1919).

- Corporation declares a dividend of $40,000. It has a class of preferred stock with a dividend preference of $2; there are 2,000 outstanding shares in this class. Corporation also has 10,000 common shares outstanding. The 2,000 preferred shares are entitled to their $2 preference first, before the common shares get anything. So multiply the 2,000 shares times the $2 preference. This is a total of $4,000, which is paid to the preferred shares. That leaves $36,000 (from the pool of $40,000) to go to the common shares. Because there are 10,000 of those, each common share gets $3.60.

So in this hypothetical, the common shares get more money than the preferred. That is fine; remember, preferred does not mean pay more. But if that is the case, why do people want to hold preferred stock? Because they know that they are first in line. Suppose, for example, in the previous hypothetical, that Corporation declared a dividend of $10,000. There, the preferred shares would get the first $4,000, as we just saw. That would leave $6,000 for the common stock. Because there are 10,000 such shares, the common would only get 60 cents per share. Whether the preferred shares get more money than common will depend upon the size of the dividend pool. But they have the comfort of knowing that they are first in line if the corporation pays a dividend.

Remember, there is no right to a dividend until the board declares it; so having preferred stock does not entitle the shareholder to compel payment. It is not like holding debt, in which case the holder is a creditor and can demand payment in accordance with the debt agreement, as we saw in section B. In practice, preferred stock usually does not carry voting rights, but the articles can provide whatever the corporation wants in this regard. Also, it is typical to have different classes of preferred stock, often designated by letter: Class A preferred, Class B preferred, etc.

Preferred stock can also have other characteristics. Specifically, it can be participating or cumulative. These characteristics are discussed below, and are in addition to the entitlement to be paid first among the classes of stock.

Preferred Participating Stock. Participating means "pay again." So preferred participating stock not only gets paid first, it also gets paid again—meaning that it participates with the common shares after the preference has been paid.

- Corporation declares a dividend of $40,000. It has a class of preferred stock with a dividend preference of $2

> *that is also participating*; there are 2,000 outstanding
> shares in this class. Corporation also has 10,000 com-
> mon shares outstanding. The 2,000 preferred shares are
> entitled to their $2 preference first—before the common
> shares get anything. So we multiply the 2,000 shares
> times the $2 preference. This is a total of $4,000, which
> is paid to the preferred shares. That leaves $36,000
> (from the pool of $40,000).

Here, the $36,000 does not go to the common stock alone (as it
did in the hypothetical we did before). Instead, because the 2,000
shares of preferred are *also* participating, they participate with the
common stock in the $36,000. So that $36,000 is divided by 12,000
shares—this consists of the 10,000 common *plus* the 2,000 preferred
participating. Dividing $36,000 by 12,000 shares equals $3 per
share. So here, the common get $3 per share. The preferred partici-
pating get $5 per share. Why? Because they got $2 in their preferred
capacity and $3 more in their participating capacity.

Holders of common stock do not like the fact that the preferred
shares are participating because it means the common holders must
share "their" dividend with shares that have already been paid. By
contrast, holders of preferred stock love to have participating shares
as well because they not only get paid a set amount first, but get to
share in what is left. Again, all of this is set up in the articles.

Cumulative Preferred Stock. Cumulative means "pay again."
This means that a preferred dividend accrues from year-to-year.
Most dividends are not cumulative, so if they are not declared in a
given year, the shareholder never gets it. But holders of a preferred
cumulative dividend need not worry—the "meter is running" on their
preference, and it adds up each year until the board finally does order
a dividend.

> • Corporation declares a dividend of $40,000. It has a
> class of preferred stock with a dividend preference of $2
> *that is also cumulative*; there are 2,000 outstanding
> shares in this class. Corporation also has 10,000 com-
> mon shares outstanding. The corporation does not pay a
> dividend in 2011, 2012, and 2013. It finally declares a
> dividend in 2014. Those 2,000 shares of preferred cumu-
> lative stock are entitled to be paid first (after all, that's
> what preferred means), and they are entitled to be paid
> for *four years of their $2 preference* (because it was add-
> ing up for the cumulative shares for 2011, 2012, and
> 2013—plus the corporation owes them the preference for
> 2014, when it declared the dividend).

- So the corporation owes the preferred cumulative shares $8 each (that is, four years of the $2 preference). There are 2,000 such shares. Multiply the 2,000 shares times the $8 per share, and we get a total of $16,000. So the first $16,000 goes to the preferred cumulative stock. That leaves $24,000 (from the pool of $40,000). That $24,000 goes to the common stock. There are 10,000 common shares, so they get $2.40 per share.

If we wanted to do so (and provided for it in the articles), we could also give those preferred cumulative shares a right to participate. There, the $24,000 left after paying the cumulative preferred dividend would be divided by 12,000 shares. This would consist of the 10,000 common plus the 2,000 preferred cumulative participating shares.

Again, there is no right to a dividend until it is declared. So unpaid cumulative preferred dividends are not a debt owed by the corporation. Instead, they have a continued right to priority when dividends are declared in the future. The board of directors may defer preferred cumulative dividends indefinitely if it is willing to forego dividends on the common shares as well. Usually, common stock is the only voting stock, so doing so may make the electorate angry. On the other hand, it is possible to provide in the articles that holders of preferred cumulative stock have the right to elect a certain number of directors if dividends are not paid for a specified period.[59]

Other Terminology—Series and Convertible. A corporation may have *series* of preferred stock. A series is a sub-class, so the corporation could have preferred stock "series A" and "series B," etc. The difference between a series and a class is usually the manner of creation. Classes of preferred stock are created in the articles, while series may be in the articles or created by the board on its own (if the articles allow).[60]

When the board creates a series, it carves out a sub-class of preferred shares from an authorized class of preferred stock. Such shares are also called "blank shares" because no terms are specified in the articles provision that creates the class. The board may vary the substantive terms of each series to take into account changing economic conditions. The importance of the power to create series of preferred shares escalated in the 1980s with the development of the

---

[59] It is possible to have partially cumulative dividends. These are usually "cumulative to the extent of earnings," which means it adds up to the extent the corporation had earnings sufficient to pay a dividend. It would not be cumulative, though, to the extent that earnings fail to cover the dividend.

[60] *See* RMBCA § 6.02.

so-called "poison pill" defensive tactic against unwanted takeover attempts. A poison pill creates a new series of preferred stock, triggered by some external event. Usually, the trigger is when an outside aggressor acquires a given percentage of the company's stock. To stave off the takeover attempt, the corporation issues new series of preferred stock to existing shareholders (but not to the aggressor). Doing so dilutes the percentage of stock held by the aggressor, and makes it more difficult for her to take over the corporation.

Preferred stock may be *convertible* into common shares at a specified price or specified ratio. Typically, the original conversion ratio is established when the class of preferred is created; the conversion price is usually set at a level that requires the common to appreciate substantially in value before it becomes profitable to convert the preferred. When the price of the common rises above the conversion price, the preferred shares will thereafter fluctuate in price in tandem with price fluctuations of the common. A conversion is said to be "forced" when shares are called for redemption at a time when the value of the shares obtainable on conversion exceeds the redemption price.

Historically, statutes in some states prohibited conversion from one class of stock to a class with superior rights or preferences in dividends or upon liquidation. These statutes thus prohibited "upstream" conversions, while allowing "downstream" conversions—conversions, for instance, from preferred to common stock. The RMBCA and the law of most states no longer impose such restrictions.[61]

5. Repurchases and Redemptions

Here we consider two ways a corporation can reacquire stock that it has issued. First, it may negotiate to repurchase stock from individual shareholders. Second, it may have a right to redeem stock from a class of shareholders at a price set in the articles. Each is a "distribution" because the corporation is making a payment to a shareholder in her capacity as a shareholder. In each, the purpose of the distribution is to buy back her stock. Either transaction decreases the worth of the corporation because it makes a distribution for which it receives no assets in return. It simply receives what is now unsold stock.

Repurchases. Repurchases are individually negotiated. If the corporation reacquires a proportional part of each shareholder's stock, the result is the equivalent of a dividend; each shareholder gets a pro-rata distribution. But most repurchases are not proportional.

---

[61] *See* RMBCA § 6.01(c)(2); DEL. GEN. CORP. LAW § 151(b).

The result is to increase the proportional ownership of those share-holders whose stock is not repurchased.

- A, B, C, D, and E each own 20 percent of the stock of Corpo-ration. If Corporation buys all of E's stock, the remaining four shareholders will each own 25 percent of the stock.

As discussed in section B, reacquired stock, or "treasury stock," is not considered "outstanding" for purposes of shareholder voting or dividends. So after the corporation repurchases these shares, it does not vote them, and does not receive dividends on them.[62]

- S owns 100 shares of Corporation. On June 8, Corporation buys S's stock from S. June 10 is the record date for voting at the annual meeting and for a dividend. Because S was not the record owner on the record date, S has no right to vote at the annual meeting and has no right to the dividend. Though Corporation was the record owner of this "treasury" or "reac-quired" stock on the record date, Corporation is not entitled to vote the stock or to receive a dividend.

The corporation can then sell these shares. The sale is an issu-ance, and must comport with the issuance requirements we saw in section C. The corporation's assets are increased by the purchase price. If the sale is to the present shareholders in their current pro-portion, their interests will not be diluted. If, however, the sale is to third parties, present shareholders' ownership and voting power will be diluted. Remember that pre-emptive rights may permit the pre-sent shareholders to avoid such dilution by purchasing their current percentage of this issuance.[63]

Because repurchases usually are not proportional, they provide a distribution to one shareholder and not another. In closely held cor-porations, repurchases may be the only hope a shareholder has of a return on her investment. Usually, there are no dividends and, obvi-ously, there is no public market on which she can sell her stock. So unless she can get the corporation to buy her stock, she may be stuck with an illiquid asset.[64]

Corporations must be careful not to engage in unfair behavior in repurchasing stock. Under the "equal opportunity" doctrine— followed in some states—a corporation offering to buy back one shareholder's stock must make the same proportional offer to others.

---

[62] The shares are not considered outstanding. *See, e.g.,* RMBCA § 6.31(a).

[63] Note further than states take different approaches to whether pre-emptive rights attach to an issuance of treasury stock.

[64] This is one reason the parties should consider a buy/sell agreement, as we saw in Chapter 8(C). The agreement will facilitate sale of her stock to the corporation.

In *Donahue v. Rodd Electrotype Company of New England, Inc.,*[65] management of a closely held corporation bought back about half the stock owned by the founder of the company. The founder was 77 years old, wanted to retire, and needed the money. Management, which consisted of his children, was happy to facilitate, and had the corporation pay $36,000 to their father for his stock. At this point, a minority shareholder offered to sell her stock back to the corporation at the same price per share. Management refused, and the minority shareholder brought a direct action against the corporation and managers for oppression.[66]

The Massachusetts Supreme Judicial Court upheld the claim, noting that shareholders in a closely held corporation owe each other a fiduciary duty of good faith and fair dealing akin to that in a partnership.[67] That duty requires the corporation to provide "equal opportunity" to the minority shareholder to resell her stock.[68] That court has retreated a bit from the broad language of the *Donahue* opinion, but the case stands as a cautionary beacon on repurchases. Unfair treatment of similarly situated shareholders concerning distributions may invite litigation over possible breaches of fiduciary duty.

Publicly held corporations may repurchase their own shares to retire them. Here, the company judges that the market has for some reason undervalued its stock. Retiring the shares at a bargain price will increase the earnings per share of the remaining shares. This often results in raising the price of the stock as well, since the market sees it as a very good sign that management is buying back stock. On the other hand, a corporation may buy its own stock for other reasons, such as to evade a hostile takeover. By driving up the price of the stock, the corporation hopes to make it more difficult for an aggressor to succeed in a tender offer. Or the insurgent group may be willing to accept "greenmail" (a colorful name for blackmail), which means the corporation will buy the insurgents' stock to make them go away.

Redemption of Stock. Shares can be made redeemable at a specified price. The redemption is a forced sale, usually at the behest of the corporation, at a price set in the articles.[69] When the board exer-

---

[65] 328 N.E.2d 505, 508 (Mass. 1975).

[66] *Id.* at 511.

[67] *Id.* at 515.

[68] *Id.* at 519.

[69] The articles could also specify that the shares are redeemable at the owner's (rather than the corporation's) option. *See* RMBCA § 6.01(c)(2)(i). Indeed, preferred stock is sometimes redeemable at the option of the shareholder at a specified price. Such stock has the general economic characteristics of a demand promissory note, so it is an example of an equity security that functions like a debt security.

cises the redemption power, the shareholders' rights shift from holding an equity interest in the corporation to holding a contractual right to receive the redemption price.

Historically, only preferred stock could be redeemable. The fear with redeemable common stock is that management could call for redemption to eliminate antagonistic shareholders. The RMBCA does not prohibit redeemable common stock, but remember that the corporation must always have at least one class of stock entitled to receive the net corporate assets upon dissolution, so not all stock can be redeemable.

F. Statutory Limitations on Distributions and Liability for Improper Distributions

1. Background

All states limit a corporation's power to declare distributions. In some states, the rules vary a bit depending on the type of distribution, so the rules for dividends are slightly different from those for repurchases and redemptions. In general, however, the limitations are the same for all forms of distribution, be it dividend, repurchase, or redemption. The limitations are intended to protect creditors. In theory, they ensure that the corporation cannot dole out money to its shareholders to the detriment of creditors.

The law has changed dramatically in this area. Historically, states imposed "fund" restrictions on when a corporation could declare a distribution. That is, distributions could be paid from certain funds and not from others. As we will see, the fund restrictions reflect the historic use of par stock. Because par stock has waned in importance, the fund restrictions are now relevant in fewer and fewer states. Nonetheless, some important commercial states, including Delaware, New York, and Texas, still use it.[70] We consider it immediately below. After discussing the fund restrictions, we will address the modern view, which permits distributions unless the corporation is "insolvent."

2. Traditional ("Fund") Limitations

Among the dwindling number of states in which the fund restrictions are relevant, there is some variation in how the rules work. What we discuss here is the typical model. It recognizes three funds: earned surplus, stated capital, and capital surplus. To start with a conclusion, distributions can be paid from earned surplus and capital surplus, but never from stated capital. These funds require us to fo-

---

[70] *See* RMBCA § 6.40(c).

cus on two ways in which a corporation can make money. One, it can do well in the real world, by selling widgets (or doing whatever the company does). The "earned surplus" fund is relevant to this. Two, it can raise capital by issuing stock. The "stated capital" and "capital surplus" funds are relevant to this.

Earned surplus is a composite income item determined by combining all net profits, income, gains, and losses during each accounting period going back to the creation of the corporation, then reducing that number for expenses, prior dividends, and transfers to other accounts. In short terms, then, it consists of all earnings minus all losses minus distributions previously made. If a corporation has earned surplus, it is doing well in the real world. It is selling widgets. It is a success in its market. Distributions may always be paid from earned surplus.

Stated capital and capital surplus are funds generated by the issuance of stock. Remember from section C that issuance is when the corporation sells its own stock, and it must receive consideration from that sale. Every penny of consideration is then allocated between stated capital and capital surplus. The allocation is important because capital surplus may be used for a distribution, but stated capital cannot. How is the allocation made?[71]

If the distribution is of par stock, the par value of the issuance is stated capital and the excess over par value is capital surplus. If it is a no-par issuance, the board allocates between stated capital and capital surplus. Usually, the board must act within a given period—say, 60 days—after the issuance and may allocate any part, but not all, to capital surplus. If the board does not act, the entire consideration from the no-par issuance goes into stated capital.

- Corporation issues 10,000 shares of $2 par stock for $50,000. Of this, $20,000 is allocated to stated capital. Why? Because that is the par value of the issuance (10,000 shares multiplied by $2 par). The excess over par value (here, $30,000) goes into capital surplus.

- Corporation issues 4,000 shares of no-par stock for $40,000. If the board does nothing, the entire $40,000 will be allocated to stated capital. If it desires, however, the board can allocate the $40,000 as it sees fit between stated capital and capital surplus.

Stated capital cannot be used for a distribution because it is a cushion to protect creditors. But it might not be much of a cushion.

---

[71] *See* DEL. GEN. CORP. LAW § 154.

After all, the corporation may set par value of par stock at a fraction of a penny. Or it may simply issue no-par stock and allocate the vast majority of the issuance to capital surplus. It is not clear, then, that the traditional fund approach ever did what it was supposed to do.

Under the fund approach, distributions are proper from "surplus"—either earned surplus or capital surplus. Again, earned surplus is generated by business success, while capital surplus is generated by issuing stock. A distribution may always come from earned surplus. But some states impose restrictions on the use of capital surplus. Commonly, the shareholders must be informed if their distribution is being paid from capital surplus.[72] In some states, the articles must provide that distributions may be paid from capital surplus. One typical use of capital surplus is to pay holders of cumulative preferred stock to discharge the cumulative rights. This permits the company to avoid building up preferred arrearages during the early years of operation when there may be no earned surplus.

In some states, there is no distinction between "earned" and "capital" surplus.[73] In those jurisdictions, they are not separate funds. Instead, there is just "surplus" and "stated capital." Surplus consists of net assets minus stated capital. Stated capital is exactly as defined above. And, of course, distributions may be paid from surplus but not from stated capital.

Some states permit distributions from current profits even if there is an earnings deficit from the operations during prior periods.[74] In other words, even though there is no earned surplus, the company is making some money currently. Payment of a dividend from this current profit is called a "nimble dividend." The leading case is *Goodnow v. American Writing Paper Co.*,[75] which permitted the corporation to use current earnings to pay a dividend rather than pay down debts. Some states do not permit nimble dividends.

States adopting the fund approach to distributions also impose a further requirement: a distribution is improper if the corporation was insolvent or would be rendered insolvent by the distribution. These states adopt only the "equity" test for insolvency, which will be discussed in the next subsection.

---

[72] *See* LA. REV. STAT. § 63(A).

[73] *See* MO. STAT. § 351.220; N.Y. BUS. CORP. LAW § 506(a).

[74] *See* DEL. GEN. CORP. LAW § 170(a).

[75] 69 A. 1014, 1016 (N.J. Ct. Err. & App. 1908).

3. The Modern ("Insolvency") Approach

The RMBCA has changed the law on distributions dramatically. A majority of states now adopts the RMBCA approach, in which the various funds we just considered are irrelevant. The fund limitations are replaced by insolvency limitations. Thus, a distribution is improper only if the corporation is insolvent at the time of the distribution or if the distribution will render it insolvent.[76]

The RMBCA prescribes two tests for insolvency. They are alternatives, so the distribution is improper if either is met at the time of the distribution. First is what some courts call the "equity test" for insolvency: the corporation is insolvent if it is unable to pay its debts as they become due in the ordinary course of business.

Second is what many call the "bankruptcy" or "balance sheet" test for insolvency: the distribution is unlawful if the corporation's assets exceed its liabilities plus the amount that would be needed to pay liquidation preferences if the company dissolved today. As we saw in section E, a preference means that this class of stock is to be paid first, before other shares. A liquidation preference is paid when the corporation dissolves, after it has paid its creditors.[77]

- Corporation has assets of $250,000 and liabilities of $200,000. Corporation has a class of stock of 1,000 shares with a $5 liquidation preference. If Corporation dissolved today, it would need $5,000 to pay the liquidation preferences (1,000 shares multiplied by $5 preference). The balance sheet test for insolvency equates liquidation preferences with liabilities. So Corporation has $250,000 in assets. It has liabilities of $200,000 and the liquidation preference would be $5,000. Assets ($250,000) minus liabilities plus liquidation preferences ($205,000) equals $45,000. So under this test, Corporation can make a distribution of up to $45,000.

---

[76] RMBCA § 6.40(c)(1)–(2). "The board of directors may base a determination that a distribution is not prohibited under subsection (c) either on financial statements prepared on the basis of accounting practices and principles that are reasonable in the circumstances or on a fair valuation or other method that is reasonable in the circumstances." RMBCA § 6.40(d).

[77] Thus, a liquidation preference works the same as a dividend preference—the holder is entitled to be paid first, before the holders of common stock. The difference between a dividend preference and a liquidation preference is timing. A dividend preference is paid when the corporation pays a dividend. A liquidation preference is relevant when the corporation is going out of business. It liquidates its assets, pays its creditors, and distributes the remainder to shareholders. See Chapter 12(H). Dividend and liquidation preferences are established in the articles.

4. Liability for Improper Distributions

Directors who assent to the declaration of a distribution are liable to the extent the distribution was improper.[78] For instance, in the hypothetical immediately above, Corporation may properly declare a distribution of $45,000. Suppose the board of directors approved a distribution of $60,000. It would be unlawful to the extent of $15,000. Directors would be jointly and severally liable for that $15,000. The suit to recover that money would be derivative because it is brought on behalf of the corporation. If a plaintiff sued one of several directors, and recovered a judgment which that director paid, that director may seek contribution from other board members who also assented to the distribution. In this regard, remember that directors are presumed to have concurred with board action unless they dissent in writing. So any director who dissented in writing would not be liable. In addition, directors may rely in good faith on information provided by officers and professionals. This defense may be especially relevant in cases concerning improper distributions.

Historically, director liability for improper distributions has been strict. That is still the rule in many states. There is a trend, however, led by the RMBCA, toward holding directors liable only upon proof that they breached a duty to the corporation by making the distribution. Section 8.33(a) provides that directors who approved what turns out to be an unlawful distribution are liable only if the plaintiff "establishes that when taking the action the director did not comply with section 8.30," which, as we saw in Chapter 7, imposes the duties of care and loyalty and the obligation of good faith.

Shareholders generally are liable for unlawful distributions only to the extent that they knew *when they received it* that it was improper. To that extent, the shareholder must return the distribution to the corporation.[79] If a shareholder finds out after the fact that the distribution was unlawful, she does not have to return it.

What we discussed to this point are statutory limitations on distributions. Many restrictions, however, will be contractual. Creditors of a corporation may be nervous about dissipation of corporate assets through distributions. It is common, therefore, for businesses entering deals or borrowing money to agree to restrict distributions. Such restrictions vary widely. If the debtor is publicly held with an established history of regular dividend payments, the agreement may

---

[78] The board of directors must only use a valuation method that is "reasonable under the circumstances." *See* RMBCA 6.40(d).

[79] *See* RMBCA § 8.33(b)(2) (directors are entitled to "recoupment from each shareholder of the pro-rata portion of the amount of the unlawful distribution the shareholder accepted").

permit dividends of specified amounts provided that certain ratios are maintained between assets and liabilities, or between current assets and current liabilities. Closely held corporations may agree to prohibit all distributions, or even to impose restrictions on salaries, as a condition of entering a contract or getting a loan.

The corporation's articles may address distributions. For example, articles may protect preferred shares by limiting the amount that can be paid to common shares, or by requiring that a portion of earnings be set aside as a sinking fund to be used to retire a portion of the preferred dividend each year. Preferred shareholders otherwise receive scant protection, because, as we discussed above, claims to dividends—even preferred cumulative dividends—are not corporate debts. They are merely a priority position in future distributions that may never be declared.

Chapter 11

POTENTIAL LIABILITY IN SECURITIES TRANSACTIONS

Analysis

A. Introduction
B. State Law
    1. From Fraud to a Fiduciary Duty to Disclose
    2. Insider Trading in the Market
C. Rule 10b–5—Background and Elements
    1. The Provision and Who Can Enforce It
    2. Potential Defendants
    3. Elements in a Rule 10b–5 Claim
    4. Types of Fraudulent Behavior Covered
D. Section 16(b)
    1. Differences from Rule 10b–5
    2. Application of § 16(b)

A. Introduction

In Chapter 9(B), we addressed aspects of federal securities law in the public corporation—registration and reporting requirements, Sarbanes-Oxley, proxy solicitation, and hostile takeover rules. We noted that the underlying policy of federal securities law is disclosure—that truthful information protects the investing public. In this Chapter, we focus on state and federal law aimed at fraudulent behavior in the trading of securities. This behavior might occur not only in connection with the initial issuance by the corporation, but also in the secondary market for resales.

Common law fraud allows one to sue if another has made a material misrepresentation (a lie) on which the victim reasonably relies to her detriment.[1] This applies in securities transactions as much as in the sale of cars. But fraud does not apply to someone who trades on the basis of something she knows and that the other side to the deal does not know. This person, who trades on "inside information," does not tell a lie. Indeed, she doesn't say anything—and thus cannot

---

[1] There can also be an action for fraud if someone has a duty to disclose but remains silent. In our discussion of common law fraud throughout this Chapter, we will assume that there was no duty to disclose and thus that the claim would be for an affirmative misrepresentation.

be liable for fraud. But the law has developed to impose liability in
some situations on this "insider trader." State common law made the
first steps here, and federal law has gone much farther by imposing
upon the "insider" (and we need to define that) a duty either to disclose what she knows or to forego trading.

The first cousin to insider trading is "tipping." Here, the insider
does not use the information to trade on her own account. Instead,
she "tips" a friend or acquaintance, who trades on the tip. State and
federal law may impose liability on the "tipper" and the "tippee."

We start this Chapter with a discussion of state law in section B.
Then we address two important federal provisions, Rule 10b–5,
promulgated by the SEC under § 10(b) of the 1934 Act as a general
anti-fraud measure, and § 16(b) of the same Act. Section 16(b) is expressly aimed at insider trading. Rule 10b–5 was not, but has been
interpreted to proscribe insider trading and tipping more effectively
than § 16(b). Rule 10b–5 has generated a great deal of litigation.
Fears about baseless claims led Congress, through legislation like the
Private Securities Litigation Reform Act, to impose procedural protections for defendants.

B. State Law

1. From Fraud to a Fiduciary Duty to Disclose

State law of securities fraud is largely common law. The starting point is the basic claim for fraud. This is a claim asserted by
someone who was victimized by a misrepresentation on which she
reasonably relied to her detriment. It is a difficult claim to win. The
plaintiff must show that the defendant knowingly misrepresented a
material fact with the intent to induce reliance, that she (the plaintiff) reasonably relied upon the misrepresentation, and that she suffered damage as a consequence.

- X owns stock in a close corporation. The stock is worth
  $1,000. X tells a friend: "I own stock in this corporation.
  This company is about to take off because of a new product. I
  need some cash right away, so I need to sell the stock, and
  because you are my friend, I'll let you have it for $10,000."
  The friend buys the stock, which turns out to be worth only
  $1,000. The friend can sue X for fraud and seek a recovery of
  $9,000.

Fraud works well when, as here, the defendant lies. But what if
she does not?

- D is a director. Because of her position, she learns that the company has developed a new product that will revolutionize the market. The financial officers at the company estimate that the company's value will double within weeks of the introduction of the new product. D plays golf with Shareholder, who owns $10,000 worth of stock in the company. Shareholder says, "I don't think the company's doing anything great; I'd like to sell my stock." D says, "OK. I'll buy it from you for $10,000." Shareholder sells to D. A month later, the new product hits the market and the value of the stock doubles.

Shareholder cannot sue for fraud because D did not tell a lie. Instead, D used her superior knowledge (nonpublic information gained by being a director) to buy Shareholder's stock. The traditional common law view is that the insider owes no duty to disclose to the shareholder. [2] This view reflects a conclusion that fiduciaries owe duties when they manage, but not when they are engaged in personal financial transactions. Under this view, Shareholder cannot sue D.

Courts have recognized two inroads on the traditional rule. Some conclude that an insider (like a director or officer, and a managing shareholder of a close corporation) holds nonpublic information "in trust" for the benefit of shareholders. These courts impose a strict duty on the insider to disclose the nonpublic information to the shareholder before dealing with her. If she cannot divulge the information because it must be kept secret, then she must abstain from trading. This view is usually called the "Kansas rule," after cases like *Hotchkiss v. Fischer,*[3] which held that a director has a duty to shareholders "to communicate . . . all material facts in connection with the transaction which the director knows or should know."[4] Kansas has not retreated from this rule.[5] At least some older case law in other states supports this strict approach as well.[6] These courts conclude that fiduciaries owe duties not only to the corporation

---

[2] *See, e.g.,* Fleetwood Corp. v. Mirich, 404 N.E.2d 38 (Ind. Ct. App. 1980) ("Where a director of a corporation sells his personal shares or buys stock from other shareholders for his personal ownership, and such sale does not affect the general well being of the corporation, he owes no fiduciary duty to disclose information he possesses regarding the value of the stock to other shareholders.").

[3] 16 P.2d 531 (Kan. 1932).

[4] *Id.* at 531.

[5] Sampson v. Hunt, 564 P.2d 489, 492 (Kan. 1997) ("We hold that the rule of law to be followed in Kansas is that where knowledge of facts affecting the value or price of stock comes to an officer or director of a corporation by virtue of his office or position, he is under a fiduciary duty to disclose such facts to other stockholders before dealing in company stock with them. . . .").

[6] *See, e.g.,* Taylor v. Wright, 159 P.2d 980 (Cal. Ct. App. 1945); Oliver v. Oliver, 45 S.E. 232 (Ga. 1903).

while managing, but also to individual shareholders when trading on their (the fiduciaries') personal account.

Other courts take a position between the Kansas rule and the traditional common law approach. They impose upon insiders a duty to disclose "special facts" (sometimes called "special circumstances"). The leading special facts case is *Strong v. Repide*.[7] There, the director of a sugar company in the Philippines knew that the company planned to sell its land to the United States at a profit (in fact, he helped negotiate the deal). He also knew that the company would then dissolve and distribute cash to the shareholders. The director did not disclose this inside information when he bought the plaintiff's stock.. The plaintiff won because the defendant breached the duty to disclose "special facts" in dealing with shareholders.[8] The Court was less than clear about what constituted a special fact. It is an elastic concept, but certainly includes information—like that held by the defendant in *Strong*—that would have a notable effect on the value of the stock. It also included the fact that the defendant was someone (a director) with access to inside corporate information, which he also failed to disclose to the plaintiff.[9]

One can find cases embracing all three of these approaches. But the majority view is probably the special facts approach. The requirement of a special fact mirrors a requirement under federal Rule 10b–5 that an omission concern a "material" fact. That has been interpreted as a fact that a reasonable investor would consider important in making an investment decision.[10] This is as good a definition of a "special fact" as any.

Note, however, that the Kansas and "special facts" approaches hold that the insider owes a duty *to a shareholder*. If the person with whom the insider trades is not a shareholder, apparently there is no duty to disclose the nonpublic information.

- D is a director. Because of her position, she learns devastating corporation news. When the news goes public, the value of the company's stock will plummet. D plays golf with X, who is *not* a shareholder. X says: "D, that company of yours

---

[7] 213 U.S. 419 (1909).

[8] *Id.* at 431.

[9] *Id.* at 431–33. "The plaintiff never had any negotiations for the sale of the stock herself, and was ignorant that it was sold until some time after the sale, the negotiations for which took place between an agent of the plaintiff and an agent of defendant, the name of the defendant being undisclosed." *Id.* at 421.

[10] *See* TSC Industries, Inc. v. Northway, Inc., 426 U.S. 438, 449 (1976) ("An omitted fact is material if there is a substantial likelihood that a reasonable shareholder would consider it important in deciding how to vote.").

seems interesting. I'd like to buy some stock." D says: "OK—I'll sell you some of mine." X buys the stock. The next day, the news goes public and the stock becomes worthless.

Again, X cannot sue for fraud because D did not lie. On the other hand, D plainly traded on the basis of nonpublic information and took advantage of X. But arguably neither the Kansas nor special facts rule applies. Why? Because X was not a shareholder at the time of the transaction, so D owed no duty to her. We are unlikely to get a definitive resolution on this score because state law is not used much. Instead, cases such as this (and the earlier hypo when D dealt with Shareholder) can be pursued under federal Rule 10b–5.[11]

2. Insider Trading in the Market

The hypotheticals above involved face-to-face transactions. What happens if the insider trades on a market? In *Goodwin v. Agassiz*,[12] the plaintiff sold stock in a mining company on a public stock exchange. These are faceless transactions, so one has no idea who is on the other side of a public stock trade. By going back through the records, however, the plaintiff was able to discover that the person who bought his stock was an insider of the mining company. The insider had learned of a geology report that an area in Michigan was likely rich in ore. The company was engaged in buying up land in the area. The plaintiff sued the insider under the special facts doctrine.

The court upheld judgment for the defendant for two reasons. First, the geology report was so speculative that it did not constitute a special "fact."[13] Second, and more importantly, the court refused to permit suit for trades on a public exchange. Doing so would impose an untenable burden—an insider, before trading, would have to seek out the person on the other side of the deal and inform her of the inside information.[14] Thus, the common law claims under the Kansas and special facts rules appear to apply only in face-to-face transactions, and not when an insider trades on a public exchange. So the person on the other side of a public trade cannot sue.

---

[11] *Cf.* Gratz v. Claughton, 187 F.2d 46, 49 (2d Cir. 1951) ("When [insiders] sold shares, it could indeed be argued that they were not dealing with a beneficiary, but with one whom his purchase made a beneficiary. That should not, however, have obscured the fact that the director or officer assumed a fiduciary relation to the buyer by the very sale; for it would be a sorry distinction to allow him to use the advantage of his position to induce the buyer into the position of a beneficiary, although he was forbidden to do so, once the buyer had become one.").

[12] 186 N.E. 659 (Mass. 1933).

[13] *Id.* at 660.

[14] *Id.*

In some states, however, the corporation (not the other party to the stock trade) may sue insiders who publicly trade in its stock. In *Diamond v. Oreamuno*,[15] a director and an officer had inside information of impending bad news for their corporation. They unloaded their stock on the public market before the bad news was made public. They sold at $28 per share. After the news became public, the stock price fell to $11. The New York Court of Appeals held that the two had breached a duty to the corporation and were liable for the $17 per share that they "saved" by selling before the news became public.[16] First, the court concluded that the defendants had profited by using corporate property (information). Second, it also concluded that even though the defendants' acts did not harm the corporation financially, they harmed the company's reputation.[17] This position has some support among economists. The idea is that such insider trading makes potential investors nervous and thus drives down the amount they are willing to invest. This, in turn, harms the corporation's ability to raise capital. *Diamond* has been accepted by some courts and rejected by others.[18]

C. Rule 10b–5—Background and Elements

1. The Provision and Who Can Enforce It

The Securities and Exchange Commission (SEC) promulgated Rule 10b–5 in 1948. Its statutory authority for doing so is § 10(b) of the Securities Exchange Act of 1934, which is a broad antifraud provision.[19] Rule 10b–5 has been interpreted and applied in thousands of cases. Its language is deceptively simple, and is worth studying with care:

> It shall be unlawful for any person, directly or indirectly, by the use of any means or instrumentality of interstate commerce, or

---

[15] 248 N.E.2d 910 (N.Y. 1969).

[16] *Id.* at 912–13.

[17] *Id.* at 913. "When officers and directors abuse their position in order to gain personal profits, the effect may be to cast a cloud on the corporation's name, injure stockholder relations and undermine public regard for the corporation's securities." *Id.* at 912.

[18] *See, e.g., In re* ORFA Securities Litigation, 654 F. Supp. 1449, 1454–55 (D.N.J. 1987) (agreeing with the *Diamond* analysis). *But see* Freeman v. Decio, 584 F.2d 186, 194 (7th Cir. 1978) (finding that the injury to corporate goodwill is speculative and may not form an adequate basis for a cause of action).

[19] "Section 10(b) of the Securities Exchange Act of 1934 forbids the 'use or employ, in connection with the purchase or sale of any security . . . , [of] any manipulative or deceptive device or contrivance in contravention of such rules and regulations as the [SEC] may prescribe as necessary or appropriate in the public interest or for the protection of investors.' " Tellabs, Inc. v. Makor Issues & Rights, Ltd., 551 U.S. 308, 318 (2007) (citing 15 U.S.C. § 78j(b)).

of the mails or of any facility of any national securities exchange,

(1) to employ any device, scheme, or artifice to defraud;

(2) to make any untrue statement of a material fact or to omit to state a material fact necessary in order to make the statements made, in light of the circumstances under which they were made, not misleading, or

(3) to engage in any act, practice, or course of business which operates or would operate as a fraud or deceit upon any person,

in connection with the purchase or sale of any security.

The SEC can enforce this provision by seeking civil penalties and injunctions. It can refer cases to the Department of Justice for criminal prosecution. The Rule says nothing, however, about whether a private citizen may sue for damages. Over time, the federal courts inferred the existence of such a claim.[20] There is, however, an important limitation on standing: one may assert a private right of action under Rule 10b–5 only if she bought or sold securities because of some bad act by the defendant. If the would-be plaintiff neither bought nor sold, she cannot sue. The rule was first imposed by the Second Circuit in *Birnbaum v. Newport Steel Co.*[21] The Supreme Court embraced the rule in *Blue Chip Stamps v. Manor Drug Stores.*[22]

- Shareholder owns 100 shares of XYZ Corp. She is thinking about selling them because the company has not been doing very well. The company issues a press release full of lies. It says that the company has new business prospects and that the stock price will go up. In reliance on the press release, Shareholder does not sell her stock. After the lies are exposed, the value of the stock plummets. Shareholder has been hurt by the fraudulent act of XYZ Corp., but she can-

---

[20] Basic, Inc. v. Levinson, 485 U.S. 224, 230–31 (1988) ("Judicial interpretation and application, legislative acquiescence, and the passage of time have removed any doubt that a private cause of action exists for a violation of § 10(b) and Rule 10b–5, and constitutes an essential tool for enforcement of the 1934 Act's requirements."). In 1988, Congress amended the 1934 Act by adding § 20A. It creates an express private right of action for violation of that Act by insider trading.

[21] 193 F.2d 461, 463–64 (2d Cir. 1952).

[22] 421 U.S. 723, 731 (1975). It is still occasionally referred to as the "*Birnbaum* rule."

not bring a private action for damages under Rule 10b–5. She did not buy or sell, so she cannot sue.[23]

On the other hand, as we will see below, persons who bought XYZ Corp. stock on the market after the press release will be able to sue under the "fraud on the market" theory.[24]

Claims under Rule 10b–5 seek recovery for harm suffered by the person buying or selling securities. Because the claim belongs to the victim of fraudulent behavior, it is personal to the plaintiff. It is thus a direct, and not a derivative, suit.[25] Such claims invoke exclusive federal jurisdiction and cannot be asserted in state court.[26] The plaintiff will sue for damages to compensate her for harm caused by the fraudulent behavior. Punitive damages, however, are not recoverable under the rule.[27] Rule 10b–5 claims are often asserted in class actions—that is, by a representative on behalf of a group of investors similarly situated. As we will see, Congress has acted to curb what it considered to be abusive class action litigation.

2. Potential Defendants

The Rule forbids "any person" from doing the things proscribed. This includes individuals and entities. Though the *plaintiff* in a civil 10b–5 case must have bought or sold securities, the same is not true of the defendant. For example, someone who lies to another to get that person to buy her stock may be sued. But the defendant is not required to be a buyer or seller. A corporation that issues a misleading press release violates Rule 10b–5, even though it did not buy or sell securities. Moreover, a "tipper," who is an insider with inside information, violates Rule 10b–5 by giving that information to a "tippee," who then trades. Both the tipper and the tippee are in trouble, even though only one of them actually traded in securities.[28]

Because it applies to "any person," Rule 10b–5 can be implicated in any business form. Thus, it might be implicated in the purchase

---

[23] Though Shareholder may not sue, the SEC may take administrative action and may refer the matter to the Department of Justice for criminal prosecution.

[24] *See* notes 498–50 and accompanying text. These persons bought stock and the "fraud on the market" theory, when applicable, permits them to raise a presumption that they relied on the misstatements.

[25] Derivative suits seek to vindicate claims by the corporation itself, usually for harm inflicted by breach of fiduciary duties by a director or officer. *See* Chapter 7.

[26] 15 U.S.C. § 78aa; *see* Gross v. Weingarten, 217 F.3d 208, 224 (4th Cir. 2000)("A direct action alleging violations of section 10(b) and Rule 10b–5 is subject to exclusively federal jurisdiction.").

[27] *See* Woods v. Barnett Bank of Ft. Lauderdale, 765 F.2d 1004, 1013 (11th Cir. 1985) ("Punitive damages are not available in a 10b–5 action.").

[28] *See* notes 734–80 and accompanying text.

and sale of securities in partnerships, limited partnerships, closely held corporations, publicly traded corporations, limited liability companies—anything. As we will see in section D, this is quite different from § 16(b), which applies only in publicly traded entities.

3. Elements in a Rule 10b–5 Claim

What must the plaintiff (or the government, when it sues or prosecutes) establish in a Rule 10b–5 case? The key element will be that the defendant committed one of the types of fraudulent behavior prohibited by the Rule. We will discuss these in detail below. For now, let's just say that such behavior may involve a misrepresentation or an omission. The defendant may lie (a misrepresentation) or, with insider trading, may fail to say something that the law required her to say (an omission). Beyond that, there are additional elements.

Instrumentality of Interstate Commerce. Rule 10b–5 is triggered by the use of facilities of interstate commerce, including the mail or facilities of a national exchange. This is easy to meet. The transaction does not have to cross state lines—even *intrastate* phone calls are covered.[29] The fraudulent behavior need not involve the instrumentality of interstate commerce—one must simply be used at some point in the overall transaction.

- D, a director of ABC Corp., lies to X in a face-to-face meeting in an effort to get X to buy stock in ABC. X then goes online and buys ABC stock. The interstate nexus is met.

- Suppose D lies to X face-to-face to get X to buy D's stock. X then writes a check to D to pay for the stock and D endorses the stock certificate to X. Interstate commerce is met by the fact that the check must clear through banking channels.[30]

About the only kind of transaction that would not satisfy this nexus is a face-to-face meeting in which the buyer pays cash and the seller endorses the certificates to the buyer. This probably does not happen very often (at least not in the real world; exam questions might be another thing).

Materiality. The defendant's fraudulent behavior must concern a "material" fact. The Supreme Court defines a fact as material if "there is a substantial likelihood that a reasonable [investor] would

---

[29] Dupuy v. Dupuy, 511 F.2d 641, 644 (5th Cir. 1975).

[30] *See, e.g.*, McLaury v. Duff and Phelps, Inc., 691 F. Supp. 1090, 1095 (N.D. Ill. 1988) ("[U]se of our system for clearing checks also should be considered use of an 'instrumentality of interstate commerce' for purposes of Section 10(b).").

consider it important in deciding [whether to buy or sell securities]."[31] Materiality will usually be clear—the defendant will say (or omit to say) something that a reasonable investor would think important to the value of the stock.

Materiality may be problematic, however, when statements are made about something that may (but not necessarily will) happen. In *Basic, Inc. v. Levinson*,[32] an aggressor corporation started buying stock in a publicly traded company; it hoped ultimately to acquire the "target" company through a merger. The target company issued misleading press releases denying that it was being pursued.[33] When the acquisition was announced, those who had sold stock in the target when the press releases came out sued under Rule 10b–5. They sought damages for their lost value—if the target had told the truth, they would not have sold their stock, and would have gotten more money for their stock through the acquisition.

Were the misstatements in the press releases "material?" The Court adopted the reasoning of an influential lower court opinion that had addressed nearly identical facts, *SEC v. Texas Gulf Sulphur Co.*[34] It employed a sliding scale approach that considers (1) the probability that the event will occur (e.g., the acquisition will go through) and (2) the magnitude of the possible event.[35] Because a merger is of enormous importance (it ends the existence of the target corporation), statements about it will become material at a lower level of probability. The Court remanded to let the district court apply the standard.

In 1995, Congress passed the Private Securities Litigation Reform Act (PSLRA).[36] Congress was concerned with weak or frivolous securities cases, filed to extort settlements from defendants.[37] The PSLRA imposes various procedural hurdles on the plaintiff in securities cases, including those brought under Rule 10b–5, whether assert-

---

[31] TSC Industries, Inc. v. Northway, Inc., 426 U.S. 438, 449 (1976) (this case was about proxy solicitation, but "material" is defined the same as in Rule 10b–5).

[32] 485 U.S. 224 (1988).

[33] It did so to tamp down rumors of the possible acquisition; if news got out, the public would buy the target's stock and thereby drive the price up. This might have stymied the deal. *Id.* at 227.

[34] 401 F.2d 833 (2d Cir. 1971).

[35] *Id.* at 849–50.

[36] Pub. L. 104–67, 109 Stat. 737. The Act is codified throughout various sections in Title 15 of the United States Code.

[37] The legislative history noted "abusive practices committed in private securities litigation," including "routine filing" of securities cases "without regard to any underlying culpability." The expense of discovery impelled defendants to settle such cases. H.R. Rep. No. 104–369, at p. 41.

ing individual claims or class actions.[38] For example, the plaintiff must allege elements of fraudulent behavior with particularity so as to create a "strong inference" that the defendant acted with scienter.[39] Another requirement, discussed below, is that the plaintiff must prove "loss causation."[40]

Importantly, the PSLRA established a "safe harbor" for "forward-looking" oral or written statements that are "accompanied by meaningful cautionary statements identifying important factors that could cause actual results to differ materially from those in the forward-looking statements."[41] This provision applies only to publicly traded corporations. The effect of such cautionary language is to render the statement non-material for purposes of Rule 10b–5. Because materiality is an element of a Rule 10b–5 case, the effect is to require dismissal of any such case.

Thus, in a public corporation, one cannot be sued under Rule 10b–5 if the alleged misrepresentation on which the case would be based (1) was a "forward-looking" statement and (2) was accompanied by appropriate cautionary language. The first requirement shields statements about the future, but not statements about the present.[42] The second requirement ensures that the statement about the future must be made along with the warning that it might be wrong. This cautionary language must be specific to the risk involved, and not simply some blanket warning like "we don't have a clue if any of this will really happen."

An example is *EP Medsystems, Inc. v. Echocath, Inc.*[43] There, Echocath developed ultrasound medical devices generically referred to as "women's health products." As part of its initial public offering of stock, it issued a prospectus setting forth details about the company and its financial data.[44] In addition, Echocath executives made various written and oral statements to representatives of EP Medsystems in an effort to get EP Medsystems to buy Echocath stock. EP Medsystems bought $1,400,000 worth of the stock. It did so largely because Echocath represented that it was close to entering

---

[38] The Act imposes special rules for class actions, including a requirement that the court appoint as "lead plaintiff" the person with the largest financial stake in the case. *See* 15 U.S.C. §§ 77z–1, 78u–4.

[39] 15 U.S.C. § 78u–4(b)(2).

[40] *See* note 58 and accompanying text.

[41] 15 U.S.C. § 78u–5(i)(1).

[42] The PSLRA defines "forward-looking" statements to include, *inter alia*, projections of revenues and objectives for future operations. 15 U.S.C. § 78u–5(i)(1)(A)–(B).

[43] 235 F.3d 865 (3d Cir. 2000).

[44] Federal law requires such prospectuses to accompany the public offering of securities. *See* Chapter 9(C).

into contracts to sell its products to medical concerns. When the products failed to sell (and the Echocath stock turned out not to be worth much), EP Medsystems sued.

Echocath claimed that it was protected by the safe harbor for "forward-looking" statements under the PSLRA. The court rejected the defense.[45] First, the statements by various Echocath representatives about hoping to sell the new products were not "forward-looking." Those statements, such as that Echocath "was on the verge of signing contracts with a number of companies," were, instead, statements of present fact. Saying that sales were "imminent" likewise were statements of the situation at the moment, and not about the future. Thus, they were not protected as forward-looking.

Second, though the company had included plenty of cautionary language in its prospectus, the language was not closely enough related to the statements about potential sales to medical products companies. The Echocath prospectus warned that an investment in the company "is speculative in nature and involves a high degree of risk," and set forth risk factors, including "there can be no assurance . . . that the company will be able successfully to reach agreements with any strategic partners."[46] This kind of language is ubiquitous in prospectuses these days. It did not avail Echocath, however, because it was not specifically aimed at the statements about being able to sell the products.[47]

Reliance. The plaintiff asserting common law fraud must demonstrate that she relied on the misstatement made by the defendant. Such reliance must be reasonable under the circumstances. Reasonable reliance is also an element in Rule 10b–5 cases, but it is often not much of a problem. In cases of misrepresentation, indirect reliance is sufficient. For example, if you buy securities because your investment adviser recommended them, and she, in turn, recommended them because she read some misrepresentation in corporate documents, you may claim reliance.

Indeed, courts go beyond this in cases of mass misrepresentation. In *Basic, Inc. v. Levinson,*[48] discussed above regarding materiality, the Court adopted a "fraud on the market" theory—applicable in public corporations—that basically results in a presumption of reli-

---

[45] The Third Circuit opinion addressed the "bespeaks caution" doctrine, which is the common law analog to the PSLRA safe harbor for forward-looking statements. 235 F.3d at 874–80. There appears to be no substantive difference between the two doctrines.

[46] *Id.* at 868.

[47] *Id.* at 874–76.

[48] 485 U.S. 224 (1988).

ance.[49] That case was a class action on behalf of people who sold their stock after the company issued misleading press releases. Defendants argued that each member of the class should be required to show that she read the press release and relied upon it in selling her stock.

The Court rejected the argument and emphasized that all investors rely on the integrity of prices set by the securities exchanges. Because misleading statements affect prices in the public markets, they constitute a fraud on the market. Courts will presume reliance in such cases. Defendant can rebut the presumption, but doing so seems difficult. For example, the court in *Basic* said the defendant could escape liability by showing that news of the merger discussion entered the market and "dissipated the effects of the misstatements."[50]

The Supreme Court has also created a presumption of reliance in cases of omission—where the defendant fails to disclose something the law required her to disclose. In such a case, "proof of reliance is not a prerequisite to recover. All that is necessary is that the facts withheld be material. . ."[51]

Scienter. Section 10(b) of the '34 Act, on which Rule 10b–5 is based, makes unlawful the use of "manipulative or deceptive device or contrivance." Such language "connotes intentional conduct designed to deceive or defraud investors," and thus cannot cover mere negligence.[52] Because an SEC rule cannot exceed the scope of the statute on which it is based, Rule 10b–5 cases cannot be based upon negligence. Plaintiff must show scienter, which the Court described as an intent to "deceive, manipulate, or defraud."

In *Ernst & Ernst v. Hochfelder*,[53] the Supreme Court refused to decide whether recklessness could support a 10b–5 claim. The majority view in the lower federal courts seems to accept that recklessness may suffice, though some appear to make it something like a "recklessness plus." In one case, the court spoke of "an extreme departure from the standards of ordinary care, . . . which presents a danger of misleading buyers and sellers that is either known to the defendant or is so obvious that the actor must have been aware of it."[54] Obvious-

---

[49] *Id*. at 246–50.

[50] *Id*. at 249.

[51] Affiliated Ute Citizens of Utah v. United States, 406 U.S. 128, 153 (1972).

[52] Ernst & Ernst v. Hochfelder, 425 U.S. 185, 199 (1976).

[53] *Id*.

[54] Sundstrand Corp. v. Sun Chemical Corp., 533 F.2d 1033, 1045 (7th Cir. 1977).

ly, drawing a line between "recklessness" and "recklessness plus" is more art than science.

Whatever standard of proof at trial, as noted above, the PSLRA makes it more difficult for plaintiffs to get past the pleading stage by stating a claim. It imposes a requirement that the plaintiff must plead "with particularity facts giving rise to a strong inference that the defendant acted with the required state of mind." The requirement of particularity means details, not conclusions. In *Tellabs, Inc. v. Makor Issues & Rights, Ltd.*,[55] the Supreme Court held that a "strong" inference of scienter is more than merely plausible or reasonable. It must be cogent and at least as compelling as any inference of non-fraudulent intent.[56] This requirement augments that in Federal Rule of Civil Procedure 9(b), which requires that allegations of the circumstances constituting fraud be detailed.

Causation. A Rule 10b–5 plaintiff must prove causation of two types. First is "but-for" causation, which developed in common law fraud cases. Generally under Rule 10b–5, the plaintiff must show that she did what she did (buy or sell securities) *because* the defendant engaged in fraudulent behavior.[57]

The PSLRA adds another requirement—plaintiff must show "loss causation."[58] This means that the defendant's fraudulent behavior actually caused the loss about which plaintiff complains. Suppose, for instance, Corporation tells an enormous lie in its prospectus or annual report. Plaintiff reads the lie and decides to buy stock in Corporation. She does so. Later, Corporation suffers huge losses for some totally unrelated reason—perhaps a downturn in the macroeconomic market or maybe some executive stole all of the assets. Plaintiff cannot show loss causation here. True, her investment has decreased in value, but that decrease had nothing to do with Corporation's lie.

"In Connection with the Purchase or Sale of Any Security." Defendant's fraudulent behavior must be in connection with a purchase

---

[55] 551 U.S. 308 (2007).

[56] *Id.* at 310.

[57] This is not so, however, in insider trading cases. Section 20A of the 1934 Act, which was passed in 1988, creates a private right of action for insider trading. It requires that the plaintiff bought or sold "contemporaneously" with a defendant who traded on inside information. It requires no showing of but-for causation. The provision also limits recovery to the profits made or losses avoided by the defendant because of her trading on inside information.

[58] 15 U.S.C. § 78u–4(b)(4)(plaintiff "shall have the burden of proving that the act or omission of the defendant . . . caused the loss for which the plaintiff seeks to recover damages").

or sale of securities. This requirement is reflected in the *Birnbaum* rule[59] that a civil 10b–5 plaintiff must have bought or sold securities. In many cases of misrepresentation or omission, this will be clear—the defendant said something or failed to say something that led directly to the plaintiff buying or selling securities.

Sometimes, however, it is not as clear. In *SEC v. Sandford,*[60] a stockbroker urged an elderly man to open an account and to give a power of attorney to trade securities for the man and his handicapped daughter. The broker traded in the account and absconded with the proceeds. Each trade was part of the dealer's plan to bilk the clients, so the fraudulent scheme was "in connection with" securities transactions.[61] It might be a different case if the broker had decided—after having traded in the account—to steal the money. In *Sandford,* the reason for the trades was the fraudulent scheme.

Under Rule 10b–5, the purchase or sale may be of "any security." Though most cases involve transactions in equity securities (stock), the Rule applies to deals concerning debt securities as well. This is different from § 16(b), which, as we will see in section D, applies only to the purchase and sale of equity securities.

Other. Privity is not a Rule 10b–5 requirement. Thus, the plaintiff need not have dealt directly with the defendant. This is one reason insider trading on the public exchanges can be pursued under the rule, as we will see in the next subsection.

4. Types of Fraudulent Behavior Covered

Background. We have just discussed the elements of a claim under Rule 10b–5. In this section, we focus on the types of behavior that can violate the Rule. All the elements we have just seen—materiality, scienter, and the like—must concern some actionable fraudulent act or omission. In this section, we will assume that the elements discussed above are satisfied, and will focus on the types of behavior that violate Rule 10b–5. We start with two important points.

First, 10b–5 only prohibits *deception*, not unfairness. So a transaction (like a merger) that is adequately disclosed cannot be attacked under Rule 10b–5, even if its terms are unfair.

---

[59] *See* notes 21–22 and accompanying text.
[60] 535 U.S. 813 (2002).
[61] *Id.* at 813–14.

Second, there is no liability in a private Rule 10b–5 case for "aiding and abetting." Suppose a corporation violated the rule by making misleading statements in its prospectus. Defrauded investors can sue the corporation. Because the corporation might have no assets, plaintiffs for years joined "secondary" or "collateral" participants, such as the accountants and bankers who may be said to have aided the corporation's fraud. The Supreme Court put a (surprising) end to the practice in *Central Bank of Denver, N.A. v. First Interstate Bank*.[62] Congress changed the result in the PSLRA—but only for cases brought by the SEC. So aiding and abetting is *not* a viable theory in private actions. The Court reiterated this point in *Stoneridge Investment Partners, LLC v. Scientific-Atlanta, Inc.*[63]

Terms of the Rule. Review the language of the Rule at Chapter 11(C)(1). It has three parts. Parts (1) and (3) seem to compete for ways to say "do not defraud folks." Clearly, behavior that would constitute common law fraud will be actionable under Rule 10b–5.

- Close Corporation is issuing stock. President tells you that the company already has contracts to provide services for hundreds of clients. A brochure published by Close Corporation says the same thing. It is a lie. You buy the stock. You can sue Close Corporation and the President under Rule 10b–5.

Nothing in the Rule limits its application to issuances (sales by the corporation itself). Indeed, it is likely that most cases invoking Rule 10b–5 involve resales of stock.

- Susie owns stock in Corporation. She tells you that the company is about to introduce a revolutionary new product and that the stock will increase in value. Because she needs cash, she says, she will sell it to you for "only" $10,000. You buy it. It turns out to be worthless. Everything Susie said was a lie. You can sue Susie under Rule 10b–5.

As we saw above, the defendant in a Rule 10b–5 case need not have bought or sold securities. So, for example, the corporation that issues a misleading press release violates the Rule and can be sued by all who buy or sell in reliance on it. Indeed, reliance will be presumed in this type of case under the "fraud on the market" theory.[64]

---

[62] 511 U.S. 164, 191–92 (1994).

[63] 552 U.S. 148, 157–58 (2008).

[64] *See, e.g.*, Basic Inc. v. Levinson, 485 U.S. 224, 241–43 (1988).

The most important developments under Rule 10b–5 concern its application to insider trading. Again, look at the language of the Rule. The only part that seems to address insider trading expressly is (2), and it seems quite limited.[65] It imposes liability for "omit[ting] to state a material fact"—but *only* if the fact would be necessary to make something already said "not misleading." In other words, if the defendant makes a statement that implies something material, the Rule expressly requires her to make an ameliorative statement.

- Close Corporation is issuing stock. The President tells you: "the last four quarterly reports by our accountants show profitability." This is true. What she does not say is that for the most recent quarter, the audit is not complete, but the accountant called this afternoon and said it was a disaster—the company had lost a ton of money.

The President did not lie to you. But she made a statement that implied something that isn't so. To make what she said "not misleading," she should have told you about today's conversation with the accountant. This fact pattern falls within the literal terms of part (2) of the Rule.

Insider Trading. On its face, Rule 10b–5 seems to impose a duty to disclose only if the defendant has already said something. To fix a misunderstanding, the defendant would have to speak. Thus, nothing in the Rule seems to apply to the classic insider trading case in which the defendant says nothing at all. Review the hypotheticals above. They do not seem to implicate Rule 10b–5 as written.

But they do violate Rule 10b–5 as interpreted. This is the most important area of Rule 10b–5 jurisprudence, and it is the result of case law. The first hint that trading on the basis of inside information might violate Rule 10b–5 came in *In re Matter of Cady, Roberts & Co.*[66] The proceeding was an administrative disciplinary case against a broker, and the SEC concluded that anyone with direct or indirect access "to information intended to be available only for a corporate purpose" may not take "advantage of such information knowing it is unavailable to those with whom he is dealing," including the investing public.[67]

---

[65] The other parts of the Rule conceivably apply because common law fraud includes failure to disclose when there is a duty to disclose. *See* note 1. But nowhere does the Rule attempt to define who might have a duty to disclose or the circumstances in which such a duty arises.

[66] 40 S.E.C. 907 (1961).

[67] *Id.* at 912.

This decision was a game-changer. From now on, at least according to the SEC, failing to disclose inside information in a securities transaction violates Rule 10b–5. *Cady, Roberts* establishes a duty to disclose, so trading on silence constitutes an act that "operates . . . as a fraud" under Rule 10b–5(3). (It is probably an "artifice to defraud" under Rule 10b–5(1) as well.) The SEC's view of this duty was very broad—it applied to insiders like directors and officers and to anyone with access to confidential information. Thus, according to *Cady, Roberts,* even low-level employees had a duty not to trade on the basis of non-public corporate information. The question now became whether the courts would agree with the SEC's position regarding insider trading.

The first major case was *SEC v. Texas Gulf Sulphur Co.*[68] A mining company (TGS) was looking for mineral sites in Canada. Core samples at one site were very favorable, and the company started buying up land in the area. TGS wanted to keep news of the mineral strike quiet so it could buy the land cheaply. During this time, insiders bought TGS stock and call options based upon their inside information about the core samples. The court held that these insiders violated 10b–5 by trading on the inside information. Insiders cannot trade until the information is divulged and the market has had a chance to digest the information—that means, until the stock market reacts to the inside information.[69]

In addition, the case involved "tipping." This is where insiders do not use their inside information to trade for their own account. Instead, they pass the information to others, who then trade in the stock. In *Texas Gulf Sulphur,* insiders "tipped" their friends, who then bought the TGS stock. When the news of the mineral strike became public, these people were able to sell the stock at a considerable profit. The court held this to be a violation of Rule 10b–5 as well. According to the court (and the SEC in *Cady, Roberts*), the purpose of Rule 10b–5 is to assure that all traders have relatively equal access to information.[70]

Development of the law now shifted to the Supreme Court. *Chiarella v. United States*[71] was a criminal 10b–5 case brought against a blue collar employee of a printing company. Chiarella prepared the documents relating to a tender offer. Though the names of the aggressor and target companies were left blank on the documents on which he worked, Chiarella did some homework and figured out

---

[68] 401 F.2d 833 (2d Cir. 1968).

[69] *Id.* at 853–54.

[70] *Id.* at 848.

[71] 445 U.S. 222 (1980).

what companies were involved. He bought stock in the target on the public market. When the news of the tender offer went public, he sold the stock at a $30,000 profit. He was convicted of criminal violations of Rule 10b–5. The Second Circuit affirmed the convictions.[72]

The Supreme Court reversed. *Chiarella* establishes a very important point: not everyone in possession of nonpublic information owes a duty to disclose it. Because the defendant was not an insider of the company whose stock he bought, Rule 10b–5 did not prohibit his trading. Stated another way, the *"Cady, Roberts* duty"—to disclose nonpublic information or else abstain from trading—did not attach to Chiarella.

The decision presents a fundamental disagreement between the SEC and lower courts, on the one hand, and the Supreme Court, on the other. The SEC and lower courts concluded that Rule 10b–5 is implicated whenever one person has inside or nonpublic information that the other party to a trade does not have. When Chiarella bought stock on the public market, he knew that the company was a target in a tender offer. The people who sold the stock to him did not know this. Thus, the SEC and lower courts concluded that he violated Rule 10b–5. To them, it did not matter who Chiarella was or how he got the information. He had inside information that the others did not have.

The Supreme Court rejected that view but in other respects embraced *Cady, Roberts*. According to the Court, the Rule 10b–5 proscription on insider trading is not triggered by mere possession of nonpublic information. The Rule is aimed at fraud. Silence constitutes fraud only if there is a duty to disclose the information the trader has. A duty to disclose arises when the parties to a trade have a relationship of trust and confidence. In *Chiarella,* the Court made clear that insiders (such as directors, officers, and controlling shareholders) have such a relationship with shareholders of their corporation. Thus, *Chiarella* adopts the SEC's view that Rule 10b–5 applies to insider trading by imposing a duty to disclose. But it imposes that duty on a narrower circle of potential defendants than the SEC would. Instead of imposing the duty on anyone in possession of confidential information, the Court imposes it on corporate insiders. Because Mr. Chiarella was not an insider of the company in which he bought stock (he was not a director, officer, controlling shareholder, nor was he an employee with access to confidential information), Rule 10b-5 did not apply to his trades.

---

[72] *Id.* at 236–37. Chiarella was convicted on 17 counts of insider trading, which reflects the fact that he traded in stock of the target company 17 times.

Chief Justice Burger dissented in *Chiarella*. He argued that the defendant should be convicted under Rule 10b–5 because "a person who has misappropriated nonpublic information has an absolute duty to disclose that information or to refrain from trading." The majority of the Court did not consider this argument because the Justices concluded that it was not properly raised in the trial court. We will see that a version of the misappropriation theory was to succeed later.

Shortly after *Chiarella*, the SEC adopted Rule 14e–3, which prohibits anyone from trading on the basis of undisclosed information about pending tender offers. It applies even to eavesdroppers who happen to hear about a tender offer and trade on the basis of that information. The defendant in *Chiarella* today would run afoul of Rule 14e–3, even though he did not violate Rule 10b–5. The Supreme Court upheld the validity of Rule 14e–3 in *United States v. O'Hagan*,[73] which we discuss below.

The next big case, *Dirks v. SEC*,[74] involved "tipping." Secrist had been insider of Equity Funding Corporation, a life insurance and mutual fund company. He was concerned about massive fraud in the company. He contacted Dirks, who was a broker, to tell him about the fraud and to ask him to investigate. Dirks did, and found that Secrist was right. Dirks advised his clients to sell their Equity Funding stock and then "blew the whistle" by going to the SEC with evidence of the fraud. The SEC rewarded Dirks by charging him with violating Rule 10b–5. (Some people think the SEC was being spiteful because it had failed to follow up on allegations by former employees about fraud at Equity Funding.)

Specifically, the SEC charged that Secrist was a "tipper" and that Dirks was a "tippee" of nonpublic information. Moreover, when Dirks used that information to tell his clients to sell their Equity Funding stock, Dirks was a "tipper" and his clients were "tippees." The SEC's theory, as in *Chiarella*, was that these people were using nonpublic information. The Court's holding, as in *Chiarella*, is that Rule 10b–5 is only implicated if there is fraud, and silence constitutes fraud only if there is a duty to disclose the non-public information on which one trades. That duty arises from a fiduciary (or otherwise confidential) relationship between the parties. The Rule does not "require equal information among all traders." Rather, "only some persons, under some circumstances, will be barred from trading while in possession of material nonpublic information."[75]

---

[73] 521 U.S. 642 (1997).

[74] 463 U.S. 646 (1983).

[75] *Id.* at 657.

Dirks sets out clear rules. First, one is a tipper only if she passes along nonpublic information in breach of a duty to her corporation and receives some benefit for doing so.[76] This breach occurs, according to the Court, when the person receives a personal benefit from giving the tip. In other words, she passes information to another for the purpose of gaining some personal benefit. This benefit might be pecunitary (like money) or it might consist simply of something non-monetary, including making a gift or enhancing one's reputation. On the facts of the case, Secrist was not a tipper. His motivation was to expose fraud, and he did not benefit from giving the information to Dirks.

Second, without a tipper, there can be no tippee.[77] So once it determined that Secrist was not a tipper, Dirks cannot be in trouble as a tippee. If there had been a tipper, a tippee violates Rule 10b–5 if he trades on the tip and knew or should have known that the information was given to him wrongfully.

Third, while a tippee can "inherit" a fiduciary duty from an insider and breach it by tipping a third party, that did not happen here. Dirks did not inherit a fiduciary duty from Secrist because Secrist violated no duty when he gave the information to Dirks. "[S]ome tippees must assume an insider's duty to the shareholders not because they receive inside information, but rather because it has been made available to them improperly."[78]

In footnote 14, the Court in *Dirks* suggested that outsiders performing services for the corporation who receive corporate information in a legitimate manner (such as underwriters, accountants, attorneys, or consultants) should be viewed as temporary insiders and not as tippees. Hence, if they disclose confidential information, it is as a tipper and not as a tippee.

Carpenter v. United States[79] offered a chance to consider the "misappropriation theory" first suggested by Chief Justice Burger in *Chiarella.* In *Carpenter,* a reporter for the *Wall Street Journal* (Winans) wrote a daily column that discussed stocks. Favorable mention of a stock in this column usually led to a run-up in the price of that stock. Winans gave information about which stocks he would feature to some associates, who bought stock before the column was published. The associates profited from these trades.

---

[76] *Id.* at 662–64.

[77] *Id.* at 664.

[78] *Id.* at 660.

[79] 463 U.S. 646 (1983).

Because Winans received no information from the corporations themselves, he could not be held liable under the "traditional" or "classical" approach to insider trading put forth in *Chiarella*. As we have seen, that applies only to persons in a relationship of trust and confidence with the shareholders of the corporation. The government prosecuted Winans under a misappropriation theory. Specifically, he was using information that "belonged" to the *Wall Street Journal*, not to the companies referred to in his column. Winans was convicted of criminal violations under the mail fraud statute, § 10(b), and Rule 10b–5. The Second Circuit affirmed. The Supreme Court affirmed the conviction under Rule 10b–5 by an equally divided court, thus leaving the status of the misappropriation theory unclear. At the same time, though, the Court unanimously upheld Winans's convictions for mail fraud.

Next is the sad case of *United States v. O'Hagan*.[80] O'Hagan was a partner in a major Minneapolis law firm. The firm represented Grand Met, an English company, and was working with it in its effort to acquire Pillsbury through a tender offer. O'Hagan was not involved in that matter but learned about it. Based on this information, O'Hagan bought Pillsbury stock and call options. When news of the takeover went public, he sold his holdings at a profit of $4,300,000. After being disbarred and prosecuted in state court, O'Hagan was hit with a 57-count federal indictment, including violations of Rules 10b–5 and 14e-3. He was convicted, and the Supreme Court affirmed. As in *Carpenter,* the government could not proceed under the "traditional" approach. O'Hagan was not an insider of Pillsbury, and thus could not have violated any duty to it. (What O'Hagan did is sometimes called "outsider trading," because he trades in the stock of a company to which he owes no fiduciary duty.)

Nonetheless, the Court concluded, O'Hagan violated the "misappropriation" theory of insider trading. Instead of focusing on a duty owed by insiders to the shareholders of the corporation, this theory is based upon a duty of confidentiality owed to the source of the information. O'Hagan owed such a duty to two entities: his employer (the law firm) and to his employer's client (Grand Met). Trading on that information breached the duty and qualified as insider trading under Rule 10b–5. *O'Hagan* resolved a split among lower courts about whether trading on misappropriated information violates Rule 10b–5.

We note two things about *O'Hagan*. First, the Court made clear that it was not deciding whether the misappropriation theory should apply in private civil actions. It clearly applies in criminal prosecu-

---

[80] 521 U.S. 642 (1997).

tions but, at least at the Supreme Court level, it is an open question whether it should apply in private cases.

Second, the version of the misappropriation doctrine adopted by the Court is narrower than that suggested by Chief Justice Burger in his dissent in *Chiarella*. The Chief Justice asserted that the duty not to trade on misappropriated information "ran to those with whom the misappropriator trades."[81] In this view, O'Hagan would have violated some duty to those who were on the other side of his market trades in Pillsbury. In *O'Hagan,* the Court held that the obligation runs to "the source of the information"—in that case, the law firm and its client.

The development of the law of insider trading under Rule 10b–5 has implicated different policies. The SEC originally asserted that the prohibition of insider trading was based upon equality of access to information. The Court rejected this in *Chiarella* and *Dirks*, and shifted the focus from equal access to preventing a breach of fiduciary duty owed to the shareholders of the company whose securities are traded. With misappropriation, liability is imposed on one who takes information in breach of a duty of confidentiality owed to the source of the information. Disclosure to the person on the other side of the trade is irrelevant. The breach of duty under this theory is the failure to disclose the proposed trading to the person with the proprietary right to the information. In other words, O'Hagan would not have committed a criminal violation if he had advised his law firm and Grand Met that he proposed to speculate in Pillsbury stock.

Policy Debate. Insider trading and tipping are illegal. Should they be? Law and economics scholars make a serious argument for deregulation in this area. Dean Henry Manne is the leading voice, and has opened a debate based upon economics. Dean Manne argues that insider trading promotes accuracy in stock prices because it results in moving stock prices to what they would be if the nonpublic information were divulged. In addition, insider trading might be an efficient means of compensating insiders who have produced information. This, in turn, gives the insiders a greater incentive to generate valuable information.

On the other side of the debate is a strong appeal to "fairness." More concretely, it may be said, especially in light of the Court's embrace of the misappropriation theory, that insider trading is a form of theft—of stealing information to which the insider does not have a right.

---

[81] *Chiarella,* 445 U.S. at 240.

D. Section 16(b)

1. Differences from Rule 10b–5

In contrast to Rule 10b–5, § 16(b) of the 1934 Act expressly addresses insider trading. Indeed, it applies to nothing but insider trading. But, as we will see, it sets forth a strange definition of insider trading. Cases under § 16(b), like Rule 10b–5 cases, must be brought in federal court. Beyond that, the two provisions are more different than they are similar.

First, § 16(b) applies only to trading in registered securities. That means it applies only in public corporations. Rule 10b–5 applies to "any person," so it can apply in any business, including closely held and publicly held corporations.

Second, § 16(b) applies only to trading in equity securities. Thus, it applies only to one who is trading stock, and not to one trading in debt securities.[82] Rule 10b–5, in contrast, applies to "any security" (equity or debt).

Third, § 16(b) imposes strict liability. If one makes a profit from trading securities under the very mechanical terms of the statute, that person must disgorge the profit, regardless of her intent. As we discuss in more detail below, there is an absolute statutory presumption that trading under § 16(b) was done on the basis of inside information. Rule 10b–5 is radically different because it requires a showing that the defendant acted with scienter.

Fourth, § 16(b) creates a claim for the corporation, while Rule 10b–5 creates a claim for the person injured by fraudulent behavior in a securities transaction. The corporation may assert the § 16(b) claim or a shareholder may assert it in a derivative suit.[83] The standing requirement of the regular derivative suit is relaxed a bit. For instance, the shareholder under § 16(b) need not have owned stock when the claim arose; merely owning stock at the time the suit is filed is sufficient.[84]

---

[82] The statute specifically refers to the purchase and sale of "any equity security."

[83] Gollust v. Mendell, 501 U.S. 115, 122 (1991) ("It is . . . the security holders of an issuer who have the ultimate authority to sue for enforcement of § 16(b). If the issuer declines to bring a § 16(b) action within 60 days of demand by a security holder, or fails to prosecute the action 'diligently,' 15 U.S.C. § 78p(b), then the security holder may 'institute' an action to recover insider short-swing profits for the issuer.").

[84] *Id.* at 123 ("[T]he terms of the statute do not even require that the security owner have had an interest in the issuer at the time of the defendant's short-swing trading, and the courts to have addressed this issue have held that a subsequent purchaser of the issuer's securities has standing to sue for the prior short-swing trading.").

Fifth, the SEC plays no role in enforcing § 16(b). The provision is enforced through a civil action brought by or on behalf of the corporation. In contrast, the SEC may undertake administrative proceedings for violations of Rule 10b–5.[85]

Sixth, § 16(b) applies only to three kinds of defendants. These "statutory insiders" are (1) directors of the corporation whose stock is traded, (2) officers of the corporation whose stock is traded, and (3) holders of more than 10 percent of the stock in the corporation whose stock is traded.[86] No one else can run afoul of § 16(b). This group of potential defendants is far more limited than Rule 10b–5, which, as we saw, applies to "any person."

2. Application of § 16(b)

Section 16(b) applies when a "statutory insider" buys *and* sells stock in her own corporation within six months. Thus, she must engage in at least two transactions: she must buy and sell stock of the corporation in which she serves as director or officer, or in which she owns more than ten percent of the stock. The purchase *and* the sale must be "within any period of less than six months."[87] This is called "short-swing" trading. The fact that a potential defendant under § 16(b) engages in short-swing trading will never be a surprise. Under § 16(a), the three types of defendants in § 16(b) are required to report to the SEC any "purchase" or "sale" of the company's stock. This information must be posted to a publicly accessible website by the end of the following business day. So the public has access to this information.

If a statutory insider buys and sells stock in her company within six months and makes a profit, the corporation is entitled to recover the profit. Remember that § 16(b) imposes strict liability. There is a conclusive presumption that the statutory insider bought and sold the stock on the basis of inside information. The plaintiff need not show intent. She need not even show that the defendant actually had inside information. Moreover, the defendant cannot escape liability by showing that she did not have inside information. Her state of knowledge and her intent are irrelevant.

---

[85] As noted above, the SEC may refer violations to the Department of Justice for criminal prosecution. In addition, Rule 10b–5 can be enforced by a civil action for damages brought by a buyer or seller of securities.

[86] The statute refers to such a holder as a "beneficial owner," and defines that person as one holding more than ten percent "of any class of any equity security" that is registered for public trading. 15 U.S.C. § 78p(a).

[87] *Id.*

The purpose of § 16(b) is to discourage statutory insiders from buying and selling their company's stock (within six months). The statute discourages the activity by taking away any profit the statutory insider makes in such trades. The fact that § 16(b) imposes strict liability means that the defendant's motivation for trading stock is irrelevant.

- D is a director of Corporation. On February 1, she bought 1,000 shares of Corporation's stock at $30 per share. In June, her husband suffered a heart attack. D desperately needed cash to pay her husband's extraordinary medical bills. In late June, D sold the 1,000 shares at $40 per share (thereby making a profit of $10,000). Corporation is entitled to her entire profit of $10,000. She bought and sold stock in her company within six months and made a profit. Under § 16(b), it is presumed that she traded on inside information and the profit must be disgorged.

The six-month window is entirely arbitrary and can be avoided by being careful.

- Same facts as in the preceding hypothetical, except that here D's husband suffers the heart attack in August. She sells the 1,000 shares at $40 per share on August 4. She makes a profit of $10,000. Because the purchase on February 1 and the sale on August 4 were more than six months apart, § 16(b) does not apply. The corporation has no claim to the profit.

Anyone with a calendar should be able to structure her buying and selling to avoid liability under § 16(b). Most cases involving liability involve inadvertence or confusion. In fairness, figuring out whether the statue applies can be confusing in some situations. For example, it may be that the actual trades were undertaken by a business and not by the statutory insider.

- Partnership buys and sells stock in Corporation within six months and makes a profit. One of the partners of Partnership is a director of Corporation. Does § 16(b) apply to disgorge her share of the profit? The general answer appears to be yes.[88]

---

[88] *See* Blau v. Lehman, 368 U.S. 403, 414 (1962) (when partnership made a profit in short-swing trading, a portion of the profit allocable to a director of the corporation was subject to § 16(b)). Note also that SEC Rule 16a–1(a)(2)(ii)(A) creates a rebuttable presumption that a statutory insider will have an interest in stock traded by

Another area of confusion is what constitutes a "purchase" and a "sale" under the statute. For example, are options to buy stock[89] covered by § 16(b)? What about redemptions[90] of stock by the corporation? What about acquisitions of the stock because of a fundamental change, such as a merger?[91] The SEC has removed some of the uncertainty regarding some, but not all, of these atypical sorts of transactions. For example, courts reached inconsistent conclusions about whether conversions of stock[92] constituted purchases or sales under § 16(b). The SEC resolved the issue in Rule 16b–9, which provides generally that conversions are neither purchases nor sales. Similarly, Rule 16b–3 brings some clarity by providing that stock options, at least when used as compensation, are not subject to § 16(b).[93]

In areas not covered by SEC rule, however, the Supreme Court has taken a rather surprising "pragmatic" approach.[94] It is surprising simply because the statute ordinarily is applied in a relentlessly mechanical way, as we have seen. The Supreme Court established the test for atypical transactions in *Kern County Land Co. v. Occidental Petroleum Corp.*,[95] which involved rather complicated facts. Company A launched a hostile takeover to acquire Company B. Through a tender offer, it acquired about 20 percent of the Company B stock. Some of those purchases would be covered by § 16(b).[96] Company B resisted and, as a defensive measure, merged with Company C. The merger resulted in Company A receiving stock in Com-

---

family members. Accordingly, short-swing profits made by a statutory insider's spouse or children may create liability for the statutory insider.

[89] We discuss such options in Chapter 10(B)(4).

[90] Redemptions are forced sales to the corporation at a price set in the articles. *See* Chapter 10(E)(5).

[91] In one case, the court concluded that an inside director whose shares were exchanged in a merger that he helped engineer was subject to § 16(b), while an outside director (whose shares were also exchanged) was not. Gold v. Sloan, 486 F.2d 340, 344 (4th Cir. 1973).

[92] Convertible securities allow the holder to change them to another type. For instance, a holder of one class of stock may be permitted to convert it into another class.

[93] When options are not given as compensation, the general rule is that § 16(b) is triggered when the buyer's or seller's obligation becomes fixed, and not when the option is actually exercised. Thus, shares would be deemed bought when the defendant acquired the option that established the price and number of shares that she could acquire. Magma Power Co. v. Dow Chem. Co., 136 F.3d 316, 320 (2d Cir. 1998).

[94] *See generally* Thomas L. Hazen, *The New Pragmatism Under Section 16(b) of the Securities Exchange Act,* 54 N.C. L. REV. 1 (1975).

[95] 411 U.S. 582 (1973).

[96] We will see below that only those purchases made after the defendant already owned more than ten percent are subject to § 16(b).

pany C. Not wanting to own that stock, and having failed in its take-over effort, Company A gave Company C an option to buy its Company C stock. Company C bought the stock, which meant that Company A had bought and sold stock within 6 months. But the purchases were not typical—they were the result of a merger and the exercise of an option. The Court prescribed the following approach:

> In deciding whether borderline transactions are within the reach of the statute, the courts have come to inquire whether the transaction may serve as a vehicle for the evil which Congress sought to prevent—the realization of short-swing profits based upon access to inside information—thereby endeavoring to implement congressional objectives without extending the reach of the statute beyond its intended limits.[97]

Applying this test, the Court concluded that the exchange of stock pursuant to the merger between Company B and Company C was not covered by § 16(b). In the Court's view, the transaction presented no potential for abuse of inside information by Company A.

We have noted that there are three types of defendants in § 16(b) cases: directors, officers, and holders of more than ten percent of the company's stock. Generally, there is no problem in determining whether someone is a director.[98] There can be some uncertainty, however, about who qualifies as an "officer." There is a tendency in some corporations toward "title inflation," which means that someone with no particular authority or responsibility is called a "vice president." The application of § 16(b) depends upon the person's actual responsibilities, and not on her title.[99]

It is clear that one can be pursued under § 16(b) if she were a director or an officer either at the time she buys or at the time she sells the stock. She need not be serving as a director or officer at both times.

- D is a director of Corporation on February 1, when she buys 100 shares of Corporation stock at $30 per share. She ceases being a director on April 1. She sells the stock on May 1 at

---

[97] 411 U.S. at 594–95 (footnote omitted).

[98] *But see* Feder v. Martin Marietta Corp., 406 F.2d 260, 263 (2d Cir. 1969) (when Company A designates someone to sit as its representative on the board of Company B, Company A may be treated as the "director" under § 16(b)).

[99] *See* Merrill Lynch, Pierce, Fenner & Smith, Inc. v. Livingston, 566 F.2d 1119, 1122 (9th Cir. 1978) ("[T]he court must look behind the title of the purchaser or seller to ascertain that person's real duties. Thus, a person who does not have the title of an officer may, in fact, have a relationship to the company which gives him the very access to insider information that the statute was designed to reach."). SEC Rule 16a–1(f) requires an "officer" to be engaged in policy making in the corporation.

$40 per share. She is liable to Corporation for her profit. It was made within six months, and she was a director during one of the events—here, the purchase. The result would be the same if she were an officer at either time.

Things are different, however, when the defendant is merely a shareholder. Section 16(b) applies only if she holds more than ten percent *both* at the time she buys and at the time she sells.[100] To determine this status, courts use a "snap shot" approach—asking how much she owned immediately *before* the purchase or the sale.[101] The percentage of her holding *after* the buy or the sale is irrelevant.

- S owns zero percent. She buys 11 percent of Corporation's stock. That purchase is not covered by § 16(b) because immediately before the purchase, S owned less than ten percent.[102] Now assume that S buys six percent more. That purchase is covered by § 16(b) because immediately before it was made, S owned more than ten percent. Within six months of this, if she sells all 17 percent, that sale will be covered because immediately before the sale, she held more than 10 percent.

No matter what kind of defendant is involved, the most vexing issue in applying § 16(b) can be the math. The goal of § 16(b) is to disgorge the statutory insider's *profit*. It is a universal principle that a profit can only be made if one buys something for a lower price and sells it for a higher price. So § 16(b) is only a problem when the statutory insider buys at a lower price than the price at which she sells (assuming the transactions are within six months). In the real world, the purchase will be before the sale—you buy something for $50 and, afterward, you sell it for $60. Everyone in the world agrees that you made a profit of $10.

---

[100] Remember that § 16(b) applies only to publicly held corporations. Very few individuals hold more than ten percent of the stock of a public corporation. Such a shareholder will almost always be another business organization. Typically, it will be an aggressor trying to takeover a target by buying the target's stock in the public market.

[101] *See Feder*, 406 F.2d at 267 ("The act expressly sets forth that the liability of a 10% shareholder to surrender his short-swing profits is conditional upon his being such both at the time of purchase and at the time of sale, but there is no such limitation in the case of officers and directors.").

[102] Foremost-McKesson, Inc. v. Provident Securities Co., 423 U.S. 232, 239–50 (1976). In *Reliance Electric Co. v. Emerson Electric Co.,* 404 U.S. 418 (1972), the defendant did not press the argument that its purchase taking it from zero percent to over ten percent should not be included for purposes of § 16(b). The Court in that case assumed that the purchase was covered. After *Foremost-McKesson*, it is clear that the statute does not apply to such a purchase.

The tricky part of § 16(b) is that the order of the purchase and sale is irrelevant. So long as the defendant bought the stock for a lower price than that at which she sold it, there is a profit—even if the purchase was after the sale!

- D is a director of Corporation. Two years ago, she bought 2,000 shares of Corporation stock at $30. On February 1 of this year, she sold 2,000 shares at $25. On June 1 of this year, she bought 1,500 shares at $19.

In the real world, D has made no profit. She bought at $30 two years ago and sold that stock for $25—that's a loss. Then, in June, she bought some more at $19. She has not sold those shares. Once again, in the real world, D has not made a profit. But under § 16(b) she has. She is strictly liable to Corporation for $9,000.[103]

Here is a foolproof way to apply § 16(b).

First, focus on the sale. Here the sale is February 1 of this year, when she sold at $25.[104]

Second, ask whether she bought for less than $25 within six months either before or after the sale. Here, she did nothing within six months before February 1. But within six months after that date (June 1), she bought at $19. So § 16(b) essentially says "you bought at $19 and you sold at $25; that is a profit of $6 per share." Believe it or not, that is the way it works! It is irrelevant that she sold before she bought. It is irrelevant that she has not sold the shares that she bought on June 1.[105]

Third, we must calculate the total "profit." She "made" $6 per share, and we multiply that by 1,500 shares. Why? We use the largest number of shares that she both bought and sold within the six months. Within the six months, she sold 2,000 shares (on February 1) and she bought 1,500 shares (on June 1). We use the 1,500 because that is the largest number common to both the buy and the sell. Suppose instead she had sold 2,000 shares on February 1 and bought only 500 on June 1. We would multiply by 500 shares because 500 is the largest number common to both the buy and the sell.

---

[103] Of course, the purchase does not have to be after the sale. The statute applies just as readily to the classic profit scenario of buying before selling.

[104] If there are multiple sales, repeat the exercise with each sale.

[105] If there are multiple sales and purchases, match the highest sales price with the lowest purchase price. In other words, maximize the "profit" to be expunged.

Chapter 12

FUNDAMENTAL CORPORATE CHANGES

Analysis

A. Introduction
B. Procedure for Fundamental Changes
C. Dissenting Shareholders' Right of Appraisal
D. Amendment to the Articles of Incorporation
E. Different Ways to Combine Businesses: Merger, Consolidation, and the Share Exchange
F. Disposition of All or Substantially All Assets
G. Conversion
H. Dissolution

A. Introduction

As we have seen, management in the corporation generally is vested in the board of directors. Shareholders elect directors, but do not ordinarily have a direct voice in management decisions. In this Chapter, we will focus on certain corporate acts that are so profound—that so fundamentally alter the entity—that the law requires approval both by the board of directors and by the shareholders. These "fundamental corporate changes" typically include: (1) amendment of the articles of incorporation, (2) merger of one corporation into another corporation, (3) acquisition of the company's stock in a "share exchange," (4) sale of substantially all the assets of the corporation, (5) conversion to another form or business, and (6) dissolution. All of these can be undertaken voluntarily by the corporation, assuming approval by both the board of directors and the shareholders. In addition, a court may order involuntary (judicial) dissolution of a corporation in certain circumstances.

Two preliminary points are important. First, statutes on fundamental changes vary considerably from state to state, so one must be careful to consult the appropriate legislation. Second, fundamental changes can implicate tax and regulatory considerations that are beyond the scope of this book. While knowledge of the legal aspects of fundamental changes, which we address in this Chapter, is essential, it is not sufficient for the practitioner in the field.

B. Procedure for Fundamental Changes

Each voluntary fundamental corporate change[1] generally requires five steps.

First, the board of directors approves the matter.[2] There have
been scholarly calls to increase the shareholders' power to initiate
fundamental changes.[3] Indeed, in a few states, shareholders have
some limited power to initiate a fundamental change.[4] For the most
part, though, there will be no fundamental change without action by
the board.

Second, the board informs the shareholders that it recommends
the fundamental change.[5]

Third, the board calls a special meeting of shareholders to consider the change. If the shareholders approve, the proposal will be
effected. If they reject it, the fundamental change will not be made.

Fourth, if the fundamental change is approved, shareholders
who opposed it may have a "dissenting shareholder's right of appraisal." As discussed in section C of this Chapter, this allows them
to force the corporation to buy their stock.

Fifth, in most fundamental changes, the corporation must inform the state by delivering a document summarizing the change,
which is filed with the secretary of state's office.[6]

We need to consider the third requirement in more detail. As we
saw in Chapter 6(C)(4), shareholders may take an act at a meeting
only if there is a quorum of shares. Unless the articles say otherwise,
this requires a majority of the shares entitled to vote. Interestingly,
in a few states, such as Ohio, the notice of the special meeting to consider a fundamental change must be sent to all shareholders—even

---

[1] That is, all fundamental changes except involuntary (judicial) dissolution.

[2] It will do so just as it takes any act: by unanimous written decision or by appropriate vote at a proper meeting. *See* Chapter 6(C)(3).

[3] *See, e.g.,* Lucian Arye Bebchuk, *The Case for Increasing Shareholder Power*, 118
HARV. L. REV. 833, 836 (2005).

[4] In Pennsylvania, ten percent of the voting shares can initiate amendment of the
articles. 15 PA. CONS. STAT. § 1912.

[5] *See, e.g.,* DEL. GEN. CORP. LAW § 242(b)(1).

[6] *See, e.g.,* RMBCA § 10.06 (concerning amendments to the articles); § 14.01 (concerning voluntary dissolution).

those who do not have voting rights.[7] In most states, however, notice goes only to those shareholders who have voting rights.[8]

Assuming there is a quorum at the shareholder meeting, the vote required to approve the fundamental change varies from state to state. There are three approaches: the traditional, the majority, and the most liberal. Under the traditional view, a proposal for fundamental change must be approved by two-thirds of the shares entitled to vote. This requirement is extraordinary for two reasons: it requires a supermajority (two-thirds), and it requires a supermajority of the shares *entitled* to vote—not simply of the shares present at the meeting.

- X Corp. has 6,000 shares entitled to vote on a fundamental change. Assume that 4,500 shares attend the meeting. At least 4,000 of those must vote "yes" to approve the proposal. This is because there must be approval by two-thirds of the 6,000 entitled to vote, and not two-thirds of the 4,500 present. Thus, if 3,800 shares attended the meeting, the change could not be approved because it would be impossible to get the "yes" votes of 4,000 shares.

Though the clear trend has been to relax this requirement, several states—including Texas,[9] Ohio,[10] and Massachusetts[11]—still require approval by two-thirds of the shares entitled to vote.

Today, the majority view requires approval by a majority of the shares entitled to vote. Note, however, that the majority has to be of those *entitled* to vote, and not simply of those present or actually voting.[12]

- X Corp. has 6,000 shares entitled to vote. At the meeting, 3,100 shares attend (so we have a quorum). At least 3,001 must vote "yes" to approve the fundamental change.

Recently, there has been a move toward an even more liberal view. Pennsylvania is emblematic of this move, which requires only

---

[7] *See, e.g.,* OHIO REV. CODE § 1701.41. This rule recognizes that every shareholder will be affected by a fundamental change, and permits non-voting shareholders to attempt to lobby their voting counterparts concerning the issue.

[8] *See, e.g.,* DEL. GEN. CORP. LAW § 242.

[9] TEX. BUS. ORGS. CODE § 21.45.

[10] OHIO REV. CODE § 1701.71.

[11] MASS. GEN. LAWS. ch. 156D, § 10.03.

[12] *See, e.g.,* DEL. GEN. CORP. LAW § 242(b)(1)(amendment of articles requires a "majority of the outstanding stock entitled to vote"); MICH. COMP. LAWS § 450.1611 (majority of outstanding shares entitled to vote); N.Y. BUS. CORP. LAW § 803 (same).

approval by a majority of the shares *actually voting* on the fundamental change.[13]

- X Corp. has 6,000 shares entitled to vote. At the meeting,
  3,100 shares attend (so we have a quorum), but only 2,800
  shares actually vote on whether the fundamental change
  should be approved (the other 300 shares do not vote). All
  that is required under this view is for 1,401 shares to vote
  "yes"—that would be a majority of the shares actually voted.

C. Dissenting Shareholders' Right of Appraisal

In the nineteenth century, the law required that fundamental
changes had to be approved by *every* shareholder. This rule gave
each shareholder a right to veto a proposed change.[14] Modern law
rejects this concept, and requires approval by only a designated percentage of the shares. Shareholders who dissent from the fundamental change, however, may be given a "right of appraisal." In other
words, modern law replaces a shareholder's right to veto with a right
of appraisal.[15]

Despite the name, the right of appraisal is really more than the
right to have one's stock appraised. Instead, it is the right to force
the corporation to buy one's stock at "fair value." If the corporation
and the shareholder cannot agree on that value, the issue will be litigated, and the court will determine the value. Statutes in each state
create the right of appraisal and prescribe detailed steps for exercising it.[16] Failure to adhere to the precise rules will result in waiver of
the right to be bought out.

Not all fundamental changes trigger the right of appraisal. As a
general rule, the right exists for (1) shareholders of the disappearing
corporation in a merger, (2) shareholders of a corporation that transfers substantially all of its assets, and (3) shareholders of a company
whose shares are acquired in a "share exchange." But the matter
varies from state to state. In a few states, for instance, some

---

[13] *See* 15 PA. CONS. STAT. § 1914.

[14] *See generally* VICTOR MORAWETZ, A TREATISE ON THE LAW OF PRIVATE CORPO-
RATIONS § 951 (2d ed. 1886).

[15] "At common law, unanimous shareholder consent was a prerequisite to fundamental changes in the corporation. This made it possible for an arbitrary minority to
establish a nuisance value for its shares by refusal to cooperate. To meet the situation, legislatures authorized the making of changes by majority vote. This, however,
opened the door to victimization of the minority. To solve the dilemma, statutes
permitting a dissenting minority to recover the appraised value of its shares were
widely adopted." Voeller v. Neilston Warehouse Co., 311 U.S. 531, 535 (1941). *See
also* William J. Carney, *Fundamental Corporate Changes, Minority Shareholders,
and Business Purposes*, 1980 AM. B. FOUND. RES. J. 69, 82.

[16] *See, e.g.,* RMBCA § 13.02(a); DEL. GEN. CORP. LAW § 262(a).

amendments to the articles give rise to a right of appraisal, though in most states amendments will not.[17] And in some states shareholders of both corporations in a merger (the disappearing corporation and the surviving corporation) will have a right of appraisal, while in most only the shareholders of the disappearing corporation will have it.[18] In most states, only shareholders who are entitled to vote on the fundamental change will have a right of appraisal.[19] In a few states, however, even holders of non-voting stock will be able to exercise the right.[20]

But even if a corporation undertakes an act that ordinarily will trigger a right of appraisal, most states recognize an important exception: appraisal is not available if the company's stock is publicly traded or if the corporation has a large number of shareholders (usually 2,000 or more).[21] This means, essentially, that the right of appraisal exists only in closely held corporations. And this makes sense. If the corporation's stock is publicly traded, or if there is a large number of shareholders, the disgruntled shareholder need not force the corporation to buy her stock. She can simply sell her stock on the public market (or to one or more of the other shareholders).[22] Accordingly, the right of appraisal is necessary only for shareholders in small corporations.

In most states, shareholders must take three steps to exercise their right of appraisal. First, before the shareholder vote on the matter, the shareholder must file with the corporation a statement of her objection to the proposed change and of her intent to demand

---

[17] *Compare* RMBCA § 13.02(a)(4)(appraisal rights available for some amendments to articles); ALA. CODE § 10A–2–13.02(a)(4)(appraisal rights for amendments that "materially and adversely" affect rights of shareholders); MASS. GEN. LAWS ch. 156D, § 13.02(a)(4)(same); N.Y. BUS. CORP. LAW § 806(b)(6)(similar) *with* DEL. GEN. CORP. LAW § 251(c)(no appraisal rights for amendment of certificate unless certificate provides otherwise).

[18] *Compare* RMBCA § 11.04(g)(shareholders of surviving corporation need not approve merger) *with* DEL. GEN. CORP. LAW § 251(c)(approval required from shareholders of "each constituent" corporation).

[19] *See, e.g.,* RMBCA § 13.02. There are exceptions when a shareholder's rights are affected by amendments to the articles. *See also* RMBCA § 13.02(a)(4); GA. CODE § 14–2–1302.

[20] OHIO REV. CODE § 1701.85; MASS. GEN. LAWS ch. 156D, § 13.02.

[21] This is called a "stock market exception" or "market-out exception." *See generally* RMBCA § 13.02, Official Comment 2 (market exception is based on the principle that the market price will be an adequate proxy for fair value where an efficient market exists). *See also* DEL. GEN. CORP. LAW § 262(b)(no appraisal rights where shares are "held of record" by more than 2,000 shareholders).

[22] This is why appraisal statutes generally speak of a shareholder's recovering the "fair value," and not the "fair market value," of her stock. In a closely held corporation, there is no market for the stock, and therefore no market value. *See generally* Joseph W. Anthony & Karlyn V. Boraas, *Betrayed, Belittled . . . But Triumphant: Claims of Shareholders in Closely Held Corporations,* 22 WM. MITCHELL L. REV. 1173, 1186 (1996). *See also* note 28.

payment if the deal is approved. Second, the shareholder must abstain or vote against the proposed change. And third, within a set time (usually 20 days) after official notification from the corporation that the change has been approved, the shareholder must make a written demand to be bought out at a particular price and must tender her stock to the corporation.[23]

The corporation may accede to the shareholder and pay her demanded price, or it may reject the demand and offer to pay a lower amount.[24] Then the shareholder may accept that lesser figure or reject it. At some point, depending upon the statute, either the corporation or the shareholder will file suit for an appraisal. One common provision requires the corporation to sue within 60 days of the shareholder's demand.[25] Failure to file suit may mean that the corporation is bound to pay the shareholder what she demanded.

When the matter is litigated, the courts in most states will appoint an appraiser to assess the value of the stock. But how does an appraiser or a judge calculate the value of the stock? The goal is to determine the value "immediately before" the fundamental change took place—so, for example, immediately before the company merged or sold off all of its assets.[26] Courts in some states may award attorney's fees either to or against the corporation depending upon the good faith with which the parties set their estimates of fair value.[27]

Delaware courts developed a means of calculation known as the "Delaware block" or "weighted averages" method. This method looks to three factors—net asset value, earnings per share, and market value of the company before the fundamental change took place.[28] The court then weights these factors as it sees fit on the facts of the

---

[23] *See, e.g.*, RMBCA ch. 13; DEL. GEN. CORP. LAW § 262.

[24] In Massachusetts, the corporation makes the first determination of the value, and proffers that amount to the shareholder; if she rejects it, she then states what she thinks the value is. MASS. GEN. LAWS ch. 156D, §§ 13.24, 13.25, 13.26(a).

[25] *See, e.g.*, RMBCA § 13.30(a).

[26] *See, e.g.*, COLO. REV. STAT. § 7–113–101; MINN. STAT. § 302A.473(c); VT. STAT. 11A, § 13.01; WYO. STAT. § 17–16–1301; *see also* DEL. GEN. CORP. LAW § 262(h) (stating that the fair value of shares will be determined "exclusive of any element of value arising from the accomplishment or expectation of" a merger or sale of assets); N.Y. BUS. CORP. LAW § 623(h)(4) (fair value is to be calculated on the close of business the day before the shareholder authorization); CAL. CORP. CODE § 1300 (stating that fair market value shall be determined "as of the day before the first announcement of the terms of" the proposed merger or reorganization.)

[27] *See, e.g.*, MINN. STAT. § 302A.473(c); N.J. STAT. § 14A:11–10; N.Y. BUS. CORP. LAW § 623(h)(7).

[28] We said above that there is no market value of the stock of a close corporation. But there will always be a market value *of the corporation itself,* which is what this factor in the Delaware block method refers to. This means the price the overall business would command if it were offered for sale to the public.

case. So, for example, it might multiply net asset value by 40 percent, earnings per share by 30 percent, and market value by 30 percent. Academic literature has criticized this method, principally for being too subjective.[29]

As a consequence, courts have moved away from the Delaware block method and embraced other accounting models for setting the appraisal price. A generation ago, even the Delaware Supreme Court held that the block method shall no longer "exclusively control" in appraisal proceedings.[30] The court in that case instructed judges to take "a more liberal approach," including "proof of value by any techniques or methods [that] are generally considered acceptable in the financial community and otherwise admissible in court."[31] Such valuation techniques are studied in detail in business schools, but not so much in law schools. Most lawyers consider the topic a "black box," and readily engage accounting experts to assist them in litigation.[32]

After determining the value of the dissenting shareholder's stock, some courts discount that value in one of two ways. A "minority discount" reduces the valuation because the shareholder does not hold enough stock to affect corporate decision-making.[33] A "lack of marketability" discount reduces the valuation because there is no market on which a shareholder can sell her stock.[34] Neither discount makes sense.[35] By definition, the shareholder in this situation will hold a minority of the stock. If she held a majority, she could have blocked the fundamental change from being approved. And by definition, there is no market for her stock because we are dealing here with closely held corporations. So both discounts are inconsistent with the statutory goal of setting the fair value of the stock, which should simply be the shareholder's pro-rata share of the value of the

---

[29] See Note, *Using Capital Cash Flows to Value Dissenters' Shares in Appraisal Proceedings,* 111 HARV. L. REV. 2099 (1998).

[30] Weinberger v. UOP, Inc., 457 A.2d 701, 713 (Del. 1983).

[31] *Id.*

[32] *See, e.g.,* Bernhard Grossfield, *Lawyers and Accountants: A Semiotic Competition,* 36 WAKE FOREST L. REV. 167 (2001).

[33] *See* Moore v. New Ammest, Inc., 630 P.2d 167, 177 (Kan. Ct. App. 1981).

[34] *See* Perlman v. Permonite Mfg. Co., 568 F. Supp. 222 (N.D. Ind. 1983), aff'd, 734 F.2d 1283 (7th Cir. 1984).

[35] *See, e.g.,* James Edward Harris, *Valuation of Closely Held Partnerships and Corporations: Recent Developments Concerning Minority Interest and Lack of Marketability Discounts,* 42 ARK. L. REV. 649 (1989); Bobbie J. Hollis II, *The Unfairness of Applying Lack of Marketability Discounts to Determine Fair Value in Dissenters' Rights Cases,* 25 J. CORP. L. 137 (1999). *But see* Zenichi Shishido, *The Fair Value of Minority Stock in Closely Held Corporations,* 62 FORDHAM L. REV. 65 (1993)(arguing that such discounts are proper because the existence of disgruntled minority shareholders contributes to a decline in the value of the stock).

company. Accordingly, courts increasingly reject minority and lack of marketability discounts.[36]

The assertion of appraisal rights can create severe cash drains for the corporation. After all, the company must find the money with which to buy back the dissenting shareholders' stock. Sometimes, the demand is too great for the corporation to meet. Accordingly, sophisticated businesses provide an escape provision in merger and other agreements, which obviates the fundamental change upon the exercise of appraisal rights by a particular percentage of shares.

One important question is whether the right of appraisal is the shareholder's exclusive remedy for any of the various fundamental changes. In most states, appraisal seems to be exclusive unless the fundamental change "is unlawful or fraudulent with respect to the shareholder or the corporation."[37] The typical argument is that the change was undertaken not for some legitimate corporate purpose, but to squeeze out minority shareholders. Most cases involve mergers in which minority shareholders claim that they should be able to sue for rescission. If the fundamental change has already been effected, the shareholders may sue for "rescissory damages," which is a monetary recovery that would put them in the position they would have been in had the change not occurred.

An example is *Coggins v. New England Patriots Football Club, Inc.*[38] In that case, Sullivan borrowed millions of dollars to purchase all of the voting stock of the corporation that owned the New England Patriots (he was already the majority shareholder). As a condition of the loan, however, banks insisted that Sullivan reorganize the corporation so that its income would be devoted to repaying the loan. In addition, they insisted that the loan be secured by corporate assets (not just the stock). To do this, Sullivan had to get rid of minority shareholders—who owned nonvoting stock. He put together a merger, under which the minority shareholders received a cash payment of $15 per share. The merger was approved through the requisite procedure. A group of minority shareholders sued Sullivan for oppressive behavior, which, they said, breached a fiduciary obligation allegedly owed to them by Sullivan.

The Supreme Judicial Court of Massachusetts held for the shareholders. First, the court held that the right of appraisal is not

---

[36] HMO-W, Inc. v. SSM Health Care System, 611 N.W.2d 250, 255 (Wisc. 2000) (rejecting the minority discount but not ruling on the lack of marketability discount because it was not properly raised on appeal).

[37] RMBCA § 13.02(b).

[38] 492 N.E.2d 1112 (Mass. 1986).

exclusive if plaintiffs show a breach of fiduciary duty.[39] Second, the court found that the merger constituted such a breach because it was not supported by a legitimate business reason. The purpose of the merger was to permit Sullivan to get a personal loan so that he could buy all of the voting stock. Thus, the controlling shareholder had breached a duty to the minority.[40] Finally, while the normal remedy would have been an injunction against the merger or rescission, here neither of these alternatives would work. Why? The case did not get to the court until a decade after the merger, so undoing the deal was impossible.[41] Instead, the plaintiffs could recover "rescissory damages," which would be the present value of the minority shareholders' stock. Because the Patriots had increased markedly in value over that decade, the minority shareholders recovered far more than the $15 merger cash-out price.

Under *Coggins,* the plaintiff bears the initial burden of showing self-dealing by the defendant. If she does this, the burden shifts to the defendant to show: (1) a legitimate business (as opposed to personal) purpose for the transaction and (2) that the transaction was fair to the minority shareholders. Because Sullivan could not show a business reason for the merger, the court did not have to address the question of fairness.[42]

Delaware courts also permit minority shareholders to sue for breach of duty in the context of fundamental corporate changes. Interestingly, though, Delaware does not assess whether the change was made for a legitimate business purpose. Instead, as established in *Weinberger v. UOP, Inc.,*[43] after the plaintiff shows self-dealing, the defendant has the burden of showing that the deal was fair under the "entire fairness" test (sometimes called the "intrinsic fairness" test).[44] This is a rigorous standard, under which the defendant must show that the transaction was: (1) procedurally fair (looking at the overall course of dealing, such as who initiated the deal) and (2) substantively fair (looking at the price).[45] Few defendants can meet this test.[46]

---

[39] *Id*. at 1118.

[40] *Id*.

[41] *Id*. at 1119.

[42]*Id*.

[43] 457 A.2d 701, 713 (Del. 1983).

[44] The "entire fairness" test is essentially the same as the "intrinsic fairness" test. *See* Tanzer v. Int'l Gen. Indus. Inc., 402 A.2d 382, 386 (Del. Ch. 1979).

[45] *Weinberger,* 457 A.2d at 711.

[46] Because this is true, a court's decision to employ the entire fairness test is often determinative: defendants lose. On the other hand, if the court employs the business judgment rule, defendants almost always win.

It is worth emphasizing that not every objection to a fundamental change will justify a suit for rescission or rescissory damages. Indeed, as the Delaware Supreme Court recognized in *Weinberger*, if the shareholder's complaint is that the financial terms of a cash-out merger are inadequate, appraisal should be her only remedy.[47] States also take differing approaches on whether claims of fraudulent or otherwise unlawful behavior may be addressed in the appraisal proceeding, or whether they have to be litigated separately. Most courts seem to reach the common-sense conclusion that the questions may be litigated in a single proceeding.[48]

D. Amendment to the Articles of Incorporation

The articles of incorporation is a document of singular importance; filing it is what formed the corporation itself. Not surprisingly, then, amending this document is a fundamental corporate change, which can be accomplished only though the procedure discussed in section B.[49] Recall that the articles set forth, *inter alia,* the number of shares that the corporation is authorized to issue. So if the corporation has issued all of the stock authorized in its original articles, it will be required to amend its articles if it wishes to raise capital by issuing more stock. Another common reason to amend the articles is to include an exculpatory clause to shield directors from liability for damages.[50]

What happens if an amendment is harmful to a particular group of shareholders? For instance, the articles might be amended to delete dividend rights or voting rights for a specific class of stock. In relatively early times, some courts concluded that shareholders had a "contractual" or "vested" right in articles provisions, and that such provisions could not be amended over the objection of those shareholders.[51] Modern law expressly rejects this theory.[52]

---

[47] *Weinberger,* 457 A.2d at 703–04.

[48] *See, e.g.,* HMO-W, Inc. v. SSM Health Care System (Wis. 2000). *But see* Cede & Co. v. Technicolor, 542 A.2d 1182, 1189 (Del. 1988) (judicial expansion of appraisal proceeding to include a fraud claim would create "unforeseen administrative and procedural problems").

[49] In some states, relatively minor changes—such as changing the registered agent —may be accomplished by the board without shareholder approval. *See, e.g.,* RMBCA § 10.05(3); N.C. GEN. STAT. § 55–10–02(3).

[50] *See* Chapter 13(H).

[51] *See, e.g.,* Keller v. Wilson & Co., 21 Del. Ch. 391 (1936). *See generally* FRANKLIN A. GEVURTZ, CORPORATION LAW 780–81 (2d ed. 2010) ("[H]istorically, . . . courts refused to interpret ambiguous provisions . . . as authorizing article amendments which would take away financial rights from an objecting minority.").

[52] *See* RMBCA § 10.01(b) ("A shareholder of the corporation does not have a vested property right resulting from any provision in the articles of incorporation. . . .")

This does not mean that shareholders are powerless in the face of amendments that harm their interests. Most states seem to provide one of two potential protections. One, provided in some states, is the right of appraisal, which we saw in section C. Specifically, if an amendment "materially and adversely affects" a shareholder, she has the right to force the corporation to buy her out (assuming the various requirements of the appraisal statute are satisfied).[53] The other, provided by states in lieu of a right of appraisal, is "class voting." This requires that the amendment be approved not only by the appropriate percentage of all shares, but by a like percentage of shares in the affected class.[54] Under this regime, if the class affected does not approve the amendment, the amendment fails.[55]

A shareholder aggrieved by an amendment may attempt to sue for breach of fiduciary duty. Some courts may entertain claims challenging vindictive or other harmful amendments that serve no purpose other than to oppress minority shareholders. In *Byelick v. Vivadelli*,[56] majority shareholders engineered an amendment that reduced the plaintiff's ownership from 10 to one percent. The federal court, purporting to apply Virginia law, held that the "dilutive transaction can be challenged under the Virginia common law of fiduciaries."[57] It imposed upon the defendants the burden of demonstrating that the amendment was fair.[58] Undoubtedly, some states would not permit such suits, but would instead find the statutory protections of appraisal rights or class voting to be exclusive.

E. Different Ways to Combine Businesses: Merger, Consolidation, and the Share Exchange

A great deal of corporate activity concerns acquisitions of one company (or multiple companies) by another. In common terms, the "acquirer" wishes to take over the "target." There are several ways to accomplish such a combination of businesses. We summarize them in this section. It is important to understand, however, that the choice

---

[53] *See, e.g.*, MINN. STAT. § 302A.471.

[54] *See, e.g.*, RMBCA § 10.04 (requiring approval from each class of shares adversely affected by the amendment).

[55] Some states do not provide such protection to non-voting stock. *See, e.g.*, DEL. GEN. CORP. LAW § 251(c). Moreover, class voting will not afford protection when majority shareholders of stock benefited by the proposed amendment also hold a majority of the shares harmed by it. They can outvote the disgruntled minority. *See, e.g.*, Lacos Land Co. v. Arden Gp., Inc., 517 A.2d 271, 275–76 (Del. Ch. 1986).

[56] 79 F. Supp. 2d 610 (E.D. Va. 1999).

[57] *Id.* at 627.

[58] *Id.* at 629.

of method will be affected in the real world by a host of other considerations, including tax and regulatory law.[59]

Technically, a *merger* involves the combination of two existing corporations, one of which will survive and one of which will cease to exist. So if Target Co. merges into Acquirer Co., Target disappears and Acquirer survives. Essentially, Target is folded into Acquirer. Technically, a *consolidation* involves two existing corporations, both of which disappear to form a new entity. So if X Corp. and Y Corp. consolidate to form Z Corp., both X Corp. and Y Corp. disappear and Z Corp. is created. Increasingly, states consider consolidation obsolete because it is usually advantageous to have one of the extant corporations survive. Moreover, if a new entity is desired, the proprietors can simply form it and merge the other corporations into it. Accordingly, the law in many states and under the RMBCA simply does not provide for consolidations. Delaware, however, retains the consolidation.[60] For convenience, we will refer to "mergers," but our discussion applies to consolidations as well.

A merger is always a fundamental change for a corporation that will cease to exist. Indeed, it is difficult to imagine a more fundamental change, since it results in the termination of that corporation's legal existence. Accordingly, the transaction must be approved not only by the board of directors, but also by the shareholders of that corporation under the procedure detailed in section B. Increasingly, a merger is not considered a fundamental change for the surviving corporation.[61] Thus, the shareholders of that corporation will not vote and will not have the right of appraisal. In Delaware, shareholders of a surviving corporation must approve a merger only if the transaction will amend that company's articles and the corporation will issue an additional 20 percent of stock in consummating the deal.[62]

One abiding characteristic of a merger is "successor liability." This means that the surviving company will succeed to the assets, rights, and liabilities of the corporation that ceases to exist. The doctrine protects creditors. Any creditor holding a claim against a corporation that was terminated in a merger automatically holds the claim against the surviving company. The surviving company has an economic incentive to assume the liabilities of the disappearing constituent. By assuming the liabilities, the acquirer pays less to obtain the

---

[59] An entire course in the law school curriculum, Mergers and Acquisitions, is devoted to the topic.

[60] DEL. GEN. CORP. LAW § 251(a).

[61] *See, e.g.,* RMBCA § 11.04(g).

[62] *See, e.g.,* DEL. GEN. CORP. LAW § 251(f).

target company. In other words, the price it pays to acquire the target company will reflect the survivor's assumption of liabilities.

In a *leveraged buy-out,* "LBO," the acquirer uses borrowed funds to finance the merger. Thus, it acquires the target without committing much, if any, of its own capital. To obtain a loan for this purpose, obviously, the acquirer will have to offer some form of collateral to the entity from which it borrows.[63] Usually, in an LBO, the acquirer uses the assets of the disappearing corporation for this purpose. If all goes well, the surviving corporation is able to pay off the loan using earnings from the business itself.[64]

The classic merger is a stock-for-stock transaction in which two similarly sized corporations combine. The shareholders of the target corporation give up their stock in that company and receive stock of the acquirer in exchange. For generations, this was the only form a merger could take. Today, however, things have changed. Modern statutes are far more flexible, and permit paying off the shareholders of the target corporation in stock or other securities, in options to acquire stock or other securities, or in "cash, other property, or any combination of the foregoing."[65] These modern provisions open the door for creative machinations, as well as for some colorful terminology.

Suppose the acquirer (A Co.) wants to take over the target (T Co.). The companies could simply set up a merger, with T Co. merging into A Co. Then, however, under the doctrine of successor liability, A Co. would assume the obligations of T Co.

Instead, the parties can engineer a *triangular merger.* Here, A Co. forms a wholly-owned subsidiary ("Sub Co."). A Co. capitalizes Sub Co. with cash or with A Co. stock. A Co. owns all of the stock of Sub Co. Then T Co. merges into Sub Co. The shareholders of T Co. receive the cash or A Co. stock with which Sub Co. was capitalized. Sub Co. receives all of the stock of T Co. As a result, (1) A Co. effectively acquires all of the stock of T Co. (because A Co.'s subsidiary now owns all of that stock); (2) the shareholders of T Co. get either stock in A Co. or cash (in which case they hold no stock in any of the

---

[63] After the upswing of activity in the 1970s and 1980s, LBOs became lukewarm during the 1990s to early 2000s. However, with the recent corrections seen in the market and the general economy, lower valuations seem more realistic, and thus, LBOs seem to be making a comeback.

[64] The success based on a leveraged investment is only one side of the coin, as there are considerable risks attached to such an operation. This is, after all, a debt-financed venture almost wholly dependent upon the performance of the acquired entity. If the earnings of the business are not sufficient to pay off the loan, then debt levels are bound to turn excessive.

[65] *See, e.g.,* RMBCA § 11.02(c)(3).

companies); and (most importantly) (3) A Co. does not assume responsibility for the liabilities of T Co. (Sub Co., as survivor of the merger, does that).

Why go through all this? In most of these deals, A Co. and T Co. are publicly traded corporations with widely held stock, and the subsidiary is formed solely to facilitate the acquisition. The transaction may be substantially cheaper than a direct merger between A Co. and T Co. because the parties do not have to bear the expense of a shareholder vote of the publicly traded A Co. More significantly, this arrangement allows A Co. to acquire T Co. without assuming direct liability for T Co.'s obligations.

Another possibility is the *reverse triangular merger*. Here, A Co. forms a wholly-owned subsidiary (Sub Co.), but Sub Co. then merges *into* T Co. In the merger between Sub Co. and T Co., shareholders of T Co. get the stock of Sub Co., which is exchanged for cash or perhaps for stock in A Co. As a result, T Co. ends up being a wholly owned subsidiary of A Co.[66] The critical point is that both triangular and reverse-triangular mergers involve three way transactions by which T Co. becomes a wholly owned subsidiary of A Co. without a transfer or assignment directly between the two corporations. T Co.'s shareholders receive cash or shares of A Co. even though the merger is with a subsidiary of A Co.

An increasing number of states recognize a fundamental corporate change called the *share exchange*.[67] It is essentially a substitute for the reverse triangular merger. The name is misleading—it is not an exchange of shares, but a device that compels a sale of stock. In other words, it forces the shareholders of a target company to sell its stock to the acquiring company. The result is that the acquirer gets all of the stock of the target, and the shareholders of the target end up with cash or other property.

The share exchange is a fundamental change only for the target company. Accordingly, the transaction must be approved through the procedure discussed in section B. If it is, all shareholders must relinquish their stock under the terms of the exchange—even those who opposed the deal.[68] A dissenting shareholder of the target company may assert appraisal rights. But, because the share exchange is not

---

[66] By way of comparison, in a regular merger, the acquirer will retain the stock it owns of the subsidiary. In a reverse triangular merger, the acquirer will receive shares of the target in exchange for the stock it owned in the subsidiary.

[67] *See, e.g.,* RMBCA § 11.03; MASS. GEN. LAWS ch. 156D, § 11.03.

[68] *See generally* RMBCA § 11.04, Official Comment.

a fundamental change for the acquiring company, its shareholders do not vote on the transaction and do not have a right of appraisal.[69]

Many mergers are between parent and subsidiary corporations. If the parent will be the surviving company, it is an *upstream merger*. If the subsidiary survives, it is a *downstream merger*. A downstream merger can be used to change the state of incorporation of a publicly held corporation. The corporation creates a wholly-owned subsidiary in the new state of incorporation, and then merges itself into its subsidiary. The stock and financial interests of the parent are mirrored in the stock and financial structure of the subsidiary. When the merger occurs, the shareholders and creditors of the old publicly held corporation incorporated in State A become shareholders and creditors in a corporation incorporated in State B.

Many states have adopted statutes that provide a special summary merger procedure—called a *short-form merger*—for upstream or downstream mergers when the parent owns a large majority (usually 90 percent or more) of the stock of the subsidiary. The short-form merger allows a parent to merge its subsidiary into it (or vice versa) without a shareholder vote in either corporation. Moreover, the board of directors of the subsidiary is not required to approve the merger.[70] The short-form procedure is based on the reality that the minority shareholders of the subsidiary simply cannot block approval of the merger; the parent corporation owns at least 90 percent of the stock of the subsidiary, so the outcome of a shareholder vote is clear. In some states, the minority shareholders of the subsidiary will have appraisal rights, even though they did not have the right to vote on the transaction.[71]

Finally, a *cash-out merger* is exactly what it sounds like: shareholders of the target company give up their stock in the target in exchange for cash. Such transactions are also called *freeze-out* or *squeeze-out* mergers because they freeze or squeeze these shareholders out of their equity interest. Before the deal goes through, they are equity holders; afterward, they no longer hold an equity interest.

In a typical cash-out merger, T Co. is merged into A Co. The majority shareholders of T Co. receive stock in A Co. and the minority shareholders of T Co. receive cash or other property as consideration. This procedure can be used to force out unwanted minority shareholders, or to eliminate public ownership as part of a "going private"

---

[69] *See generally* RMBCA § 11.04, Official Comment (approval of shareholders is not required if the corporation will survive the merger or is acquiring another corporation in a share exchange).

[70] *See, e.g.,* RMBCA § 11.05.

[71] *See, e.g.,* DEL. GEN. CORP. LAW § 253.

transaction. The latter occurs when management decides to avoid various requirements imposed on publicly traded corporations. There are legitimate reasons to cash out the minority shareholders.[72]

On the other hand, the cash-out merger (like any corporate change) can be used to oppress minority shareholders. For example:

- X, Y, and Z are the shareholders of XYZ Corp. Each owns one-third of the stock. After a disagreement, X and Y cause XYZ Corp. to merge into XY Co., which they own. Under the terms of the merger, X, Y, and Z receive equal cash consideration. After the merger, X and Y (through XY Co.) now have complete control of what used to be XYZ Corp. Z is out of luck. He has cash, but has no equity position in any company.

What can Z do? The starting point is her statutory right of appraisal, by which she can force the corporation to buy her stock at fair value. That may be a higher figure than the cash-out price she was paid in the merger. The big question will be whether the right of appraisal is the exclusive remedy. As we discussed above, in some states Z may be able to sue if the transaction was tinged with fraud or oppression.

F. Disposition of All or Substantially All Assets

Selling all or substantially all of a business's assets, "not in the ordinary course of business," is a fundamental corporate change[73] which must be approved by the procedure detailed in section B above. Though it may seem counterintuitive that a company would sell off its assets, there are good reasons for doing so. Usually, a corporation sells its assets before undergoing a voluntary dissolution and going out of business. In the voluntary dissolution, it will use the proceeds of the sale of assets to pay creditors. Any amount left over will then be distributed to its shareholders. Thus, often, the disposition of assets is the first step in ending the company's existence. In contrast, corporations sometimes sell their assets to raise cash to fund business operations or to invest in other ventures.

The sale of assets is a fundamental change only for the company actually disposing of its assets. It is not a fundamental change for the company buying the assets. This makes sense. When one invests

---

[72] Doing so may rid the company of internecine dissention between majority and minority factions. Or there may be tax reasons for doing so, particularly in the parent-subsidiary context. *See* John Hetheringon, *Defining the Scope of Controlling Shareholders' Fiduciary Responsibilities,* 22 WAKE FOREST L. REV. 9 (1987)(discussing the redemption of minority shareholders' interests).

[73] *See, e.g.,* RMBCA § 12.02.

in a company, she expects it to acquire things; there is nothing extraordinary about your company's buying up assets from other businesses. On the other hand, you do not expect your company to jettison as large portion of its assets. You, as shareholder, should have a voice in such an extraordinary event. And you do. Because the disposition of all assets is a fundamental change, the corporation must go through the approval process discussed in section B. This includes, of course, a shareholder vote and the dissenting shareholders' right of appraisal.[74] Because the purchase of assets is not a fundamental change, however, the buying company need not get approval as discussed in section B. Shareholders of the buying company have no vote on the matter and no right of appraisal.

We focus on three statutory terms. First, what is a "disposition" of all assets? Everyone agrees that a *sale* qualifies. Most states seem to agree that leasing or exchanging the assets for other property is also a "disposition." On the other hand, mortgaging or pledging the assets (for a loan, for instance) is not a "disposition." [75] Accordingly, it need not be approved by the shareholders.

Second, while a disposition of "all" assets is covered, what would qualify as a disposition of "substantially all" of the assets? Courts have not been consistent on this score.[76] They have been flexible,[77] and have required shareholder approval when significant components of the company are disposed of, even though other significant components are retained.

Third, the disposition of all or substantially all assets is only a fundamental change if it is "not in the ordinary course of business."[78] Some corporations are in the business of selling their assets—for example, a company that buys and sells real estate. But most companies are not, and it will usually be obvious when this is true.

There is an important distinction between disposition of assets, on the one hand, and mergers and consolidations, on the other. With such combinations, at least one business entity ceases to exist. Thus, we expect successor liability—that is, the surviving company succeeds to the assets, rights, and liabilities of the entities that disappear. In the sale of assets, however, no entity disappears. The com-

---

[74] *See* RMBCA §§ 12.02(a), 13.02(3).

[75] *See, e.g.,* Resnick v. Karmax Camp Corp., 149 A.2d 709 (N.Y. 1989).

[76]*See* Gimbel v. Signal Cos, 316 A.2d 599, 607 (Del. Ch. 1974) (transaction involving the sale of 41% of assets did not qualify as substantially all assets), *aff'd in part* 316 A.2d 619 (Del. 1974); *see also* Katz v. Breman, 431 A.2d 1274 (Del. Ch. 1981).

[77] *See* N.Y. BUS. CORP. LAW § 909; *see also* Eisen v. Post, 3 N.Y.2d 518 (1957) (relevant inquiry is not the dollar amount, but, instead, is whether the transaction is outside the normal and ordinary course of business).

[78] *See, e.g.,* RMBCA § 12.02.

pany that sold its assets still exists—and, indeed, now it should have considerable cash, because it just sold all of its assets. That means that a creditor of the selling corporation can sue it. And if the selling corporation dissolves, it will have to discharge its liabilities before distributing assets to shareholders. Accordingly, as a general rule, we do *not* expect successor liability in a sale of assets.

There are exceptions. For one, the parties are free to agree to the contrary. Thus, the company buying assets may agree to assume liabilities of the selling company. Presumably, doing so would permit the buyer to purchase the assets for a lower price. Another exception is the "mere continuation" doctrine. Under this, if the buyer is a mere continuation of the selling company, the court will apply successor liability. For example, if the buying company has the same management and engages in the same business as the selling company, a court may equate the two corporations and find the buyer to have assumed the seller's obligations.[79] Another exception is the "de facto merger" doctrine, by which a court concludes that what was structured as a sale of assets was "really" a merger.[80] Invoking this doctrine means that the transaction must be approved by the procedure discussed in section B.

Many cases dealing with these exceptions to the general rule involve product liability claims. For instance, in *Franklin v. USX Corp.*,[81] plaintiff's wife died of lung cancer, allegedly caused by exposure to asbestos when she was a child. Her parents worked for Western Pipe & Steel Shipyard (WPS) in the 1940s, and allegedly were exposed to asbestos, which they brought home unwittingly on their clothing, thereby exposing the plaintiff's wife. WPS sold its assets to Consolidated of California (Con Cal) in 1945 for $6.2 million in cash, and the buyer agreed to assume the liabilities of WPS. Con Cal sold its assets to Consolidated of Delaware (Con Del) in 1948 for $17 million. Later, Con Del was merged into United States Steel (USX). Plaintiff argued that WPS's liability from the 1940s was assumed by the subsequent companies, and thus that USX was liable for the product liability claim filed decades later.

Clearly, Con Cal was liable for claims against WPS because the deal between them said so. And clearly USX is liable for Con Del's claims because successor liability would attach to their deal (it was a merger). The question was whether Con Del assumed the liabilities of Con Cal when it bought its assets in 1945. The trial court held

---

[79] *See, e.g.,* Ed Peters Jewelry Co. v. C & J Jewelry Co., 124 F.3d 252 (1st Cir. 1997).

[80] The leading case on the doctrine is *Farris v. Glen Alden Corp.*, 143 A.2d 25 (Pa. 1958).

[81] 87 Cal. Ct. App. 4th 615 (2001).

that it did.[82] Although the transaction was a sale of assets and not a merger, the trial court found that it was a "de facto merger" and thus that successor liability attached.

The California Court of Appeal reversed.[83] It reviewed the case law on "mere continuation" and de facto merger and reached an interesting conclusion: no case had ever imposed successor liability in a sale of assets if the sale was for adequate consideration.[84] Stated another way, courts will impose successor liability in a sale of assets only if the sale involved insufficient consideration to cover reasonably foreseeable prospective liabilities. The court found that the purchase of assets for $17 million in 1945 was adequate. Indeed, plaintiff did not argue that there was insufficient consideration to meet the claims of creditors at the time Con Cal sold to Con Del and subsequently dissolved.

Successor liability in a sale of assets might be analogized to piercing the corporate veil on the basis of undercapitalization. Just as shareholders of a closely held corporation might be personally liable for corporate debts if they failed to invest enough capital to cover prospective liabilities when forming the company, so too a buyer of assets who fails to pay sufficient capital may be hit with successor liability. In each situation, limited liability is effectively "purchased" by parting with sufficient capital to cover prospective liabilities.

G. Conversion

Suppose the managers of a corporation decide that they would rather run their business as a limited liability company, or as a partnership. Historically, they would have to dissolve the corporation and form a new business. Increasingly, this is unnecessary because states permit a new fundamental change: the conversion. It is exactly what it sounds like. A corporation can convert to any other form of business by going through the procedure discussed above for any fundamental change. Those states permitting conversion generally provide that a dissenting shareholder has appraisal rights.[85]

H. Dissolution

Dissolution is the ultimate corporate change; it terminates the corporation's existence. Dissolution is a process that may take con-

---

[82] *Id.* at 620.

[83] *Id.* at 629.

[84] *Id. at* 625 (stating that the crucial factor in determining whether a corporate acquisition constituted a de facto merger or a mere continuation is whether adequate cash consideration was paid for the predecessor's assets).

[85] Under the RMBCA, the procedure is called "entity conversion," and it triggers appraisal rights. §§ 9.50–9.56, 13.02(a)(8).

siderable time. Assets must be gathered and sold, liabilities must be paid, and any remaining surplus must be distributed to shareholders. At the end of the process, the corporate existence will cease. Some recent statutes, such as the Texas Business Organizations Code, use "termination"[86] instead of dissolution, but the process is the same.[87] There are three types of dissolution.

Voluntary Dissolution. Here, the entity "decides" to dissolve and undertakes the process detailed above. In most states, the board of directors and the shareholders must approve the voluntary dissolution.[88] The corporation must give notice to creditors to ensure the orderly payment of obligations.[89] Moreover, the board of directors must ensure that all franchise and other taxes have been paid.[90] After the liquidation process (discussed below), the corporation files a certificate of dissolution, which ends the corporate existence.[91]

There is no right of appraisal from a voluntary dissolution. Because the corporation is ceasing its existence and will distribute its net assets to shareholders, it would make no sense to permit a shareholder to force the company to buy her stock. It is clear, however, that voluntary dissolution can be used (as mergers can be used) to freeze out minority shareholders unfairly. For example, controlling shareholders might cause dissolution in an effort to keep minority shareholders from sharing in a profitable business. Upon dissolution, some other entity—owned by the controlling shareholders—would take over the business. In such cases, courts should be willing to step in to provide protection for the minority owners by permitting them to sue for breach of fiduciary duty owed directly to them.[92]

Administrative Dissolution. With administrative dissolution, the appropriate state office terminates the corporate existence. The state does not have to go to court or get an order. It simply issues a certificate of dissolution. The reasons and procedures vary from state to state, but administrative dissolution usually arises when the proprietors abandon a business and fail to pay franchise taxes, file annual reports, or to do other things required of corporations.[93] The statutes require that the state give notice of its intention to shut the

---

[86] Tex. Bus. Orgs. Code § 11.101.

[87] Tex. Bus. Orgs. Code §§ 11.101–105.

[88] In some states, the pattern is different. For instance, in New York, voluntary dissolution is effected by vote of the shares, and does not require board of director action. N.Y. Bus. Corp. Law § 1001.

[89] *See, e.g.,* RMBCA § 14.06.

[90] *See, e.g.,* RMBCA § 14.09.

[91] *See, e.g.,* RMBCA § 14.03.

[92] *See, e.g., In re* Security Finance Co., 49 Cal.2d 370, 376 (1957); Noakes v. Schoenborn, 841 P.2d 682, 688 (Or. Ct. App. 1982).

[93] *See, e.g.,* RMBCA § 14.20.

corporation down, and give the proprietors an opportunity to fix the problems (or to demonstrate that the state office is incorrect). After administrative dissolution, it is possible for the proprietors to seek reinstatement of corporate status.

Involuntary Dissolution. Statutes permit specified persons to seek a judicial order dissolving a corporation. In most states, a creditor can do so if the corporation is insolvent and either the creditor has a judgment against the corporation or the company admits the debt in writing.[94] In some states, but not under the RMBCA, a director can petition for involuntary dissolution in limited circumstances.[95]

Most important, however, are provisions permitting shareholders to petition for dissolution. In many states, as in RMBCA § 14.30(a)(2), any shareholder may seek dissolution on various grounds, including (1) director deadlock, inability to break the deadlock, and the corporation is suffering or will suffer irreparable injury, (2) shareholder deadlock and inability for at least two consecutive annual meetings to fill a vacant seat on the board, (3) waste or misapplication of corporate assets, or (4) management is engaged in "illegal, oppressive, or fraudulent" behavior.[96]

Generally, such a shareholder petition will be made in a closely held corporation. Indeed, under RMBCA § 14.30(b), the shareholder petition is only available in closely held corporations. In some states, only specified percentages of shares can seek involuntary dissolution. In New York, for example, at least 20 percent of the shares in a closely held corporation must petition based upon illegal, oppressive, or fraudulent acts by management.[97]

In Chapter 8(F), we discussed oppressive behavior in the closely held corporation. Some courts have recognized a common law right to sue for such behavior. And, as we noted there, many states provide that such acts will support a petition to dissolve the closely held corporation. One important question is whether these statutes permit any other remedy. The principal alternative remedy would be a buy-out of the complaining shareholder. This course of action is often preferable to dissolution. It provides the minority shareholder with a fair return on her investment and allows a business (possibly a thriving business) to continue to operate.

In some states, the dissolution statute expressly allows the court to order alternative remedies and thus to avoid the harshness of end-

---

[94] *See, e.g.,* RMBCA § 14.30(a)(3).
[95] *See, e.g.,* CAL. CORP. CODE § 1800.
[96] *See, e.g.,* RMBCA § 14.30(a)(2).
[97] N.Y. BUS. CORP. LAW § 1104–a.

ing corporate existence.[98] In others, however, the statute is silent as to any remedy other than dissolution. Some courts have interpreted such statutes to forbid alternative remedies. In such states, the court is powerless to order the lesser remedy of a buy-out.[99] But other courts have concluded that they may order remedies other than dissolution.[100] In a few states, the involuntary dissolution statute permits the corporation or other shareholders to avoid dissolution by purchasing the stock of the petitioning shareholder.[101] The court must approve the purchase to ensure that the price is fair.

The Liquidation Process. We have seen that various events— such as approval of voluntary dissolution or a court order of involuntary dissolution—trigger dissolution. The corporation remains in existence after this triggering event, but only for the process of liquidation (or "winding up"). The board of directors usually oversees this process, although the court may appoint a receiver to do so in cases of involuntary dissolution if the directors have engaged in misconduct.[102]

This process consists of four steps.[103] First, those in charge collect all of the corporate assets. This includes claims the corporation may have against others. So the corporation may bring suit to perfect those claims in an attempt to gather the assets. Second, the assets usually are sold to generate cash. Third, creditors must be paid, and an appropriate amount must be set aside to cover prospective liabilities. Finally, any remaining funds are distributed to the shareholders.

As holders of the equity interest in the company, shareholders receive this liquidating distribution only after the creditors—the holders of debt interests—are paid off. Directors can be personally liable for distributions wrongfully made to shareholders before debts are discharged.[104] Shareholders receive the liquidating distribution just as they receive dividends—that is, pro rata by share. The articles may provide for a "liquidation preference" for a particular class, which will work just as a dividend preference works—the preferred shares are paid first, before the common shares. So if there were a

---

[98] *See, e.g.*, RMBCA § 14.34; MINN. STAT. § 302A.751 subd. 1–2 ("any equitable relief"); N.J. STAT. § 14A: 12–7(1)(providing nonexclusive list, including buy-out).

[99] *See, e.g.*, Giannotti v. Hamway, 387 S.E.2d 725, 734 (Va. 1990) (interpreting VA. CODE § 13.1–747(A)(1)(b)).

[100] See, e.g., Bedore v. Familian, 125 P.3d 1168, 1172 (Nev. 2006); Baker v. Commercial Body Builders, Inc., 507 P.2d 387, 395–96 (Or. 1973).

[101] *See, e.g.*, CAL. CORP. CODE § 2000; N.Y. BUS. CORP. LAW § 1118.

[102] *See, e.g.*, RMBCA § 14.32.

[103] *See, e.g.*, RMBCA § 14.05.

[104] *See, e.g.*, RMBCA § 8.33.

class of 1000 shares of stock with a liquidation preference of $2, the first $2000 would be paid to those shares.

After the debts are paid or provided for, and the remaining money distributed to shareholders, the directors certify these facts to the appropriate state officer, who then files a certificate formally ending the existence of the corporation.

Chapter 13

SHAREHOLDER AS PLAINTIFF: DERIVATIVE LITIGATION

Analysis

A. Introduction
B. Determining Whether a Case is Derivative
C. Overview of Derivative Litigation
D. Procedural Requirements for Derivative Litigation
    1. Contemporaneous Ownership
    2. Adequacy of Representation
    3. Security for Expenses
    4. Demand that the Corporation Bring Suit
E. Motions to Dismiss and Special Litigation Committees
F. Discontinuance or Settlement of a Derivative Suit
G. Indemnification Statutes
H. Exculpatory Provisions and Insurance

A. Introduction

As we have seen, shareholders are the owners of the corporation. That status allows them to do several things, including elect and remove directors, vote on fundamental changes, and inspect the books and records. In this Chapter, we focus on the right to bring a "shareholder's derivative suit." In such a case, the shareholder sues to vindicate the *corporation's* claim, and not her own personal claim. The suit is "derivative" because the shareholder's right to bring it "derives" from the corporation's right to sue.

But why should a shareholder be able to do this? After all, whether to have the corporation assert a claim is a management decision, which should be made by the board of directors. In two situations, though, the board might not have the corporation sue. First, there might be good business reasons not to sue. For example, suppose the corporation has an ongoing relationship with a supplier, and a contract dispute arises. The corporation could sue, but it values the relationship with the supplier and decides that the parties will work out the problem in the future. A derivative suit here seems questionable because it second-guesses the kind of business decision directors are hired to make.[1]

Second, the board may choose not to have the corporation pursue litigation because the directors themselves (or some of them) would be defendants in the case. The best examples are when directors breach the duty of care or duty of loyalty. Those duties are owed to the corporation, so breach of either harms the corporation. These are corporate claims, and the board has a conflict of interest—if it decides to have the corporation bring suit, they are acquiescing to a suit against themselves (or some of them). In such a case, a derivative suit may make great sense, because we have some question about whether the board will pursue such a claim with diligence.

The law permits a shareholder to initiate derivative suits in either situation. It imposes strict procedural requirements on the plaintiff, however, as we will see in section D. And it is not always clear that the shareholder will be permitted to prosecute the derivative suit to judgment. As we will see in section E, the corporation may move to dismiss because the claim is not in the company's best interest. In an effort to avoid abusive derivative litigation, courts must oversee the settlement or other discontinuance of such cases, as discussed in section F. It is worth remembering that derivative suits seek to impose personal liability on the defendants. One of the most significant developments in the past generation is the availability of protection for directors and officers from liability and from the expense of such litigation. We will discuss the layers of protection available in sections G and H.

B. Determining Whether a Case is Derivative

Whenever one sues in her capacity as a shareholder, her case will either be derivative or direct. With a derivative suit, she is suing to vindicate the corporation's claim. So, in a derivative suit, the corporation is the real party in interest.[2] With a direct suit, she sues to vindicate her own claim. If it is a derivative suit, the shareholder must satisfy all of the procedural requirements imposed in such cases, which we will see in section D. In a direct suit, in contrast, the plaintiff need not jump through any special procedural hoops.

---

[1] "[I]t is arguable that a refusal by the Board of Directors, however unreasonable, should always prevent a derivative suit against a third-party wrongdoer." Ash v. International Business Machines, Inc., 236 F. Supp. 218, 220 (E.D. Pa. 1964).

[2] See Ross v. Bernhard, 396 U.S. 531, 538 (1970) (in a derivative suit, the corporation "is the real party in interest, the stockholder being at best the nominal plaintiff").

As a rule of thumb, to determine whether a claim is derivative, ask: could the corporation have brought this suit? If so, it is probably a derivative suit because the plaintiff is vindicating the entity's claim.[3]

- S, a shareholder of C Corp., sues Third Party because Third Party allegedly breached its contract with C Corp. This is derivative because C Corp. could sue Third Party.

The best example of a derivative suit is a claim that directors or officers have breached the duty of care or loyalty (or both). Those fiduciary duties, as we saw in Chapter 7, are owed *to the corporation*.[4] So when a manager breaches such a duty, the corporation is the aggrieved party. Most derivative suits assert breach of these duties.

- The board of directors of XYZ Corp. approves a corporate purchase of land without undertaking any evaluation of the land. The property turns out to be worthless. This breach of the duty of care by the board has hurt XYZ Corp. A shareholder may bring a derivative suit against the directors to recover from them personally for the losses suffered by the corporation.

A derivative suit generally will be brought against either a third party or against individuals who have breached a duty to the corporation.[5] The suit seeks to impose personal liability on such defendants. These cases would have been brought by the corporation itself had the board decided to have the entity sue.

When a shareholder sues to vindicate her own claim (and not that of the corporation), she brings a "direct" suit. Such a case is just a "regular" lawsuit, and the plaintiff need not satisfy the procedural requirements imposed in derivative suits.

- S, a shareholder of C Corp., sues C Corp. because it issued stock without honoring her preemptive rights. This is a direct suit. C Corp. could not bring this suit because C Corp. has not been harmed. The harm is to the shareholder.

---

[3] "[Whether a stockholder's claim is derivative or direct] must turn *solely* on the following questions: (1) who suffered the alleged harm (the corporation or the suing stockholders, individually); and (2) who would receive the benefit of any recovery or other remedy (the corporation or the stockholders, individually)?" Tooley v. Donaldson, Lufkin & Jenrette, Inc., 845 A.2d 1031, 1033 (Del. 2004) (emphasis original).

[4] *See, e.g.,* RMBCA §§ 8.30(a), 8.42(a)(3) (". . . reasonably believes to be in the best interests of the corporation").

[5] *See, e.g.,* Wood v. Baum, 953 A.2d 136, 139 (Del. 2008); Auerbach v. Bennett, 419 N.Y.S.2d 920, 923 (1979).

These would also be direct: suits to force the corporation to allow a shareholder to inspect the books and records,[6] to honor a dividend preference when the corporation declared a dividend,[7] to force dissolution of the corporation,[8] and suits for violation of Rule 10b–5.[9] The latter is direct because it gives a private right of action for damages by a buyer or seller of securities who is defrauded by misleading statements or omissions. Notice that most direct suits are against the corporation itself—the claim is that the corporation is not living up to some agreement with the shareholder.

Sometimes it is not obvious whether a claim is derivative. In those cases, the defendant will invariably argue that the case is derivative. She does so to force the plaintiff to jump through the procedural hoops required of derivative suits. A well-known example is *Eisenberg v. Flying Tiger Line, Inc.*[10] There, plaintiff held stock in a corporation that operated an airline. After a series of mergers, plaintiff ended up owning stock in a holding company that *owned* an airline. Plaintiff challenged the mergers as depriving him (and other minority shareholders) of having a vote or influence on a corporation that ran an airline. In other words, his power as a shareholder was diluted: he bought stock to participate in a company that ran an airline, not one that simply owned an airline. The defendant argued that it was a derivative suit, and thus that plaintiff had to post a bond (which is a requirement for derivative suits in some states, as we will see in section D). Because plaintiff refused to post a bond, the trial court dismissed the case.

The Second Circuit, applying New York law, held that the claim was direct.[11] This meant that plaintiff did not have to post the bond, and the case could proceed. The court emphasized that a derivative suit is one regarding injury to the corporation. Here, the injury (if any) was to minority shareholders. The court discussed the case of *Gordon v. Elliman*[12] in which the New York Court of Appeals held that a suit to force the board to declare a dividend was derivative. That court concluded that the failure to pay dividends was a failure to discharge a duty owed to the corporation, not to the shareholders. As the court in *Eisenberg* pointed out, the decision in *Gordon* was widely criticized, and led to a statutory change in New York law to define a derivative suit as one in which plaintiff seeks a judgment "in

---

[6] *See* RMBCA § 16.04

[7] *See, e.g.,* Staats v. Biograph Co., 236 F. 454, 457 (2d Cir. 1916).

[8] *See, e.g.,* Read v. Read, 556 N.W.2d 768, 771–72 (Wisc. Ct. App. 1996).

[9] *See, e.g.,* Medkser v. Feingold, 307 Fed. Appx. 262, 265 (11th Cir. 2008).

[10] 451 F.2d 267, 268 (2d Cir. 1971).

[11] *Id.* at 272.

[12] 119 N.E.2d 331 (N.Y. 1954).

[the corporation's] favor."[13] This statute abrogated the result in *Gordon*. Today, a suit for the declaration of a dividend would likely be seen as direct because it seeks to put money in the pockets of the shareholders, and not to assert a right belonging to the corporation.[14]

Clever lawyers may argue that derivative claims are actually direct. Again, they will do so to avoid having to satisfy the strict procedural requirements of a derivative suit. At some level, anything that harms the corporation might be said to hurt the shareholders too. And if it hurts the shareholders—one might argue—it is a direct claim. Courts are careful, however, not to allow such bootstrap arguments. In most cases, the simple question we posed at the beginning of this section will yield a satisfactory answer.

It is important to distinguish between a derivative suit and a class action. In a class action, a representative sues on behalf of similarly situated persons to enforce their individual claims. In other words, a class action is a *direct* suit involving so many potential plaintiffs that they satisfy the class action requirements of Federal Rule of Civil Procedure 23 (or the state equivalent). *Eisenberg* was a class action, brought on behalf of other minority shareholders who opposed the mergers.[15] All of those people had direct claims, and no one was asserting the interest of the corporation. The corporation had not been wronged. A derivative suit is entirely different because it is not brought by a representative on behalf of others similarly situated. It is brought by a shareholder on behalf of the *corporation*.[16]

Why does anyone—whether a representative in a class action or the plaintiff in a derivative suit—take on the burden of litigating for someone else? One answer is altruism—the plaintiff wants to do the right thing, to vindicate a right. But a more realistic (and troubling) possibility is that the moving force behind the litigation is the plaintiff's lawyer. In many cases, it is the lawyer who recruits a shareholder to bring the derivative suit (and the representative in a class action). We worry that the lawyer is motivated not by altruism, but by the desire to make money. A "suit" is one intended to gain a quick

---

[13] N.Y. BUS. CORP. LAW § 626.

[14] *See* Knapp v. Bankers Securities Corp., 230 F.2d 717, 721 (3d Cir. 1956).

[15] 119 N.E.2d at 269–70.

[16] *See* Felzen v. Andreas, 134 F.3d 873, 875 (7th Cir. 1998) (shareholder in derivative suit, unlike class member in class action, is not the injured party). Derivative suits and class actions are alike, however, in an important way—in each, someone purports to sue on behalf of someone else. In the class action, the fate of the class members' direct claims will sink or swim with the representative. In the derivative suit, a shareholder is suing on behalf of the corporation, and the corporation's interest will sink or swim depending on how the shareholder does.

settlement for the plaintiff's lawyer, rather than to rectify a corporate wrong.[17]

In response to this potential for abuse, the law of every state imposes a series of procedural safeguards, as we will see. In addition, a derivative suit can be settled only with court approval. The court is thrust into a direct supervisory role to ensure that the settlement is not made to line the pockets of the plaintiff's lawyer.[18]

C. Overview of Derivative Litigation

If a derivative suit is successful, the recovery goes to the corporation. This makes sense, because the suit asserted the corporation's claim. On the other hand, the shareholder did all the work of bringing and prosecuting the case. So what does she get? As a general matter, she recovers her litigation costs from the other side. This is consistent with the normal rule in civil procedure that the prevailing party shall recover her costs from the losing party.[19] "Costs," however, is a term of art, and usually consists of various expenses of litigation (such as filing fees, discovery costs, expert witness fees), but not attorney's fees. Under the American Rule, subject to some exceptions, each party bears her own attorney's fees. Because the successful derivative plaintiff has conferred a benefit on the corporation (by vindicating the corporate claim), usually she will recover attorney's fees from the corporation, often from the recovery she won. Even if there was no monetary recovery (as, for example, a case that resulted in equitable relief), the plaintiff may be entitled to recover her attorney's fees from the corporation—so long as the suit conferred a benefit on the corporation.[20]

In some circumstances in the closely held corporation, the derivative suit model might not make sense. Suppose, for example, that a corporation has three shareholders—X, Y, and Z—each of whom owns one-third of the stock and serves as a director. Assume that X causes the company to buy supplies from another business, which she owns. And suppose this interested director deal causes the corporation to overpay for supplies by $30,000. X has clearly breached her duty of

---

[17] Strike suits are derivative suits filed "by people who might be interested in getting quick dollars by making charges without regard to their truth so as to coerce corporate managers to settle worthless claims in order to get rid of them." Surowitz v. Hilton Hotels Corp., 383 U.S. 363, 371 (1966).

[18] "Thus, a continuing debate surrounding derivative actions has been over restricting their use to situations where the corporation has a reasonable chance for benefit." Joy v. North, 692 F.2d 880, 887 (2d Cir. 1982).

[19] See FED. R. CIV. P. 54(d).

[20] See, e.g., RMBCA § 7.46(1)(court may order the corporation to pay plaintiff's expenses and attorney's fees if the case "resulted in a substantial benefit to the corporation").

loyalty to the corporation, and has caused damages of $30,000. If another shareholder brings a derivative suit and wins, the $30,000 judgment will go to the corporation. Because X owns one-third of the corporation, however, this recovery in essence returns one-third of the judgment to X, the wrongdoer.

For this reason, some courts will treat the case as a direct suit, and thus allow the "innocent" shareholders to recover directly their pro-rata share of the harm done.[21] The Corporate Governance Project of the American Law Institute suggested this approach, and some states have adopted it. For instance, in Texas, derivative claims in corporations having 35 or fewer shareholders may be treated as direct. Thus the plaintiffs need not satisfy the procedural requirements of a derivative suit, and the recovery goes to them, not to the corporation.[22]

What happens when the plaintiff loses the derivative suit? First, she will bear her own attorney's fees and probably will have to pay the defendant's litigation costs. Second, in most states, the court can order her to pay the defendant's attorney's fees if she sued "without reasonable cause or for an improper purpose."[23] And third, a judgment on the merits is entitled to claim preclusion (res judicata) effect, which means that no other shareholder can sue the same defendant on the same transaction or occurrence. This is because that claim—on behalf of the corporation—has already been asserted. Claim preclusion prohibits a second assertion of the same claim.

Is the corporation itself a litigant? Yes, it must be joined as a party. And though the suit is brought to assert the corporation's claim, the corporation is joined as a defendant.[24] This is because the corporation did not actually sue, and the law has always been reluctant to force someone to litigate as an involuntary plaintiff. In the litigation itself, the corporation may play an active role or a passive role. It may side with the individual defendants and urge that their conduct did not harm the company, or it may champion the plaintiff's cause.[25]

---

[21] See Thomas v. Dickson, 301 S.E.2d 49, 51(Ga. 1983).

[22] TEX. BUS. ORGS. CODE § 21.563.

[23] See, e.g., RMBCA § 7.46(2).

[24] "The corporation is a necessary party to the action; without it the case cannot proceed. Although named as a defendant, it is the real party in interest. . . ." Ross v. Bernhard, 396 U.S. 531, 538 (1970); see also Grosset v. Wenaas, 42 Cal.4th 1100, 1108 (2008) ("When a derivative suit is brought to litigate the rights of the corporation, the corporation is an indispensable party and must be joined as a nominal defendant.").

[25] If the corporation champions the plaintiff's cause, however, it could opt to file suit itself.

The New York Business Corporation Law has an interesting provision that allows a director or officer to sue another director or officer to force her to account for breach of a duty to the corporation. The plaintiff sues in her own name, though any recovery goes to the corporation, and need not satisfy the prerequisites of a derivative suit.[26]

D. Prerequisites for a Derivative Suit

1. Contemporaneous Ownership

Generally, the person bringing a derivative suit must have owned stock *when the claim arose* or must have gotten stock "by operation of law" from someone who owned the stock when the claim arose. The purpose of this "contemporaneous ownership" requirement[27] is to prevent someone from essentially purchasing a lawsuit by buying a share of stock in the corporation after the claim becomes apparent.[28]

Section 7.41(1) of RMBCA is typical of the statutes imposing the contemporaneous ownership requirement, as is Rule 23.1 of the Federal Rule of Civil Procedure. For purposes of these provisions, "operation of law" includes inheritance and divorce decrees, but not simply the purchase of the stock.

- P brings a derivative suit to vindicate a claim belonging to XYZ Corp. P did not own stock in XYZ when the claim arose, but her uncle did. In the meantime, her uncle passed away and she inherited the stock from him. She has standing under the contemporaneous ownership requirement because she received the stock by operation of law from someone who owned the stock when the claim arose.

- In contrast, if P's uncle had not died, and P bought the stock from her uncle after the claim arose, P would not have standing to bring a derivative suit. She did not own the

---

[26] N.Y. BUS. CORP. LAW § 720.

[27] A handful of states do not always insist on contemporaneous ownership. For instance, California permits a court to allow any shareholder to prosecute a derivative suit if various conditions are met, including a strong prima facie case in favor of the claim and the likelihood that no similar suit will be filed. CAL. CORP. CODE § 800(b)(1).

[28] *See* Cadle v. Hicks, 272 Fed. Appx. 676, 678 (10th Cir. 2008). Moreover, a shareholder who buys stock after the claim arose will pay relatively less for her stock, because the stock price should reflect the fact that the corporation has been harmed. Allowing her to recover on the claim would thus arguably amount to a windfall.

stock when the claim arose and did not get it "by operation of law" from someone who did.

When a claim occurs over time, some courts have adopted the "continuing wrong" theory to permit a shareholder to sue if she held stock (or got it by operation of law) at any point during a continuing wrong. For example, in *Palmer v. Morris,*[29] the plaintiff bought stock after a wrongful transaction was entered into, but before the payments under the deal were made. The court upheld standing. California law embodies this approach by permitting a shareholder to sue if she owned stock during the alleged wrong "or any part thereof."[30]

The contemporaneous ownership requirement does not mandate that the plaintiff own a particular amount of stock; neither does it require that the shareholder know anything about the claim when it arises.[31] Accordingly, statutes impose further requirements in addition to stock ownership.

2. Adequacy of Representation

In most states, the derivative plaintiff must *also* demonstrate that she will adequately represent the interests of the corporation.[32] Because the result of the litigation will bind the corporation, the plaintiff must demonstrate to the court that she has the proper motivation and stake in the case. The court should ensure that the plaintiff's lawyer is not the real party, and that the shareholder actually has some interest in pursuing the claim.[33]

Part of ensuring adequacy of representation is an ongoing interest in the corporation. Though most statutes are silent on the point, courts insist that the plaintiff continue to own stock when the case is brought and throughout the litigation.[34] If the plaintiff divests her holding during the case, she loses standing, although the court might permit recruitment of another plaintiff.[35]

---

[29] 316 F.2d 649, 651 (5th Cir. 1963).

[30] CAL. CORP. CODE § 800(b)(1).

[31] *See, e.g.,* DEL. GEN. CORP. LAW § 327.

[32] *See, e.g.,* RMBCA § 7.41(2).

[33] *See In re* Fuqua Industries, Inc. Shareholder Litigation, 752 A.2d 126, 133 (Del. Ch. 1999) ("The allegation that attorneys bring actions through puppet plaintiffs while the real parties in interest are the attorneys themselves in search of fees is an oft-heard complaint from defendants in derivative suits.").

[34] Lewis v. Anderson, 477 A.2d 1040, 1046 (Del. 1984).

[35] RMBCA § 7.41 provides that "[a] shareholder may not commence or *maintain* a derivative proceeding unless . . . ." This language of section 7.41 makes it clear that if the plaintiff ceases to be a shareholder, the proceeding should be dismissed.

3. Security for Expenses

Derivative litigation raises the possibility of "strike suits"—that is, cases aimed at extorting a favorable settlement for the plaintiff (or her lawyer). One way to avoid such suits is to require plaintiffs to put up some of their own money as security for the defendants' litigation costs. Usually, this means that the plaintiff must post a bond—that is, deposit money with the court—from which defendants may recover their litigation expenses (often including attorney's fees) if the claim turns out to be a loser.

Relatively few states still require security for expenses. Section 627 of the New York Business Corporation Law is perhaps the best known provision. It gives the corporation a right to demand that the plaintiff post security for expenses unless she owns at least five percent of any class of the corporation's stock, or unless the stock she owns is worth at least $50,000.[36] The court sets the size of the bond, which depends upon the estimated expenses for the corporation. This figure may include expenses to individual defendants for which the corporation may be liable for indemnification, which we discuss in section G. The security requirement is a significant hurdle for plaintiffs. Indeed, as happened in *Eisenberg v. Flying Tiger Line, Inc.*, a plaintiff required to post a bond may simply abandon the derivative suit.

4. Demand that the Corporation Bring Suit

This is the major procedural prerequisite for derivative suits. The idea makes sense: whether a corporation should pursue litigation is a business decision, so a shareholder should not be permitted to proceed without giving the corporation a chance to press the claim.[37] Statutes thus require the shareholder to make a written demand that the corporation bring suit.[38] And because corporation decisions are made by the board of directors, the demand must be made on it.[39] The demand must state with reasonable specificity what the claim is and against whom it exists.

---

[36] *See also* PA. CONS. STAT. § 1782 (similar, with the exception that plaintiff's stock must be worth at least $200,000).

[37] "Inaction by the Board will not excuse the failure to make a demand because it would deprive the Board of the opportunity to be 'prodded' into action, which is a fundamental goal of the demand requirement." McCall v. Scott, 239 F.3d 808, 824 (6th Cir. 2001).

[38] *See, e.g.*, GA. CODE § 14–2–742(1).

[39] Some older statutes also required the plaintiff to make a demand on *shareholders* that the corporation bring suit. These shareholder-demand statutes are largely a thing of the past. Massachusetts was one of the last states to hold onto this requirement, but abandoned it in 2004.

Must this demand always be made? There are two general views: (1) the traditional approach, which is still followed in many states, and (2) the RMBCA "universal demand" approach, which is increasing in popularity.

The Traditional Approach. Under this view, the plaintiff need not make the demand if doing so would be "futile." The archetype is when a majority of the board is interested in the challenged transaction. Suppose, for instance, that the derivative claim is against the sitting directors for engaging in an interested director transaction or for awarding themselves excessive bonuses. The requirement of a demand in such a case amounts to telling directors to have the company sue themselves; doing so would be futile.

Under Delaware law, the demand is futile if the plaintiff can allege detailed facts creating a "reasonable doubt" either that the directors were disinterested or that the challenged act was the product of valid business judgment.[40] Moreover, in Delaware, the plaintiff cannot use discovery to ferret out facts supporting futility. Rather, she may only employ her right to inspect corporate books and records.

The New York Court of Appeals found the "reasonable doubt" language in Delaware law confusing, and therefore avoided it.[41] Beyond that, though, its definition of when a demand would be futile is basically consistent with Delaware law. New York will excuse demand when a majority of directors is implicated in the acts alleged (or is under the control of one who is implicated) and where the board's decision was not reasonably informed or the result of sound business judgment.

In these "demand excused" cases, the plaintiff files suit without making a demand. But it would be easy for a plaintiff simply to allege that the board is tainted and thus that demand would be futile. So the law requires that the plaintiff's derivative complaint allege "with particularity" either her efforts to get the board to bring suit or her reasons for concluding that such demand would be futile.[42] Thus, she must allege in detail why board members could not be trusted with making the decision of whether to have the corporation sue. In addition, some states require that the complaint be "verified"—which means signed under penalty of perjury.[43]

---

[40] Aronson v. Lewis, 473 A.2d 805, 808 (Del. 1984).

[41] Marx v. Akers, 666 N.E.2d 1034, 1038 (N.Y. 1996).

[42] *See, e.g.,* RMBCA § 7.44(c).

[43] *See* UTAH CODE § 16–6a–612(3)(b)(i).

What are the consequences of the plaintiff's making a demand on the board? First, the board may accept it as a recommendation and authorize the corporation to bring suit. If this happens, the case is brought by the corporation itself and is not a derivative suit; there is no further role for the shareholder. Second (and far likelier), the board may reject the demand. If this happens, either the shareholder will give up or (far likelier) assert that the board erred in concluding that the case should not be filed. This course is almost always a loser because the shareholder is simply disagreeing with a decision by the board. The board's judgment will be upheld unless the shareholder can show that the board's decision was tainted by self-interest (and if that were true, the demand would have been excused in the first place).[44] Indeed, under Delaware law, the shareholder will always lose in this "demand rejected" scenario, because making the demand on directors constitutes an admission that the board was disinterested.[45] This means that the board's decision is protected by the business judgment rule.

What happens, though, if the plaintiff sues without making a demand on the board? Most likely, the board will seek dismissal on the ground that the plaintiff should have made the demand. On this motion, the court faces one issue: would a demand on the board have been futile? In most cases, the decision will depend upon whether a majority of the directors is tainted. If the court determines that the demand was not futile—that it should have been made—the derivative suit will be dismissed.[46] On the other hand, if it determines that the demand was excused, the derivative suit continues.[47]

The RMBCA "Universal Demand" Approach. Under the modern approach, the plaintiff in a derivative suit must always make a demand on the board; a demand is never excused. Section 7.42 of the RMBCA leads the way on this point, and has been adopted in many states.[48] The universal demand requirement recognizes that (1) litigation over whether a demand is excused is expensive and time-consuming and (2) making a demand—even if a majority of the board is tainted—will give the board a chance to consider the claim and do the right thing in the context of potential litigation.

---

[44] "The board's rejection of the shareholder's demand will not be disturbed unless it is wrongful." Stepak v. Addison, 20 F.3d 398, 402 (11th Cir. 1994).

[45] Spiegel v. Buntrock, 571 A.2d 767, 777 (Del. 1990).

[46] *See, e.g.,* Beam ex rel. Martha Stewart Living Omnimedia, Inc. v. Stewart, 845 A.2d 1040, 1057 (Del. 2004).

[47] *See, e.g.,* Rales v. Blasband, 634 A.2d 927, 937 (Del. 1993).

[48] *See, e.g.,* MASS GEN. LAWS ch. 156D, § 7.42; NEB. REV. STAT. § 21–2072(1); R.I. GEN. LAWS § 7–1.2–711(c).

Under RMBCA § 7.42, a plaintiff must make a demand and then wait at least 90 days before filing a derivative suit. She may sue before 90 days if the board rejects the demand, or if waiting that long will cause "irreparable injury" to the corporation. For example, if the statute of limitations on the claim is about to expire, the plaintiff may be permitted to sue earlier. The corporation may accept the demand and have the corporation bring suit. Or, if the shareholder has filed suit, the corporation may take over the case. More likely, though, the corporation will reject the demand and move to dismiss the derivative suit.

E. Motions to Dismiss and Special Litigation Committees

Here, we assume that a derivative suit is pending and that the corporation wants it dismissed. Its motion will assert that the case should be dismissed because it is not in the corporation's best interest. This might be true, for instance, because the expense of litigation will exceed any recovery, or because litigation will create publicity that will be more harmful to the business than the trouble on which the suit is based. Clearly, this determination must be made by disinterested, independent people, and not by those who are the defendants in the derivative suit.

The law of every state permits boards of directors to appoint committees (consisting of one or more directors) to perform various tasks. One function commonly undertaken by committees is the review of whether pending derivative litigation should be dismissed. These are usually called "special litigation committees," or SLCs. (The word "special" connotes that the committee is formed to consider a specific pending case or cases, and not litigation generally.) Often, members of the committee will be new directors, brought onto the board specifically to serve on the SLC. This committee is required to investigate and determine whether the case is in the company's best interest. If it concludes that suit is not in the company's interest, the corporation may move to dismiss.

Such a motion raises an interesting clash of policies dealing with the difference between the right to *file* a derivative suit and the right to *maintain* that suit. On the one hand, the law permits shareholders to file a derivative suit. On the other hand, whether the corporation should maintain the case is a business decision, properly addressed to the expertise of the board. But if the suit is against the directors, we are nervous that they will seek dismissal for selfish reasons. So the law must balance the shareholder's undoubted right to initiate the case with management's right to determine whether the suit should proceed. This balance will be affected by the type of claim asserted.

When the derivative suit is against a third party, such as a supplier who breached a contract with the corporation, courts are very deferential to the SLC. Because in these cases no director or officer is a defendant, the SLC's conclusion that the case should be dismissed is supported by the business judgment rule. Unless the plaintiff can show that the SLC members were so lacking in diligence that they breached the duty of care, the court will honor the SLC's conclusion and dismiss the case. But when the case is against present managers, we are nervous that members of the SLC might try to help their fellow directors. This is the fear of "structural bias"—that even independent directors will look at the defendants, will say "there but for the Grace of God go I," and will try to get the case dismissed.

Historically, everyone seemed to assume that the plaintiff in a derivative suit against directors or officers had a right to initiate and to pursue the case. This view started to change, however, with *Gall v. Exxon Corp.*,[49] in which a federal court permitted a disinterested SLC to seek dismissal based upon its conclusion that the case was not in the company's best interest. The court assessed whether the SLC consisted of truly disinterested persons and whether it had undertaken a reasonable investigation.

Today, motions to dismiss derivative suits against directors or officers based upon SLC determinations are common. But the level of intrusiveness of a court's inquiry in such motions varies from state to state. In section D of this Chapter, we noted that a shareholder, before filing a derivative suit, is supposed to make a demand on the board that it authorize the corporation to sue. Under the traditional approach, however, this demand is excused if it would be futile.

In Delaware, in a "demand required" case—that is, one in which making a demand on the board was not futile—the court generally will grant the motion to dismiss based upon the SLC's recommendation. This makes sense. If the demand was required, there was no conflict of interest and the corporate decision should be protected by the business judgment rule.

Things are different, however, in a "demand excused" case—that is, one in which making the demand on the board would have been futile. There, under Delaware law, as established in *Zapata Corp. v. Maldonado*,[50] the court must assess two things—one procedural and

---

[49] 418 F. Supp. 508, 517 (S.D.-N.Y. 1976).

[50] 430 A.2d 779, 788–89 (Del. 1981).

one substantive. First, the court must review the "the independence and good faith" of the SLC. The corporation has the burden on this point, and must show not only that members of the SLC were independent of the defendants, but that the committee undertook a reasonable investigation and had reasonable bases for its findings and recommendation. The court may permit limited discovery on these topics. Second, assuming the first requirement is met, the court undertakes an independent review of the substance of the SLC's recommendation. The court is to apply its "own independent business judgment" to determine whether the case should be dismissed as not in the best interest of the corporation. This substantive assessment is surprising because it seems to enmesh the court in making precisely the types of business judgments that courts are not trained to undertake.[51]

Many states part company with Delaware on this second prong of its analysis in "demand excused" cases. That is, many courts will grant the motion to dismiss if they are satisfied that the SLC members were truly independent of the defendants and that they undertook a reasonable investigation.[52]

Again, every state requires that members of the SLC must be independent and disinterested.[53] One nagging problem, however, is whether tainted directors (those who are defendants in the litigation) may appoint members of the SLC. Should we be nervous that these people owe their positions on the SLC (or even on the board) to people who have been accused of breach of duty? In a perfect world, SLC members would be appointed by untainted people. In practical terms, however, it may be impossible to do that, and the law does not require it. Our nervousness about "structural bias" generally is abated only by the requirement that members of the SLC be independent of the derivative suit defendants.

What is the review the procedure under the RMBCA? Recall that demand on the board is never excused under the RMBCA. Accordingly, there is no bifurcation between "demand required" and "demand excused" cases. Section 7.44(a) *requires* a court to dismiss if these underlying requirements are met: (1) an appropriate group determines (2) in good faith after a reasonable inquiry that (3) the derivative suit is not in the corporation's best interest. Unlike Delaware law in *Zapata,* the RMBCA does not permit the court to undertake an independent investigation and to use its own business judg-

---

[51] *See* Kahn v. Kohlberg Kravis Roberts & Co., L.P., 23 A.3d 831, 842 (Del. 2011) (reversing the lower court's independent business judgment).

[52] *See, e.g.,* Johnson v. Hui, 811 F. Supp. 479, 489–90 (N.D. Cal. 1991).

[53] *See, e.g.,* Blohm v. Kelly, 765 N.W.2d 147, 155 (Minn. 2009).

ment to determine whether the case should be dismissed. Rather, it focuses wholly on the procedural components of independence and reasonable investigation.[54]

Section 7.44(b) defines the appropriate group who may make a recommendation to dismiss—and focuses on the notion of a "qualified" director. This is defined in RMBCA § 1.43 as a director without a material interest in the outcome and without a close relationship with such a person. In addition, § 7.44(e) permits the court, on motion by the corporation, to appoint a panel of qualified persons to make the determination. So if there are no qualified directors on the board, § 7.44(e) avoids the need to recruit people to become directors so that they may serve on the SLC.

If the plaintiff filed the derivative suit after the board rejected her demand, § 7.44(c) requires that she allege in detail facts showing either that a majority of the board was tainted or that the underlying requirements of § 7.44(a) were not met. More interestingly, § 7.44(d) allocates the burden of proof in a way reminiscent of the "demand required"/"demand excused" bifurcation under traditional law. If—when the board rejected the demand—a majority of the board was qualified, the plaintiff must prove that the underlying requirements of § 7.44(a) were not met. If, however, a majority of the board was tainted and therefore unqualified, the corporation must demonstrate that the underlying requirements of § 7.44(a) were satisfied.

F. Discontinuance or Settlement of a Derivative Suit

In section B, we saw the potential abuse of derivative suits in "strike" cases. These are derivative suits aimed at leading to a quick settlement essentially to buy off the plaintiff to ignore a wrong done to the corporation and to line the plaintiff's lawyer's pockets. This evil was promoted by secret settlements, which the parties reached without court supervision. Today such secret settlements are a thing of the past. Statutes uniformly provide that a derivative suit "may not be discontinued or settled without the court's approval."[55] In addition, most statutes provide that if a court determines that a proposed discontinuance or settlement will "substantially affect" the interests of shareholders, "the court shall direct that notice be given to the shareholders affected."[56]

---

[54] See In re UnitedHealth Group Inc. Shareholder Derivative Litigation, 754 N.W.2d 554, 559 (Minn. 2008).

[55] RMBCA § 7.45.

[56] See, e.g., VA. CODE § 13.1–672.2(A); MICH. COMP. LAWS § 450.1496.

Most derivative suits—like most cases generally—are settled and do not go to trial. In reviewing proposed settlements, courts consider several factors, including the size of the potential recovery in litigation versus the size of the proposed settlement, the possibility of success in litigation, the financial position of the defendants, and the reasonableness of the proposed fee to be paid to the plaintiff's lawyer (the plaintiff's lawyer usually works on a contingent fee in derivative suits).[57] The settlement should lay out responsibility for various litigation expenses.

One reason for giving notice to shareholders is to solicit their input on the proposed discontinuance or settlement. Shareholders may appear at the hearing on the proposed settlement to object. The exercise, however, is not one in democracy, and the decision whether to approve the settlement is entirely for the judge. As a practical matter, if the plaintiff's lawyer, the corporation, and the individual defendants support a proposed settlement, the court will usually approve it.

G. Indemnification Statutes

One should not take on the responsibilities of being a director or officer lightly. The jobs are rigorous and the fiduciary duties exacting. Moreover, such people are targets for litigation—sometimes justified and sometimes baseless. Litigation expenses and attorney's fees can be catastrophic, so many people refuse to serve in corporate management positions unless they are protected from exposure—both to liability and to the costs of litigation. Every state permits corporations to protect directors and officers from such risks.

Corporations today may provide three layers of protection. Whether to do so—and, to a degree, to what extent—are business decisions to be answered by each company. As a general rule, however, publicly held corporations provide all three to the maximum extent permitted. One layer is a provision in the articles exculpating or exonerating managers from personal liability. The second is liability insurance. Each of these is discussed in the next section. The focus in this section is the third layer of protection: indemnification statutes.

For this purpose, indemnification means reimbursement—the corporation reimburses its director or officer for expenses and attorney's fees incurred because she was sued. Usually, she will have been sued "by or on behalf of the corporation." This means that she was sued directly by the company or derivatively for allegedly breach-

---

[57] *See, e.g.,* Shlensky v. Dorsey, 574 F.2d 131, 150 (3d Cir. 1978).

ing a duty to the corporation. Indemnification statutes may apply in other cases as well, such as criminal prosecutions of a manager, but, for the most part, we are concerned with civil litigation brought against someone because of her role as a director or officer.

These matters are handled by statute in each state. Though the terms vary somewhat, the provisions of the RMBCA are typical. If you study the provisions of particular states, however, be careful about whether they apply to both directors and officers.[58] The RMBCA provisions discussed below refer only to directors, but RMBCA § 8.56(a)(1) provides that a corporation may indemnify officers to the same extent. (So throughout our discussion we will refer to directors, but could also speak about officers.) Also be careful to note whether the corporation can opt out of certain provisions in the indemnification statutes.[59] We will assume that the corporation has done nothing to limit the protection potentially available under the statutes.

When a director is sued for some alleged breach of duty, she incurs litigation expenses and attorney's fees. She may settle the litigation, in which case she will write a check in return for dismissal. Or perhaps the litigation resulted in her having to pay a judgment to the corporation or a fine to some regulatory body. She may seek indemnification (reimbursement) of these amounts. The RMBCA and the laws of most states provide for three categories of cases.

Category 1: when indemnification is required. Under RMBCA § 8.52, the corporation must indemnify the director if she "was wholly successful, on the merits or otherwise," in defending the suit brought against her. In short-hand terms, this means that the underlying case resulted in a judgment in her favor. Indemnification here makes sense because the litigation vindicated her.

Note that she did not have to win on the merits of the case. In other words, winning on a technicality—such as improper venue, or the plaintiff lacked standing to bring a derivative suit, or the statute of limitations had run—is just as good as winning after a jury trial. Notice also that under the RMBCA she must win the entire case— she must be "wholly successful." Not all states are so stringent. In

---

[58] See, e.g., DEL. GEN. CORP. LAW § 145 ("Indemnification of officers, directors, employees and agents"); VA. CODE § 13.1–700.1(A) ("An individual who is made a party to a proceeding because he is a director . . .").

[59] See, e.g., ORE. REV. STAT. § 62.464(6)(b) ("[A] cooperative may eliminate or impair a director's right to indemnification if at the time the act or omission occurred the cooperative's articles of incorporation or bylaws explicitly authorized the cooperative to eliminate or impair the right").

some, she is entitled to reimbursement "to the extent" that she was successful.[60]

- D was sued on three claims and the court entered judgment in her favor on two of them; D settled the third claim. She does not qualify for mandatory indemnification under the RMBCA because she was not "wholly successful"—she only won two of three claims. But in states mandating indemnification "to the extent" she was successful, she is entitled to be reimbursed for all expenses and attorney's fees incurred in litigating the two claims that she won.

Category 2: when is indemnification prohibited? In most states, the corporation is prohibited from indemnifying the director if she was "held" liable to the corporation. "Held" means that this issue was actually adjudicated or adjudged by the court. In other words, there was a court finding of liability. Such a holding means that the director was found to have breached a duty to the corporation. In such a case, the director should have to pay the judgment and her own expenses and attorney's fees.

Some provisions are narrower in this regard, however. Under RMBCA § 8.51(d)(2), the corporation cannot reimburse if the director was "adjudged liable on the basis that [she] received a financial benefit to which [she] was not entitled." In Texas, indemnification is prohibited only if the director was held liable for "willful or intentional misconduct" in performing a duty to the corporation.[61]

Category 3: when is indemnification permitted (or, in RMBCA terms, "permissible")? Every situation that does not satisfy Category 1 and does not satisfy Category 2 will fall into Category 3. The best example is when the case against the directors is settled.

- D settled the derivative suit brought against her. She paid $50,000 to the corporation to settle the case, and incurred various legal expenses of $25,000 and attorney's fees of $200,000. So she is out of pocket $275,000. She seeks reimbursement of that amount from the corporation. The case does not fall within Category 1 because a judgment was not entered in D's favor. It does not fall within Category 2 because there was no holding of liability by the court. Thus the

---

[60] *See, e.g.*, MICH. COMP. LAWS § 450.1563 ("To the extent that a director or officer of a corporation has been successful on the merits or otherwise . . . the corporation shall indemnify him. . . .").

[61] TEX. BUS. ORGS. CODE § 8.102.

case falls within Category 3, and the corporation may—but is not required to—reimburse her.

To be eligible, the director must show that she satisfied the standard for permissive indemnification. In most states, the standard is the same as in RMBCA § 8.51(a)(1)—she must demonstrate that (1) she acted in good faith and (2) with the reasonable belief that she acted in the corporation's best interest.[62] By statute, the fact that the underlying case ended in settlement or a judgment or conviction is not itself determinative of whether the director had met this standard.[63] In other words, none of those creates a presumption that the director did not act in good faith.

Every state defines with care who may determine whether the director is entitled to permissive indemnification. Under RMBCA § 8.55(b), the decision can be made by (1) a majority vote of qualified directors or a committee of two or more qualified directors, or (2) by a vote of shareholders, not counting the shares held by an interested director, or (3) by special legal counsel.

If a proper group determines that the director is entitled to permissive indemnification, what sums are reimbursed? Most statutes speak of "expenses" as including attorney's fees, so in the hypothetical above, D's $25,000 in various expenses and $200,000 in attorney's fees could be reimbursed. The bigger question, though, concerns the amount she spent to settle the case. Settlements are inherently ambiguous—we do not know who would have won had the case been tried. Moreover, allowing D to recover the $50,000 she paid to settle the claim results in a curious circularity. That is, D was accused of breaching a duty to the corporation. To settle the claim, she wrote a check to the corporation for $50,000. If the corporation reimburses her for this, the corporation receives nothing for the alleged breach by D. Indeed, if the corporation pays D the full $275,000, it is actually worse off than if no suit had been brought—the corporation is out-of-pocket $275,000. If no suit had been brought, the corporation would have that $275,000.

Recognizing this problem, most states seem to prohibit reimbursement for amounts paid to settle the underlying case—at least if the case against the director was for breach of duty to the corporation (which it almost always will be).[64] If the case were for something

---

[62] The required showing is the same as the duty of loyalty. RMBCA § 8.30(a).

[63] RMBCA § 8.51(c).

[64] *See* TLC Beatrice Int'l Holdings, Inc. v. CIGNA Ins. Co., No. 97–Civ. 8589(MBM), 1999 WL 33454, at *5 (S.D.-N.Y. Jan. 27, 1999) ("To permit a corporation to indemnify an officer or director for amounts paid in settlement or satisfaction of judgment in a derivative action would permit the management of the corporation

else—say, liability to a third party incurred in one's role as a director or officer—perhaps the corporation should reimburse her, assuming she meets the standard for permissive indemnification.[65]

The indemnification statutes discussed to this point are augmented in most states by provisions allowing a *court* to order the corporation to indemnify a director. Section 8.54(a)(3) of the RMBCA is instructive. It allows the court to order indemnification if it is "fair and reasonable" under the circumstances of the case. The authority to do so is strikingly broad. The court may order indemnification even of one who was adjudged liable to the corporation for breach of fiduciary duty! Such indemnity would be limited to expenses, including attorney's fees, and could not include the judgment entered against her.

Finally, states also permit (but do not require) the corporation to advance litigation expenses to a director during the litigation.[66] This permits the defendant in a derivative case, for example, to avoid potentially enormous personal outlays for expenses and fees. The problem for the corporation, of course, is that advances are made before much is known about the merits of the litigation. The statutes permit such advances only if the director gives a written affirmation of her good faith belief that she has satisfied the requirements for permissive indemnification. In addition, she must provide a written undertaking to repay funds advanced if it is determined that she did not satisfy the requirements. This undertaking need not be secured and the corporation may accept it without regard to the financial ability of the director to repay.[67] The purpose of this latter provision is to avoid discrimination against less well-to-do directors.

Statutes also specify who may approve such advances—qualified directors or shareholders, not counting the shares of the interested director.[68] Corporations may make advances for expenses by a provision in the articles or bylaws, or by action by the directors or shareholders.

---

to deprive the corporation, as ultimate plaintiff, of the very benefit it is meant to receive.").

[65] Section 8.51(d)(1) of the RMBCA prohibits indemnification in a case brought by or on behalf of the corporation. It provides an exception, though, for reasonable "expenses," which can be reimbursed if the director meets the standard for permissive indemnification. The Official Comment to that provision makes clear that expenses in this context do not include settlement amounts. Under § 8.51(a), one can get indemnification from "liability"—which includes settlement—but not in cases brought by or on behalf of the corporation.

[66] *See, e.g.*, ARK. CODE § 4–28–627; 805 ILL. COMP. STAT. § 5/8.75(f).

[67] *See* RMBCA § 8.53(b).

[68] *See* RMBCA § 8.53(c).

H. Exculpatory Provisions and Insurance

Indemnification statutes, discussed above, provide significant protection from the risk of director (and usually officer) liability and expense of litigation. In this section, we consider two other layers of protection for corporate managers: exculpation clauses and insurance. In Chapter 7(C)(3), we discussed *Smith v. Van Gorkom*,[69] which sent shock waves through the corporate world because it imposed liability for breach of the duty of care in circumstances in which few observers expected it. In the wake of that decision, every state eventually passed a statute permitting the corporation to provide in its articles that directors (and in some states officers) will not be liable for damages in certain circumstances. These provisions vary from state to state, but RMBCA § 2.02(b)(4) is typical. It says that the articles may include a provision "eliminating or limiting the liability of a director to the corporation or to its shareholders for money damages for any action taken, or any failure to take any action, as a director."

These "exculpation clauses" are widespread. Indeed, it is difficult to see why anyone would agree to serve as a director without such protection in the articles. In every state, however, the power to exculpate from liability is limited. Under the RMBCA, it cannot apply to cases involving (1) receipt of an improper financial benefit, (2) intentional infliction of harm on the corporation or shareholders, (3) approval of an unlawful distribution, or (4) intentional violation of criminal law.[70] Other states word the exceptions differently, but the upshot is similar in most states: the articles can exculpate directors for liability for damages for breach of the duty of care, but not for breach of the duty of loyalty.

Corporations can also protect directors and officers (and themselves) with "D & O" liability insurance. This is purchased from third-party providers (insurance companies) and is not cheap. But it can help at various levels. For instance, it can provide a source of money for managers who are entitled to indemnification but whose corporation may lack funds to pay it. It may also cover claims the corporation elects not to indemnify.

The language of D & O policies varies considerably from issuer to issuer. Indeed, there is no standard-form policy for D & O insurance. Generally, D & O insurance can cover claims based on negligence, misconduct not involving dishonesty or knowing bad faith, and false or misleading statements in disclosure documents. Deliberately

---

[69] 488 A.2d 858 (Del. 1983).

[70] RMBCA § 2.02(b)(4).

wrongful misconduct, dishonest acts, acts in bad faith with knowledge thereof, or violations of statutes such as § 16(b) are not covered. Policy applications require extensive disclosure of contingent or possible claims and a failure to disclose known claims may permit the insurer to void the entire policy. Policies usually provide that expenses advanced by the insurer reduce the amount of insurance coverage provided.

Most states have statutes expressly permitting corporations to purchase D&O insurance.[71] Even without such authorization, the power to obtain such insurance is implicit in the universal corporate power to provide executive compensation.

---

[71] *See, e.g.*, RMBCA § 8.57.

Chapter 14

THE LIMITED PARTNERSHIP

Analysis

A. Introduction
B. Formation
C. Management and Operation
D. Financial Rights and Obligations
E. Entity Status
F. Limited Liability
    1. The Control Rule
    2. Control of the Entity General Partner
G. Fiduciary Duties
    1. General Partners
    2. Limited Partners
H. Ownership Interests and Transferability
I. Dissociation and Dissolution
    1. Dissociation
    2. Dissolution
J. A Final Look

A. Introduction

Like a corporation, a limited partnership is a creature of statute. Unlike a general partnership, which can be created simply by the owners behaving in a certain manner ("carrying on as co-owners a business for profit"), a limited partnership can only be created by complying with the formation requirements of the relevant statute.

A limited partnership is comprised of at least one general partner and at least one limited partner. While a general partner in a limited partnership has unlimited liability for the obligations of the firm, a limited partner has no liability for the debts of the venture beyond the loss of his investment. As we will see, however, in certain circumstances that limited liability can be forfeited if a limited partner participates in the control of the business. Like a general partnership, a limited partnership provides its owners with pass-through tax treatment[1] and structural flexibility (i.e., the parties

---

[1] In response to the use of limited partnerships as vehicles for evading the double tax on corporations, § 7704 of the Internal Revenue Code now mandates that, for federal income tax purposes, a "publicly traded partnership" shall be taxed as a corporation. *See* I.R.C. § 7704. A "publicly traded partnership" is defined as "any partnership if (1) interests in such partnership are traded on an established securities

can contractually arrange to run the business largely as they see fit).

The limited partnership has a long history in the United States. New York and Connecticut adopted the first limited partnership statutes in 1822, followed by Pennsylvania in 1836. The adoption of these statutes was motivated by a desire to avoid the liability of the general partnership form and by a related effort to facilitate investment and business development.

The first uniform act on limited partnerships was the 1916 Uniform Limited Partnership Act ("ULPA"). ULPA was drafted by the National Conference of Commissioners on Uniform State Laws ("NCCUSL"), and the Act was widely adopted in this country. In 1976, NCCUSL promulgated the Revised Uniform Limited Partnership Act ("RULPA (1976)"). Modern limited partnerships had become much more sophisticated, and many of ULPA's provisions were outdated. As one authority explained:

> While the 1916 Act was motivated largely by the underutilization of its predecessors, the 1976 Act was motivated largely by the overutilization of its predecessor. Rising prosperity and high income-tax rates coupled with numerous special deductions and credits led to the creation and growth of a major tax shelter industry from the 1960s onward. The limited partnership was the favorite vehicle. . . Into it the syndicator or promoter (who often became or selected the general partner) put the oil and gas lease, apartment complex, or other asset. Shares were sold to investors in the form of interests (often called units) in the limited partnership. Investors thus could enjoy the tax benefits [such as interest expense, depletion, depreciation, and ultimate capital gain treatment] attached to ownership or development of the asset (until restricted by legislative changes) but with limited liability. The 1916 Act, which contemplated small numbers of limited partners, simple financial arrangements, and local operations, was not well suited to the hundreds or thousands of limited part-

---

market, or (2) interests in such partnership are readily tradable on a secondary market (or the substantial equivalent thereof)." *Id.* § 7704(b). An exception to the rule exists "if 90 percent or more of the gross income of such [publicly traded] partnership for such taxable year consists of qualifying [passive-type] income," such as interest, dividends, or rent. *Id.* § 7704(c)(2), (d)(1). Publicly traded partnerships meeting the exception, in other words, will avoid corporation tax treatment.

ners, intricate financial arrangements, and multistate operations in some of the modern firms.[2]

RULPA (1976) made a number of important changes to limited partnership law, including, among others, increasing the relative importance of the limited partnership agreement over the certificate of formation, and reducing the circumstances under which a limited partner could be liable for participating in the control of the enterprise.

In 1985, NCCUSL significantly amended the 1976 act ("RULPA (1985)"). RULPA (1985) further established the limited partnership agreement as the more important organizational document, and it continued to reduce the circumstances under which a limited partner could be liable for the venture's obligations. The limited partnership statutes of most states today are based upon RULPA (1985).

In 2001, NCCUSL approved a new Uniform Limited Partnership Act ("ULPA (2001)"). In contrast to its predecessors, ULPA (2001) is a stand-alone act that does not link to any general partnership statute. (We will discuss the concept of "linkage" shortly.) As a result, the Act is considered to be more than a mere revision, and the term "revised" was dropped from its title. Among other changes, ULPA (2001) completely eliminates a limited partner's liability for participating in the control of the business, and it removes buyout rights for dissociating general and limited partners. As of this writing, only eighteen states (plus the District of Columbia) have adopted ULPA (2001). Limited partnerships in most of the country, therefore, are still governed by earlier versions of the Act. Consequently, the discussion below focuses on RULPA (1985), although the corresponding provisions of ULPA (2001) are examined as well.

For many years, the limited partnership stood alone as the only business form that provided the best of both worlds—the corporate trait of limited liability, and the partnership traits of pass-through taxation and structural flexibility. With the birth of the limited liability partnership ("LLP") and the limited liability company ("LLC"), however, the modern business owner now has multiple options that fuse limited liability, operational flexibility, and favorable tax treatment. As a result, a number of commentators have predicted that the usage of the limited partnership will dramatically wane. Nevertheless, keep the following in mind: (1) the relatively long history of use of limited partnerships in this country has pro-

---

[2] III ALAN R. BROMBERG & LARRY E. RIBSTEIN, BROMBERG AND RIBSTEIN ON PARTNERSHIP § 11.02(c), at 11:26 to 11:27 (13th ed. 2005).

duced a level of comfort among many attorneys and business owners with that form; (2) that same history of use has generated a significant body of common-law precedent that makes the limited
partnership's operation more "predictable" than newer business
structures; (3) the legal framework of other business forms (particularly the LLC) is derived, in large part, from limited partnership
law; and (4) limited partnerships are still popular in certain specialized areas (e.g., estate planning, real estate, venture capital, oil and
gas). Consequently, limited partnerships—and the law of limited
partnerships—are likely to remain relevant for many years to come.

Limited partnership statutes have historically been "linked" to
general partnership statutes. Because of this linkage, a jurisdiction's general partnership law often applies to a limited partnership
issue when that issue is not covered by the limited partnership
statute. For example, UPA § 6(2) states that "this act [UPA] shall
apply to limited partnerships except in so far as the statutes relating to such partnerships are inconsistent herewith." Correspondingly, ULPA § 1 specifically defines a limited partnership as a
"partnership," and § 9 states that a general partner, with some exceptions, "shall have all the rights and powers and be subject to all
the restrictions and liabilities of a partner in a partnership without
limited partners."

In contrast, RUPA § 202(b) indicates that "[a]n association
formed under a statute other than this [Act], a predecessor statute,
or a comparable statute of another jurisdiction is not a partnership
under this [Act]," and the comment specifically states that "[a] limited partnership is not a partnership under this definition." The
comment to RUPA § 101, however, states that the language of
§ 202(b) "was not intended to preclude the application of any RUPA
general partnership rules to limited partnerships where limited
partnership law otherwise adopts the RUPA rules." Further, the
comment notes that "[t]he effect of these definitions leaves the scope
and applicability of RUPA to limited partnerships to limited partnership law, not to sever [sic] the linkage between the two Acts in
all cases." It is important to note, therefore, that § 101(7) of RULPA
(1976) and RULPA (1985) defines a limited partnership as a "partnership," § 403 provides that a general partner in a limited partnership has the rights, powers, restrictions, and liabilities "of a partner
in a partnership without limited partners," and § 1105 indicates
that "[i]n any case not provided for in this [Act] the provisions of the
Uniform Partnership Act govern."[3]

---

[3] "States enacting R.U.P.A. have typically amended [RULPA (1985)] § 1105 to say
that R.U.P.A. rather than U.P.A. governs, and courts are likely to construe it this

This linkage between limited partnership and general partnership statutes is useful to the extent that general partnership law can be used to answer questions when the limited partnership statute is silent. At times, however, general partnership law may be inappropriate for the limited partnership context. For example, consider the issue of whether limited partners owe fiduciary duties. RULPA (1985) is silent on this question; thus, the general partnership statute applies, and RUPA § 404(a) indicates that a "partner" owes fiduciary duties.[4] This linkage-based analysis, however, results in a poor fit, as most limited partners do not exercise the degree of control over the business that typically calls for the imposition of fiduciary duties.

Moreover, there is often uncertainty about whether linkage should occur in a dispute, particularly when RULPA (1985) addresses a general topic but not every issue within that topic. That is, a court's conclusion that RULPA (1985) does "not provide[] for" (RULPA (1985) § 1105) a particular issue turns in large part on how narrowly or broadly the court frames the issue. For example, assume that a limited partnership dispute centers on whether an assignee can petition for judicial dissolution. If the issue is framed broadly as a "judicial dissolution" dispute, linkage seems inappropriate, as RULPA (1985) § 802 addresses judicial dissolution. If the issue is framed narrowly as a "judicial dissolution by an assignee" dispute, linkage is arguably appropriate, as § 802 addresses judicial dissolution by partners and partner representatives, but does not address judicial dissolution by assignees. Thus, there is ambiguity associated with linkage that can make the concept difficult to apply.

Significantly, ULPA (2001) explicitly "de-links" itself from the general partnership statutes with the purpose of standing alone as a comprehensive limited partnership act. The "Prefatory Note" to ULPA (2001) sheds some light on this decision:

> The Committee saw several substantial advantages to delinking. A stand alone statute would:
>
> • be more convenient, providing a single, self-contained source of statutory authority for issues pertaining to limited partnerships;

---

way even if the state has not amended [RULPA (1985)] § 1105." IV *id.* § 17.01(b)(2), at 17:11.

[4] *See also* RULPA (1985) § 101(8) (defining "partner" to include general and limited partners).

- eliminate confusion as to which issues were solely subject to the limited partnership act and which required reference (i.e., linkage) to the general partnership act; and

- rationalize future case law, by ending the automatic link between the cases concerning partners in a general partnership and issues pertaining to general partners in a limited partnership.

As stated above, ULPA (2001) has not been widely adopted. For most of the limited partnerships in this country, therefore, "linkage" is still an important concept—one that may determine the applicable law in a particular limited partnership dispute.

B. Formation

Unlike general partnerships, limited partnerships can only be formed by filing a certificate of limited partnership with the secretary of state (or equivalent official) of the appropriate jurisdiction. The certificate is a relatively skeletal document that includes basic information about the company, including, among other items, the name of the limited partnership and the identity of the general partners.[5] Of course, you should always check a state's limited partnership statute for precisely what is required in a particular jurisdiction.

The real detail on the rights and duties of partners and on the overall operation of a limited partnership is contained in the partnership agreement—a separate, non-public document that the parties draft (or, more precisely, the parties' lawyers draft) to govern their particular firm.[6] In general, a partnership agreement can be tailored to suit the specific needs of a limited partnership, and the agreement's terms will displace the default provisions of the statute. Interestingly, neither RULPA (1985) nor ULPA (2001) requires a limited partnership to have a partnership agreement. The default rules of the limited partnership statute (and, when RULPA (1985) is silent, the general partnership statute) would provide the operative terms. Nevertheless, most limited partnerships have a detailed partnership agreement, and an attorney will likely need to draft one to meet the needs of his client.

In general, the function of a certificate of limited partnership is to provide notice to the public that certain owners (the limited part-

---

[5] *See, e.g.*, RULPA (1985) § 201; ULPA (2001) § 201.

[6] Under RULPA (1985) § 101(9), a limited partnership agreement can be written or oral. Under ULPA (2001) § 102(13), a limited partnership agreement can be written, oral, or implied.

ners) are protected by limited liability.[7] The partnership agreement, rather than the certificate, is intended to govern the partners' rights and duties to each other. Indeed, noncompliance with formation requirements is rarely important in suits between the partners themselves.[8]

With respect to non-partners, what happens if the relatively simple formation requirements of a limited partnership are not complied with? Section 201(b) of RULPA (1985) states that "[a] limited partnership is formed at the time of the filing of the certificate of limited partnership in the office of the Secretary of State . . . if . . . there has been substantial compliance with the requirements of this section."[9] This "substantial compliance" language gives some wiggle room if there is less-than-perfect compliance with the requirements of the statute. If there is not substantial compliance, however, then a limited partnership has not been formed, and presumably all partners would be liable as in a general partnership. Interestingly, some courts reach this liability conclusion only if a third party seeking to impose liability had no knowledge that the business was a limited partnership. The logic of these decisions seems to be something like the following: if the plaintiff third party knew that some of the partners had limited liability, yet chose to transact with the limited partnership, the plaintiff has assumed the risk of non-recovery from the limited partners. (This is similar to the third branch of the estoppel doctrine in corporate law.) Under this view, actual knowledge effectively trumps the substantial compliance standard. That is, even without substantial compliance with the statutory formation requirements, a third party's actual knowledge of limited partnership status would prevent him from recovering from the limited partners.[10]

---

[7] *See, e.g.,* Garrett v. Koepke, 569 S.W.2d 568, 570 (Tex. Civ. App. 1978) ("The purpose of the filing requirements under the [limited partnership] act is to provide notice to third persons dealing with the partnership of the essential features of the partnership arrangement. . . . [The legislature's] intent was to provide notice of limited liability of certain partners to third parties dealing with a partnership.").

[8] *See, e.g.,* Fujimoto v. Au, 19 P.3d 699, 728 (Haw. 2001) ("[T]he purpose underlying the statutes requiring that a certificate of limited partnership be filed in order to form a limited partnership is to ensure notice to third persons, and failure to comply with the filing requirement does not affect the rights, among themselves, of the parties to the partnership agreement.").

[9] Earlier limited partnership statutes had a similar provision, as does ULPA (2001) § 201(c).

[10] *See, e.g., Garrett,* 569 S.W.2d at 570–71 ("Appellees [limited partners] admit that they had failed to file a certificate of limited partnership as required . . . . Since appellants [creditors of the limited partnership] knew that the entity with which they were dealing was a limited partnership, as well as the consequences of dealing with such an entity, they were in no way prejudiced by the failure to comply with the statute. . . . We hold, therefore, that where a party has knowledge that the entity with which he is dealing is a limited partnership, that status is not changed by failing to file . . . ."); *see also* Direct Mail Specialist, Inc. v. Brown, 673 F. Supp. 1540,

On the other hand, failing to hold partners accountable for noncompliance with statutory formation requirements may lead the organizing partners to disregard those requirements. Moreover, is it arguably improper for a court to effectively override the legislature's substantial compliance standard with an actual knowledge finding. Under this view, actual knowledge of limited partnership status should be irrelevant.[11]

RULPA (1985) § 304 also mitigates the effect of defective formation. Section 304(a) provides protection to a person who makes a contribution to a business enterprise under the mistaken (but good faith) belief that he is a limited partner. According to the statute, such a person "is not a general partner in the enterprise and is not bound by its obligations" if, upon ascertaining the mistake, he either (1) "causes an appropriate certificate of limited partnership or a certificate of amendment to be executed and filed," or (2) "withdraws from future equity participation in the enterprise by executing and filing in the office of the Secretary of State a certificate declaring withdrawal under this section." If these requirements are met, § 304(b) indicates that the mistaken person is only liable as a general partner to any third party who transacts business with the enterprise before (1) or (2) above are accomplished. Even then, liability is only imposed "if the third party actually believed in good faith that the person was a general partner at the time of the transaction." Although § 304 is typically used to mitigate the effect of a limited partnership's defective formation, the statute has also been applied in the general partnership context.[12]		ULPA (2001) § 306 is similar to RULPA (1985) § 304.

1542 (D. Mont. 1987) ("Where there is a failure substantially to comply with the statutes authorizing limited partnerships, the parties remain liable as general partners as to third persons having no knowledge of the limited nature of the partnership.").

[11] *See, e.g.,* Dwinell's Central Neon v. Cosmopolitan Chinook Hotel, 587 P.2d 191, 194 (Wash. Ct. App. 1978) ("[A] third party's knowledge regarding the status of a limited partnership is irrelevant when at the time of contracting, the partners have made no attempt to comply with the statutory information and filing requirements of the Limited Partnership Act. . . . A creditor has a right to rely upon there being substantial compliance . . . before the protection of [the statute's] provisions are afforded to any member of a partnership. Here there was no compliance."); *see also* DANIEL WM. FESSLER, ALTERNATIVES TO INCORPORATION FOR PERSONS IN QUEST OF PROFIT 229 (3d ed. 1991) ("[There are] two irreconcilable lines of judicial reasoning. One stresses the theme that limited partnerships are the creature of statutory law, and concludes that the benefits and protections of that association may be claimed only by those who have complied with the relevant statutes. The expectations of creditors are irrelevant since limited liability is not conferred by contract but results from a statutory status. The contrary authorities argue that creditor expectations, not abstract notions of public policy, should govern individual liability claims.").

[12] *See, e.g.,* Briargate Condo. Ass'n v. Carpenter, 976 F.2d 868, 870–71 & n.6 (4th Cir. 1992) (involving a partner who mistakenly believed that he was a limited part-

C. Management and Operation

As RULPA (1985) § 403(a) indicates, a general partner in a limited partnership typically has the same rights and powers (and is subject to the same restrictions) as a general partner in a general partnership. The statute explicitly links to general partnership law, in other words, on the subject of a general partner's management rights and powers. Those rights and powers would include, among others, the right to participate in management (UPA § 18(e); RUPA § 401(f)), the ability to bind the partnership to transactions in the ordinary course of business via apparent authority (UPA § 9(1); RUPA § 301(1)), the right to vote (UPA § 18(h); RUPA § 401(j)), the right to inspect the venture's records (UPA § 19; RUPA § 403), and the right to information about the partnership (UPA § 20; RUPA § 403). As § 403(a) makes clear, however, these linked rights and powers are only default rules, so a partnership agreement can restrict or alter them.

RULPA (1985) does not explicitly grant or deny management rights to limited partners. Nevertheless, several cases have stated that limited partners cannot take part in the management of the business,[13] and partnership agreements tend to explicitly deny management rights to limited partners. As discussed in Chapter 14(F)(1), limited partners who participate in the control of the business risk liability for some or all of the obligations of the venture. Indirectly, therefore, this control restriction helps to restrain limited partners from exercising substantial management rights.

RULPA (1985) does not speak to the issue of whether a limited partner is an agent of the limited partnership who can bind the venture, via apparent authority, to transactions in the ordinary course of business. Because the statute is silent, linkage might be used to conclude that a limited partner is an agent, as the language in the relevant general partnership statute indicates that every "partner" is an agent with the ability to bind the venture.[14] Such a conclusion would be misguided, however, as an agent classification based merely on limited partner status would be inconsistent with the passive role of limited partners contemplated by the statutory provisions.[15]

---

ner in a limited partnership, even though he was actually a general partner in a business that was intentionally formed as a general partnership).

[13] *See, e.g.,* Goodman v. Epstein, 582 F.2d 388, 408 (7th Cir. 1978).

[14] *See* UPA § 9(1); RUPA § 301(1); *see also* RULPA (1985) § 101(8) (defining "partner" to include limited and general partners).

[15] *See, e.g.,* Berman v. Herrick, 231 F. Supp. 918, 921 (E.D. Pa. 1964) ("It should be observed at this point that although Kupin was a limited partner . . . that status

A limited partner has very few default voting rights under RULPA (1985),[16] even on issues of significance. Removing a general partner or amending a partnership agreement, for example, are clearly important matters. General partners make management decisions for the firm, and amendments to the partnership agreement can directly affect the rights of limited partners. Nevertheless, unless a right to vote is provided in a partnership agreement, limited partners cannot vote on these matters.[17] In practice, however, many partnership agreements do provide voting rights to limited partners on selected issues of importance. Such issues might include the removal of the general partner, the election of a successor general partner, the amendment of the partnership agreement, the extension of the term of the partnership, or the approval of a merger or sale of assets.

RULPA (1985) § 305 provides limited partners with the right to inspect the limited partnership's records and the accompanying right to obtain information about the limited partnership. These rights allow limited partners to monitor the operation of the business and the status of their investments. Because limited partners are typically passive investors who are uninvolved in the management and conduct of the business, they depend on information from the general partners (and the limited partnership itself) to gauge how the general partners are performing and whether their investments are secure. As the comment to RULPA (1985) § 305 states, "Section 305, which should be read together with Section 105(b),

---

alone did not vest Kupin with authority to act for or bind the partnership or the general partners.").

[16] Technically, it is not accurate to say that limited partners have "no" default voting rights. To avoid a person ceasing to be a general partner under § 402, for example, "all partners," which would include limited partners under § 101(8), have to approve in writing. See RULPA (1985) § 402 ("Except as approved by the specific written consent of all partners at the time, a person ceases to be a general partner of a limited partnership upon the happening of any of the following events . . . .").

[17] See, e.g., RULPA (1985) §§ 302, 402(3). With respect to removing a general partner, keep in mind that other provisions of § 402 can result in removal. For example, § 402(4) indicates that, subject to a contrary provision in a written partnership agreement, a general partner's bankruptcy (or comparable proceeding) causes the removal of that partner. The general partner can be retained, however, if all of the partners (including the limited partners) agree in writing. See note 16; see also Curley v. Brignoli Curley & Roberts Assocs., 746 F. Supp. 1208, 1221 (S.D.N.Y. 1989) (involving a court that used its equitable powers to remove a general partner).

With respect to amending the limited partnership agreement, could linkage be used to argue that the limited partners' consent is necessary for the amendment to be effective? See, e.g., RUPA § 401(j) (requiring the consent of "all of the partners" to amend the partnership agreement); see also RULPA (1985) § 101(8) (defining "partner" to include limited and general partners). This seems doubtful. RULPA (1985) § 302 does cover limited partner voting rights by indicating that they must be specified in a partnership agreement. Under the language of § 1105, it may be difficult to convince a court that the subject of limited partner voting rights was "not provided for" in RULPA (1985).

provides a mechanism for limited partners to obtain information about the partnership useful to them in making decisions concerning the partnership and their investments in it."[18]

Consistent with its effort to "de-link" from general partnership law, ULPA (2001) addresses a general partner's rights and powers within the statute itself. Section 402 provides for a general partner's agency authority, § 406 discusses a general partner's right to participate in management and the accompanying right to vote, and § 407 addresses a general partner's inspection and information rights.

With respect to a limited partner's rights and powers, ULPA (2001) § 302 indicates that a limited partner lacks management rights and agency authority. The section states that "[a] limited partner does not have the right or the power as a limited partner to act for or bind the limited partnership," and the comment clarifies that "[i]n this respect a limited partner is analogous to a shareholder in a corporation; status as owner provides neither the right to manage nor a reasonable appearance of that right." ULPA (2001) does provide limited partners with default voting rights on a number of significant matters, including the right to vote on the expulsion of a general partner (under certain circumstances), and the right to vote on amending the partnership agreement. Outside of these specified circumstances, however, a limited partner has no voting rights (other than rights provided by agreement).[19] Finally, under § 304, limited partners are provided with defined inspection and information rights.

D. Financial Rights and Obligations

RULPA (1985) § 503 and § 504 state that, unless otherwise agreed in a written partnership agreement, the profits, losses, and distributions of a limited partnership shall be allocated "on the basis of the value . . . of the contributions made by each partner to the extent they have been received by the partnership and have not been returned."[20] This default rule differs from the "equal sharing" default rule of general partnership law. As discussed in Chapter

---

[18] Limited partner information rights under § 305(2) are triggered solely "upon reasonable demand." There is no explicit statutory requirement in RULPA (1985) for a general partner or a limited partnership to provide information to limited partners without a demand. Nevertheless, such a requirement may exist under the common law. *See* Appletree Square I Ltd. P'ship v. Investmark, Inc., 494 N.W.2d 889, 892–93 (Minn. App. 1993) (concluding that partners in a limited partnership are in a fiduciary relationship that requires disclosure of material facts to each other, even without a demand).

[19] *See, e.g.,* ULPA (2001) §§ 302 & cmt., 406(a), (b)(1), 603(4); *see also id.* § 102(12) (defining "partner" to include general and limited partners).

[20] *See also* RULPA (1985) §§ 101(2), 501 (defining "contribution" broadly).

3(C)(1), when owners have unlimited personal liability for a firm's obligations, as in a general partnership, a default equal sharing rule arguably makes sense because the owners are providing more than a mere financial contribution to the firm—they are providing their personal credit as well. In other words, personal liability gives owners a stake in the business that exceeds their contributions of financial capital.

With limited liability for limited partners, however, a default pro rata rule based upon contributions may be sensible because limited partners make no "extra" contribution of personal credit. Further, along with their capital and credit contributions, general partners often provide management services to the firm. Limited partners, by contrast, usually make only capital contributions and serve primarily as passive investors. Thus, both general and limited partners would typically expect general partners to earn something additional in return for their credit and service contributions. Stated differently, in a limited partnership, general partners take more risk and participate more actively than limited partners. As a consequence, a default equal sharing rule makes less sense than a default contribution-based sharing rule that can account for at least some of these additional contributions.

RULPA (1985) § 601 states that "[e]xcept as provided in this Article, a partner is entitled to receive distributions from a limited partnership before his [or her] withdrawal from the limited partnership and before the dissolution and winding up thereof to the extent and at the times or upon the happening of the events specified in the partnership agreement." Ordinarily, therefore, a partner (general or limited) has no default right to demand pre-withdrawal or pre-dissolution distributions, as the partnership agreement governs. Section 604, however, does provide general and limited partners with a default buyout right upon withdrawal.

RULPA (1985) contains several provisions that are designed to prevent partners from abusing their financial rights to the detriment of creditors. Section 502 gives a creditor the right, under certain circumstances, to enforce a limited partner's promise to contribute to the venture. Under § 607, a distribution to a partner is prohibited if it would leave the firm insolvent. Finally, § 608 makes partners liable to the limited partnership for wrongful distributions and, in some instances, for rightful distributions. These creditor protections can be viewed as a trade-off of sorts for the limited liability granted by the statute.

Like RULPA, ULPA (2001) § 503 also allocates distributions on the basis of partner contributions, although it does so without regard to whether a limited partnership has returned any of those contributions.[21] ULPA (2001) is silent, however, on the allocation of profits and losses. The comment to § 503 suggests that the drafters of ULPA (2001) believed that a default rule for profit and loss allocation was inappropriate: "Nearly all limited partnerships will choose to allocate profits and losses in order to comply with applicable tax, accounting and other regulatory requirements. Those requirements, rather than this Act, are the proper source of guidance for that profit and loss allocation."[22]

ULPA (2001) § 504 states that "[a] partner does not have a right to any distribution before the dissolution and winding up of the limited partnership unless the limited partnership decides to make an interim distribution." The comment to § 504 adds that "[u]nder Section 406(a), the general partner or partners make this decision for the limited partnership." Thus, under ULPA (2001), there is no default right to a distribution before the dissolution and winding up of the venture. Moreover, in sharp contrast to RULPA (1985), ULPA (2001) does not provide general or limited partners with a default buyout right upon withdrawal.[23]

ULPA (2001) § 502 retains a creditor's right, under certain circumstances, to enforce a contribution obligation, and § 508 retains the prohibition on distributions that would render the firm insolvent. ULPA (2001) § 509 makes partners liable for wrongful distributions but, unlike RULPA (1985) § 608, § 509 does not impose liability for distributions that were rightfully made.

E. Entity Status

RULPA (1985) does not directly address the question of whether a limited partnership is a separate legal entity. Nevertheless, limited partnerships possess a number of characteristics that suggest a separateness between the partners and the business itself. As examples, limited partners possess limited liability for the obligations of the business (§ 303(a)), limited partners can bring derivative lawsuits on behalf of the limited partnership (§ 1001), and the dissociation of a partner (general or limited) does not necessarily result in the dissolution of the limited partnership (§ 801). Perhaps not surprisingly, therefore, courts have generally treated RULPA limited partnerships as legal entities distinct from their owners.[24]

---

[21] *See also* ULPA (2001) §§ 102(2), 501 (defining "contribution" broadly).

[22] As a practical matter, the financial rights of general partners and limited partners are almost always specified in a partnership agreement. As a result, any default rules relating to the allocation of profits, losses, and distributions seldom apply.

[23] *See* ULPA (2001) § 505; *see also* Chapter 14(I)(1) (discussing dissociation).

[24] *See, e.g.,* Barr Lumber Co. v. Old Ivy Homebuilders, Inc., 40 Cal. Rptr. 2d 717, 719–21 (Cal. App. Dep't Super. Ct. 1995) (denying relief to the plaintiff in entity-like

Under ULPA (2001), the question is more easily answered, as § 104(a) explicitly states that "[a] limited partnership is an entity distinct from its partners." Even if a limited partnership is recognized as an entity under limited partnership law, however, a court may conclude that a limited partnership will not be treated as a distinct entity when policy considerations outside of limited partnership law are compelling.[25]

F. Limited Liability

1. The Control Rule

A central feature of the limited partnership is the limited liability provided to limited partners. As mentioned, limited partners have no liability for the debts of the venture beyond the loss of their investments. A limited partner can lose his limited liability protection, however, if he participates in the "control" of the business—an inquiry that is the subject of much litigation.

What function(s) does the control rule serve? Consider the following: (1) The control rule protects creditors who might be misled by a limited partner's participation in control into thinking that the limited partner was actually a general partner. The control rule allows creditors to recover from the persons who are actually making the decisions for the business regardless of their "label" as limited or general partner. (2) The control rule protects general partners (who are personally liable for partnership obligations) by discouraging limited partners from interfering with their managerial decisions. For example, a limited partner with limited liability may prefer the business to engage in riskier conduct for the potential of higher returns, while a general partner with unlimited liability may prefer a more conservative approach. The control rule provides some assurance to general partners that they will be able to control their exposure by having management authority over the firm. (3) Similarly, the control rule helps to ensure that only those with per-

---

fashion by concluding that a lawsuit against the general partner was distinct from a lawsuit against the limited partnership itself).

Linkage might support an argument that a limited partnership is not an entity to the extent that UPA is the governing general partnership statute. Indeed, to the extent that entity status is "not provided for" in RULPA (1985), § 1105 might defer to UPA's aggregate orientation. See Chapter 3(B)(3). As discussed, however, this would result in a poor fit given the number of characteristics that suggest that a limited partnership is distinct from its owners. Linkage to RUPA, of course, would result in an entity characterization, as RUPA § 201 states that a partnership is an entity.

[25] See, e.g., Currier v. Amerigas Propane, L.P., 737 A.2d 1118, 1119–20 (N.H. 1999) (concluding that a general partner's immunity from suit under the workers' compensation laws extended to the limited partnership itself).

sonal liability, and thus with a strong desire to be careful, will exercise management powers. This protects creditors to the extent that managerial authority will be exercised by those who have the strongest incentive to avoid insolvency. (4) The control rule helps to preserve specialization of function. The general partners typically have the business "know-how" and they make the business decisions. The limited partners, by contrast, are usually mere providers of capital. The control rule helps prevent those without management expertise from interfering with those with management expertise.

On the other hand, the control rule has some drawbacks: (1) Limited partners may have valuable skills and abilities and their assistance in matters related to the firm may be beneficial. The control rule discourages such assistance, however, because it may be construed as participation in control. (2) The control rule could weaken the quality of management because limited partners may be deterred from monitoring the general partners out of fear that monitoring activities will be construed as participation in control. (3) The control rule is outcome-uncertain and it leads to considerable litigation over what constitutes participation in control.

With each version of NCCUSL's limited partnership statute, the control rule has become progressively more protective of limited partners. Section 7 of the 1916 ULPA stated, in its entirety, that "[a] limited partner shall not become liable as a general partner unless, in addition to the exercise of his rights and powers as a limited partner, he takes part in the control of the business." There was considerable doubt under this sparse language as to how much activity by the limited partner would constitute "tak[ing] part in the control of the business" with the corresponding liability of a general partner. For example, could limited partners advise general partners and consult with them on business issues? Could a limited partner act as an employee, agent, or surety of the limited partnership? Could limited partners retain the power to remove a general partner and to elect another person for the position? Finally, could a limited partner be granted the power to vote for or against amendments to the limited partnership agreement? Under ULPA, one could not be sure whether engaging in this type of conduct or providing these or similar rights would be viewed as "tak[ing] part in the control of the business." This uncertainty made the limited partnership somewhat dangerous for investors relying on limited liability, and it played a substantial role in the decision to modernize the 1916 ULPA.

RULPA (1976) § 303(a) retained the control rule and added a new second sentence that narrowed the scope of a limited partner's liability: "However, if the limited partner's participation in the control of the business is not substantially the same as the exercise of the powers of a general partner, he [or she] is liable only to persons who transact business with the limited partnership with actual knowledge of his participation in control." RULPA (1976) § 303(b) also added a "safe harbor"—i.e., a list of protected limited partner activities that did not constitute "participat[ion] in the control of the business." The list included, among other activities, "consulting with and advising a general partner with respect to the business of the limited partnership," "being a contractor for or an agent or employee of the limited partnership or of a general partner," "acting as surety for the limited partnership," and voting on various listed matters.

RULPA (1985) § 303(a) retained the control rule and altered the second sentence to further restrict a limited partner's liability: "However, if the limited partner participates in the control of the business, he [or she] is liable only to persons who transact business with the limited partnership reasonably believing, based upon the limited partner's conduct, that the limited partner is a general partner." RULPA (1985) § 303(b) also expanded the safe harbor list of protected limited partner activities.

ULPA (2001) § 303 completed the pro-limited partner evolution by wholly eliminating the control rule: "A limited partner is not personally liable, directly or indirectly, by way of contribution or otherwise, for an obligation of the limited partnership solely by reason of being a limited partner, even if the limited partner participates in the management and control of the limited partnership." As the comment to ULPA (2001) § 303 explains: "In a world with [limited liability partnerships], [limited liability companies] and, most importantly, [limited liability limited partnerships], the control rule has become an anachronism. The Act therefore takes the next logical step in the evolution of the limited partner's liability shield and renders the control rule extinct."[26]

---

[26] Even before ULPA (2001) was promulgated, a few states had eliminated the control rule in their limited partnership statutes. *See, e.g.*, GA. CODE § 14–9–303 ("A limited partner is not liable for the obligations of a limited partnership by reason of being a limited partner and does not become so by participating in the management or control of the business."); MO. REV. STAT. § 359.201 (same). The comment to the Georgia statute is particularly revealing:

The following is a summary of the reasons for eliminating the "control" rule: (1) The control rule has, over the years, been greatly watered down, so that in its current version in RULPA there is no liability without creditor reliance and [there is] a broad safe harbor as to what constitutes control. (2) Even in a watered down form, the control rule leaves some uncertainty as to liability of limited partners, and therefore operates as an important disincentive to limited partnership investments. In particular, many of the "safe harbor" categories of non-control acts are open to interpretation. (3) Even without a control rule,

To get a sense of the changes brought about by the statutory developments, consider the decision of *Gateway Potato Sales v. G.B. Investment Co.*[27] Sunworth Packing was a limited partnership with a general partner, Sunworth Corporation, and a limited partner, G.B. Investment Company. Robert Ellsworth was the president of Sunworth Corporation, and Darl Anderson and Thomas McHolm were employees of G.B. Investment. Gateway Potato Sales, a creditor of Sunworth Packing, sued Sunworth Packing, Sunworth Corporation, and G.B. Investment to recover on an unpaid account. G.B. Investment moved for summary judgment, arguing that its limited partner status shielded it from liability. The trial court agreed and granted G.B. Investment's motion.

Arizona's applicable statute was based on the 1976 version of RULPA § 303. The *Gateway* court explained that, under the statute, there were two ways to establish "control" liability for a limited partner. First, a creditor could prove that the limited partner's participation in control was "substantially the same as the exercise of the powers of a general partner." Under this clause, the creditor did not have to possess any knowledge of the limited partner's control and there was no need for contact between the creditor and the limited partner. Second, even if the limited partner's participation in control was not "substantially the same as . . . a general partner," the limited partner would still be liable to any creditor who transacted business with the limited partnership "with actual knowledge of his [the limited partner's] participation in control." Under this clause, the court concluded that direct contact between the creditor and the limited partner was required.

The court observed that all of Gateway's dealings were with Ellsworth, and that Gateway had no contact with G.B. Investment prior to entering into the potato sale transaction. Nevertheless, the court reversed the trial court's grant of summary judgment. As the court explained, the trial court's ruling may have been based on a

---

third parties are protected if (despite their ability to check the certificate) they are misled by a limited partner's participation in control into believing that he is a general partner. Thus, a limited partner may be liable on [partner by estoppel] or fraud grounds, or on general equitable grounds under a "veil-piercing" theory. Fraud liability may be imposed, for example, if the limited partner's name is used in the name of the partnership [as in RULPA (1985) § 303(d)]. This Section only eliminates liability imposed solely because a limited partner participates, as such, in control of the business. (4) The control rule is not effective in fulfilling the objective of ensuring that only those with personal liability, and thus a strong incentive to be careful, will manage the business. General partners can always incorporate or delegate control to individuals other than limited partners. The control rule may actually serve to weaken the quality of management since the risk of liability for participation in control deters limited partners from monitoring the generals.

[27] 822 P.2d 490 (Ariz. Ct. App. 1991).

belief that a limited partner could never be liable "unless the creditor had contact with the limited partner and learned directly from him of his participation and control of the business." This belief, according to the court, was erroneous, as the Arizona statute did not require contact between the creditor and the limited partner for purposes of the "substantially the same as . . . a general partner" clause. Because "[t]he affidavit testimony of Ellsworth raise[d] the issue [of] whether he was merely a puppet for the limited partner, G.B. Investment," the court reversed the judgment of the trial court and remanded for further proceedings.[28]

A number of issues are presented by the *Gateway* opinion. First, why was Ellsworth assisting Gateway in its efforts to hold G.B. Investment liable? Ellsworth was the president of the general partner, Sunworth Corporation. Perhaps he was assisting Gateway because he wanted another party to be liable—aside from the corporate general partner and the limited partnership itself—in the event that Gateway won a judgment. Indeed, perhaps Ellsworth feared personal liability on some cause of action if Gateway's debt was not satisfied. For example, Ellsworth might have been worried about being individually named in a fraud or negligent misrepresentation claim based on his assurances to Gateway's owner "that he was in partnership with a large financial institution, G.B. Investment Company, and that G.B. Investment was providing the financing, was actively involved in the operation of the business, and had approved the purchase of the seed potatoes." Perhaps Ellsworth was worried about his reputation (the opinion indicated that Gateway's owner knew of Ellsworth's prior bankruptcy and was hesitant to do business with him in the first place) and he was trying to "make good" on his assurances.[29] Finally, perhaps Ellsworth was just angry with Anderson and McHolm for the way that they micro-managed him.

Second, what was G.B. Investment's alleged participation in control? According to Ellsworth's affidavit, some examples included the following: (1) Anderson/McHolm directed the operation of the business and instructed Ellsworth to make certain operating changes; (2) G.B. Investment negotiated a line of credit for the business (i.e., it obtained financing for the partnership) and guaranteed the loan; (3) significant business decisions had to be approved by Anderson/McHolm, and Anderson/McHolm directed Ellsworth to carry out certain decisions; (4) Anderson/McHolm dictated the accounting procedures to be followed by the partnership; (5) Anderson/McHolm had to approve all partnership expenditures and Anderson had to

[28] *See id.* at 491, 495–97.
[29] *See id.* at 492.

approve and sign partnership checks; (6) Anderson/McHolm selected equipment, chose contractors and suppliers, and approved bids
for the partnership; and (7) Anderson was able to withdraw partnership funds. Moreover, the opinion mentioned the testimony of
Gateway's owner that "Ellsworth had informed him that G.B. Investment's employees, McHolm and Anderson, were at the partnership's office on a frequent basis, that Ellsworth reported directly to
them, that daily operations of the partnership were reviewed by
representatives of G.B. Investment, and that Ellsworth had to get
their approval before making certain business decisions."[30] These
allegations strongly suggested that G.B. Investment, through Anderson and McHolm, called the shots for the limited partnership
and participated in control that was "substantially the same as . . .
a general partner." Just as a general partner possesses ultimate
decision-making authority and the corresponding power to direct
the limited partnership's affairs, so too did Anderson and McHolm
exercise management authority over the limited partnership and
direct its business operations.[31]

Third, it is worth considering whether any of the alleged conduct of Anderson and McHolm could fall within the safe harbor of
RULPA (1976) § 303(b). Some of their conduct might be characterized as "consulting with and advising a general partner" under
§ 303(b)(2), but the allegations in Ellsworth's affidavit that they
"directed" and "instructed" him sound like more than "advising."
Guaranteeing a loan falls under § 303(b)(3), although directly negotiating and obtaining the loan does not seem to be protected. (Obtaining a loan arguably constitutes participation in control because
it affirmatively commits the limited partnership to a binding transaction.) The § 303(b)(1) language of "being . . . an agent" of the limited partnership is broad and might encompass G.B. Investment's
initiating transactions for the partnership. Of course, this safe harbor presumably covers situations where the agent was authorized

---

[30] See id. at 492–93 & n.1.

[31] One might think of control as a continuum running from "passive" or indirect
control on one end (i.e., the power to stop things from happening, such as the power
to veto decisions) to "active" or direct control on the other (i.e., the power to affirmatively make things happen, such as the power to initiate transactions). Both passive
and active control are forms of control, but courts tend to be more reluctant to find
that the control rule has been violated when only passive control is present. In
Gateway, however, there was significant evidence of active control.

The control issue in this context can be related to the control issue that arises in
assessing whether an agency relationship has been created or whether a general
partnership has been formed. See Chapters 2(B)(1), 3(B)(1). In all three contexts,
"control" can be described as a continuum with evidence of active control (the ability
to initiate transactions, the ability to direct conduct, the possession of ultimate decision-making authority) being more persuasive than evidence of passive control.
Even passive control, however, is a form of control, and in certain circumstances it
may be sufficient on its own to persuade a factfinder.

by the limited partnership to enter into the transactions. Anderson and McHolm seem to have acted on their own without a grant of authority—more like principals than agents. Section 303(c) indicates that the absence of protection under § 303(b) does not necessarily mean that the limited partner's actions constitute participation in the business,[32] but the overall control possessed by Anderson and McHolm is pretty damning.

Fourth, the *Gateway* court indicated that even if a limited partner's participation in control was not "substantially the same as . . . a general partner," the limited partner would still be liable to any creditor who transacted business with the limited partnership "with actual knowledge of his [the limited partner's] participation in control." As mentioned, under this clause, the court concluded that direct contact between the creditor and the limited partner was required. This conclusion, however, can be questioned. Indeed, it would seem that a person could gain actual knowledge about a limited partner's participation in control by simply being told about that participation (as occurred in *Gateway* itself when Ellsworth informed Gateway's owner of G.B. Investment's role). On the other hand, the comment to RULPA (1976) § 303 suggests that a limited partner could evade liability under the actual knowledge clause by "avoiding any direct dealings with third parties." Such language might imply that direct dealings between the limited partner and the third party creditor are necessary to establish the creditor's actual knowledge. Of course, this is a comment and not statutory text. Further, the comment itself may only be illustrating an example of actual knowledge (direct dealings) rather than the sole example. The resolution of this issue will presumably turn on how much protection a court wishes to grant to a limited partner who is active in the business.

Finally, what result in *Gateway* if RULPA (1985) had governed the dispute? As opposed to the two methods of establishing control liability under the 1976 version of RULPA § 303(a), there is only one method under the 1985 version. A limited partner who participates in the control of the business is liable only to persons "who transact business with the limited partnership reasonably believing, based upon the limited partner's conduct, that the limited partner is a general partner." The *Gateway* court believed that this language "reflect[ed] a reluctance to hold a limited partner liable if the limited partner had no direct contact with the creditor."[33] If direct contact is a requirement, then Gateway would have lost un-

---

[32] *See* RULPA (1985) § 303 cmt. ("Section 303(c) makes clear that the exercise of power beyond the ambit of Section 303(b) is not ipso facto to be taken as taking part in the control of the business.").

[33] *Gateway*, 822 P.2d at 496.

der the facts of the case because it had no direct contact with G.B. Investment until after the potato sale transaction was concluded.

On the other hand, similar to the discussion under the 1976 statute, one could argue that the language "based upon the limited partner's conduct" does not necessarily require direct contact between the creditor and the limited partner. As mentioned, Gateway's owner testified that Ellsworth told him that "G.B. Investment's employees, McHolm and Anderson, were at the partnership's office on a frequent basis, that Ellsworth reported directly to them, that daily operations of the partnership were reviewed by representatives of G.B. Investment, and that Ellsworth had to get their approval before making certain business decisions." This information addressed G.B. Investment's conduct, and arguably Gateway formed a reasonable belief from the information that G.B. Investment was a general partner (indeed, Gateway thought that it was doing business with a general partnership). Admittedly, Gateway learned of G.B. Investment's conduct through hearsay rather than through direct contact or observation, but the statute does not seem to define how a conduct-based belief must be formed. Simply put, does "based upon the limited partner's conduct" mean that the limited partner participated in some general partner-like conduct, and the creditor came to know of it through direct contact with the limited partner? Or does it mean more broadly that the limited partner participated in some general partner-like conduct, and the creditor came to know of it by any means? Once again, this interpretive issue will presumably turn on how much protection a court wishes to grant to a limited partner who is active in the business.[34]

Aside from the "limited partner's conduct" restriction, notice that RULPA (1985) (as well as part of RULPA (1976)) imposes liability on limited partners only for the benefit of those who "transact

---

[34] What if Gateway learned about the general-partner-like conduct of G.B. Investment through direct contact, but then was explicitly told that G.B. Investment was a limited partner? While G.B. Investment's actions would seem to create a reasonable belief in Gateway, based upon G.B. Investment's conduct, that G.B. Investment was a general partner, the explicit statement that G.B. Investment was a limited partner would undercut that belief. *See, e.g.,* Shimko v. Guenther, 505 F.3d 987, 992 (9th Cir. 2007) (suggesting that, upon learning of a partner's status as a limited partner, a plaintiff "could not have reasonably believed that [defendant] was a general partner, whatever role [defendant] played in the control of the business"). *But see In re* Adelphia Commc'ns Corp., 376 B.R. 87, 96 (Bankr. S.D.N.Y. 2007) ("[T]he focus of Section 17–303 is at all times on the conduct of the limited partner. At first glance, it may seem illogical to ignore the actual knowledge of the third party. Under this interpretation of Section 17–303, a third party could be held to have a 'reasonable belief' that a limited partner was acting as the *de facto* general partner notwithstanding the fact that third party actually knew of the limited partner's status in public filings. Yet that is what the plain language of Section 17–303(a) mandates by inclusion of the words 'reasonably believing, *based upon the limited partner's conduct,* that the limited partner is a general partner.'").

business" with the limited partnership. This language suggests that only voluntary creditors have a chance of succeeding in an action against limited partners—i.e., creditors who affirmatively choose to transact business with the limited partnership. The typical voluntary creditor is a contract claimant. Tort claimants, by contrast, are usually involuntary creditors who, due to the tortious conduct, are thrust into a relationship with the limited partnership that they did not desire. In many tort situations (particularly those involving personal injury), it is hard to say that a tort victim "transact[ed] business" with the limited partnership with some reasonable belief about the limited partners.[35] Thus, the "transact business" restriction suggests that limited partners will rarely be vicariously liable for the limited partnership's tort obligations.[36]

2. Control of the Entity General Partner

By definition, a limited partnership has at least one general partner who is subject to unlimited personal liability for the debts of the venture.[37] In modern practice, the general partner is almost always a business entity with limited liability of its own (e.g., a corporation). The implications of such a structure are discussed in the following passage:

> A limited partnership with a corporation as the sole general partner creates a totally different kind of entity than the traditional limited partnership. If the general partner is only marginally capitalized, the limited partnership becomes a lim-

---

[35] For example, in a lawsuit by a pedestrian injured by the negligent driving of a limited partnership vehicle, it is difficult to assert that the pedestrian "transact[ed] business" with the limited partnership in any manner. (Moreover, the pedestrian likely has no knowledge whatsoever about the conduct of the limited partners; in fact, there is a good chance that the pedestrian has never heard of the limited partnership.) On the other hand, in a lawsuit by a supplier claiming that it was fraudulently induced to enter into a supply contract with the limited partnership, the supplier did "transact business" with the partnership, and it is possible that the supplier had a reasonable conduct-based belief that a limited partner was a general partner. This type of tort victim (one who was injured through a voluntary transaction with the partnership) might have a chance of recovery against a limited partner.

[36] Aside from control rule liability, limited partners might also face liability under a piercing the veil theory. For example, if a limited partner commingled partnership funds with personal funds, it would seem that a piercing claim should be available. See, e.g., C.F. Trust, Inc. v. First Flight Ltd. P'ship, 580 S.E.2d 806, 810 (Va. 2003) (suggesting that veil-piercing principles were applicable to limited partnerships). But see Pinebrook Props., Ltd. v. Brookhaven Lake Prop. Owners Ass'n, 77 S.W.3d 487, 499–500 (Tex. App. 2002) ("Alter ego is inapplicable with regard to a partnership because there is no veil that needs piercing, even when dealing with a limited partnership, because the general partner is always liable for the debts and obligations of the partnership to third parties."). Of course, a piercing claim against a limited partner would be necessary only if a control rule claim failed, perhaps because the creditor is unable to establish the "transact business" or "limited partner conduct" requirements of § 303(a).

[37] See, e.g., RULPA (1985) §§ 101(7), 403(b).

ited liability entity not unlike a corporation. No individual is personally liable for the firm's debts. ... A corporate general partner differs from an individual general partner in several basic respects. ... First, a corporate general partner is subject to the control of somebody else. With an individual as a general partner, there is no doubt as to whose decisions will be evaluated under applicable principles of fiduciary duty. Where a corporate general partner is involved, the decision maker may be a panel of individuals or a single person whose identity may or may not be known to the limited partners and whose financial interest in the limited partnership may be great or may be small.

Second, it is relatively easy to control transfers of managerial authority to third persons when individual general partners are involved. Restrictions on the transfer of general partnership interests without the consent of the limited partners appear both in statutes and in limited partnership agreements. While it may be possible to evade these limitations through a delegation of duties rather than an assignment of the interest itself, such a delegation does not eliminate the continuing responsibility of the general partner. In contrast, a corporate general partner is inherently an economic entity which itself may be purchased or sold. The individuals involved in the ownership and management of the business of the corporate general partner may change without a change in the identity of the general partner itself. The simplest example is the sale of shares by the shareholders of the general partner to an unrelated third person. The same result may be achieved through mergers or other transactions that arguably do not involve a sale or transfer at all. Thus, a corporate general partner is unlike an individual general partner in that control may be shifted from one group to another without apparently affecting the corporate general partner's continuous existence. From the standpoint of the inactive investors who are the limited partners, the identity of those in control of the general partner is usually more important than the formal identity of the general partner itself.

Third, a corporate general partner may be entirely acceptable and responsible as a general partner even though its assets are nominal or relatively insignificant in comparison to the size of the business it is managing. This is likely where the shareholders or managers of the corporate general partner also own substantial limited partnership interests. A claim of breach of fiduciary duty against a general partner is not worth very much if the general partner itself is a corporation with nominal assets . . .

Fourth, even if a corporate general partner is reasonably capitalized at the outset, subsequent transactions may bleed off these assets to the owners of the corporation without the consent of the limited partnership and without involving a fraudulent conveyance but greatly increasing the potential risks to the limited partners.[38]

When a limited partnership has an entity general partner, the individual managers of the general partner may also be limited partners in the limited partnership. Can the control exercised by the managers over the entity general partner—in their positions as managers of the entity general partner—be "imputed" to them in their limited partner roles? If so, the control rule may be violated. Alternatively, perhaps liability for the limited partnership's obligations extends only to the entity general partner itself.

Some courts resisted the concept of entity general partners and the notion of limited liability for limited partners who participated in the control of such entities (usually as managers or controlling owners). The case of *Delaney v. Fidelity Lease Ltd.*[39] is illustrative. In *Delaney*, a limited partnership was formed with a corporate general partner, Interlease Corporation. Interlease's sole officers, directors, and shareholders were W.S. Crombie, Jr., Alan Kahn, and William D. Sanders—individuals who were also limited partners in the limited partnership. Creditors of the limited partnership sued for breach of a lease agreement, naming as defendants the limited partnership itself, Interlease, and all of the limited partners. The creditors alleged that Crombie, Kahn, and Sanders controlled the business of the limited partnership through their managerial roles in Interlease. In response, Crombie, Kahn, and Sanders argued that they acted only as representatives of Interlease and that the corporation, Interlease, actually controlled the business of the limited partnership. The court expressed concern that "the statutory requirement of at least one general partner with general liability in a limited partnership [could] be circumvented or vitiated by limited partners operating the partnership through a corporation with minimum capitalization and therefore minimum liability." Moreover, the *Delaney* court held that "the personal liability, which attaches to a limited partner when 'he takes part in the control and manage-

[38] Robert W. Hamilton, *Corporate General Partners of Limited Partnerships*, 1 J. SMALL & EMERGING BUS. L. 73, 79–87 (1997).

[39] 526 S.W.2d 543 (Tex. 1975).

ment of the business,' cannot be evaded merely by acting through a corporation."[40]

These days, the use of entity general partners, and the provision of limited liability to limited partners who participate in the control of such entities, is far less controversial. Indeed, due in no small part to the evolution of limited partnership statutes, *Delaney*-like antagonism has largely disappeared.[41] For example, RULPA (1985) now explicitly permits entity general partners. Section 101(5) defines a "general partner" as a "person," and § 101(11) includes a natural person, general partnership, limited partnership, association, or corporation within the definition of a "person." Further, RULPA (1985) § 303(b)(1) explicitly states that a limited partner "does not participate in the control of the business" by "being . . . an agent or employee . . . of a general partner or being an officer, director, or shareholder of a general partner that is a corporation."[42] Even under § 303(a), creditors can only hold limited partners liable if they reasonably believed, based upon the limited partners' conduct, that the limited partners were general partners. If the creditors were aware that the limited partners were acting as managers of the general partner, then they probably did not believe that the limited partners were general partners themselves.[43] Finally, from a policy standpoint, problems with minimally capitalized entities are not unique to the limited partnership setting. They arise when-

---

[40] *See id.* at 544–46.

[41] For cases refusing to impose personal liability on limited partners who participated in the control of an entity general partner, *see* Western Camps, Inc. v. Riverway Ranch Enterprises, 138 Cal. Rptr. 918 (Cal. Ct. App. 1977); Zeiger v. Wilf, 755 A.2d 608 (N.J. Super. Ct. App. Div. 2000); Frigidaire Sales Corp. v. Union Properties, Inc., 562 P.2d 244 (Wash. 1977).

[42] RULPA (1985) was drafted before the limited liability company ("LLC") existed in most states. As a consequence, there is no reference to an LLC in the definition of "person" in § 101(11) or in the safe harbor of § 303(b)(1). Nevertheless, a number of states have amended their versions of RULPA (1985) to include a reference to the LLC. *See, e.g.,* N.Y. P'SHIP LAW § 121–101(n) (defining "person" to include a "limited liability company (domestic or foreign)"); *id.* § 121–303(b)(1) ("A limited partner does not participate in the control of the business . . . by virtue of doing one or more of the following: (1) being . . . a member, manager or agent of a limited liability company that is a general partner of the limited partnership . . . .").

[43] For this reason, limited partners who participate in the control of an entity general partner should seek to ensure that third parties are aware that they are acting solely in their capacity as managers of the entity general partner. *See, e.g.,* Zeiger v. Wilf, 755 A.2d 608, 619 (N.J. Super. Ct. App. Div. 2000) (involving a manager of a corporate general partner who failed to consistently identify himself as a manager of the general partner when he acted on behalf of the limited partnership, but refusing to impose personal liability because "plaintiff was at all times fully aware of what [the manager] was doing and how [the manager] was doing it"); *id.* at 618–19 ("[T]here is no claim that plaintiff was misled, or that he relied on some impression that [the manager] was a general partner . . . . A failure to comply with some designated formality might have had some significance if, at any time or in any way, it misled plaintiff or prejudiced him. But, as we have noted several times, that is simply not the case.").

ever a creditor is dealing with a separate legal entity. Moreover, because business entities can only function through their individual managers, it is usually more accurate to say that limited partners were exercising control merely in their managerial capacities, not in their limited partner capacities.[44]

G. Fiduciary Duties

1. General Partners

RULPA (1985) does not explicitly address general partner fiduciary duties. Instead, as a result of the linkage created by RULPA (1985) § 403 (as well as § 1105), general partnership law is imported to deal with the topic. UPA § 21 and RUPA § 404, in other words, wind up governing fiduciary duty issues for general partners in limited partnerships. Consistent with its "de-linkage" theme, ULPA (2001) § 408 specifically addresses general partner fiduciary duties. It does so, however, in a manner that is nearly identical to RUPA § 404.[45]

Despite the parallels between general partner fiduciary duties in the general partnership and limited partnership settings, some commentators have suggested that the application of these duties should not be equivalent:

---

[44] *See, e.g.*, Frigidaire Sales Corp. v. Union Props., Inc., 562 P.2d 244, 247 (Wash. 1977) ("There can be no doubt that respondents, in fact, controlled the corporation. However, they did so only in their capacities as agents for their principal, the corporate general partner. Although the corporation was a separate entity, it could act only through its board of directors, officers, and agents. . . . In the eyes of the law, it was Union Properties [the corporate general partner], as a separate corporate entity, which . . . controlled the limited partnership.").

[45] RULPA (1985) § 107 states that "[e]xcept as provided in the partnership agreement, a partner may lend money to and transact other business with the limited partnership and, subject to other applicable law, has the same rights and obligations with respect thereto as a person who is not a partner." *See also* ULPA (2001) § 112 (substantially the same); RUPA § 404(f) (substantially the same). In *BT-I v. Equitable Life Assurance Society*, 89 Cal. Rptr. 2d 811 (Ct. App. 1999), the court indicated that this section does not alter a general partner's fiduciary duties:

We cannot discern anything in the purpose of Corporations Code section 15617 [analogous to RULPA (1985) § 107] that suggests an intent to affect a general partner's fiduciary duty to limited partners. Under the prior limited partnership rule, limited partners were prohibited from making secured loans to the partnership and any collateral received could be set aside as a fraud upon creditors. Corporations Code section 15617 is identical to Uniform Limited Partnership Act (1976) section 107, which was enacted to remove the fraudulent conveyances prohibition from the limited partnership law and leave the question to the general fraudulent conveyances statute. This change hardly sanctions Equitable's self-dealing.

Id. at 818; *see also* ULPA (2001) § 112 cmt. ("This section has no impact on a general partner's duty . . . [to] refrain[] from acting as or for an adverse party . . . and means rather that this Act does not discriminate against a creditor of a limited partnership that happens also to be a partner.").

It is helpful to compare limited partnership with other fiduciary relationships. Fiduciary duties in the general partnership arguably should be less extensive than those in other agency or trust relationships because of the greater availability in the general partnership of extrajudicial controls, including joint management and control by the partners, the relatively equal expertise of the partners, the terminability of the relationship, and the alignment of incentives of the partners through profit sharing and personal liability for partnership debts. Fiduciary duties of a general partner in limited partnerships arguably should be more intense than those of a general partner in a general partnership, because the limited partners do not participate in management and control, typically lack the expertise of the general partner and may have restrictions on terminability of the relation. Rather, fiduciary duties in limited partnerships should be quite similar to those in other relationships without the balance of power accorded by the general partnership characteristics just listed. It follows that fiduciary duties of general partners in limited partnerships should be at the same level as those in principal-agent and director-corporation relationships. . .[46]

As discussed in the general partnership chapter, partners have broad latitude to modify traditional fiduciary duties by contract. This latitude applies to the limited partnership context as well:

Delaware's limited partnership jurisprudence begins with the basic premise that, *unless limited by the partnership agreement*, the general partner has the fiduciary duty to manage the partnership in its interest and in the interests of the limited partners. That qualified statement necessarily marries common law fiduciary duties to contract theory when it comes to considering actions undertaken in the limited partnership context. Thus, I think it a correct statement of law that principles of contract preempt fiduciary principles where the parties to a limited partnership have made their intentions to do so plain. . . In short, I think that under Delaware limited partnership law a claim of breach of fiduciary duty must first be analyzed in terms of the operative governing instrument—the partnership agreement—and only where that document is silent or ambiguous, or where principles of equity are implicated, will a Court begin to look for guidance from the statutory default rules, traditional

---

[46] IV ALAN R. BROMBERG & LARRY E. RIBSTEIN, BROMBERG & RIBSTEIN ON PARTNERSHIP § 16.07(a)(2), at 16:93 (13th ed. 2005) (footnotes omitted).

notions of fiduciary duties, or other extrinsic evidence. . . .[47]

Until 2004, § 17–1101(d)(2) of the Delaware Revised Uniform Limited Partnership Act ("DRULPA") stated that a "partner's or other person's duties and liabilities may be expanded or restricted by provisions in the partnership agreement." In *Gotham Partners, L.P. v. Hallwood Realty Partners*,[48] the Supreme Court of Delaware strongly suggested that this statutory language did not permit the *elimination* of fiduciary duties:

> The Vice Chancellor's summary judgment opinion in this case, however, creates a separate problem. We refer to one aspect of the Vice Chancellor's discussion of the [DRULPA] in his summary judgment opinion in this case where he stated that section 17–1101(d)(2) "expressly authorizes the *elimination*, modification or enhancement of . . . fiduciary duties in the written agreement governing the limited partnership." It is at least the second time the Court of Chancery has stated in dicta that DRULPA at 6 *Del. C.* § 17–1101(d)(2) permits a limited partnership agreement to *eliminate* fiduciary duties. . . . Section 17–1101(d)(2) states: "the partner's or other person's duties and liabilities may be *expanded* or *restricted* by provisions in the partnership agreement." There is no mention in § 17–1101(d)(2), or elsewhere in DRULPA at 6 *Del. C.*, ch. 17, that a limited partnership agreement may *eliminate* the fiduciary duties or liabilities of a general partner.

> Finally, we note the historic cautionary approach of the courts of Delaware that efforts by a fiduciary to escape a fiduciary duty, whether by a corporate director or officer or other type of trustee, should be scrutinized searchingly. Accordingly, although it is not appropriate for us to express an advisory opinion on a matter not before us, we simply raise a note of concern and caution relating to this dubious dictum in the Vice Chancellor's summary judgment opinion.[49]

Two years after *Gotham Partners*, the Delaware legislature amended DRULPA § 17–1101. The statute now provides that "a

---

[47] Sonet v. Timber Co., 722 A.2d 319, 322, 324 (Del. Ch. 1998) (footnote omitted); *see also* Continental Ins. Co. v. Rutledge & Co., 750 A.2d 1219, 1236 n.37 (Del. Ch. 2000) ("Many opt for the limited partnership form in Delaware precisely in order to embrace this [contractual] flexibility. . . . [P]arties, otherwise unwilling to shoulder fiduciary burdens, maintain the opportunity to form limited partnerships precisely because the parties can contract around some or all of the fiduciary duties the general partner typically owes the limited partners.").

[48] 817 A.2d 160 (Del. 2002).

[49] *Id.* at 167–68 (footnotes omitted).

partner's or other person's duties may be expanded or restricted or eliminated by provisions in the partnership agreement; provided that the partnership agreement may not eliminate the implied contractual covenant of good faith and fair dealing."[50] The statute also states that "[i]t is the policy of this chapter [on limited partnerships] to give maximum effect to the principle of freedom of contract and to the enforceability of partnership agreements."[51]

The Uniform Acts do not go as far as Delaware. RULPA (1985) does not address limits on partners' contractual freedom; thus, linkage would presumably make the limitations in RUPA § 103 applicable to the extent that RUPA was the governing general partnership statute.[52]   RUPA § 103(b)(3) and § 103(b)(4) would not allow a partnership agreement to eliminate the fiduciary duties of loyalty and care. ULPA (2001) § 110(b) limits partners' contractual freedom in a manner similar to RUPA § 103(b) by providing an explicit list of restrictions. For example, a partnership agreement is not permitted to eliminate the fiduciary duties of loyalty and care.

When a general partner of a limited partnership is a business entity, managers of the entity may personally owe fiduciary duties to the limited partners and the limited partnership. In *In re USACafes, L.P. Litigation*,[53] USACafes was a limited partnership with a corporate general partner, USACafes General Partner, Inc. Sam and Charles Wyly owned all of the stock of the general partner, sat on its board, and owned 47% of the limited partnership units. The lawsuit arose out of a purchase by Metsa Acquisition Corp. of substantially all of the assets of the limited partnership. Plaintiffs were holders of limited partnership units who brought a class action alleging breach of fiduciary duty against the Wyly brothers and other directors of the general partner.

---

[50] DRULPA § 17–1101(d); *see id.* § 17–1101(f). Although the only statutory limitation is the inability to eliminate the implied contractual covenant, some Delaware courts have suggested that public policy is also available to police abuses. *See, e.g.,* Abry Partners V, L.P. v. F&W Acquisition LLC, 891 A.2d 1032, 1036 (Del. Ch. 2006) ("For these reasons, when a seller intentionally misrepresents a fact embodied in a contract—that is, when a seller lies—public policy will not permit a contractual provision to limit the remedy of the buyer to a capped damage claim. Rather, the buyer is free to press a claim for rescission or for full compensatory damages. By this balance, I attempt to give fair and efficient recognition to the competing public policies served by contractual freedom and by the law of fraud."); *cf.* R&R Capital, LLC v. Buck & Doe Run Valley Farms, LLC, Civ. A. No. 3803–CC, 2008 WL 3846318, at *8 (Del. Ch. Aug. 19, 2008) (concluding that parties can contractually eliminate their right to petition for judicial dissolution based not only on freedom of contract principles and an analysis of the statutory language, but also based on a consideration of public policy arguments).

[51] DRULPA § 17–1101(c).

[52] *See* RULPA (1985) § 1105; *see also id.* § 101(7) (noting that a limited partnership is a "partnership").

[53] 600 A.2d 43 (Del. Ch. 1991).

The defendants moved to dismiss the breach of fiduciary duty claims. They asserted that while the corporate general partner owed fiduciary duties to the limited partners, they as directors of the general partner owed no such duties. The court disagreed, analogizing to trust law in concluding that the directors of a corporate general partner do owe fiduciary duties to the limited partners and the limited partnership itself.[54]

The holding in *USACafes* is controversial. On the one hand, the court's conclusion disregards the separate entity status of the corporate general partner to the extent that the corporation's duties as a general partner are being imputed, in a sense, to its directors. Moreover, the holding places managers of an entity general partner into a position where their fiduciary obligations may conflict. Under corporate law, for example, the director of a corporate general partner owes a fiduciary duty to the corporation, but under *USACafes*, that same director also owes a fiduciary duty to the limited partners and the limited partnership. It is not clear how these conflicting duties should be reconciled when the interests of the general partner and the limited partnership diverge.[55] On the other hand, the corporate general partner has complete control over the management of the limited partnership, and the managers of the corporation have complete control over the general partner. Thus, it seems plausible to impose the fiduciary duties owed by the general partner upon those managers. In other words, because the managers of the corporate general partner effectively have complete control over the management of the limited partnership, they should have responsibility for abuse of that control.[56]

---

[54] *See id.* at 45–50.

[55] It is also useful to compare the holding in *USACafes* to the control rule decisions discussed earlier. While RULPA (1985) § 303(b)(1) explicitly states that "being [a] . . . director . . . of a general partner that is a corporation" does not constitute participation in control, *USACafes* holds that such a director may nevertheless owe fiduciary duties to the limited partners and the limited partnership. Are these positions consistent? Does it make sense to say that a director of a corporate general partner owes a fiduciary duty to the limited partnership, even though carrying out director responsibilities does not constitute participation in control of the limited partnership?

[56] Courts have used other theories to impose fiduciary duty (or related) liability on the controllers of an entity general partner. The *USACafes* court itself, for example, mentioned the possibility of aider and abettor liability—i.e., the officers and directors of an entity general partner could be personally liable for aiding and abetting the general partner's breach of its fiduciary duties. *See USACafes*, 600 A.2d at 49; *see also* Wilson v. Friedberg, 473 S.E.2d 854, 856–57 (S.C. Ct. App. 1996) (applying a piercing the corporate veil theory and concluding that the sole shareholder of a corporate general partner owed a fiduciary duty to the limited partners). Keep in mind, of course, that the entity general partner itself is clearly liable for breaches of fiduciary duty. If the general partner has sufficient assets, there may be no need to pursue an additional theory of liability against the general partner's managers or owners.

2. Limited Partners

RULPA (1985) does not address the fiduciary duties of limited partners. In such circumstances, § 1105 indicates that general partnership law applies, but the general partnership statutes also fail to specifically address the duties of limited partners. Because RULPA (1985) § 101(8) defines "partner" to include a limited partner, one might argue (via linkage) that the general partnership law of "partner" fiduciary duties (e.g., UPA § 21; RUPA § 404) applies to limited partners as well. For example, in *KE Property Management Inc. v. 275 Madison Management Corp.*,[57] the court cited the Delaware equivalent to RULPA (1985) § 1105 and stated that, "although the Delaware Revised Uniform Limited Partnership Act does not specifically state that a limited partner owes a fiduciary duty to a general partner it, by reference to the Delaware Uniform Partnership Act, so provides."[58]

This linkage argument results in a poor fit, however, as most limited partners do not exercise the degree of control over the business that typically calls for the imposition of fiduciary duties. Indeed, in the later Delaware decision of *Bond Purchase, L.L.C. v. Patriot Tax Credit Properties, L.P.*,[59] the court rejected the contention that a limited partner (Bond) owed a fiduciary duty because the limited partner lacked the power to manage and control the business:

> [A] fiduciary is typically one who is entrusted with the power to manage and control the property of another. As the holder of 5 BUC$ [essentially 5 out of the 38,125 limited partnership units] and in the absence of a provision in the Partnership Agreement granting [limited partners] the right to manage or control Partnership property, Bond stands in no such relationship to the other limited partners. . . Therefore, in the absence of any provision in the Partnership Agreement engrafting fiduciary duties onto Bond, I conclude that Bond owes no fiduciary duties to the other limited partners . . .[60]

Although the court acknowledged the linkage analysis of *KE Property*, it stated that its refusal to impose a fiduciary duty on Bond

---

[57] Civ. A. No. 12683, 1993 WL 285900 (Del. Ch. July 27, 1993).

[58] *Id.* at 8–9 (citations omitted); *see also id.* at 9 (noting that "[u]nder the Delaware Uniform Partnership Law all partners owe each other fiduciary obligations").

[59] 746 A.2d 842 (Del. Ch. 1999).

[60] *Id.* at 864 (footnotes omitted). On whether a partnership agreement can impose fiduciary duties on limited partners, *see Cantor Fitzgerald, L.P. v. Cantor*, No. 16297, 2000 WL 307370, at *19 (Del. Ch. Mar. 13, 2000) ("Nothing in DRULPA or our case law expressly prohibits a limited partnership agreement from providing that limited partners are subject to duties that the common law or equity does not independently impose upon them.").

was consistent with that decision: "It is clear . . . that the *K.E. Property Management* Court was not adopting that proposition [that all partners, including limited partners, owe fiduciary obligations] in its entirety but was limiting it to situations in which a 'partnership agreement empowers a limited partner discretion to take actions affecting the governance of the limited partnership.'"[61] As the *Bond Purchase* court suggests, most courts in RULPA jurisdictions are likely to hold that a limited partner owes a fiduciary duty only when the limited partner participates in the management and control of the limited partnership—i.e., when a limited partner acts like a general partner by exercising management power.[62]

Section 305(a) of ULPA (2001) states that "[a] limited partner does not have any fiduciary duty to the limited partnership or to any other partner solely by reason of being a limited partner." Under § 305(b), however, a limited partner "shall discharge the duties to the partnership and the other partners under this [Act] or under the partnership agreement and exercise any rights consistently with the obligation of good faith and fair dealing." The comment to § 305 states, in part, the following:

> Fiduciary duty typically attaches to a person whose status or role creates significant power for that person over the interests of another person. Under this Act, limited partners have very limited power of any sort in the regular activities of the limited partnership and no power whatsoever justifying the imposition of fiduciary duties either to the limited partnership or fellow partners. It is possible for a partnership agreement to allocate significant managerial authority and power to a limited partner, but in that case the power exists not as a matter of status or role but rather as a matter of contract. The proper limit on such contract-based power is the obligation of good faith and fair dealing, not fiduciary duty, unless the partnership agreement itself expressly imposes a fiduciary duty or creates a role for a limited partner which, as a matter of other law, gives rise to a fiduciary duty. For example, if the partnership agreement makes a limited partner an agent for the limited partnership as to particular matters, the law of agency will impose fiduciary

---

[61] *Bond Purchase*, 746 A.2d at 864 (quoting *KE Property*, 1993 WL at *9).

[62] *Cf.* Goldwasser v. Geller, 684 N.Y.S.2d 210, 210 (App. Div. 1999) ("Defendants-appellants, all limited partners in the partnership in which the nonappealing defendants were the general partners, assumed a fiduciary duty to plaintiff, also a limited partner aggrieved by the general partners' nonfeasance, when they took over managerial control of the partnership.").

duties on the limited partner with respect to the limited partner's role as agent.[63]

H. Ownership Interests and Transferability

As previously discussed, partners in limited partnerships may
have management and financial rights (although limited partners
are rarely given substantial management rights).   Like general
partnerships, the default rule in limited partnerships is that financial rights are unilaterally transferable by a partner, but management rights are not.   In other words, in the absence of a contrary
agreement, the unanimous consent of the other partners is required
before a transferee can become a full-fledged partner in the venture
with all of the rights and obligations that partner status conveys.[64]

For general partner interests, these default restrictions on
transferability are sensible.   General partners tend to participate
actively in the management of the business and face personal liability for the obligations of the firm.   As a consequence, they probably
expect to have some control over the identity of their fellow general
partners.   After all, other general partners have a default right to
participate in management (and you don't want just "anyone" participating in management), and they can engage in misconduct that
imposes liability on the partnership and the general partners themselves.

These rationales, however, do not apply to limited partner interests.   Limited partners typically have little or no management
rights, and they are protected by limited liability.   Thus, it is less
obvious why limited partners are unable, as a default matter, to
unilaterally transfer their full ownership interests.   (Indeed, limited
partners are like corporate shareholders in these respects, and the
default corporate rule is that shareholders can unilaterally transfer
their full ownership interests.)   Put differently, limited partners
would not seem to need a veto right over the admission of new lim-

---

[63] Notice that this comment suggests that when a partnership agreement allocates
significant control to a limited partner, the exercise of that control is subject to the
obligation of good faith and fair dealing, but not to a fiduciary duty. By contrast, the
KE Property court stated that, "to the extent that a partnership agreement empowers
a limited partner discretion to take actions affecting the governance of the limited
partnership, the limited partner may be subject to the obligations of a fiduciary, including the obligation to act in good faith as to the other partners." *KE Property*,
1993 WL at *9.

It should be noted that RULPA (1985) and ULPA (2001) explicitly authorize derivative lawsuits. *See* RULPA (1985) §§ 1001–1004; ULPA (2001) §§ 1001–1005.

[64] *See, e.g.*, RULPA (1985) §§ 101(10), 702; ULPA (2001) §§ 102(22), 701–702; *see
also* RULPA (1985) § 301 (addressing the admission of limited partners); ULPA
(2001) § 301 (same); RULPA (1985) § 401 (addressing the admission of general partners); ULPA (2001) § 401 (same).

ited partners.[65] Of course, all of these transfer restrictions are simply default rules; thus, the partners can contract around the ones that do not suit the needs of their venture.[66]

Entity general partners present interesting issues related to ownership and transferability. For example, the transfer of shares of a corporate general partner is technically distinct from the transfer of a general partner interest. That is, the corporation maintains its identity as the general partner even if 100% of its shares are sold to a third party. One could argue, therefore, that limited partners have no basis for objecting when shareholders of a corporate general partner sell all or a controlling block of their shares in the corporation to a third party. Selling a controlling block of shares, however, shifts control of a corporate general partner to new owners, even if the identity of the corporate general partner remains the same. Such a result may adversely affect the interests of limited partners, although the use of broad anti-transfer clauses can help to alleviate this problem.[67]

A merger involving an entity general partner may also shift control of the general partner to new owners and may change the identity of the general partner itself. As a result, a merger might constitute a "transfer" or "assignment" that violates the statutory prohibition against partners unilaterally transferring their management powers (or a contractual prohibition against transfer in a limited partnership agreement). A leading case is *Star Cellular Telephone Co. v. Baton Rouge CGSA, Inc.*[68] The agreement provid-

---

[65] Restrictions on the transferability of limited partner interests were important in the pre-check-the-box days, as they helped to combat a corporate-like "free transferability of ownership interests" finding. *See* Chapter 16(A). This may explain their inclusion in RULPA (1985). Their inclusion in ULPA (2001), however, is probably explained by the fact that limited partners are given more default management rights in that statute. *See, e.g.,* ULPA (2001) § 302 cmt.; *see also id.* § 303 (eliminating the control rule). As a consequence, in an ULPA (2001) jurisdiction, there may be more of a need for a veto power over the admission of new limited partners. As mentioned, you don't want just "anyone" exercising management rights.

[66] RULPA (1985) § 703 provides a charging order procedure whereby "the court may charge the partnership interest of the partner with payment of the unsatisfied amount of the judgment with interest," but "[t]o the extent so charged, the judgment creditor has only the rights of an assignee of the partnership interest." *See also* ULPA (2001) § 703 (providing for charging orders).

[67] *See, e.g., In re* Asian Yard Partners, No. 95–333–PJW, 1995 WL 1781675, at *7 (Bankr. D. Del. Sept. 18, 1995) (concluding that language in a limited partnership agreement that barred transfer of a partnership interest "directly or indirectly, or by operation of law or otherwise" prevented the transfer of a controlling stock interest in a corporate general partner: "By using the words 'directly or indirectly' the parties obviously meant that a partner could not do indirectly that which it was prohibited from doing directly. In my view, the plain meaning of the language encompasses a situation where there is a transfer of a controlling interest in a partner entity, because such a transaction effectively transfers a partner interest to the control of the party acquiring the controlling interest of the partner entity.").

[68] Civ. A. No. 12507, 1993 WL 294847 (Del. Ch. Aug. 2, 1993).

ed that "[t]he General Partner may transfer or assign its General Partner's interest only after written notice to all the other Partners and the unanimous vote of all the other Partners to permit such transfer and to continue the business of the Partnership with the assignee of the General Partner as General Partner." The court concluded that the word "transfer" could not be read to encompass a merger, although it noted that the parties could have provided otherwise (e.g., by explicitly defining transfer to include transfers "by operation of law"). Significantly, however, the court rested its decision on an analysis of the effect of the merger in the context of the relationships of the parties. It concluded that the merger created no material change in control or operations—i.e., the change was in form and not in substance:

> Antiassignment clauses are normally included in contracts to prevent the introduction of a stranger into the contracting parties' relationship and to assure performance by the original contracting parties. ... Here, in contrast, no "stranger" has been "forced" upon the plaintiffs in any meaningful sense. The defendants retained the same partner, but in a different corporate form.

> The record establishes that the Merger did not adversely impact the plaintiffs' position or rights. After the Merger, operational control of the Partnership remained in the hands of BellSouth, which made no material changes in the Partnership's management. ... In short, the Merger created no material change in the control of the general partner or in the operations of the Partnership. The change was purely formal—the substitution of a new corporate entity for the entity that was the original general partner. That effected a change, to be sure, but one of legal form, not of substance. It altered none of the pre-Merger realities that were crucial to the limited partners' economic interests.[69]

The *Star Cellular* court seemed to consider both contract interpretation and a functional analysis based on material changes in management and operation. Both considerations pointed in the direction of approving the transfer. One can imagine more difficult cases, of course, where the contract interpretation and functional analyses do not suggest the same outcome.[70]

---

[69] *Id.* at *3, 5–11.

[70] In *In re Asian Yard Partners*, No. 95–333–PJW, 1995 WL 1781675 (Bankr. D. Del. Sept. 18, 1995), the limited partnership agreement barred transfer of a partnership interest "directly or indirectly, or by operation of law or otherwise." *Id.* at *7. The court distinguished the *Star Cellular* conclusion that the word "transfer" did not encompass a merger by noting that the parties clearly defined prohibited transfers as

I. Dissociation and Dissolution

1. Dissociation

Section 402 of RULPA (1985) specifies the events of withdrawal (what RUPA calls "dissociation") for a general partner, including, among others, voluntary withdrawal, removal, and bankruptcy. Section 602 allows a general partner to withdraw at any time by giving written notice to the other partners, but if withdrawal violates the partnership agreement, the limited partnership may recover damages. Pursuant to § 604, a withdrawing partner (general or limited) is entitled to receive any distribution provided for in the partnership agreement. If the partnership agreement is silent, § 604 specifies that a partner shall receive, "within a reasonable time after withdrawal, the fair value of his [or her] interest in the limited partnership as of the date of withdrawal based upon his [or her] right to share in distributions from the limited partnership."

Section 603 of RULPA (1985) allows a limited partner to withdraw under circumstances specified in a written partnership agreement. If the agreement is silent, "a limited partner may withdraw upon not less than six months' prior written notice to each general partner." As noted above, when withdrawal occurs, § 604 provides for a "fair value" buyout.

Why can general partners withdraw at any time from a limited partnership under RULPA (1985) § 602, but limited partners can withdraw only upon six months' notice under § 603? General partners have unlimited liability for the obligations of the limited partnership. They need the right to withdraw at any time in order to cut off their vicarious liability. By contrast, limited partners have limited liability. As a result, there is no liability-driven need for limited partners to be able to withdraw at any time. The withdrawal of a partner, however, triggers the fair value buyout of RULPA (1985) § 604, which could pose a problem for financially strapped firms. Thus, the six months' notice provision for limited partner withdrawal is presumably designed to give the limited partnership time to organize its financial affairs in order to minimize the disruption of a buyout. (Notice that general partner with-

---

including transfers "by operation of law or otherwise." *Id.* at *8. The court also suggested that any substantive inquiry into whether the merger caused a material change of control was unnecessary: "It may fairly be inferred from the broad scope of the description of a 'transfer' set forth in . . . the Partnership Agreement that the parties here intended to eliminate the need for a determination (including a litigated one) of whether a transfer by operation of law (such as by merger) would result in a material change in control of the general partner or in the operation of the partnership. They carried out that intent by providing a blanket prohibition to transfer . . . .") *Id.*

drawal causes the same cash drain concerns, but the need to cut off potential liability seems to trump any negative financial ramifications to the partnership.)

The primary issue posed by the limited partnership dissociation provisions is their effect on the family limited partnership ("FLP"). An FLP is an estate planning device involving a business owner who creates a limited partnership with family members as the limited partners. The goal of the FLP, at least in part, is to ultimately transfer the business to the family members while minimizing estate and gift taxes. As part of the tax minimization effort, an owner of a limited partnership interest will frequently claim that the value of his ownership position should be reduced to reflect (1) that the interest is difficult to liquidate, and (2) that purchasers will generally pay less for illiquid positions. This is known as the "marketability discount," and it is commonly applied when valuing closely held business interests for tax purposes (a lower value generally results in lower taxes owed). Federal tax law, however, eliminates the ability to apply a marketability discount when state statutes provide default withdrawal and buyout rights to limited partners. In the FLP context, in other words, the presence of exit rights under state law hinders the effort to minimize taxes.[71] As a result, many jurisdictions have modified RULPA (1985) § 603 by eliminating a limited partner's default right to withdraw, upon six months' notice, from the business.[72] Because RULPA (1985) § 604 provides for a fair value buyout upon withdrawal, the elimination of the default right to withdraw prevents a limited partner from invoking § 604 to cash out of the business (unless a right to withdraw is provided in the limited partnership agreement).

This elimination of default withdrawal and buyout rights for limited partners has some benefits. As mentioned, if the elimination is carried out via state statute, it makes it easier to obtain marketability discounts when valuing transferred limited partnership interests for tax purposes. Moreover, the possibility of a cash drain on the limited partnership caused by limited partners withdrawing and demanding a fair value buyout is eliminated. (The possibility of a limited partner threatening withdrawal and an accompanying cash drain unless certain demands are met is also eliminated.) On the other hand, without a means of liquidating the investment, the capital of limited partners remains trapped within

[71] See I.R.C. § 2704(b); Robert T. Danforth, *The Role of Federalism in Administering a National System of Taxation,* 57 TAX LAW. 625, 633–34 (2004).

[72] See, e.g., TEX. BUS. ORGS. CODE § 153.110 ("A limited partner may withdraw from a limited partnership only at the time or on the occurrence of an event specified in a written partnership agreement."). Many states are eliminating default exit rights in the LLC setting as well. See Chapter 16(I). In both contexts, this elimination facilitates the business organization's use as an estate planning vehicle.

the enterprise, similar to a shareholder's investment in a closely held corporation. If the managers of the partnership engage in misconduct or otherwise act oppressively towards the limited partners, the limited partners have no easy exit from the situation. They cannot cash out their investments and redeploy their capital elsewhere.

The provisions of ULPA (2001) reflect this trend towards restricting or eliminating default exit rights in the limited partnership. Section 601(a) eliminates the *right* of a limited partner to dissociate before the firm's termination. Section 601(b)(1), however, recognizes a limited partner's *power* to dissociate by express will.[73] Under § 602(a)(3), the effect of dissociation is that the former limited partner becomes a transferee of his own transferable interest. A right to payment upon dissociation is not provided. Pursuant to § 603 and § 604, a general partner has dissociation rights and powers similar to those in RUPA. Under § 605(a)(5), the effect of dissociation is that the former general partner becomes a transferee of his own transferable interest. Once again, a right to payment upon dissociation is not provided.[74]

2. Dissolution

Under RULPA (1985) § 801, a limited partnership is dissolved (1) at the time specified in the certificate of limited partnership; (2) upon the occurrence of events specified in a written partnership agreement; (3) upon the written consent of all partners; (4) upon an event of withdrawal of a general partner under § 402 (except when certain requirements are met); and (5) by the entry of a decree of judicial dissolution under § 802. Notice that dissolution is not caused by the dissociation of a limited partner. This comports with the typical structure of limited partnerships—i.e., limited partners are passive owners who mainly provide financing to the venture. Their departure does not normally cause a substantial change in the business.

---

[73] NCCUSL's "Summary" of ULPA (2001) states the following: "Under RULPA a limited partner could theoretically withdraw from the partnership on six months notice unless the partnership agreement specified the withdrawal events for a limited partner. Due to estate planning concerns, the new ULPA default rule affords no right to disassociate as a limited partner before the termination of the limited partnership. The power to disassociate is expressly recognized, but may be exercised only through the partnership agreement or those events listed in section 601(b) of this Act."

[74] *See also* ULPA (2001) § 505 ("A person does not have the right to receive a distribution on account of dissociation."). Sections 606 and 607 address, in a RUPA-like fashion (*see* Chapter 3(G)(2)), the effect of dissociation on a general partner's power to bind the limited partnership and a general partner's liability for the obligations of the limited partnership.

RULPA (1985) § 802 provides that a court "may decree dissolution of a limited partnership whenever it is not reasonably practicable to carry on the business in conformity with the partnership agreement." Courts have applied this language to various forms of general partner misconduct, including the general partner's operation of the venture in a manner that violates the partnership agreement. Keep in mind that the standard is "not reasonably practicable," which presumably differs from "impossible."

ULPA (2001) § 801 states the grounds for non-judicial dissolution. The section provides that a limited partnership will not ordinarily dissolve upon the withdrawal of a general partner if another general partner remains (unless partners owning a majority of the distribution rights consent to dissolution). In addition, dissolution by partner consent does not require the consent of all of the limited partners. Instead, along with the consent of all of the general partners, only the consent of limited partners owning "a majority of the rights to receive distributions as limited partners" is required. Like RULPA (1985) § 802, ULPA (2001) § 802 provides for judicial dissolution "if it is not reasonably practicable to carry on the activities of the limited partnership in conformity with the partnership agreement."

In some limited partnerships, the partnership agreement specifies how distributions should be made in the event of the company's dissolution. When a partnership agreement is silent, however, the statute provides a distribution scheme.[75]

J. A Final Look

In a world of LLPs and LLCs, what role remains for the limited partnership? The Prefatory Note to ULPA (2001) provides some insight:

> The new Act has been drafted for a world in which limited liability partnerships and limited liability companies can meet many of the needs formerly met by limited partnerships. This Act therefore targets two types of enterprises that seem largely beyond the scope of LLPs and LLCs: (i) sophisticated, manager-entrenched commercial deals whose participants commit for the long term, and (ii) estate planning arrangements (family limited partnerships). This Act accordingly assumes that, more often than not, people utilizing it will want:
>
> • strong centralized management, strongly entrenched, and

---

[75] See, e.g., RULPA (1985) § 804; ULPA (2001) § 812.

- passive investors with little control over or right to exit the entity

The Act's rules, and particularly its default rules, have been designed to reflect these assumptions.

Chapter 15

THE LIMITED LIABILITY PARTNERSHIP

Analysis

A. Introduction
B. Formation
C. Limited Liability
D. The Limited Liability Limited Partnership

A. Introduction

The limited liability partnership ("LLP") is typically a general partnership that, depending on the relevant statute, provides the partners with limited liability for the firm's tort obligations or for both its tort and contract obligations. Because the LLP is ordinarily a general partnership rather than a limited partnership,[1] all of the partners have the right to participate in the management of the venture without risking a loss of their limited liability. More generally, because partnership statutes often provide that an LLP is a "partnership,"[2] general partnership law is applicable to LLPs when it is not explicitly altered by LLP-specific provisions.

The LLP form of business organization is a relatively recent development. Texas passed the first LLP statute in 1991 as a result of leading the nation in bank and savings and loan failures in the 1980s. The Federal Deposit Insurance Corporation and related governmental entities brought lawsuits against hundreds of shareholders, directors, and officers of these failed financial institutions in an effort to recover funds. When the amounts recovered from the principal wrongdoers amounted to only a tiny fraction of the total losses, malpractice lawsuits were then directed against the lawyers and accountants who had represented the failed institutions. The fear of massive personal liability on the part of "innocent" partners for the banking work of fellow partners spurred a vigorous lobbying effort that ultimately resulted in the passage of the first LLP stat-

---

[1] In some jurisdictions, limited partnerships can register as LLPs. *See* Chapter 15(D).

[2] *See, e.g.,* RUPA § 101(5).

ute. Other states followed suit, and the LLP quickly became a viable business option across the country.

Is the LLP a positive development? In today's litigious climate, lawsuits are a fact of life. In a general partnership, partners have vicarious liability for the misconduct of their fellow partners. If a judgment is large enough to exhaust the firm's assets (including insurance), the partners' personal assets are at risk. Many believe that it is unfair to impose personal liability on innocent partners and that such unfairness justifies the provision of limited liability. Indeed, this sense of unfairness is what spurred the LLP's creation.

The provision of limited liability to general partners, however, may affect their incentives to monitor one another. Smaller firms own few assets of significance, although the individual partners may have substantial personal wealth. Unlimited liability, therefore, encourages partners to monitor their co-partners' work to prevent misconduct and possible personal liability. Limited liability removes this incentive to monitor, and may actually discourage active monitoring due to the risk of being personally implicated as a directly liable party (e.g., a negligent supervision claim).

On the other hand, unlimited liability may impose unreasonable burdens to monitor on partners, particularly in larger firms where partners may be in different cities (or countries) from where the wrongful conduct is occurring. Moreover, while limited liability may reduce the liability-driven incentives to monitor, other incentives to monitor exist (e.g., concerns about the firm's reputation would encourage partners to monitor one another to help avoid wrongful conduct). Finally, in larger firms, clients may be adequately protected by the firm's assets and reputational capital. Clients may not need the additional protection of unlimited liability. In fact, unlimited liability might restrict the size of a firm (we can't grow too large or the risk of potential liability from a partner's wrongdoing increases—it will be impossible to monitor what everyone is doing). A restriction on firm growth will likely decrease the amount of asset and reputational protection that a firm can provide.

In short, to the extent that limited liability results in a disincentive to monitor the work of fellow partners, one could argue that LLP provisions are a negative development. Presumably the quality of professional or other work improves to some degree if partners are incentivized to collaborate and to help one another. As mentioned, however, reputational concerns still exist to encourage monitoring and assistance. Further, even before the LLP, professional firms could achieve limited liability by using the professional corporation structure. Thus, the LLP is not the first business organization to raise monitoring concerns in the professional firm setting. As far as we know, there has been no hue and cry from clients of professional corporations that the quality of work has suffered due to a purported lack of monitoring.[3]

B. Formation

Partnership statutes typically provide that an LLP is a "partnership."[4] With respect to formation, therefore, an LLP must fall within the statutory definition of a partnership—i.e., an association of two or more persons to carry on as co-owners a business for profit.[5] Beyond meeting the partnership definition, an LLP must satisfy certain statutory formalities. Most importantly, an LLP is required to file a document (generally called an application, registration, or certificate) with the secretary of state or other designated official. The document must provide prescribed information, which usually includes, among other items, the firm's name (which ordinarily must contain the "LLP" abbreviation or the "limited liability partnership" term), the firm's address, and a statement of its business or purpose.[6] Because of legislative variations, one should always check the relevant statute for the precise informational requirements.

In addition, some jurisdictions require an LLP to provide a specified amount of liability insurance or, alternatively, a pool of funds designated and segregated for the satisfaction of judgments against the partnership.[7] An LLP that fails to comply with the in-

---

[3] Admittedly, some professional corporation statutes explicitly impose supervisory liability, which would obviously encourage monitoring. Other statutes, however, furnish broad limited liability, much like many LLP provisions. *See, e.g.,* TEX. BUS. ORGS. CODE § 303.002 (stating that "[a] shareholder of a professional corporation is not required to supervise the performance of duties by an officer or employee of the corporation," and further noting that "[a] shareholder of a professional corporation is subject to no greater liability than a shareholder of a for-profit corporation").

[4] *See* note 2 and accompanying text.

[5] *See* Chapter 3(B)(1).

[6] *See, e.g.,* RUPA § 1001 (prescribing the contents of the "statement of qualification"); *id.* § 1002 (addressing the LLP's name). An LLP is simply a partnership that has availed itself of statutory procedures altering the traditional rule of partner liability. Thus, the registration filed with the state is not a document effectuating or evidencing formation of the entity in the same sense as articles of incorporation or a certificate of limited partnership. The partnership is formed with or without an effective LLP registration; it is the same entity as it was prior to registration. The filing merely changes the rule regarding the personal liability of the partners.

[7] *See, e.g.,* N.M. STAT. § 54–1–47 ("A registered limited liability partnership shall carry at least five hundred thousand dollars ($500,000) per occurrence and one million dollars ($1,000,000) in the aggregate per year of liability insurance, beyond the amount of any applicable deductible, covering the partnership for errors, omissions, negligence, wrongful acts, misconduct and malpractice for which the liability of partners is limited . . . ."); *id.* ("A registered limited liability partnership is . . . in substantial compliance with . . . this section if the partnership provides an amount of funds equal to the amount of insurance required . . . [that is] specifically designated

surance/segregated funds requirement presumably loses its limited liability protection, at least up to the amount that insurance or segregated funds should have provided.[8] Even if there is no LLP-specific insurance/segregated funds provision, an LLP may still be subject to similar requirements under licensing or other statutes.

A number of issues arise with respect to the formation of an LLP. First, what vote of the partners is needed to approve LLP registration? Depending on the statute, unanimous, "majority in interest," or majority approval may be required. Some statutes (such as RUPA § 1001(b)) provide that approval by the vote necessary to amend the partnership agreement is required, and some LLP statutes are silent on the issue. Regardless of the specified vote, these approval requirements can raise some thorny issues:

> Statutes that permit registration by majority or other subunanimous vote raise difficult policy and constitutional issues. LLP registration may, in effect, redistribute exposure to liability from the partners generally to those partners who are closely enough involved in the liability-generating aspects of the practice to be exposed to direct liability for monitoring or supervision lapses. Directly affected partners arguably ought to be able to block the registration. On the other hand, a default unanimity rule might so greatly increase the bargaining costs associated with registration that some firms may be unable to become LLPs. The appropriate balance between these competing considerations may vary from firm to firm. . . . [P]ermitting LLP registration is a new development that partnerships in existence on adoption of the LLP statute did not anticipate in drafting their agreement. It is reasonable to suppose that many partnerships would have contracted for limited liability from the outset if they had been allowed to do so.[9]

Second, most LLP statutes provide that limited liability begins as soon as the registration statement is filed.[10] Nevertheless, the

---

and segregated for the satisfaction of judgments against the partnership or its partners . . . .").

[8] *See, e.g.*, OKLA. STAT. tit. 54, § 1–309(g) ("If a limited liability partnership . . . fails to comply with this [insurance/segregated funds] section, the partners thereof shall be liable jointly for the debts, obligations and liabilities of the partnership . . . ; provided, however, that the aggregate amount for which the partners are jointly liable shall be limited to the difference between the amount of security required to be maintained . . . and the amount of security actually maintained by the partnership.").

[9] ALAN R. BROMBERG & LARRY E. RIBSTEIN, BROMBERG AND RIBSTEIN ON LIMITED LIABILITY PARTNERSHIPS, THE REVISED UNIFORM PARTNERSHIP ACT, AND THE UNIFORM LIMITED PARTNERSHIP ACT (2001) § 2.04(b), at 59 (2010).

[10] *See, e.g.*, RUPA § 1001(e).

effect of LLP registration on existing contracts and relationships is
not entirely clear:

> Since LLP registration continues the pre-existing partner-
> ship entity, it apparently does not affect the firm's contracts ei-
> ther among the partners or between the partnership and third
> parties. But there are many unanswered questions with respect
> to attributing liabilities to the pre- or post-registration period.
> Are post-registration loans pursuant to a pre-registration line of
> credit subject to the LLP liability limitation (under statutes
> that limit liability for contract debts)? Is a partner's malprac-
> tice covered by the registration if it was committed prior to reg-
> istration but results in an injury afterward? Is a creditor who
> agreed to a lease or a line of credit prior to registration stuck
> with limited liability as to subsequent loans or rent?

> One possible place to look for answers to these questions is
> cases that have considered whether new partners are personally
> liable, or former partners not liable, for interest or other pay-
> ments on preexisting partnership contracts or debts that accrue
> after dissociation or admission. The reasoning in these cases for
> and against liability, which is based on the creditors' expecta-
> tions as to who would be liable on the loan, arguably also ap-
> plies to the effect of the LLP liability limitation on post-
> registration charges or liabilities that accrue on pre-registration
> contracts or misconduct.

> Creditors can, of course, deal with these issues in their
> agreements with the partnership. The problem, of course, is
> that older agreements could not have anticipated the LLP.[11]

Finally, most states require LLPs to pay registration fees. In
Texas, for example, an LLP must pay $200 per partner, per year.[12]
When a state requires an LLP to renew its registration, a failure to
comply may jeopardize the partners' limited liability. In *Apcar Investment Partners VI, Ltd. v. Gaus*,[13] a partnership (Smith & West)
registered as a Texas LLP on March 6, 1995. The LLP failed to
subsequently renew its registration. On August 11, 1999, the LLP
entered into a lease agreement. Apcar ultimately sued the LLP and
its two individual partners (Gaus and West) for breach of the lease
agreement. Gaus and West filed a summary judgment motion as-

---

[11] Larry E. Ribstein, Unincorporated Business Entities 499–500 (3d ed.
2004) (citation omitted).

[12] *See* Tex. Bus. Orgs. Code §§ 4.158(1)–(2), 152.802(a), (e), (g) (noting that the
fee for filing an initial LLP application is "$200 for each partner," and the fee for
filing the required annual renewal of the application is "$200 for each partner on the
date of renewal").

[13] 161 S.W.3d 137 (Tex. App. 2005).

serting that the Texas partnership statute shielded them from personal liability for the LLP's obligations. The trial court granted the motion, but the Court of Appeals reversed:

> ... Apcar contends that the lease obligations were not incurred while Smith & West, L.L.P. was a registered limited liability partnership because Smith & West, L.L.P.'s status as a registered limited liability partnership expired in 1996—three years before the lease was executed. Therefore, Apcar asserts that Gaus and West are personally liable for the lease obligations. Gaus and West contend that Smith & West, L.L.P.'s initial registration as a registered limited liability partnership in 1995 protects them from individual liability in this case. To support their argument, Gaus and West rely on cases involving the statutory filing requirements for limited partnerships. They assert that, based on the reasoning of the limited partnership cases, Smith & West, L.L.P. did not need to comply with statutory renewal requirements for maintaining its status as a registered limited liability partnership in order to protect them from individual liability under the lease. ... In the context of limited partnerships, courts have held that it is not necessary for limited partnerships to strictly comply with statutory filing requirements for its limited partners to receive limited liability protection. [*See, e.g.,* Garrett v. Koepke, 569 S.W.2d 568 (Tex. App. 1978)]. In each of these cases, the courts held that limited partners did not lose their limited liability status when the partnership failed to comply with filing requirements.

> . . .

> The limited partnership cases are distinguishable from registered limited liability partnership cases for two reasons. First, the clear language of Article 6132b–3.08(a)(1) [now TEX. BUS. ORGS. CODE § 152.801] provides that partners are protected from individual liability only for debts and obligations that are incurred while the partnership is a registered limited liability partnership. Article 6132b–3.08(b)(5) and (b)(7) [now TEX. BUS. ORGS. CODE § 152.802] provides that registration expires in one year unless it is renewed prior to the expiration date. To apply the reasoning of the limited partnership cases would conflict with the clear language of Article 6132b–3.08.[14] Second,

---

[14] The former Texas statute (Article 6132b–3.08(a)(1)) clearly stated that a partner in an LLP had limited liability "while the partnership is a *registered* limited liability partnership" (emphasis added). The current § 152.801 of the Texas Business Organizations Code states that a partner in an LLP has limited liability "while the partnership is a limited liability partnership." Does the omission of the term "registered" have any significance? Is it possible to now argue that an LLP that fails to renew its registration under § 152.802(e) and (g) is still a limited liability partner-

the Texas Revised Limited Partnership Act . . . contains a ["substantial compliance" provision analogous to RULPA (1985) § 201(b)] that is not present in Article 6132b–3.08. . . . Article 6132b–3.08 does not contain a "substantial compliance" section, nor does it contain a grace period for filing a renewal application. We hold that a partnership must be in compliance with the registration requirements in Article 6132b–3.08(b) for its partners to receive protection from individual liability under Article 6132b–3.08(a)(1). Smith & West, L.L.P. was not a registered limited liability partnership when it incurred the lease obligations; therefore, Gaus and West are not protected from individual liability for the lease obligations under Article 6132b–3.08(a)(1).[15]

C. Limited Liability

When the first wave of LLP statutes were enacted, most protected partners from vicarious liability for the firm's tort obligations, but not from vicarious liability for the firm's contract obligations.[16] The emphasis on vicarious liability is important; indeed, no LLP statute (and, for that matter, no statute related to any business organization) provides protection to a partner for his own direct liability (i.e., liability stemming from the partner's own wrongful acts).

Providing limited liability for a firm's tort obligations, but not for its contractual obligations, seems counter-intuitive. Contract

---

ship that provides limited liability protection to its partners? At the very least, the argument seems easier to make than before.

[15] Apcar, 161 S.W.3d at 140–42 (citations omitted).

[16] For example, the Utah statute presently states, in relevant part, the following:

(1) Except as provided in Subsection (2), all partners are liable [for partnership obligations] . . . .

(2)(a) A partner in a limited liability partnership is not liable, directly or indirectly, including by way of indemnification, contribution or otherwise, for a debt, obligation, or liability chargeable to the partnership arising from negligence, wrongful acts, or misconduct committed while the partnership is registered as a limited liability partnership and in the course of the partnership business by another partner, or an employee, agent, or representative of the limited liability partnership.

(b) Notwithstanding Subsection (2)(a), a partner in a limited liability partnership is liable for his own negligence, wrongful acts, or misconduct.

UTAH CODE § 48–1–12. Notice that subsection (1) of the Utah statute is written to say that an LLP partner is liable for the obligations of the LLP, except in circumstances provided in subsection (2). Subsection (2) then indicates that an LLP partner has no liability for the firm's tort obligations ("for a debt, obligation, or liability chargeable to the partnership arising from negligence, wrongful acts, or misconduct"). Because subsection (2) does not shield a partner from the LLP's contractual obligations, the general rule of liability in subsection (1) applies.

creditors, to a large degree, voluntarily assume the risk of dealing with a limited liability entity. If a contract creditor is concerned about the effect of limited liability, the creditor can contract for personal liability (e.g., guarantees from the owners and/or managers) or negotiate for additional protection (such as collateral or a higher interest rate). Alternatively, the creditor can choose to forego dealing with the limited liability entity all together.

In contrast, the typical tort victim does not have the ability to bargain for protection before becoming a creditor of the firm. Tort victims are often involuntarily thrust into a creditor relationship with the business with no opportunity to secure additional protection (think about a person who is suddenly injured when a company truck runs a red light). Thus, "partial-shield" statutes that provide limited liability only for the firm's tort obligations seem almost backward in design. The creditor least able to bargain for advance protection from limited liability (the tort victim) is restricted to the partnership's assets, while the creditor with the greatest ability to mitigate the effect of limited liability (the contract creditor) is not.

Of course, the "birth" of the LLP arose out of the savings and loan crisis and partners' concerns about exposure due to their fellow partners' malpractice. Thus, the early statutes focused on providing limited liability to partners for the firm's tort obligations. Partner exposure for the contractual obligations of the business was, as an initial matter, simply not a primary concern.[17]

Over time, the design of most LLP statutes evolved from partial-shield (i.e., providing partners with limited liability only for the firm's tort obligations) to full-shield (i.e., providing partners with limited liability for the firm's tort and contract obligations). For example, RUPA § 306(c) provides, in relevant part, the following:

---

[17] The lack of initial concern may have also been due to the fact that partners have historically been able to circumvent personal liability for a partnership's contractual obligations by explicitly contracting for non-recourse liability with a particular creditor.

Under a partial-shield statute that provides limited liability only for a firm's tort obligations, what result if a malpractice claim is instead pled as a breach of a contract action (e.g., an implied warranty claim, or a claim for breach of an attorney-client engagement letter)? Does this "artful pleading" of a tort claim as a contract claim circumvent the limited liability protection? Some statutes attempted to combat this pleading creativity by adding language indicating that there is no liability for any claim arising "from" negligence, wrongful acts, omissions, misconduct, or malpractice, even though such claim may arise "in" tort or contract. For example, before Illinois switched to full-shield protection, its LLP provision stated that there is no liability "for debts, obligations, and liabilities of or chargeable to the partnership, whether arising in tort, contract or otherwise, arising from negligence, wrongful acts, omissions, misconduct, or malpractice." 805 ILL. COMP. STAT. 205/15 (repealed).

An obligation of a partnership incurred while the partnership is a limited liability partnership, whether arising in contract, tort, or otherwise, is solely the obligation of the partnership. A partner is not personally liable, directly or indirectly, by way of contribution or otherwise, for such an obligation solely by reason of being or so acting as a partner.[18]

Despite the movement to full-shield protection, many statutes carve out circumstances in which a partner is still exposed to personal liability. As mentioned, a partner is always subject to direct liability for his own wrongful acts. Some LLP provisions explicitly state this,[19] while others reach the same result by indicating that a partner is only insulated from liability that is based upon his mere status as a partner. A liability theory based upon something other than partner status, therefore, such as the partner's own misconduct, is not affected by the LLP provisions.[20]

More importantly, many LLP provisions specify that a partner is liable for the misconduct of others under the partner's supervision and control. For example, the Connecticut statute states that LLP protection "shall not affect the liability of a partner in a registered limited liability partnership for his own negligence, wrongful acts or misconduct, or that of any person under his direct supervision and control."[21]

This supervisory liability raises a number of interesting issues. First, supervisory liability appears sensible because it imposes liability on those in a position to help prevent malpractice or other wrongful acts. Ideally, this potential for liability encourages better monitoring. As mentioned, however, one might argue that supervisory liability is unnecessary to encourage monitoring, even in a limited liability business, because other incentives to monitor exist (e.g., concerns about the firm's reputation would encourage partners to monitor one another to help avoid wrongful conduct). Moreover, supervisory liability may impose unreasonable burdens to monitor on partners, particularly in larger firms where partners may be in different geographic locations from where the wrongful conduct is

---

[18] What is meant by the language "by way of contribution or otherwise?" Assume that an LLP owes money to a third party and that the LLP is insolvent. The third party demands that partners contribute to the LLP to provide the LLP with funds to pay the obligation. Under most LLP statutes, the contribution reference is intended to make clear that partners do not have to contribute to the LLP to satisfy obligations that they are not otherwise personally liable for.

[19] See, e.g., note 16 (quoting the Utah statute).

[20] See, e.g., RUPA § 306(c) (imposing no liability for LLP obligations "solely by reason of being or so acting as a partner"); id. cmt. ("As with shareholders of a corporation and members of a limited liability company, partners remain personally liable for their personal misconduct.").

[21] CONN. GEN. STAT. § 34–327.

occurring, or where partners handle a large number of files. Even worse, supervisory liability may cause partners to attempt to avoid supervisory roles (at least without indemnification protection from the firm or the other partners, greater compensation, or perhaps an insistence that the firm maintain large amounts of insurance or cash on hand), which could be problematic for a firm with junior partners, associates, or employees that need some level of guidance.

Second, under supervisory liability provisions, is a partner liable only for negligent supervision? Or is the partner liable for any wrongful acts committed by a supervisee, even if the supervision is non-negligent? The Connecticut provision, for example, states that an LLP partner is liable for his own negligence and wrongful acts, which would presumably include negligent supervision. The fact that the next clause goes on to say that the partner is also liable for the misconduct of persons under his direct supervision and control suggests that something beyond negligent supervision was meant to be covered—i.e., non-negligent supervision. Indeed, what is the point of the second clause if it was only meant to cover negligent supervision given that the first clause seems to cover negligent acts?

Of course, the first clause covering the partner's own negligence would only impose liability for negligent supervision if the partner had some common law duty to supervise. Perhaps, in certain situations, an individual partner owes no common law duty to do so. In such situations, the second clause could be viewed as imposing a statutory duty to supervise. Under this interpretation, the second clause would have an independent meaning even if it only imposed liability for negligent supervision. Such liability, in other words, would not already be covered by the first clause.

As a policy matter, liability for non-negligent supervision seems harsh. Other than providing another pocket from which a third party may recover, it is hard to see the point of imposing liability on partners who act reasonably and competently in their supervision—particularly because liability for non-negligent supervision defeats the vicarious liability protections of the LLP statute.[22]

---

[22] *Cf.* BROMBERG & RIBSTEIN, *supra* note 9, § 3.04(a), at 124 ("It is uncertain under the supervision-type of provision whether the partner must be negligent or at fault in order to be held liable. Stating that the LLP provisions 'shall not affect' the partner's liability [for his own negligence or for the negligence of those under his supervision] suggests that the statute only continues any liability partners may have had for their own misconduct or for negligently failing to monitor or supervise others. But it is not clear to what preexisting supervisory liability the statute might be referring other than partners' *vicarious* liability under traditional partnership law, which is supposedly eliminated by LLP registration.").

Finally, how far does supervisory liability extend? Does the managing partner of a law firm have supervisory liability over all of the partners and employees of a firm? While this seems like a stretch, an argument could be made that everyone works under the "actual supervision and control" of the managing partner—the language used in the Wisconsin statute.[23] Compared to the Wisconsin provision, the Connecticut statute seems more favorable to the managing partner by limiting his exposure to persons working under his "*direct* supervision and control." The level of "closeness" required for "direct" supervision and control is, of course, unclear, but the notion that some degree of closeness is required is helpful to the managing partner.[24] Similar issues can be raised with respect to other supervisory positions, such as billing partners, firm executive committees, or firm committees that review opinion letters.[25]

The LLP unquestionably protects partners from liability for partnership obligations owed to outside creditors. It is not clear, however, that similar protection is provided for partnership obligations owed to the partners themselves. In *Ederer v. Gursky*,[26] Ederer was a partner in Gursky & Ederer, LLP. He withdrew from the firm before it ceased operations. Pursuant to a withdrawal agreement, the LLP was obligated to pay Ederer various sums of money. When those sums were not forthcoming, Ederer sued the LLP and its partners for breach of the agreement. The individual partners moved to dismiss on the ground that New York's LLP liability provision (§ 26(b)) shielded them from personal liability for the firm's obligations.[27]

The Court of Appeals held that § 26(b) did not shield a partner in an LLP from personal liability for partnership obligations owed to other partners. The court was influenced by the fact that § 26 "has always governed only a partner's liability to third parties, and,

---

[23] WIS. STAT. 178.12(3)(b).

[24] Perhaps "actual," like "direct," was meant to convey some level of closeness and to exclude attenuated supervision and control. The term "direct," however, seems a bit clearer. Until it was repealed in September 2011, the Texas statute imposed liability for persons working under the "supervis[ion] and direct[ion]" of the defendant. TEX. BUS. ORGS. CODE § 152.801(b)(1) (repealed). The absence of modifying terms such as "actual," "direct," and "control" would pose even more difficulties for a managing partner or other supervisory defendant.

[25] Conflicts between LLP partners can arise depending upon their personal liability exposure. For example, a conflict as to distributions can arise between partners who can be sure of limited liability and partners who are exposed to liability for negligent supervision or other misconduct. The partners without the risk of personal exposure may prefer the partnership to distribute more of its assets, while the partners with the risk of personal exposure may prefer the firm to retain more. After all, if the firm has insufficient assets to pay a claim, the partners with personal liability for that claim will have to satisfy it out of their own pockets.

[26] 881 N.E.2d 204 (N.Y. 2007).

[27] *See id.* at 205–07.

in fact, is part of article 3 of the Partnership Law ('Relations of Partners to Persons Dealing with the Partnership'), not article 4 ('Relations of Partners to One Another')." According to the court, "[t]he logical inference, therefore, is that 'any debts' [language used in § 26(b)] refers to any debts owed [to] a third party, absent very clear legislative direction to the contrary."[28]

The dissent argued that § 26(b) eliminated partner liability for "any debts" of the partnership, and it asserted that the New York legislature carved out only two exceptions to this limited liability— neither of which was at issue in the dispute. According to the dissent: "The statute contains two specific exceptions, applicable when a partner acts wrongfully or when partners agree to vary the liability scheme (Partnership Law § 26[c], [d]), but there is no exception for liabilities to former partners claiming a share of the partnership's net assets. We should not create an exception that the Legislature did not." Moreover, the dissent criticized the majority's distinction between liabilities owed to third parties and liabilities owed to former partners. A former partner, according to the dissent, "is a third party where the partnership is concerned, and there is no good reason to treat him more favorably than any other third party."[29]

By concluding that the LLP does not protect partners from liability for partnership obligations owed to the partners themselves, the *Ederer* court provides better collection rights to partner creditors than non-partner creditors. Moreover, partners in an LLP have less liability protection than shareholders in a corporation or members in an LLC, as shareholders and members are not vicariously liable for claims by their fellow owners. Do these results make sense? They do if one focuses on the fact that the LLP is not a stand-alone entity that is distinct from a general partnership. Instead, the LLP liability provision was simply grafted onto the general partnership statute that imposed personal liability on partners for all partnership obligations. Because of the placement of the provision in the statute ("Relations of Partners to Persons Dealing with the Partnership"), the graft is arguably limited to protecting partners from vicarious liability to third parties. All other aspects of general partnership liability are unchanged—including a partner's personal liability for partnership obligations to other partners (and, apparently, withdrawn partners). The court suggested that a partnership agreement could change this result by making clear that partners were not liable for firm obligations to other partners, but there was no such agreement in the case.

---

[28] *Id.* at 211.

[29] *Id.* at 212 (Smith, J., dissenting).

What about the dissent's argument that a withdrawn partner is a third party as far as the partnership is concerned? Put differently, isn't a former partner a "Person[] Dealing with [the] Partnership?" This argument seems quite plausible, but it appears to have gotten no traction with the majority.

Following the logic of the *Ederer* court, one would think that the same conclusion would be reached under RUPA § 306(c). After all, the section is in article 3 of RUPA ("Relations of Partners to Persons Dealing with [the] Partnership") and not in article 4 ("Relations of Partners to Each Other and to [the] Partnership"). Thus, the same argument could be made that the provision was intended to limit the liability of partners to third-party creditors, but not to partner-creditors.

As a final issue related to partner liability in an LLP, recall that general partnership law is applicable to LLPs when it is not explicitly altered by LLP-specific provisions. Given that partners have limited liability in the LLP form, however, one can question whether general partnership law is suitable for the LLP setting. As a few specific examples, consider the following:

Management rights: Partnership law provides a default rule that each partner has a right to participate in the management of the business.[30] When partners have personal liability for the obligations of the partnership, this rule can be justified on the ground that poor management decisions threaten a partner with substantial liability. As a consequence, each partner needs the ability to participate in (and hopefully influence) management decisions. When limited liability is present, however, the risk of personal liability from poor management decisions is lessened. Correspondingly, one can argue that the need to participate in management is lessened as well.

Profit sharing: Under partnership law, the default rule is that partners share profits equally.[31] When partners have unlimited personal liability for partnership debts, this rule can be justified on the ground that each partner's "credit" contribution to the partnership (i.e., putting one's personal assets at risk) largely makes up for any inequality in financial contributions. When credit contributions are eliminated as a result of limited liability, however, this justification for equal sharing is weaker. Similarly, an LLP partner who practices in a high-risk area (e.g., a law firm partner who writes opinion letters and/or supervises a significant number of associates)

---

[30] *See* UPA § 18(e); RUPA § 401(f).
[31] *See* UPA § 18(a); RUPA § 401(b).

may demand an increased share of the profits if, as a result of limited liability, his fellow partners no longer share in the risk.

Admitting new partners: Under partnership law, the default rule is that a unanimous vote of the partners is required to admit a new partner.[32] At least part of the rationale for this rule is that the misconduct of a new partner can create partnership obligations and, therefore, personal liability for the partners. When limited liability is present, of course, this justification for unanimity is less compelling.

Even if these general partnership principles are applicable to the LLP setting, keep in mind that they are merely default rules. Thus, the partners in an LLP can contract around any unsuitable provisions.

D. The Limited Liability Limited Partnership

Some states allow limited partnerships to register as LLPs. In effect, this creates a limited liability limited partnership ("LLLP")— a limited partnership where all of the partners have limited liability. (The alphabet soup seemingly never ends.)

Because an LLLP is a limited partnership, a firm that is not a limited partnership—such as a firm that fails to comply with the filing requirements of a limited partnership statute—cannot be an LLLP. In general, if a limited partnership wishes to become an LLLP, it must comply with the registration and insurance/segregated funds requirements of the relevant LLP statute. Statutes typically specify the partner vote that is necessary to become an LLLP, and they usually provide for special name requirements as well.[33]

In contrast to a general partner in a traditional limited partnership, a general partner in an LLLP is liable for the obligations of the business only when a general partner in an LLP would be liable.[34] A limited partner in an LLLP is often granted the same pro-

---

[32] *See* UPA § 18(g); RUPA § 401(i).

[33] *See, e.g.*, TEX. BUS. ORGS. CODE § 153.351 (noting that a limited partnership can register as an LLP "as permitted by its partnership agreement" or, if the agreement is silent, "with the consent of partners required to amend its partnership agreement"); *id.* § 5.055 (stating that the name of a limited partnership must include the word "limited," the phrase "limited partnership," or an abbreviation of that word or phrase, and further indicating that the name of a limited partnership that is an LLLP "must also contain the phrase 'limited liability partnership' or an abbreviation of that phrase"); *see also* RUPA § 101 cmt. (suggesting an LLLP provision that specifies the necessary partner vote and that mandates compliance with the name requirements of the LLP statute).

[34] *See, e.g.*, GA. CODE § 14–9–403(c) ("If a limited partnership is a limited liability partnership . . . , then . . . the liabilities of each general partner of such limited part-

tection.[35] In practical terms, this seems to reduce the importance of the control rule for limited partner liability in LLLPs. A limited partner who would be liable for violating the control rule in a non-LLLP, in other words, has no liability in an LLLP unless the situation would also result in liability for an LLP partner.[36]

Some LLLP provisions, however, speak only of general partners receiving LLP liability protection. In these jurisdictions, limited partner liability in an LLLP is presumably no different from limited partner liability in a traditional limited partnership. Notice, however, that this results in a peculiarity. In a RULPA (1985) limited partnership, a limited partner who participates in the control of the business can become personally liable for at least some of the venture's obligations. When a limited partnership has elected LLLP status, however, a general partner can participate in the control of the business without becoming personally liable for any of the venture's obligations.[37] LLLP status in a RULPA (1985) jurisdiction, therefore, may provide general partners with more liability protection than limited partners.

The drafters of RUPA clearly recognized this peculiarity. The Comment to RUPA § 101 states, in part, the following:

> . . . [According to RULPA (1985) § 303(a),] [u]nless also a general partner, a limited partner is not liable for the obligations of a limited partnership unless the partner participates in the control of the business and then only to persons reasonably believing the limited partner is a general partner. Therefore, arguably limited partners in a LLLP will have the specific RULPA Section 303 [(a)] liability shield while general partners will have a superior [RUPA] Section 306(c) liability shield [the

---

nership shall be determined by reference to the provisions . . . regarding limited liability partnerships.").

[35] *See, e.g.,* ARIZ. REV. STAT. § 29–1026(D) ("If a limited partnership is a limited liability partnership, [LLP liability protection] applies to its general partners and to any of its limited partners who . . . are liable for the debts or obligations of the partnership.").

[36] When applicable to limited partners, LLLP provisions are designed to make limited partners better off than limited partners in traditional limited partnerships. Thus, no consideration should be given to a limited partner's liability under the LLP provisions unless the limited partner would otherwise be liable under limited partnership law—most likely for violating the control rule. Put differently, liability should only be imposed on a limited partner in an LLLP if the limited partner's conduct (1) violates the control rule *and* (2) results in liability under the LLP provision. *See, e.g.,* TEX. BUS. ORGS. CODE § 153.353 (stating that the LLP liability protection applies to "a limited partner *who is liable under other provisions of this chapter* [on limited partnerships] for the debts or obligations of the limited partnership" (emphasis added)).

[37] *See, e.g.,* RUPA § 306(c).

LLP liability shield]. In order to clarify limited partner liability and other linkage issues, states that have adopted RUPA, these limited liability partnership rules, and RULPA may wish to consider an amendment to RULPA. A suggested form of such an amendment is:

§ 1107. Limited Liability Limited Partnership. . . .

(c) Sections 306(c) and 307(b) of the Uniform Partnership Act (1994) apply to both general and limited partners of a limited liability limited partnership.

ULPA (2001) provides for LLLPs. If a limited partnership wishes to become an LLLP, it must state that it is an LLLP in its certificate of limited partnership.[38] If an LLLP is created, a full status-based liability shield is provided for the firm's general and limited partners.[39] Under ULPA (2001), therefore, the above-described peculiarity disappears.

---

[38] See ULPA (2001) §§ 102(9), 201(a)(4); see also id. § 108(c) (setting forth name requirements for LLLPs).

[39] See id. §§ 303, 404(c).

Chapter 16

THE LIMITED LIABILITY COMPANY

Analysis

A. Introduction
B. Formation
C. Management and Operation
    1. General Governance and Actual Authority
    2. Apparent Authority
    3. Inspection and Information Rights
D. Financial Rights and Obligations
E. Entity Status
F. Limited Liability
G. Fiduciary Duties
    1. The Basic Duties
    2. The Role of Contract
H. Ownership Interests and Transferability
I. Dissociation and Dissolution
J. The Nature of the LLC
K. A Final Look

A. Introduction

The limited liability company ("LLC") is a noncorporate business structure that provides its owners, known as "members,"[1] with several benefits: (1) limited liability for the obligations of the venture, even if a member participates in the control of the business; (2) pass-through tax treatment; and (3) contractual freedom to arrange the internal operations of the venture. Because of this favorable combination of attributes, the LLC has emerged as the preferred business structure for many closely held businesses.[2] Keep

---

[1] Many LLC statutes formerly required LLCs to have at least two members, suggesting that LLCs were viewed more as partnerships than corporations. Modern-day statutes have largely eliminated this two-member requirement, however, and single-member LLCs are now permissible.

[2] As one commentator noted:

> The [LLC] is now undeniably the most popular form of new business entity in the United States. . . . Rising from near obscurity in the 1990s, the LLC has now taken its place as the new "king-of-the-hill" among business entities, utterly dominating its closest rivals. As the research reported in this article indicates, the number of new LLCs formed in America in 2007 now outpaces the number of new corporations formed by a margin of nearly two to one. In sever-

in mind, however, that the LLC is a relatively new form of business organization in this country. Although its "birth" dates back to 1977, its widespread use is more recent. Compared to other forms of business organization, therefore, the LLC is less established, and lawyers and courts continue to wrestle with many open questions.

The LLC was the product of innovative professionals creating solutions when the legal system failed to meet client needs. Hamilton Brothers Oil Company had been involved in international oil and gas exploration using foreign business organizations, primarily the Panamanian "limitada." Limitadas provided limited liability for all owners and the ability to secure partnership classification for tax purposes. Because no similar domestic entity existed in the United States, representatives of Hamilton Brothers suggested legislation that authorized the creation of an unincorporated domestic entity that resembled the limitada. An initial effort to obtain enactment in Alaska failed, but the same legislation was enacted in Wyoming on March 4, 1977, apparently without controversy. The critical question then became whether the Internal Revenue Service would permit partnership taxation for an unincorporated entity that provided limited liability to all of its owners. A favorable ruling on the question was obtained in 1988.[3] Once the tax issue was resolved, states quickly adopted LLC statutes to take advantage of the flexibility of the new business form. By 1995, all 50 states had adopted an LLC statute.

Because of concerns that diversity in state law might create serious problems for interstate LLCs, attempts to develop prototype or uniform LLC statutes began almost immediately after the LLC's tax status was recognized. The rush by states to enact LLC legislation was underway, however, and most states enacted an LLC statute before efforts to develop standardized statutes came to fruition. The first standardized product was a "Prototype Limited Liability Company Act" that was proposed in 1992 by a committee of the American Bar Association. Concepts developed in this prototype act were incorporated into many state statutes.

---

al "bellwether" states, the numbers are even more impressive. . . . Other business forms have fared no better against the LLC. While data for hybrid and newer business structures is more difficult to compile, the data in this Article relating to limited partnerships (LPs) demonstrate that the LLC's dominance of these entities is even more staggering. For example, the number of new LLCs formed in 2007 outpaced the number of new LPs formed in that same year by a margin of over 34 to 1.

Rodney D. Chrisman, *LLCs are the New King of the Hill*, XV FORD. J. OF CORP. & FIN. L. 459, 459–62 (2010).

[3] *See* Rev. Rul. 88–76, 1988–2 C.B. 360.

The Uniform Limited Liability Company Act ("ULLCA") was promulgated by the National Conference of Commissioners on Uniform State Laws ("NCCUSL") in 1996. As of this writing, ULLCA is the governing law in only eight states and the U.S. Virgin Islands. ULLCA's limited acceptance may be due in part to the fact that it incorporates more partnership concepts than many existing LLC statutes. For example, ULLCA retains the "at-will" versus "term" distinction for the LLC as well as the related dissociation and dissolution consequences that flow from that distinction.[4]   In 2006, ULLCA was substantially revised and updated. Only seven states and the District of Columbia, however, have presently adopted the revised Act ("RULLCA").[5] Nevertheless, ULLCA and RULLCA (the "Uniform Acts") serve as useful templates for studying and debating LLC provisions, and the text below will discuss both statutes. Many provisions of the Delaware LLC Act ("DLLCA") will also be referenced in the text, as DLLCA and the Uniform Acts differ on a number of significant points and serve, to some extent, as competing statutory models.

Due to this developmental history of LLC legislation, LLC statutes tend to be less uniform than statutes governing other business forms. Indeed, even ULLCA's prefatory note points out that "state limited liability company acts display a dazzling array of diversity." Because LLC statutes often reflect a mishmash of corporation, partnership, and limited partnership principles, courts frequently analogize to existing doctrines from other business forms when confronting LLC issues—particularly when the LLC statute itself offers little guidance.[6]

---

[4] *See* Chapter 3(G).

[5] The prefatory note to RULLCA states the following:

Eighteen years have passed since the IRS issued its gate-opening Revenue Ruling 88–76, declaring that a Wyoming LLC would be taxed as a partnership despite the entity's corporate-like liability shield. More than eight years have passed since the IRS opened the gate still further with the "check the box" regulations. It is an opportune moment to identify the best elements of the myriad "first generation" LLC statutes and to infuse those elements into a new, "second generation" uniform act.

[6] One court explained its analytical approach as follows:

It is important to keep the history of LLC development in perspective when working with LLCs and court interpretations of LLC acts. . . . The typical LLC act is usually a hybrid of provisions culled from the individual state's partnership statutes and business corporation law. . . . [W]hen a court is interpreting an LLC act or agreement, the court will focus on the particular aspect of the LLC that gives rise to the problem, with emphasis on the foundational business form from which that characteristic originated. Usually, the particular aspect can be traced to either the corporate components or the partnership components of the LLC act or agreement. In such cases where the characteristic originated from the partnership aspects of the LLC, the court will use the established [principles] and precedent of the partnership law to resolve the issue . . . . In such cases where the characteristic originated

As noted above, a primary reason for forming an LLC is to create an entity that offers investors the protections of limited liability and the pass-through tax status of partnerships. The Treasury regulations in effect when the original LLC statutes were enacted provided that an unincorporated business organization such as an LLC would be taxed as a corporation (with the undesirable double taxation on distributions) if it possessed more "corporate" characteristics than "noncorporate" characteristics. More specifically, these so-called "Kintner regulations" provided that a firm would be taxed as a corporation rather than a partnership if it had three or more of the following "corporate" characteristics: (1) continuity of life; (2) free transferability of ownership interests; (3) centralized management; and (4) limited liability. Because LLC statutes provided limited liability and, typically, the possibility of centralized management, a state wanting to ensure partnership tax treatment for LLCs organized under its statute needed to deny both of the remaining corporate characteristics. As a result, early versions of LLC statutes tended to restrict the members' ability to transfer their ownership interests in order to deny the free transferability characteristic. Further, to deny the continuity of life characteristic, LLC statutes usually provided for dissolution of an LLC upon a member's withdrawal or other dissociation from the business. As critics of the Kintner regulations argued, these statutory provisions were driven largely by tax concerns rather than by broader business considerations.

In 1997, the IRS replaced the Kintner regulations with the new "check-the-box" regulations.[7] Under these new rules, an unincorporated business entity such as an LLC simply elects to be taxed as a partnership (pass-through taxation) or a corporation (entity taxation). (Technically, the unincorporated entity receives pass-through taxation by default and must only make an affirmative election if it wishes to be taxed as a corporation.) Certain entities, however, must be taxed as corporations. Such businesses include: (1) entities organized under a federal or state statute that refers to the entity as "incorporated" or a "corporation"; (2) certain foreign entities that are specifically listed in the regulations as per se corporations; and (3) business entities that are taxable as corporations under other provisions of the Internal Revenue Code, such as publicly traded firms and regulated investment companies. As a result of the

---

from the corporate aspects of the LLC, the court will utilize the established [principles] and precedent of corporate law to resolve the issue.

Anderson v. Wilder, No. E2003–00460–COA–R3–CV, 2003 WL 22768666, at *4 (Tenn. Ct. App. Nov. 21, 2003) (quoting Annotation, *Construction and Application of Limited Liability Company Acts,* 79 A.L.R.5TH 689, 698 (2000)). In all likelihood, many courts, either explicitly or implicitly, follow this analytical approach.

[7] *See* Treas. Reg. §§ 301.7701–1 to –3; Chapter 3(B)(5).

check-the-box regulations, the federal income tax treatment of LLCs is now determined by a simple taxpayer choice rather than by the fact-specific "corporateness" inquiry called for by the Kintner regulations.

B. Formation

Like corporations, limited partnerships, and LLPs, LLCs are formed by publicly filing a document, usually known as the "certificate of formation" or "articles of organization," with the secretary of state or equivalent official of the appropriate jurisdiction. The articles of organization are relatively skeletal and typically include only basic information about the company. (For the precise requirements of any given state, of course, check that state's LLC statute.) In Delaware, for example, the certificate of formation is required to include only the name of the LLC, the address of its registered office, and the name and address of its registered agent for service of process.[8] ULLCA demands slightly more content in the articles of organization (e.g., the articles must specify whether the LLC is to be manager-managed), but the information required is still relatively basic.[9] The legal existence of the LLC usually commences at the time of the filing of the certificate/articles, unless a later date is specified.[10]

---

[8] *See* DEL. CODE tit. 6, § 18–201(a) [hereinafter DLLCA].

[9] *See* ULLCA § 203; RULLCA § 201(b).

[10] *See* DLLCA § 18–201(b); ULLCA § 202. Under RULLCA, the legal existence of an LLC begins when the Secretary of State has filed the certificate and the LLC has at least one member, unless a later date is specified in the certificate. *See* RULLCA § 201(d)(1).

Many practitioners and clients wish to have an LLC formed and on the public record before the precise identity and relationship of the members has been determined. When the prospective members complete the negotiation of their business deal, the LLC can be "waiting on the shelf" and business can commence without any filing delay. This concept of a "shelf LLC"—i.e., an LLC formed without having at least one member upon formation—poses difficulties under the statutes of some jurisdictions, as the statutes presuppose that the LLC has a member upon formation. *See, e.g.,* ULLCA § 202(a). RULLCA permits shelf LLCs, but two filings have to be made. First, the certificate of organization must be filed, and it must explicitly state that the LLC will have no members when the Secretary of State files the certificate. *See* RULLCA § 201(b)(3). Second, within ninety days from the filing of the certificate, an organizer of the LLC must file a notice stating that the LLC has at least one member and the date on which the person or persons became the LLC's initial member or members. If this second filing is properly made, the LLC is deemed formed as of the date of initial membership stated in the notice. If the second filing is not properly made, the certificate lapses and is void. *See id.* § 201(e)(1)–(2).

Is it possible to form a shelf LLC in Delaware? Section 18–201 seems to allow the formation of an LLC without any members. On the other hand, § 18–101(6) defines a "limited liability company" as "a limited liability company formed under the laws of the State of Delaware and having 1 or more members." Given this uncertainty, the prudent course is to have a member upon formation.

The real detail on the governance of an LLC is usually provided in a separate document known as an "operating agreement" or a "limited liability company agreement." The operating agreement is a nonpublic document (i.e., it is not filed with any state official) similar to a partnership agreement or a corporation's bylaws. It contains specifics on the rights, duties, and obligations of the LLC's members and managers and on the operation of the LLC as a whole. In general, the operating agreement can be tailored to suit the particular needs of an LLC's members, and the operating agreement's terms will displace most, if not all, of the related statutory provisions. Freedom of contract, in other words, is central to the LLC.[11] Moreover, LLC statutes usually contain far fewer governance rules than the statutory schemes of other business forms (e.g., LLC statutes typically contain few or no default rules on meetings, quorums, and notice). As a consequence, the operating agreement of the parties is often the only supplier of basic governance terms.

Despite the importance of an operating agreement, LLC statutes in some jurisdictions do not seem to require one. For example, ULLCA § 103(a) merely states that the members "may" enter into an operating agreement.[12] Similarly, in the New York decision of *In re Spires*,[13] the court observed:

---

[11] In fact, a number of LLC statutes explicitly promote freedom of contract and encourage the enforcement of the parties' private arrangements. *See, e.g.*, DLLCA § 18–1101(b); *cf.* RULLCA § 102 cmt. (noting that "a key function of the operating agreement is to override statutory default rules").

[12] The text of RULLCA is not clear on the necessity for an operating agreement, but the comments suggest that an operating agreement will always be present upon the formation of an LLC:

> An agreement to form an LLC is not itself an operating agreement. The term "operating agreement" presupposes the existence of members, and a person cannot have "member" status until the LLC exists. However, the Act's very broad definition of "operating agreement" means that, as soon as a limited liability company has any members, the limited liability company has an operating agreement. For example, suppose: (i) two persons orally and informally agree to join their activities in some way through the mechanism of an LLC, (ii) they form the LLC or cause it to be formed, and (iii) without further ado or agreement, they become the LLC's initial members. The LLC has an operating agreement. "[A]ll the members" have agreed on who the members are, and that agreement—no matter how informal or rudimentary—is an agreement "concerning the matters described in Section 110(a)." (To the extent the agreement does not provide the *inter se* "rules of the game," this Act "fills in the gaps." Section 110(b).)
>
> The same result follows when a person becomes the sole initial member of an LLC. It is not plausible that the person would lack any understanding or intention with regard to the LLC. That understanding or intention constitutes an "agreement of all the members of the limited liability company, including a sole member."

RULLCA § 102 cmt.; *see also id.* § 110 cmt. ("A limited liability company is as much a creature of contract as of statute, and Section 102(13) delineates a very broad scope for 'operating agreement.' As a result, once an LLC comes into existence and has a

> There is no provision in the [New York] Limited Liability Company Law imposing any type of penalty or punishment for failing to adopt a written operating agreement. The statute does not require an operating agreement prior to the formation of this type of entity. There is no statute or common law that leads to the conclusion that the failure to enter into an operating agreement transforms a limited liability company into a partnership... Lighthouse Solutions LLC was formed at the time of the filing of the Articles of Organization ... with the Department of State. According to the statute, the filing is conclusive evidence of the formation of the limited liability company. ...[14]

Even if an operating agreement is not required, the lack of default governance rules in many LLC statutes strongly suggests that state legislatures contemplated that the members would enter into some type of operating agreement. Otherwise, a great deal of uncertainty about basic governance matters would exist.[15]

As in the limited partnership context, some LLC statutes provide that an LLC is created so long as there has been "substantial compliance" with the formation requirements of the statute.[16] Other statutes omit the substantial compliance language but provide that the filing of the articles is "conclusive proof" that formation requirements have been satisfied.[17] The conclusive proof language should eliminate any uncertainty about whether an error in the articles prevents the formation of an LLC.[18]

---

member, the LLC necessarily has an operating agreement. Accordingly, this Act refers to 'the operating agreement' rather than 'an operating agreement.' ").

DLLCA § 18–201(d) states that an LLC agreement "shall" be entered into "either before, after or at the time of the filing of a certificate of formation." An operating agreement seems to be required, therefore, although it does not have to exist at the inception of the venture.

[13] 778 N.Y.S.2d 259 (Sup. Ct. 2004).

[14] *Id.* at 262–63 (citation omitted).

[15] Does an operating agreement have to be in writing? DLLCA § 18–101(7) provides that an LLC agreement may be written, oral, or implied. ULLCA § 103(a) indicates that the operating agreement "need not be in writing." RULLCA § 102(13) states that an operating agreement may be "oral, in a record, implied, or in any combination thereof."

[16] *See, e.g.*, DLLCA § 18–201(b).

[17] *See, e.g.*, ULLCA § 202(c); RULLCA § 201(d)(3), (e)(3).

[18] Interestingly, unlike limited partnership statutes, LLC statutes do not typically provide any amendment/withdrawal protection for members who mistakenly believe in good faith that an LLC has been formed. *Cf.* RULPA (1985) § 304 (providing amendment/withdrawal protection); ULPA (2001) § 306 (same).

C. Management and Operation

1. General Governance and Actual Authority

As a default rule, most LLC statutes assign all management functions to members.[19]   This member-managed structure resembles a general partnership, as each of the owners has management rights. In contrast, a few statutes default to management by a separate group of managers, who may or may not be members. This manager-managed structure resembles a corporation, as management is centralized in a smaller subset of actors. Because these are only default rules, member-managed jurisdictions allow the owners to elect manager-managed governance, and manager-managed jurisdictions allow the owners to elect member-managed governance.[20]

Why might LLC owners choose member-management or manager-management for their venture? Unlike in public corporations, LLC members cannot exit by cashing out of the business whenever they are dissatisfied with the direction of the LLC. Indeed, LLC interests cannot be freely transferred, and there is usually no market for LLC interests. As a consequence, members may want an active management role (member-management) to have some "say" in the direction of the business and to help protect the value of their investments. Moreover, before the check-the-box regulations were enacted, member-management helped to avoid corporation tax status, as centralized management was a corporate element. Today, of course, this rationale is inapplicable.

On the other hand, members may not have the skills, experience, or time to participate effectively in the management of an LLC. A manager-managed LLC with professional management may be preferred, especially because limited liability makes this passive role more palatable.[21] In addition, as is the case in general partnerships, the greater the number of members, the harder it is to have a member-managed structure where everyone is entitled to

---

[19] *See, e.g.*, DLLCA § 18–402; ULLCA §§ 101(11)–(12), 203(a)(6); RULLCA §§ 102(10), (12), 407.

[20] An LLC may not have to be entirely member-managed or manager-managed. Some LLC statutes allow the management functions to be divided between members and managers. *See, e.g.*, VA. CODE § 13.1–1024(A) ("The articles of organization or an operating agreement of a limited liability company may delegate full or partial responsibility for managing a limited liability company to or among one or more managers."). Even without explicit statutory authorization, the members could presumably divide up management authority between members and managers in the operating agreement. For example, an LLC may choose manager-management for ordinary business decisions but member-management for some or all of the firm's extraordinary business decisions.

[21] By contrast, in a general partnership, a passive role risks personal liability as a result of the poor decisions of others.

participate in management (the "too many cooks" problem). Simply
put, a governance structure that requires the vote of large numbers
of members for ordinary business decisions is both cumbersome and
inefficient.[22]

The default rules for voting in an LLC differ among the states.
About half of the LLC statutes default to members voting on a per
capita basis (one vote per member), while the other half default to
members voting on a pro rata basis (by financial or other contribution to the firm). For ordinary matters, majority rule (whether on a
per capita or pro rata basis) typically carries the decision. For extraordinary matters, however, some statutes require a specified supermajority vote. In manager-managed LLCs, decisions are usually
made by a majority vote of the managers (by number), although certain extraordinary decisions will often require a specified vote of the
members as well.[23] If the requisite consent is obtained according to
these rules, a member or manager has actual authority to bind the
LLC to the transaction at issue. Actual authority can also be established by other conduct of the company (or the members collectively)
that makes it reasonable for the member or manager to believe that
he is authorized (e.g., language in an operating agreement, a title,
or a position).

As you might expect, a pro rata rule—a rule based on contributions to the firm—is typically preferred when the contributions of
the members are substantially different. A per capita rule is typically preferred when the contributions of the members are relatively equal.[24] As discussed in the general partnership materials, when
owners have unlimited personal liability for a firm's obligations, the
owners are providing more than a mere financial contribution to the
firm—they are providing their personal credit as well.[25] Thus, even
if financial contributions differ among the members, the overall fi-

---

[22] The choice of member-management or manager-management may also affect
who has agency authority to bind the LLC to third-party transactions. *See, e.g.,*
ULLCA § 301; Chapter 16(C)(2). This may influence how the members want the firm
to be structured.

[23] *See, e.g.,* ULLCA § 404(c); RULLCA § 407(c). With respect to manager-managed
LLCs, ULLCA § 404(b)(3)(i) and RULLCA § 407(c)(5) indicate that managers are
elected and removed by a majority of the members. DLLCA § 18–402 states that,
when an operating agreement provides for manager-management, managers shall be
chosen and removed as provided in the operating agreement. Thus, Delaware provides no statutory default rule for the election and removal of managers.

[24] A per capita rule may also be preferred when it is simply too difficult to value
the contributions that members make. A pro rata rule is based on contributions to
the firm; consequently, the rule requires the contributions of the members to be valued. Non-financial contributions such as services, however, can be difficult to quan-
tify. Because a per capita rule avoids valuation issues by simply assuming that the
contributions of the members are relatively equal, such a rule may be desirable in
firms where the members' contributions are difficult to measure.

[25] *See* Chapter 3(C)(1).

nancial and credit contributions of members might be deemed to be relatively equal such that a per capita rule is sensible. With the limited liability of the LLC, however, the members make no "extra" contribution of personal credit to "even out" varying financial contributions. Thus, a pro rata rule may be preferred. Of course, even if LLC members do not make credit contributions stemming from a rule of unlimited liability, they may enter into personal guarantees for the firm or participate actively in the management of the venture. To this extent, they are making credit and service contributions that exceed their contributions of financial capital to the firm, and they may expect their overall contribution to be viewed as relatively equivalent to the contributions of other members. Following this logic, a per capita rule would be desired.

2. Apparent Authority

Under some statutes, members in member-managed LLCs and managers in manager-managed LLCs possess partnership-like apparent authority to bind the company. For example, ULLCA § 301 follows the structure of RUPA § 301 by indicating that each member in a member-managed LLC, and each manager in a manager-managed LLC, is an agent of the company with the apparent authority to bind the LLC to transactions within the ordinary course of the company's business. (The transaction is not binding if the third party knows or has notice that the member or manager lacks actual authority.) Members in manager-managed LLCs are usually not considered to be agents solely because of their member status, and they typically have no statutory apparent authority to bind the venture.[26] On this point, notice that an ULLCA-based manager-managed LLC is superior to a general partnership. The ability to bind the LLC via statutory apparent authority can be limited to the managers of the venture and denied to the members. In a general partnership—even a partnership with centralized management—all of the partners retain their ability to bind the partnership via statutory apparent authority.[27]

DLLCA § 18–402 indicates that "[u]nless otherwise provided in a limited liability company agreement, each member and manager has the authority to bind the limited liability company." To say that this sentence is cryptic is an understatement. It appears that, even in a manager-managed LLC, a member is an agent of the LLC

---

[26] *See, e.g.,* ULLCA § 301(a)–(b). *But see* DLLCA § 18–402 ("Unless otherwise provided in a limited liability company agreement, each member and manager has the authority to bind the limited liability company."). One might be able to argue that a member in a manager-managed LLC is an agent with apparent authority, but that argument would come from agency law and would need to stem from something beyond the person's status as a member.

[27] *See* Chapter 3(C)(2).

with the authority to bind the company. Moreover, the first clause suggests that authority can be restricted in an LLC agreement. Is this meant to include apparent authority? While members should be allowed to restrict actual authority in an agreement between themselves, it seems conceptually inconsistent to suggest that a third party's rights to sue on apparent authority grounds could be affected by a non-public agreement between the members. After all, apparent authority is based on the principal's conduct and how such conduct is reasonably interpreted by a third party. The reasonableness of the interpretation should presumably be unaffected by private information that the third party neither knows nor can easily discover in a public filing. As one commentator observed:

> Does [the above sentence from DLLCA § 402] mean that a member that has been outvoted by fellow members still binds the LLC when the member enters a contract with a third party that knows of the opposition of the majority? Does the initial phrase in the sentence mean that if the operating agreement deprives a member or manager of actual authority to carry out a particular transaction, the doctrine of apparent authority will not apply either to protect a third party who has been misled? The Delaware courts do not appear to have yet interpreted this section.[28]

In a sharp break from prior Uniform Acts, RULLCA eliminates the concept of statutory agency and its accompanying apparent authority. Section 301(a) states that "[a] member is not an agent of a limited liability company solely by reason of being a member," and there is no provision addressing the agency authority of managers.[29] The comments to RULLCA § 301 provide the rationale for this elimination:

> Most LLC statutes, including the original ULLCA, provide for what might be termed "statutory apparent authority" for members in a member-managed limited liability company and managers in a manager-managed limited liability company. This approach codifies the common law notion of apparent authority by position and dates back at least to the original, 1914 Uniform Partnership Act. . . . This Act rejects the statutory apparent authority approach . . .

---

[28] Howard M. Friedman, *The Silent LLC Revolution—The Social Cost of Academic Neglect,* 38 CREIGHTON L. REV. 35, 79 (2004).

[29] *See also* RULLCA § 407 cmt. (stating that "[t]he actual authority of an LLC's manager or managers is a question of agency law," and further noting that "[t]he common law of agency will also determine the apparent authority of an LLC's manager or managers").

The concept [of statutory apparent authority] still makes sense both for general and limited partnerships. A third party dealing with either type of partnership can know by the formal name of the entity and by a person's status as general or limited partner whether the person has the power to bind the entity.

Most LLC statutes have attempted to use the same approach but with a fundamentally important (and problematic) distinction. An LLC's status as member-managed or manager-managed determines whether members or managers have the statutory power to bind. But an LLC's status as member- or manager-managed is not apparent from the LLC's name. A third party must check the public record, which may reveal that the LLC is manager-managed, which in turn means a member as member has no power to bind the LLC. As a result, a provision that originated in 1914 as a protection for third parties can, in the LLC context, easily function as a trap for the unwary. The problem is exacerbated by the almost infinite variety of management structures permissible in and used by LLCs.

The new Act cuts through this problem by simply eliminating statutory apparent authority.

Codifying power to bind according to position makes sense only for organizations that have well-defined, well-known, and almost paradigmatic management structures. Because:

- flexibility of management structure is a hallmark of the limited liability company; and

- an LLC's name gives no signal as to the organization's structure,

it makes no sense to:

- require each LLC to publicly select between two statutorily preordained structures (i.e., manager-managed/member-managed); and then

- link a "statutory power to bind" to each of those two structures.

Under this Act, other law—most especially the law of agency—will handle power-to-bind questions.

RULLCA's elimination of statutory agency has not escaped criticism:

RULLCA essentially abandons the careful compromise and distinctive features embodied in the dominant state statutory approach, as well as seeking to halt its evolution, by imposing brand new agency rules on LLCs. While RULLCA preserves the distinction between member-managed and manager-managed LLCs, it undercuts the effect of the distinction. The firm need not disclose its status in the articles and, more importantly, members and managers have no statutory default agency power to bind the LLC. By eliminating positional agency power, RULLCA unmoors itself not only from every other LLC statute, but also from the LLC's partnership antecedents clarified in generations of partnership precedents. At the same time, RULLCA does not align the LLC with any other model. The RULLCA LLC becomes a sui generis business form regarding the important category of agency rules.

The reporters' main rationale for the change was that the standard LLC rule is a trap for the unwary because third parties may not be aware of whether an LLC is member-managed or manager-managed. . . .

The reporters exaggerated the third party's plight. The costs of checking the public record are low. A third party who checks and learns that the LLC is manager-managed is on notice that only a manager can bind the LLC. If a person represents herself to third parties as a manager, the third party usually can rely on this person having at least the power to bind as to ordinary business unless the third party is aware of limitations or circumstances limiting authority. . . .[30]

At some level, these varying statutory approaches are efforts to wrestle with the tension between (1) the desire of members to limit the actual and apparent authority of members or managers who might bind the LLC to unfavorable transactions, and (2) the desire to facilitate transactions by not requiring a third party to perform an excessive investigation into who has authority to bind the company. Most statutes accept the notion that if a third party has actual knowledge of a restriction on authority, the third party is bound by that restriction. The hard question, of course, is whether third parties should be bound by restrictions on authority when they do not have actual knowledge of the restrictions. Some considerations: (1) From the standpoint of ease of access to information, it is easier to justify holding third parties to restrictions that are contained in public articles of organization versus non-public operating agreements. (2) If restrictions in the articles or operating agree-

---

[30] Larry E. Ribstein, *An Analysis of the Revised Uniform Limited Liability Company Act*, 3 VA. L. & BUS. REV. 35, 59 (2008).

ment are binding on third parties, it decreases the monitoring costs of LLC members who may otherwise feel compelled to check up on fellow members or managers to ensure that unauthorized transactions are not occurring. (3) If restrictions are binding, it presumably will increase a creditor's cost of doing business with an LLC, as a creditor (or, more likely, the creditor's attorney) will have to inspect the articles and the operating agreement even for routine transactions, or bear the risk that the transaction will be invalidated due to a lack of authority. This cost will likely be passed on to the LLC. Is it significant enough to make a difference? It depends on how burdensome it is for third parties to obtain the public articles and the private operating agreement, and to subsequently review them. (4) To the extent that restrictions in the operating agreement are binding, keep in mind that an operating agreement can be oral in many jurisdictions. An oral agreement raises the possibility of fraud on creditors who will have difficulty proving that an oral restriction on authority did not exist at the time of the transaction.

The decision of *Taghipour v. Jerez*[31] involves yet another statutory approach to the tension between limiting authority and facilitating third-party transactions. Jerez was the manager of an LLC. The operating agreement stated that no loans could be entered into on behalf of the LLC unless authorized by a resolution of the members. Jerez, on his own and without a member resolution, borrowed $25,000 from Mt. Olympus and pledged the LLC's real estate as collateral. Jerez absconded with the loan, and Mt. Olympus foreclosed on the property.

The LLC and its members (collectively "Taghipour") filed suit against Mt. Olympus claiming that the loan agreement and foreclosure were invalid because Jerez lacked authority under the operating agreement. Mt. Olympus moved to dismiss the claims, asserting that the LLC was bound by § 48–2b–127(2) of the Utah Code. That section stated the following:

> Instruments and documents providing for the acquisition, mortgage, or disposition of property of the limited liability company shall be valid and binding upon the limited liability company if they are executed by one or more managers of a limited liability company having a manager or managers or if they are executed by one or more members of a limited liability company in which management has been retained by the members.

The trial court granted Mt. Olympus's motion, and the Court of Appeals affirmed.

---

[31] 52 P.3d 1252 (Utah 2002).

On appeal, the Utah Supreme Court held that § 48–2b–127(2) trumped a related statute, § 48–2b–125(2)(b), which stated that "[i]f the management of the [LLC] is vested in a manager or managers, any manager has the authority to bind the [LLC], unless otherwise provided in the articles of organization or operating agreement." The court affirmed the dismissal of Taghipour's claims.[32]

In light of the *Taghipour* court's holding, how should the members of the LLC have protected themselves against Jerez's (the manager's) unauthorized disposition of the LLC's property? This is a difficult question to answer. Pursuant to § 48–2b–125(2)(b), the members properly limited Jerez's authority in the operating agreement, but they were thwarted by the language of § 48–2b–127(2). Ideally, the members could have filed some public document that placed creditors on notice of restrictions on the manager's authority,[33] but the Utah statute did not provide for such a procedure. Perhaps the members should nevertheless have included the restriction on Jerez's authority in the articles of organization, and then filed the articles with the real property records in the county where the real estate parcel was located. The goal would have been to convey at least constructive knowledge of the manager's limited authority to third parties. Even doing this, however, may not have overcome the plain language of § 48–2b–127(2), as the section binds the LLC without providing an explicit exception for a third party's knowledge of the manager's lack of authority.

The members should certainly have put something in the operating agreement requiring the manager to indemnify the LLC for any unauthorized action. Indemnification is likely required under agency law even in the absence of an operating agreement provision.[34] An action for indemnification, of course, is unlikely to do much good when the manager is bankrupt or gone.

What is the purpose of a statutory provision like Utah Code § 48–2b–127(2)? The provision seems designed to facilitate the disposition of the LLC's property without third parties having to worry about whether a manager (in a manager-managed LLC) or a member (in a member-managed LLC) had actual authority to effectuate the transaction. While there are often special LLC provisions dealing with real estate transactions, the Utah provision encompasses all property—real or personal. Even in real estate transactions, one might argue that such a provision is unnecessary, as parties to real estate transactions are often sophisticated enough to know that they may need to consult the articles and the operating agreement

---

[32] *See id.* at 1253–57.

[33] *See, e.g.,* ULLCA § 301(c); *cf.* RUPA § 303(a), (e).

[34] *See* Chapter 2(D)(2).

to determine if authority is present. One wonders whether this sort of statutory language is sought by real estate interests (title companies, etc.) who may worry about title problems arising from unauthorized transactions.

Taghipour was a decision by the Supreme Court of Utah. A concurring judge in a lower court opinion in the case was also perplexed by § 48–2b–127(2):

> ... I must note that I find the policy reflected in sections 48–2b–125(2)(b) and –127(2) to be quite curious. If, as in this case, there are restrictions in a limited liability company's organic documents on its managers' ability to unilaterally bind the company, those restrictions will be effective across the range of mundane and comparatively insignificant contracts purportedly entered into by the company, but the restrictions will be ineffective in the case of the company's most important contracts. Thus, if the articles of organization or operating agreement provide that the managers will enter into no contract without the approval of the company's members, as memorialized in an appropriate resolution, the company can escape an unauthorized contract for janitorial services, coffee supplies, or photocopying, but is stuck with the sale of its property for less than fair value or a loan on unfavorable terms.

> Surely this is at odds with the expectations of the business community. A manager or officer typically can bind the company to comparatively unimportant contracts, but, as is provided in the Operating Agreement in this case, needs member or board approval to borrow against company assets. Financial institutions know this and are able to protect themselves by insisting on seeing articles of incorporation, bylaws, and board resolutions—or the limited liability company equivalents—as part of the mortgage loan process. A cursory review of such documents in this case would have disclosed that Jerez lacked the authority to bind the company to the proposed loan agreement.

> In short, I suspect that the strange result in this case is not so much the product of carefully weighed policy considerations as it is the product of a legislative oversight or lapse of some kind. That being said, I readily agree that the language of both statutory sections is clear and unambiguous and that it is not the prerogative of the courts to rewrite legislation. If the laws which dictate the result in this case need to be fixed, the repairs

must come via legislative amendment rather than judicial pronouncement.[35]

Is the concurrence correct to observe that "if the articles of organization or operating agreement provide that the managers will enter into no contract without the approval of the company's members . . . the company can escape an unauthorized contract for janitorial services, coffee supplies, or photocopying, but is stuck with the sale of its property for less than fair value or a loan on unfavorable terms?" That is, while § 48–2b–125(2)(b) certainly allows the articles or an operating agreement to restrict a manager's *actual* authority, it is not so clear that these documents can also restrict the manager's *apparent* authority. Moreover, to the extent that the concurrence acknowledges that § 48–2b–127(2) trumps any limitations on authority in the company's articles or operating agreement, § 48–2b–127(2) encompasses the LLC's "acquisition" of "property," which would seem to cover a contract for the acquisition of coffee supplies as well as any other manager-authorized acquisition of property.[36] Nevertheless, the concurrence's suggestion that § 48–2b–127(2) was some sort of legislative goof is supported by the fact that the section was repealed in Utah's revision to its LLC Act. Substantially similar provisions, however, are still found in other LLC statutes.[37]

If the Uniform Acts had governed the dispute in *Taghipour*, would the result have changed? Under ULLCA, § 301(c) would need to be examined, but it is not the clearest of provisions. It seems to indicate that a member (in a member-managed LLC) or a manager (in a manager-managed LLC) has the authority to engage in a binding transaction involving the LLC's real property. The opening clause, however, provides that the articles of organization can limit this authority, and the comment makes clear that this limitation "is effective when filed, even to persons without knowledge of the agent's lack of authority." Thus, ULLCA provides a procedure where limitations on authority (with respect to the LLC's real property) contained in a public filing (the articles) will bind third parties—even third parties who fail to actually read the articles. Un-

---

[35] Taghipour v. Jerez, 26 P.3d 885, 889 (Utah Ct. App. 2001) (Orme, J., concurring).

[36] The language of § 48–2b–127(2) might not cover contracts for janitorial services or photocopying, as those are predominately contracts for the acquisition of services rather than property.

[37] *See, e.g.*, NEB. REV. STAT. § 21–2617 ("Instruments and documents providing for the acquisition, mortgage, or disposition of property of the limited liability company shall be valid and binding upon the limited liability company if executed by a manager of a limited liability company having a manager or, if management has been retained by one or more classes of members, by a member of any such class."); OHIO REV. CODE § 1705.35 (substantially the same); R.I. GEN. LAWS § 7–16–68 (substantially the same).

der ULLCA, therefore, persons dealing with an LLC in a real property transaction must review the articles for restrictions on authority or bear the risk.[38]

ULLCA § 301(c) would not have changed the result in *Taghipour*, however, because the limitation on Jerez's authority was in the operating agreement rather than in the articles. This is likely a significant difference, as part of the rationale for binding third parties under § 301(c) is surely that the limitation of authority is contained in a public document. Thus, the second sentence of § 301(c) would have protected Mt. Olympus assuming that it gave value without actual knowledge of Jerez's lack of authority.

Even though ULLCA § 301(c) would not have changed the result in *Taghipour*, what about § 301(b)? Jerez would have had apparent authority to enter into the transaction so long as the transaction was considered to be "in the ordinary course of the company's business or business of the kind carried on by the company." Borrowing money would seem to be within the ordinary course of the company's business, but would pledging the only significant asset of the company as security for the loan take the transaction outside of the ordinary course? One would think so, but some expert testimony may be needed here.

RULLCA has a procedure similar to ULLCA § 301(c) where a "statement of authority" may be filed with the Secretary of State. The statement can restrict the authority of designated persons or positions to transfer real property, and third parties will be deemed to know of the restriction if a certified copy of the statement is filed in the office for recording transfers of that real property.[39] In *Taghipour*, of course, the restriction on Jerez's authority was in a non-public operating agreement; thus, Mt. Olympus would not have deemed knowledge of the restriction. As under ULLCA, the dispute

---

[38] Admittedly, the second sentence of § 301(c) is mysterious. It allows a third party to rely on the instrument affecting the company's real property if the third party gives value without "knowledge" of the lack of the signer's authority. ULLCA § 102(a) states that a person "knows a fact if the person has actual knowledge of it." Thus, the second sentence appears to protect a third party so long as the third party has no actual knowledge of a restriction on authority. The comment to § 301 indicates, however, that actual knowledge of a restriction on authority (with respect to matters covered in § 301(c)) is *not* required when the restriction is in the articles. In effect, third parties are deemed to have knowledge of restrictions in the articles, but restrictions found anywhere else (e.g., operating agreement restrictions) are seemingly not binding on third parties in the absence of actual knowledge. As mentioned, it is not the clearest of provisions.

[39] *See* RULLCA § 302(a), (g). Note that the required filings under this procedure are separate from the filing of a certificate of organization.

would ultimately turn on the application of apparent authority principles.[40]

3. Inspection and Information Rights

Similar to partnership and corporation statutes, LLC statutes often provide members and managers with defined rights to inspect the records of the venture.[41] The rights provided under LLC statutes, however, may differ in meaningful ways from the corresponding rights provided under other business organization statutes. For example, in *Kasten v. Doral Dental USA, LLC*,[42] the Supreme Court of Wisconsin contrasted a shareholder's inspection right under the state's corporation statute with a member's inspection right under the LLC statute:

> However, consideration of the WLLCL's [Wisconsin Limited Liability Company Law] inspection provision in light of its corporate counterpart only serves to highlight the differences between the statutes. The corporation statute includes a host of explicit requirements not provided in the WLLCL's inspection statute, including that the requester either hold at least five percent of the company's shares or be a shareholder for at least six months prior to the request; that the request be made in writing, and at least five days prior to the desired inspection date; and that the records requested be directly connected to the purpose of the request.
>
> Additionally, the corporation statute limits shareholder inspection rights to the types of records enumerated in Wis. Stat. § 180.1602(2)(a) [e.g., excerpts from minutes or records that the corporation is required to keep as permanent records, accounting records of the corporation, and the list of shareholders]. The WLLCL, by contrast, contains no explicit restrictions on the time and place of inspection, and allows access to "any . . . limited liability company record," unless otherwise provided by the operating agreement. . .
>
> By the plain language of Wis. Stat. § 183.0405(2) [the LLC inspection statute], an LLC member may inspect anything that is a "record," and access will be granted to the member "upon reasonable request." Thus, the scope of a member's right of inspection under the default inspection provisions of § 183.0405(2) is exceptionally broad, and hinges on what constitutes an LLC

---

[40] Under RULLCA, of course, those apparent authority principles would derive from the common law of agency rather than from any statutory apparent authority.

[41] *See, e.g.,* DLLCA § 18–305; ULLCA § 408; RULLCA § 410.

[42] 733 N.W.2d 300 (Wis. 2007).

"record," and the degree and kind of restrictions on access that "upon reasonable request" may impose.[43]

Although the LLC inspection statute in Wisconsin does not explicitly include a "proper purpose" requirement, the *Kasten* court noted that a member's purpose for inspecting the records was still relevant to the "reasonable request" requirement of the statute:

> We note that while Wis. Stat. § 183.0405(2) does not require that a member's inspection request be made for a "proper purpose," the reason for the request may be a relevant factor in determining whether the request is reasonable under § 183.0405(2). Thus, a request that is made for an improper purpose may well be unreasonable. However, for a request to meet the reasonableness requirement, the requester need not always show that the request was submitted for a "proper purpose," or even give a reason for the request.[44]

Aside from inspection provisions, many LLC statutes also impose a duty upon members, managers, or the LLC itself to disclose information to the members. For example, similar to RUPA § 403(c), ULLCA § 408(b)(1) requires an LLC to furnish to a member "without demand, information concerning the company's business or affairs reasonably required for the proper exercise of the member's rights and performance of the member's duties under the operating agreement or this [Act]." Moreover, § 408(b)(2) requires the LLC to furnish, "on demand, other information concerning the company's business or affairs, except to the extent the demand or the information demanded is unreasonable or otherwise improper under the circumstances." RULLCA § 410 follows a similar approach.[45] Under the Delaware statute, however, there is no comparable provision.[46]

---

[43] *Id.* at 313 (citations omitted).

[44] *Id.* at 320 n.19.

[45] Under ULLCA, the statutory duty to disclose is clearly not a "fiduciary" duty, as § 409(a) states that the "only" fiduciary duties are those of loyalty and care. RULLCA, by contrast, does not contain this "cabining in" language. Although RULLCA does not describe the statutory duty to disclose as fiduciary in nature (in contrast to the "fiduciary" duties of loyalty and care described in RULLCA § 409(a)), the comment to§ 410 observes that, "[i]n some situations, some courts have seen owners' information rights as reflecting a fiduciary duty of those with management power." Moreover, the comment reiterates that "[t]his Act's statement of fiduciary duties is not exhaustive."

[46] Why does a jurisdiction need both an inspection statute and a disclosure statute? Put differently, if management has an obligation to provide information to members, why does a member need a right to inspect the LLC's records? Perhaps a member would want to see relevant documents to confirm what he is being told. Similarly, perhaps the inspection statute serves as a safety net so that a member does not have to rely on management complying with its disclosure duties. Finally, a

Can an operating agreement eliminate a member's rights to inspection and information? In Delaware, LLC members have a statutory inspection right, but not a statutory disclosure obligation. DLLCA § 18–305(a) indicates that the inspection right may be limited by "reasonable" standards in an operating agreement. Similarly, § 18–305(g) states that a member's or manager's rights to obtain information may be "restricted" in an operating agreement. Would a contractual elimination of the inspection right be considered "unreasonable" and beyond a mere "restriction?" One would think so. The argument is complicated, however, by § 18–1101. Section 18–1101(b) conveys the legislative policy to give "maximum effect to the principle of freedom of contract," and § 18–1101(c) allows for an elimination of "duties" owed to members. Would the obligation to comply with an inspection request be considered a "duty" that could be eliminated? Presumably the more specific language of § 18–305 should prevail over the more general language of § 18–1101, but the Delaware courts have not yet spoken to the issue.

Under ULLCA § 103(b)(1), the operating agreement may not "unreasonably restrict" the right to access records (the inspection statute) or the right to information (the disclosure statute) under § 408. The wholesale elimination of these rights would presumably constitute an unreasonable restriction.

Under RULLCA § 110(c)(6), an operating agreement may not "unreasonably restrict" the right to access records or the right to information under § 410. As under ULLCA, the wholesale elimination of these rights would presumably constitute an unreasonable restriction.[47]

D. Financial Rights and Obligations

With respect to the sharing of profits and losses, LLC statutes tend to provide either a partnership-like equal allocation or a corporate/limited partnership-like pro rata allocation based upon contributions to the firm. For example, DLLCA § 18–503 states that profits and losses of an LLC are allocated in the manner provided by an LLC agreement. If the LLC agreement does not provide an allocation scheme, profits and losses are allocated on the basis of the agreed value (as stated in the LLC's records) of the contributions made by each member to the extent they have been received by the

---

particular jurisdiction might allow the parties' contract to modify or eliminate the disclosure statute, but not the inspection statute. *Cf.* note 47 (discussing RUPA).

[47] Under RUPA, the inspection right of partners may not be "unreasonably restrict[ed]," but the right to information under § 403(c) may be eliminated. *See* RUPA §§ 103(b)(2), 403. Thus, ULLCA and RULLCA stand in sharp contrast to RUPA on this point.

LLC and have not been returned.[48] Because statutory provisions governing the sharing of profits and losses are typically default rules, members have the ability to contract around them. Like partners in a general partnership, LLC members typically establish capital accounts and specify the division of profits and losses in their operating agreement.[49]

Although LLC statutes provide members with limited liability, the statutes often include provisions that protect creditors (to some extent) from member actions that can damage a creditor's position. For example, many statutes provide that a member may be liable to a creditor for an unpaid contribution to the firm, even if the other members have decided to waive that contribution obligation.[50] Many statutes also indicate that members may have liability for receiving distributions that render the LLC insolvent.[51] Fraudulent transfer law, however, offers similar protection.

Should an operating agreement allow members to make additional contributions to an LLC? When financial and voting rights are determined on a pro rata basis (i.e., based on contributions to the firm), additional contributions can affect the existing balance of power within the company. Moreover, if additional contributions are mandatory, members may be faced with sudden financial burdens. Such mandatory contributions may also provide the basis for creditor suits against the members to enforce contribution obligations. On the other hand, mandatory contributions do help to ensure future funding if and when it is needed.

Does a member have a right to compel the LLC to distribute some of its profits before dissolution? Under DLLCA § 18–601, a member can receive an interim profit distribution to the extent provided in an LLC agreement. Further, according to § 18–504, distributions are allocated in the manner provided by an LLC agreement.

---

[48] DLLCA § 18–305(a)(5) requires the LLC to provide "information regarding the amount of cash and a description and statement of the agreed value of any other property or services contributed by each member" upon a member's reasonable demand. The LLC, therefore, is apparently required to keep such information.

Unlike the Delaware statute, the Uniform Acts do not contain a default rule for allocating profits and losses. See ULLCA § 405(a); RULLCA § 404(a); see also id. § 404 cmt. ("This Act has no provision allocating profits and losses among the partners. Instead, the Act directly apportions the right to receive distributions. Nearly all [LLCs] will choose to allocate profits and losses in order to comply with applicable tax, accounting and other regulatory requirements. Those requirements, rather than this Act, are the proper source of guidance for that profit and loss allocation.").

[49] Many operating agreements provide that profits and losses (as well as voting rights) shall be allocated among the members according to an agreed "sharing ratio," which is usually based upon a member's financial contributions to the firm (but not always, particularly in the case of firms with service-providing members).

[50] See, e.g., DLLCA § 18–502(b); ULLCA § 402(b); RULLCA § 403.

[51] See, e.g., DLLCA § 18–607; ULLCA §§ 406–407; RULLCA §§ 405–406.

If the LLC agreement does not provide an allocation scheme, distributions are made on the basis of the agreed value (as stated in the LLC's records) of the contributions made by each member to the extent they have been received by the LLC and have not been returned.

ULLCA § 404(c)(6) indicates that, in a member-managed LLC, a member can receive an interim profit distribution only if all of the members consent. Section 405(a) provides that distributions are to be made in equal shares. RULLCA § 404(b) states that a person has the right to a distribution before the dissolution and winding up of the LLC only if the company decides to make an interim distribution. Thus, it is left to the LLC's management to make the decision pursuant to the company's voting rules. If a distribution is made before the dissolution and winding up of the LLC, RULLCA § 404(a) indicates that the distribution should be made in equal shares.

E. Entity Status

Under most statutes, an LLC is characterized as a separate legal entity whose identity is distinct from that of its owners.[52] As a separate "legal person," an LLC can exercise rights and powers in its own name. For example, an LLC can bring a lawsuit (or be a defendant in one), and it can own property.[53] Nevertheless, judicial treatment of the LLC's entity status is not always predictable. In *Premier Van Schaack Realty, Inc. v. Sieg*,[54] for example, a brokerage fee agreement stated that if Sieg's real estate parcel (the "property") were sold or exchanged during the listing period, Sieg would owe a 7% brokerage fee. Sieg became a member of an LLC ("MJTM") and conveyed the property to MJTM in return for a 40% interest in MJTM and a preferential return of 9% on future profits. The operating agreement also provided that Sieg had a beginning balance of $670,000 in his capital account and that MJTM assumed $580,000 of Sieg's debt. The other members of MJTM agreed not to encumber the property without Sieg's approval.[55]

The broker ("Premier") claimed that the conveyance constituted a sale or exchange of the property, and it demanded its commission. Sieg argued that his contribution of property was an investment as opposed to a sale or exchange. The trial court granted summary judgment to Sieg. The Court of Appeals noted that, to have either a sale or exchange, there must be consideration. The court concluded that Sieg did not receive consideration, primarily because "Sieg re-

[52] *See, e.g.,* DLLCA § 18–201(b); ULLCA § 201; RULLCA § 104(a).

[53] *See, e.g.,* ULLCA § 112(b); RULLCA § 105.

[54] 51 P.3d 24 (Utah Ct. App. 2002).

[55] *See id.* at 26–27.

tained a substantial ownership interest in the property that caused him to assume the risks of an investor instead of the risks of a seller." According to the court, Sieg's ownership interest in the property was demonstrated by his interest in the property's future sale and by his right to prevent MJTM from encumbering the property without his permission. The court also determined that the debt relief could not constitute consideration to Sieg because MJTM "did not actually relieve Sieg of debt, but rather caused him to personally incur nearly three times more debt than he owed on the Property prior to joining MJTM." As the court concluded, "because the facts in this case show Sieg continued to have substantially the same ownership interest in the Property after the deed to MJTM was executed, there was no consideration and a sale or exchange as contemplated in the Agreement did not occur." The judgment of the trial court was affirmed.[56]

In its opinion, the *Sieg* court repeatedly stated that Sieg, post-transfer, retained a significant ownership interest in the property. That assertion, however, is incorrect. The relevant Utah statutes at the time of the dispute provided that an LLC was a separate legal entity and that a member had no interest in specific property of an LLC.[57] While it is true that Sieg was interested in the property's future sale, his interest was not because he was still the owner of the property. It was simply because his ownership interest in the LLC would appreciate in value to the extent that the LLC prospered through a sale of its primary asset. It is also true that the property could not be encumbered without Sieg's permission. Nevertheless, this should be characterized merely as a veto power that Sieg had been granted by the other members on a particular LLC transaction. LLC owners (as well as closely held business owners generally) can agree among themselves to allocate voting power in any way that they choose, even if that voting power affects the LLC's assets. The fact remains, however, that the LLC owns the assets.

The court's conclusion that Sieg did not receive consideration for the conveyance to the LLC also seems flawed. In exchange for conveying the property to the LLC, Sieg received (1) a 40% interest in MJTM; (2) a preferential return of 9% on future profits; (3) a beginning balance of $670,000 in his capital account; and (4) an assumption by MJTM of $580,000 of Sieg's debt. Any one of these items should constitute valid consideration. While it may be true that Sieg accrued more debt after he joined MJTM, MJTM appar-

---

[56] *See id.* at 27–30.

[57] *See* UTAH CODE § 48–2c–104 ("A company formed under this chapter is a legal entity distinct from its members."); *id.* § 48–2c–701(2) ("A member has no interest in specific property of a company."); *cf.* DLLCA § 18–701; ULLCA § 501(a); RULLCA § 501 cmt.

ently did assume $580,000 of Sieg's preexisting debt. Just because Sieg voluntarily guaranteed a later loan does not change the fact that a portion of his debt was assumed by the LLC. As mentioned, that assumption should count as valid consideration.

The *Sieg* court relied on two partnership decisions involving the conveyance of property to a UPA-governed partnership.[58] These decisions concluded that a partner who conveyed property to the partnership retained an ownership interest in the property. According to the opinions, the conveyance resulted merely in a change in the form of ownership and did not constitute a transfer of the property to another entity. These decisions, however, are easily distinguishable. UPA jurisdictions adopt an aggregate view of the partnership.[59] Thus, when an individual partner conveys property to the partnership, there is an argument that no transfer has actually occurred, as the partner still owns the property to some degree. It could be characterized as a mere change in the form of ownership.[60] By statute, however, the LLC is a separate legal entity and its members have no interest in the LLC's property. A conveyance to an LLC, in other words, is legally equivalent to a transfer to a third party.

In contrast to *Sieg*, consider the decision of *Hagan v. Adams Property Associates, Inc.*[61] In *Hagan*, Ralph and Maureen Hagan (collectively "Hagan") owned the Stuart Court Apartments. On April 30, 1994, Hagan executed an agreement with Adams Property Associates, Inc. giving Adams the exclusive right to sell the property for $1,600,000. The agreement provided that if the property were "sold or exchanged" within one year, with or without Adams' assistance, Hagan would pay Adams a fee of six percent of the "gross sales amount." Before the year expired, Hagan, Roy Tepper, and Lynn Parsons formed an LLC called Hagan, Parsons, & Tepper, LLC ("HPT"). By deed dated April 23, 1995, Hagan transferred the property to HPT. When Hagan refused to pay a commission to Adams, Adams sued. The Supreme Court of Virginia held that a sale of the property had occurred and that a commission was required:

> When Hagan transferred the property to HPT, he received more than an interest in the new company. Under the terms of the operating agreement executed in conjunction with the for-

---

[58] *See Sieg*, 51 P.3d at 28–29 (citing Cooley Inv. Co. v. Jones, 780 P.2d 29 (Colo. App. 1989), *and* Dahdah v. Continent Realty, Inc., 434 So.2d 997 (Fla. Dist. Ct. App. 1983)).

[59] *See* Chapter 3(B)(3).

[60] *See* UPA § 25(1). If all of the partners are now co-owners of the property as tenants in partnership, however, it would seem as if ownership of the property has transferred, at least in part, to others.

[61] 482 S.E.2d 805 (Va. 1997).

mation of HPT, HPT agreed to assume all liabilities existing on the property, which included the $1,028,000 unpaid balance on a first deed of trust note on the property. The record does not indicate whether the holder of the first deed of trust note released Hagan and substituted HPT as the obligor on the note. Even assuming such substitution did not occur, Hagan nevertheless received substantial relief from his debt obligation because, upon assuming all liabilities on the property, HPT became liable to Hagan for any amount Hagan would have had to pay the holder of the first deed of trust note. Also as part of the property transfer transaction, HPT executed a second deed of trust on the property securing a note payable to Hagan for $323,000. This note was due and payable when the property was subsequently sold, and it had priority over payments to anyone other than the beneficiary of the first deed of trust. Thus, in exchange for transfer of title to the property, Hagan received relief from his debt on the first deed of trust note as well as the benefit of a second deed of trust note and an interest in HPT. These benefits received by Hagan constituted valid consideration.

Furthermore, the cases relied on by Hagan for the proposition that the contribution of property to a limited liability company is not a sale but the capitalization of a new company are inapposite. Those cases involved the capitalization of a *partnership* or entity governed by partnership law. As noted in those cases, a partnership is not an entity separate from the partners themselves; thus, in such circumstances, there is no transfer of property from one person to another, but only a change in the form of ownership. In this case, however, the new venture was a limited liability company, not a partnership. Under the Virginia Limited Liability Company Act, a limited liability company is an unincorporated association with a registered agent and office. It is an independent entity which can sue and be sued and its members are not personally liable for the debt or actions of the company. In contrast to a partnership, a limited liability company in Virginia is an entity separate from its members and, thus, the transfer of property from a member to the limited liability company is more than a change in the form of ownership; it is a transfer from one entity or person to another. Accordingly, we agree with the trial court's conclusion that Hagan transferred the title of the property in exchange for valuable consideration and that this transfer was a sale of the property.[62]

---

[62] *Id.* at 806–07 (citations omitted).

In *Elf Atochem North America, Inc. v. Jaffari*,[63] the operating agreement contained an arbitration clause covering all disputes. The agreement was signed by the two members of the LLC, Malek, Inc. and Elf, but not by the LLC itself. Elf attempted to avoid arbitration by bringing a derivative action on behalf of the LLC. Although the LLC was not a signatory to the operating agreement, the Supreme Court of Delaware concluded that the LLC was bound by the agreement, including the arbitration provision:

> . . . Because Malek LLC never expressly assented to the arbitration and forum selection clauses within the Agreement, Elf argues it can sue derivatively on behalf of Malek LLC . . .

> We are not persuaded by this argument. Section 18–101(7) defines the limited liability company agreement as "any agreement, written or oral, *of the member or members* as to the affairs of a limited liability company and the conduct of its business." Here, Malek, Inc. and Elf, the members of Malek LLC, executed the Agreement to carry out the affairs and business of Malek LLC and to provide for arbitration and forum selection.

> Notwithstanding Malek LLC's failure to sign the Agreement, Elf's claims are subject to the arbitration and forum selection clauses of the Agreement. The Act is a statute designed to permit members maximum flexibility in entering into an agreement to govern their relationship. It is the members who are the real parties in interest. The LLC is simply their joint business vehicle. This is the contemplation of the statute in prescribing the outlines of a limited liability company agreement.[64]

As this passage reveals, the *Elf Atochem* court viewed the LLC in an aggregate-like manner and effectively concluded that the LLC was bound to the operating agreement because its two members were bound. Such a conclusion is hard to square with the statutory pronouncement in DLLCA § 18–201(b) that an LLC "shall be a separate legal entity." Delaware courts would presumably limit this aggregate conception to situations involving an *inter se* agreement like the one that existed in *Elf Atochem*—i.e., an agreement between all of the members addressing their rights and obligations to each other.[65] Interestingly, this issue is now addressed by statute,

---

[63] 727 A.2d 286 (Del. 1999).

[64] *Id.* at 287–89, 293 (footnotes omitted).

[65] For a counterpoint to *Elf Atochem*, see Bubbles & Bleach LLC v. Becker, No. 97 C 1320, 1997 WL 285938 (N.D. Ill. May 23, 1997) ("There is no indication from this definition that the Wisconsin legislature anticipated that operating agreements would bind limited liability companies as entities distinct from their constituent members. Nor is there any case law holding the same. In fact, it is this characteris-

as DLLCA § 18–101(7) provides that "[a] limited liability company is bound by its [LLC] agreement whether or not the [LLC] executes the [LLC] agreement."[66]

F. Limited Liability

Like many of the other business entities, the LLC provides its owners with limited liability for the venture's obligations. For example, ULLCA § 303(a) indicates that "the debts, obligations, and liabilities of a limited liability company, whether arising in contract, tort, or otherwise, are solely the debts, obligations, and liabilities of the company," and it further states that "[a] member or manager is not personally liable for a debt, obligation, or liability of the company solely by reason of being or acting as a member or manager."[67] Keep in mind that limited liability protects members and managers only from vicarious liability for the obligations of the LLC. In other words, members and managers are not personally liable for the obligations of the LLC simply because of their status as members or managers. Limited liability provisions, however, do not insulate members or managers from direct liability for their own personal wrongdoing.[68]

---

tic of limited liability companies—their distinct legal existence as an entity apart from their constituent members—which allows them to shield their members from personal liability and distinguishes them from both general and limited partnerships. Indeed, defendants admit that [the LLC] is not a party to the Agreements, and did not take part in the drafting of the Agreements or sign them. Thus, in the instant case, there appears to be no basis flowing from the Agreements that would subject [the LLC] to the arbitration clause [in the Agreements].").

[66] See also RULLCA § 111(a) ("A limited liability company is bound by and may enforce the operating agreement, whether or not the company has itself manifested assent to the operating agreement.").

For federal diversity jurisdiction purposes, the LLC is also viewed from an aggregate perspective. A number of courts have concluded that an LLC's citizenship is determined by looking at the citizenship of its individual members, regardless of whether state law views the LLC as a separate legal entity. See, e.g., Cosgrove v. Bartolotta, 150 F.3d 729, 731 (7th Cir. 1998) ("Given the resemblance between an LLC and a limited partnership, and what seems to have crystallized as a principle that members of associations are citizens for diversity purposes unless Congress provides otherwise (as it has with respect to corporations, in 28 U.S.C. § 1332(c)(1) [deeming that a corporation is a citizen of the state where it incorporated and the state where it has its principal place of business]), we conclude that the citizenship of an LLC for purposes of the diversity jurisdiction is the citizenship of its members." (citations omitted)).

[67] See also DLLCA § 18–303(a) (substantially the same); RULLCA § 304(a) (substantially the same).

[68] See, e.g., ULLCA § 303 cmt. ("A member or manager, as an agent of the company, is not liable for the debts, obligations, and liabilities of the company simply because of the agency. A member or manager is responsible for acts or omissions to the extent those acts or omissions would be actionable in contract or tort against the member or manager if that person were acting in an individual capacity."); RULLCA § 304 cmt.

In *Pepsi-Cola Bottling Co. v. Handy*,[69] the court seemed to overlook this point. Pepsi-Cola purchased real property from an LLC, Willow Creek. Pepsi alleged that Handy, a member and manager of Willow Creek, fraudulently failed to disclose that wetlands existed on the property. The other members, Ginsburg and McKinley, were also alleged to have participated in the wrongdoing. Technically, these wrongful actions occurred before the LLC was formed and before the property was acquired by the LLC.

The individual defendants moved to dismiss on the basis of limited liability. The court examined DLLCA § 18–303(a) and teed up the issue as "whether the defendants here are being sued 'solely by reason of being a member' of Willow Creek (the LLC) where the claim is based upon fraudulent acts committed by the LLC members before the LLC was formed and took title to the Property." The court noted that "[b]ecause the facts alleged in the complaint establish that the LLC was not formed (and the Property was not acquired by the LLC) until after the allegedly critical wrongful acts had been committed, it follows that the defendants could not have been acting '*solely* as members of the LLC when they committed those acts.'" As a result, the court concluded that the individual defendants were not protected by the limited liability of § 18–303.[70]

Would the result in Handy have changed if the LLC had been formed (and if it had acquired the property) well before Pepsi-Cola became interested in purchasing the land? Of course not. The temporal analysis of the court seems unnecessary. When a member gets sued for personally committing a tort or other wrongdoing, the member is not being sued "solely by reason of being a member." The member is being sued for his own misconduct. Similarly, liability in *Handy* is premised on more than member status. It is premised on alleged fraud—an act of personal misconduct that is not shielded by limited liability provisions.

DLLCA § 18–215 provides an additional form of limited liability protection. An operating agreement can designate a "series" or specified group of members, managers, LLC interests, or assets that have "separate rights, powers or duties with respect to specified property or obligations of the limited liability company or profits and losses associated with specified property or obligations." If the operating agreement creates one or more of these series, and if certain requirements are met, then "the debts, liabilities, obligations and expenses incurred, contracted for or otherwise existing with

[69] No. 1973–S, 2000 WL 364199 (Del. Ch. Mar. 15, 2000).
[70] *See id.* at *1–2, 4.

respect to a particular series shall be enforceable against the assets of such series only, and not against the assets of the limited liability company generally or any other series thereof." Similarly, "none of the debts, liabilities, obligations and expenses incurred, contracted for or otherwise existing with respect to the limited liability company generally or any other series thereof shall be enforceable against the assets of such series."

Some other states have followed Delaware's lead in authorizing "series LLCs." RULLCA, however, does not include such a provision. As the Prefatory Note to RULLCA explains:

> The new Act also has a very noteworthy omission; it does not authorize "series LLCs." Under a series approach, a single limited liability company may establish and contain within itself separate series. Each series is treated as an enterprise separate from each other and from the LLC itself. Each series has associated with it specified members, assets, and obligations, and—due to what have been called "internal shields"—the obligations of one series are not the obligation of any other series or of the LLC.

> Delaware pioneered the series concept, and the concept has apparently been quite useful in structuring certain types of investment funds and in arranging complex financing. Other states have followed Delaware's lead, but a number of difficult and substantial questions remain unanswered, including:

> • *conceptual*—How can a series be—and expect to be treated as—a separate legal person for liability and other purposes if the series is defined as part of another legal person?

> • *bankruptcy*—Bankruptcy law has not recognized the series as a separate legal person. If a series becomes insolvent, will the entire LLC and the other series become part of the bankruptcy proceedings? Will a bankruptcy court consolidate the assets and liabilities of the separate series?

> • *efficacy of the internal shields in the courts of other states*— Will the internal shields be respected in the courts of states whose LLC statutes do not recognize series? Most LLC statutes provide that "foreign law governs" the liability of members of a foreign LLC. However, those provisions do not apply to the series question, because those provisions pertain to the liability of a member for the obligations of the LLC. For a series LLC, the pivotal question is entirely different—namely, whether some assets of an LLC should be immune from some of the creditors of the LLC.

- *tax treatment*—Will the IRS and the states treat each series separately? Will separate returns be filed? May one series "check the box" for corporate tax classification and the others not?

- *securities law*—Given the panoply of unanswered questions, what types of disclosures must be made when a membership interest is subject to securities law?

... Given the availability of well-established alternate structures (e.g., multiple single member LLCs, an LLC "holding company" with LLC subsidiaries), it made no sense for the Act to endorse the complexities and risks of a series approach.

Should courts allow "piercing the veil" in the LLC context? Several judicial decisions and state statutes explicitly provide that piercing doctrines should apply in LLC disputes.[71] Nevertheless, there are differences between the corporation and LLC settings that could affect the inquiry. For example, many LLC statutes directly impose liability on members for withdrawing funds from failing firms.[72] Such direct liability can be used to rectify inadequate capitalization problems rather than having to resort to a piercing analysis. Even if a piercing analysis is applied, many LLC statutes impose far fewer management formalities (e.g., no requirement for an annual meeting, no prescribed notice or quorum procedures) than their corporate counterparts. Consequently, corporate piercing precedents on the failure to follow formalities may be of little applicability.[73] In fact, because informal management and operation is very common in the LLC setting, a failure to comply with formalities should arguably play no role at all in an LLC piercing analysis.[74]

---

[71] *See, e.g.*, Hollowell v. Orleans Reg'l Hosp., No. Civ.A. 95–4029, 1998 WL 283298, at *9–10 (E.D. La. May 29, 1998); Kaycee Land & Livestock v. Flahive, 46 P.3d 323, 327–28 (Wyo. 2002); *see also* MINN. STAT. § 322B.303(2) ("The case law that states the conditions and circumstances under which the corporate veil of a corporation may be pierced under Minnesota law also applies to [LLCs]."); WASH. REV. CODE § 25.15.060 ("Members of a limited liability company shall be personally liable for any act, debt, obligation, or liability of the limited liability company to the extent that shareholders of a Washington business corporation would be liable in analogous circumstances. In this regard, the court may consider the factors and policies set forth in established case law with regard to piercing the corporate veil . . .").

[72] *See, e.g.*, DLLCA § 18–607; ULLCA §§ 406–407; RULLCA §§ 405–406.

[73] *See, e.g.*, *Kaycee Land*, 46 P.3d at 328 ("Certainly, the various factors which would justify piercing an LLC veil would not be identical to the corporate situation for the obvious reason that many of the organizational formalities applicable to corporations do not apply to LLCs. The LLC's operation is intended to be much more flexible than a corporation's.").

[74] Indeed, under some statutes, an LLC piercing analysis cannot consider a firm's failure to follow formalities. *See, e.g.*, ULLCA § 303(b) ("The failure of [an LLC] to observe the usual company formalities or requirements relating to the exercise of its

G. Fiduciary Duties

1. The Basic Duties

In contrast to many corporation statutes, several LLC statutes address the concept of fiduciary duty. The statutes often state that members (in member-managed LLCs) and managers (in manager-managed LLCs) owe fiduciary duties of care and loyalty to the LLC, and at least some of the statutes indicate that those duties also run to the individual members.[75]

LLC statutes that explicitly define the duty of care provide either that a member or manager must act as a prudent person in similar circumstances, or that a member or manager must refrain from engaging in grossly negligent conduct.[76] Is there a substantive difference between these articulations? The "ordinarily prudent person" language sounds like an ordinary negligence standard. The gross negligence language is, obviously, a gross negligence standard. Nevertheless, it is not clear whether these articulations will lead to different results in lawsuits, as the application of the busi-

---

company powers or management of its business is not a ground for imposing personal liability on the members or managers for liabilities of the company."); RULLCA § 304(b) (substantially the same); *see also id.* § 304 cmt. ("In the corporate realm, 'disregard of corporate formalities' is a key factor in the piercing analysis. In the realm of LLCs, that factor is inappropriate, because informality of organization and operation is both common and desired.").

As discussed in the corporation materials, one can argue that a failure to follow formalities should also play no role in a corporate piercing analysis, as there is rarely a link between a lack of formalities and a third party's injury. *See* Chapter 8(E).

[75] *See, e.g.,* ULLCA § 409; RULLCA § 409. In *McGee v. Best*, 106 S.W.3d 48 (Tenn. Ct. App. 2002), the court concluded that the Tennessee LLC statute "define[d] the fiduciary duty of members of a member-managed LLC as one owing to the LLC, not to individual members." *Id.* at 64. In contrast, the same Court of Appeals concluded in *Anderson v. Wilder*, No. E2003–00460–COA–R3–CV, 2003 WL 22768666 (Tenn. Ct. App. Nov. 21, 2003), that a majority member of an LLC did owe a fiduciary duty to a minority member by relying on partnership and closely held corporation precedents. *See id.* at *4–6. Perhaps these seemingly disparate conclusions can be reconciled by noting that the Tennessee statute does not purport to be exclusive—i.e., it does not state that the *only* fiduciary duties owed in an LLC run between a member and the LLC. The statute, in other words, does not speak to the issue of fiduciary duties between members, and arguably there is room for a court to impose such duties as a matter of common law (as has been done in the closely held corporation setting). *See also In re* Allentown Ambassadors, Inc., 361 B.R. 422, 461–62 (Bankr. E.D. Pa. 2007) (observing that the North Carolina LLC statute indicated that managers owed a fiduciary duty to the LLC but not to individual members, but nevertheless concluding that managers do owe a fiduciary duty to individual members based on closely held corporation precedents).

[76] *See, e.g.,* N.Y. LTD. LIAB. CO. LAW § 409(a) (act as a prudent person in similar circumstances); ULLCA § 409(c) (refrain from gross negligence); *see also* RULLCA § 409(c) (stating that, "[s]ubject to the business judgment rule," the duty of care "is to act with the care that a person in a like position would reasonably exercise under similar circumstances and in a manner the member reasonably believes to be in the best interests of the company").

ness judgment rule may, in many circumstances, result in a gross negligence standard under either articulation.[77]

The duty of loyalty in the LLC setting likely addresses the same issues that it covers in other business contexts—i.e., regulating conflict of interest transactions, preventing competition with the firm, restricting personal use of the firm's assets, and prohibiting the misappropriation of LLC business opportunities.[78] With respect to conflict of interest transactions, some LLC statutes state, in a partnership-like manner, that such transactions require the consent of members or managers.[79] Other statutes bear a closer resemblance to the corporate model, as a conflict of interest transaction can be validated through the consent of disinterested members or managers, or upon a showing of fairness.[80]

Following other Uniform Acts, ULLCA § 409(a) states that the "only" fiduciary duties owed by members and managers are the duties of loyalty and care set forth in the statute. Moreover, pursuant to § 409(b), the duty of loyalty is "limited to" the circumstances described in the statute. In a sharp break from prior practice, RULLCA § 409 "uncabins" fiduciary duty by removing the "only" and "limited to" restrictions. As the Comment to RULLCA § 409 explains:

> Until the promulgation of RUPA, it was almost axiomatic that: (i) fiduciary duties reflect judge-made law; and (ii) statutory formulations can express some of that law but do not exhaustively codify it. The original UPA was a prime example of this approach.

---

[77] What is the purpose of the RULLCA formulation in the prior note? Perhaps it is a way of saying that the standard will be gross negligence in the decision-making context (i.e., when the business judgment rule applies), but will be ordinary negligence in the oversight context (i.e., when the business judgment rule does not apply). *See* Chapter 7(C)(3).

[78] *See, e.g.,* ULLCA § 409(b), (h) (addressing the duty of loyalty); RULLCA § 409(b), (g) (same).

[79] *See, e.g.,* CONN. GEN. STAT. § 34–141(e); OKLA. STAT. tit. 18, § 2016(5); *see also* ULLCA §§ 103(b)(2)(ii), 404(c)(2) (indicating that all of the members must consent to a transaction that would otherwise violate the duty of loyalty, unless some lower number is specified in the operating agreement).

[80] *See, e.g.,* OHIO REV. CODE § 1705.31(A)(1). RULLCA seems to borrow from both the partnership and corporation models. Section 409(f) states that "[a]ll of the members of a member-managed limited liability company or a manager-managed limited liability company may authorize or ratify, after full disclosure of all material facts, a specific act or transaction that otherwise would violate the duty of loyalty." Further, with respect to claims under § 409(b)(2) (i.e., conflict of interest transactions), § 409(e) states that "[i]t is a defense to a claim under subsection (b)(2) and any comparable claim in equity or at common law that the transaction was fair to the limited liability company."

In an effort to respect freedom of contract, bolster predictability, and protect partnership agreements from second-guessing, the Conference decided that RUPA should fence or "cabin in" all fiduciary duties within a statutory formulation. That decision was followed without re-consideration in ULLCA and ULPA (2001).

This Act takes a different approach. After lengthy discussion in the drafting committee and on the floor of the 2006 Annual Meeting, the Conference decided that: (i) the "corral" created by RUPA does not fit in the very complex and variegated world of LLCs; and (ii) it is impracticable to cabin all LLC-related fiduciary duties within a statutory formulation.

As a result, this Act: (i) eschews "only" and "limited to"— the words RUPA used in an effort to exhaustively codify fiduciary duty; (ii) codifies the core of the fiduciary duty of loyalty; but (iii) does not purport to discern every possible category of over-reaching. One important consequence is to allow courts to continue to use fiduciary duty concepts to police disclosure obligations in member-to-member and member-LLC transactions.

RULLCA's "uncabining" of fiduciary duty is quite controversial. The most important implication is that courts will be allowed to use fiduciary duty doctrine to police conduct that does not otherwise fit nicely under the statutory articulations of the duties of care and loyalty. For example, as the comment above suggests, disclosure violations might be characterized as a breach of fiduciary duty under RULLCA.[81] This result cannot be reached, however, under ULLCA (assuming that the statute is literally followed). ULLCA § 409(a) states that the "only" fiduciary duties are the duties of loyalty and care under § 409(b) and (c), and disclosure violations do not seem to fall within those subsections. Failure to disclose could be a statutory violation under ULLCA § 408, but that violation could not be considered a breach of fiduciary duty.

What difference does it make if a failure to disclose is characterized as a breach of fiduciary duty versus a statutory violation? If the conduct is not characterized as a breach of fiduciary duty, a plaintiff may lose out on a favorable jury instruction that the jurisdiction uses for fiduciary actions. Moreover, while a jurisdiction may have doctrines providing for a liberal statute of limitations and the possibility of punitive damages (or other remedies) for breach of fiduciary duty claims, such benefits may not be extended to "mere" statutory claims.

---

[81] *See also* note 45 (discussing whether the duty to disclose is fiduciary in nature).

RULLCA also eliminates the RUPA § 404(e) and (f) subsections that ULLCA § 409 had adopted for the LLC setting. As the comment to RULLCA § 409 explains:

Section 409 omits a noteworthy provision, which, beginning with RUPA, has been standard in the uniform business entity acts. RUPA, ULLCA, ULPA (2001) each placed the following language in the subsection following the formulation of the obligation of good faith:

A member . . . does not violate a duty or obligation under this [act] or under the operating agreement merely because the member's conduct furthers the member's own interest.

This language is inappropriate in the complex and variegated world of LLCs. As a proposition of contract law, the language is axiomatic and therefore unnecessary. In the context of fiduciary duty, the language is at best incomplete, at worst wrong, and in any event confusing.

. . .

This Act also omits, as anachronistic and potentially confusing, any provision resembling ULLCA, § 409(f). . . Those provisions originated to combat the notion that debts to partners were categorically inferior to debts to non-partner creditors. That notion has never been part of LLC law, and so a modern uniform LLC act need not include language combating the notion. Moreover, to the uninitiated the language can be confusing, because the words might: (i) seem to undercut the duty of loyalty, which they do not; and (ii) deflect attention from bankruptcy law and the law of fraudulent transfer, which assuredly can look askance at transactions between an entity and an "insider."

In Delaware and other jurisdictions where fiduciary duty is not defined by statute, the courts have a significant role, as they must shape the contours of fiduciary duty doctrine in the LLC setting without any legislative aid.[82] For example, in *VGS, Inc. v. Castiel*,[83]

---

[82] Regardless of whether fiduciary duty is defined by statute, most LLC statutes explicitly authorize derivative lawsuits. *See, e.g.*, DLLCA §§ 18–1001 to 18–1004; ULLCA §§ 1101–1104; RULLCA §§ 902–906. The statutes (and the courts) typically prescribe rules that are similar to the rules applied to derivative lawsuits in the corporation setting. *See, e.g.*, Wood v. Baum, 953 A.2d 136, 138–41 (Del. 2008) (applying corporate law demand requirements and demand futility standards to a derivative lawsuit in the LLC setting). Even when derivative lawsuits are not explicitly authorized by statute, courts have allowed them. *See, e.g.*, Weber v. King, 110 F. Supp. 2d 124, 131 (E.D.N.Y. 2000) ("[I]t seems peculiar that in drafting New York's Limited Liability Company Law, the New York State legislature chose not to include a provision expressly permitting derivative lawsuits by members of an LLC on behalf

the Delaware Court of Chancery addressed a breach of fiduciary duty claim in a dispute among managers of a manager-managed LLC. David Castiel formed Virtual Geosatellite LLC. The members were Holdings (a corporation controlled by Castiel), Ellipso (a corporation controlled by Castiel), and Sahagen Satellite (an LLC controlled by Peter Sahagen). Holdings owned 63.46% of the LLC, Satellite owned 25%, and Ellipso owned 11.54%. Management of the LLC was vested in a three-member board of managers. As the majority unitholder, Castiel (through Holdings) had the power to appoint, remove, and replace two of the three members of the Board of Managers. Castiel, therefore, had the power to prevent any board decision with which he disagreed.

Castiel named himself and Tom Quinn to the board of managers. Sahagen named himself as the third member of the board. Sahagen convinced Quinn that Castiel must be ousted from management. Without notice to Castiel, Sahagen and Quinn acted by written consent to merge the LLC into VGS, a Delaware corporation (this written consent was permissible under the literal language of DLLCA § 18–404(d)). As a result of the merger, Sahagen and Quinn took over the management of the business, and Castiel was excluded from management. Holdings and Ellipso went from having a 75% combined interest in the LLC to a 37.5% combined interest in VGS. Sahagen Satellite went from a 25% interest in the LLC to a 62.5% interest in VGS.[84]

The court determined that notice to Castiel was not required before Sahagen and Quinn could act by written consent, and it observed that "[t]he LLC Agreement [did] not purport to modify the statute in this regard."[85] The actions of Sahagen and Quinn, therefore, did not violate any express provisions of the LLC Act or the LLC agreement. Nevertheless, after broadly declaring that "Sahagen and Quinn each owed a duty of loyalty to the LLC, its in-

---

of the LLC. . . . We do not believe that the legislature's failure to include a derivative action provision in the [LLC statute] prevents us from recognizing such a right at common law."); *accord* Tzolis v. Wolff, 884 N.E.2d 1005, 1005 (N.Y. 2008).

[83] No. C.A. 17995, 2000 WL 1277372 (Del. Ch. Aug. 31, 2000).

[84] *See id.* at *1–2.

[85] *Id.* at *4. After parsing the LLC agreement, the court also concluded that a unanimous vote of the managers was not required to effectuate the merger. *See id.* at *3. This issue arose because the LLC agreement did not expressly state whether the managers voted on a majority or unanimous basis. Moreover, DLLCA has no statutory default rule for manager voting in manager-managed LLCs. *See* DLLCA §§ 18–402, 18–404(b). This can be a serious problem for a statutory scheme that depends so heavily on private ordering—what does a court do with incomplete operating agreements? As a practical matter, failing to include a voting rule in the operating agreement of a manager-managed LLC is a colossal oversight—one that could have drastic consequences.

vestors and Castiel, their fellow manager," the court held that Sahagen and Quinn "failed to discharge their duty of loyalty to Castiel in good faith" by acting to effectuate the merger without notice to Castiel. According to the court, Sahagen and Quinn knew that Castiel's protection against actions adverse to him was his right to remove and appoint two managers at will; thus, their effort to circumvent that right (by acting secretly) was seen as a breach of their duty of loyalty.[86] Notice the broader proposition that *VGS* supports—technical compliance with statutes and operating agreements may not protect parties from liability for conduct that a court deems inequitable.[87]

What if Sahagen and Quinn truly believed that their secret course of action to remove Castiel from power was the only feasible way of protecting the LLC from financial ruin? Had there been other investors, could Sahagen and Quinn have been sued for breaching their fiduciary duties if they failed to proceed with their scheme? Perhaps Sahagen and Quinn should have given notice to Castiel of their plans, and if Castiel tried to block them, he could be sued for breach of duty (assuming that Castiel was, in fact, driving

---

[86] *See id.* at *3–4. The court focuses on a duty owed to Castiel, but Castiel was not a member himself. Holdings and Ellipso—corporations controlled by Castiel—were members. Unless the court implicitly engaged in a piercing analysis, the only duty that would run to Castiel individually would be a duty from manager to manager. This is a duty that the law has not clearly recognized in other contexts. It may be easier to conceptualize the court's result as managers (Sahagen and Quinn) owing duties to members (Holdings and Ellipso), which were breached by Sahagen's and Quinn's secret actions. The reference to Castiel individually may simply have been shorthand for Holdings and Ellipso.

[87] In *Nixon v. Blackwell*, 626 A.2d 1366 (Del. 1993), the Supreme Court of Delaware refused to create special common-law rules to protect minority shareholders in closely held corporations who agreed to a governance structure (majority rule), but who failed to foresee all of its consequences (e.g., the majority can terminate the minority from employment, remove the minority from a management position, and prevent the minority from receiving dividends). The court had little sympathy for a minority shareholder who could have protected his participatory and financial rights by contract, but who failed, for one reason or another, to do so. *See* Chapter 8(F). In *VGS*, however, the Delaware Court of Chancery comes to the aid of a majority investor who agreed to a governance structure (majority-of-managers rule, but the majority investor has the right to remove and appoint two of the three managers), but who failed to foresee all of its consequences (e.g., the other two managers could act in secret without notifying the majority investor). The majority investor could have contracted for notice in every situation involving action by the other managers, but the majority failed to do so. Nevertheless, the court comes to the majority's aid with common-law fiduciary duty doctrines. Why the difference in approach? Why didn't the court tell Castiel that he should have protected himself with a better-drafted agreement? Is Delaware just more friendly to majority investors?

the business into ruin).[88] These are not easy issues to resolve, and Vice-Chancellor Steele largely ducks them in the *VGS* opinion.[89]

The court cites no authority for its pronouncement that "Sahagen and Quinn each owed a duty of loyalty to the LLC, its investors and Castiel, their fellow manager." As mentioned, DLLCA has no provision defining the fiduciary duties of LLC members and managers. Further, the operating agreement in *VGS* did not state anything on point. Thus, the pronouncement is purely a matter of judicial lawmaking, just as fiduciary duty has largely been a matter of common law in the corporate setting.

As a final note, it is worth considering whether differences between the LLC and other business organizations might affect the need for a vigorous application of fiduciary duties. Limited liability, owner participation in management, and the existence of exit rights are all relevant to this inquiry. For example, if owners have personal liability for the obligations of the firm, there is arguably a greater need for the protections of fiduciary duty doctrine. After all, decisions made by fellow owners and managers can negatively impact the firm and, because of unlimited liability, the owners themselves. When limited liability exists, however, as in the LLC context, the impact of owner and manager decisions is felt by the LLC, but not directly by the members (at least to the extent that the members' personal assets are not at risk). Thus, there is less of a need for the protection of fiduciary duty doctrine.

On the other hand, curbing poor managerial decisions that affect the LLC itself is also important, and fiduciary duty doctrine can help. Moreover, because of the existence of limited liability, owners may be less inclined to be directly involved in management. They may not feel a personal need to monitor managerial decisions as much as they would in a business organization where poor decisions can create unlimited liability for the owners. In these passive investment situations, the members may expect fiduciary duty, rather than their direct involvement in governance, to protect them from poor managerial decisions.

An owner's ability to exit a firm with the value of his investment is also significant. When owners can leave a firm without suf-

---

[88] There was at least circumstantial evidence that Castiel was doing a lousy job; after all, Sahagen was able to convince Quinn (Castiel's own nominee) that Castiel needed to be ousted.

[89] *Cf. VGS*, 2000 WL at *5 ("Perhaps, had notice been given and an attempt then made to block Castiel's anticipated action to replace Quinn, the allegedly disinterested and independent member that Castiel himself had appointed, the analysis might be different. However, this, as all cases, must be reviewed as it is presented, not as it might have been.").

fering significant losses, there is a less of a need for the protection offered by fiduciary duty doctrine, as investors can protect themselves through exit. In the LLC, however, there typically is no easy exit.[90] On the other hand, the lack of easy exit tends to make investors take a more active role in the management of the firm, as the firm's overall direction becomes more important to an owner when his investment cannot be quickly and easily liquidated. An active management role may result in less of a need for the protection of fiduciary duty because the owners are protecting themselves from managerial misconduct through their direct involvement in the firm's governance.

2. The Role of Contract

Freedom of contract and the enforcement of the parties' private arrangements are central to the LLC. In *Elf Atochem North America, Inc. v. Jaffari*,[91] the Supreme Court of Delaware underscored this point:

> The basic approach of the Delaware Act is to provide members with broad discretion in drafting the Agreement and to furnish default provisions when the members' agreement is silent. The Act is replete with fundamental provisions made subject to modification in the Agreement (e.g. "unless otherwise provided in a limited liability company agreement . . .").

> . . .

> Section 18–1101(b) of the Act, like the essentially identical Section 17–1101(c) of the [limited partnership] Act, provides that "[i]t is the policy of [the Act] to give the maximum effect to the principle of freedom of contract and to the enforceability of limited liability company agreements." Accordingly, the following observation relating to limited partnerships applies as well to limited liability companies:

>> The Act's basic approach is to permit partners to have the broadest possible discretion in drafting their partnership agreements and to furnish answers only in situations where the partners have not expressly made provisions in their partnership agreement. Truly, the partnership agreement is the cornerstone of a Delaware limited partnership, and effectively constitutes the entire agreement among the partners with respect to the admission of partners to, and the creation, operation and termination of, the

---

[90] *See* Chapter 16(I).
[91] 727 A.2d 286 (Del. 1999).

limited partnership. Once partners exercise their contractual freedom in their partnership agreement, the partners have a great deal of certainty that their partnership agreement will be enforced in accordance with its terms. [Martin I. Lubaroff & Paul Altman, *Delaware Limited Partnerships* § 1.2 (1999) (footnote omitted)].

In general, the commentators observe that only where the agreement is inconsistent with mandatory statutory provisions will the members' agreement be invalidated. Such statutory provisions are likely to be those intended to protect third parties, not necessarily the contracting members.[92]

Elf Atochem reflects the deference that many courts are willing to give to contractual arrangements between LLC owners. This deference, however, gives rise to the thorniest question in the legal development of the LLC—should freedom of contract have any limits? This question tends to arise in the context of fiduciary duties when the parties' operating agreement seeks to limit, or eliminate all together, the fiduciary duties otherwise owed.[93]

DLLCA § 18–1101(c) clearly indicates that fiduciary duties may be eliminated by agreement. Similarly, § 18–1101(e) allows elimination of liability for breach of duties.[94] The only statutory limitation on this freedom of contract is the inability to eliminate

---

[92] *Id.* at 291–92 (footnotes omitted).

[93] For example, in *McConnell v. Hunt Sports Enterprises,* 725 N.E.2d 1193 (Ohio. Ct. App. 1993), Columbus Hockey Limited ("CHL") was an LLC formed to obtain and operate a National Hockey League franchise in Columbus, Ohio. The members of CHL included, among others, McConnell and Hunt Sports Group. The franchise was ultimately awarded to a separate ownership group headed by McConnell and not to CHL.
Section 3.3 of the CHL operating agreement stated that "Members shall not in any way be prohibited from or restricted in engaging or owning an interest in any other business venture of any nature, including any venture which might be competitive with the business of the Company." McConnell filed a complaint for declaratory judgment requesting a declaration that section 3.3 allowed CHL members to compete with CHL for the NHL franchise. Hunt Sports Group filed a counterclaim asserting that McConnell's competition had breached his fiduciary duty to CHL.
The trial court found that section 3.3 was clear and unambiguous and that McConnell's competition was permissible. The Court of Appeals agreed: "[The] evidence shows that appellees obtained the NHL franchise to the exclusion of CHL. This constituted direct competition with CHL. However, appellees were permitted under the operating agreement to compete with CHL and . . . this in and of itself cannot constitute a breach of fiduciary duty." *See id.* at 1200, 1202–03, 1206, 1216.

[94] The difference between eliminating duties and "liability" for duties is that eliminating liability means that money damages cannot be sought against those owing fiduciary duties, but equitable relief for breaches of fiduciary duty can be pursued. Eliminating the duty itself, however, eliminates the fiduciary obligation all together such that neither monetary nor equitable relief can be sought.

the "implied contractual covenant of good faith and fair dealing."[95] Thus, the contractual concept of good faith—murky in the contracts area—becomes very important to LLC law as well.

The contractual good faith obligation is generally understood to protect the spirit of the parties' actual bargain. That is, the good faith obligation is often explained as follows: (1) it is difficult to write a contract that covers every possible contingency and situation; (2) as a result, contracts often provide the possibility for one party to take opportunistic advantage of another (such as when one party has received the benefits of the contract but is in a position to deny the other party his expected benefits—think of firing an employee the day before his pension vests); (3) the good faith obligation is designed to protect the spirit of the actual deal reached by the parties to ensure that all parties get the fruits of the bargain that they negotiated for. The key point is that fiduciary duty is a background obligation that is often viewed as somewhat of a free-floating selflessness (or at least fairness) norm. By contrast, the implied contractual covenant of good faith and fair dealing is explicitly tethered to the parties' bargain. It neither requires selflessness nor polices for generalized fairness—it seeks to give effect to the actual bargain that the parties struck, whether that bargain seems fair or unfair to one side.[96]

This description of the implied covenant highlights the conclusory nature of statements that the mere exercise of one's contractual rights, without more, cannot constitute a breach of the covenant. Assume that a member has the contractual power to expel another member. Does this mean that expulsion can occur solely for the purpose of stealing the value of the expelled member's inter-

---

[95] Although the only statutory limitation is the inability to eliminate the implied contractual covenant, *see* DLLCA § 18–1101(c), (e), some Delaware courts have suggested that public policy is also available to police abuses. *See, e.g.*, Abry Partners V, L.P. v. F&W Acquisition LLC, 891 A.2d 1032, 1036 (Del. Ch. 2006) ("For these reasons, when a seller intentionally misrepresents a fact embodied in a contract—that is, when a seller lies—public policy will not permit a contractual provision to limit the remedy of the buyer to a capped damage claim. Rather, the buyer is free to press a claim for rescission or for full compensatory damages. By this balance, I attempt to give fair and efficient recognition to the competing public policies served by contractual freedom and by the law of fraud."); *cf.* R&R Capital, LLC v. Buck & Doe Run Valley Farms, LLC, Civ. A. No. 3803–CC, 2008 WL 3846318, at *8 (Del. Ch. Aug. 19, 2008) (concluding that parties can contractually eliminate their right to petition for judicial dissolution based not only on freedom of contract principles and an analysis of the statutory language, but also based on a consideration of public policy arguments).

[96] *Cf.* RULLCA § 409 cmt. ("The obligation of good faith and fair dealing is not a fiduciary duty, does not command altruism or self-abnegation, and does not prevent a partner from acting in the partner's own self-interest. . . . To the contrary . . . the obligation should be used only to protect agreed-upon arrangements from conduct that is manifestly beyond what a reasonable person could have contemplated when the arrangements were made.").

est? Merely stating that expulsion generally is within the scope of the member's contractual rights begs the question—did the member bargain for the contractual right to expel for this opportunistic purpose? This is the interpretative question that the implied covenant is designed to answer. Broadly stating that the mere exercise of contractual rights cannot constitute a breach of the covenant misleadingly suggests that the covenant has no role in these circumstances because the contract generally states that expulsion is permissible.

In contrast to Delaware's approach, the Uniform Acts are somewhat more reserved in the freedom afforded to parties to alter their fiduciary duties. In brief, ULLCA provides that the parties may (1) alter, but not eliminate, the fiduciary duty of loyalty, if not manifestly unreasonable; (2) alter, but not eliminate, the fiduciary duty of care, if the duty is not "unreasonably reduce[d]"; and (3) alter, but not eliminate, the obligation of good faith and fair dealing by prescribing the standards by which to measure whether the obligation has been met, if the standards are not manifestly unreasonable.[97] RULLCA provides, in a somewhat cumbersome manner, that the parties may, subject to an "if not manifestly unreasonable" restriction: (1) alter or eliminate the fiduciary duty of loyalty; (2) alter, but not eliminate, the fiduciary duty of care, except that it is impermissible to authorize intentional misconduct or a knowing violation of law; and (3) alter, but not eliminate, the implied contractual obligation of good faith and fair dealing by prescribing the standards by which to measure whether the obligation has been met. Because RULLCA "uncabins" fiduciary duty, it also provides that any "other" fiduciary duty may be altered, including eliminating particular aspects of that duty.[98]

Even in jurisdictions that allow contract to modify or eliminate fiduciary duties, courts may differ in how broadly or narrowly they are willing to construe a contract that purports to displace such duties. Unless a contract clearly and explicitly permits some type of conduct—even arguably inequitable conduct—to occur, there is frequently room for a court to say that the contract does not unambiguously speak to the situation and that fiduciary duty is not displaced. Whether a court construes a contract broadly or narrowly is likely based, at least in part, on the extent of the court's willingness to give up its policing powers in deference to the private arrangements of the parties.

---

[97] *See* ULLCA § 103(b)(2)–(4).
[98] *See* RULLCA § 110(c), (d).

For example, in *Fisk Ventures, LLC v. Segal*,[99] Genitrix, LLC (a Delaware LLC) was attempting to raise money from investors. Dr. Andrew Segal owned 55% of the Class A membership interests. H. Fisk Johnson owned a sizable portion of the Class B membership interests along with Fisk Ventures, LLC and Stephen Rose. The Class B members had contracted for a put right that allowed them to force the company to purchase their membership interests at any time at a price determined by an independent appraisal. The put, if exercised, would subrogate senior claims of new investors to the company's obligation to pay the purchase price. As a result, Segal believed that the put right would scare off potential investors (investors would not want to contribute money to an LLC just to watch their money get paid to the Class B members who had exercised their put rights), and he asked the Class B members on several occasions to suspend the right. The Class B investors refused to do so.

Efforts to raise money from investors failed. By the summer of 2007, Genitrix had run out of money. Fisk Ventures filed a lawsuit seeking the dissolution of Genitrix. Segal counterclaimed against Fisk Ventures and filed third-party claims against Johnson, Rose, and others. He claimed that the counterclaim/third-party defendants breached their duties to Segal and to the company by, among other actions, failing to waive their put right.[100]

The court dismissed Segal's breach of fiduciary duty claim primarily because the court believed that the members had eliminated fiduciary duties by contract. According to the court, the LLC agreement eliminated fiduciary duties by stating that "members have no duties other than those expressly articulated in the Agreement," and that "[b]ecause the Agreement does not expressly articulate fiduciary obligations, they are eliminated." This conclusion, however, seems questionable. The LLC agreement stated that members were still liable for their gross negligence, fraud, or intentional misconduct. This would appear to retain some vestige of fiduciary duty; indeed, fiduciary duty in Delaware is often measured by gross negligence. Second, the language cited by the court that purportedly eliminated fiduciary duties spoke of duties owed by members to members. It did not address duties owed by members to the company. Thus, even if the court's interpretation were correct, it would seem that Segal's claim of breach of fiduciary duty to the company should have survived.

Perhaps the court simply believed that the Class B members were being sued for nothing more than asserting (or failing to relin-

---

[99] Civ. A. No. 3017–CC, 2008 WL 1961156 (Del. Ch. May 7, 2008).

[100] *See id.* at *1–2, 4, 6.

quish) the contractual rights for which they negotiated. In other words, perhaps the court believed that there just weren't sufficient allegations of gross negligence, fraud, or intentional misconduct. Indeed, this was the court's second rationale for dismissing the breach of fiduciary duty claim. Nevertheless, the court gave a first rationale based on contractual language, and this first rationale seems problematic in too quickly concluding that fiduciary duties were eliminated.[101]

The Tennessee decision of *Anderson v. Wilder*[102] is a nice contrast to *Fisk Ventures*. In *Anderson*, the operating agreement of FuturePoint Administrative Services, LLC permitted expulsion of a member (with or without cause) upon a majority vote of the members, and it required a buyout of the expelled member's interest. On September 10, 2001, two outside offers to purchase ownership units at $250 per unit were discussed by the members. Four days later, plaintiffs were expelled from the LLC by the defendants pursuant to a majority vote of the members. Under the operating agreement, the plaintiffs' ownership units were purchased by the defendants for $150 per unit. Shortly thereafter, the defendants sold ownership units to a third party for $250 per unit. As one plaintiff alleged, the intent was to "expel us at a low price and sell the interests taken at a high price."

The plaintiffs sued, alleging breach of fiduciary duty and breach of the duty of good faith and fair dealing. Defendants moved for summary judgment, arguing that the expulsion and the $150 per unit buyout were expressly permitted under the operating agreement.[103] Given that the parties had agreed to an expulsion procedure, and given that the defendants had complied with that procedure, isn't the defendants' position correct? Once again, the issue turns on the court's construction of the agreement between the parties. Did the agreement clearly manifest an intention to permit ex-

---

[101] *See id.* at *9, 11. The court also dismissed Segal's breach of the implied covenant of good faith and fair dealing claim. The claim was not dismissed on the ground of contractual elimination in the LLC agreement because DLLCA does not permit contractual elimination of the covenant. Instead, the claim was dismissed because the court believed that the members had specifically contracted for the Class B members to have the right to veto Segal's proposals. (The LLC agreement provided that a Board of Member Representatives would manage the company, and the Class B members appointed three of the five board members.) The members' intent, in other words, was clear—Segal did not have the right to unilaterally make decisions about financing for the company, and asserting that he did have such a right was contrary to the intent of the parties. The court simply believed that everything the Class B members did was "within the bounds of rights granted by the LLC agreement" and was not, therefore, in violation of the spirit of the parties' bargain. *See id.* at *2, 11.

[102] No. E2003–00460–COA–R3–CV, 2003 WL 22768666 (Tenn. Ct. App. Nov. 21, 2003).

[103] *See id.* at *1–2, 8.

pulsion for any reason—displacing any related fiduciary duty challenges—or was it meant to have a narrower application?

On appeal, the *Anderson* court concluded that "there exists a genuine issue of material fact regarding whether the Defendants' actions in expelling the minority Plaintiffs were taken in good faith, as required by the LLC Act, or whether they expelled Plaintiffs solely in order to force the acquisition of their membership units at a price of $150.00 in order to sell them at $250.00 per unit, in violation of their fiduciary duty."[104] In effect, the court did not believe that the agreement was intended to permit expulsion for any reason; instead, the court construed the agreement to permit expulsion in various circumstances, but not for the purpose of stealing the value of a member's interest. This approach seems sensible; after all, it is hard to believe that the parties intended their agreement to permit taking opportunistic advantage of one another. In short, a court should not draw the conclusion that the parties intended to permit opportunism and to displace fiduciary duty in all circumstances unless that intent is explicitly conveyed in the agreement (e.g., expulsions are permitted "for any reason, with or without cause, and regardless of whether the reason is viewed as unfair, opportunistic, or otherwise inequitable to the expelled member").

Notice that the concepts of fiduciary duty and the implied covenant overlap here. If a party acts for a particular purpose, and if the parties' agreement does not explicitly permit conduct for that purpose, then two conclusions can be reached. First, a court may determine that the background fiduciary duties have not been displaced by agreement because the contract does not permit conduct for this purpose. Thus, the conduct may be a breach of fiduciary duty. Second, because the contract does not permit conduct for this purpose, the conduct could be viewed as a breach of contract— specifically as a breach of the implied contractual covenant of good faith. In *Anderson*, for example, the spirit of the parties' bargain was likely that expulsions with accompanying buyouts were permissible, but not for the purpose of stealing from a fellow member.

Despite the fact that the concepts of fiduciary duty and the implied covenant overlap, it is important to recognize them as distinct doctrines. For one reason, a fiduciary duty claim is generally better for most plaintiffs, particularly because it is a tort with the possibility of punitive damages. In addition, a jurisdiction such as Delaware may allow the parties' agreement to eliminate fiduciary duties, but not the implied covenant. In such circumstances, the im-

---

[104] *Id.* at *10.

plied covenant may be the only remaining doctrinal "hook" for the plaintiff.

H. Ownership Interests and Transferability

An ownership interest in an LLC entitles a member to (1) the right to receive distributions and to share in the profits and losses of the venture (financial rights), and (2) the right to participate in the management and control of the business (management rights). Like partnerships, all LLC statutes provide that a transfer of an LLC ownership interest conveys a member's financial rights, but not his management rights.[105] Indeed, the statutes usually specify that a transferee can acquire a member's management rights only with the consent of the nontransferring members.[106] Unlike a shareholder but like a partner, therefore, an LLC member cannot unilaterally transfer his full ownership interest (i.e., both his financial and management rights) to an outsider. Ordinarily, however, this restriction on transferability is simply a default rule that the parties can modify to suit their needs.

Are restrictions on the transferability of ownership interests appropriate in the LLC setting? In privately held businesses, owners often work closely with one another. As a result, they may prefer to select their own co-owners and to prevent the introduction of unwanted persons. In addition, LLC members may have agency authority to bind the firm.[107] Control over the admission of new members, therefore, may be desirable. On the other hand, unlike in a general partnership, LLC owners are not personally liable for the debts of the venture that are caused by the conduct of their fellow owners.[108] To this extent, there is less of a need to be concerned about the admission of new owners. Further, if an LLC is manager-managed with passive members, members may have less reason to care who their fellow members are. Finally, under the check-the-

---

[105] *See, e.g.,* DLLCA §§ 18–702, 18–704; ULLCA §§ 101(6), 501–503; RULLCA §§ 102(21), 501–502. The transfer of all of a member's financial rights can result in the dissociation of the member. *See, e.g.,* DLLCA § 18–702(b)(3); ULLCA §§ 601(3), 601(5)(ii), 603(b)(1); RULLCA §§ 602(4)(B), 603(a). The rationale for this result is presumably that the remaining members may not want a fellow member with management (including inspection) rights who is no longer financially motivated to act in the venture's best interest.

[106] *See, e.g.,* DLLCA §§ 18–702(a), 18–704(a); ULLCA § 503(a), (d); *cf.* RULLCA § 401(d) (discussing the admission of members). *But see* RULLCA § 502 cmt. ("However, consistent with current law, a member may transfer governance rights to another member without obtaining consent from the other members. Thus, this Act does not itself protect members from control shifts that result from transfers among members (as distinguished from transfers to non-members who seek thereby to become members).").

[107] *See* Chapter 16(C)(1)–(2).

[108] *See* Chapter 16(F).

box regulations, mandatory restrictions on transferability are no longer needed to help avoid a corporation tax classification.

Most LLC statutes provide a charging order remedy that creditors can use against a member's interest.[109]   In *Herring v. Keasler*,[110] the court prevented a judgment creditor plaintiff from seizing and selling defendant's LLC membership interests pursuant to a writ of execution. The trial court had denied defendant's request to seize and sell the LLC interests, and had instead granted a charging order.[111] The Court of Appeals affirmed:

> Generally, a trial court
>
> may order any property, whether subject or not to be sold under execution (except the homestead and personal property exemptions of the judgment debtor), in the hands of the judgment debtor or of any other person, or due to the judgment debtor, to be applied towards the satisfaction of [a] judgment.
>
> N.C.G.S. § 1–362 (2001). North Carolina General Statutes § 57C–5–03, however, provides that with respect to a judgment debtor's membership interest in a limited liability company, a trial court "may charge the membership interest of the member with payment of the unsatisfied amount of the judgment with interest." This "charge" entitles the judgment creditor "to receive ... the distributions and allocations to which the [judgment debtor] would be entitled." N.C.G.S. § 57C–5–02 (2001). The "charge" "does not dissolve the limited liability company or entitle the [judgment creditor] to become or exercise any rights of a member." *Id.* . . .
>
> In this case, despite Plaintiff's attempts to have Defendant's membership interests in the LLCs seized and sold, his only remedy is to have those interests charged with payment of the judgment under N.C.Gen.Stat. § 57C–5–03. Accordingly, the trial court did not err in ordering that the judgment be satisfied through the application of the distributions and allocations of Defendant's membership interests in the LLCs and

---

[109] *See, e.g.*, DLLCA § 18–703; ULLCA § 504; RULLCA § 503.

[110] 563 S.E.2d 614 (N.C. Ct. App. 2002).

[111] *See id.* at 615 ("With respect to the charging order, the trial court directed: Defendant's membership interests in the LLCs to be charged with payment of the judgment, plus interest; the LLCs to deliver to Plaintiff any distributions and allocations that Defendant would be entitled to receive on account of his membership interests in the LLCs; Defendant to deliver to Plaintiff any allocations and distributions he would receive; and Plaintiff to not obtain any rights in the LLCs, except as those of an assignee and under the respective operating agreement.").

in denying Plaintiff's motion to have Defendant's membership interests seized and sold.[112]

As *Herring* illustrates, a charging order procedure is generally understood to trump the state's general execution statute. Indeed, despite the facts that (1) an LLC ownership interest is personal property, and (2) non-exempt personal property is typically subject to execution, allowing a judgment creditor to involuntarily seize and sell a debtor-member's ownership interest would be undesirable, as it would suggest that the buyer is now a full-fledged member with governance rights. Such a result would be contrary to the closely held nature of the LLC, as the remaining members did not consent to the admission of a new owner.

In *Olmstead v. Federal Trade Commission*,[113] however, the Supreme Court of Florida held that, in a single-member LLC, the statutory charging order procedure did not preclude a creditor from executing on an ownership interest. The court acknowledged that a charging order provision is generally designed to preserve a nondebtor member's right to block the admission of a new member (and the exercise of accompanying management rights), but it implied that this right was not implicated when the debtor was the sole member of the LLC. The court was particularly influenced by the fact that the Florida LLC statute did not indicate that a charging order was a creditor's exclusive remedy, while the Florida general partnership and limited partnership statutes did so provide. Although the court appeared to limit its holding to disputes involving a single-member LLC, the dissent noted that the court's emphasis on the lack of exclusivity language in the statute would seem to extend its holding to multi-member LLCs.[114]

I. Dissociation and Dissolution

LLC statutes typically state that a member dissociates from a venture upon the occurrence of certain specified acts—e.g., withdrawal, resignation, death, or bankruptcy.[115] When a member dissociates from a member-managed firm, does he retain the right to participate in management? What happens to the agency powers of a dissociated member? Many LLC statutes do not answer these

---

[112] *Id.* at 615–16 (citation omitted).

[113] 44 So. 3d 76 (Fla. 2010).

[114] *See id.* at 78, 81–82; *id.* at 84 (Lewis, J., dissenting). It is worth noting that the Delaware and Uniform LLC Acts explicitly provide that a charging order is a creditor's exclusive remedy. *See* DLLCA § 18–703(d); ULLCA § 504(e); RULLCA § 503(g).

[115] *See, e.g.,* ULLCA § 601; RULLCA § 602. Delaware has no dissociation provision other than § 18–603, which states that a member may not resign from an LLC prior to dissolution unless an LLC agreement provides otherwise.

questions, but the Uniform Acts do. Under ULLCA, for example, § 603(b) indicates that a member's right to participate in management terminates upon dissociation, except for the purpose of winding up the LLC's business. Under § 703, a dissociated member still has apparent authority agency power to bind the LLC in certain circumstances for two years after dissociation. Section 704 mitigates this post-dissociation agency power by allowing the member or the LLC itself to file a statement of dissociation, which gives constructive notice to the world of the member's dissociation ninety days after filing. Such constructive notice terminates the member's agency power under § 703(3). Section 803(a) provides that a member who has not wrongfully dissociated may participate in the winding up of the LLC's business.[116]

With respect to dissolution, LLC statutes generally include both voluntary and involuntary dissolution provisions. For example, dissolution is often triggered by the expiration of the venture's term, the consent of all or a specified percentage of the members, or a judicial decree based upon fraud, oppression, or other specified grounds.[117]

Until relatively recently, member dissociation usually resulted in (1) a buyout of the dissociating member's ownership interest, or (2) dissolution of the LLC. If dissolution did not occur because the requisite percentage of the remaining members voted to continue the venture, then a buyout was required. If dissolution occurred, however, the dissociating member would receive his share of the company's dissolution value, and a buyout was no longer needed. As a default matter, therefore, an LLC member could easily exit the venture with the value of his capital, either through a buyout or through receipt of his proportionate share of the company's dissolution value.

---

[116] There is a peculiarity with the operation of ULLCA §§ 603, 703, and 803. Assume that a member rightfully dissociates without causing dissolution. Ten years pass. Under §§ 603 and 703, the dissociated member has no right to participate in management and no agency power. The LLC then dissolves. Under § 803, does the long-gone (and possibly fully bought-out) LLC member spring back into a management role for the purposes of winding up? The statute seems to indicate as much, although this would be an odd result.

RULLCA § 603 conveys that a member's dissociation ends his right to participate in the management of the company and converts his status to "transferee." Because RULLCA does not address the agency powers of members and managers, see notes 29–30 and accompanying text, it has no provisions addressing the agency powers of a dissociated member. Section 702 indicates that a dissolved LLC shall wind up its activities. This suggests that winding up is a task entrusted to the management of the LLC. Thus, under RULLCA, a dissociated member (who no longer has the right to participate in management) cannot take part in the winding up of the venture.

[117] See, e.g., DLLCA §§ 18–801, 18–802; ULLCA § 801; RULLCA § 701.

With the passage of the check-the-box regulations, there was no longer a tax-driven need for member dissociation to trigger a dissolution of the LLC.[118] As a result, many states curtailed the buyout and dissolution rights that had previously arisen upon the dissociation of a member. Although statutes today continue to provide other triggers of dissolution, the easy exit and accompanying liquidity provided by dissociation-triggered buyouts and dissolution has been eliminated in many jurisdictions.[119]

Although one could attempt to justify the curbing of buyout and dissolution rights on the ground that "locking-in" capital helps to facilitate business development, the movement to restrict exit rights appears to have been motivated primarily by a desire to make the family-owned LLC an attractive business structure for estate and gift tax purposes. To minimize the tax value of an ownership interest in a closely held business, an investor will frequently claim that the value of his ownership position should be reduced to reflect (1) that the interest is difficult to liquidate, and (2) that purchasers will generally pay less for illiquid positions. This well-accepted "marketability discount" is premised on empirical evidence indicating that investors will "extract a high discount relative to actively traded securities for stocks or other investment interests that lack [a]

---

[118] In other words, there was no longer a need to combat a continuity of life finding under the Kintner regulations. *See* Chapter 16(A).

[119] *See, e.g.*, ALA. CODE § 10–12–30(b), (c) (1995) (providing for a buyout upon withdrawal); *id.* § 10–12–30 (1998) (eliminating the buyout right upon withdrawal); *id.* cmt. ("This section makes a major change in the limited liability company law by providing that the company is not obligated to buy the interest of a withdrawing member unless the articles or the operating agreement provide for a buyout. This reverses the previous rule, which provided for a buyout and provided terms for the buyout if the operating agreement did not have such terms."); *id.* §§ 10–12–36, 10–12–37 (1995) (providing for dissolution upon "an event of dissociation of a member," and defining those events to include, among others, withdrawal, death, and bankruptcy); *id.* § 10–12–37 (1998) (eliminating the dissolution upon dissociation of a member ground); *id.* cmt. ("This section has been amended to eliminate the rule that a limited liability company will dissolve upon the withdrawal of a member. Unless the articles of organization or the operating agreement provide otherwise, the withdrawal of a member has no effect on the company.").
A number of states do not expressly eliminate the right to a buyout upon withdrawal or other dissociation, but they do restrict a member's ability to withdraw before the dissolution of the LLC. These statutes, therefore, have the same effect of "locking-in" a minority member for the duration of the venture. *See, e.g.*, DLLCA §§ 18–603, 18–604 (providing that, "upon resignation any resigning member is entitled to receive . . . the fair value of such member's [LLC] interest," but also stating that "unless [an LLC] agreement provides otherwise, a member may not resign from [an LLC] prior to the dissolution and winding up of the [LLC]").
Some states continue to provide buyout rights when a member withdraws or otherwise dissociates from an LLC. *See, e.g.*, 15 PA. CONS. STAT. § 8933 (granting a member a right to be bought out at "fair value" upon dissociation); ULLCA §§ 603, 701 (granting a member a right to be bought out at "fair value" upon dissociation, and indicating that the timing of the buyout will vary based upon the "at will" or "term" status of the LLC at issue).

high degree of liquidity."[120] To qualify for a marketability discount in a family-owned LLC, however, state law must restrict an owner's ability to cash out of a business through withdrawal or dissolution. As a result, and with the blessing of estate tax planners, many jurisdictions amended their LLC statutes to restrict a member's ability to liquidate his ownership position.[121] While perhaps accomplishing an estate tax goal, the elimination of default exit rights in many jurisdictions leaves minority members vulnerable to oppressive majority actions, as the minority can no longer easily exit the venture with the value of his investment.

The Wyoming decision of *Lieberman v. Wyoming.com LLC*[122] illustrates the restrictions on exit rights that now exist in many LLC statutes. Lieberman was a member of Wyoming.com LLC. After being terminated as vice-president, Lieberman asserted that he had been expelled. He presented the LLC and its members with a formal notice of withdrawal, but the parties could not agree on the financial consequences of withdrawal. Lieberman demanded $400,000, which he claimed was his share of the current value of the company. The remaining members offered the return of Lieberman's $20,000 capital contribution.

The parties filed a petition for declaratory judgment. The district court, via summary judgment, ordered a buyout of Lieberman's ownership interest at its capital account value as of the date of his withdrawal. (Lieberman's capital account value was negative.) The Supreme Court reversed:

> The Wyoming LLC Act contains no provision relating to the fate of a member's equity interest upon the member's dissociation. Thus, it was entirely up to the members of Wyoming.com to contractually provide for terms of dissociation. Upon careful review of all the agreements entered into by the parties regarding Wyoming.com, we determine that the agreements contain no provision regarding the equity interest of a dissociating member. Since we can find no provision mandating a different result, Lieberman retains his equity interest. Lieberman is under no obligation to sell his equity interest, and Wyoming.com is under no obligation to buy Lieberman's equity interest.[123]

---

[120] SHANNON P. PRATT ET AL., VALUING A BUSINESS: THE ANALYSIS AND APPRAISAL OF CLOSELY HELD COMPANIES 333 (3d ed. 1996).

[121] *See* note 119 and accompanying text. *See generally* Douglas K. Moll, *Minority Oppression & The Limited Liability Company: Learning (or Not) From Close Corporation History*, 40 WAKE FOREST L. REV. 883, 931–40 (2005) (discussing the statutory changes).

[122] 82 P.3d 274 (Wyo. 2004).

[123] *See id.* at 275–77.

Understanding the court's conclusion requires an analysis of the Wyoming dissociation and dissolution provisions. Under the Wyoming LLC statute at the time, dissociation did not trigger a buyout of the member's interest. Dissociation did trigger dissolution of the LLC, but the statute allowed for the avoidance of dissolution if all of the remaining members consented to the continuation of the LLC under a provision in the articles. If continuation occurred, there was no statutory requirement for a buyout. Lieberman's withdrawal did not result in dissolution because the remaining members voted to continue the LLC pursuant to a provision in the Articles of Organization.[124] Thus, Lieberman's dissociation neither resulted in a buyout of his interest nor in the dissolution of the venture.

Do you think Lieberman was happy with the result of this decision? On the one hand, the district court apparently ruled that Lieberman no longer had an equity interest in the company. That is, the district court concluded that Lieberman was entitled to the balance of his capital account (which was negative) in return for his equity interest. The end result of the district court's ruling, therefore, was that Lieberman lost his ownership interest completely and received nothing in return. To the extent that the Supreme Court gave him his ownership interest back, Lieberman was probably "happy" with the result.

On the other hand, the majority's ruling gave the remaining members all of the leverage in the dispute. They had no obligation to buy Lieberman's interest and, because of his withdrawal, Lieberman was no longer a member (and presumably no longer had the rights of a member). His capital was tied up in the LLC for as long as the remaining members saw fit, and he had no say in the management of the business. In effect, he was frozen out of the venture. To this extent, it is hard to see how Lieberman could have been truly happy with the result of this litigation. After all, he alleged that he was entitled to $400,000 for his ownership interest. As a result of the court's ruling, he has his ownership interest, but he has no ability to get any value from it.[125]

If the parties had explicitly considered the rights of dissociated members at the time they formed the venture, they might very well have agreed that a buyout was required in the event that dissocia-

---

[124] See Lieberman v. Wyoming.com LLC, 11 P.3d 353, 357–58 (Wyo. 2000).

[125] It should be noted that, in an earlier decision, the Supreme Court of Wyoming did rule that Lieberman was entitled to the return of his $20,000 initial capital contribution. See id. at 358. Given that Lieberman believed that his contribution had appreciated to $400,000 in value, the receipt of $20,000 was likely of little consolation.

tion did not result in the dissolution of the LLC. Otherwise, a member's investment could be tied up in the LLC until the other members saw fit to release it. Indeed, on remand from an earlier ruling, all of the members seemed to believe that Lieberman was entitled to a buyout of his equity interest upon withdrawal, as the LLC requested the district court to determine how Lieberman's interest should be valued.[126] But there are so many questions related to a buyout (a buyout as of when? a buyout at what price? a buyout paid immediately or over time? a buyout with discounts or not?) that one can sympathize with the majority's reluctance to provide this remedy in the absence of statutory authorization or an explicit agreement between the parties.

A strong dissent in *Lieberman* argued that because the articles allowed the remaining members to continue the business after a member's withdrawal, the remaining members must have intended to compensate the withdrawing member for his interest in some manner. If such compensation were not required, the dissent observed that a majority member could oppress a minority member by expelling him from the LLC and by refusing to negotiate for a buyout of the expelled member's interest. In the dissent's view, therefore, a member's withdrawal required a buyout of his interest "at what he would have received had the business been dissolved on the day he terminated his membership in the LLC." The dissent acknowledged, however, that "fair market value . . . would be a reasonable alternative estimate of the departing member's share."[127]

Is the dissent's position a radical one? It is to the extent that there was no statutory support for a dissociation buyout or even for a dissolution-for-oppression remedy. Further, the dissent was, effectively, writing a buyout provision that the parties neglected, for good or bad reasons, to draft themselves. On the other hand, the dissent seemed sensitive to the potential for oppression that the court's ruling created, as the majority opinion drew no distinction between expulsion and withdrawal as dissociation events. Indeed, as the dissent noted, a majority member who unjustifiably expelled a minority member from the venture may be able to continue the LLC's business while refusing to buy out the terminated member.

The dissent's position hearkens back to closely held corporation precedents like *Donahue* and *Wilkes*.[128] Just as in those decisions, the dissent may simply be creating a common-law remedy to deal with the problem of freezeouts. Of course, in *Donahue* and *Wilkes*, the oppression doctrine was premised on a breach of fiduciary duty

---

[126] *See Lieberman*, 82 P.3d at 277.

[127] *See id.* at 283–85 (Kite, J., dissenting).

[128] *See* Chapter 8(F)(2).

owed between shareholders, but courts have analogized to those precedents in disputes between LLC members.[129] Moreover, the notion of a fiduciary duty owed between LLC members is an explicit part of many LLC statutes.[130] Thus, the dissent's position is arguably consistent with *Donahue* and its progeny.[131]

How would *Lieberman* have been resolved under the Delaware and Uniform Acts? DLLCA § 18–603 states that a member may not resign from an LLC prior to dissolution unless an LLC agreement provides otherwise. Thus, Lieberman may not have been able to withdraw if such a right wasn't provided in the operating agreement. Other than § 18–603, DLLCA seems to have no dissociation provision.

Pursuant to DLLCA § 18–101(7), an LLC agreement may be oral. When Lieberman served his notice of withdrawal and the other members accepted Lieberman's withdrawal, this might have constituted an LLC agreement that allowed Lieberman to resign under § 18–603. If so, § 18–604 would allow Lieberman to receive any distribution that the LLC agreement provided. If the LLC agreement were silent, Lieberman would be entitled to receive, "within a reasonable time after resignation, the fair value of such member's limited liability company interest as of the date of resignation based upon such member's right to share in distributions from the limited liability company." This provision would make Lieberman very happy, but he could get to it only if he had the right to withdraw or resign under § 18–603.

Significantly, Lieberman would have no right to dissolve the LLC. DLLCA § 18–801(a) provides for dissolution rights as specified in an LLC agreement, upon member consent, and in circumstances not applicable to the dispute. DLLCA § 18–801(b) makes clear that Lieberman's withdrawal (or resignation or expulsion), if permitted, would not result in the dissolution of the LLC. DLLCA § 18–802 provides for judicial dissolution under certain circumstances, but it does not seem applicable to Lieberman's situation.

---

[129] *See, e.g., Anderson v. Wilder*, No. E2003–00460–COA–R3–CV, 2003 WL 22768666, at *4–6 (Tenn. Ct. App. Nov. 21, 2003) (concluding that a majority member of an LLC did owe a fiduciary duty to a minority member by relying on partnership and closely held corporation precedents).

[130] *See, e.g.,* ULLCA § 409(a); RULLCA § 409(a).

[131] Keep in mind, however, that the dissent would seem to allow a buyout whenever dissociation did not result in dissolution, even in the absence of oppression or breach of fiduciary duty. This is far more radical than *Donahue* and other oppression precedents, which require some showing of oppression or breach of fiduciary duty before remedies are provided. *See* Chapter 8(F)(2).

With respect to the Uniform Acts, ULLCA borrows heavily from partnership concepts and specifies different consequences depending upon whether the LLC is an "at-will company" or a "term company."[132]   Assuming that Wyoming.com LLC was an at-will company, Lieberman's withdrawal would constitute an event of dissociation under § 601(1). Under § 602(b), Lieberman's withdrawal would not be wrongful. Under § 603(a)(1) and § 701(a)(1), the LLC would have to purchase Lieberman's interest at its "fair value determined as of the date of the member's dissociation." Under § 801, Lieberman's withdrawal would not result in the dissolution of the company.[133]

If the LLC were a term company, Lieberman's withdrawal would still constitute an event of dissociation, but it would likely be wrongful.[134]   Under § 602(c), Lieberman would be liable for any damages caused by the wrongful dissociation. Assuming that the company did not "dissolve and wind up its business on or before the expiration of its specified term," Lieberman would be entitled under § 603(a) to have his interest purchased "on the date of the expiration of the term specified at the time of the member's dissociation." (Notice that, in contrast to a buyout in an at-will company, a term company buyout occurs only at the expiration of the term.) Under § 701(a)(2), the purchase price would be "fair value determined as of the date of the expiration of the specified term that existed on the date of the member's dissociation if the expiration of the specified term does not result in a dissolution and winding up of the company's business under Section 801." Pursuant to § 801, Lieberman's withdrawal, by itself, would not result in the dissolution of the company, but he could argue for judicial dissolution under § 801(4) or (5) if any of those grounds (e.g., oppressive conduct) were present.[135]

In short, under the partnership concepts of ULLCA, Lieberman's interest will be bought out regardless of whether the LLC is

---

[132] *See* ULLCA § 101(2), (19).

[133] ULLCA takes an interesting hybrid approach to restricting exit rights in the LLC. An easy dissolution right may be problematic because of the instability that it injects into the business form and the freezeout possibilities that it raises (e.g., a wealthy member may dissolve and purchase the business for himself without the other member(s)). Buyout rights may pose less difficulties. Thus, a case could be made for eliminating easy dissolution rights but preserving buyout rights. This is the choice that ULLCA has made—a member of an at-will LLC is entitled to a buyout upon withdrawal, but he has no right to compel the dissolution of the company. *See* ULLCA §§ 603, 701, 801.

[134] *See id.* §§ 601(1), 602(b).

[135] ULLCA § 801(4) is available to members or dissociated members. Section 801(5) is only available to transferees, but § 603(b)(1) indicates that a dissociated member "ceases to be a member and is treated the same as a transferee of a member."

at-will or term. The buyout may be delayed for some time, however, in a term LLC.

Under RULLCA § 601(a) and § 602(1), Lieberman's withdrawal would likely be considered a dissociation by express will. Such a dissociation would be considered wrongful under § 601(b) because it occurred before the termination of the LLC. Under § 601(c), a wrongful withdrawal would subject Lieberman to liability to the LLC and to the other members for any damages caused by the dissociation.

Pursuant to § 603, Lieberman's dissociation would end his right to participate in the management of the company (as well as his fiduciary duties), and he would have the status of a transferee. Under § 701, Lieberman's withdrawal, by itself, would not result in the dissolution of the company, but if Lieberman believed that his termination rose to the level of oppressive conduct, he could bring an action for judicial dissolution of the company.[136] Finally, § 404 makes clear that Lieberman's dissociation would not entitle him to a distribution.[137] Absent a contrary provision in the operating agreement, therefore, a dissociation by express will of a member under RULLCA will not result in the member receiving any money (assuming that the company is not dissolving). In fact, it will be considered a wrongful dissociation that subjects the member to damages.

As previously mentioned, LLC statutes in many jurisdictions allow a member to petition for involuntary dissolution on various grounds.[138] For example, ULLCA § 801(4) allows a court to decree dissolution when (a) the economic purpose of the company is likely to be unreasonably frustrated; (b) another member has engaged in conduct that makes it not reasonably practicable to carry on the company's business with that member; (c) it is not otherwise reasonably practicable to carry on the company's business in conformity with the articles or the operating agreement; or (d) those in control of the company are acting in a manner that is illegal, oppressive, fraudulent, or unfairly prejudicial to the petitioner.

---

[136] Under RULLCA, only a "member" may bring an action for oppressive conduct. As a consequence, Lieberman would not want to dissociate, as that would end his "member" status under § 603. As mentioned, the comparable provision under ULLCA is available to both members and dissociated members. *See* note 135.

[137] Indeed, § 404(b) states that a person has the right to a distribution before the dissolution and winding up of the company only if the company decides to make an interim distribution.

[138] *See, e.g.*, DLLCA § 18–802; ULLCA § 801; RULLCA § 701.

In *Dunbar Group, LLC v. Tignor*,[139] the court addressed the somewhat murky dissolution ground of "not reasonably practicable" to carry on in conformity with the LLC's governing documents. Xpert was an LLC with two 50% members—The Dunbar Group, LLC and Archie Tignor. Dunbar and Tignor were the sole managers of Xpert. Edward Robertson was the sole member and manager of Dunbar.

Disputes arose between Robertson and Tignor over matters primarily related to the management and disbursement of Xpert's assets. Dunbar filed an amended bill of complaint against Tignor requesting, among other items, the entry of an order "expelling and dissociating Tignor as a member of Xpert pursuant to Virginia Code § 13.1–1040.1(5) [which provides grounds for judicial expulsion]." Dunbar alleged that Tignor engaged in "numerous acts of misconduct as a member and manager of Xpert." Tignor filed a separate "Application for Judicial Dissolution" against Dunbar and Xpert. Tignor requested, among other things, the dissolution of Xpert under Code § 13.1–1047 on the ground that "it is not reasonably practicable to carry on the business of [Xpert] in conformity with the Articles of Organization and [the] Operating Agreement."[140]

The Chancellor found that Tignor had engaged in various acts of misconduct which violated § 13.1–1040.1(5). As a result, the Chancellor ordered that Tignor be "immediately expelled as an active member of Xpert." The Chancellor also ordered that Robertson "shall continue to operate Xpert" until Xpert's contract with Samsung terminated, at which point Xpert would be dissolved.[141]

Dunbar appealed the portion of the order providing for dissolution. It argued that "the record fail[ed] to show that after the expulsion of Tignor as a member of Xpert, it would not be reasonably practicable to carry on Xpert's business." The court agreed: "Although Tignor's actions in those capacities [as a member and manager of Xpert] had created numerous problems in the operation of Xpert, his expulsion as a member changed his role from one of an active participant in the management of Xpert to the more passive role of an investor in the company. The record fails to show that after this change in the daily management of Xpert, it would not be reasonably practicable for Xpert to carry on its business pursuant to its operating authority." Moreover, the court observed that the

---

[139] 593 S.E.2d 216 (Va. 2004).

[140] Why was Tignor seeking dissolution? Because of the disagreements between Robertson and Tignor, Tignor may have wanted to liquidate his investment and to separate from Dunbar and Robertson. Presumably, Tignor had no right to a buyout under the operating agreement or the Virginia LLC statute; thus, dissolution was probably the only option for liquidating his interest.

[141] *See id.* at 216–18.

Chancellor's directive for Xpert to continue operating until the termination of its Samsung contract "indicate[d] that he [the Chancellor] concluded that Tignor's expulsion from Xpert would make it reasonably practicable for Xpert to continue to operate for an extended period of time." The court affirmed the part of the Chancellor's judgment expelling Tignor as a member of Xpert, but reversed the part of the judgment ordering the dissolution of Xpert.[142]

Given that Robertson and Tignor clearly had serious problems with one another, why did the court decline to order dissolution? As mentioned, Tignor requested dissolution on the ground that "it is not reasonably practicable to carry on the business of [Xpert] in conformity with the Articles of Organization and [the] Operating Agreement."[143] Serious disagreement between the members, however, does not necessarily meet the standard. Even with discord, in other words, it may still be reasonably practicable to carry on the business. Dunbar (not Tignor) "conducted the daily operations of the company"; thus, Tignor's expulsion arguably did not substantially affect the operation of the business. Moreover, the lower court's order of operation (until the Samsung contract terminated) followed by dissolution recognized that it was reasonably practicable for Xpert to continue to operate for an extended period of time, even with Tignor's expulsion.

What circumstances would suggest that it is not reasonably practicable to carry on the business in conformity with the governing documents? The Delaware courts have provided some guidance. In *Fisk Ventures, LLC v. Segal*,[144] the court made the following observations:

> The text of § 18–802 does not specify what a court must consider in evaluating the "reasonably practicable" standard, but several convincing factual circumstances have pervaded the case law: (1) the members' vote is deadlocked at the Board level; (2) the operating agreement gives no means of navigating around the deadlock; and (3) due to the financial condition of the company, there is effectively no business to operate. These factual circumstances are not individually dispositive; nor must they all exist for a court to find it no longer reasonably practicable for a business to continue operating. ... If a board deadlock prevents the limited liability company from operating or from furthering its stated business purpose, it is not

[142] *See id.* at 218–20.

[143] The Delaware LLC statute and the Uniform LLC Acts all have similar provisions. *See* DLLCA § 18–802; ULLCA § 801(4)(iii); RULLCA § 701(a)(4)(B).

[144] Civ. A. No. 3017–CC, 2009 WL 73957 (Del. Ch. Jan. 13, 2009).

reasonably practicable for the company to carry on its business.[145]

On the facts before it, the *Fisk Ventures* court concluded that "[w]hen . . . a company has no office, no employees, no operating revenue, no prospects of equity or debt infusion, and when the company's Board has a long history of deadlock as a result of its governance structure, more than ample reason and sufficient evidence exists to order dissolution."[146] Other decisions grappling with the "not reasonably practicable" language have granted dissolution when the purpose of the company has been frustrated.[147]

Should members of an LLC be permitted to contractually waive their rights to petition for judicial dissolution? In *R&R Capital, LLC v. Buck & Doe Run Valley Farms, LLC*,[148] the court upheld the following provision in an LLC agreement:

Waiver of Dissolution Rights. The Members agree that irreparable damage would occur if any member should bring an action for judicial dissolution of the Company. Accordingly each member accepts the provisions under this Agreement as such Member's sole entitlement on Dissolution of the Company and waives and renounces such Member's right to seek a court decree of dissolution or to seek the appointment by a court of a liquidator for the Company.

As part of its rationale for enforcing the provision, the court stated the following:

---

[145] *Id.* at *4 (footnotes omitted).

[146] *Id.* at *1.

[147] *See, e.g., In re* Silver Leaf, L.L.C., No. Civ. A. 20611, 2005 WL 2045641, at *10–11 (Del. Ch. Aug. 18, 2005) (granting dissolution under DLLCA § 18–802: "Silver Leaf was formed for the specific purpose of marketing the vending machines of Tasty Fries. . . . Thus, at the time the dispute between the parties began, the only asset of Silver Leaf was the SMA [a sales and marketing agreement giving Silver Leaf the right to market the vending machines] . . . . Now, the SMA is no longer an asset of Silver Leaf because Tasty Fries terminated that contract. . . . Clearly, the business of marketing Tasty Fries's machines no longer exists for Silver Leaf. . . . The vote of the members is deadlocked and the Operating Agreement provides no means around the deadlock. Moreover, Silver Leaf has no business to operate. Therefore, upon application of a member . . . the court dissolves Silver Leaf."); McConnell v. Hunt Sports Enters., 725 N.E.2d 1193, 1220, 1222 (Ohio Ct. App. 1999) ("[T]he evidence does support the trial court's conclusion that it was no longer practicable to carry on the business of CHL [an LLC formed for the purpose of obtaining a National Hockey League franchise in Columbus, Ohio]. . . . The above evidence shows that the cause of it being no longer practicable to carry on the business of CHL was the fact that CHL was not the ownership group awarded the NHL franchise. . . . June 9, 1997 was the deadline for the ownership group to be identified. This ownership group was not CHL. Hence, as of June 9, 1997, the reason for CHL's existence was gone.").

[148] Civ. A. No. 3803–CC, 2008 WL 3846318 (Del. Ch. Aug. 19, 2008).

In addition to Delaware's general policy promoting the freedom of contract, there are legitimate business reasons why members of a limited liability company may wish to waive their right to seek dissolution or the appointment of a receiver. For example, it is common for lenders to deem in loan agreements with limited liability companies that the filing of a petition for judicial dissolution will constitute a noncurable event of default. In such instances, it is necessary for all members to prospectively agree to waive their rights to judicial dissolution to protect the limited liability company. Otherwise, a disgruntled member could push the limited liability company into default on all of its outstanding loans simply by filing a petition with this Court.[149]

J. The Nature of the LLC

Is an LLC more like a partnership or a corporation? The question is an important one, particularly because the applicability of various regulatory statutes may turn on the answer. Many of these statutes were enacted when partnerships and corporations were the only options for business organizations with more than one owner. As a result, the statutes tend to refer only to partnerships and corporations, leaving considerable uncertainty about whether newer business forms, such as the LLC, fall within the statutory coverage.

This uncertainty is nicely illustrated by *Meyer v. Oklahoma Alcoholic Beverage Laws Enforcement Commission*.[150] Meyer applied to the Oklahoma Alcoholic Beverage Laws Enforcement Commission ("ABLE") for a retail package store license for an LLC. ABLE concluded that an LLC was ineligible to hold such a license. On appeal, the district court reversed ABLE's ruling based on a literal reading of a provision from the Oklahoma Constitution that prohibited the licensing of "corporations, business trusts, and secret partnerships." The LLC was not one of these three business forms; thus, according to the district court, it was not prohibited from holding a liquor license. The Court of Appeals agreed that the Oklahoma Constitution prohibited the licensing of corporations, business trusts, and secret partnerships, but it also cited another constitutional provision that allowed the licensing of "any person or general or limited partnership" (presumably if "non-secret"). The court concluded that the "evident purpose" of these constitutional provisions "was the assignment of personal responsibility for compliance with

---

[149] *Id.* at *3, 6–7. In the closely held corporation setting, a New York court reached a contrary conclusion. The court held that a provision in a shareholders' agreement that waived the shareholders' statutory and common-law rights to petition for judicial dissolution violated public policy and was unenforceable. *See In re* Validation Review Assocs., Inc., 646 N.Y.S.2d 149, 149, 152 (App. Div. 1996), *rev'd on other grounds*, 690 N.E.2d 487 (N.Y. 1997).

[150] 890 P.2d 1361 (Okla. Ct. App. 1995).

the liquor laws." Thus, "business forms that did not insure such personal responsibility were excluded from eligibility for licensing."[151] Because the LLC provided limited liability, the court held that the trial court erred in reversing ABLE's decision. In effect, the court upheld ABLE's determination that an LLC was ineligible to hold a liquor license.[152]

What result in *Meyer* if the business organization at issue was a limited partnership with an individual general partner? The Oklahoma Constitution allowed non-secret general and limited partnerships to hold liquor licenses. Because a limited partnership always has at least one general partner with unlimited personal liability, a limited partnership with an individual general partner is consistent with both the language of the Constitution and the concern for personal responsibility. The court would likely allow such an organization to hold a liquor license.

What about a limited partnership with a corporate general partner? Once again, a limited partnership is consistent with the language of the Oklahoma Constitution, but there is some question about the personal responsibility concern. While it is true that a corporate general partner will have "personal responsibility" for the venture's obligations, there is no individual who will typically be on the hook. When the Oklahoma Constitution referred to a "person or general or limited partnership" holding a liquor license, was it contemplating that some individual would be liable? If so, the court would not allow a liquor license in this situation (or in the situation of a general partnership with limited liability entities as partners). Indeed, perhaps the prohibition on "secret partnerships" is designed to prevent partnerships where the individual principals are "concealed" behind limited liability entities from holding a liquor license.

A similar analysis would apply to LLPs and LLLPs. An LLP is a general partnership, and an LLLP is a limited partnership.[153] As a literal matter, therefore, they meet the language of the Oklahoma Constitution for holding a liquor license. Because they provide limited liability to all of their owners, however, these entities would implicate the concern for personal responsibility. Presumably this concern would trump the constitutional language, and a court would not allow an LLP or LLLP to hold a license. After all, the

---

[151] Why is personal responsibility important in this context? Presumably because personal responsibility is thought to make owners more likely to comply with the legal rules related to liquor sales. Fear of financial sanctions is presumably less likely to motivate shareholders, members, and other owners of limited liability entities.

[152] *See id.* at 1362–64.

[153] *See* Chapter 15.

constitutional language was likely drafted when LLPs, LLLPs, and possibly limited partnerships with corporate general partners did not exist.

As *Meyer* suggests, there are likely numerous statutes, on both the state and federal levels, that were enacted when only partnerships and corporations existed. To the extent these statutes are premised on the notion that all multiple-owner businesses are partnerships or corporations, how should they apply, if at all, to LLCs? At least three possibilities are worth considering: (1) have a legislature revise each statute to add "limited liability company" where appropriate; (2) provide a legislative "quick fix" by including a statutory provision indicating that the words "corporation" or "partnership" will always include an LLC; or (3) leave courts to make these decisions on individual, statute-by-statute bases in litigated disputes.

In a world of unlimited time and resources, the first possibility is probably the ideal approach. A legislature would consider the statutory purpose behind each provision and would choose whether to amend. This would take a tremendous amount of time, however, and state legislatures presumably have more important things to do.

The second possibility is a more efficient way of extending the coverage of statutes to LLCs, but some problems will undoubtedly arise. Some statutes that address "corporations" or "partnerships" will not make sense when extended to LLCs, although this issue could be addressed with prefatory language such as "except as otherwise required by the context."[154] Of course, this prefatory language makes the second and third possibilities nearly identical.

Another decision raising similar characterization issues is *Poore v. Fox Hollow Enterprises.*[155] Douglas Campbell did not have a license to practice law in Delaware. He drafted an answer on behalf of a Delaware LLC named Fox Hollow Enterprises. Because Fox Hollow was an LLC and not a corporation, Campbell believed that he could represent the LLC in Delaware Superior Court without a Delaware-licensed attorney. Appellant Tammy Poore filed a motion to strike for failure to properly file an answer through Delaware counsel.

[154] *See, e.g.*, S.C. CODE § 33–44–1205 ("Except (1) as otherwise required by the context, (2) as inconsistent with the provisions of this chapter, and (3) for this chapter . . . the term 'partnership' or 'general partnership,' when used in any other statute or in any regulation, includes and also means "limited liability company.").
[155] No. C.A. 93A–09–005, 1994 WL 150872 (Del. Super. Mar. 29, 1994).

The Superior Court cited precedent from the Supreme Court of Delaware holding that a corporation could not appear in court without representation by Delaware counsel. The Supreme Court's rationale focused on the fact that a corporation is an "artificial or fictional entity," and that although a natural person may represent himself in court without a licensed attorney, an artificial entity could not. The Superior Court framed the issue as whether "a Limited Liability Company more closely resembles a partnership, which may represent itself in Court, or a corporation, which requires representation by legal counsel."

The court noted that the LLC is treated as a partnership for federal income tax purposes, but it also observed that (1) an LLC is largely a creature of contract; (2) an LLC is a separate legal entity; (3) "the interest of a member in the LLC is analogous to shareholders of a corporation"; (4) a member has no interest in specific assets owned by the LLC; and (5) members and managers have limited liability for the LLC's obligations. Given these characteristics, the Superior Court concluded that the LLC is a "distinct, but artificial entity under Delaware law." The court thus analogized the LLC to a corporation for representation purposes and applied the rule requiring representation by a Delaware-licensed attorney. Appellant's motion to strike was granted.[156]

As mentioned, Delaware precedent stated that an "artificial entity" could not represent itself in court. The *Poore* court indicated that a partnership could represent itself in court, presumably because the prevailing view at the time did not conceptualize the partnership as an artificial entity. Instead, a partnership was viewed as an aggregate of the individual partners themselves. Now that Delaware has adopted RUPA and recognizes a partnership as a separate legal entity,[157] a partnership presumably can no longer represent itself in a Delaware court without a Delaware-licensed attorney.

K. A Final Look

As we have seen, the LLC possesses many of the best features of other business organizations. It is worth asking, therefore, why anyone would choose to conduct a closely held business in a non-LLC form. Consider the following issues:

(1) *Differences in fees and franchise taxes.* In some states, filing and other statutory fees for LLCs are higher than for comparable business forms. In Illinois, for example, the filing fee for articles of

---

[156] *See id.* at *1–2.

[157] *See* DEL. CODE tit. 6, § 15–201.

incorporation is $150, while the filing fee for LLC articles of organization is $500. The fee for filing a corporation's annual report is $75, yet it is $250 for an LLC.[158] Moreover, some states may impose income and franchise taxes on corporations and LLCs, but not on partnerships.

(2) *Other taxes.* Federal social security and self-employment taxes, including Medicare taxes, may be higher in LLCs and partnerships than in corporations.

(3) *The relative complexity of the LLC.* A corporation is an established business form and corporate statutes provide numerous default governance rules that may very well be acceptable to the founders of a business. While the LLC has the advantage of flexibility, that flexibility also creates the need, in most instances, for a detailed operating agreement that is tailored to the wishes of the founders. This is particularly true given that most LLC statutes contain few or no default rules on basic governance procedures. This complexity may result in higher legal fees to form an LLC.

(4) *Attorney and business owner inertia.* Lawyers trained in the use of corporations and other closely held structures (and comfortable with existing shareholder and partnership agreements) may be reluctant to recommend a more unfamiliar business form and hesitant to tinker with "tried and true" operative documents. Similarly, business owners who have prior experience with corporations and other non-LLC ventures may prefer to avoid an unfamiliar business form.

(5) *Sparse case law.* Compared to the amount of judicial precedent on partnerships and corporations, there is less case law on LLC issues. Lawyers and business owners may feel less comfortable with LLCs because of this relative absence of judicial guidance. Given the number of LLC formations, however, this problem will lessen with the passage of time. Nevertheless, in light of the differences in LLC statutes, judicial opinions may have little precedential value in other jurisdictions.

(6) *Lack of exit rights.* LLC statutes often limit a member's ability to dissociate, dissolve the firm, or otherwise recover invested capital from the venture. Partnership default rules, however, provide broad dissociation and dissolution rights.

---

[158] *See, e.g.,* Friedman, *supra* note 28, at 55–58 (discussing fee differentials in various states and observing that "[m]any LLCs are extremely small businesses with limited capital" such that "[a] few hundred dollars at the time of formation plus a few hundred dollars differential each year may be sufficient to affect the choice of entity").

(7) *The desire to "go public."* Because the Internal Revenue Service taxes all publicly held business organizations as corporations (subject to a few narrow exceptions), a publicly traded LLC has no income-tax advantage over a corporation. Further, public investors are generally more familiar with the corporation than the LLC. Founders who desire to sell all or part of a business to the public, therefore, may prefer the corporate form.

(8) *Ease of reorganization.* Some businesses may hope to be acquired in the future by a larger, publicly held corporation. The Internal Revenue Code allows a corporation to engage in a merger or other reorganization with another corporation on a tax-free basis. A merger or other reorganization between a corporation and an LLC, however, does not qualify for such tax-free treatment. Although an LLC could convert to a corporation at the time of the merger or other reorganization, it may be easier for a business to form as a corporation from inception to avoid the delay and expense of conversion (especially because pass-through tax treatment can be obtained in the S-corporation form).

Table of Cases

Cases

1250 Broadway Parking Corp. v. 38–32 Assocs., 655 N.Y.S.2d 958 ------------------------------ 335

68th Street Apts., Inc. v. Lauricella, 362 A.2d 78 (N.J. Super. Ct. Law Div. 1976) - 121

A. Gay Jenson Farms Co. v. Cargill, Inc., 309 N.W.2d 285 (Minn. 1981) ---------------- 15, 18

A.P. Smith Manufacturing Co. v. Barlow, 98 A.2d 581 (N.J. 1953)---------------------------- 147

Abetter Trucking Co. v. Arizpe, 113 S.W.3d 503 (Tex. Ct. Civ. App. 2003) --------------------- 273

Abry Partners V, L.P. v. F&W Acquisition LLC, 891 A.2d 1032 (Del. Ch. 2006) ---526, 594

Adams v. Mid-West Chevrolet Corp., 179 P.2d 147 (Okla. 1946)----------------------------- 289

Affiliated Ute Citizens of Utah v. United States, 406 U.S. 128 (1972)--------------------------- 434

AFSCME v. American International Group, Inc., 462 F.3d 121 (2d Cir. 2006) ----- 366

Ag Servs. of Am., Inc. v. Nielsen, 231 F.3d 726 (10th Cir. 2000) 75

Alliance Steel, Inc. v. Piland, 134 P.3d 669 (Kan. Ct. App. 2006) ------------------------------------ 172

Amanda Acquisition Corp. v. Universal Foods Corp., 877 F.2d 496 (7th Cir. 1989) ----- 378

Anderson Hay & Grain Co. v. Dunn, 467 P.2d 5 (N.M. 1970) ------------------------------------ 75

Anderson v. Marathon Petroleum Co., 801 F.2d 936 (7th Cir. 1986)----------------------------- 27

Anderson v. Wilder, 2003 WL 22768666 (Tenn. Ct. App. Nov. 21, 2003)----- 557, 585, 597, 607

Apcar Investment Partners VI, Ltd. v. Gaus, 161 S.W.3d 137 (Tex. App. 2005)--------542, 544

Appletree Square I Ltd. P'ship v. Investmark, Inc., 494 N.W.2d 889 ------------------------------ 508

Aronson v. Lewis, 473 A.2d 805 (Del. 1984) -- 263, 264, 265, 485

Ash v. International Business Machines, Inc., 236 F. Supp. 218 (E.D. Pa. 1964)----------- 476

Ass'n v. Carpenter, 976 F.2d 868 (4th Cir. 1992) ----------------- 505

Auer v. Dressel, 118 N.E.2d 590 (N.Y. 1954)--------------------- 193

Auerbach v. Bennett, 393 N.E.2d 994 (N.Y. 1979) --------- 267, 477

B&H Warehouse, Inc. v. Atlas Van Lines, Inc., 490 F.2d 818 (5th Cir. 1974) ----------------- 317

Badger v. Madsen, 896 P.2d 20 (Utah Ct. App. 1995)-- 203, 204

Baker v. Commercial Body Builders, Inc., 507 P.2d 387 (Or. 1973)----------------- 346, 473

Balfour v. Baker City Gas & Elec. Light Co., 41 P. 164 (Or. 1895)----------------------------- 388

Bancroft-Whitney Co. v. Glen, 411 P.3d 925, 935 (Cal. 1965) ------------------------------------ 273

Bane v. Ferguson, 890 F.2d 11 (7th Cir. 1989) --------- 105, 106

Barnes v. Andrews, 298 F. 614 (S.D.N.Y. 1924)--256, 257, 258, 300

Barr Lumber Co. v. Old Ivy Homebuilders, Inc., 40 Cal. Rptr. 2d 717 (1995)----------- 510

Basic, Inc. v. Levinson, 485 U.S. 224 (1988) --- 428, 431, 433, 437

BBF, Inc. v. Germanium Power Devices Corp., 430 N.E.2d 1221 (Mass. Ct. App. 1981)-------- 292

Beam ex rel. Martha Stewart Living Omnimedia, Inc. v. Stewart, 845 A.2d 1040 (Del. 2004)---------------------------- 486

Bedore v. Familian, 125 P.3d 1168 (Nev. 2006) ------------- 473

Bell Atlantic Tricon Leasing Corp. v. DRR, Inc., 443 S.E.2d 374 (N.C Ct. App. 1994) ---- 245

Benihana of Tokyo, Inc. v. Benihana, Inc., 906 A.2d 114 (Del. 2006) --------------------- 284

Berkey v. Third Avenue Railway Co., 155 N.E. 58 (N.Y. 1926) ---------------------------------- 330

Berman v. Herrick, 231 F. Supp. 918 (E.D. Pa. 1964) ---------- 506

Bing Crosby Minute Maid Corp. v. Eaton, 297 P.2d 5 (Cal. 1956)---------------------------- 393

Birnbaum v. Newport Steel Co., 193 F.2d 461 (2d Cir. 1952) 428

Blau v. Lehman, 368 U.S. 403 (1962)-------------------------- 447

Blohm v. Kelly, 765 N.W.2d 147 (Minn. 2009) ------------------- 489

Bloom v. Nathan Vehon Co. 173 N.E. 270 (Ill. 1930) ----------- 245

Blue Chip Stamps v. Manor Drug Stores, 421 U.S. 723 (1975) 428

Blue Cross and Blue Shield of Alabama v. Protective Life Ins. Co., 527 So. 2d 125 (Ala. Civ. App. 1987) ---------------------- 170

Bohatch v. Butler & Binion, 977 S.W.2d 543 (Tex. 1998) ---- 130, 131

Bond Purchase, L.L.C. v. Patriot Tax Credit Properties, L.P., 746 A.2d 842 (Del. Ch. 1999) ---------------------------------- 528

Brecher v. Gregg, 89 Misc.2d 457 (N.Y. Sup. Ct. 1975) --------- 305

Brenner v. Berkowitz, 634 A.2d 1019 (N.J. 1993) ------------- 347

Brown v. Pool Depot, Inc., 853 So.2d 181 (Ala. 2002)-------- 173

Brown v. W.P. Media, Inc., 17 So.3d 1167 (Ala. 2009)168, 185, 186, 188

Broz v. Cellular Information Systems, Inc., 673 A.2d 148 (Del. 1996) --------- 290, 295, 296

Bryan v. Western P. R. Corp., 28 Del. Ch. 13 (Del. Ch. 1944) 335

BT-I v. Equitable Life Assurance Society, 89 Cal. Rptr. 2d 811 (Cal. Ct. App. 1999)--- 102, 103, 523

Bubbles & Bleach LLC v. Becker, 1997 WL 285938 (N.D. Ill. May 23, 1997)------------------------ 580

Burkin v. Katz, 136 N.E.2d 862 (N.Y. 1956)---------------------- 191

Burnett v. Word, Inc., 412 S.W.2d 792 (Tex. Ct. Civ. App. 1967) ---------------------------------- 324

Burns v. Gonzalez, 439 S.W.2d 128 (Tex. Civ. App. 1969) ---- 81

Business Roundtable v. SEC, 905 F.2d 406 (D.C. Cir. 1990)--- 386

Byelick v. Vivadelli, 79 F. Supp. 2d 610 (E.D. Va. 1999) ----- 345, 348, 462

Byelick v. Vivadelli, 79 F.2d 610, (E.D. Va. 1999) --------------- 394

Byker v. Mannes, 641 N.W.2d 210 (Mich. 2002) ---------------66

C.F. Trust, Inc. v. First Flight Ltd. P'ship, 580 S.E.2d 806 (Va. 2003) ---------------------- 519

Cadle v. Hicks, 272 Fed. Appx. 676 (10th Cir. 2008)---------- 482

Cantor Fitzgerald, L.P. v. Cantor, 2000 WL 307370 (Del. Ch. Mar. 13, 2000)------------ 528

Cargill, Inc, v. Hedge, 375 N.W. 2d 477 (Minn. 1985)---------- 339

Castleberry v. Branscum, 721 S.W.2d 270 (Tex. 1986)------ 337

Castonguay v. Castonguay, 306 N.W.2d 143 (Minn. 1981)--- 317

Caswell v. Jordan, 362 S.E.2d 769 (Ga. Ct. App. 1987) ----- 303

Cede & Co. v. Technicolor, 542 A.2d 1182 (Del. 1988)-------- 461

Cede & Co. v. Technicolor, Inc., 634 A.2d 345 (Del. 1993) -- 259, 281

Center v. Hampton Affiliates, Inc., 488 N.E.2d 828 (N.Y. 1985)---------------------------- 247

Central Bank of Denver, N.A. v. First Interstate Bank, 511 U.S. 164 (1994) ---------------------- 437

Cheesecake Factory, Inc. v. Baines, 964 P.2d 183 (N.M. Ct. App. 1998)-------------------------75

Chiarella v. United States, 445 U.S. 222 (1980) --------- 439, 444

Christopher v. Sinyard, 723 S.E.2d 78 (Ga. Ct. App. 2012) ---------------------------------- 329

Citizens United v. Federal Election Commission, 130 S. Ct. 876 (2010) ------------------ 151

Clark v. Dodge, 199 N.E. 641 (N.Y. 1936)--------------- 321, 322

Clinton Inv. Co. v. Watkins, 536 N.Y.S.2d 270 (N.Y. App. 1989) ---------------------------------- 176

Coggins v. New England Patriots Football Club, Inc., 492 N.E.2d 1112 (Mass. 1986) ----- 459, 460

Collins v. Lewis, 283 S.W.2d 258 (Tex. Civ. App. 1955) ------- 127

Consumer's Co-op of Walworth County v. Olsen, 419 N.W.2d 211 (Wis. 1988) ---------------- 333

Continental Ins. Co. v. Rutledge & Co., 750 A.2d 1219 n.37 (Del. Ch. 2000) ---------------------- 525

Cookies Food Products, Inc. v. Lakes Warehouse Dist., Inc., 430 N.W.2d 447 (Iowa 1988) ---------------------------------- 284

Cooley Inv. Co. v. Jones, 780 P.2d 29 (Colo. App. 1989) -------- 578

Cope v. Pitzer, 166 S.W. 447 (Tex. Civ. Ct. App. 1914) --- 389

Corrales v. Corrales, 2011 WL 3484470 (Cal. Ct. App. Aug. 10, 2011)----------------------- 128

Cosgrove v. Bartolotta, 150 F.3d 729 (7th Cir. 1998) ---------- 581

Coupounas v. Morad, 380 A.2d 800, 803 (Ala. 1980)--------- 299

Credit Lyonnais Bank Nederland, N.V. v. Pathe Communications Corp., 1991 WL 277613 (Del. Ch. Dec. 30, 1991)---------------------------- 253

Creel v. Lilly, 729 A.2d 385 (Md. 1999)------------------------- 134

Crim Truck & Tractor Co. v. Navistar Int'l Transp. Co., 823 S.W.2d 591 (Tex. 1992) ------- 94

Crosby v. Beam, 548 N.E.2d 217 (Ohio 1989) -------------------- 345

CST, Inc. v. Mark, 520 A.2d 469 (Pa. Super. 1987) ------------- 294

CTS Corp. v. Dynamics Corp. of America, 481 U.S. 69 (1987) ----------------------------162, 378

Curley v. Brignoli Curley & Roberts Assocs., 746 F. Supp. 1208 (S.D.N.Y. 1989) -------- 507

Currier v. Amerigas Propane, L.P., 737 A.2d 1118 (N.H. 1999)---------------------------- 511

Dahdah v. Continent Realty, Inc., 434 So.2d 997 (Fla. Dist. Ct. App. 1983) ---------------- 578

Dawson v. White & Case, 672 N.E.2d 589 (N.Y. 1996) ----- 131

DeBaun v. First Western Bank & Trust, 120 Cal.Rptr. 354 (Cal. Ct. App. 1975) ---------------- 302

Delaney v. Fidelity Lease Ltd., 526 S.W.2d 543 (Tex. 1975) ----------------------------521, 522

Deutsche Credit Corp. v. Case Power & Equip. Co., 876 P.2d 1190 (Ariz. Ct. App. 1994) - 331

Dev., LLC v. 607 South Park, LLC, 71 Cal.Rptr.3d 810, 812 (Cal. Ct. App. 2008) ---------- 176

Dewitt Truck Brokers, Inc. v. W. Ray Flemming Fruit Co., 540 F.2d 681 (4th Cir. 1976) ---- 331

Diamond v. Oreamuno, 248 N.E.2d 910 (N.Y. 1969) ---- 427, 438

Direct Mail Specialist, Inc. v. Brown, 673 F. Supp. 1540 (D. Mont. 1987)-------------------- 504

Dirks v. SEC, 463 U.S. 646 (1983) ----------------------------441, 442

Disotell v. Stiltner, 100 P.3d 890 (Alaska 2004) ----------------- 134

Dodge v. Ford Motor Co., 170 N.W. 668 (Mich. 1919)------- 409

Donahue v. Rodd Electrotype Co., 328 N.E.2d 505 (Mass. 1975) ----------------- 195, 196, 343, 415

Drashner v. Sorenson, 63 N.W.2d 255 (S.D. 1954) ---122, 123, 125

Dreifuerst v. Dreifuerst, 280 N.W.2d 335 (Wis. Ct. App. 1979)----------------132, 133, 135

Dunbar Group, LLC v. Tignor, 593 S.E.2d 216 (Va. 2004)- 610, 611

Dupuy v. Dupuy, 511 F.2d 641 (5th Cir. 1975) ----------------- 430

Dwinell's Central Neon v. Cosmopolitan Chinook Hotel, 587 P.2d 191 (Wash. Ct. App. 1978) ---------------------------- 505

Ed Peters Jewelry Co. v. C & J Jewelry Co., 124 F.3d 252 (1st Cir. 1997)---------------------- 469

Ederer v. Gursky, 881 N.E.2d 204 (N.Y. 2007) --------- 548, 549

Edgar v. Mite Corp., 457 U.S. 624 (1982) --------------- 161, 378

Eisen v. Post, 3 N.Y.2d 518 (1957)---------------------------- 468

Eisenberg v. Flying Tiger Line, Inc., 451 F.2d 267 (2d Cir. 1971)---------------------------- 478

Elf Atochem North America, Inc. v. Jaffari, 727 A.2d 286 (Del. 1999)---------------------- 580, 592

Ellzey v. Fyr-Pruf, Inc., 376 So. 2d 1328 (Miss. 1979)--------- 294

Enea v. Superior Court, 34 Cal. Rptr. 3d 513 (Ct. App. 2005)99, 100

Energy Resources Corp. v. Porter, 438 N.E.2d 391 (Mass. Ct. App. 1982------------------- 294

EP Medsystems, Inc. v. Echocath, Inc., 235 F.3d 865 (3d Cir. 2000)---------------------- 432, 433

Ernst & Ernst v. Hochfelder, 425 U.S. 185 (1976) --------------- 434

Essco Geometric v. Harvard Industries, 46 F.3d 718 (8th Cir. 1995)-------------------------34

Essex Universal Corp. v. Yates, 305 F.2d 572 (2d Cir. 1962) 304

Evans v. Blesi, 345 N.W.2d 775 (Minn. Ct. App. 1984) ------- 345

Evans v. Ruth, 195 A. 163 (Pa. Super. Ct. 1937) ----------------48

Exacto Spring Corp. v. Commissioner, 196 F.3d 833 (7th Cir. 1999) ---------------- 286

Fairway Development Co. v. Title Insurance Co. of Minnesota, 621 F. Supp. 120 (N.D. Ohio 1985)------------------------------ 73

Faour, 789 S.W.2d 620 (1990) 253

Farris v. Glen Alden Corp., 143 A.2d 25 (Pa. 1958) ------------ 469

FDIC v. Claycomb, 945 F.2d 853 (5th Cir. 1991) -------------------- 85

Feder v. Martin Marietta Corp., 406 F.2d 260 (2d Cir. 1969)449, 450

Felzen v. Andreas, 134 F.3d 873 (7th Cir. 1998) ---------------- 479

Fili v. Matson Motors, Inc., 590 N.Y.S.2d 961 (App. Div. 1992) -------------------------------------- 12

First Cmty. Bank, N.A. v. Youth Ctr., 81 Va. Cir. 416 (2010) 187

Fisk Ventures, LLC v. Segal, 2008 WL 1961156 (Del. Ch. May 7, 2008) ------------------ 596

Fisk Ventures, LLC v. Segal, 2009 WL 73957 (Del. Ch. Jan. 13, 2009)------------------------ 611

Fleetwood Corp. v. Mirich, 404 N.E.2d 38 (Ind. Ct. App. 1980) ------------------------------------ 424

Fliegler v. Lawrence, 361 A.2d 218 (Del. 1976) ----------282, 284

Fogel v. U.S. Energy Systems Inc., 2007 WL 4438978 (Del. Ch. Dec. 13, 2007) ------------ 231

Foremost-McKesson, Inc. v. Provident Securities Co., 423 U.S. 232 (1976) ---------------- 450

Fought v. Morris, 543 So. 2d 167 (Miss. 1989) -------------------- 345

Fox v. 7L Bar Ranch Co., 645 P.2d 929 (Mont. 1982)------- 347

Francis v. United Jersey Bank, 432 A.2d 814 (N.J. 1981) -- 255, 256

Franklin v. USX Corp., 87 Cal. Ct. App. 4th 615 (2001) ---- 469, 470

Free Enterprise Fund v. Public Company Accounting Oversight Board, 130 S.Ct. 3138 (2010) ------------------------------------ 363

Freeman v. Decio, 584 F.2d 186 (7th Cir. 1978) ---------------- 427

Frick v. Howard, 126 N.W.2d 619 (Wis. 1964)---------------------- 180

Frigidaire Sales Corp. v. Union Properties, Inc., 562 P.2d 244 (Wash. 1977) ------------522, 523

Fujimoto v. Au, 19 P.3d 699 (Haw. 2001) -------------------- 504

Gabelli & Co. v. Liggett Group, Inc., 479 A.2d 276 (Del. 1984) ------------------------------------ 408

Gall v. Exxon Corp., 418 F. Supp. 508 (S.D. N.Y. 1976) --------- 488

Galler v. Galler, 203 N.E.2d 577 (Ill. 1964) ----------------------- 324

Gano v. Jamail, 678 S.W.2d 152 (Tex. App. 1984)------------71, 72

Garrett v. Koepke, 569 S.W.2d 568 (Tex. App. 1978) --------- 543

Gateway Potato Sales v. G.B. Investment Co., 822 P.2d 490 (Ariz. Ct. App. 1991) - 514, 515, 516, 517

Gentile v. Rossette, 906 A.2d 91 (Del. 2006) --------------------- 396

Geyer v. Ingersoll Publications Co., 621 A.2d 784 (Del. Ch. 1992)------------------------------- 253

Gianotti v. Hamway, 387 S.E.2d 725 (Va. 1990)----------- 346, 473

Gibbs v. Breed, Abbott & Morgan, 710 N.Y.S.2d 578 (Sup. Ct. 2000)---------------- 109

Gilbert v. Howard, 326 P.2d 1085 (N.M. 1958) -----------------------75

Gimbel v. Signal Cos, 316 A.2d 599 (Del. Ch. 1974) ----------- 468

Gold v. Sloan, 486 F.2d 340 (4th Cir. 1973)----------------------- 448

Goldberg v. Lee Express Cab Corp., 634 N.Y.S.2d 337 (Sup. Ct. 1995) ------------------------- 341

Goldwasser v. Geller, 684 N.Y.S.2d 210 (App. Div. 1999) ------------------------------------ 529

Gollust v. Mendell, 501 U.S. 115 (1991) ----------------------------- 445

Goodman v. Epstein, 582 F.2d 388 (7th Cir. 1978) ----------- 506

Goodnow v. American Writing Paper Co., 73 N.J. Eq. 692 (N.J. 1908) --------------------- 418

Goodwin v. Agassiz, 186 N.E. 659 (Mass. 1933) -------------------- 426

Gord v. Iowana Farms Milk Co., 60 N.W. 2d 820 (Iowa 1953)395

Gordon v. Elliman, 119 N.E.2d 331 (N.Y. 1954) ----------------- 478

Gorton v. Doty, 69 P.2d 136 (Idaho 1937) ----------------12, 13

Gotham Partners, L.P. v. Hallwood Realty Partners, 817 A.2d 160 (Del. 2002) --------- 525

Graham v. Allis-Chalmers Manufacturing Co., 188 A.2d 125 (Del. 1963)---------------- 260

Gratz v. Claughton, 187 F.2d 46 (2d Cir. 1951)----------------- 426

Grayson v. Imagination Station, Inc., 2010 WL 3221951 (Del. Ch. Aug. 16, 2010) ------------ 217

Green v. H&R Block, Inc., 735 A.2d 1039 (Md. 1999)---------11

Grimmett v. Higginbotham, 907 S.W.2d 1 (Tex. App. 1994) --- 85

Gross v. Weingarten, 217 F.3d 208 (4th Cir. 2000) ---------- 429

Grosset v. Wenaas, 42 Cal.4th 1100 (2008) -------------------- 481

Guth v. Loft, Inc., 5 A.2d 503 (Del. 1939) -------------------- 289

Guy v. Duff & Phelps, Inc., 672 F. Supp. 1086 (N.D. Ill. 1987) --------------------------------- 345

Hagan v. Adams Property Associates, Inc., 482 S.E.2d 805 (Va. 1997) ----------578, 579

Harris v. Carter, 582 A.2d 222 (Del. Ch. 1990) --------------- 252

Hartung v. Architects Hartung/Odle/Burke, Inc., 301 N.E.2d 240 (Ind. Ct. App. 1973)----------------------196, 343

Haynes v. Edgerson, 240 S.W.3d 189 (Mo. Ct. App. 2007) ---- 333

Heit v. Weitzen, 402 F.2d 909 n.3 (2d Cir. 1968) ----------------- 351

Heller v. Boylan, 29 N.Y.S.2d 653 (Sup. Ct. 1941) --------------- 286

Herring v. Keasler, 563 S.E.2d 614 (N.C. Ct. App. 2002) -- 600, 601

Hilco Prop. Servs., Inc. v. United States, 929 F. Supp. 526 (D.N.H. 1996) ------------------- 68

Hill v. Southeastern Floor Covering Co., 596 So. 2d 874 (Miss. 1992) ------------------- 290

Hirsch v. Silberstein, 227 A.2d 638 (Pa. 1967) ------------- 53, 54

HMG/Courtland Properties, Inc. v. Gray, 749 A.2d 94 (Del. Ch. 1999)-------------------------285, 307

HMO-W, Inc. v. SSM Health Care System, 611 N.W.2d 250 (Wisc. 2000) ------------------- 459

Hoddeson v. Koos Bros., 135 A.2d 702 (N.J. Super. Ct. App. Div. 1957)-------------------------46, 47

Hoggett v. Brown, 971 S.W.2d 472 (Tex. Ct. Civ. App. 1997) ------------------------------------ 345

Holland v. Nat'l Auto. Fibres, Inc., 19 A. 124 (Del. 1937) - 144

Hollowell v. Orleans Reg'l Hosp., 1998 WL 283298 ------------- 584

Hooper v. Yoder, 737 P.2d 852 n.4 (Colo. 1987)----------------- 95

Hotchkiss v. Fischer, 16 P.2d 531 (Kan. 1932) -------------------- 424

Hunt v. Rousmanier's Administrators, 21 U.S. 174 (1823)---------------------------- 213

In re Adelphia Commc'ns Corp., 376 B.R. 87 (Bankr. S.D.N.Y. 2007)----------------------------- 518

In re Allentown Ambassadors, Inc., 361 B.R. 422 (Bankr. E.D. Pa. 2007)----------------------- 585

In re Asian Yard Partners, 1995 WL 1781675 (Bankr. D. Del. Sept. 18, 1995)---------- 531, 532

In re AutoStyle Plastics, Inc., 269 F.3d 726 (6th Cir. 2001) ---- 381

In re Caremark International, Inc. Derivative Litigation, 698 A.2d 959 (Del. Ch. 1996)--- 260, 261

In re Drive-In Development Corp., 371 F.2d 215 (7th Cir. 1966) ------------------------------------ 244

In re Emerging Communications, Inc. Shareholders Litigation, 2004 WL 1305745 (Del. Ch. May 3, 2004)------------------- 257

In re Enron Corp. Securities, Derivative & ERISA Litigation, 235 F. Supp. 2d 549 (S.D. Tex. 2002) -------------- 362

In re Fuqua Industries, Inc. Shareholder Litigation, 752 A.2d 126 (Del. Ch. 1999)---- 483

In re Gaylord Container Corp. S'holders Litig., 753 A.2d 462 n.46 (Del. Ch. 2000) ---------- 375

In re Judiciary Tower Assocs., 175 B.R. 796 (Bankr. D.D.C. 1994) ------------------------------92

In re Kemp & Beatley, Inc., 473 N.E.2d 1173 (N.Y. 1984)---- 347

In re ORFA Securities Litigation, 654 F. Supp. 1449 (D.N.J. 1987)----------------------------- 427

In re Security Finance Co., 49 Cal.2d 370 (1957) ------------ 471

In re Silicone Gel Breast Implants Liability Litigation, 887 F. Supp. 1447 (N.D. Ala. 1995)----------------------------- 336

In re Silver Leaf, L.L.C., 20611, 2005 WL 2045641 (Del. Ch. Aug. 18, 2005)----------------- 612

In re Spires, 778 N.Y.S.2d 259 (Sup. Ct. 2004)---------------- 560

In re Sunpoint Securities, Inc., 377 B.R. 513 (Bankr. E.D. Tex. 2007)----------------------------- 247

In re The Walt Disney Company Derivative Litigation, 906 A.2d 27 (Del. 2006) -----270, 271, 358

In re UnitedHealth Group Inc. Shareholder Derivative Litigation, 754 N.W.2d 554, 559 (Minn. 2008) ------------- 490

In re USACafes, L.P. Litigation, 600 A.2d 43 (Del. Ch. 1991) ------------------------------526, 527

In re Validation Review Assocs., Inc., 646 N.Y.S.2d 149 (App. Div. 1996) ----------------------- 613

In re Wheelabrator Technologies, Inc. Shareholders Litig., 663 A.2d 1194 (Del. Ch. 1995)-- 282

International Textbook Co. v. Prigg, 217 U.S. 91 (1910)-- 150, 172

Ira S. Bushey & Sons, Inc. v. United States, 398 F.2d 167 (2d Cir. 1968) --------------- 26, 58

Irving Trust Co. v. Deutsch, 73 F.2d 121 (2d Cir. 1934) ----- 294

Isle of Thye Land Co. v. Shisman, 279 A.2d 484 (Md. 1971)------------------------------ 175

J&J Celecom v. AT&T Wireless Servs., Inc., 169 P.3d 823 (Wash. 2007) ------------------- 104

J.C. Snavely & Sons, Inc. v. Wheeler, 538 A.3d 324, 327 (Md. Ct. App. 1988) ---------- 172

J.I. Case Co. v. Borak, 377 U.S. 426 (1964)---------------------- 367

Jacobellis v. State of Ohio, 378 U.S. 184 (1964) ---------------- 198

Janssen v. Best & Flanagan, 662 N.W.2d 876 (Minn. 2003) -- 268

Johnson v. Hui, 811 F. Supp. 479 (N.D. Cal. 1991)-------------- 489

Johnston v. Greene, 121 A.2d 919 (Del. Ch. 1956) ---------------- 292

Jones Co., Inc. v. Burke, 117 N.E.2d 237 (N.Y. 1954) ----- 273

Jones v. H. F. Ahmanson & Co., 1 Cal.3d 93 (1969)--------------- 305

Joseph Schlitz Brewing Co. v. Missouri Poultry & Game Co., 229 S.W 813 (Mo. 1921) ---- 170

Joy v. North, 692 F.2d 880 (2d Cir. 1982) --- 265, 268, 351, 480

Judson Atkinson Candies, Inc. v. Latini-Hohberger Dhimantec, 529 F.3d 371 ------------------- 337

Kahn v. Kohlberg Kravis Roberts & Co., L.P., 23 A.3d 831 (Del. 2011)---------------------------- 489

Kahn v. Lynch Comm. Sys., 638 A.2d 1110 (Del. 1985) ------- 284

Kahn v. Sullivan, 594 A.2d 48 (Del. 1991) ---------------------- 148

Kasten v. Doral Dental USA, LLC, 733 N.W.2d 300 (Wis. 2007)---------------------------- 572

Katz v. Breman, 431 A.2d 1274 (Del. Ch. 1981) --------------- 468

Katz v. Prete, 459 A.2d 81 (R.I. 1983)------------------------- 176

Kaycee Land & Livestock v. Flahive, 46 P.3d 323 (Wyo. 2002)----------------------------- 584

KE Property Management Inc. v. 275 Madison Management Corp., 1993 WL 285900 (Del. Ch. July 27, 1993) ------------ 528

Keams v. Tempe Technical Institute, Inc., 993 F. Supp. 714 (D. Ariz. 1997) ----------- 332

Keller v. Wilson & Co., 21 Del. Ch. 391 (1936) ---------------- 461

Kemether v. Pa. Interscholastic Athletic Ass'n, Inc., 15 F. Supp. 2d 740 (E.D. Pa. 1998) --------22

Kern County Land Co. v. Occidental Petroleum Corp., 411 U.S. 582 (1973) --- 448, 449

Kessler v. Antinora, 653 A.2d 579 (N.J. Super. Ct. App. Div. 1995)--------------------------86, 87

Kidd v. Thomas A. Edison, Inc., 239 F. 405 (S.D.N.Y. 1917)--39, 40

Kim v. Grover C. Coors Trust, 179 P.3d 86 (Colo. Ct. App. 2007)----------------------------- 252

Kiriakides v. Atlas Food Sys. & Servs., Inc., 541 S.E.2d 257 (S.C. 2001) --------------------- 347

Klinicki v. Lundgren, 695 P.2d 906 (Or. 1985)----------------- 295

Knapp v. Bankers Securities Corp., 230 F.2d 717 (3d Cir. 1956)------------------------------- 479

Kortum v. Webasto Sunroofs, Inc., 769 A.2d 113 (Del. Ch. 2000) ------------------------------------ 221

Kovacik v. Reed, 315 P.2d 314 (Cal. 1957) ----------------------86

Kullgren v. Navy Gas & Supply Co., 135 P.2d 1007 (Colo. 1943) ------------------------------------ 253

Lacos Land Co. v. Arden Gp., Inc., 517 A.2d 271 (Del. Ch. 1986)------------------------------- 462

Lagarde v. Anniston Lime & Stone Co., 28 So. 199 (Ala. 1900)------------------------------- 290

Laya v. Erin Homes, Inc., 352 S.E.2d 93 (W. Va. 1986)----- 333

Lee v. Cameron, 169 P. 17 (Okla. 1917)------------------------------- 392

Lewis v. Anderson, 477 A.2d 1040 (Del. 1984)--------------- 483

Lieberman v. Wyoming.com LLC, 11 P.3d 353 (Who. 2000)---- 605

Lieberman v. Wyoming.com LLC, 82 P.3d 274 (Wyo. 2004) ---- 604

Ling & Co., Inc. v. Trinity Sav. & Loan Ass'n, 482 S.W.2d 841 (Tex. 1972) --------------------- 316

Litwin v. Allen, 25 N.Y.S.2d 667
(Sup. Ct. 1940) --------------- 268
Lofland v. DiSabatino, 1991 WL
138505 -------------------------- 203
Long Park, Inc. v. Trenton–New
Brunswick Theatres Co., 77
N.E.2d 633 (N.Y. 1948) ----- 323
Louis K. Liggett Co. v. Lee, 288
U.S. 517 (1933) --------------- 153
Lupien v. Malsbenden, 477 A.2d
746 (Me. 1984) ------------------ 70
Lyondell Chemical Co. v. Ryan,
970 A.2d 235 (Del. 2009) --- 377
Magma Power Co. v. Dow Chem.
Co., 136 F.3d 316 (2d Cir.
1998) --------------------------- 448
Malone v. Brincat, 722 A.2d 5
(Del. 1998) --------------- 253, 296
Marciano v. Nakash, 535 A.2d
400 (Del. 1987) --------------- 282
Marine Serv. Unlimited v. Rakes,
918 S.W.2d 132 (Ark. 1996) 203
Martin v. Peyton, 158 N.E. 77
(N.Y. 1927) --------- 66, 67, 69, 70
Marx v. Akers, 666 N.E.2d 1034
(N.Y. 1996) --------------------- 485
Maschmeier v. Southside Press,
Ltd., 435 N.W.2d 377 (Iowa Ct.
App. 1988) --------------------- 347
Masters v. Cobb, 431 So. 2d 540
(Ala. 1983) --------------------- 248
Matter of Hausman, 13 N.Y.3d
408 (N.Y. 2009) --------------- 183
Maul v. Kirkman, 637 A.2d 928
(N.J. Super. Ct. App. Div.
1994) --------------------------- 408
McArthur v. Times Printing Co.,
51 N.W. 216 (Minn. 1892) -- 176
McCall v. Scott, 239 F.3d 808
(6th Cir. 2001) ---------------- 484
*McConnell v. Hunt Sports
Enterprises, 725 N.E.2d 1193
(Ohio. Ct. App. 1993)* --593, 612
McCullough v. of State
Maryland, 17 U.S. 316 (1819)
------------------------------- 151
McGee v. Best, 106 S.W.3d 48
(Tenn. Ct. App. 2002) ------- 585
McInerney v. Charter Golf, Inc.,
680 N.E.2d 1347 (Ill. 1997) 248
McLaury v. Duff and Phelps,
Inc., 691 F. Supp. 1090 (N.D.
Ill. 1988) ---------------------- 430
McNeil Real Estate Fund XXVI,
L.P. v. Matthew's, Inc., 112 F.
Supp. 2d 437 (W.D. Pa. 2000)
------------------------------- 44
*McQuade v. Stoneham, 189 N.E.
234 (N.Y. 1934)*-- 196, 320, 321,
322

Md. Assocs. Ltd. P'ship v.
Sheehan, 14 S.W.3d 576 (Mo.
2000) -------------------------- 93
Medkser v. Feingold, 307 Fed.
Appx. 262 (11th Cir. 2008)- 478
Meehan v. Shaughnessy, 535
N.E.2d 1255 (Mass. 1989)- 107,
108
Meinhard v. Salmon, 164 N.E.
545 (N.Y. 1928) ---94, 95, 96, 97
Meiselman v. Meiselman, 307
S.E.2d 551 (N.C. 1983) ----- 196,
343, 347
Menard, Inc. v. Dage-MTI, Inc.,
726 N.E.2d 1206 (Ind. 2000)
------------------------------- 245
Merrill Lynch, Pierce, Fenner &
Smith, Inc. v. Livingston, 566
F.2d 1119 (9th Cir. 1978)--- 449
Meyer v. Oklahoma Alcoholic
Beverage Laws Enforcement
Commission, 890 P.2d 1361
(Okla. Ct. App. 1995) -------- 613
Miller v. A. & N. R.R. Co., 476
S.W.2d 389 (Tex. Ct. Civ. App.
1972) -------------------------- 243
Miller v. Miller, 222 N.W.2d 71
(Minn. 1974) ------------------- 293
Miller Waste Mills, Inc. v.
Mackay, 520 N.W.2d 490
(Minn. Ct. App. 1994) ------- 316
Mills v. Electric Auto–Lite Co.,
396 U.S. 375 (1970) --------- 367
Miners, Inc. v. Alpine Equip.
Corp., 722 A.2d 691 (Pa. Sup.
1998) -------------------------- 341
Minich v. Gem State Dev., 591
P.2d 1078 (Ida. 1979) -------- 184
Moore v. Dallas Post Card Co.,
215 S.W.2d 398 (Tex. Ct. Civ.
App. 1948) --------------------- 176
Moore v. New Ammest, Inc., 630
P.2d 167 (Kan. Ct. App. 1981)
------------------------------- 458
Moran v. Household
International, Inc., 500 A.2d
1346 (Del. 1985) -------------- 375
*Morris Oil Co. v. Rainbow
Oilfield Trucking, Inc., 741
P.2d 840 (N.M. 1987)* -----41, 42
National Biscuit Co. v. Stroud,
106 S.E.2d 692 (N.C. 1959) --79
Neri v. Neri, 1993 WL 7649
(Conn. Super. Jan. 12, 1993)
------------------------------- 231
Nixon v. Blackwell, 626 A.2d
1366 (Del. 1993)- 323, 325, 345,
590
NLRB v. Greater Kansas City
Roofing, 2 F.3d 1047 (10th Cir.
1993) -------------------------- 334

Noakes v. Schoenborn, 841 P.2d 682 (Or. Ct. App. 1982) ----- 471

Northeast Harbor Golf Club, Inc. v. Harris, 661 A.2d 1146 (Me. 1995)------------------------291, 297

Old Dominion Copper Mining & Smelting Co. v. Bigelow, 89 N.E. 193 (Mass. 1909)------- 180

Old Dominion Copper Mining & Smelting Co. v. Lewisohn, 210 U.S. 206 (1908)---------------- 180

Oliver v. Oliver, 45 S.E. 232 (Ga. 1903)---------------------------- 424

Olmstead v. Federal Trade Commission, 44 So. 3d 76 (Fla. 2010)----------------------601, 603

Owen v. Cohen, 19 Cal.2d 147, 119 P.2d 713 ------------------- 125

Page v. Page, 359 P.2d 41 (Cal. 1961)---------- 124, 125, 126, 127

Palmer v. Morris, 316 F.2d 649 (5th Cir. 1963) ----------------- 483

Panter v. Marshall Field & Co., 646 F.2d 271 ------------------- 374

Paramount Communications, Inc. v. QVC Network, Inc., 637 A.2d 34 (Del. 1994) ------------------ 377

Paramount Communications, Inc. v. Time, Inc., 571 A.2d 1140 (Del. 1989) ----------------376, 377

Parks v. Riverside Ins. Co., 308 F.2d 175 (10th Cir. 1962) ------ 86

Parsons Mobile Prods., Inc. v. Remmert, 531 P.2d 428 (Kan. 1975)---------------------------- 272

Paul v. Virginia, 75 U.S. 168 (1869)---------------------------- 150

People v. Ford, 128 N.E. 479 (Ill. 1920)------------------------- 181

Pepsi-Cola Bottling Co. v. Handy, 2000 WL 364199 (Del. Ch. Mar. 15, 2000) ----------------- 582

Perlman v. Feldmann, 219 F.2d 173 (2d Cir. 1955) ------301, 306

Perlman v. Permonite Mfg. Co., 568 F. Supp. 222 (N.D. Ind. 1983)---------------------------- 458

Phoenix Airline Servs. v. Metro Airlines, 397 S.E.2d 699 (Ga. 1990)---------------------------- 293

Pinebrook Props., Ltd. v. Brookhaven Lake Prop. Owners Ass'n, 77 S.W.3d 487 (Tex. App. 2002)--------------- 519

Poore v. Fox Hollow Enterprises, 1994 WL 150872 (Del. Super. Mar. 29, 1994) ----------------- 615

Premier Van Schaack Realty, Inc. v. Sieg, 51 P.3d 24 (Utah Ct. App. 2002) ---- 576, 577, 578

Quickturn Design Systems v. Shapiro, 721 A.2d 1281 (Del. 1998)---------------------------- 373

R&R Capital, LLC v. Buck & Doe Run Valley Farms, LLC, 2008 WL 3846318 (Del. Ch. Aug. 19, 2008) -----------------526, 594, 612

Railway Express Agency, Inc. v. Virginia, 282 U.S. 440 (1931) ---------------------------------- 160

Rales v. Blasband, 634 A.2d 927 (Del. 1993) ---------------------- 486

Rapistan Corp. v. Michaels, 511 N.W.2d 918 (Mich. Ct. App. 1994 ----------------------------- 289

Rapoport v. 55 Perry Co., 376 N.Y.S.2d 147 (App. Div. 1975) ---------------------------------- 116

Read v. Read, 556 N.W.2d 768 (Wisc. Ct. App. 1996) -------- 478

Reed, Roberts Assoc., Inc. v. Strauman, 353 N.E.2d 590 (N.Y. 1976) ---------------------- 273

Reliance Electric Co. v. Emerson Electric Co., 404 U.S. 418 (1972) ----------------------------- 450

Resnick v. Karmax Camp Corp., 149 A.2d 709 (N.Y. 1989) --- 468

Revlon, Inc. v. MacAndrews & Forbes Holdings, Inc., 506 A.2d 173 (Del. 1985)----------------- 376

Rhode v. Dock-Hop Co., 194 P. 11 (Cal. 1920) ---------------------- 393

Ringling Bros.-Barnum & Bailey Combined Shows v. Ringling, 53 A.2d 441 (Del. 1947) ---- 216, 217, 252

Ritchie v. Rupe, 339 S.W.3d 275 (Tex. Ct. Civ. App. 2011) --- 347

Rivercity v. American Can Co., 600 F.Supp. 908 (E.D. La. 1984)----------------------------- 282

Robertson v. Levy, 197 A.2d 443 (D.C. Ct. App. 1964)---------- 187

Rogers v. Hill, 289 U.S. 582 (1933)---------------------------- 286

Roof Depot, Inc. v. Ohman, 638 N.W.2d 782 (Minn. Ct. App. 2002) ----------------------------- 317

Ross v. Auto Club Group, 748 N.W.2d 552 n.1 (Mich. 2008330

Ross v. Bernhard, 396 U.S. 531 (1970) ---------------------- 476, 481

Salem Tent & Awning Co. v. Schmidt, 719 P.2d 819 (Or. Ct. App. 1986)----------------------- 335

Sample v. Morgan, 914 A.2d 647 (Del. Ch. 2007)---------------- 390

Sampson v. Hunt, 564 P.2d 489 (Kan. 1997) -------------------- 424

Schautteet v. Chester State Bank, 707 F.Supp. 885 (E.D. Tex. 1988)---------------------- 253

Schroder v. Scotten, Dillon Co., 299 A.2d 431 (Del. Ch. 1972) ------------------------------------ 231

SEC v. Sandford, 535 U.S. 813 (2002)---------------------------- 436

SEC v. Texas Gulf Sulphur Co., 401 F.2d 833 (2d Cir. 1971) ------------------------------431, 439

Securities & Exchange Comm. v. Transamerica Corp., 163 F.2d 511 (3d Cir. 1947) ------------ 365

Shimko v. Guenther, 505 F.3d 987 (9th Cir. 2007) ----------- 518

Shlensky v. Dorsey, 574 F.2d 131 (3d Cir. 1978) ------------------ 491

Shlensky v. Wrigley, 237 N.E.2d 776 (Ill. Ct. App. 1968)266, 267

Sims v. Western Waste Industries, 918 S.W.2d 682 (Tex. Ct. Civ. App. 1996) --- 339

Sinclair Oil Corp. v. Levien, 280 A.2d 717 (1972)--- 264, 307, 308

Singer v. Singer, 634 P.2d 766 (Okla. Ct. App. 1981) -------- 110

Smith v. Van Gorkom, 488 A.2d 858 (Del. 1985) --- 265, 266, 496

Sonet v. Timber Co., 722 A.2d 319 (Del. Ch. 1998)----------- 525

Southeast Consultants, Inc. v. McCrary Eng. Corp., 273 S.E.2d 112 (Ga. 1980) ------- 290

Southern-Gulf Marine Co. No. 9, Inc. v. Camcraft, Inc., 410 So.2d 1181 (La. Ct. App. 1982) --- 186

Spiegel v. Buntrock, 571 A.2d 767 (Del. 1990) ---------------- 486

Staats v. Biograph Co., 236 F. 454 (2d Cir. 1916) ------406, 478

Star Cellular Telephone Co. v. Baton Rouge CGSA, Inc., 1993 WL 294847 (Del. Ch. Aug. 2, 1993)---------------------------- 531

State ex rel. Carlton v. Triplett, 517 P.2d 136 (Kan. 1973) -- 182

State v. Chicago, B. & Q.R. Co., 199 N.W. 534 (Neb. 1924)-- 148

Stefano v. Coppock, 705 P.2d 443 n.3 (Alaska 1985) ------------- 347

Stepak v. Addison, 20 F.3d 398 (11th Cir. 1994) -------------- 486

Stone v. Ritter, 911 A.2d 362 (Del. 2006) ----------------261, 270

Stoneridge Investment Partners, LLC v. Scientific-Atlanta, Inc., 552 U.S. 148 (2008) ---------- 437

Strong v. Repide, 213 U.S. 419 (1909)---------------------------- 425

Summers v. Dooley, 481 P.2d 318 (Idaho 1971)---------------- 78, 79

Sundstrand Corp. v. Sun Chemical Corp., 533 F.2d 1033, 1045 (7th Cir. 1977)--------- 434

Surowitz v. Hilton Hotels Corp., 383 U.S. 363 (1966) ---------- 480

Swafford v. Berry, 382 P.2d 999 (Colo. 1963) -------------------- 180

Taghipour v. Jerez, 26 P.3d 885 (Utah Ct. App. 2001)--------- 570

Taghipour v. Jerez, 52 P.3d 1252 (Utah 2002) ------------- 567, 568

Tanzer v. Int'l Gen. Indus. Inc., 402 A.2d 382 (Del. Ch. 1979) ------------------------------------ 460

Tarnowski v. Resop, 51 N.W.2d 801 (Minn. 1952)-----------58, 59

Taser Int'l, Inc. v. Ward, 231 P.3d 921 (Ariz. 2010) ------- 273

Taylor v. Standard Gas & Electric Co., 306 U.S. 307 (1939)---------------------------- 335

Taylor v. Wright, 159 P.2d 980 (Cal. Ct. App. 1945) ---------- 424

Tellabs, Inc. v. Makor Issues & Rights, Ltd., 551 U.S. 308 (2007)---------------------- 427, 435

Templeton v. Nocona Hills Owners Ass'n, Inc., 555 S.W.2d 534 (Tex. Civ. App. 1977)--- 245

Theodora Holding Corp. v. Henderson, 257 A.2d 398 (Del. Ch. 1969) ------------------------ 148

Thomas v. Dickson, 301 S.E.2d 49 (Ga. 1983 -------------------- 481

Thomson v. Anderson, 498 P.2d 1 (Kan. 1972) -------------------- 317

Timberline Equipment Co. v. Davenport, 514 P.2d 1109 (Or. 1973)---------------------------- 182

TLC Beatrice Int'l Holdings, Inc. v. CIGNA Ins. Co., 1999 WL 33454 (S.D. N.Y. Jan. 27, 1999) ------------------------------------ 494

Tooley v. Donaldson, Lufkin & Jenrette, Inc., 845 A.2d 1031 (Del. 2004) ---------------------- 477

Topanga Corp. v. Gentile, 58 Cal. Rptr. 713 (Cal. Ct. App. 1967) ------------------------------------ 180

Towe Antique Ford Foundation v. I.R.S., 999 F.2d 1387 (9th Cir. 1993)----------------------- 338

Trustees of Dartmouth College v. Woodward, 17 U.S. 518 (1819) ------------------------------------ 143

TSC Industries, Inc. v. Northway, Inc., 426 U.S. 438 (1976)----------------367, 425, 431

Tzolis v. Wolff, 884 N.E.2d 1005 (N.Y. 2008) ---------------------- 589

U.S. v. Bestfoods, 524 U.S. 51 (1998) --------------------------- 337

United States v. O'Hagan, 521
U.S. 642 (1997) ---------441, 443
Unitrin, Inc. v. American
General Corp., 651 A.2d 1361
(Del. 1995) --------------------- 376
Unocal Corp. v. Mesa Petroleum
Co., 493 A.2d 946 (Del. 1985)
----------------------------------- 375
Van D. Costas, Inc. v. Rosenberg,
432 So. 2d 656 (Fla. Dist. Ct.
App. 1983) ----------------------- 56
Van Dyke v. DCI, Inc., 675
N.W.2d 810 (Wis. App. 2004)
----------------------------------- 176
VantagePoint Venture Partners
1996 v. Examen, Inc., 871 A.2d
1108 (Del. 2005)---------161, 162
Versata Enterprises, Inc. v.
Selectica, Inc., 5 A.3d 586 (Del.
2010)---------------------------- 373
VGS, Inc. v. Castiel, 2000 WL
1277372 (Del. Ch. Aug. 31,
2000)----------------------------- 589
Villar v. Kernan, 695 A.2d 1221
----------------------------------- 327
Virginia Bankshares, Inc. v.
Sandberg, 501 U.S. 1083 (1991)
-----------------------------367, 368
Voeller v. Neilston Warehouse
Co., 311 U.S. 531 (1941)---- 455
W&W Equip. Co. v. Mink, 568
N.E.2d 564 (Ind. Ct. App.
1991)----------------------------- 345
Walkovszky v. Carlton, 223
N.E.2d 6 (N.Y. 1966)--------- 340
Warshaw v. Calhoun, 221 A.2d
487 (Del. Ch. 1966)----------- 264
Wasserman v. Rosengarden, 406
N.E.2d 131 (Ill. Ct. App. 1980)
----------------------------------- 249
Weber v. King, 110 F. Supp. 2d
124 (E.D.N.Y. 2000)---------- 588
Weinberger v. UOP, Inc., 457
A.2d 701 (Del. 1983) --307, 309,
310, 458, 460, 461
Western Camps, Inc. v. Riverway
Ranch Enterprises, 138 Cal.
Rptr. 918 (Cal. Ct. App. 1977)
----------------------------------- 522
Whitney Arms Co. v. Barlow, 63
N.Y. 62 (1875) ---------------- 170
Whittenton Mills v. Upton, 76
Mass. 582 (1858)-------------- 171
Wilkes v. Springside Nursing
Home, Inc., 353 N.E.2d 657
(Mass. 1976)-------------312, 344
Wilson v. Friedberg, 473 S.E.2d
854 (S.C. Ct. App. 1996)---- 527
Wilson v. Louisiana-Pacific
Resources, Inc., 138 Cal.App.3d
216 (Cal. Ct. App. 1982)---- 161

Wood v. Baum, 953 A.2d 136
(Del. 2008) -------------- 477, 588
Woodruff v. Cole, 269 S.W. 599
(Mo. 1925)---------------------- 252
Woods v. Barnett Bank of Ft.
Lauderdale, 765 F.2d 1004
(11th Cir. 1985)--------------- 429
Yanow v. Teal Indus., 422 A.2d
311------------------------------- 303
Zapata Corp. v. Maldonado, 430
A.2d 779 (Del. 1981) --------- 488
Zeiger v. Wilf, 755 A.2d 608 (N.J.
Super. Ct. App. Div. 2000) - 522
Ziddell v. Ziddell, 560 P.2d 1086
(Or. 1977)---------------------- 347
Zion v. Kurtz, 50 N.Y.2d 92 (N.Y.
1980)---------------------- 323, 325

Index

References are to Pages

ACCOUNTING
Balance sheets, 402
Partnerships, 83, 98
Publicly traded corporation
    regulations, 363, **399**

AGENCY COSTS
Generally, 144

AGENCY RELATIONSHIPS
    Generally, 7 et seq.
    See also Authority, this index
Bailments distinguished, 12
Control levels, 10, 15
Corporate officers as agents, 195,
    243
Costs, agency, 144
Creation, 9
Creditor-debtor relationships
    distinguished, 15
Disclosed, partially disclosed, and
    undisclosed principals, 28
Duties, 57, 61
Fiduciary Duties, this index
Fraud or misrepresentation of
    agent, 28
General agents, 38
Independent contractors, 22
Inherent agency power, 43
Intent to create, 11
Liabilities
    Contract Liabilities, this index
    Tort, 20
Officers, agent status, 195, 243
Principles, 9
Ratification of agent's actions, 47
Restatements, 8
Termination of agent's power, 62

AGGREGATE ORGANIZATIONS
See Entity vs Aggregate
    Organizations, this index

APPRAISAL RIGHTS
Shareholders, 455

ARTICLES OF INCORPORATION
Generally, 163
Amendments, 461

ASSET SALES
Generally, 467

ASSUMED NAME
    CERTIFICATES
Generally, 1

AUTHORITY
    Generally, 7 et seq.
    See also Agency Relationships,
    this index
Actual authority
    Contract liabilities in agency
      relationships, 29
    Partnerships, 76
    Termination, 62
Apparent authority
    Contract liabilities in agency
      relationships, 31
    Estoppel compared, 44
    Ordinary course of business, 8, 81
    Partnerships, 8, 81
    Statutory apparent authority, 562
Disclosed, partially disclosed, and
    undisclosed principals, contract
    liabilities, 28
Estoppel
    Apparent authority compared, 44
    Inherent authority compared, 45
    Implied actual authority, 30
    Inherent agency power, 43
Inherent authority
    Contract liabilities in agency
      relationships, 38
    Estoppel compared, 45
Limitations, undisclosed, 34
Limited liability companies, 561
Non-agent, 31
Officers, corporate, 241
Ordinary course of business, 8, 81
Proof of corporate authority, 243
Ratification of agent's actions, 47
Revocation, renunciation, 62

Statutory apparent authority, 562
Termination, 62

BAILMENTS
Agency relationships distinguished,
12

BALANCE SHEETS
Generally, 402

BUSINESS JUDGMENT RULE
Generally, 262 et seq.
Applicability, rules of, 263
Care duties
Generally, 105
Good faith duties compared, 270
Loyalty duties compared, 264
Conflicts of interest affecting
application, 264, 269
Deference standards, 263, 267
Dividend policies, 408
Expert opinions to support board
actions, 268
Good faith obligations, 263, 269
Hostile takeover decisions, 376
Intentional dereliction of duty, 270
Loyalty vs care duties, 264
Presumption, 263
Procedural vs substantive matters,
267
Statutory modifications, 268

BUSINESS OPPORTUNITIES
See Fiduciary Duties, this index

BUYOUTS
Leveraged, 369, 463
Limited liability companies, 601

BUY-SELL AGREEMENTS
Generally, 318

BYLAWS
Generally, 167
Amendments, 192

CAPITAL
Generally, 5
Piercing the corporate veil,
inadequate capitalization as
factor,
331

CARE DUTY
See Fiduciary Duties, this index

CASH FLOW STATEMENTS
Generally, 401

CHARGING ORDERS
Generally, 117
Foreclosures of charging orders, 118
Limited liability companies, 598

**CHECK-THE-BOX
REGULATIONS**
Generally, 76, 157
Limited liability companies, 554

CLASS ACTIONS
Derivative litigation, shareholder
class actions distinguished,
478

CLASSES OF STOCK
Dividends rights, 409

**CLOSELY HELD
CORPORATIONS**
Generally, 311 et seq.
Buy-sell agreements, 318
Derivative litigation, 479
Employee-shareholders' interests,
312
Fiduciary Duties, this index
Freeze outs, 346
Illiquidity problems, 318
Involuntary dissolution remedies,
345
Limited liability companies
compared, 614
Management
Partnerships distinguished, 312
Shareholder management, 319
Statutory close corporations, 324
Oppressive Conduct, this index
Outsider problems, 314
Partnerships distinguished
Generally, 312
Fiduciary duties, 342
Publicly held corporations
distinguished, 3, 190, 195
Squeeze outs, 346
Statutory close corporations, 197,
313, 324
Sterilization agreements, 321
Stock transfer restrictions, 314
Veil Piercing, this index

CONFLICTS OF INTEREST
See Fiduciary Duties, this index

**CONSOLIDATIONS OF
ENTITIES**
Generally, 462

CONTINUITY OF EXISTENCE
Generally, 5, 141

CONTRACT LIABILITIES
Agency relationships
    Generally, 28 et seq.
    Actual authority, 29
    Agent to third party, 55
    Apparent authority, 31
    Estoppel, 43
    Implied actual authority, 30
    Inherent authority, 38
    Non-agent apparent authority, 31
    Partnerships, 90
    Principal to third party, 29 et seq.
    Ratification of agent's acts, 47
    Third party to principal, 51
Corporate officers, 245
Disclosed, partially disclosed, and
    undisclosed principals, 28
Veil Piercing, this index

CONTROL
Affirmative and negative control, 17
Agency relationships, 10, 15
Continuum of control, 515
Creditors, 15
Fiduciary duties of controlling
    shareholders. See Fiduciary
    Duties, this index
Independent contractors, 27
Liability/control relationships
    Generally, 27
    Creditors, 15
Limited liability partnerships, 544
Limited partnerships, control rule,
    510
Passive and active control, 515
Piercing the corporate veil,
    excessive control theory, 330

**CONVERSIONS OF BUSINESS
ORGANIZATIONS**
Generally, 470

CORPORATIONS
    Generally, 2, 139 et seq.
B corporations, 149
Bylaws, this index
Closely Held Corporations, this
    index
Constitutional protections, 150
De facto corporations, 182
Defective incorporation, 180
Derivative Litigation, this index
Dissolution, 470
Duration, 166
Entity status, 140
Estoppel, corporation by, 184
Foreign and domestic, 160, 172
Formation, 158 et seq.
Fundamental Corporate Changes,
    this index

Historical development of corporate
    law, 151
Holding companies, 305
Hostile Takeovers, this index
Internal affairs doctrine, 159
Limited liability companies
    compared, 552, 611
Limited partnerships distinguished,
    497
Liquidation, 473
Mergers, this index
Names requirements, 164
Powers and purposes, 169
Promoters, 159, 173
Proof of corporate authority, 243
Proxies, this index
Publicly Traded Corporations, this
    index
Purposes statements, 165
Race-to-the-bottom thesis, 153
Repurchases and redemptions of
    stock, 413
Securities Transaction Liabilities,
    this index
State corporations laws, 155
Taxation, 155
Ultra vires acts, 158, 169
Venture capital financing, 398
Winding up, 473

**CREATION OF BUSINESS
ORGANIZATIONS**
Agency relationship creations, 9

CREDITORS
Contract Liabilities, this index
Control/liability relationships, 15
Corporate fiduciaries' duties to, 253
Deep Rock doctrine, 334
Insolvency distribution limitations,
    418
Tort Liabilities, this index
Veil Piercing, this index

DEBT
Agency and creditor-debtor
    relationships distinguished, 15
Corporation financing, 379 et seq.
Corporation loans to directors, 286
Equity distinguished, 5
Shareholder loans to corporations,
    335

DEEP ROCK DOCTRINE
Piercing the corporate veil, 334

DELAWARE BLOCK METHOD
Generally, 457

DERIVATIVE LITIGATION
Generally, 474 et seq.
Adequacy of representation, 482
Attorneys' roles, 478
Bond requirements, 477
Bonds, 483
Class actions by shareholders
distinguished, 478
Closely held corporation, 479
Conflicts of interest, 475, 486
Contemporaneous ownership
requirement, 481
Demand on directors, 483, 487
Direct actions distinguished, 475
Discontinuances, 489
Dismissal motions, 486
Exculpation of officers and directors,
495
Indemnification of officers and
directors, 490
Liability insurance for directors and
officers, 495
Litigation committees, 486
Notice requirements, 489
Parties, 480
Security for expenses, 477, 483
Settlements, 489
Strike suits, 479

DILUTION OF STOCK
Generally, 394

DIRECTORS
Generally, 190, 222 et seq.
Audit committees, 353
Boards' vs individual directors'
powers, 227
Business Judgment Rule, this index
Business opportunities, usurpation,
272, 287 et seq.
Bylaw provisions affecting, 167
Classified boards, 224
Committee system, 237
Compensation committees, 357
Compensation of directors, 236
Competing ventures and loyalty
duties, 272
Exculpation provisions in articles of
incorporation, 495
Expert opinions to support board
actions, 268
Fiduciary Duties, this index
Fundamental corporate changes,
452 et seq.
Good faith, intentional dereliction of
duty, 270
Indemnification statutes, 490
Inside directors, 351
Intentional dereliction of duty, 270
Interested director transactions,
loyalty duties
Generally, 272, 274 et seq.

Ratification, 193, 274 et seq.
Interlocking boards, 237
Liabilities
Fiduciary duties, 299
Insurance, 495
Litigation committees, 486
Loans of corporations to, 286
Meetings, 229
Misfeasance, 262
Monitoring duties, 260
Nonfeasance as breach of care duty,
255
Outside directors, 236, 351
Oversight responsibility, 261
Piercing the corporate veil, 329
Prudent person standard of care,
255
Publicly traded corporations, 351
Qualifications
Generally, 223
Care duty implications, 256
Quorums, 232
Replacement of, 226
Self-dealing, loyalty duties, 272, 274
et seq.
Stacked boards, 303
Staggered boards, 222
Voting, 232

DISCLOSURE
Fictitious name certificates, 1
Fiduciary Duties, this index
Inspection and Information Rights,
this index
Principals, disclosed, partially
disclosed, and undisclosed, 28

DISSOCIATION
See also Exit Rights, this index;
Expulsion, this index
Limited liability companies, 599
Limited partnerships, 532
Partnerships, this index

DISSOLUTION
Closely held corporations,
involuntary dissolution
remedies, 345
Corporations, 470
Limited liability companies, 599
Limited partnerships, 534
Partnerships, this index
Winding Up, this index
Wrongful dissolution, 121

**DIVIDENDS AND
DISTRIBUTIONS**
Generally, 404 et seq.
Business judgment rule, dividend
policies, 408

Capital surplus funds, distribution
limitations, 417
Classes of stock and dividends, 409
Insolvency limitations, 418
Liability for improper distributions,
419
State capital funds, distribution
limitations, 417
Statutory limitations on
distributions, 416
Taxation, 407

EARNED SURPLUS FUNDS
Distribution limitations, 416

EDGAR
Publicly traded corporation
information, 351

EMPLOYEES
Independent contractors
distinguished, 20

ENTERPRISE LIABILITY
Piercing the corporate veil
distinguished, 339

**ENTITY VS AGGREGATE
ORGANIZATIONS**
Generally, 2, 142
Continuity of existence, 5, 141
Corporations, 140
Diversity jurisdiction
determinations, 579
Formal Requirements of Entity
Organizations, this index
Limited liability and, relationship of
doctrines, 140
Limited liability companies, 574,
611
Limited partnerships
Generally, 509
Entity general partners, 518, 530
Partnerships
Generally, 72
Dissociation and dissolution, 136
Piercing the corporate veil, formal
requirements of entity
operations, 331
Regulatory statutes, applicability to
hybrid business organizations,
611
Related entities, enterprise liability,
339
Social responsibilities of business
entities, 146
Taxation
Generally, 2
Check-the-Box Regulations, this
index
Kintner regulations, 555

Veil Piercing, this index

EQUITY
Corporate financing, 379 et seq.
Debt distinguished, 5

ESTOPPEL
Apparent authority compared, 44
Contract liabilities in agency
relationships, 43
Corporation by, 184
Definition, 184
Inherent authority compared, 45
Partnership by, 75

EXIT RIGHTS
See also Dissociation, this
index; Transfers of Ownership
Interests, this index
Closely held corporations, 197
Corporations, 3
Limited liability companies, 559
Limited partnerships, 4, 533
Partnerships, 2, 113, 123

EXPULSIONS
See also Dissociation, this
index
Limited liability companies, 596
Partnerships, 69, 130
Wrongful, 592

**FICTITIOUS NAME
CERTIFICATES**
Generally, 1

FIDUCIARY DUTIES
Generally, 94 et seq., 251 et
seq.
Accountings by partners, 98
Agency relationships, 57
Agent and principal, 9
Business Judgment Rule, this index
Business opportunities, usurpation,
272, 287 et seq.
Cardozo standard, 94
Care
Generally, 105 et seq.
See also Business Judgment
Rule, this index
Contractual modification, 112
Directors, 254 et seq.
Directors' specialist qualifications,
256
Expert opinions to support board
actions, 268
Good faith duties compared, 270
Loyalty duty compared, 261, 271
Monitoring duties, 260

Negligence principles applicable, 264
Nonfeasance, 255
Oversight liability of directors, 261
Proof of breach, 257
Prudent person standard, 255
Closely held corporations
Generally, 341
Controlling shareholders, 300 et seq.
Involuntary dissolution remedies, 345
Oppressive Conduct, this index
Partnerships compared, 342
Common law and statutory, 94, 104, 342
Competing ventures and loyalty duties, 272
Conflicts of interest
Generally, 100
Business judgment rule, conflicts of interest affecting application, 264, 269
Derivative litigation, 475, 486
Contractual modifications
Generally, 110, 146
Care duty, 112
Good faith and fair dealing duties, 112
Implied covenants, 596
Indemnification of officers and directors, 490
Interested director transactions, 193
Judicial restrictions, 593
Limited liability companies, 590
Loyalty duty, 103
Partnerships, 98, 103
Controlling shareholders
Generally, 300 et seq.
Looters, transfers to, 302
Parent corporations, 306
Transfers of controlling interests, 301
Corporation promoters, 179
Creditors, corporate fiduciaries' duties to, 253
Directors
Generally, 299
Care, above
Interested director transactions, below
Liabilities, 299
Loyalty, below
Disclosure
Generally, 106
Limited liability companies, 571
Loyalty distinguished, 97
Exculpation provisions in articles of incorporation, 495
Freeze outs, 346

Fundamental corporate changes, 460
Good Faith, this index
Good Faith and Fair Dealing, this index
Hostile takeovers, duties of target corporation directors, 374
Implied covenants in contracts modifying, 596
Interested director transactions
Generally, 272, 274 et seq.
Ratification, 193, 274 et seq.
Joint ventures, 96
Limited liability companies, 571, 583 et seq.
Limited partnerships
Generally, 501
General partners, 103
General vs limited partners, 522
Loans of corporations to directors, 286
Looters, transfers of controlling interests to, 302
Loyalty
Generally, 99, 271 et seq.
Business opportunities, usurpation, 272, 287 et seq.
Care duty compared, 261, 271
Competing ventures, 272
Directors, 254, 271 et seq.
Disclosure duty distinguished, 97
Good faith and fair dealing compared, 102
Good faith duty compared, 262
Interested director transactions, above
Loans of corporations to directors, 286
Self-dealing, 272, 274 et seq.
Management responsibilities creating, 252
Misfeasance, 262
Nonfeasance, 255
Officers, 249
Oppressive Conduct, this index
Parent and subsidiary corporations, 306
Partnerships
Generally, 94 et seq.
Closely held corporations compared, 342
Contractual modifications, 98
Departing partners, 107
Power relationship, 528
Promoters, 179
Public vs closely held corporations, 253
Remedies for breach, 95
Secret profit rule, 179
Securities transaction liabilities, 423
Self-dealing

Generally, 100, 272, 274 et seq.
Interested director transactions, above
Shareholders. Controlling shareholders, above
Squeeze outs, 346
Transfers of interests of controlling shareholders, 301
Trustees' duties compared, 252
Uncabining of fiduciary duty, 585

FORMAL REQUIREMENTS OF ENTITY ORGANIZATIONS
Corporations, 320
Parent and subsidiary corporations, 337
Veil piercing, 331

FORMATION OF ORGANIZATIONS
Generally, 5
Corporations, 158 et seq.
Defective incorporation, 159, 180
Limited liability partnerships, 538
Limited partnerships, 502, 504
Partnerships, 65 et seq.
Promoters of corporations, 159, 173

FRAUD
Securities Transaction Liabilities, this index

FUNDAMENTAL CORPORATE CHANGES
Generally, 192, 452 et seq.
Appraisal rights of dissenters, 455
Fiduciary duties, 460

GENERAL PARTNERSHIPS
See Partnerships, this index

GOOD FAITH
Generally, 269
Business judgment rule, 263
Care duties compared, 270
Closely held corporations, oppressive behavior, 342
Intentional dereliction of duty, 270
Loyalty duty compared, 262
Oppressive behavior, 342

GOOD FAITH AND FAIR DEALING
Generally, 98
Contractual modification of duties of, 112
Limited partnerships, 528
Loyalty duty compared, 102

GOODWILL
Partnerships, 122

HOLDING COMPANIES
Generally, 305
Parent and Subsidiary Corporations, this index

HOSTILE TAKEOVERS
Generally, 368 et seq.
Business judgment rule applicability, 376
Defenses of target corporation, 372
Fiduciary duties of target corporation directors, 374
Leveraged buyouts, 369
Proxy contests, 370
State anti-takeover laws, 377
Tender offers, 369
Williams Act, 370

HYBRID BUSINESS ORGANIZATIONS
Generally, 3
Regulatory statutes applicability, 611

INCOME STATEMENTS
Generally, 399

INDEPENDENT CONTRACTORS
Agency relationships, 22
Control factors, 27
Employees distinguished, 20
Tort liabilities, 20

INSIDER TRADING
Generally, 426
Rule 10b-5 liability, 439
Section 16(b) litigation, 445

INSOLVENCY
Distribution limitations, 418

INSPECTION AND INFORMATION RIGHTS
EDGAR database of company information, 351
Limited liability companies, 570
Partnerships, 83, 106
Shareholders, 218

INSURANCE REQUIREMENTS
Limited liability partnerships, 538

INTERESTED TRANSACTIONS
See Fiduciary Duties, this index

ISSUANCE OF STOCK
Generally, 387 et seq.

JOINT VENTURES
Generally, 95

LEVERAGED BUYOUTS
Generally, 369, 463

LIABILITIES
Abnormally dangerous activities, 28
Business organizations generally, 5
Charging Orders, this index
Contract Liabilities, this index
Contribution, 93
Control/liability relationships, 15,
    27
Directors, this index
Distributions, improper, 419
Fraud or misrepresentation of
    agent, 28
Indemnification, 93
Insider Trading, 426
Joint and several, 91
Non-delegable duties, 28
Partnerships
  Charging orders, 117
  Liabilities to third parties, 90
Proxy regulation violations, 366
Scope of employment, 26
Securities Transaction Liabilities,
    this index
Tort Liabilities, this index
Veil Piercing, this index

LIMITED LIABILITY
Generally, 3
Charging Orders, this index
Contribution and indemnification,
    93
Defective incorporation, 180
Entity vs aggregate status and,
    relationship of doctrines, 140
Tort vs contract claims, 543
Veil Piercing, this index

**LIMITED LIABILITY
    COMPANIES (LLC)**
Generally, 4, 552 et seq.
Authority, 561
Buyouts, 601
Caselaw development, 554
Charging orders, 598
Check-the-box regulations, 554
Closely held corporations compared,
    614
Corporations compared, 552, 611
Disclosure duties, 571
Dissociation, 599
Dissolution, 599
Entity status, 574, 611

Exit rights, 602
Expulsions, 592, 596
Fiduciary duties, 571, 583 et seq.
Financial rights and obligations,
    572
Formation, 556
Inspection and information rights,
    570
Limited liability principle, 142, 499,
    573, 579
Limited partnerships compared,
    499, 535, 553
Management
  Generally, 559 et seq.
  Member vs manager, 559, 564
Managers, 557
Members
  Generally, 552
  Shelf LLCs, 556
Mergers, 616
Operating agreements, 557, 615
Operation, 559
Oppressive conduct, 607
Ownership interests, 597
Partnerships compared, 611
Piercing the veil, 582
Publicly traded LLC, 616
Regulatory statutes applicability,
    611
Series LLCs, 580
Shelf LLCs, 556
Statutory apparent authority, 562
Statutory development, 553
Taxation, 156, 555
Transfers of ownership interests,
    597
Uniform acts, 103, 554
Voting, 560
Winding up, 574

**LIMITED LIABILITY LIMITED
    PARTNERSHIPS (LLLP)**
Generally, 549
Regulatory statutes applicability,
    612

**LIMITED LIABILITY
    PARTNERSHIPS (LLP)**
Generally, 4, 536
Control, 544
Formation, 538
Insurance requirements, 538
Limited liability limited
    partnerships distinguished, 549
Limited liability principle, 499, 537,
    542
Limited partnerships distinguished,
    535
Management, 548
Regulatory statutes applicability,
    612

LIMITED PARTNERSHIPS (LP)
Generally, 3, 497 et seq.
Control rule, 510
Corporations distinguished, 497
Defective formation, 504
Dissociation, 532
Dissolution, 534
Entity status, 509
Fiduciary Duties, this index
Financial rights and obligations, 507
Formation, 502
General partners
Generally, 497
Entity general partners, 518, 530
Fiduciary duties, 103, 522
General partnerships distinguished, 497
Good faith and fair dealing, 528
Limited liability companies compared, 499, 535, 553
Limited liability limited partnerships compared, 549
Limited liability partnerships compared, 535
Limited liability principle
Generally, 142
Control rule, 510
Limited partners
Generally, 497, 510
Control exercises, 516, 521
Fiduciary duties, 526
Management, 504
Operation, 504
Ownership interests, 529
Piercing the corporate veil, 518
Regulatory statutes applicability, 612
Tort liability, 517
Transfers of ownership interests, 519, 529
Uniform acts, 498
Voting, 505
Winding up, 508

LIQUIDATION
Corporations, 473
Partnerships, 119

LOYALTY
See Fiduciary Duties, this index

MANAGEMENT
Generally, 5
Closely Held Corporations, this index
Fiduciary duties, management responsibilities creating, 252
Limited liability companies, 559 et seq.
Limited liability partnerships, 548

Limited partnerships, 504
Partnerships
Generally, 76
Closely held corporations distinguished, 312
Transferability of management rights, 115
Publicly traded corporation responsibilities, 352
Shareholders
Generally, 198, 323
Active vs passive shareholders, piercing the corporate veil, 335
Closely held corporations, 319
Transferability of partnership management rights, 115

MERGERS
Generally, 462
De facto, 469
Limited liability companies, 616
Oppressive behavior, 348
Taxation, 616
Triangular mergers, 464

NEGLIGENCE
Care duty. See Fiduciary Duties, this index

OFFICERS
Generally, 190, 240 et seq.
Agent status, 195, 243
Appointments, 247
Authority, 241
Compensation, publicly traded corporations, 356
Contract liability to third parties, 245
Contract rights to offices, 248
Exculpation provisions in articles of incorporation, 495
Fiduciary duties, 249
Imputed knowledge, 247
Indemnification statutes, 490
Inside directors, officers serving as, 351
Liability insurance, 495
Multiple offices held by one person, 240
Piercing the corporate veil, 329
Publicly traded corporations, 352
Secretaries' functions, 242
Selection and removal, 247
Statutory requirements, 240
Titles, 241
Treasurers' functions, 242

OPERATION
Limited liability companies, 557, 559
Limited partnerships, 504

Partnerships, 76

OPPRESSIVE CONDUCT
Closely held corporations, 341 et
    seq.
Freeze outs and squeeze outs, 346
Involuntary dissolution remedies,
    345
Limited liability companies, 607
Mergers, 348
Reasonable expectations of
    shareholders, 346

OWNERSHIP INTERESTS
Generally, 5
Limited liability companies, 597
Limited partnerships, 529
Partnerships
    Generally, 113
    Charging orders, 117
Shareholders, this index
Transfers of Ownership Interests,
    this index

PARENT AND SUBSIDIARY
CORPORATIONS
Enterprise liability, 339
Fiduciary duties, 306
Formal requirements, 337
Piercing the corporate veil, 336
Related corporations, enterprise
    liability, 339

PARTNERSHIPS
Generally, 2, 64 et seq.
Accounting, 83
Agreements of partnership, 71
At-will, 120
Authority
    Actual, 76
    Apparent, 8, 81
Capital accounts, 83
Causes of dissolution, 124
Charging orders, 117
Closely held corporations compared
    Generally, 312
    Fiduciary duties, 342
Contribution, 93
Departing partners' fiduciary
    duties, 107
Dissociation and dissolution
    Generally, 119 et seq.
    Definitions and distinctions, 119
    Entity vs aggregate view, 136
    Revised Uniform Partnership Act,
        136
    Uniform Partnership Act, 119 et
        seq.
    Winding up, 137
Entity vs aggregate treatment
    Generally, 72

Dissociation and dissolution, 136
Estoppel, partnership by, 75
Expulsions, 69, 130
Fiduciary duties, closely held
    corporations compared, 342
Financial rights and obligations, 83
Foreclosures of charging orders, 118
Formation, 65 et seq.
Goodwill, 122
Indemnification, 93
Inspection and information rights of
    partners, 83, 106
Joint ventures, 95
Judicial dissolution, 128
Liabilities to third parties, 90
Limited liability companies
    compared, 611
Limited partnerships distinguished,
    497
Liquidation, 119
Management rights
    Generally, 76
    Transferability, 115
Operation, 76
Ownership interests
    Generally, 113
    Charging orders, 117
Profit and loss sharing, 83
Revised Uniform Partnership Act
    Generally, 65
    Dissociation and dissolution, 136
Taxation, 75, 156
Term, 120
Termination, 119
Transferability
    Management rights, 115
    Ownership interests, 114
Uniform Partnership Act
    Generally, 65
    Dissociation and dissolution, 119 et
        seq.
Winding up
    Generally, 119, 132
    Dissociation vs dissolution, 137
Wrongful dissociation, 138
Wrongful dissolution, 121

PERSONS
Definition, 11

PIERCING THE VEIL
See Veil Piercing, this index

POWER
Generally, 29, 38
    See also Authority, this index;
    Control, this index
Corporate powers and purposes, 169
Fiduciary duties relationship, 528

PRE-EMPTIVE RIGHTS TO STOCK
Generally, 394

PRIVATE SECURITIES LITIGATION REFORM ACT (PSLRA)
Securities transaction liabilities, 431

PROXIES
Hostile takeovers, 370
Regulations
Generally, 364 et seq.
Liability for violations, 366
Shareholder proposals, 365

PUBLICLY TRADED CORPORATIONS
Generally, 349 et seq.
Accounting regulations, 363, 399
Audit committees, 353
Closely held corporations
distinguished, 3
Generally, 190, 195
Fiduciary duties, 253
Compensation of officers, 356
EDGAR publication of company
information, 351
Hostile Takeovers, this index
Inside and outside directors, 351
Limited liability companies, public
trading, 616
Management responsibilities, 352
Markets for securities, 359
Mergers, this index
Officers, 352
Prospectuses, 361
Proxies, this index
Registration of securities, 359
Sarbanes-Oxley Act regulation, 362
Securities and Exchange
Commission, 351
Securities Transaction Liabilities,
this index
Voting by shareholders, 354

RATIFICATION
Authority, 47
Interested director transactions,
193, 274 et seq.

RIGHTS
Stock, options to purchase, 406

RULE 10b-5 LITIGATION
Generally, 427
Insider trading, 439

S CORPORATIONS
Taxation, 156

SALES OF INTERESTS
See Transfers of Ownership
Interests, this index

SARBANES-OXLEY ACT (SOX)
Generally, 362

SECURITIES AND EXCHANGE COMMISSION (SEC)
Generally, 351

SECURITIES REGULATIONS
See Publicly Traded Corporations,
this index

SECURITIES TRANSACTION LIABILITIES
Generally, 422 et seq.
Common law fraud, 422
Deceptive actions, 436
Fiduciary duties, 423
Insider Trading, 426
Private Securities Litigation Reform
Act, 431
Rule 10b-5 litigation, 427
Section 16(b) litigation, 445
State law, 423
Unfairness, 436

SELF-DEALING
See Fiduciary Duties, this index

SHAREHOLDERS
Generally, 190, 198 et seq.
Active vs passive shareholders,
piercing the corporate veil, 335
Appraisal rights of dissenters, 455
Buy-sell agreements, 318
Closely Held Corporations, this
index
Controlling shareholders
Generally, 300 et seq.
See also Fiduciary Duties, this
index
Looters, transfers to, 302
Transfers of controlling interests,
301
Cumulative voting, 207
Derivative Litigation, this index
Exchanges of shares, 465
Fiduciary Duties, this index
Fundamental corporate changes,
452 et seq.
Illiquidity problems, closely-held
corporations, 318
Inspections of corporate records, 218
Loans to corporations, 335

Looters, transfers of controlling
    interests to, 302
Management
    Generally, 198, 323
  Active vs passive shareholders,
    piercing the corporate veil, 335
  Closely-held corporations, 319
  Shareholders, managing, 300
Meetings, 202
Minority shareholders, duties owed
    Generally, 300 et seq.
    See also Fiduciary Duties, this
        index
Pools, voting, 213
Powers, 191
Proxies, this index
Quorums for voting purposes, 205
Reasonable expectations, oppressive
    behavior, 346
Securities Transaction Liabilities,
    this index
Transfer restrictions, closely-held
    corporations, 314
Trusts, voting, 214
Veil Piercing, this index
Voting rights, 199

SOCIAL RESPONSIBILITIES OF
    BUSINESS ENTITIES
Generally, 146

SOLE PROPRIETORSHIPS
Generally, 1

STERILIZATION AGREEMENTS
Closely-held corporations, 321

STOCK OPTIONS
Generally, 386, 406

STRIKE SUITS
Generally, 479

TAXATION
    Generally, 5
  Check-the-Box Regulations, this
    index
  Corporate governance, tax rules
    affecting, 357
  Corporations, 155
  Dividends and distributions, 407
  Entity vs aggregate business
    associations, 2
  Executive compensation, 357
  Franchise taxes, 3, 143
  Kintner regulations, 555
  Limited liability companies, 156,
    555
  Mergers, 616
  Partnerships, 75, 156

S corporations, 156

TENDER OFFERS
Generally, 369

TERMINATION
    See also Dissolution, this index
Authority, 62
Partnerships, 119

TORT LIABILITIES
  Agency relationships, 20
  Employees, 20
  Independent contractors, 20
  Limited liability principles, 543
  Limited partnerships, 517
  Veil Piercing, this index

TRANSFERS OF OWNERSHIP
    INTERESTS
    See also Exit Rights, this index
  Closely-held corporations, stock
    transfer restrictions, 314
  Controlling shareholders' fiduciary
    duties, 301
  Hostile Takeovers, this index
  Illiquidity problems, closely-held
    corporations, 318
  Leveraged buyouts, 369, 463
  Limited liability companies, 597
  Limited partnerships, 519, 529
  Partnerships, 114
  Proxy contests, 370
  Securities Transaction Liabilities,
    this index
  State anti-takeover laws, 377
  Tender offers, 369

ULTRA VIRES ACTS
Generally, 158, 169

UNIFORM ACTS
Limited liability companies, 103

VEIL PIERCING
    Generally, 328
  Active vs passive shareholders, 335
  Alter ego theory, 330, 331
  Capitalization, inadequacy as factor,
    331
  Choice of law issues, 337
  Commingling of assets, 334
  Contract vs tort liability, 330
  Deep Rock doctrine, 334
  Directors, 329
  Domination theory, 330
  Enterprise liability distinguished,
    339
  Excessive control theory, 330

Formal requirements of entity
    operations, 331
Horizontal piercing, 340
Limited liability companies, 582
Limited partnerships, 518
Mere instrumentality theory, 330
Officers, 329
Parent and subsidiary corporations,
    336
Reverse piercing, 338
Stripping of assets, 334
Terminology, 330
Tort vs contract liability, 330
Unity of ownership theory, 330
Vertical piercing, 340

VENTURE CAPITAL FINANCING
Generally, 398

VOTING
Elections of directors, 222
Limited liability companies, 560
Limited partnerships, 505
Proxies, this index
Publicly traded corporations, 354

WARRANTS
Stock, options to purchase, 406

WATERED STOCK
Generally, 392

WILLIAMS ACT
Generally, 370

WINDING UP
    See also Dissolution, this index
Corporations, 473
Limited liability companies, 574
Limited partnerships, 508
Partnerships, this index